LAW AND PRACTICE IN MATRIMONIAL CAUSES

SECOND EDITION

By

BERNARD PASSINGHAM, O.B.E., T.D.

Solicitor, Clements Inn and Broderip Prizeman,
Scott and Travers-Smith Scholar,
Lately a member of the Board of Management
of the College of Law

LONDON
BUTTERWORTHS
1974

This book is also available as part of Butterworths Annotated Legislation Service

ENGLAND: BUTTERWORTH & CO. (PUBLISHERS) LTD.
     LONDON: 88 Kingsway, WC2B 6AB
AUSTRALIA: BUTTERWORTHS PTY. LTD.
     SYDNEY: 586 Pacific Highway, Chatswood, NSW 2067
     MELBOURNE: 343 Little Collins Street, 3000
     BRISBANE: 240 Queen Street, 4000
CANADA: BUTTERWORTH & CO. (CANADA) LTD.
     TORONTO: 14 Curity Avenue, 374
NEW ZEALAND: BUTTERWORTHS OF NEW ZEALAND LTD.
     WELLINGTON: 26–28 Waring Taylor Street, 1
SOUTH AFRICA: BUTTERWORTH & CO. (SOUTH AFRICA) (PTY.) LTD.
     DURBAN: 152–154 Gale Street

First Edition	..	..	September 1971
Second Edition	..	..	June 1974
Reprinted	..	..	March 1975

©

BUTTERWORTH & CO. (PUBLISHERS) LTD.
1974

ISBN—Casebound: 0 406 63702 4
Limp: 0 406 63703 2

PREFACE

At the time when I completed my work on the first edition of this book, the Divorce Reform Act 1969 and the Matrimonial Proceedings and Property Act 1970 had been in operation for only six months. The Nullity of Marriage Act 1971 was not yet in operation and the Recognition of Divorces and Legal Separations Act 1971 had not yet received the Royal Assent. There was little authority upon the way in which the Acts of 1969 and 1970 would operate in practice because, during the early months of 1971, the courts had been mainly engaged in clearing away the back-log of petitions which had been filed before January 1, 1971. The Matrimonial Causes Rules 1971 were about to come into operation. I could only set out the provisions of the new Acts and Rules, and do my best to anticipate what their effect might be.

The position today is very different. The Matrimonial Causes Act 1973 came into operation on January 1, 1974. As will be seen from the Table of Derivations in Appendix I, pp. 379–381, it consolidates, with little amendment, the provisions of the Divorce Reform Act 1969, the Nullity of Marriage Act 1971, and the Matrimonial Causes (Polygamous Marriages) Act 1972, together with most of the provisions of the Matrimonial Causes Act 1965 and the Matrimonial Proceedings and Property Act 1970. The sections of these two Acts which have not been repealed, together with the Recognition of Divorces and Legal Separations Act 1971 and the Domicile and Matrimonial Proceedings Act 1973, which have escaped consolidation, will also be found in that Appendix. To complicate matters still further, all the previous Rules and Forms have been replaced, as from January 11, 1974, again with some amendment, by the Matrimonial Causes Rules 1973. The alteration of the numbers of virtually every section and sub-section, and not a few of the Rules and Forms, has, I confess, proved a formidable and wearisome task.

Of much greater interest has been the very considerable body of case law and Practice Directions. So much which was formerly doubtful is now clear and this, far more than the statutory changes, has meant that much has had to be rewritten. Hardly a Chapter remains unchanged. That on Transitional Provisions has gone and Chapter 9, on matters affecting financial provision and adjustment of property rights, is entirely new, as is much of Chapter 2 on the ground for divorce and Chapter 6 on the jurisdiction of the English courts.

In effect I have been able to make a fresh start. In planning I have kept to my original object, to provide a description of the law and practice as it now is rather than an exhaustive and complete book of reference. But the character of legal professional examinations is changing, with much greater emphasis, in both branches of the profession, upon practical training rather than upon theoretical knowledge alone. Indeed the Law Society has now embarked upon a pilot scheme of a year's practical training in lieu of articles of clerkship, which

will begin in the near future. Thus the needs of the student and those of the
practitioner are closer than they were three years ago and whilst the increase
in length of this edition, as compared with its ancestor, is modest, the emphasis
has, I hope rightly, moved towards the needs of the practitioner and of the
student who is seeking to become one.

Again, I have received much help in what I have set out to do. I must
acknowledge my gratitude for the many helpful suggestions of those who
reviewed the first edition, which I have tried to adopt. Next, I have gathered
much help from the deliberations of the Law Society's Sub-Committee on Family
Law, of which I am privileged to be a member, and from many members of the
Administrative Staff of the Society. My so-called handwriting has occasioned,
as I grow older, more trouble than ever to the Publishers, whose advice and
help has been so readily given, and to my daughter, Ann, who still bravely
continues to type, correct and criticise my handiwork. I can only hope that the
result may meet the needs of those for whom it is intended.

February 1974   BERNARD PASSINGHAM

TABLE OF CONTENTS

TABLE OF STATUTES

References in this Table to "*Stats.*" are to Halsbury's Statutes of England (Third Edition) showing the volume and page at which the annotated text of the Act will be found. Page references printed in bold type indicate where the Act is set out in part or in full.

xi

TABLE OF CASES

In the following Table references are given to the English and Empire
Digest showing where a digest of the case will be found.

xix

PAGE

PAGE

Q

R

CHAPTER 1

HISTORICAL AND INTRODUCTORY

1. Historical

The purpose of this book is to provide an outline of the law as it now is. But for years to come it will be necessary to know something of what it formerly was. This is so first because there will be topics on which it will be necessary to refer to cases decided before the changes took place, and the judgments in those cases cannot be properly understood and applied without some understanding of the law as it was when the judgments were given. Secondly, there are still in existence many decrees and orders which had already been made before the law was changed, and some reference will be required to the effect of the changes upon them. Finally, a brief description of the more recent developments in this branch of the law is not without historical and social interest.

Prior to the Matrimonial Causes Act 1857 the Ecclesiastical Courts had exclusive jurisdiction in England over all matters of marriage and matrimonial causes. The courts of first instance were the Consistory Courts of the Bishop in each diocese, from which an appeal lay to the Provincial Courts of the Archbishops—the Court of the Arches in the Province of Canterbury and the Chancery Court in the Province of York. After the Judicial Committee Act 1833 the ultimate appeal was to the Judicial Committee of the Privy Council.

These courts did not grant decrees of divorce in the modern sense of the word—*a vinculo matrimonii*—since the Church regarded a marriage as indissoluble. They did grant decrees of divorce *a mensa et thoro*, in effect our modern decrees of judicial separation, on grounds of adultery, cruelty and actual or attempted unnatural crime. They granted decrees of nullity on grounds which included the incapacity of either party to consummate the marriage, a prior subsisting marriage, want of age or of consent and consanguinity or affinity. Such decrees are, of course, available today, though the grounds differ. They also granted decrees of restitution of conjugal rights and of jactitation of marriage. The former were granted in cases of desertion; the latter were available when the petitioner complained that the respondent had falsely boasted that he or she was married to the petitioner and resulted in an order forbidding the respondent from repeating the assertion.

Prior to the Matrimonial Causes Act 1857, the only method by which a valid marriage could be dissolved was by private Act of Parliament, which was available only on the ground of adultery. The applicant had first to obtain a decree of divorce *a mensa et thoro* from the Ecclesiastical Courts. He had then to bring an action for criminal conversation in the common law courts and obtain a judgment for damages against the man with whom his wife had

committed adultery. Only then could the Bill be presented and it is easy to
appreciate the delay and expenses which this procedure involved. From 1715
to 1852 the total number of such dissolutions was, according to the Report of
the Royal Commission of 1850, only 244. This procedure was normally available only to a husband, but there were apparently four cases in which Parliament dissolved a marriage on a wife's petition where the husband had committed adultery "in circumstances of aggravated enormity".[1]

The Matrimonial Causes Act 1857 was based upon the Report of the Royal
Commission of 1850. Its main effect was twofold. It abolished the jurisdiction
of the Ecclesiastical Courts in matrimonial causes and transferred it to a new
Court for Divorce and Matrimonial Causes, and it introduced into English law
petitions for divorce in the modern sense of the word. But the distinction
between the rights of husband and wife which existed in relation to legislative
divorce was preserved. A husband could petition for divorce on the ground of
his wife's adultery. She could seek divorce only if her husband's offence was
aggravated, i.e. if he had been guilty of (i) incestuous adultery, (ii) bigamy with
adultery, (iii) rape, sodomy or bestiality, or (iv) adultery coupled with desertion
for two years or upwards, or with cruelty. If on the other hand the petition
was for judicial separation[2] instead of for divorce, the grounds were the same
without distinction between the sexes. They included not only the grounds
on which the former decree of divorce *a mensa et thoro* could have been pronounced, but also desertion for two years or upwards. The action for criminal
conversation was abolished, and the husband was instead enabled, in his
petition for divorce or judicial separation or in a separate petition, to claim
damages from the man with whom his wife committed adultery. A wife has
never been given a corresponding right to claim damages against an adulteress.

The life of the Court for Divorce and Matrimonial Causes was short. When
the Judicature Act 1873 came into operation in 1875 the jurisdiction which that
court formerly exercised was transferred to the newly established High Court
of Justice and assigned to the Probate, Divorce and Admiralty Division.
Appellate jurisdiction was vested in the Court of Appeal subject, in certain
cases only, to a further appeal to the House of Lords. But the grounds on which
matrimonial decrees could be granted remained substantially unchanged for
many years, save that the Matrimonial Causes Act 1884 abolished the power to
enforce obedience to a decree of restitution of conjugal rights by attachment,
but made such disobedience an additional ground for judicial separation. A
change of much greater substance was made by the Matrimonial Causes Act
1923. The part played by women during the First World War had led to a
much clearer appreciation of their proper position in the life of the community,
as was exemplified by the Sex Disqualification (Removal) Act 1919. This was
recognised by the Act of 1923, which abolished the distinction between the
grounds on which a husband and wife respectively could petition for divorce,
and enabled a wife to seek a decree on the ground of her husband's adultery
without proof of additional aggravating circumstances.

The next important change came with the Matrimonial Causes Act 1937.

---

[1] Rayden on Divorce, 11th Edn., p. 6.
[2] Which replaced the former decree of divorce *a mensa et thoro*.

The theory that divorce and judicial separation should in general be based upon the commission of a matrimonial offence was preserved, but to the offences of adultery and, in the case of a wife petitioner, that her husband had since the marriage been guilty of rape, sodomy or bestiality, were added those of cruelty, and desertion for a continuous period of at least three years. But one further ground was added which was in no sense dependent upon any offence—that the respondent was incurably of unsound mind and had been continuously under care and treatment for five years immediately preceding the presentation of the petition. The Act also introduced new grounds for nullity, to which reference (together with the changes resulting from the Nullity of Marriage Act 1971, now repealed and replaced by the Matrimonial Causes Act 1973) will be made in Chapter 5, and a new decree of presumption of death and dissolution, which could be granted when there were reasonable grounds for supposing that the other party to the marriage was dead. For the first time also this Act contained a statutory provision aimed at discouraging over hasty divorce proceedings. It provided that no such petition could be presented within three years from the date of the marriage without leave of a judge, to be granted only if the case was one of exceptional hardship to the petitioner or exceptional depravity by the respondent, and required the judge in reaching his decision to consider whether there was a reasonable probability of reconciliation within the three years. No restriction was placed on proceedings for judicial separation. These provisions of the Act of 1937 were incorporated in the consolidating Matrimonial Causes Act 1965.

No reference has yet been made to the subject of defences to divorce proceedings. The Act of 1857 laid down three absolute bars—connivance at or condonation of the adultery, and collusion—and five discretionary bars—the petitioner's own adultery, unreasonable delay, cruelty, desertion or wilful neglect or misconduct conducing to the respondent's adultery. These bars were preserved by the Act of 1937, with appropriate variations in respect of the new grounds for divorce introduced by that Act. But some of these bars acted as deterrents to reasonable attempts at reconciliation, and provisions aimed at avoiding this difficulty were made in the Matrimonial Causes Act 1963. Agreements reached between the parties might, if the marriage ultimately foundered, be regarded as collusive and, if the marriage could not be saved, agreements which might have taken some of the bitterness out of the proceedings, to the advantage of the parties and still more that of their children, would have been more than likely to prove an absolute bar to a decree. This problem was met by making collusion a discretionary rather than an absolute bar and by enabling the parties to bring any agreement or arrangements made or proposed to be made between them before a judge for consideration. The judge could not, as the Court of Appeal observed in *Gosling* v. *Gosling*[3] (where the principles were examined) "approve" a collusive agreement: he could "grant leave to implement it". A more serious difficulty arose in relation to condonation which remained an absolute bar to proceedings based upon adultery or cruelty. Reconciliation would be difficult without some resumption of cohabitation: yet

---

[3] [1968] P. 1.

if that attempt failed it would be the end of chances of divorce unless the condoned offence was later revived. The Act sought to overcome this difficulty by permitting a continuance or resumption of cohabitation for one single period not exceeding three months. But this laudable attempt to enable the parties to seek to preserve their marriage was largely defeated by the decision in *Brown* v. *Brown*[4] where it was held that since the Act referred only to cohabitation "with a view to effecting a reconciliation" the bar of condonation must operate if at any time, whether before or after the cohabitation was resumed, the parties became reconciled, but later parted.

Over the period from 1837 to 1965 many statutory provisions were introduced relating to such matters as financial provision for spouses and children in the event of a breakdown of marriage. Some of the resulting inconsistencies and anomalies are briefly described on page 7. Since they were all swept away by the Matrimonial Proceedings and Property Act 1970 it seems unnecessary to consider them further at this stage, save to mention that the various forms of ancillary relief now available in suits for divorce, nullity and judicial separation are available to husband and wife without distinction. Provisions enabling the High Court to order a husband to make periodical payments to his wife on the ground of his wilful failure to provide reasonable maintenance were first introduced by the Law Reform (Miscellaneous Provisions) Act 1949.[5]

One further stage in the development of the law over this period dates from the Matrimonial Proceedings (Children) Act 1958. Before that Act the court was not required to concern itself with their welfare in matrimonial proceedings unless an application concerning it was made to the court. Thereafter no decree of divorce or nullity could be made absolute, and no decree of judicial separation could be made, unless the judge had declared himself satisfied as to matters concerning their care and upbringing. These requirements, and provisions concerning their custody and maintenance, were also extended to cover not only a child of both the parties to the marriage but also a child of either who had been accepted by the other as one of the family.

So far as proceedings for divorce, nullity or judicial separation are concerned, the remaining matters to be noticed concern the courts which administer the law, rather than the law itself. The greatly increased number of divorce petitions led to difficulties in providing for the prompt despatch of the business of the courts, and trial in the High Court involved considerable cost to the Legal Aid Fund. The size of the problem is shown by the fact that the petitions filed in 1966 totalled 45,610, a figure which rose to 60,134 in 1969. These difficulties were met by the Matrimonial Causes Act 1967. As from April 11, 1968, all matrimonial causes were required to be commenced in one of the divorce county courts designated as such by the Lord Chancellor. If the proceedings remained undefended, they were to be tried in one of the divorce county courts which had also been designated as a court of trial, but if they were defended transfer to the High Court was obligatory.[6] Finally, by virtue of the Administration of Justice

---

[4] [1967] P. 105.
[5] See now Act of 1973, s. 27—Chapter 10.
[6] Matrimonial Causes Act 1967, s. 1 (1) and (3).

Act 1970, s. 1, the Probate, Divorce and Admiralty Division of the High Court ceased to exist. It was replaced by the Family Division and all matrimonial causes in the High Court are now assigned to it, together with many other matters of family law in a wide sense which are set out in the First Schedule to that Act.

This brief survey would not be complete without some mention of matrimonial proceedings in magistrates' courts, which are dealt with in detail in Chapter 17. These proceedings are governed by the Matrimonial Proceedings (Magistrates' Courts) Act 1960, an Act of comparatively recent origin, which did much to ensure that the relief which could be granted was equally available to husband and wife and that these courts had ample powers to protect the welfare of children of the family. The matrimonial orders which they have power to make can include a clause whereby the complainant is no longer bound to cohabit with the defendant, provisions for payments (unlimited in amount since the Maintenance Orders Act 1968) for the maintenance of spouse or child, and for custody of and access to children. Unfortunately, however, the reforms instituted by recent legislation, and particularly by the Divorce Reform Act 1969, have not as yet been extended to these courts, with the result that there is a most inconvenient and unsatisfactory disparity between the law which they administer and that applicable in divorce county courts and in the High Court.

2. The Present Law

(a) *The principal decrees*

Item XIX of the Law Commission's Second Programme of Law Reform[7] consists of a comprehensive examination of the whole subject of Family Law with a view to its systematic reform and eventual codification. The subject of Matrimonial Causes with which this book is concerned is but one part of Family Law, but it is a part in which the reforms which must precede eventual codification have already made considerable progress.

The first stage involved a reconsideration of the decrees which the court grant and the grounds upon which they should be based. The Commission concluded that a good divorce law should seek to achieve two objects:—

"(i) To buttress, rather than to undermine, the stability of marriage; and

(ii) When, regrettably, a marriage has irretrievably broken down, to enable the empty legal shell to be destroyed with the maximum fairness, and the minimum bitterness, distress and humiliation."[8]

Of these objects the first required that divorce should not be so easy that the parties had no incentive to make a success of their marriage—to overcome temporary difficulties. It also required that everything possible should be done to encourage reconciliation. The second required that when the marriage was dead it should not merely be buried, but buried "with decency and dignity and in a way which will encourage harmonious relationships between the parties and their children in the future."[9]

---

[7] Law. Com. No. 14, dated November 14, 1967.
[8] Reform of the Grounds of Divorce: The Field of Choice (Cmnd. 3123), para. 15.
[9] *Ibid.*, paras. 16 and 17.

The Commission considered that the law as it then was did not adequately achieve these objectives. It did not do all it might to aid the stability of marriage, but tended rather to discourage attempts at reconciliation. It did not enable all dead marriages to be buried, or secure such burial with the minimum of distress and humiliation. It did not achieve the maximum fairness, for a spouse might be branded as guilty in law though not the more blameworthy in fact. The insistence on guilt and innocence tended to embitter relationships, with particularly damaging results to the children. Its principles were widely regarded as hypocritical.[10]

The solution adopted to meet these criticisms is to be found in the Divorce Reform Act 1969, which came into operation on January 1, 1971. Its provisions are now repealed and consolidated, with little amendment of substance, in the Matrimonial Causes Act 1973.[11] It represented a somewhat uneasy compromise. Irretrievable breakdown of the marriage replaced the former matrimonial offences and is the sole ground for divorce. But the court is precluded from holding that there has been such a breakdown except upon proof of one or more of five specified facts. Of these the first three closely resemble the former grounds for divorce, but the remaining two were novel, involving respectively two years of life apart if the respondent consents to the grant of a decree, and five years of life apart without the need for such consent. A decree of judicial separation is available on proof of any one or more of the specified facts, and for this purpose it is not necessary to prove that the breakdown is irretrievable.

The necessity for leave to petition for divorce within three years of the date of the marriage was retained,[12] but the former absolute and discretionary bars to divorce,[13] including those of condonation, connivance, collusion and the petitioner's own adultery, were abolished. The Act contained provisions aimed at encouraging reconciliation, and overcame the difficulties resulting from the decision in *Brown* v. *Brown*[14] by enabling the parties to live together for one or more periods not exceeding six months in all, whether or not they in fact became reconciled, without prejudicing their chances of obtaining a decree if their attempts at reconciliation failed.

The law governing decrees of divorce and judicial separation will be found in Chapters 2, 3 and 4.

The changes made by the Nullity of Marriage Act 1971 were less extensive. The grounds upon which a decree could be granted in respect of a marriage celebrated before August 1, 1971, were left unchanged, but some changes were made (as explained in Chapter 5) as to marriages celebrated on or after that date, and in relation to possible defences.

Of the remaining decrees which were available before the year 1971, that for restitution of conjugal rights has been abolished.[15] Indeed such proceedings were already virtually obsolete. In the years 1965 to 1968, both inclusive, there

---

[10] *Ibid.*, para. 28.
[11] See *post*, p. 9.
[12] See *ante*, p. 3.
[13] See *ante*, p. 3.
[14] See *ante*, p. 4.
[15] Matrimonial Proceedings and Property Act 1970, ss. 20, 42 (1) and Sched. 3.

were only 121 petitions and only 37 decrees were granted. The decree of jactitation of marriage, prohibiting the respondent from falsely boasting that he or she is married to the petitioner, still survives, despite provisional proposals for its abolition in a Working Paper published by the Law Commission in 1971.[16] The procedure has been little used, only six cases having been reported since 1900. However, in a subsequent Working Paper,[17] the Commission was impressed with the argument that abolition would mean that the law provided no remedy in cases of this kind, and took the view that if suits for jactitation were to be abolished it should only be done after a general review of civil remedies available in respect of injurious statements.

It would have been anomalous if, in view of the departure from the theory of divorce for a matrimonial offence, a husband should still have been permitted to claim damages from the man with whom his wife had committed adultery, particularly since she had never been given a corresponding right against the woman who had committed adultery with him. His right to claim such damages was abolished by the Law Reform (Miscellaneous Provisions) Act 1970, s. 4. Incidentally, though it is not a matter strictly relevant to the subject of matrimonial causes, this Act also abolished actions for breach of promise of marriage, and those for enticement, seduction and harbouring of a spouse or child.

The increasing number of immigrants to this country from places in which polygamy is permitted led to the Matrimonial Proceedings (Polygamous Marriages) Act 1972. This enabled the High Court, a divorce county court or a magistrates' court to grant almost all forms of matrimonial relief notwithstanding that the marriage in question was entered into under a law which permits polygamy.

(b) Ancillary and other relief

As a result of over 100 years of piecemeal legislation which was consolidated by the Matrimonial Causes Act 1965, and of subsequent amendments to that Act, the law governing such matters as financial provision for spouses and children in the event of a breakdown of marriage became filled with illogical inconsistencies. Under the Act of 1965 the names given to the type of provision available varied with the nature of the proceedings: in suits for divorce or nullity it was styled maintenance: in those for judicial separation it was permanent alimony: in those for restitution of conjugal rights it might be either permanent alimony or periodical payments. Some types of payment, such as maintenance, could be ordered to be secured; others, such as permanent alimony, could not. Even when security was ordered it could sometimes last for the wife's life and sometimes only for the joint lives of the spouses. A lump sum payment could be ordered in some proceedings but not in others: a wife could be ordered to settle part of her own property in certain cases, but a husband could never be

---

[16] Working Paper No. 34.
[17] Working Paper No. 48, Declarations in Family Matters, para. 63.

ordered to do so. A secured provision for children always terminated at full age, but periodical payments could usually, but not always, continue beyond that age. Some types of provision could be ordered only in favour of children of the marriage, whereas others could benefit some, but not all, children who could rightly be regarded as members of the family.

Enough has been said to remind practitioners of the difficulties which, until January 1, 1971, beset those who had to unravel this antiquated tangle. As from that date this part of English matrimonial law was rationalised and simplified by the Matrimonial Proceedings and Property Act 1970, and a knowledge of the law as it previously was is relevant only in relation to transitional provisions and the variation or orders made before 1971. The main provisions of the Act thus came into operation on the same date as the Divorce Reform Act 1969, though a few provisions, mainly embodied in Part II of the Act, operated from an earlier date.[18]

Broadly, the principal effect of Part I of the Act was to repeal the whole of Part II of the Act of 1965, which dealt with ancillary relief, with the exception of sections 26 to 28A, which enabled the court to order financial provision out of the estate of a deceased former spouse. The previous powers of the court were replaced by much wider powers which can in general be exercised irrespective of the nature of the proceedings. In most cases the financial resources of the spouses are likely to be such as to preclude the exercise of many of these powers. But the court is, in its discretion, able to make use of them in all cases to which they may properly apply.

As a result of the Act of 1970, the main forms of financial provision which have replaced those formerly available under the Act of 1965 are as follows:—

(a) Maintenance pending suit, replacing the former alimony pending suit.

(b) Financial provision for a spouse ancillary to proceedings for some other decree, replacing the former orders for maintenance and permanent alimony.

(c) A similar ancillary financial provision for children, replacing the former orders for maintenance of children.

(d) Orders for various forms of property adjustment consequent upon decrees of divorce, nullity or judicial separation, covering the transfer and settlement of property and variation of settlements.

(e) Non-ancillary financial provision for a spouse or child in cases where there has been wilful neglect to maintain them.

(f) Provision out of the estate of a former spouse whose marriage has been dissolved or annulled.

The Act did not affect proceedings in magistrates' courts except in so far as amendment was required to bring the law into line with the changes relating to the powers of the High Court and of divorce county courts. Such further changes as may be necessary in relation to matrimonial proceedings in magis-

---

[18] See s. 43 (2).

trates' courts are the subject of a Working Paper of the Law Commission,[19] which contains the proposals of a joint committee of the Home Office and the Commission.

(c) Consolidation

The Matrimonial Causes Act 1973, with effect from January 1, 1974, has repealed and consolidated, with some minor amendments, virtually all the then subsisting legislation to which reference has already been made. In particular it has replaced almost all that remained of the Matrimonial Causes Act 1965 (except the sections dealing with provision out of the estate of a former spouse) the whole of the Divorce Reform Act 1969, the Matrimonial Proceedings and Property Act 1970 (except for certain sections relating to magistrates' courts and the property of married persons), the Nullity of Marriage Act 1971 and the Matrimonial Proceedings (Polygamous Marriages) Act 1972, in so far as that Act applies to England and Wales. The provisions of the Matrimonial Causes Act 1973 will be found in Appendix I to this book and, unless otherwise stated, a reference in Parts I and II of this book to "the Act" or "the Act of 1973" will be to this Act and a reference to a section (e.g. "section 1", or "s. 1") to that section in the Act. Appendix I also contains those provisions of the Matrimonial Proceedings and Property Act 1970 which remain unrepealed.

The consolidation does not affect the statutes relating to the recognition of foreign decrees and the jurisdiction of the English Courts. These Acts—the Recognition of Divorces and Legal Separations Act 1971 and the Domicile and Matrimonial Proceedings Act 1973—are dealt with in Chapter 6. The former Act is already in force, the latter is operative as from January 1, 1974. The text of both Acts will be found in Appendix I.

(d) Conclusion

In conclusion it seems worthwhile to summarize some of the trends which have appeared in the development of the law governing matrimonial causes since 1857. The main points seem to be as follows:—

(1) The abolition of distinctions between the claims of husband and wife respectively, both as regards grounds for a decree and matters ancillary to the grant of a decree.

(2) The shift from divorce on the ground of the commission of a matrimonial offence to divorce on the ground that the marriage has irretrievably broken down.

(3) The greater emphasis upon attempts at reconciliation—that the marriage should not end unless the breakdown is truly irretrievable.

(4) The increased concern for the welfare of the children of a broken marriage, and the widening of the classes of children with whose welfare the court should be concerned.

---

[19] Law Commission's Working Paper No. 53, "Family Law: Matrimonial Proceedings, in Magistrates' Courts".

(5) The great increase in the number of divorces, as is shown by the following examples of decrees nisi granted

1867	119
1900	494
1913	870
1920	2,985
1939	8,248
1947	52,249
1954	27,353
1969	54,151

These increases, save in the case of the aftermath of two World Wars, were not necessarily indicative of a corresponding increase in the number of broken marriages, but reflect also the extension of the grounds for dissolution, the availability of legal aid, and the virtual disappearance of the stigma which divorce formerly attracted.

As was to be expected the changes effected by the Divorce Reform Act 1969 have led to still greater increases. The figures for the first year of its operation, 1971, are not truly representative of the results of the Act, since they were affected by a backlog of petitions already filed before that Act came into force. In the year 1972,[20] the number of divorce petitions filed had risen to 109,822 and decrees granted to 106,560. Of these decrees no less than 20,475 were based upon two years' separation coupled with the respondent's consent and 22,030 on five years' separation without that consent, i.e. in cases in which no relief might have been available before the Act of 1969. The extent to which that Act has succeeded in avoiding the bitterness engendered by the public hearing of defended cases is evident from the fact that of the 115,292 petitions disposed of during 1972, only 2,355 were defended, though much bitterness does still result from subsequent applications for ancillary relief.

---

[20] Civil Judicial Statistics 1972, Cmnd. 5333.

PART I

THE PRINCIPAL DECREES

CHAPTER 2

THE GROUND FOR DIVORCE

Since the Divorce Reform Act 1969 came into operation on January 1, 1971, and now by virtue of section 1 of the Matrimonial Causes Act 1973, the sole ground on which a petition for divorce may be presented to the court by either party to a marriage is that the marriage has broken down irretrievably. The difficulty of determining in practice whether or not this has occurred is met by laying down, in section 1 (2), that the court shall not hold that the marriage has broken down irretrievably unless the petitioner satisfies the court of one or more of five specified facts. These facts, though some of them closely resemble the former grounds for divorce, must no longer be regarded as grounds, since irretrievable breakdown is the sole ground. They must instead be treated as the essentials which will alone enable the court to determine whether or not that ground exists. If the court is satisfied on the evidence of any of the facts mentioned in this sub-section, it is provided by section 2 (4) that it shall grant a decree nisi "unless it is satisfied on all the evidence that the marriage has not broken down irretrievably." This is subject to a special defence of grave hardship available in certain cases only under section 5 of the Act,[1] and to the provisions of section 3 (3), which is concerned with cases in which leave has been granted to petition for divorce within three years of the date of the marriage.

Leave to Petition for Divorce.

Section 3 of the Act requires the leave of a judge to be obtained before a petition for divorce can be filed within three years of the date of marriage, and provides that this leave shall only be given on the ground that the case is one of exceptional hardship suffered by the petitioner or of exceptional depravity by the respondent. This does not mean that a petition cannot be based upon matters which occur during this period[2] but only that unless the circumstances are exceptional proceedings must be delayed until the three years have expired and the parties will thus be deterred from overhasty attempts to end their marriage at the first signs of discord.

Applications under the section are heard in chambers and the decisions are therefore usually not reported, but some indication of the way in which the discretion is exercised can be gathered from reports of appeals to the Court of Appeal. These make it clear that the discretion is that of the judge who hears the application, and that the Court of Appeal will not interfere with his decision unless he has applied some wrong principle, or failed to have regard to some

---

[1] See *post*, p. 54.
[2] S. 3(4).

consideration which is relevant, or some grave injustice has been done.[3] The emphasis in reported decisions is upon the word "exceptional". There is always hardship in the early breakdown of a marriage, but the hardship or depravity must be something beyond that which is ordinary. The test of hardship is subjective, so that possible injury to the health of the proposed petitioner is relevant,[4] and the word "depravity" is not confined to sexual perversions.[5] Thus adultery in the early stages of the marriage is not exceptional, nor is the fact that this adultery has led to the birth of a child of whom the husband is the father, or that as a result the wife is pregnant by another man.[6] There must in addition be some aggravating circumstances, such as violence, or promiscuous adultery by a husband with several women, or his adultery with his wife's sister.[7]

Having reached a decision that the case is exceptional, the judge is then expressly required by the section to have regard:—

(1) to the interests of any child of the family as defined in section 52 of the Act, which is fully considered on p. 113. It suffices at this point to note that it can include not only a child of both the parties to the marriage but also any other child, no matter who the parents may be, who has been treated by both of these parties as a child of their family;

(2) to the question whether there is reasonable probability of a reconciliation between the parties during the three years.

But the above matters are not exclusive of other matters so that, for example, the court could give weight to the fact that an applicant unreasonably refuses to entertain any overtures for reconciliation.[8]

Where the parties have separated before the expiration of the three year period, but the facts are such that leave to petition for divorce cannot be obtained, a wife who is in need of maintenance can apply to a divorce county court under section 27 of the Act[9] or to a magistrates' court under the Matrimonial Proceedings (Magistrates' Courts) Act 1960[10] for financial provision on the ground of her husband's wilful failure to provide reasonable maintenance for her or any child of the family. Indeed, since the need for leave relates only to suits for divorce, she could petition without leave for a decree of judicial separation, or apply for a matrimonial order from a magistrates' court, on the very facts on which she would have wished to rely in a suit for divorce. Such a decree or order would enable the court to make suitable financial provision for her or a child of the family, would in no way prejudice her chances of divorce on the same facts when the three year period was completed, and would indeed facilitate the proof of her case when her divorce petition came to be heard.[11]

Section 3 (3) provides that if it appears to the court, at the hearing of a

---

[3] *Winter* v. *Winter*, [1944] P. 72; *Charlesby* v. *Charlesby* (1947), 176 L.T. 532.
[4] *C.* v. *C.*, [1967] P. 298.
[5] *G.* v. *G.* (1968), 112 Sol. Jo. 481.
[6] *W.* v. *W.*, [1967] P. 291.
[7] *Bowman* v. *Bowman*, [1949] P. 353.
[8] *C.* v. *C. supra, per* Sir JOCELYN SIMON, P.
[9] See *post*, Chapter 10.
[10] See *post*, Chapter 17.
[11] See s. 4 (2) and *post*, p. 43.

petition for divorce presented in pursuance of such leave, that the leave was obtained by the petitioner by any misrepresentation or concealment of the nature of the case, the court may either (a) dismiss the petition, without prejudice to the right to petition again upon the same, or substantially the same, facts after the expiration of a period of three years from the date of the marriage; or (b) if it grants a decree, direct that no application to make the decree absolute shall be made during that period. It has been held, however, in *Stroud* v. *Stroud (No. 2)*[12] that these restrictions on the powers of the trial judge apply only when the petitioner has been guilty of some deliberate misrepresentation or concealment. If, as in that case, the court considers that the petitioner honestly believed in her charges that her husband had been guilty of perverse sexual practices which led to the grant of leave, but at the trial she has proved only an ordinary case of cruelty, the decree nisi granted to her can be directed to be made absolute within the ordinary time without awaiting the end of the three year period.

THE PROOF OF IRRETRIEVABLE BREAKDOWN

There are two matters of which the court must be satisfied before it can grant a decree of divorce. The only ground is that the marriage has broken down irretrievably; the only way in which the breakdown may be proved is by satisfying the court of one or more of the five facts specified in section 1 (2) of the Act. The Act lays down that it is the duty of the court to inquire, so far as it reasonably can, into the facts alleged by the petitioner and into any facts alleged by the respondent.[13] If the court is satisfied on the evidence of any of the five facts, then the Act requires that it "shall grant a decree of divorce, unless it is satisfied on all the evidence that the marriage has not broken down irretrievably".[14] This is subject to the defence of grave hardship under section 5 (see *post*, p. 54) and to the special situation which arises when it appears at the trial that leave to petition for divorce within three years of the date of the marriage was wrongly obtained.[15] Subject to these provisions, a petition may therefore fail for one of two reasons.

(1) *That the petitioner has failed to prove any of the facts mentioned in section 1 (2) of the Act.*

Section 1 (2) of the Act deals clearly with the onus of proof of these facts; it says that the court shall not hold that the marriage has broken down irretrievably unless the petitioner satisfies the court of one or more of the facts specified in the sub-section. The Act is less clear as to the standard of proof. The wording of section 1 (3) and (4) corresponds closely to that of section 5 (1) and (3) of the Matrimonial Causes Act 1965, which is now repealed. Both Acts provide that on a petition for divorce "it shall be the duty of the court to inquire, so far as it reasonably can" into the facts alleged. The Act of 1965 laid

---

[12] [1963] 3 All E.R. 539.
[13] S. 1 (3).
[14] S. 1 (4).
[15] *Supra.*

down that the court shall grant a decree "if satisfied on the evidence that the case for the petition has been proved" and of the absence of any bars. The Act of 1973, s. 1 (4), likewise provides that the court shall grant a decree nisi "if satisfied on the evidence of any such fact as is mentioned in sub-section (2) of this section" unless satisfied on all the evidence that the breakdown is not irretrievable.

In spite of the close similarity in wording, experience since the Act of 1969 came into force indicates that a change has been effected in the standard of proof required. At one time there were decisions, following the practice of the ecclesiastical courts, that since adultery was a serious offence—a quasi-crime—it had to be proved beyond reasonable doubt, with the same strictness as a criminal charge in criminal proceedings.[16] Certainly, proof beyond reasonable doubt was required in cases in which proof of adultery would bastardize a child born to the wife.[17] Some dicta in the House of Lords in *Blyth* v. *Blyth*[18] (where the point was not directly in issue) suggested that, apart from cases where legitimacy was involved, this standard was too high. But the Court of Appeal in *Bastable* v. *Bastable*[19] considered that although proof beyond reasonable doubt might not be essential, these dicta went too far. There were similar difficulties as to the need for corroboration of charges of cruelty.[20]

But the object of the Act of 1969 was to sweep away the matrimonial offence as the basis for divorce and it seems clear that in consequence all previous decisions, based upon the gravity of these offences, are no longer law. Certainly as regards adultery, the standard required can be no more than proof upon a balance of probabilities, as is instanced by the *Practice Direction* referred to on p. 20, *post*. The Family Law Reform Act 1969, s. 26, which took effect from January 1, 1970, provides that any presumption of law as to the legitimacy or illegitimacy of any person may in any civil proceedings be rebutted by evidence which shows that it is more probable than not that the person is illegitimate or legitimate, as the case may be, and it shall not be necessary to prove that fact beyond reasonable doubt in order to rebut the presumption. It would be strange indeed if the court were to hold that more cogent evidence was needed to prove the fact of adulterous intercourse which led to the child's conception. If this view be accepted, it would seem to follow that the same must be true of the other facts specified in section 1 (2), none of which have hitherto, in their guise of matrimonial offences, been regarded as more serious than adultery.

(2) *That despite the proof of one or more of the specified facts the court should not be satisfied that the breakdown is irretrievable.*

The onus of proof here is presumably upon the respondent, though the Act does not expressly say so. Nor is it specific as to the standard of proof, saying only that a decree nisi shall be granted unless the court "is satisfied on

---

[16] E.g. *Ginesi* v. *Ginesi*, [1948] P. 179; *Fairman* v. *Fairman*, [1949] P. 341.
[17] *F.* v. *F.* (*No. 2*), [1968] P. 506.
[18] [1966] A.C. 643.
[19] [1968] 3 All E.R. 701.
[20] *Kafton* v. *Kafton*, [1948] 1 All E.R. 435; *Hodgkins* v. *Hodgkins*, [1950] P. 183.

all the evidence" that the breakdown is not irretrievable. But having regard to what has been said in respect of the standard of proof of such matters as adultery, it seems unlikely that the standard required here is more than the same balance of probabilities.

Viewed from another angle, the question of whether the breakdown is irretrievable depends upon whether or not there is any prospect of reconciliation, and experience hitherto has shown that once the spouses have reached the stage of proceedings for divorce the chances of reconciliation are slim. In accordance with section 6 (1) of the Act, the Rules provide that where a solicitor is acting for a petitioner for divorce, a certificate in Form 3 must be filed with the petition. This form will be found in Appendix II, *post.* It will be seen that it requires the solicitor to certify whether he has discussed with the petitioner the possibility of reconciliation and given him the names and addresses of persons qualified to help effect a reconciliation between parties to a marriage who have become estranged. The Act does not require him to certify in all cases that he *has* discussed the matter with the petitioner, for there are obviously cases in which it would be ludicrous to do so, as where a deserting wife is living with another man by whom she has borne several children. A *Practice Direction*[1] emphasises that

> "The object of the section and of the rule made pursuant to it is to ensure that parties know where to seek guidance when there is a sincere desire for a reconciliation; it is important that reference to a marriage guidance counsellor or a probation officer should not be regarded as a formal step which must be taken in all cases irrespective of whether or not there is any prospect of a reconciliation."

Section 6 (2) provides that if at any stage of proceedings for divorce it appears to the court that there is a reasonable possibility of reconciliation between the parties to the marriage, it may adjourn the proceedings to enable attempts to be made to effect such a reconciliation, this power being additional to any other power of the court to adjourn proceedings. It seems unlikely that this power would be exercised where the parties had lived apart for five years, or where they had lived apart for two years and the respondent consented to a decree being granted, particularly if they had lived together during the relevant periods in unsuccessful attempts at reconciliation. The power appears more appropriate to cases falling within the first three "facts", particularly if there are children of the marriage, but little advantage appears to have been taken of it in practice.

The Act is not specific as to the date on which irretrievability must be established, though at first sight the wording of section 1 (1) suggests that it must be established at the date when the proceedings are begun, since it provides that "a petition for divorce may be presented ... on the ground that the marriage has broken down irretrievably." But in *Pheasant* v. *Pheasant*[2] ORMROD, J., took the view that the provisions as to reconciliation, and as to the court's power to adjourn the case for that purpose, showed clearly that this was

---

[1] [1972] 3 All E.R. 768.
[2] [1972] Fam. 202.

not the intention, and that it is sufficient if the petitioner establishes that the breakdown has become irretrievable by the date of the hearing. A similar conclusion was reached in *Goodrich* v. *Goodrich*,[3] where a husband obtained a decree notwithstanding the fact that he had been willing to consider the possibility of reconciliation right up to the last moment.

It might also seem that if the petitioner goes into the witness box and declares on oath "I will never live with this man (or this woman) again" the court could hardly refuse to hold that the breakdown was irretrievable. It may well be, however, that this view will not prevail. In *Roper* v. *Roper* FAULKS, J., dealing with the not dissimilar point under section 1 (2) (a) of whether the petitioner found it intolerable to live with the respondent, held that the court was not required to accept the petitioner's word in this respect. When the Act says "the petitioner finds it intolerable" it does not mean "the petitioner says she finds it intolerable".[4]

IRRETRIEVABLE BREAKDOWN: "THE FIVE FACTS"

(a) *That the respondent has committed adultery and the petitioner finds it intolerable to live with the respondent.*

There are thus two matters here which require separate consideration—adultery and intolerability.

(i) *Adultery.*

In effect the court is here required to consider one of the former grounds for divorce, not as a ground, but as an indication of breakdown of the marriage. In fact, as the Law Commission has observed, the commission of such a matrimonial offence normally follows the breakdown of marriage and is not the cause of it. To quote the favourite dictum of VAISEY, J., in ward of court cases—"it takes three to commit adultery".[5]

Adultery may be defined as voluntary sexual intercourse between two persons who are not married to each other but one or both of whom are married to a third person. Section 1 (2)(a) does not expressly require that the adultery upon which reliance is placed should have occurred since the celebration of the marriage. Nevertheless it seems unlikely that the court would allow the petitioner to rely on the respondent's adultery before the marriage since this would lead to the illogical result that reliance could be placed on pre-marital intercourse with a third person who was already married, but not upon such intercourse with an unmarried third party.

To amount to adultery the intercourse must be voluntary. It follows that a wife who is the victim of rape is not guilty of adultery, though the onus is upon her to prove that she did not consent ;[6] the man who raped her is of course guilty of adultery. For the same reason it was held in *S.* v. *S.*[7] that a person who is insane within the meaning of the M'Naghten rules, in that he did not

[3] [1971] 2 All E.R. 1340.
[4] [1972] 3 All E.R. 668 at p. 670.
[5] Quoted by ORMROD, J., in *Wachtel* v. Wachtel, [1973] 2 W.L.R. 84, 90.
[6] *Redpath* v. *Redpath and Milligan*, [1950] 1 All E.R. 600.
[7] [1962] P. 133.

know the nature and quality of his act or (if he knew this) that he did not know that what he was doing was morally wrong, could not be found guilty of adultery. It is not necessary to a finding of adultery that the act of intercourse should have been completed, but there must have been at least some penetration.[8] The fact that a woman is found to be virgo intacta is not necessarily inconsistent with such partial penetration as would constitute adultery, though the burden of proof upon the petitioner in such a case would be heavy.[9]

The general question of the burden and standard of proof of the various facts set out in section 1 (2) of the Act has already been considered.[10] It is at this point, however, convenient to refer to certain matters particularly affecting proof of adultery.

In the nature of things, the direct evidence of eye-witnesses is seldom available, and reliance must be placed upon circumstantial evidence. This should be directed to showing both intention or inclination and the opportunity to gratify it, and proof will be required of the actual adultery alleged in the petition, though evidence of adultery, or undue familiarity falling short of adultery, between the same parties on other occasions, is admissible as indicating what inference the court should draw from the evidence concerning the occasions to which the petition refers.[11] The inference of adultery will normally be drawn from the fact that the parties concerned have spent the night together in the same bedroom.[12] But it is not an inference which must be drawn, and the court will sometimes accept evidence of some other and innocent explanation, such as the illness of one of the parties[13] or might reach the conclusion that no intercourse had in fact taken place but an attempt had been made to fabricate evidence in an effort to expedite the dissolution of the marriage. Despite the changes in the law, there will still be some temptation to do this rather than to accept the delay occasioned by awaiting the completion of, for example, two years' separation under section 1 (2) (d).

Confessions of adultery are admissible in evidence, though they may be viewed with some suspicion.[14] They not infrequently result from investigations by an inquiry agent who will often find that, for example, a husband who has left his wife is living with another woman whom he wishes to be free to marry. In practice an inquiry agent will normally caution a person whom he wishes to interview. In *Hathaway* v. *Hathaway*[15] the President, after observing that there seems to be no rule of law or practice which renders an admission to an inquiry agent inadmissible in evidence unless such a caution is given, added that he wished to say nothing to discourage the practice of giving such cautions. Where, however, as in that case, a person who has been cautioned refuses to make any statement, no adverse inference can be drawn from his failure to deny adultery, save in exceptional circumstances.

---

[8] *Dennis* v. *Dennis*, [1955] P. 153; *Sapsford* v. *Sapsford and Furtado*, [1954] P. 394.
[9] *Thompson* v. *Thompson*, [1939] P. 1.
[10] See *ante*, p. 15 *et seq.*
[11] *Wales* v. *Wales*, [1900] P. 63.
[12] *Woolf* v. *Woolf*, [1931] P. 134.
[13] As in *England* v. *England*, [1953] P. 16.
[14] The possibility of obtaining admissions of adultery by means of interrogatories is discussed in Chapter 16.
[15] [1970] 2 All E.R. 701.

In many cases a respondent spouse will have signed an admission of adultery in the form of a statement in writing to an inquiry agent or a letter to the petitioner. In such cases proof of the adultery will usually present little difficulty. By a *Practice Direction*,[16] in undefended proceedings for divorce a statement in writing signed by the respondent admitting the adultery can be put in at the hearing, the respondent's signature being identified by the petitioner. Where this is done it should normally be unnecessary either to call as a witness, or to put in affidavit evidence from, the inquiry agent or other person who merely took the statement from the respondent. It is obviously advantageous for a respondent who does not wish to defend the proceedings to save costs by providing such a statement. Where for some special reason the evidence of an inquiry agent is necessary in an undefended case it should normally be given by affidavit, and leave to do this may be sought from the judge at the hearing without the need for a prior application to the registrar. Although a confession of adultery by a respondent spouse with a named person may under the Civil Evidence Act 1968 be admissible evidence against that person[17] the trial judge has to decide under section 6 of that Act what weight is to be attached to it. The *Practice Note* is not intended to disturb the recognised practice of obtaining a confession from the named person as well as from the respondent spouse.

This *Practice Direction* clearly demonstrates the departure from the rule which at one time existed whereby adultery was required to be proved with the same strictness as a criminal charge in criminal proceedings, so that even if the wife gave evidence of her adultery in the witness box, she was regarded as the accomplice of the man with whom she admitted it and a finding of adultery against him based upon that evidence could not stand unless the judge had indicated the danger of accepting her evidence without corroboration.[19] There is no such strict rule in matrimonial proceedings today, though the wife's evidence might be received with some suspicion if the court thought that it resulted from the fury of a "woman scorned".

Adultery can sometimes be established by showing that the respondent spouse is suffering from venereal disease. If the disease existed at the date of the marriage it may be a ground for nullity.[20] If it was contracted subsequently, otherwise than from the petitioner, it is prima facie evidence of adultery, the onus being upon the respondent to rebut the presumption that it was contracted as a result of intercourse with some person other than the petitioner.[1]

In some cases a husband may seek to rely upon the birth of a child to his wife after a period of non-access by him as sufficient proof of her adultery. In such cases, although the House of Lords agreed in *Preston-Jones* v. *Preston-Jones*[2] that the court can take judicial notice of the fact that there is a normal period of gestation of 270 to 280 days, it was recognised that considerable variations occurred in practice, and doubts must be determined by medical evidence. In

---

[16] [1973] 3 All E.R. 180.
[17] The decision in *Rutherford* v. *Richardson*, [1923] A.C. 1 is thus no longer law.
[19] *Galler* v. *Galler*, [1954] P. 252; *Fairman* v. *Fairman*, [1949] P. 341.
[20] See *post*, pp. 75 and 78.
[1] *Butler* v. *Butler*, [1917] P. 244; *Anthony* v. *Anthony* (1919), 35 T.L.R. 559.
[2] [1951] A.C. 391.

that case the House declined to hold that a period so long as 360 days could of itself create a presumption of adultery, but held that the evidence of a general medical practitioner that such a period was impossible should have been accepted as sufficient. Medical evidence based on such matters as the size of the child at birth may account for the fact that adultery was presumed in a case where the period of non-access was 340 days[3] but not in a case where it was so long as 349 days.[4]

Where the parties have been living apart under a decree of judicial separation or a matrimonial order of a magistrates' court containing a provision that the parties are no longer bound to cohabit,[5] there is a presumption that the husband has not had intercourse with the wife since the date of the decree or order, the onus being then upon the wife to rebut the presumption.[6] But there is no such presumption when the parties are separated by agreement, or under a magistrates' order for maintenance only,[7] and in such cases it is for the husband to prove that he has not had intercourse with his wife during the relevant period. Both husband and wife are competent and compellable to give evidence as to whether or not marital intercourse took place between them during any period, and have no longer any privilege entitling them to refuse to answer questions the answers to which might tend to show that they have committed adultery.[8]

In cases in which the husband seeks to rely upon the birth of a child to his wife after a period of non-access by him, advantage may be taken of another recent statute, Part III of the Family Law Reform Act 1969, in order to prove by means of blood tests that the child was conceived in adultery. Subject to numerous safeguards, section 20 of this Act provides that in any civil proceedings in which the paternity of any person falls to be determined by the court hearing the proceedings, the court may, on the applications of any party to the proceedings, give a direction for the use of blood tests to ascertain whether such tests show that a party to the proceedings is or is not thereby excluded from being the father of that person, and for the taking, for the purpose of these tests, of blood samples from that person, the mother of that person and any person alleged to be the father of that person. The decision in *W.* v. *W. (No. 4)*[9] to the effect that an adult cannot be ordered to provide a blood sample, remains, and section 21 provides that a blood sample shall not be taken from a person without his consent. The consent of a minor aged 16 or over is as effective as if he were of full age, and no other consent is required. If the minor has not reached the age of 16, the consent of the person who has the care and control of him suffices. Special provision[10] is made for the case of persons suffering from mental disorders.

---

[3] *M.-T.* v. *M.-T. and Official Solicitor,* [1949] P. 331.
[4] *Hadlum* v. *Hadlum,* [1949] P. 197.
[5] See *post,* p. 44, and Chapter 17.
[6] *Ettenfield* v. *Ettenfield,* [1940] P. 96.
[7] *Ibid.*
[8] S. 48 (1). For the history of this matter see the Law Commission's Report on consolidation of the law, upon which the Matrimonial Causes Act 1973 is based (Law Com. No. 51, para. 10).
[9] [1964] P. 67.
[10] S. 21 (4).

Provision is also made for the possibility that a person may fail to take some step required of him for the purpose of giving effect to the court's directions. This might arise from, for example, complete refusal to provide a blood sample. In such a case, section 23 (1) provides that the court may draw such inferences, if any, from that fact as appear proper in the circumstances, the normal inference obviously being that that person has good reason to fear what the test may show. Yet another possibility is covered by section 23 (2). It might well happen that a wife might refuse to comply with the court's directions because, should it prove that her husband was thereby excluded from being the father of her child, he could not be compelled to maintain that child; or a husband might refuse because he was fond of the child, and should he be excluded from being the child's father, he might not be granted custody of or access to the child. The sub-section therefore provides that if a party who is claiming relief in any proceedings, and who is entitled for that purpose to rely on a presumption of law that the child is legitimate, fails to comply with the court's directions, the court may adjourn the hearing for such period as it thinks fit to enable him to do so and, if he fails to comply, may dismiss his claim for relief notwithstanding the absence of evidence to rebut the presumption.

Regulations have been made under the Act[11] as to the manner of giving effect to the court's directions. It provides also for the report to be made, and the right to call as a witness the person who made it,[12] and for the question of costs.[13]

Finally, it should be observed that section 20 does not provide that the court *must* give directions for the use of blood tests if a party applies for such a direction, but only that it *may* do so. Before the Act the tendency, in cases concerning the inherent power of the High Court to order a blood test on an infant, was to hold that such an order should only be made when it was in the best interests of the child. Thus in *B.(B.R.)* v. *B.(J)*,[14] where it was clear that the father was either the husband or the co-respondent, an order was made because it would be in the infant's interests to know who his father was. In *M.(D.)* v. *M.(S.)*,[15] where the father was either the husband or a man unknown, the order was refused since, should the tests prove that the husband was not the father, the infant would know he was illegitimate but have no idea who his father might be. This approach was condemned by the House of Lords in *S.* v. *S.*,[16] as being based upon the provisions relating to custody of infants where, in accordance with the Guardianship of Minors Act 1971, s. 1, the welfare of the minor is the first and paramount consideration. When the issue before the court is the legitimacy of a child, and the inference of adultery which will follow if the child is illegitimate, it is in the interests of justice that the court shall have before it the best evidence available, and the interests of the child are best served if the truth is ascertained. To quote Lord HODSON[17]

---

[11] The Blood Test (Evidence of Paternity) Regulations 1971. See also R.S.C. Ord. 112, C.C.R. Ord. 46, r. 23 and Magistrates' Courts (Blood Tests) Rules 1971.

[12] S. 20, (2)–(5).

[13] S. 20 (6).

[14] [1968] P. 466.

[15] [1969] 2 All E.R. 243.

[16] [1972] A.C. 24.

[17] *Ibid.*, at p. 57.

"whatever may have been the position in the past the general attitude towards illegitimacy has changed and the legal incidents of being born a bastard are now almost non-existent"

and again

"there must be few cases where the interests of children can be shown to be best served by the suppression of the truth"

In the result the decision was that the court ought to permit a blood test of a young child to be taken, not only in cases in which it would be in the best interests of the child, but unless the court was satisfied that this would clearly be against the child's interest—by no means a distinction without a difference.

Three of the Law Lords[18] also considered the position under section 20 (1) of the Family Law Reform Act which was not then in operation. They were of opinion that the courts which were called upon to exercise the discretion conferred by this section, which would include county courts and magistrates' courts as well as the High Court, should not regard their discretion as unfettered. The principles settled by superior courts must be regarded as binding, and will presumably follow the general lines laid down by the House of Lords in *S. v. S.*

(ii) *Intolerability.*

The Divorce Reform Act 1969 introduced for the first time the concept that there are other matters more destructive of marriage than a single act of adultery (which had previously sufficed as a ground for divorce), and that many marriages have survived such a set-back. This view-point was, perhaps inaptly, put forward in the Committee Stage of the Bill by a Member of Parliament who suggested that a spouse should not be divorced for adultery "pure and simple".

Nevertheless it is difficult to see that the Act has effectively dealt with this problem by the additional requirement that the petitioner must find it intolerable to live with the respondent. The words "the petitioner" show clearly that the test is subjective—that of the feelings of this petitioner himself or herself—and not those of a supposedly reasonable petitioner who rides to and from Clapham on an omnibus.

The Act is silent upon the question of whether or not the intolerability must result from the adultery, and there were conflicting decisions on this point. In *Goodrich* v. *Goodrich*[19] the petitioning husband did not find it intolerable to live with his wife because of her adultery but because of her adamant refusal to consider a reconciliation. LLOYD-JONES, J., held that the requirements are independent of each other and granted a decree. But in *Roper* v. *Roper*,[20] where there were cross-prayers for divorce based on adultery, FAULKS, J., held that the meaning of the section was that "in consequence of the adultery the petitioner finds it intolerable to live with the respondent". He further held that the words "the petitioner finds it intolerable" do not mean "the petitioner says she finds it intolerable" and refused the wife a decree because he did not believe her evidence on the point but thought that she merely found there was another man who was more sexually attractive. The doubt has been resolved by the

---

[18] Lords REID, HODSON and GUEST.
[19] [1971] 2 All E. R. 1340.
[20] [1972] 3 All E.R. 668.

decision in the Court of Appeal in *Cleary* v. *Cleary*[21] that since the subsection does not contain the words "in consequence of the adultery", it is not permissible to read those words into it.

The Act contains a number of provisions aimed at ensuring that the parties shall not be deterred from attempts at reconciliation by the fear that, should these attempts fail, they will be fatal to the chances of a subsequent petition for divorce. In relation to adultery section 2 of the Act contains two provisions:—

(1) One party to a marriage shall not be entitled to rely for the purposes of section 1 (2) (*a*) on adultery committed by the other if, after it became known to him that the other had committed that adultery, the parties have lived with each other for a period exceeding, or periods together exceeding, six months. Thus if the parties have lived together for more than the permitted six months, this will constitute an absolute bar to consideration of prior adultery as an indication of breakdown, and resort must be had, if breakdown is to be proved, to some other provision in section 1 (2).

(2) Where the above provision does not apply, as where the periods of life together after discovery of the adultery do not amount to six months, the fact that they have lived together after it became known to one party that the other had committed adultery is to be disregarded in determining for the purposes of section 1 (2) (*a*) whether the petitioner finds it intolerable to live with the respondent.

By virtue of section 2 (6), references in the section to the parties to the marriage living with each other are to be construed as references to their living with each other in the same household. Section 2 appears to have avoided difficulties which arose from a somewhat similar provision in sections 1 (2) and 42 (2) of the Act of 1965. Both these sub-sections referred to the parties cohabiting for one period not exceeding three months, which was to be disregarded in calculating a period of desertion and in determining whether adultery or cruelty has been condoned if it was proved that they did so "*with a view to reconciliation*". It was held in *Brown* v. *Brown*[1] that if cohabitation was resumed because they were reconciled, or they became reconciled during the period of three months and later parted before its expiration, advantage could not be taken of either subsection. The provision in the present Act makes no reference to the reason why they have lived together, so that it will be immaterial whether they did so in the hope of, or because of, a reconciliation. What is more, the reference to one single period is replaced by one or more periods, and their duration together extended from three to six months.

(b) *That the respondent has behaved in such a way that the petitioner cannot reasonably be expected to live with the respondent.*

When the Divorce Reform Act 1969 came into operation there was little or no direct authority upon how this "guide line" to irretrievable breakdown would operate in practice. Clearly it comprises much of the ground covered by

---

[21] [1974] All E.R. 498, C. A.
[1] [1967] P. 105; see also *Quinn* v. *Quinn*, [1969] 3 All E.R. 1212.

the former matrimonial offences, but with very important variations. Thus it can cover the former grounds of:—

(i) *Cruelty*, but without the requirement laid down by the House of Lords in *Russell* v. *Russell*[2] that the conduct complained of must have been such as to cause injury, or a reasonable apprehension of injury, to life, limb or health, bodily or mental. Proof of such injury must always be highly relevant in determining what can be expected of the petitioner, but it is no longer essential to support charges of cruelty by medical evidence.

(ii) *Constructive desertion*, consisting, to use the words of Sir Jocelyn SIMON, P.,[3] of "such grave and weighty misconduct that the only sensible inference is that he [the respondent] knew that the complainant would in all probability withdraw permanently from cohabitation with him if she acted like any reasonable person in her position". It seems unlikely that a petitioner who has been driven to separation by conduct of this nature will in future await the completion of the period of two years' desertion required by section 1 (2) (c) of the Act. Instead he can, if he wishes, proceed immediately under section 1 (2) (b) and constructive (as opposed to actual) desertion has ceased to figure as such in divorce proceedings, though it will still be relevant in a magistrates' court.[4]

(iii) *The husband's sodomy or bestiality*, at all events since the celebration of the marriage, in that his wife could hardly be expected to live with him thereafter. The provisions of the Civil Evidence Act 1968, s. 11, will enable the fact that he has been convicted of these offences to be given in evidence[5] as in the case of conviction for rape, which constitutes adultery on his part though not on the part of his victim. Moreover proof of, or convictions for, attempts to commit these offences, which previously were not of themselves sufficient grounds for a wife's petition for divorce, are likely to constitute conduct within the ambit of this guideline, as are also unnatural practices by a wife with another woman, which have not hitherto been grounds for a husband's petition, unless in the circumstances his health suffered, so that he could allege cruelty.[6]

(iv) *Behaviour resulting from forms of unsoundness of mind*, without the former requirement that it should be incurable and accompanied by five years' care and treatment.

This list is in no way intended to be exhaustive: there might yet fall within the ambit of this heading such matters, at present largely unresolved in England, as the conduct of a wife who, without her husband's consent, submits to artificial insemination by a donor, or that of a spouse who, after the marriage, elects to undergo an operation resulting in a change of sex.

As in the case of adultery provision is made by section 2 (3) of the Act to ensure that the parties are not deterred from attempts at reconciliation. Where the petitioner relies upon this "fact" but the parties to the marriage have lived with each other for a period or periods after the date of the occurrence

---

[2] [1897] A.C. 395.
[3] In *Saunders* v. *Saunders*, [1965] P. 499, 504.
[4] See *post*, Chapter 17.
[5] *Post*, p. 48.
[6] *Gardner* v. *Gardner*, [1947] 1 All E.R. 630; *Spicer* v. *Spicer*, [1954] 3 All E.R. 208.

of the final incident relied on by the petitioner and held by the court to support his allegation, that fact is to be disregarded in determining whether the petitioner cannot reasonably be expected to live with the respondent if the length of that period or of those periods together was six months or less. The wording is different from that of section 2 (1) in relation to adultery, whereby after a period or periods of life together exceeding six months in all reliance cannot be placed upon that adultery for the purposes of section 1 (2) (*a*). Section 2 (3) does not say that after periods of life together exceeding six months in all no earlier behaviour can be relied upon for purposes of section 1 (2) (*b*). It says only that lesser periods of life together are to be disregarded in determining whether the petitioner cannot reasonably be expected to live with the respondent. It would still be open to the court to find that despite longer periods of life together the total effect of the respondent's behaviour during the marriage, including adultery which was no longer available under section 1 (2) (*a*), was such that the requirements of section 1 (2) (*b*) had been satisfied. Indeed in *Bradley* v. *Bradley*[7] it was held that it might be possible for a wife to obtain a decree although her family circumstances were such that she was still compelled to live with her husband and share a bed with him at the date when the petition was heard.

But although this "fact" may cover what have hitherto been regarded as matrimonial offences, it is essential to appreciate that it is no longer to be regarded in this light. As ORMROD, J. observed in *Pheasant* v. *Pheasant*,[8] "It would be consistent if this problem were to be approached more from the point of view of breach of obligation than in terms of the now out-moded idea of the matrimonial offence."

The most convenient way in which to examine the problem in practice is to sub-divide it and examine the essential elements separately.

1. *The behaviour*

If the court is to be satisfied that this "fact" has been proved, there must have been some action or conduct by the one spouse which affects the other. Behaviour is something more than a mere state of affairs or a state of mind. It may take the form of an act or omission or may be a course of conduct, and must have some reference to the marriage.[9] Thus a repugnance to sexual intercourse would not of itself suffice and neither would a husband's feeling that his wife against whom he made no specific charges was unable to show him the spontaneous, demonstrative affection which his nature demanded.[10]

As ORMROD, J., observed in *Pheasant* v. *Pheasant*, the test to be applied is closely similar to, but not necessarily identical with, that formerly used in relation to constructive desertion. His Lordship however, added[11]

"I would not wish to see carried over into the new law all the technicalities which accumulated round the idea of constructive desertion but rather to

---

[7] [1973] 3 All E.R. 750, C. A.
[8] [1972] Fam. 202, 208.
[9] *Katz* v. *Katz*, [1972] 3 All E.R. 219, 223.
[10] *Pheasant* v. *Pheasant, supra.*
[11] [1972] Fam. 202, 208.

use the broader approach indicated by PEARCE, J.,·in *Lissack* v. *Lissack*[12] and consider whether it is reasonable to expect this petitioner to put up with the behaviour of this respondent bearing in mind the characters and difficulties of each of them, trying to be fair to both of them, and expecting neither heroic virtue nor selfless abnegation from either."

2. *"Reasonably"*

It is important to appreciate that the test to be applied is what can "reasonably be expected" of the petitioner. To quote again from ORMROD, J.[13]

"The question is not whether the respondent has behaved unreasonably and the court is no longer required, except marginally, to pass judgment on whether a person's behaviour is right or wrong, good or bad."

The question is whether, having regard to the behaviour, it is reasonable to expect the petitioner to go on living with the respondent.

It follows that a decree will not be refused merely because the respondent's behaviour resulted from mental illness. As was the case in relation to the former matrimonial offence of cruelty, it is not essential to prove a malign intention to injure or inflict misery on the petitioner,[14] and the fact that through insanity the respondent is incapable of forming such an intention is no bar to the grant of a decree.[15] A decree was granted to a wife under the new law in *Katz* v. *Katz*[16] although his behaviour resulted from a manic depressive illness, though the test of "breach of obligation" proposed in *Pheasant* v. *Pheasant*[17] is difficult to apply in a case of this kind. The question is, of course, one of fact and degree in each individual case, and due allowance must be made for the fact that the respondent's behaviour resulted from ill-health, whether mental or physical. It was, no doubt, for this reason that a decree was refused in *Richards* v. *Richards*,[18] where the behaviour, and the illness, were less severe. Nor must it be supposed from what has been said on this subject that the respondent's intention is irrelevant in reaching a decision, a point which was well expressed by Lord NORMAND in *Jamieson* v. *Jamieson*,[19] when he said

"Actual intention to hurt is a circumstance of peculiar importance because conduct which is intended to hurt strikes with a sharper edge than conduct which is the consequence of mere obtuseness or indifference."

3. *"The petitioner" and "the respondent"*

In one sense the phrase "cannot reasonably be expected to live with the respondent" poses an objective test, in contrast to the expression "the petitioner finds it intolerable to live with the respondent" in section 1 (2) (*a*). But the words "the petitioner" and "the respondent" do not refer to ordinary reasonable

[12] [1951] P. 1.
[13] *Carew-Hunt* v. *Carew-Hunt* (1972), *Times*, June 28.
[14] *Gollins* v. *Gollins*, [1964] A.C. 644.
[15] *Williams* v. *Williams*, [1964] A.C. 698.
[16] [1972] 3 All E.R. 219.
[17] *Ante*, p. 26.
[18] [1972] 3 All E.R. 695.
[19] [1952] A.C. 525, 535.

spouses who are placed in that position, but to the actual persons concerned in the case. This was made clear by BAGNALL, J., in *Ash* v. *Ash*[20]

> "The general question may be expanded thus: can this petitioner with his or her character and personality, with his or her faults and other attributes, good and bad, and having regard to his or her behaviour during the marriage, reasonably be expected to live with this respondent?"

His Lordship added—

> "Then, if I may give a few examples, it seems to me that a violent petitioner can reasonably be expected to live with a violent respondent; a petitioner who is addicted to drink can reasonably be expected to live with a respondent similarly addicted; a taciturn and morose spouse can reasonably be expected to live with a taciturn and morose partner; a flirtatious husband can reasonably be expected to live with a wife who is equally susceptible to the attractions of the opposite sex; and if each is equally bad, at any rate in similar respects, each can reasonably be expected to live with the other."

Examples

As SCARMAN, L.J., said in *Trippas* v. *Trippas*,[1] "In construing a reforming statute it is wrong, in my view, to pay regard to cases that were decided before the Act was enacted."

As was formerly the case in relation to cruelty[2] and in relation to constructive desertion,[3] the courts have refrained from any attempt at an exhaustive definition of behaviour which would, or would not, suffice. Indeed such a definition would be impossible. Each case raises a question of fact and degree.

Nevertheless it may be helpful to take some examples of conduct which justified the grant of a decree before the Act of 1969 came into operation, and which would be likely to suffice today.

Serious violence in the shape of kicks and blows obviously suffices[4] though an occasional blow struck in temper might not, of itself, and nor would mere frailty of temper.[5] Whether drunkenness will suffice is a question of degree: sometimes it may fall within the no-man's land where it must be a question of fact: sometimes it may make matrimonial cohabitation virtually impossible.[6] A wife petitioner might succeed on proof of her husband's inordinate sexual demands,[7] or the fact that he had denied her the chance of bearing a child by insistence upon the practice of coitus interruptus[8] or upon the use of contraceptives, or by undergoing an operation for sterilisation without her consent.[9]

---

[20] [1972] Fam. 135, 140.
[1] [1973] 2 W.L.R. 585, 593.
[2] *Russell* v. *Russell*, [1897] A.C. 395, 420, 439; *Jamieson* v. *Jamieson*, [1952] A.C. 525, 550; *Lauder* v. *Lauder*, [1949] P. 277, 286.
[3] *Weatherley* v. *Weatherley*, [1947] A.C. 628, 631.
[4] *Fromhold* v. *Fromhold*, [1952] 1 T.L.R. 1522, 1525.
[5] *Yeatman* v. *Yeatman* (1868), L.R. 1 P. & D. 489.
[6] *Hall* v. *Hall*, [1962] 3 All E.R. 518.
[7] *Holborn* v. *Holborn*, [1947] 1 All E.R. 32.
[8] *White* v. *White*, [1948] P. 330; *Cackett* v. *Cackett*, [1950] P. 253.
[9] *Bravery* v. *Bravery*, [1954] 3 All E.R. 59.

A husband might rely on his wife's refusal, by insistence on contraceptive measures, to bear him the heir for whom he longed, coupled with taunts which endangered his health.[10] The refusal by one spouse of ordinary matrimonial intercourse could suffice,[11] unless there is good reason for it, as in the case of a wife's invincible repugnance following childbirth,[12] or the fact that the husband is grossly undersexed.[13] Sometimes the case may be one of mental cruelty, as in cases of persistent nagging[14] or prolonged insults, slights and unkindness.

Much more difficult are the cases in which it has been held that one spouse may be justified in leaving or remaining apart from the other for the time being, but not necessarily for ever. An example is to be found in the case of *G. v. G.*[15] where the husband's mental condition was such that he terrified the children. It was held that this constituted just cause for his wife's decision that she could not live with him for the time being, though had she shown an intention never in any circumstances to resume cohabitation with him, she would herself have been guilty of desertion. The Act requires only that the respondent "has behaved in such a way that the petitioner cannot reasonably be expected to live with the respondent" and does not say that it must be such as to justify a *permanent* refusal. Presumably, however, the court would avoid this difficulty by refusing a decree, in such a case, on the ground that it was not satisfied that the breakdown was irretrievable.[16]

A similar difficulty arises with regard to cases in which it has been held that a spouse is guilty of constructive desertion if he behaves in such a way as to lead the other spouse reasonably to believe that he has committed adultery[17] and that this constitutes just cause for leaving or remaining apart.[1] These decisions are subject to the provisoes that the belief must have resulted from the conduct of the other spouse[2] and not merely from statements by third parties,[3] and that the belief cannot be regarded as reasonable unless, within a reasonable time, an opportunity has been given to the other spouse to explain.[4] There are several problems here. First, these cases were in part based on the fact that to remain in such circumstances might have constituted condonation of the adultery, should satisfactory evidence of it later be forthcoming, and condonation is no longer a bar to a divorce. Secondly, it is another example of conduct which would not necessarily justify permanent departure because, for example, the court might later find that the suspicions, though reasonable, were groundless.[5] Thirdly, section 1 (2) (*a*) provides that, in the case of *actual* adultery, the petitioner must find it intolerable to live with the respondent and presumably,

---

[10] *Forbes* v. *Forbes,* [1956] P. 16.
[11] *Hutchinson* v. *Hutchinson,* [1963] 1 All E.R. 1; *Sheldon* v. *Sheldon,* [1966] P. 62; *Slon* v. *Slon,* [1969] P. 122.
[12] *Beevor* v. *Beevor,* [1945] 2 All E.R. 200.
[13] *P.* v. *P.,* [1964] 3 All E.R. 919.
[14] *Atkins* v. *Atkins,* [1942] 2 All E.R. 637.
[15] [1964] P. 133.
[16] See s. 6 (2) and *ante,* p. 16 *et seq.*
[17] *Baker* v. *Baker,* [1954] P. 33.
[1] *Glenister* v. *Glenister,* [1945] P. 30.
[2] *Beer* v. *Beer,* [1948] P. 10.
[3] *Elliott* v. *Elliott,* [1956] P. 160.
[4] *Marsden* v. *Marsden,* [1968] P. 544.
[5] *Allen* v. *Allen,* [1951] 1 All E.R. 724.

by inference, this must be equally true of suspicions of adultery. Should the court find that the adultery was not in fact committed, the unfounded suspicions cannot themselves continue to provide good reason for life apart.[6] But there will no doubt be cases where the conduct which led to the suspicions was of itself so outrageous as to satisfy the requirements of section 1 (2) (b).

It is not easy, also, to forecast the effect that the present law may have on a case such as *France* v. *France*.[7] There the wife told the husband that she no longer loved him, but loved another man, and told him to leave the matrimonial home, which he did. Presumably in these circumstances he could not reasonably be expected to live with her again. Subsequently, the parties met on six occasions and had sexual intercourse, and treating the case as one of constructive desertion, the Court of Appeal held that the principle of condonation must apply and the petition must fail. Condonation will no longer be a bar to divorce, and periods of life together (even were these acts of intercourse to be regarded as life in one household) are to be ignored, by virtue of section 2 (3), since they do not amount to six months in all. Yet it is not easy to feel that the case is one in which a petition would be certain of success. Possibly the solution would lie in the court adjourning the case under section 6 (2) of the Act,[8] to enable attempts to be made to effect a reconciliation.

(c) *That the respondent has deserted the petitioner for a continuous period of at least two years immediately preceding the presentation of the petition.*

In contrast to head (b), above, there is ample judicial authority on the subject of desertion, and this "fact" differs from the former ground for divorce only in that the period required is reduced from three years to two years. The requirement of leave to petition for divorce within three years of the date of the marriage[9] is of course in no way affected by the reduction in the period of desertion required.

Since the circumstances of different cases may vary greatly the courts have refrained from and discouraged any attempt to give a comprehensive definition of desertion.[10] But among the essential elements are the cessation of cohabitation, the respondent's intention to desert the petitioner and the absence of consent by the petitioner.[11] To these may be added the fact that the respondent must not have had good cause or excuse for leaving or remaining apart and that, to be a ground for divorce, the desertion must have continued for a period of at least two years. These elements provide convenient headings under which to examine the law on this subject.

(i) *The cessation of cohabitation.*

Desertion involves a departure from a state of affairs rather than from a place.[12] It can occur although the parties have never had a matrimonial home, as where the husband left his wife, who was expecting a child, at the church

---

[6] *Ibid.*
[7] [1969] P. 46.
[8] *Ante,* p. 17.
[9] *Ante,* p. 13.
[10] *Weatherley* v. *Weatherley,* [1947] A. C. 628, 631; *Cohen* v. *Cohen,* [1940] A.C. 631, 645.
[11] *Williams* v. *Williams,* [1939] P. 365, 368.
[12] *Pulford* v. *Pulford,* [1923] P. 18.

door and refused to return to her,[13] or where they separated by agreement for a limited time, and one refused to rejoin the other when that time expired.[14] Equally it can exist although the parties are living under the same roof, as Lord DENNING explained in *Hopes* v. *Hopes*[15]

> "The husband who shuts himself up in one or two rooms of his house, and ceases to have anything to do with his wife, is living separately and apart from her as effectively as if they were separated by the outer door of a flat. They may meet on the stairs or in the passageway, but so they might if they had separate flats in the same building. If that separation is brought about by his fault, why is that not desertion? He has forsaken and abandoned her as effectively as if he had gone into lodgings."

His Lordship continued

> "It is most important to draw a clear line between desertion . . . and gross neglect or chronic discord. . . . That line is drawn at the point where the parties are living separately and apart. In cases where they are living under the same roof that point is reached when they cease to be one household and become two households. . . ."

In such cases, therefore, the common life and the common home must have altogether ceased to exist. It is not essential that there should be physical separation between the parts of the house. In *Walker* v. *Walker*[16] the wife withdrew to a separate bedroom, which she kept locked, and refused to cook for her husband or perform any household duties for him, communicating with him by notes. It was held that the fact that necessity drove him at times to make use of the same kitchen did not alter the fact that she had deserted him. By way of contrast, in *Littlewood* v. *Littlewood*[17] where the wife, who was also in employment, refused her husband sexual intercourse and held little conversation with him, but occasionally cooked a meal for him and took some part in household duties, they constituted one (unhappy) household rather than two, and there was no desertion.

The test of cohabitation is therefore the same as that of "living with each other" for the purposes of section 2 of the Act of 1973, which is to be construed, by virtue of sub-section (6), as referring "to their living with each other in the same household". Whilst they do so, it was held by the House of Lords in *Wheatherley* v. *Weatherley*,[18] the mere fact that one spouse, without reasonable excuse, is refusing to have sexual intercourse with the other does not constitute desertion. If, however, the refusal leads to separation this may, according to the circumstances, amount to constructive desertion, or to good cause for leaving, or to conduct falling within section 1 (2) (*b*) of the Act of 1973.[19]

---

13 *De Laubenque* v. *De Laubenque*, [1899] P. 42.
14 *Shaw* v. *Shaw*, [1939] P. 269.
15 [1949] P. 227, 235.
16 [1952] 2 All E.R. 138; see also *Wilkes* v. *Wilkes*, [1943] P. 41.
17 [1943] P. 11.
18 [1947] A.C. 628.
19 See *ante*, p. 22.

It will already be clear from what has been said about that sub-section that the party guilty of desertion is not necessarily the party who withdraws from cohabitation without good cause or excuse, but may be the party whose conduct caused the separation. So far as proceedings for divorce are concerned it seems unnecessary to add to what has already been said on the subject of constructive desertion because, as has already been pointed out, a petitioner who had been driven to withdraw from cohabitation by the respondent's conduct would be likely to rely upon section 1 (2) (*b*), rather than awaiting the completion of the necessary period of two years and relying upon section 1 (2) (*c*). Where the period of two years has in fact elapsed it may be advisable, however, until the working of the Act has been fully considered by the courts, to rely upon both guidelines in drafting a petition, in case some unforeseen problems may arise.

Where the separation has resulted from the failure of the parties to agree upon a home, it was held by the Court of Appeal in *Dunn* v. *Dunn*[20] that it is the party who has acted unreasonably who is guilty of desertion. A husband has today no absolute right to dictate to his wife upon the choice of a home though no doubt, when he alone is the breadwinner, he can properly insist that the home shall be conveniently near to his place of employment and reasonably in keeping with his earnings. But when both are working, as in *King* v. *King*[1] even this consideration is absent: the matter must be settled by agreement between them, and if the husband unreasonably insists on a move to a place so distant that he cannot keep his promise that his wife shall continue with her business, he may be guilty of desertion. Circumstances may arise where both are unreasonable, where neither will even listen to the viewpoint of the other, much less attempt to understand it. In such a case it was held by WILLMER, J. in *Walter* v. *Walter*[2] that neither can prove desertion. This decision was criticised by DENNING, L.J. in *Hosegood* v. *Hosegood*[3] where he considered (obiter) that both parties should have been granted decrees, and supported (again obiter) by Lord MERRIMAN, P. in *Simpson* v. *Simpson*.[4] Since then the question of whether both spouses can be guilty of desertion at one and the same time has never been clearly decided. In the latest case, *Price* v. *Price*,[5] all three members of the Court of Appeal expressly refused to discuss the point, save that SACHS, L.J. did remark[6]

> "I would, however, add that it would need persuasive argument before I was prepared to hold that the views expressed in turn by all three judges of this court in *Lang* v. *Lang, The Times*, July 7, 1953 . . . were wrong, and that there could be twin decrees for desertion."

This is a difficulty which may be resolved in some cases by reliance upon

---

[20] [1949] P. 98.
[1] [1942] P. 1.
[2] (1949), 65 T.L.R. 680.
[3] (1950), 66 (Pt. 1) T.L.R. 735, 740.
[4] [1951] P. 320, 330.
[5] [1970] 2 All E.R. 497.
[6] *Ibid.*, at p. 997.

section 1 (2) (*b*). There is no reason why, as in *Wachtel* v. *Wachtel*,[7] both parties should not be held to have behaved in such a way that neither can reasonably be expected to live with the other, and in such a case the marriage has obviously irretrievably broken down and decrees can be granted to both parties.

(ii) *The intention to desert.*

Desertion is not established until the petitioner has proved both the cessation of cohabitation and the intention of the respondent, at the time when that cessation commenced or continues, permanently to desert the petitioner. It is obvious that a separation which is involuntary, such as that resulting from imprisonment, or mental or physical illness, or the requirements of business or service in the Armed Forces, cannot of itself amount to desertion, though it may in some circumstances amount to living apart for the purposes of section 1 (2) (*d*) or (*e*) of the Act of 1973.[8] There is no reason, however, why desertion should not commence during a period of involuntary separation, as where a husband whose business commitments have taken him to another country informs his wife that he never intends to return to her. This is well illustrated by the case of *Beeken* v. *Beeken*.[9] The husband and wife, having both been captured by the Japanese, were interned in 1941 in the same prison camp. Although they shared the same bedroom, the husband knew that his wife had formed a friendship with another internee, and she refused her husband sexual intercourse. Subsequently, whilst they were interned in different camps in 1944, she told her husband that she never intended to return to him. The Court of Appeal held that she was in desertion from that date in 1944. The question whether the desertion commenced at an earlier date, when they were compelled to live in the same room against the wishes of the wife, did not require consideration, and was the subject of a difference of judicial opinion. The point is perhaps unlikely to arise in practice, but section 1 (2) (*b*) does not require that the parties should have separated, and in similar circumstances a court might, under this subsection, be satisfied that a wife had behaved in such a way that her husband could not reasonably be expected to live with her.

Just as desertion may commence during a period of involuntary separation, if there is proof of the necessary intention, so also desertion which has already started may continue although there are circumstances which prevent the respondent from returning, if the intention to desert continues. This is illustrated by *Drew* v. *Drew*[10] where a husband who had deserted his wife was subsequently arrested and imprisoned. The court took the view that he would not have returned to her even had he been free to do so, and that his desertion continued despite the imprisonment.

A different situation arises where the respondent is, by reason of mental incapacity, unable to form the necessary intention. In these circumstances it was held by the House of Lords in *Crowther* v. *Crowther*[11] that desertion cannot

---

[7] [1973] Fam. 72, C.A.
[8] As to this, see *post*, p. 39 *et seq.*
[9] [1948] P. 302.
[10] (1888), 13 P.D. 97.
[11] [1951] A.C. 723.

commence.   There is no irrebuttable presumption that a spouse who is under-going hospital treatment for insanity is incapable of forming the intention to desert, but the onus lies upon the petitioner to prove that the respondent is able to, and in fact did, do so.[12]   The position is different when the insanity com-mences after the desertion has started.   Section 2 (4) of the Act of 1973 provides[13] that for the purpose of section 1 (2) (c) the court may treat a period of desertion as having continued at a time when the deserting party was incapable of con-tinuing the necessary intention if the evidence before the court is such that, had that party not been so incapable, the court would have inferred that his deser-tion continued at that time.   It must be noticed that this provision is limited to proceedings for divorce and judicial separation (to which section 1 (2) (c) alone applies) and has no application in a magistrates' court, where the onus lies upon the complainant to prove that the defendant was able to continue, as well as to form, the necessary *animus deserendi*.

It seems clear that the decision of the House of Lords in *Williams* v. *Williams*[14], that the respondent's insanity is not necessarily a defence to a charge of cruelty, does not have any bearing on the relationship of insanity to desertion, since the statutory provision on the subject mentioned above, would in that event have been unnecessary.   There is no reason, however, why, in a case in which the respondent's insanity leads him to behave in such a way that the petitioner cannot reasonably be expected to live with him, reliance should not be placed upon section 1 (2) (b) rather than 1 (2) (c), which would obviate the necessity of waiting for two years before filing a petition.[15]

(iii) *The absence of consent by the petitioner.*

It is self-evident that if the parties are living apart by agreement neither can successfully allege that the other is guilty of desertion.   The agreement may be formal or informal.   But it must be a true agreement to separate and not a mere maintenance agreement, as in *Crabtree* v. *Crabtree*,[16] where the husband agreed to pay maintenance to his wife "if they shall so long live separate and apart from each other"—words which merely defined the duration of the maintenance.   The agreement must be freely and voluntarily entered into and not, as in *Holroyd* v. *Holroyd*[17] practically forced upon a reluctant wife without legal advice because she thought it was the only way in which to make her husband maintain her.   The fact that one spouse is glad to see the other go is not of itself the same thing as a consent to their parting.   As BUCKLEY, L.J. said in *Harriman* v. *Harriman*[18]

> "Desertion does not necessarily involve that the wife desires her husband to remain with her.   She may be thankful that he has gone, but he may nevertheless have deserted her."

---

[12] *Kaczmarz* v. *Kaczmarz*, [1967] 1 All E.R. 416—a case of a chronic schizophrenic.
[13] Re-enacting a provision introduced by the Divorce (Insanity and Desertion) Act 1958, s. 2.
[14] [1964] A.C. 698.
[15] See *Katz* v. *Katz*, [1972] 3 All E.R. 219 and *ante*, p. 27.
[16] [1953] 2 All E.R. 56.
[17] (1920), 36 T.L.R. 479.
[18] [1909] P. 123, 148.

Were this not so, the worse his behaviour the harder it would be for her to complain of his desertion.

Although the existence of a separation agreement suffices to prevent the commencement of desertion, or to terminate desertion which has already started, this is only so whilst the agreement remains in force. It would end if the parties resumed cohabitation, i.e. if they once again lived together in one household[19] and a subsequent departure by one spouse without the consent of the other could constitute desertion. It is possible for a separation which began by being consensual to be changed into desertion without a resumption of cohabitation, but for this to be so it must lose its consensual element on both sides. This may occur, as in *Pardy* v. *Pardy*,[20] when one party repudiates the agreement and the other can show that during the relevant period he or she had no intention of relying on the agreement and was always ready and willing, in spite of it, to resume cohabitation. A mere failure by a husband to make some of the payments for which the agreement provided would not of itself amount to repudiation,[21] but it would be otherwise if he evinced an intention to make no further payments, as he did in *Pardy* v. *Pardy*. There must in effect be something which goes to the root of the agreement, such as a refusal by a wife to allow her husband the access to their child for which the agreement provided.[1] It is not essential for the party alleging desertion, as in the case of a commercial contract, to notify the other party expressly that he or she has accepted the repudiation as terminating the agreement. It is sufficient that no attempt has been made to enforce the terms agreed, so that both parties, to use the words of Lord Greene in *Pardy* v. *Pardy*[2] "are during the relevant period in truth regarding the agreement as a dead letter, which no longer regulates their matrimonial relations".

When it is said that the separation must be against the wishes of the petitioner, this does not mean that the petitioner must make efforts to persuade the respondent to return.[3] The position was well explained in *Sifton* v. *Sifton*[4]

"When the spouse is deserted, he or she is in the position that the presumption is in his or her favour and against the deserting spouse, and it is not until some offer to return is made by the other side that the question arises whether that is an offer which ought, in all the circumstances, to be accepted."

When such an offer is made, however, the refusal of it without good reason has the effect, not only of terminating the desertion of the party who made the offer, but of making the party who refuses guilty of desertion.[5] The offer must, of course, be genuine and not a mere stratagem to interrupt the running of the period required by statute,[6] but there is no rule that an offer by letter will not suffice: it could not be expected that a deserting wife must make an unheralded

---

[19] *Bull* v. *Bull*, [1953] P. 224, and see *post*, p. 38.
[20] [1939] P. 288.
[21] *Smith* v. *Smith*, [1915] P. 288, 289; *Ratcliffe* v. *Ratcliffe*, [1938] 3 All E.R. 41, 43.
[1] *Stockley* v. *Stockley*, [1939] 2 All E.R. 707.
[2] [1939] P. at p. 307.
[3] *Brewer* v. *Brewer*, [1962] P. 69, 80.
[4] [1939] P. 221, 226.
[5] *Thomas* v. *Thomas*, [1946] 1 All E.R. 170; *Ogden* v. *Ogden*, [1969] 2 All E.R. 135.
[6] *Ware* v. *Ware*, [1942] P. 49.

entry to her husband's house.[7] Whether the offer is genuine is in every case a question of fact. It must not be accompanied by unreasonable conditions, as in *Slawson* v. *Slawson* where a wife's offer to return on condition that there should be no sexual intercourse was described as "an offer to return merely as a housekeeper".[8] In cases of constructive desertion, the offer must be accompanied by suitable assurances of future good behaviour,[9] and there may be conduct so gross that no spouse could ever be expected to resume cohabitation.[10] Indeed, just as there is conduct which constitutes good cause for leaving or remaining apart, as will be explained shortly, so that conduct may also constitute sufficient reason for refusing an otherwise genuine offer to return. Thus, the fact that the respondent has committed adultery may justify refusal of his offer, provided that the court is satisfied that it was the real reason for the refusal but not otherwise,[11] and even the respondent's conduct which leads the petitioner reasonably to believe that the respondent has committed adultery may suffice.[12]

The subsistence of a valid agreement to separate for life necessarily precludes the need for acceptance of an offer to return, since such an agreement cannot be terminated unilaterally, and the same is true of an agreement to separate for a fixed but limited time which has not expired, or for a purpose not yet fulfilled.[13] But a mere informal agreement to separate for an indefinite time is terminable at the will of either party, and if one party refuses without good reason a bona fide offer by the other to resume cohabitation[14] and still more if such an offer is rejected out of hand without any consideration of the terms which are offered,[15] the party refusing is guilty of desertion.

(iv) *The absence of good cause.*

The Matrimonial Causes Act 1965, s. 1 (1) (*a*) required expressly that the respondent should have deserted the petitioner "without cause". These words do not appear in section 1 (2) (*c*) of the Act of 1973[16] because it is clear that a spouse who has good cause for leaving, or remaining apart from the other, is not in any event guilty of desertion. It seems unnecessary here to multiply examples of conduct which will suffice, since in effect any behaviour such that the petitioner cannot reasonably be expected to live with the respondent within the meaning of section 1 (2) (*b*) of the Act would preclude a finding of desertion against the petitioner.[17] But as has already been indicated,[18] there may be cases where the behaviour has been due to mental illness which would justify

---

[7] *Pratt* v. *Pratt*, [1939] A.C. 417.
[8] *Per* BUCKNILL, J., [1942] 2 All E.R. 527, 528.
[9] *Thomas* v. *Thomas*, [1924] P. 194, 201.
[10] *Edwards* v. *Edwards*, [1948] P. 268, 272, *per* Lord MERRIMAN, P.
[11] *Day* v. *Day*, [1957] P. 202.
[12] *Everitt* v. *Everitt*, [1949] P. 374.
[13] *Nutley* v. *Nutley*, [1970] 1 All E.R. 410.
[14] *Hall* v. *Hall*, [1960] 1 All E.R. 91.
[15] *Gallagher* v. *Gallagher*, [1965] 2 All E.R. 967.
[16] Or in the Matrimonial Proceedings (Magistrates' Courts) Act 1960, s. 1 (1) (*a*).
[17] For some examples, see *ante*, p. 28.
[18] See *ante*. p. 29, and *G.* v. *G.*, [1964] P. 133.

the other spouse in withdrawing temporarily from cohabitation but not the inference that the marriage has irretrievably broken down. An example is to be seen in *Lilley* v. *Lilley*.[19] The wife's mental disorder was such that were she to have returned to her husband this would, through no fault on his part, have been likely to result in a serious breakdown in her health. It was held that, although this might justify her refusal to return for the time being, it could not justify her settled decision never to return to him and that she was guilty of desertion.

(v) *The duration of the desertion.*

The period of two years' desertion, like that of the three years required by the Act of 1965, must be a continuous period immediately preceding the presentation of the petition, i.e. the date when the petition[20] (or in the case of answer claiming cross-relief, the answer[1]) was filed. A petitioner cannot add to a petition, in which he relies upon other facts, a claim to rely upon a period of two years' desertion completed since that petition was filed, either by way of supplemental petition[2] or by way of amendment.[3] In such a case, if he feels that he may be unable to satisfy the court of the facts already alleged, his best course could be to apply for leave to present a further petition, since it is not permissible to have two petitions relating to the same marriage on the file at the same time without such leave.[4]

In pursuance of the same policy of encouraging attempts at reconciliation which has already been considered in relation to section 1 (2) (*a*) and (*b*), section 2 (5) of the Act provides that in considering, for the purposes of section 1 (2), whether the period of two years' desertion has been continuous, no account is to be taken of any one or more periods, not exceeding six months in all, during which the parties have resumed living with each other. But it must be emphasised that this relates only to the *continuity* of the desertion, and not the calculation of the period of two years, and section 2 (5) expressly provides that these periods shall not count as part of the period of desertion. Thus if the husband deserted his wife two years ago and during those two years they have lived together in the unsuccessful hope of reconciliation, first for two months and then for one month, the wife is not precluded from reliance upon the desertion, but cannot do so until her husband has remained apart from her for a further three months.

(vi) *Termination of desertion.*

Many of the ways in which desertion can be terminated have already been considered, or will be considered elsewhere, but it seems desirable to gather them together, with some further examples, by way of conclusion.

Thus desertion will be precluded or terminated:—

---

[19] [1960] P. 158. See also *Clark* v. *Clark*, [1956] 1 All E.R. 823.
[20] *Alston* v. *Alston*, [1946] P. 203.
[1] *Faulkner* v. *Faulkner*, [1941] 2 All E.R. 748.
[2] *Spawforth* v. *Spawforth*, [1946] P. 131.
[3] *Blacker* v. *Blacker*, [1960] P. 146.
[4] Rule 12 (4).

(1) By a decree of judicial separation, which ends the duty to cohabit.[5]
(2) By a matrimonial order of a magistrates' court containing a provision that the complainant is no longer bound to cohabit with the defendant, which has the same effect.[6]
(3) By a separation agreement, so long as it is valid and subsisting.[7]
(4) By the refusal, without reasonable cause, of a bona fide offer to return.[8]
(5) By a resumption of cohabitation. The effect of periods of life together upon the continuity of desertion has already been noted,[9] as has the fact that for this purpose living with each other means, as does a resumption of cohabitation, living with each other in the same household. Residence under the same roof in separate households would not suffice.[10] A resumption of sexual intercourse is not essential, and isolated and casual acts of intercourse, without any intention on the part of either, or both, of the parties of reconciliation, would not amount of themselves to a resumption of cohabitation or of living together.[11]

In addition, desertion *may* be precluded or terminated:—

(a) By the respondent's insanity,[12] though the petitioner's insanity is immaterial.[13]
(b) By the petitioner's own adultery. This is no longer a discretionary bar to divorce, but it may still constitute a good reason for the respondent leaving the petitioner, or desisting from any attempts to return, provided that the court is satisfied that it was the real reason for their parting or remaining apart. In such a case the onus lies upon the petitioner to prove that the respondent was ignorant of the adultery or that he was in no way influenced by it into behaving as he did—that he would still have left or remained away from the petitioner even if he had known of it.[14]
(c) By the institution by the petitioner, during the relevant period of two years, of unsuccessful proceedings for divorce[15] or nullity[16] on other grounds. The respondent in such cases will not unnaturally feel that it is difficult for the petitioner to allege that the separation is without his consent when he has commenced proceedings with a view to ending the marriage. But the House of Lords took the view in *Cohen* v. *Cohen* that the relevant question was whether the respondent would have attempted to return had the proceedings not been

[5] See *post*, p. 64.
[6] See *post*, p. 44.
[7] See *ante*, p. 35.
[8] See *ante*, p. 35.
[9] See *ante*, p. 37.
[10] See *ante*, p. 31.
[11] *Mummery* v. *Mummery*, [1942] P. 107; *Perry* v. *Perry*, [1952] P. 203.
[12] See *ante*, p. 34.
[13] *Sotherden* v. *Sotherden*, [1940] P. 73.
[14] *Herod* v. *Herod*, [1939] P. 11.
[15] *Cohen* v. *Cohen*, [1940] A.C. 631.
[16] *W.* v. *W.*, (No. 2), [1954] P. 486.

instituted. If so, the desertion was terminated: if his decision was unaffected by the proceedings, the desertion continued.

(d) *That the parties to the marriage have lived apart for a continuous period of at least two years immediately preceding the presentation of the petition and the respondent consents to a decree being granted.*

It is at this point that the Divorce Reform Act, so far as English law is concerned, broke entirely new ground, though in New Zealand, where divorce on this basis has been available for some time, with a period of separation of three years instead of two,[17] some 46 per cent. of all divorces have been granted for this reason. It seems likely that in the course of time a similar pattern may emerge in this country and that in cases where there is no chance of reconciliation practitioners will, where. possible, encourage intending petitioners to consider this head before the others. In the year 1972 this was the basis upon which some 19 per cent. of all English decrees were granted. Certainly it is the one most likely (to use again the words of the Law Commission) "to take the heat out of the disputes between husband and wife and certainly not further embitter the relationships between them or between them and their children".[18]

The requirement that the parties should have "lived apart" for a continous period of at least two years under section 1 (2) (*d*) (and the similar requirement of life apart for at least five years under section 1 (2) (*e*)) involves both a physical and a mental element.

The physical element is clearly described in section 2 (6) whereby for the purposes of the Act a husband and wife are to be treated as living apart "unless they are living with each other in the same household". The section does not say "in the same house" so that it is possible, as it is in cases of desertion,[19] for the court to find that they are living apart despite the fact that they are residing under the same roof, where their life is in two households rather than one. Such a finding will be possible only if the common home and the common life have altogether ceased.[20] A good example is to be found in *Fuller* v. *Fuller*,[21] where after the wife had left her husband to live with another man, he became incapable through illness of continuing to live alone and went to live as a mere lodger in the house in which his wife was living, paying her rent for so doing. The Court of Appeal held that the words "with each other" mean "living with each other as man and wife", and the parties were living apart. The case of *Mouncer* v. *Mouncer*[22] was distinguished on the ground that the mere cessation of sexual intercourse does not suffice if the parties are otherwise living in the same household.

The Act is silent upon the question of the reason why parties have lived apart, so that it might at first sight appear that absences resulting from illness,

---

[17] Recently reduced to two years.
[18] Cmnd. 3123, para. 17.
[19] See *ante*, p. 31.
[20] *Mouncer* v. *Mouncer*, [1972] 1 All E.R. 289, following *Hopes* v. *Hopes*, [1949] P. 227, C.A.
[21] [1973] 2 All E.R. 650, C.A.
[22] *Supra*.

whether physical or mental, from service in the armed forces or from the exigencies of business, might of themselves suffice. But it is clear from the decision of the Court of Appeal in *Santos* v. *Santos*[23] that mere physical separation is not of itself sufficient to constitute "living apart" and that in addition a mental element is required. In the vast generality of cases there is no life apart whilst both parties recognise the marriage as still subsisting. It is necessary for the petitioner to prove in addition that he or she has for the requisite period recognised that the marriage is in truth at an end, and has become a "mere shell".

The difficulty of determining the moment at which this occurred is self-evident, and the more so in view of the decision of the Court of Appeal that not only is this element capable of being unilateral, but also that communication of the petitioner's state of mind to the respondent by word or conduct is not essential. The court recognised the difficulty that this might often cause in practice in cases, for example, of long terms of imprisonment or illness. Sometimes the moment when the mental element was first present can be identified by a letter, by the cessation or reduction of visits, or by the petitioner starting to live with some other person. Sometimes the oral evidence of the petitioner will not of itself suffice without some corroboration; in others it will be obvious that some grave or incurable disability has made a resumption of any form of married life impossible. Finally, from the use of the words "in the vast generality of cases", the Court of Appeal has left open the question of some wholly exceptional case which could only be dealt with when it arose, such as a case under section 1 (2) (*e*) where misfortune has caused both spouses to be of unsound mind for more than five years.

The concluding words of the judgment of the Court of Appeal in *Santos* v. *Santos*[1] were as follows:—

> "It is clear from our examination of the issues inherent in petitions founded on heads (*d*) and (*e*) that the bulk of such cases need careful judicial scrutiny and ought not (as might else be suggested) to be determined on affidavit evidence or otherwise than by a judge. . . . Whilst sympathising from experience with those judges who have to take the undefended list, it is still the case that the legislature, in our judgment, intended the procedure before them to involve judicial care as opposed to rubber stamping."

The judgment of the Court of Appeal was delivered on February 16, 1972. In the light of what was then said the amendments to the Rules which came into operation on December 1, 1973[2] represent a surprising divergence from the unanimous judgment of the Court of Appeal. The details are considered in Chapter 16. But briefly, in any case in which the only fact upon which the petitioner relies in his petition is that mentioned in 1 (2) (*d*) of the Act, and there are no children of the family to whom section 41 of the Act applies[3] (so that a

---

[23] [1972] Fam. 247.
[1] [1972] Fam. 247 at pp. 263, 264.
[2] Matrimonial Causes (Amendment No. 2) Rules 1973, and see now Rules 33 (3) and 48.
[3] See *ante*, p. 184.

decree of divorce could not be made absolute unless the judge had by order declared himself satisfied as to the arrangements for their welfare) the case will be entered for trial in the special procedure list. This can be done only if the respondent's consent to the grant of a decree has been given in writing, and an affidavit by the petitioner has been filed as to the circumstances of the separation and the time and circumstances in which he came to the conclusion that the marriage was in fact at an end. The registrar considers the evidence filed by the petitioner and if satisfied makes and files a certificate to that effect. A day is then fixed for the decree nisi to be pronounced by the judge in open court, but neither party is required to attend before the registrar or before the judge.

The procedure cannot exactly be described as "rubber stamping", since the registrar can refuse his certificate if not satisfied that the case has been proved. But it is contrary not only to the letter but also to the spirit of the judgment of the Court of Appeal and probably also, as was stressed in that judgment, to the intentions of the legislature, save that it applies only to cases based upon two years' separation and not those based upon separation for five years. Again, as in the case of the guidelines already considered, the Act is so framed as to encourage attempts at a reconciliation. In considering whether the period for which the parties to the marriage have lived apart has been continuous (as in the case of a period of desertion[4]), no account is to be taken of any one period (not exceeding six months) or of any two or more periods (not exceeding six months in all) during which the parties living with each other, though periods of life together cannot be counted as part of the period of life apart.[5]

It has been argued that the period of two years is not in any case of sufficient length to exclude all hopes of saving the marriage. On the other hand, if a longer period were required the parties might be tempted to fabricate evidence of say, adultery, in order to shorten the period of waiting. The Act does not require that the period of life apart shall have resulted from any matrimonial offence or disagreement. There is nothing to prevent them from separating by agreement, with a view to divorce two years thereafter, if they remain of the like mind, or from coming together for trial periods (not exceeding six months in all), to discover whether they have changed their minds. It must also be remembered that even if this (or any other) guideline is established by the evidence, the court is only required to grant a decree "unless it is satisfied on all the evidence that the marriage has not broken down irretrievably".

The Act does not merely require that the respondent should not object to the grant of a decree: a positive consent is required which cannot be implied or given on his behalf by any other person.[6] In cases in which the respondent suffers from some mental incapacity, the test for his capacity to give a valid consent to the dissolution of his marriage is exactly the same as the test for determining the validity of a marriage propounded in *In the Estate of Park, Park* v. *Park*[7]—is he capable of understanding the nature of the consent which he is expressing and capable of appreciating the effect of expressing such consent,

---

[4] See *ante*, p. 37.
[5] S. 2 (5).
[6] *McG. (formerly R.)* v. *R.*, [1972] 1 All E.R. 362.
[7] [1954] P. 89.

and the burden of establishing that consent is upon the petitioner.[8] Further, by section 2 (7), provision is to be made by rules of court to ensure that, where the petitioner alleges that such consent has been obtained, the respondent has been given such information as will enable him to understand the consequences to him of consenting to a decree being granted, and the steps which he must take to indicate that he consents to the grant of a decree. A reference to paragraph 4 of the Notice of Proceedings[9] which will be served on the respondent together with the petition will show the information which a respondent spouse will receive in such a case. It is probable that the decision as to whether to consent or not by a respondent who has been properly advised will depend largely upon satisfactory terms being agreed as to questions of financial provision, property and children.

(e) *That the parties to the marriage have lived apart for a continuous period of at least five years immediately preceding the presentation of the petition.*

It is this "fact" which has produced the most controversy, since it will enable a party whose conduct has led to the breakdown of the marriage to seek a divorce against the wishes of a spouse who is in no way to blame. Nevertheless, since the Act is based on the principle that irretrievable breakdown is the sole ground for divorce, there can hardly be clearer evidence that there is no hope of retrieving the marriage. It must not be supposed, however, that the description "a Casanova's charter", which has so often been applied to it, is well merited—that this provision will benefit only philandering husbands who have deserted their ageing and blameless wives. As Lady Gaitskill said in debate "I do not believe that Casanovas are marrying men", and as Lord Stow Hill added "Casanovas do not bother with charters".[10]

It is true that a husband who has left his wife and lived with another woman for five years could seek a divorce in order to marry the other woman, although his wife had persisted throughout in her refusal to set him free to do so. Conversely it might affect a husband who refused to petition on the ground of the adultery of his deserting wife. The Civil Judicial Statistics suggest that husbands and wives are almost equally to blame for the breakdown of marriages. There has been little difference between the number of decrees nisi based on adultery obtained by husbands and wives respectively—in 1966 there were 10,769 obtained by husbands and 10,369 by wives; in 1972 husbands obtained 14,407 such decrees and wives 16,956. What must be clearly understood is that the guideline is in no way confined to one kind of case.

Proceedings might be brought under it by parties who have for a long time been separated by agreement, to whom divorce on the ground of desertion is denied because their separation is consensual. A decree could be granted under section 1 (2) (*d*) if the respondent spouse consented or under section 1 (2) (*e*), although that consent was refused, if the separation had lasted for five years or more. No express provision is contained in the Act for cases of incurable

---

[8] *Mason* v. *Mason*, [1972] Fam. 302.
[9] Form 5, in Appendix II, Part 1, *post.*
[10] (1969), *The Times*, July 1.

unsoundness of mind which before the Act of 1969 were grounds for divorce only if accompanied by five years' care and treatment as defined in section 1 (3) of the Act of 1965. Under the Act of 1973, five years of life apart by reason of unsoundness of mind would suffice, without proof of the continuity or nature of any care and treatment, or of the fact that the insanity was incurable, unless the court considered that the breakdown of the marriage was nevertheless not irretrievable, which seems unlikely. There must of course, be the necessary mental element in addition to the fact of physical separation.[11]

The provisions of section 2 (5) of the Act as to periods of life together, not in all exceeding six months, which have already been noted in relation to desertion[12] and two years of life apart,[13] are equally applicable to the period of five years required by this guideline.

DIVORCE AFTER PREVIOUS PROCEEDINGS

In many cases there will already have been previous proceedings in relation to the marriage. It is therefore necessary to consider how far, if at all, the existence of those proceedings may affect the chances of a subsequent petition for divorce, and how far any findings in those proceedings may assist, or hinder, the proof of the case which the petitioner now seeks to establish.

1. The existence of previous proceedings.

Among the information which is required to be included in every petition for divorce[14] is a statement of whether or not there have been any previous proceedings in any court in England or Wales or elsewhere with reference to the marriage and if so, the nature of those proceedings, the date and effect of any decree or order, and whether there has been any resumption of cohabitation since it was made.

The position if there have been previous proceedings for judicial separation or for a matrimonial order of a magistrates' court, is dealt with by section 4 of the Act. The section provides that a person shall not be prevented from presenting a petition for divorce, or the court from granting a decree of divorce, by reason only that the petitioner or respondent has at any time, on the same or substantially the same facts as those proved in support of the petition, been granted a decree of judicial separation or a matrimonial order of a magistrates' court.[15] In such a case, by section 4 (2), the court is *permitted*, but not necessarily *required*, to treat the existing decree or order as sufficient proof of the adultery, desertion, or other ground on which it was granted, but cannot grant a decree of divorce without receiving evidence from the petitioner. The result is that if the previous decree or order was based upon facts upon which a petitioner would be entitled to rely as proof of irretrievable breakdown under section 1 (2) of the Act, he can convert that decree or order into a decree of divorce.

Where the decree of judicial separation was granted on a petition presented on or after January 1, 1971, there will be little difficulty in conversion, since the

---

[11] See *ante*, p. 40.
[12] *Ante*, p. 37.
[13] *Ante*, p. 41.
[14] Rule 9 and Form 2 in Appendix II, Part 1, *post*.
[15] Including orders made in Northern Ireland, the Channel Islands or the Isle of Man.

facts specified in section (1) (2) of the Act of 1973 will be the *grounds* for judicial separation.[16] Nor is there likely to be much difficulty in the case of decrees granted before 1971. These were available, since the Matrimonial Causes Act 1937, on the same grounds as those for divorce—adultery, cruelty, three years' desertion, incurable insanity coupled with five years' care and treatment and, in the case of a wife's petition, that her husband had been guilty of rape, sodomy or bestiality, all of which would clearly fall within one or other of the "facts" specified in section 1 (2). To these were added the failure to comply with a decree for restitution of conjugal rights, and any other ground upon which a decree *a mensa et thoro* could have been granted before the Matrimonial Causes Act 1857. These grounds no longer suffice, and were seldom relied upon, but conversion of a decree based on non-compliance with a restitution decree, which could be granted for desertion without awaiting completion of the three year period, would not be possible. The decree of judicial separation would have terminated the desertion, and unless it had already lasted for the two years required by section 1 (2) (*c*), reliance could be placed only on one of the other facts specified in section 1 (2).

The grounds for a matrimonial order of a magistrates' court are by no means the same as the guidelines to breakdown in section 1 (2) though, as explained in Chapter 17, many of them would satisfy one or other of these guidelines. But, as in the case of non-compliance with a decree of restitution of conjugal rights, the magistrates might make an order in respect of desertion which had not lasted for two years, and if that order contained a clause providing that the complainant was no longer bound to cohabit with the defendant it would, as would a decree of judicial separation, terminate that desertion. To some extent these difficulties as to desertion are overcome by section 4 (3) of the Act of 1973. This provides that where it is sought to obtain a decree of divorce and a decree of judicial separation (including a decree obtained abroad[17]) or a magistrates' order exempting one party to the marriage from the obligation to cohabit with the other is already in force, a period of desertion immediately preceding the institution of proceedings for the decree or order shall, if the parties have not resumed cohabitation and the decree or order has been continuously in force since it was granted, be deemed immediately to precede the presentation of the petition for divorce. The result is best illustrated by examples:—

(1) After H had deserted W for three months, she obtained a decree of restitution of conjugal rights. That decree would not have terminated the desertion. Four months later W obtained a decree of judicial separation on the ground's of H's non-compliance with the restitution decree. The desertion was then terminated after it had lasted for seven months only and section 4 (3) cannot assist W. If she seeks divorce she must rely upon some fact other than desertion, such as the fact that she and H have lived apart for two years and H consents to the grant of a decree, if he is willing to do so.

---

[16] S. 17, and see *post*, p. 62.
[17] *Tursi* v. *Tursi*, [1958] P. 54.

(2) The same result would follow if W had obtained a magistrates' order containing a non-cohabitation clause, which would have terminated the desertion after it had lasted for three months only. For that reason such a clause is not usually inserted in an order based upon desertion.

(3) If the magistrates' order had not contained a non-cohabitation clause the desertion, which had already lasted for three months, would have continued despite the order, and W could rely upon section 1 (2) (c) after a further twenty-one months which, added to the three months before the proceedings were started, would complete the necessary period of two years. She would have no need to rely upon section 4 (3) of the Act of 1973.

(4) If at the time when W commenced her proceedings for judicial separation in case (1) above or for a magistrates' order in case (2) above the desertion had already lasted for two years, she can rely upon that desertion for the purposes of her petition for divorce because it is deemed, by virtue of section 4 (3), immediately to precede the presentation of her divorce petition.

More difficulty has been occasioned by cases in which the magistrates' order originally contained a non-cohabitation clause, but this was later struck out. In *Cohen* v. *Cohen*,[18] although the magistrates had not ordered the inclusion of this clause, their clerk failed to strike it out from the printed form of order. It was held that the clause was a nullity since it was no part of the order made by the magistrates, and that it had not prevented the continuance of the desertion upon which the order was based. In *Thory* v. *Thory*[1] the magistrates had ordered the inclusion of the clause when it was in no way necessary for the wife's protection, and on leave being given to appeal from the refusal of the magistrates to delete the clause, a Divisional Court ordered it to be struck out. It was held that, unless the court otherwise directed, the deletion of the clause operated from the date of the original order, so that again the desertion had never ceased. A decision of more doubtful validity is that in *Green* v. *Green*,[2] to the effect that a period of less than two years' desertion before the institution of proceedings before the magistrates could be added to a further period of desertion after the magistrates had ordered the deletion of the clause so as to complete the period of two (then three) years' desertion required for divorce. It is difficult to see how this decision can be justified because the Act then in force, which was worded in the same way as section 4 (3) of the Act of 1973, provided that the earlier period should be deemed "immediately to precede" the presentation of the divorce petition, so that it could hardly be added to the later period after the deletion of the clause, which in fact immediately preceded the presentation, to complete a continuous period of two or three years.

Where proceedings before the Act of 1969 were for divorce (or for nullity) it follows that they must have been unsuccessful, since the marriage still continues. But the fact that the previous petition was dismissed does not necessarily signify

---

[18] [1947] P. 147.
[1] [1948] P. 236.
[2] [1946] P. 112.

that a petition based upon the Act of 1973 will meet with the same fate, even though the facts are unchanged, since the law both as to the grounds for, and defences to, a petition is now very different.   Where the failure of the previous proceedings was due to failure to prove the facts alleged, then despite some change in the standard of proof now required,[3] the petitioner will usually be estopped *per rem judicatam* from proceeding again on the same facts.   But it is in most cases unlikely that the parties will have resumed cohabitation after unsuccessful divorce proceedings, and once they have lived apart for a continuous period of five years (some part of which period may well have been completed before the previous petition) the irretrievable breakdown of the marriage can be proved by reliance upon section 1 (2) (*e*).   Indeed, if consent to a decree were forthcoming, reliance on section 1 (2) (*d*) could ensure success after only two years of life apart.   There will, however, be many cases in which a petition failed because of the existance of bars rather than the absence of grounds. Thus, for example, a petition based on adultery might have been dismissed because of connivance, one based on adultery or cruelty by reason of condonation, and one based upon any ground because of collusion, the petitioner's adultery or his unreasonable delay in presenting or prosecuting the petition. All these bars have now been swept away, and the breakdown of that marriage is at least as irretrievable as it then was.   There seems to be no reason why the same adultery should not be alleged again in reliance on section 1 (2) (*a*), or the same cruelty as behaviour within section 1 (2) (*b*), or why proceedings found to be collusive could not be the subject of decrees by consent under section 1 (2) (*d*).   The length of time which has elapsed since the former proceedings seems immaterial, since delay is now no bar, and if it amounts to five years of life apart additional reliance could be placed on section 1 (2) (*e*), though a petitioner might wish to avoid this because of a possible defence of grave hardship under section 5 of the Act.[4]

Where the previous proceedings did not take place in England or Wales it is still necessary to disclose them in the petition, and the petitioner may be uncertain as to whether a decree of divorce or nullity obtained abroad will be recognised as valid here, and whether or not his marriage is regarded as still existing.   The circumstances in which a decree obtained elsewhere will be recognised here are discussed in Chapter 6.[5]   A *Practice Direction* dated November 30, 1970,[6] draws attention to the fact that it is incorrect to pray in the same petition for a declaration as to the validity of a purported divorce and in the alternative for dissolution of the marriage.   Though the latter relief is within the competence of a divorce county court, the former is not.   In such cases of doubt the petition should pray only for divorce, and the county court will have power to determine the validity of the marriage or the invalidity of a divorce under section 74 of the County Courts Act 1959, as a necessary preliminary to consideration of the prayer for divorce.   The Law Commission has published

---

[3] See *ante*, p. 16.
[4] As to which see *post*, p. 54.
[5] See *post*, pp. 93 *et seq*.
[6] [1970] 3 All E.R. 1024; [1971] 1 W.L.R. 29.

a Working Paper (No. 48) on "Declarations in Family Matters" and if the proposals were accepted and implemented a divorce county court would have jurisdiction to grant such declarations.

2. Findings in other proceedings.

The findings of the court in previous proceedings may sometimes assist the petitioner in proving the facts upon which he relies.

Before the Civil Evidence Act 1968, as a result of the decision in *Hollington* v. *Hewthorn & Co. Ltd.*[7] a finding of guilt, whether of a criminal or matrimonial offence, was not admissible in evidence unless the parties to the present and former proceedings were the same. By section 12 of that Act, in any civil proceedings, the fact that a person has been found guilty of adultery in any matrimonial proceedings, or has been adjudged to be the father of a child in affiliation proceedings before any court in the United Kingdom, shall (so long as the finding subsists) be admissible in evidence to prove that he committed the adultery or was the father of that child, as the case may be, whether or not he defended the original proceedings or he is a party to the subsequent civil proceedings. He is then to be taken to have committed that adultery or to be the father of that child, unless the contrary is proved. It was held in *Sutton* v. *Sutton*[8] that the effect of this latter provision was to cast upon him the onus of disproving the adultery to which the finding related, and that as regards the standard of proof he had only to discharge the burden of disproving that adultery on a balance of probability.

For the purposes of this section "matrimonial proceedings" are defined[9] as meaning "any matrimonial cause in the High Court or a county court in England and Wales or in the High Court of Northern Ireland, any consistorial action in Scotland, or any appeal arising out of any such cause or action". It will be observed that this expression does not include matrimonial proceedings in a magistrates' court, though the findings of such a court in affiliation proceedings are admissible. Some examples may serve to show how these provisions will operate in practice.

(1) Mrs. P obtains a decree of divorce in the High Court, or in a divorce county court, on the ground of her husband's adultery with Mrs. Q. That finding would, by virtue of section 12, be admissible in subsequent divorce proceedings brought by Mr. Q on the ground of his wife's adultery with Mr. P, and the finding would be conclusive against them unless they could disprove their adultery upon a balance of probability.

(2) Miss R has obtained an affiliation order in a magistrates' court against Mr. T. Should Mrs. T petition for divorce on the ground of her husband's adultery, she could rely upon the affiliation order as evidence that he was the father of Miss R's child, and by virtue of section 12 the onus will be upon Mr. T to prove the contrary. True, the section does not expressly say that the finding is evidence that he committed

---

[7] [1943] K.B. 587, C.A.
[8] [1969] 3 All E.R. 1348.
[9] By s. 12 (5).

adultery, but a judge could hardly hold that his liability to maintain the child resulted from adultery that he did not commit.

(3) Mrs. X has obtained a matrimonial order from a magistrates' court on the ground of her husband's adultery with Mrs. Y. Since the expression "matrimonial proceedings" in section 12 does not include such proceedings in a magistrates' court, there would be no way in which Mr. Y could rely upon this finding in support of his own petition for divorce on the ground of that adultery. A different position would arise if Mrs. X were later to take advantage of section 4 (1) of the Act of 1973, which has already been considered[10] and herself petition for divorce on the basis of the same adultery with Mrs. Y upon which the magistrates' order was based. The High Court or a divorce county court would then be able to accept the magistrates' order as sufficient proof of Mr. X's adultery by virtue of section 4 (2) of that Act, which provides that in such a case the court *may* treat the order as sufficient proof of the adultery for which it was granted. But this subsection merely permits the court to accept that evidence, and does not make it conclusive unless the contrary is proved; and it further provides that in such a case the court cannot grant a decree without also receiving evidence from the petitioner; she must also satisfy the court that life together is intolerable.

A similar provision to that in section 12 of the Civil Evidence Act 1968 is contained in section 11 of that Act, whereby in any civil proceedings the fact that a person has been convicted of an offence by or before any court in the United Kingdom or by a court martial there or elsewhere shall be admissible in evidence (whilst the conviction subsists) for the purpose of proving, where to do so is relevant to any issue in those proceedings, that he committed that offence, whether he was convicted upon a plea of guilty or otherwise and whether or not he is a party to the civil proceedings. Once again, he is to be taken to have committed the offence unless he proves the contrary. Advantage could be taken of this section, for example, when a husband had been convicted of rape, which would constitute adultery by him though not by his victim or when, as in *Taylor* v. *Taylor*,[11] he had been convicted of incestuous adultery with his daughter. Once again, the effect of this section is to shift the legal burden of proof, leaving the husband in such cases to prove, on a balance of probability, that he was not guilty of the offence of which he was convicted.[12] What is more, the view has been expressed that the very fact of conviction is entitled to very great weight.[13]

Where a petitioner in reliance upon section 11 or 12 of the Civil Evidence Act 1968 intends to adduce evidence of a conviction, a finding of adultery, or a finding of paternity in affiliation proceedings, a statement of that intention with particulars of the finding or conviction and of the issue to which it is relevant

---

[10] See *ante*, pp. 43 *et seq.*
[11] [1970] 1 W.L.R. 1148.
[12] See *Stupple* v. *Royal Insurance Co.*, [1971] 1 Q.B. 50, 72 and 74.
[13] *Per* DAVIES, L.J., [1970] 1 W.L.R. at p. 1152; *per* Lord DENNING, [1971] 1 Q.B. 50, 72, *per contra* BUCKLEY, L.J., at p. 75.

must be included in the petition.[14] This rule likewise applies to a respondent's answer, and if he wishes to deny the conviction or finding or allege that it was erroneous, or deny that it is relevant to any issue in the proceedings, he must make the denial or allegation in his answer.[15]

The Civil Evidence Act may also enable a transcript of the evidence given in the previous proceedings to be admitted in evidence under section 2 (1) or 4 (1) and a transcript of the judge's summing up under section 4 (1). There are detailed rules as to giving notice to the other party in advance and as to his right to object to the use of a transcript of evidence unless for some reason such as death, illness, or absence abroad, the witness cannot be called. But the court can waive the requirement of notice in advance and no notice is required in an undefended matrimonial cause, unless the court otherwise directs.[16]

Thus far consideration has been given only to the admissibility in evidence of findings in previous proceedings and not to the extent to which the doctrine of estoppel *per rem judicatam* may prevent a party from alleging that these findings were wrong. The court which is trying a suit for divorce, though it will always give due weight to a previous finding, can never be bound to accept it as sufficient proof of the matter to which it relates. Section 1 (3) of the Act of 1973 requires the court to inquire, so far as it reasonably can, into the facts alleged by the parties. Section 1 (4) provides that if the court is *satisfied* on the evidence of any such fact as is mentioned in section 1 (2) it shall grant a decree of divorce unless it is *satisfied* on all the evidence that the marriage has not broken down irretrievably. No previous finding can absolve the court from this statutory duty to be satisfied that the case for the petitioner has been proved.[17] If the court does decide to re-open the matter there is no longer any estoppel on either party.[18] Subject to this, the plea of *res judicata* may be stated as follows[19]

"Every judgment is conclusive proof against parties . . . of facts directly in issue in the case, actually decided by the court, and appearing from the judgment itself to be the ground on which it is based."

This involves several points:—

(1) The same persons must have been parties to both the present and the previous proceedings. It is true that the Civil Evidence Act 1968 makes certain findings admissible in evidence although the previous proceedings were between different parties. But in these cases there is no *estoppel*. The previous finding of, for example, adultery, is conclusive only "unless the contrary is proved".

(2) The precise point must have been in issue in the previous case, and the subject of litigation must have been the same. Thus if a magistrates' court, in proceedings under the Matrimonial Proceedings (Magistrates' Courts) Act 1960, rejected a wife's complaint that her husband had been guilty of wilful neglect

---

[14] Rule 9 (5).
[15] Rule 21 (5) and (6).
[16] Rule 42, applying with modifications R.S.C. Ord. 38, rr. 20–33, and see *Taylor* v. *Taylor*, supra, where these matters are discussed at length.
[17] *Harriman* v. *Harriman*, [1909] P. 123.
[18] *Thompson* v. *Thompson*, [1957] P. 19.
[19] *Tumath* v. *Tumath*, [1970] P. 78.

to maintain her on the ground that she had herself committed adultery, she
would not be estopped from denying that adultery were he to rely upon it in a
subsequent petition for divorce against her,[20] though the finding might have
strong probative value.[1] The first litigation was aimed at maintenance of the
wife during the marriage, the second at ending that marriage, two completely
different "subjects".

(3) If the subject of litigation is the same there is an estoppel as to all points
actually decided. Thus if W petitioned for divorce in reliance upon an allegation of H's adultery, and the petition was dismissed by the High Court or a
divorce county court on the ground that she had failed to prove that adultery,
she could not again rely upon it by way of any subsequent petition or answer.
If, on the other hand, H did not defend the case, and a divorce county court
found the adultery proved and granted W a decree nisi, H would be estopped,
in subsequent applications by W for ancillary relief, from denying that the
adultery was committed.

(4) A plea of *res judicata* cannot be raised in respect of matters which were
not before the court in the previous proceedings, so that the court never adjudi-
cated upon them. Thus it was held in *Tumath* v. *Tumath*[2] that a husband who
does not choose to defend his wife's petition for divorce based upon his adultery,
which he is not in a position to deny, is not precluded thereafter, when the
question of financial provision comes to be considered, from raising charges
relating to her conduct which he might, had he wished to do so, have raised in
answer to her prayer for divorce. As Sir GORDON WILLMER pointed out in
that case[3]

> "I cannot think that there is any room for a rule of public policy inhibiting
> parties from raising in maintenance proceedings matters relating to the
> conduct of the parties, even where such matters could have been raised
> at the trial of the suit, provided that there is no ground for holding that
> there is an estoppel *per rem judicatam* as between the parties. This is a
> matter which, I apprehend, is likely to become one of increasing import-
> ance when the new Divorce Reform Act 1969 comes into force: it is likely
> that when decrees of divorce can be granted upon mere proof of the
> breakdown of the marriage, the real disputes between the parties will only
> emerge in the course of subsequent ancillary proceedings."

And as SALMON, L.J. said[4]

> "Everyone knows that until comparatively recently divorce cases have
> habitually been hotly contested in public at great expense to the parties
> or to the legal aid fund solely for the purpose of securing a supposed benefit
> for one or other of the parties in future maintenance or custody proceed-
> ings. This cannot in my view serve any useful purpose and may indeed
> be properly regarded as contrary to modern concepts of public policy."

---

[20] *Winnan* v. *Winnan*, [1949] P. 174.
[1] *Turner* v. *Turner*, [1962] P. 283.
[2] [1970] P. 78.
[3] *Ibid.*, at p. 94.
[4] *Ibid.*, at p. 86.

DIVORCE AFTER SEPARATION AGREEMENT

The effect of a separation agreement as terminating or precluding desertion has already been noted,[5] as has the fact that separation by agreement in no way precludes a petition based upon two or five years of life apart.[6] Where, however, such an agreement has been entered into and a petitioner wishes to rely upon the respondent's adultery, or upon behaviour such that the petitioner cannot reasonably be expected to live with the respondent, it will sometimes be found that the agreement contains a so-called *Rose* v. *Rose*[7] or *L.* v. *L.*[8] clause. Such a clause in its usual form provides for absolute forgiveness of past offences, and that no offence or misconduct committed before the execution of the agreement shall be pleaded or alleged by either party or be admissible in evidence in case either party should thereafter commence or prosecute any proceedings against the other. It was held in the above-mentioned cases that such a clause is in no way contrary to public policy, as tending to oust the jurisdiction of the court or pervert the course of justice, and that it is valid and effective.

The abolition of the absolute bar of condonation will in no way affect the validity of such a clause, and it will prevent either party from relying upon matters which occurred before the agreement was made. It cannot, presumably, contain a licence to commit adultery in the future which, despite the abolition of such bars as connivance and collusion, would still seem to be contrary to public policy.[9] Thus if, after a deed containing such a clause has been executed, the husband files a petition alleging his wife's adultery with the co-respondent after the date when it was executed, the clause would in no way bar the success of his petition and neither the wife nor the co-respondent could rely by way of defence upon any matters which occurred before the deed was made.[10] The exact effect of each clause must, of course, depend upon the wording employed, as for example in *Gooch* v. *Gooch*[11] where a covenant "not to commence or present" proceedings was held not to prevent matters being pleaded by way of answer.

What has been said as to these clauses in no way affects the quite different rule of public policy which renders void any agreement purporting to restrict any right of a wife to apply to a court for an order for financial provision for herself[12] or a child of the family.[13] So far as agreements in writing are concerned, this rule has statutory force by virtue of section 34 of the Act of 1973.

PRESUMPTION OF DEATH AND DISSOLUTION

By section 19 of the Act of 1973, any married person who alleges that reasonable grounds exist for supposing that the other party to the marriage is dead may present a petition to the court to have the death presumed and the marriage

---

[5] See *ante*, p. 35.
[6] See *ante*, p. 42.
[7] (1883), 8 P.D. 98.
[8] [1931] P. 63.
[9] *Harrison* v. *Harrison*, [1910] 1 K.B. 35.
[10] *N.* v. *N. & L.*, [1957] P. 333.
[11] [1893] P. 99.
[12] *Hyman* v. *Hyman*, [1929] A.C. 601.
[13] *Bennett* v. *Bennett*, [1952] 1 K.B. 249.

dissolved, and the court may, if satisfied that such reasonable grounds exist, make a decree of presumption of death and dissolution of the marriage. This procedure meets the dilemma of, say, a wife who has heard nothing of her husband for several years, or last heard of him when he embarked upon some hazardous adventure, and wishes to re-marry. If she is right in her assumption that he is dead, although her reasonable belief in the death of her husband is a defence to a charge of bigamy,[14] her second "marriage" will have been void *ab initio*.

By section 19 (3) of this Act, in any proceedings under this section the fact that for a period of seven years or more the other party to the marriage has been continuously absent from the petitioner, who has no reason to believe that the other party has been living within that time, is to be evidence that the other party is dead unless the contrary is proved. This does not mean that a petition cannot be presented until the absence has lasted for seven years, but merely determines the moment at which the onus of proof shifts. Before the period of seven years has elapsed, the petitioner must adduce evidence of valid reasons for assuming that the death has occurred. When that period has elapsed, even though the matter may be one of speculation, the petition will succeed "if nothing has happened within that time to give the petitioner reason to believe that the other party was then living".[15] Even then, the failure to make reasonable enquiries will usually result in the court's refusal to exercise its discretion to grant a decree.[16] There may well be cases in which the petitioner would stand a greater chance of success if the petition was based upon the irretrievable breakdown of the marriage in reliance upon section 1 (2) (e) of the Act of 1973 after five years of life apart, instead of seeking a decree of presumption of death and dissolution.

The marriage is not dissolved until the decree nisi is made absolute, so that if after a decree nisi has been granted and before it is made absolute, the respondent is found to be alive, the decree nisi will be rescinded.[17] If the party who has been presumed to be dead is found to be alive after the decree has been made absolute, since the decree is a decree dissolving the marriage, financial provision can be ordered to be made in favour of that party in the same manner, and to the same extent, as in other suits for divorce.[18]

---

[14] *R.* v. *Tolson* (1889), 23 Q.B.D. 168.
[15] *Thompson* v. *Thompson*, [1956] P. 414, 425.
[16] *Bullock* v. *Bullock*, [1960] 2 All E.R. 307; *Bradshaw* v. *Bradshaw*, [1956] P. 274.
[17] *Manser* v. *Manser*, [1940] P. 224.
[18] *Deacock* v. *Deacock*, [1958] P. 230.

CHAPTER 3

BARS TO DIVORCE

1. DEFENCES

Since the Divorce Reform Act 1969 came into operation, all the former absolute and discretionary bars to the success of a petition have been completely abolished. The reason for their abolition becomes clear if it is remembered that a decree of divorce no longer indicates the guilt or innocence of the parties, but only that their marriage is no longer viable. Thus the petitioner's own adultery, cruelty, desertion or wilful neglect may make it more, rather than less, likely that the breakdown is irretrievable, and the fact that there has been collusion (unless it took the form of an agreement to present a false case) can no longer be objectionable. Unreasonable delay in petitioning might suggest that there could be some hope of reconciliation, as might condonation of adultery or cruelty: the petitioner's own adultery, or his connivance at the respondent's adultery, might go to show that the petitioner did not find that adultery intolerable: but of themselves these matters are otherwise irrelevant with one exception. As has already been mentioned[1] the fact that the parties have lived together for one or more periods amounting in all to more than six months after the respondent's adultery became known to the petitioner, will be an absloute bar to reliance upon that adultery.

But despite these provisions, the conduct of the parties, including these matters, will still to some extent be relevant when the time comes for consideration of questions of financial provision, property and the interests of the children. They have, with one exception[2] been withdrawn from the publicity of divorce proceedings in open court into the privacy of chambers where they may yet, in relation to questions of ancillary relief, engender all the bitterness which they have so often done in the past.

The effect of periods of life together, which differ according to the facts alleged, have already been considered. There appears to be one defence only which is applicable to all cases. **Irrespective of the facts proved in support of the petition, it will be a defence to show that the court should not be satisfied that the marriage has broken down irretrievably.**

The problems which arise in relation to proof of irretrievable breakdown have already been considered (see *ante*, p. 15).

The only other defence, which is applicable only to cases founded upon section 1 (2) (*e*) of the Act, is that of grave hardship.

---

[1] See *ante*, p. 24.
[2] Under s. 5 of the Act, *infra*.

By section 5 of the Act the respondent to a petition for divorce in which the petitioner alleges five years' separation may oppose the grant of a decree on the ground that the dissolution of the marriage will result in grave financial or other hardship to him and that it would in all the circumstances be wrong to dissolve the marriage.

Where the grant of a decree is opposed by virtue of this section, the court must first find, if the defence is to succeed, that the petitioner is entitled to rely in support of his petition on the fact of five years' separation and make no such finding as to any other fact mentioned in section 1 (2) of the Act. The wording of section 5 of the Act of 1973 here differs (as a result of a Report of the Law Commission[3]) from that of section 4 of the Divorce Reform Act 1969, whereby the defence could only apply if the court was satisfied that the *only* fact on which the petitioner was entitled to rely was that of five years' separation. If strictly interpreted, this required two findings, that he was entitled to rely upon five years' separation and that he was not entitled to rely upon any other fact. This difficulty was avoided in *Rule* v. *Rule*[4] by holding that a petitioner was "entitled to rely" upon a particular fact only if it was both pleaded and proved, so that if, for example, a petitioner might have been able to rely (in addition to reliance upon five years' separation) upon adultery or unreasonable behaviour, but had chosen not to do so, the defence could still be pleaded. Doubts about the validity of this sensible decision led to the change in wording whereby it is only necessary that the court should make "no such finding" in relation to any other fact. A similar change in wording has been made in sections 10 (1) and (2) (as to which see *post*, pp. 57 and 59).

Assuming that the court is satisfied on this preliminary point and would, apart from section 5, grant a decree on the petition, it is required to consider all the circumstances, including the conduct of the parties to the marriage and the interests of those parties and of any children or other persons concerned. If it is then of opinion that the dissolution of the marriage will result in grave financial or other hardship to the respondent and that it would in all the circumstances be wrong to dissolve the marriage, it is required to dismiss the petition. It is expressly provided[5] that for the purposes of this section hardship is to include the loss of the chance of acquiring any benefit which the respondent might acquire if the marriage was not dissolved.

The operation of this section in practice involves a number of points.

(i) *There must be financial or other hardship*

It is clear from the wording of the section that if the defence is to succeed the hardship must be one which will result from the dissolution of the marriage, and not one which has already been suffered from the five or more years of life apart. In almost all the reported cases the hardship alleged has taken the form of the loss of pension rights which would result from the wife's loss of her opportunity of surviving her husband as his widow. Sometimes, as in *Parker* v.

---

[3] By s. 5 (3).
[4] [1971] 3 All E.R. 1368.
[5] Law Com. No. 51. Cmnd. 5167, para. 1.

Parker,[6] this hardship can be avoided by some other form of financial provision—in that case by the purchase of a deferred annuity with the obligation to pay the annual premiums secured by a second mortgage on the husband's house. In others, such as *Julian* v. *Julian*,[7] the husband's assets may be insufficient to compensate the wife for the loss of pension rights, and it may be necessary to refuse a decree.

There has been little authority on the subject of hardship other than financial hardship, save for two cases in which social hardship was alleged. In the first, *Banik* v. *Banik*,[8] a rehearing was ordered so that there might be a thorough investigation of the allegation of the wife, who had been married by a Hindu ceremony in India, that divorce would render her a social outcast in the society in which she lived in India, and dying as an unmarried woman would be anathema in her religious beliefs. A similar point arose in the second case, *Parghi* v. *Parghi*,[9] where a decree nisi was granted, not on the ground that divorce could not cause grave hardship to any Hindu wife, but on the ground that in this case, among educated Hindus, the approach to marriage had changed and was now similar to that in the West.

(ii) *The hardship must be grave*

The adjective "grave" qualifies both "financial" and "other hardship".[10] There is always some hardship on a young wife with a child where neither party is a wealthy person, but the husband has expectations.[11] Obviously the hardship cannot be grave in cases such as *Parker* v. *Parker*,[12] where it can be substantially mitigated by other financial arrangements. Where it is said to arise from loss of prospective pension rights, much will depend upon the age of the wife. Such a loss might be grave hardship to a wife in her late forties, as in *Parker* v. *Parker*. It might not be so to a younger wife in her early thirties, as in *Mathias* v. *Mathias*,[13] where the wife was healthy, would be able to obtain employment, and might eventually re-marry.

(iii) *The matters for consideration*

Very little seems to have turned, in the cases so far reported, on the requirement that the court should consider all the circumstances of the case, including not only the interests of the parties to the marriage but also the conduct of the parties and the interests of any children or other persons concerned. In *Dorrell* v. *Dorrell*,[14] Sir George BAKER, P., took the view that conduct in relation to this section cannot mean conduct in the sense of the old matrimonial offence. This dictum was, however, overruled by the Court of Appeal in *Brickell* v. *Brickell*.[15]

---

[6] [1972] Fam. 116.

[7] (1972), 116 Sol. Jo. 763.

[8] [1973] 3 All E.R. 45; on this re-hearing the defence failed (1973), 117 Sol. Jo. 874.

[9] (1973), *Times*, May 8.

[10] *Parker* v. *Parker*, [1972] 1 Fam. 116, 118; *Dorrell* v. *Dorrell*, [1972] 3 All E.R. 343, 1090.

[11] *Mathias* v. *Mathias*, [1972] Fam. 287, *per* KARMINSKI, L.J., at p. 300.

[12] *Supra*.

[13] *Supra*.

[14] [1972] 1 W.L.R. 1087, 1092.

[15] [1973] 3 W.L.R. 602, 606.

Conduct in the context of the section is not confined to a matrimonial offence in the old sense, but must clearly include it. Nevertheless in the earlier case of *Chapman* v. *Chapman*[16] the Court of Appeal held that it is wrong for a petitioner who seeks a divorce on the ground of five years' separation to charge the respondent with a matrimonial offence: if he wishes to make such a charge, he should proceed on some other ground, such as adultery, unreasonable behaviour or desertion. In particular, and this was the point of that case, a petition based upon five years' separation should not contain any allegation of fault for the purpose of seeking an order for costs,[17] and the question of fault should not be investigated at the hearing. Logically, this should also be so in relation to the defence of grave hardship, and indeed the tendency of the courts in dealing with matters of financial provision and adjustment of property rights is, in general, to disregard questions of conduct.[18]

As to the interests of other persons concerned, it seems that prospects of re-marriage and new commitments are accepted as irrelevant.[19] The fact that social security benefit will be available to a wife and that the pension which will be lost is so small that it will be swallowed up in social security, does not alter the fact that the loss of that pension will still be a grave hardship to the wife.[20]

(iv) *The petition must be dismissed only if it would be wrong in all the circumstances to dissolve the marriage*

It is at this final stage, when all the remaining matters have been considered, that weight must be given to the element of public policy. A balance must be maintained between on the one hand upholding the sanctity of marriage and avoiding hardship, and on the other the public interest in the dissolution of a marriage which has hopelessly broken down, and enabling one, or both, of the spouses, to make a fresh start in life. Indeed in *Mathias* v. *Mathias*,[21] where the wife was young and cohabitation had lasted some two and three-quarter years and separation for seven and three-quarter years, the Court of Appeal took the view that it would be wrong not to dissolve the marriage.

In cases of this nature it must not be supposed that a wife is left without a remedy. She has still available to her the additional protection of section 10 (2) of the Act (as to which see *post*, p. 57) whereby she can ask the court to decline to make absolute the decree nisi which has been granted unless it is satisfied that the financial provision which has been made for her is reasonable and fair or the best which can be made in the circumstances. Indeed it is wise for a wife who intends to raise the defence available under section 5 of the Act also to give notice of her intention to apply to the court to consider her financial position under section 10 (2) should her defence under section 5 fail.[1] These

---

[16] [1972] 3 All E.R. 1089, C.A.
[17] See *post*, p. 192.
[18] See *Wachtel* v. *Wachtel*, [1973] Fam. 72 and *Trippas* v. *Trippas*, [1973] Fam. 134, and *post*, p. 138.
[19] *Dorrell* v. *Dorrell*, *supra*, at p. 1092.
[20] *Dorrell* v. *Dorrell*.
[21] *Supra*.
[1] See *post*, pp. 58, 59.

alternatives are neatly illustrated by *Parkes* v. *Parkes*.[2] The wife had raised the defence of grave financial hardship to her husband's petition based upon five years' separation, but had agreed to allow the petition to go undefended upon the terms of an apparent agreement reached between the parties, subject to the court's approval of the terms agreed. Subsequently, before the decree nisi had been made absolute, it appeared that there were disputes as to the meaning of the terms agreed, as to whether the maintenance payable was to be clear of tax and as to whether the husband had fully disclosed his financial position. The Court of Appeal gave the wife the option of having the decree nisi set aside owing to mistake, and raising the defence of grave financial hardship, or of allowing the decree nisi to stand and applying to the court to consider her financial position before allowing the decree to be made absolute.

The Law Commission has reported[3] that the ways of protecting a divorced wife's expectations under her husband's pension scheme is a problem which remains unsolved, and added "after full consultation, we believe it to be incapable of direct and complete solution".

2. MATTERS AFFECTING THE MAKING ABSOLUTE OF A DECREE NISI

In the strict sense of the word the matters considered under this heading are not defences, since they do not lead to the dismissal of the petition but only to the rescission of a decree nisi already obtained, or a refusal to make that decree absolute. Nevertheless, since the petitioner's object is to be free from the marriage bond, it seems convenient to consider them at this point. Their application varies according to the facts upon which the petitioner relies. The relevant provisions are as follows:

(a) *In all cases, that the court is not satisfied with the arrangements for the welfare of children of the family.*

This matter is dealt with in detail in Chapter 13.[4] At this point it is only necessary to mention that section 41 provides that if the court makes absolute a decree of divorce or nullity, or makes a decree of judicial separation without having made an order declaring that it is satisfied as to this question of welfare, the decree will be void. This provision, unlike the remaining matters considered under this heading is not limited to decrees of divorce, and is mandatory and does not depend upon any application by the respondent for the matter to be considered.

(b) *In cases based upon two or five years' separation, that the petitioner's financial provision for the respondent is unsatisfactory.*

This allegation, which is based upon section 10 (2) of the Act of 1973, differs from that relating to children, which has already been considered,[5] in two main respects. First, it does not apply to all decrees nisi, but is limited to cases where

---

[2] [1971] 3 All E.R. 870, C.A.
[3] Report on Financial Provision in Matrimonial Proceedings Law Com. No. 25, para 112.
[4] See *post*, p. 184.
[5] *Supra*, and see p. 184, *post*.

the court has granted a decree on the basis of a finding that the petitioner was entitled to rely in support of the petition on the fact of two years' or five years' separation (as the case may be) and has made no such finding as to any other fact mentioned in section 1 (2) of the Act.[6] Secondly, it is not a matter which the court is required, or entitled, to raise of its own accord, but arises only if the respondent applies to the court under the said section to consider the respondent's financial position after the divorce.

It seems somewhat strange that a respondent who, after two years of separation, has consented to the grant of a decree, should be enabled to apply to the court, after decree nisi, to consider the financial position. Presumably the respondent was satisfied as to this before giving the consent and, if misled into so doing, can apply under section 10 (1) of the Act, as explained below, to rescind the decree nisi. If he was not misled, it seems unjust to the petitioner to permit the respondent to change his mind. The wisdom of ensuring that both parties in such cases have competent legal advice at an early stage is self-evident. In practice applications under section 10 (2) are likely to be much more frequent when the petition is based upon the fact that the parties have lived apart for five years, and the respondent has declined to consent to the grant of a decree.

If such an application is made the section requires the court[7] consider all the circumstances, including the age, health, conduct, earning capacity, financial resources and financial obligations of each of the parties, and the financial position of the respondent as, having regard to the divorce, it is likely to be after the death of the petitioner should the petitioner die first. Having considered these matters and subject to the proviso mentioned below,[8] the court shall not make absolute the decree of divorce unless it is satisfied that the petitioner should not be required to make any financial provision for the respondent or that the financial provision made by the petitioner for the respondent is reasonable and fair or the best that can be made in the circumstances. It was held in *Wilson* v. *Wilson*[9] the word "made" does not include a mere proposal. The husband had obtained a decree nisi on the basis of five years' separation and the court accepted that his proposal that the matrimonial home should be sold and that his wife should receive half the net proceeds of sale would be a reasonable and fair financial provision. But it was ordered that the decree should not be made absolute until the sale had been completed and her share of the proceeds of sale paid to the wife.

This provision must be sharply contrasted with the defence of grave financial or other hardship which, under section 5 of the Act, is available only in cases based on five years of life apart. Generally, unless the parties be wealthy, the grant of any divorce decree is likely to cause some financial hardship. The resources which formerly provided for one home have now to provide for two. If that hardship is grave, and section 5 applies, the petition may be dismissed. If less than grave, and the financial provision is the best that can be

---

[6] As to the reason for the change in wording from that in s. 6 of the Divorce Reform Act 1969, see *ante*, p. 54.

[7] Since December 1, 1973, such applications have been dealt with by a registrar, unless either party requests otherwise. See now Rule 57.

[8] See s. 10 (4).

[9] [1973] 1 All E.R. 17.

made in the circumstances, a decree nisi can be granted and made absolute despite the respondent's objection. Just as in relation to provision for children there is power to accept undertakings,[10] so section 10 (4) of the Act of 1973 enables the court to make the decree absolute without observing the above requirements if it appears that there are circumstances making it desirable that the decree should be made absolute without delay and the court has obtained a satisfactory undertaking from the petitioner that he will make such financial provision for the respondent as the court may approve—a somewhat difficult decision for him unless there are compelling reasons, such as a desire to remarry before a child is born, for avoiding delay.

(c) *In cases where the parties have lived apart for two years and the respondent has consented to the grant of a decree, that the petitioner misled the respondent into so consenting.*

This provision, which is contained in section 10 (1) of the Act, is relevant where the court has granted a decree of divorce on the basis of a finding that the petitioner was entitled to rely in support of his petition on the fact of two years' separation coupled with the respondent's consent to a decree being granted[11] and has made no finding as to any other fact mentioned in section 1 (2). In that case, and in that case only, the court may on the application of the respondent at any time before the decree is made absolute rescind the decree if it is satisfied that the petitioner misled the respondent (whether intentionally or unintentionally) about any matter which the respondent took into account in deciding to give his consent.

It will be noticed that this is not a case in which the making absolute of the decree is merely postponed, but one in which the decree nisi is actually rescinded, though presumably if the parties can reach a satisfactory adjustment of the matter the application to rescind the decree nisi could be withdrawn. The Act is silent as to the kind of matters on which the respondent may rely—it refers only to "any matter which the respondent took into account". But it seems likely that the relevant matters will be matters of finance and property—both present resources and future prospects—and perhaps matters concerning the petitioner's own conduct. A wife who had been misled into believing that her husband had never committed adultery might well claim that she would not have accepted the terms which he offered had she known the truth. In order to avoid, so far as is possible, an application of this kind, it is essential that legal advisers acting for the petitioner should impress upon him the necessity for absolute frankness in these matters.

3. AGREEMENTS AS TO FINANCIAL PROVISIONS

Much has already been said of the importance of matters of finance, of property, and of arrangements for the welfare of children, in the wording of the

---

[10] S. 41 (2), *post*, p. 184.
[11] As to the reason for the change in wording from that of the Divorce Reform Act 1969, s. 5, see *ante*, p. 54.

provisions of the Act. This is especially the case when it is sought to obtain the respondent's consent to the grant of a decree after two or more years of life apart and still more so if the court is to be persuaded to grant, or make absolute, a decree nisi after five years of life apart, often brought about by the fault of the petitioner. Even where breakdown has been established after shorter periods on the basis of what were formerly matrimonial offences, the petition will in the majority of cases be undefended and, if the parties can be persuaded to make sensible and reasonable arrangements as to these matters, much bitterness and unhappiness, especially to the children, can sometimes be avoided.

By virtue of what is now section 7 of the Act of 1973, provision can be made by rules of court to enable the parties to a marriage, or either of them, on application made either before or after the presentation of a petition for divorce, to refer to the court any agreement or arrangement made or proposed to be made between them, being an agreement or arrangement which relates to, or arises out of, or is connected with, the proceedings for divorce which are contemplated or, as the case may be, have begun, and for enabling the court to express an opinion, should it think it desirable to do so, as to the reasonableness of the agreement or arrangement and to give such direction, if any, in the matter as it thinks fit.

The Rule which formerly governed this matter[12] has, however, been omitted from the Matrimonial Causes Rules 1973. The reason is no doubt to be found in a *Practice Direction*[13] which made it clear that where the parties have reached a concluded agreement with the assistance of their legal advisers it is now rarely necessary or desirable for them to incur the considerable expense of referring the agreement to the judge prior to the hearing.

There are nevertheless, cases in which the court is required, under sections 41 or 10 (2),[14] to consider whether any particular arrangements are, or are not, reasonable. The relevant factors are discussed in some detail in Chapter 9, which deals with matters affecting financial provision and adjustment of property rights. It will no doubt be true, as it has been in the past, that the court will be reluctant to regard as reasonable an arrangement whereby a wife agrees to a term consenting to dismissal for all time to her claim for maintenance.[15]

As has already been explained, agreements purporting to oust the jurisdiction of the court to award maintenance for a wife or a child of the family are void.[16] But where such an agreement is entered into as part of the terms on which the respondent consents to the grant of a decree under section 1 (2) (*d*), there is much to be said for the view that, subject no doubt to the sanction of the court, the parties should be permitted to make a final and binding agreement which could not be the subject of variation except by agreement between them.[17]

---

[12] Matrimonial Causes Rules 1971, r. 6.
[13] [1972] 3 All E.R. 704, para. 3.
[14] See *ante*, p. 57.
[15] *M.* v. *M. (No. 1)*, [1967] P. 313, 317.
[16] *Ante*, p. 51, and see *post*, pp. 172, 173.
[17] As to embodiment of the agreed terms in an order of the court, see *post*, p. 148.

4. INTERVENTIONS

There are three circumstances in which the Queen's Proctor may take part in proceedings for divorce and these provisions are equally applicable to suits for nullity or judicial separation.[18]

Section 8 (1) (*a*) enables the court (including the Court of Appeal) to direct that all necessary papers in the matter be sent to the Queen's Proctor in order that he may, under the directions of the Attorney-General, instruct counsel to argue before the court any point which the court wishes to have fully argued. This power is usually exercised where some point of law of exceptional difficulty arises, particularly in an undefended case. The effect, as was pointed out by KARMINSKI, L.J., in *Kaur* v. *Singh*,[19] is to enable the court to be quite certain that all the relevant facts and authorities are put before it by a skilled and wholly neutral source. The Queen's Proctor is entitled to charge the costs of such a case as part of the expenses of his office.

By section 8 (1) (*b*) any person may at any time during the progress of the proceedings or before the decree nisi is made absolute give information to the Queen's Proctor on any matter material to the due decision of the case, and he may then take such steps as the Attorney-General considers necessary or expedient. The circumstances in which the Queen's Proctor will intervene during the progress of the suit by virtue of this provision are very rare.

Section 9 of the Act is a provision of a different nature. Where a decree nisi of divorce or nullity[20] has been granted but not made absolute, the Queen's Proctor or any other person who is not a party to the proceedings may show cause why the decree should not be made absolute by reason of material facts not having been brought before the court, and the court may then make the decree absolute, rescind the decree nisi, require further inquiry, or otherwise deal with the case as it thinks fit. Interventions of this nature were not uncommon when such matters as condonation, collusion and the petitioner's own adultery were bars to proceedings for divorce. They are now rare: in the year 1972 the Queen's Proctor intervened in only eleven cases.[1]

It should be noted that although section 9 enables a person other than the Queen's Proctor to show cause why a decree should not be made absolute, it gives such a person who is not a party to the suit no right to intervene before a decree nisi has been granted. Where, however, adultery with any party to the suit is alleged against any person who is not a party, or the court considers, in the interest of any person not already a party, that he should be made a party, it has a discretion to allow him to intervene on such terms, if any, as it thinks fit.[2]

---

[18] Ss. 15 and 19 (4).
[19] [1972] 1 W.L.R. 105, 109.
[20] S. 15.
[1] Civil Judicial Statistics 1972, Cmnd. 5333, Table 10.
[2] S. 49 (5).

CHAPTER 4

JUDICIAL SEPARATION

1. Grounds for and bars to judicial separation.

The Law Commission, in a report presented in July 1969,[1] recommended the abolition of the matrimonial remedy of restitution of conjugal rights which in effect ordered a deserting spouse to return to cohabitation. The order was not specifically enforceable, but if it was disobeyed the court was enabled to make orders concerning such matters as financial provision for the petitioner and the children and for custody of children. This recommendation was embodied in the Matrimonial Proceedings and Property Act 1970; section 20 provided that no person after the commencement of that Act (i.e. on or after January 1, 1971) should be entitled to petition the High Court or any county court for such a decree. Amongst the reasons given for the abolition was that the "order" had in fact no teeth and only brought the law into disrepute, and that the mere fact that the remedy was so rarely used of itself indicates that it was not an effective one. The latter argument is abundantly supported by the Civil Judicial Statistics. The Commission reported that in the three years 1965–1967 there were only 105 petitions and 31 decrees made. The downward trend continued in 1968 with a (hardly grand) total of 16 petitions and 6 decrees. The decree is of importance today only in the few cases in which orders relating to financial provision made in the proceedings still remain in force. Disobedience to the decree has not, since the Divorce Reform Act 1969, been a ground for judicial separation. By contrast the remedy of judicial separation remains available to spouses who, on religious or other grounds, do not wish to seek divorce. The totals here are higher—in the year 1972 there were 330 petitions and 115 decrees.[2]

By section 17 of the Act of 1973, a petition for judicial separation may be presented by either party to a marriage on the ground that any such fact as is mentioned in section 1 (2) exists and the court is not concerned to consider whether the marriage has broken down irretrievably. Thus these five facts, which in relation to a petition for divorce are only the means of proving that the breakdown is irretrievable,[3] are of themselves the actual *grounds* for judicial separation. The position as to proof of these facts is the same as in a divorce suit. It is the duty of the court to inquire, so far as it reasonably can, into the facts alleged by the respondent, and if it is satisfied in the evidence of any of these facts, it must grant a decree of judicial separation.[4]

---

[1] Law Com. No. 23.
[2] Civil Judicial Statistics for the year 1972, Cmnd. 5333.
[3] See Chapter 2.
[4] S. 17 (2), see *ante*, p. 15.

Save for the fact that no leave is required to petition for judicial separation within three years of the date of the marriage, and proof is not required that the marriage has broken down irretrievably, many of the matters already considered in relation to divorce apply equally to judicial separation, and in particular the provisions of sections 2, 6 and 7. Thus:—

(1) The provisions whereby the parties are permitted to live together for one or more periods not exceeding six months in all without prejudicing their chances of obtaining a decree[5] are the same, as is the meaning for this purpose of "living apart".[6]

(2) The provisions as to continuance of desertion despite the respondent's inability to continue the necessary intention[7] and as to rules of court concerning the respondent's consent to a decree after two years' separation, are equally applicable.[8]

(3) Despite the fact that there is no need to prove that the breakdown is irretrievable, the petitioner's solicitor is still required to certify whether he has discussed with the petitioner the prospects of reconciliation, and the court has the same power to adjourn the proceedings to enable attempts to be made to effect a reconciliation.[9]

(4) Agreements or arrangements may be referred by either party to the court to enable it to express an opinion as to their reasonableness and give such directions as it thinks fit.[10]

(7) A decree cannot be granted unless the court has declared its satisfaction as to the arrangements for the welfare of the children of the family.[11]

At this point the similarities end. In proceedings for judicial separation there is one final decree, and not a decree nisi as in a divorce suit. It follows that the bars to making absolute a decree of divorce because the financial provision for the respondent is unsatisfactory, or as to rescission of a decree nisi based upon two years' separation on the ground that the respondent has been misled into consenting to the grant of a decree,[12] have no application to suits for judicial separation. Since the decree does not end the marriage, the defence of grave financial or other hardship which applies to divorce suits based upon five years' separation[13] is not applicable.

Section 12 (3) of the Matrimonial Causes Act 1965 enabled a spouse against whom a decree of judicial separation had been granted to apply for rescission of the decree on the ground that it was obtained in the absence of the applicant or, if desertion was the ground of the decree, that there was reasonable cause

---

[5] S. 2 (1), (2), (3) and (5). See *ante*, pp. 24, 26, 37, 41 and 43.
[6] S. 2 (6), see *ante*, p. 24.
[7] S. 2 (4), see *ante*, p. 34.
[8] S. 2 (7), see *ante*, p. 42.
[9] S. 6, see *ante*, p. 17.
[10] S. 7, see *ante*, p. 60.
[11] Ss. 17 (2) and 41, see *post*, p. 184.
[12] S. 10, see *ante*, pp. 57, 59.
[13] S. 5, see *ante*, p. 54.

for the alleged desertion. This provision has, on the recommendation of the Law Commission,[14] been repealed and not re-enacted. Although it had existed since the Matrimonial Causes Act 1857, there had only been three reported cases on it in the last hundred years. It was illogical that there should be a special provision for judicial separation, since the court has an inherent power to rescind a decree which was granted in circumstances of procedural irregularity or contrary to the justice of the case, and because in effect it gave a right of appeal in cases of desertion without any limit of time.

2. Effect of judicial separation.

The principal effect of the decree itself is that it is no longer obligatory for the petitioner to cohabit with the respondent.[15] From this it follows, as has already been explained in relation to divorce, that if desertion has already started it will be terminated and that desertion cannot commence whilst the decree remains in force. It also follows that a wife's implied consent to intercourse, which results from the marriage, and which she cannot withdraw as and when she pleases,[16] is revoked. If, therefore, her husband has intercourse with her against her wishes whilst the decree of judicial separation remains in force, he can properly be convicted of rape, which would obviously be impossible whilst the implied consent continued. A magistrates' order containing a provision that she is no longer bound to cohabit with him has the same result.[17] It was suggested (obiter) in *R.* v. *Miller*[18] that a separation agreement containing a covenant by the husband not to molest his wife might also have this effect. But the implied consent to intercourse is not revoked by the fact that the wife has filed a petition for divorce: her husband could not in such a case be convicted of rape, but if he used force or violence he could be convicted for whatever offence the facts of the case warranted, such as an assault causing actual bodily harm or common assault.

The Matrimonial Proceedings and Property Act 1970 not only abolished the wife's agency of necessity,[19] but also revoked section 20 (4) of the Matrimonial Causes Act 1965, whereby if in a case of judicial separation alimony was ordered to be paid to the wife but was not paid, the husband was liable for necessaries supplied for the use of the wife. These methods of making good the inadequacy of financial provision which her husband was making for her were of little use to the wife in practice, since those with whom she wished to deal were reluctant to give her credit in the hope of recourse against a husband from whom she was separated. By way of compensation for the loss of these rights the court has new power to make the same orders for financial provision in favour of a wife who has obtained a decree of judicial separation as it could if she had instead obtained a decree of divorce.

---

[14] Report on the Matrimonial Causes Bill, Cmnd. 5167, para. 9.
[15] S. 18 (1).
[16] *R.* v. *Clarence* (1888), 22 Q.B.D. 23.
[17] *R.* v. *Clarke*, [1949] 2 All E.R. 448.
[18] [1954] 2 Q.B. 282.
[19] See *post*, pp. 108, 189.

Section 20 (3) of the Act of 1965 also contained a provision whereby in the case of judicial separation any property which was acquired by or devolved upon the wife after the date of the decree and whilst the separation continued would, if she died intestate, devolve as if her husband had then been dead. There was no corresponding provision in relation to the property of a husband, even though he was the party who obtained the decree of judicial separation. This provision remains in force as regards cases in which the death occurred before August 1, 1970, and, in relation to deaths before that date, applies also to cases where there was in force an order of a magistrates' court containing a non-cohabitation clause.[20] It is, however, repealed as regards deaths on or after that date and the position is now governed by section 18 (2) of the Act of 1973. This provides that if whilst a decree of judicial separation is in force and the separation is continuing either the husband or the wife should die intestate as respects all or any of his or her real or personal property, that property shall devolve as if the other party had been dead. The position is therefore now the same in respect of both parties to the marriage and no doubt represents what they would have intended had they considered the matter. But the view was taken that the existence of a magistrates' order containing a non-cohabitation clause does not mark the final end of the marriage in the same way as does a decree of judicial separation. Accordingly although such orders (which are in practice uncommon) continue to have the effect of a decree of judicial separation for other purposes, the section provides that they are to have no effect as regards intestate succession.[1]

It will be noticed that section 18 (2) uses the words "If while a decree of judicial separation is in force and the separation is continuing...". The reason is that it has never been clearly decided whether a resumption of co-habitation of itself discharges the decree automatically, though there are dicta to the effect that it does.[2] It is, however, clear that the court has power, on the application of either party, to order the discharge of the decree on this ground.[3]

---

[20] Act of 1973, Sched. 1, Pt. II, para. 13.
[1] S. 18 (3).
[2] *Per* A. L. SMITH, J., in *Haddon* v. *Haddon* (1887), 18 Q.B.D. 778, 782; *Matthews* v. *Matthews*, [1912] 3 K.B. 91, 102.
[3] *Oram* v. *Oram* (1923), 129 L.T. 159.

CHAPTER 5

NULLITY OF MARRIAGE

The Nullity of Marriage Act 1971, which came into operation on August 1, 1971, gave effect to the recommendations in the Law Commission's Report on this subject (Law Com. No. 33). Its provisions are now consolidated in the Act of 1973. The changes were not extensive. The distinction between marriages which are void and those which are voidable was preserved, though lack of consent which had hitherto made a marriage void (save perhaps in cases of duress) became a ground making it voidable only, and certain other changes were made in the grounds and defences available. Most, but not all, of these changes will apply to marriages which took place after the commencement of the Act. It is therefore necessary to consider first the distinction between void and voidable marriages, then the grounds and defences applicable to marriages which took place before August 1, 1971 and finally those which are available in respect of marriages which took place thereafter.

1. Void and voidable marriages.

The distinction between a void and a voidable marriage was explained by Lord GREENE, M.R., in *De Reneville* v. *De Reneville*[1] as follows:—

"A void marriage is one that will be regarded by every court in any case in which the existence of the marriage is in issue as never having taken place, and can be so treated by both parties to it without the necessity of any decree annulling it; a voidable marriage is one that will be regarded by every court as a valid and subsisting marriage until a decree annulling it has been pronounced by a court of competent jurisdiction."

The distinction has a number of important consequences.
(a) If the marriage was void *ab initio* the decree of nullity is declaratory only and the petitioner will seek such a decree for the purpose of dispelling doubts as to the validity of the marriage and enabling the court to exercise its power to grant ancillary relief. In the case of a voidable marriage section 16 of the Act of 1973 provides that a nullity decree granted after July 31, 1971 is to operate to annul the marriage only as respects any time after the decree has been made absolute, and that the marriage shall, notwithstanding the decree, be treated as if it had existed up to that time. The section is in general terms so that it applies, so far as English law is concerned, not only to decrees of nullity granted by the English courts but also to decrees obtained elsewhere, and is equally applicable to marriages taking place before or after the specified date. It avoids

---

[1] [1948] P. 100, 110–111.

the difficulties which have arisen in the past from the fact that, for some purposes at all events, a nullity decree in respect of a voidable marriage had retrospective effect. The wording of the decree, whether the marriage was found to be void or voidable, was the same; it declared the marriage "to have been and to be absolutely null and void to all intents and purposes in the law whatsoever".

(b) If the marriage was void *ab initio* the parties are free to re-marry without first obtaining a nullity decree. It was held in *Wiggins* v. *Wiggins*[2] that if the marriage was voidable, despite the retro-active wording of the decree, any re-marriage to a third person before the decree was made absolute would be bigamous and void. This will clearly be so, by virtue of section 16 of the Act of 1973, as to decrees granted after July 31, 1971, and earlier doubts as to correctness of the decision will no longer arise in such cases.[3]

(c) Where the marriage is void, any transactions entered into on the basis that it was valid will also be void on the ground of fundamental mistake. Prior to the Nullity of Marriage Act 1971 the retro-active effect of the decree could invalidate such transactions in respect of a voidable marriage, as in *Re Wombwell's Settlement, Clerke* v. *Menzies*,[4] where the trusts of an ante-nuptial marriage settlement failed on the decree being made absolute. The difficulties which this could cause were, however, mitigated by the rule that where the marriage was voidable rather than void transactions completed while it was still current would not be re-opened, so that any money paid or property transferred on the basis that the marriage existed could not be recovered[5] and the tax liability of the spouses in the years before the decree would not be re-adjusted on the ground that they became retrospectively single persons.[6] The effect of section 16 of the Act of 1973 is that when a nullity decree is made after July 31, 1971 in respect of a voidable marriage it will remain valid for all purposes until that decree is made absolute, and difficulties resulting from the doctrine of retro-active effect will no longer arise. The effect will in this respect to precisely the same as that of a decree of divorce.

(d) Only the parties to a voidable marriage can challenge its validity, and only by means of proceedings for nullity. It follows that once either party had died without a decree having been obtained the marriage remains valid for all purposes. Any person who has a pecuniary interest, however slight, may challenge the validity of a marriage on the ground that it is void and petition for a declaration that this is so, even after the death of one or both of the parties.[7]

(e) Where a decree of nullity was granted on or before July 31, 1971 in respect of a voidable marriage any child who would have been the legitimate child of the parties to the marriage if at the date of the decree it had been dissolved instead of being annulled is deemed to be their legitimate child.[8] As regards any decree granted after that date the child is, by virtue of section 16 of the

---

[2] [1958] 2 All E.R. 555.
[3] See Law Com. No. 33, para. 22, and the Irish case of *Mason* v. *Mason*, [1944] N.I. 134.
[4] [1922] 2 Ch. 298.
[5] *Re Eaves*, [1940] Ch. 109; *Re Dewhirst, Flower* v. *Dewhirst*, [1948] Ch. 198.
[6] *Dodworth* v. *Dale*, [1936] 2 K.B. 503.
[7] See Law. Com. No. 25, para. 87.
[8] Act of 1973, Sched. 1, Part II, para. 12, preserving Matrimonial Causes Act 1965, s. 11.

Act of 1973, both in fact and in law their legitimate child, and is not only "deemed" to be so, because the marriage is to be treated as if it had existed up to the time of decree absolute.

Prima facie the children of a void marriage are illegitimate, because their parents have never been married. But by section 2 of the Legitimacy Act 1959 such a child is to be treated as a legitimate child of his parents if the father of the child was domiciled in England at the time of the child's birth or, if the father died before the birth, was so domiciled immediately before his death and if at the time of the intercourse resulting in the birth (or at the time of the celebration of the marriage if later) both or either of the parties reasonably believed that the marriage was valid.[9] This provision is likely especially to apply in cases where a man has induced a woman to go through a ceremony of marriage with him in the belief that he is unmarried, and she only discovers that the marriage was bigamous after a child has been conceived.

The interests which children may have in the outcome of nullity proceedings can, in appropriate cases, be protected by an order, under the Matrimonial Causes Rules, that they shall be separately represented.

2. Marriages before August 1, 1971

The grounds and defences applicable to marriages entered into before the Nullity of Marriage Act 1971 came into operation depend mainly upon the common law and partly upon provisions of the Matrimonial Causes Act 1965, which are preserved by Schedule 1, Part II of the Act of 1973.

(a) Grounds rendering a marriage void.

A marriage which took place before August 1, 1971 may be held to be void on any of the following grounds:—

(i) *That the parties are within the prohibited degrees of relationship as laid down in the Marriage Act* 1949.

The prohibited degrees of relationship under canon law are set out in Part I of the First Schedule to that Act. There were a number of statutory exceptions from these prohibited degrees. Thus a man has been allowed to marry his deceased wife's sister since 1907,[10] and his deceased brother's widow since 1921,[11] and he has been permitted to marry his deceased wife's niece and a woman her deceased husband's nephew since 1931.[12] These Acts, and Part II of the First Schedule to the Marriage Act 1949, have been repealed and replaced by the Marriage (Enabling) Act 1960 which permits marriages between a man and a woman who is the sister, aunt or niece of a former wife of his (whether living or not), or was formerly the wife of his brother, uncle or nephew (whether living or not), these words of kinship applying equally to kin of the whole and half blood. The result of the change is that, for example, a man may now marry his

---

[9] See s. 2 of that Act as to titles of honour and testate and intestate succession in such cases.

[10] Deceased Wife's Sister's Marriage Act 1907.

[11] Deceased Brother's Widow's Marriage Act 1921.

[12] Marriage (Prohibited Degrees of Relationship) Act 1931.

divorced wife's sister during the lifetime of his former wife, whereas previously he could only do so after her death. The Act of 1960 applies to marriages in Great Britain or elsewhere. But it does not render valid a marriage, even if it took place in Great Britain, if either party was at the time of the marriage domiciled outside Great Britain and the law of the domicile of that party did not permit such a marriage.

(ii) *That either party was, at the date of the marriage, under the age of sixteen.*

Before the Age of Marriage Act 1929 the ages were fourteen for a boy and twelve for a girl and if either was below that age the marriage was voidable. Since that Act, and now by section 2 of the Marriage Act 1949, the age has been raised to sixteen for both sexes and if either was under that age the marriage is void. This requirement, like those concerning degrees of relationship, is a matter of capacity to marry. Accordingly a party domiciled in England cannot avoid it by going through a ceremony of marriage in another country where earlier marriage is allowed. In *Pugh* v. *Pugh*[13] the husband, who was over the age of sixteen and domiciled in England, went through a ceremony of marriage in Austria with a girl aged fifteen domiciled in Hungary. Although the marriage was valid by both Austrian and Hungarian law, she was granted a decree of nullity. The Act requires that both parties shall have reached the required age, and as regards a party domiciled in England it has extra-territorial effect.

(iii) *That the parties have inter-married in disregard of certain requirements as to the formation of the marriage.*

These requirements are laid down by the Marriage Act 1949.[14] They are at the time of writing the subject of a Report (Law Com. 53) of the Law Commission and are too complex for consideration here. It must suffice to say that in general a defect in the formalities will not invalidate a marriage unless both parties were aware of the irregularity,[15] and that in some cases even this will not make the marriage void.[16] If, for example, the parties marry without the consents required to the marriage of a person under eighteen having been obtained[17] the marriage is nevertheless valid, but as one (or both) will have been guilty of making a false statement for the purpose of procuring the marriage, that party will be criminally liable under section 3 of the Perjury Act 1911, and if convicted on indictment will be liable to imprisonment for up to seven years, or to a fine, or both.

(iv) *That at the time of the marriage either party was already lawfully married.*

In such a case the marriage is obviously void *ab initio*, irrespective of whether or not the parties or either of them knew that the marriage was bigamous, and notwithstanding that either or both may have a valid defence to a charge of bigamy, such as mistaken but honest belief on reasonable grounds that the

---

[13] [1951] P. 482.
[14] See also Marriage (Registrar General's Licence) Act 1970, permitting marriages with such licence in unregistered premises.
[15] See Marriage Act 1949, s. 49.
[16] *Ibid.,* s. 48.
[17] *Ibid.,* s. 3 and Sched. 2.

...ouse was dead,[18] or that the marriage had been validly dissolved.[19] Such ...matters will no doubt, however, be highly relevant in considering the conduct of the parties in relation to ancillary relief.

(v) *Lack of consent.*

This may result from unsoundness of mind, from certain kinds of mistake or from duress.

Unsoundness of mind can only render a marriage void if at the time of the ceremony the spouse in question was incapable of understanding the nature of the marriage and the obligations and responsibilities which it involved.[20] Thus if a person otherwise of unsound mind went through the marriage ceremony during a lucid interval the marriage is not void, though it may be voidable.[1] There seems to be little modern authority on the subject of extreme drunkenness, but no doubt it might have the same result as has unsoundness of mind.[2] It is not every mistake which will invalidate a marriage; to have that effect the mistake must relate to the nature of the ceremony or the identity of the other party. In *Mehta* v. *Mehta*,[3] where the wife believed that what was in fact a ceremony of marriage was a ceremony of conversion to the Hindu faith, and in *Kelly* v. *Kelly*[4] where the petitioner believed that the marriage ceremony was a formal betrothal ceremony, the marriages were held to be void. But mistakes as to the effect of the ceremony will not suffice. Thus in *Kassim* v. *Kassim*[5] where the husband wrongly believed that the marriage he contracted in Southern Rhodesia was potentially polygamous, so that he would be allowed to take further wives, when in fact it was monogamous, the marriage was valid. So also, had it not been for defective formalities, would have been the marriage in *Way* v. *Way*[6] where the husband's mistaken belief that he and the wife whom he married in Soviet Russia would be permitted by the authorities there to live together was insufficient to invalidate the marriage.

Mistakes concerning the other party to the marriage are only sufficient if they relate to the identity of that party as where, to take an imaginary case, a man marries one identical twin in the belief that he is marrying her sister. Such mistakes are very rare. Mistakes as to quality or fortune are insufficient, so that if the wife had deceived her husband into believing that she was a wealthy and childless spinster age twenty-two, when in fact she was an impoverished widow aged thirty with three children, he might feel that he had cause to complain, but he has no ground on which he could obtain a decree of nullity.[7]

---

[18] *R.* v. *Tolson* (1889), 23 Q.B.D. 168.
[19] *R.* v. *Gould*, [1968] 2 Q.B.D. 65; *R.* v. *Wheat* and *R.* v. *Stocks*, [1921] 2 K.B. 119 not followed.
[20] *In the Estate of Park*, [1954] P. 112.
[1] See Matrimonial Causes Act 1965, s. 9 (1) (*b*), *post*, p. 74, which is preserved by Sched. 1, Part II of the Act of 1973, para. 11 (1) (*b*).
[2] See *Sullivan* v. *Sullivan* (1818), 2 Hag. Con. 238, 246.
[3] [1945] 2 All E.R. 690.
[4] (1933), 49 T.L.R. 99.
[5] [1962] P. 224.
[6] [1950] P. 71. Decree obtained for defective formalities sub. nom. *Kenward* v. *Kenward*, [1951] P. 124.
[7] See Jackson, "Formation and Annulment of Marriage" 2nd Edn., pp. 300–304, and Ayliffe's Parergon Juris Canonici p. 361 cited in *Moss* v. *Moss*, [1897] P. 263, 271–72.

Whether, in view of the fact that the fraud preceded the marriage, he could obtain a divorce on the basis that she had behaved in such a way that he could not reasonably be expected to live with her, is a question which must await judicial determination. Decisions on duress are more numerous. In a recent case, *Szechter* v. *Szechter*[8] Sir JOCELYN SIMON, P., summarised the law (in a statement unanimously approved by the Court of Appeal in *Singh* v. *Singh*[9]) as follows:—

> "It is, in my view, insufficient to invalidate an otherwise good marriage that a party has entered into it in order to escape from a disagreeable situation, such as penury or social degradation. In order for the impediment of duress to vitiate an otherwise valid marriage, it must, in my judgment, be proved that the will of one of the parties thereto has been overborne by genuine and reasonably held fear caused by threat of immediate danger (for which the party himself is not responsible) to life, limb or liberty, so that the constraint destroys the reality of consent to ordinary wedlock."

In many cases the source of the fear and the agent of duress will be the other party to the marriage. The Law Commission[10] observed that what in effect the courts have done in such cases is to distinguish legitimate threats from illegitimate ones. They have rightly held that the threat is illegitimate if it is to make a false charge against the person threatened. They have implied that it may be legitimate if the charge is just, but have never held that it is necessarily so. Thus in *Buckland* v. *Buckland*[11] the husband, who was employed by the British authorities in Malta as a dockyard policeman, was falsely charged by a fifteen-year-old girl and her father with corrupting her and advised that he would inevitably be convicted, and sentenced to a long term of imprisonment, unless he married her. In *Parojcic* v. *Parojcic*[12] a daughter who had just contrived to leave Jugoslavia and reach England was threatened by her father on arrival that unless she married the man who accompanied him, whom she had never met before, she would be sent back to Jugoslavia. In both cases decrees of nullity were granted, though in the latter case it was suggested that duress made a marriage voidable rather than void. It is not, however, essential that the duress should emanate from the other spouse. In *Szechter* v. *Szechter*[13] it arose from the brutal inhumanity of the security police in Poland to a Jewish girl, already an invalid, who was sentenced to imprisonment which she feared she would not survive. In *H.* v. *H.*[14] it resulted from the well-founded fears of a girl in Hungary of the fate she might meet at the hands of the victorious Russian army. In both cases the girl escaped to England by the device of marriage to a man who was willing to aid her on the understanding that the marriage would not be consummated and that they would take steps to end it after she had

---

[8] [1971] P. 286.
[9] [1971] P. 226.
[10] Law Com. No. 33, para. 65.
[11] [1968] P. 296.
[12] [1959] 1 All E.R. 1.
[13] *Supra.* A terrifying story of man's inhumanity.
[14] [1954] P. 258.

escaped. The nullity decrees in these cases were obviously justified, but they must be contrasted with *Silver* v. *Silver*[15] where the wife had married a British husband in Germany with the sole object of obtaining the right of entry into England, and on the understanding that the marriage would not be consummated and they would then part. There was here no element of duress and a marriage freely entered into cannot be invalidated by mental reservations by the parties.

(vi) *That the parties are both of the same sex.*

In *Talbot* v. *Talbot*,[16] when a widow went through a ceremony of marriage with a person who purported to be a bachelor but was in fact, as it later appeared, also a woman, the marriage was held to be void. A much more difficult situation arose in *Corbett* v. *Corbett*.[17] The same judge, Mr. Justice ORMROD, had to face the difficult problem of so-called "change of sex". His conclusion was that the only cases in which this term is appropriate are those in which a mistake of sex is made at birth and subsequently revealed by further medical investigation.[18] If the respondent has been since birth a biological male, no subsequent operation by removal of the male sexual organs and construction of an artificial vagina can make him a female, and if he marries a man, in the ordinary sense of that word, the marriage is void. The fact that a decree of nullity can be granted in such a case does enable the court to exercise its powers to grant ancillary relief.[19] But these powers are in the court's discretion, and there may be circumstances in which it would not be unjust to exercise them. The alternative of a declaration as to status under Rule 109 of the Rules of 1973 would not confer such powers on the court, and is not available.

(b) Grounds making a marriage voidable.

(i) *The incapacity of either party to consummate the marriage.*

This ground, which has existed from the earliest days of the canon law and which is sometimes referred to as "canonical disability", means the inability to have, or to permit, ordinary sexual intercourse. It must not be confused with the inability to procreate children. If a husband is incapable of sexual intercourse the marriage cannot have been consummated despite the fact that the the wife has borne his child by artificial insemination;[20] if both parties are so capable the fact that through sterility their intercourse will not lead to the birth of children is no ground for nullity.

To be a ground for a decree the incapacity must have existed at the date of the marriage, and not have resulted from subsequent injury. Consummation involves complete penetration, but not necessarily ejaculation; if the penetration can be sustained only for a very short time and there is no emission it cannot properly be described as the "ordinary and complete" intercourse which is required for consummation.[1] The incapacity must be incurable, but if the party

[15] [1955] 2 All E.R. 614.
[16] (1967), 111 Sol. Jo. 213.
[17] [1971] P. 83.
[18] *Ibid.*, at p. 1323.
[19] See *post*, Part II.
[20] *R.E.L.* (*otherwise R.*) v. *E. L.*, [1949] P. 211.
[1] *D-E.* v. *A-G.* (*falsely calling herself D-E.*) (1845), 1 Rob. Ecc. 279, 298; *W.* v. *W.* (*otherwise K.*), [1967] 3 All E.R. 178.

in question declines to submit to an operation which might effect a cure the defect is regarded as incurable,[2] as it is also if the operation is likely to prove dangerous or is unlikely to be successful. It is for the petitioner to prove his case: it is not enough for him to prove that the marriage has not been consummated by reason of a defect which existed at the date of the marriage. Thus if, shortly before the hearing of a husband's petition, his wife had undergone an operation which had some reasonable prospect of effecting a cure, or even if she consented at the last moment to such an operation, his petition cannot succeed, though should the operation fail to achieve its object, he could again petition.[3] The incapacity need not be structural: invincible repugnance may suffice,[4] and it may be relative to the other party to the marriage only, as where for some psychological reason a husband is capable of intercourse with other women but incapable of intercourse with the wife whom he has chosen to marry.[5]

Even the party who is incapable of consummating the marriage is permitted to petition for nullity on this ground, provided that he was not, at the time of the marriage, aware of his own incapacity, and that it would not be unjust in the circumstances to permit him to petition.[6] An example of such injustice is to be found in *Pettit* v. *Pettit*.[7] The husband had always been impotent. His wife had borne him a child by artificial insemination and had kept the house going during the war years by paying the bills and mortgage instalments. After twenty years he sought to obtain a decree of nullity, having fallen in love with another woman, and his petition rightly failed.

(ii) *The respondent's wilful refusal to consummate the marriage.*

Before the Matrimonial Causes Act 1937, s. 7 (now preserved by Schedule 1, Part II, para. 11 (1) (a) of the Act of 1973) this was not a ground for nullity, though on the petitioner's complaint that the marriage had not been consummated within three years it was presumed that the respondent was impotent.[8] That presumption may today be regarded as obsolete, and without awaiting the completion of so long a period of time the petitioner may rely upon an allegation of wilful refusal or, if uncertain as to the real reason, upon an allegation of incapacity or wilful refusal in the alternative. In the years 1964 to 1969 inclusive the average number of petitions based upon incapacity was 148, upon wilful refusal 193, and upon both together 498, whereas the average number of decrees based upon incapacity was 349 and upon wilful refusal was 333.[9]

A decree will not be granted upon this ground unless the respondent's conduct amounts to "a settled and definite decision come to without just excuse" and the whole history of the marriage must be considered.[10] The refusal must have continued up to the date of the presentation of the petition,[11]

---

[2] *J.* (*otherwise K.*) v. *J.* (1908), 24 T.L.R. 622.
[3] *S.* v. *S.* (*otherwise W.*), [1963] P. 162.
[4] *G.* v. *G.*, [1924] A.C. 349.
[5] *C.* (*otherwise H.*) v. *C.*, [1921] P. 399.
[6] *Harthan* v. *Harthan*, [1949] P. 115.
[7] [1963] P. 177.
[8] *G.* v. *M.* (1885), 10 App. Cas. 171.
[9] Law Com. No. 33, App. B.
[10] *Horton* v. *Horton*, [1947] 2 All E.R. 871, H.L.
[11] *S.* v. *S.* (*otherwise C.*), [1956] P. 1.

but if it is clear that the respondent has come to a definite decision, and that the refusal is not the result of some indecision or shyness, there is no need to prove that it has continued for any particular period of time.[12]   Where impotence and wilful refusal are alleged in the alternative, the court must reach a definite decision as to which was the cause of the non-consummation of the marriage.[13]

In *Baxter* v. *Baxter*[14] it was held by the House of Lords that the word "consummate" was used in the Act as that word is used in common parlance and in the light of social conditions known to exist.   In the Canon Law the question of consummation was in no way dependent upon the question of whether the intercourse could result in the conception of a child and it followed that the insistence throughout the marriage on the use of contraceptive methods which prevented such conception could not amount to refusal to consummate the marriage if the intercourse was otherwise complete.   The House of Lords left open the question of whether insistence upon the practice of *coitus interruptus* could amount to refusal to consummate: in *White (otherwise Berry)* v. *White*[15] and *Cackett* v. *Cackett*[16] it was held that it would not have this result, not following *Grimes (otherwise Edwards)* v. *Grimes*[17] where the judge reached the opposite conclusion.   But it was emphasised in *Baxter* v. *Baxter* that the decision in that case did not mean that there was no relief available in cases of this nature, but only that a decree of nullity was not the appropriate form of relief. As Lord JOWITT, L.C., put it[18] ". . . the proper occasion for considering the subjects raised by this appeal is when the sexual life of the spouses, and the responsibility of either or both for a childless home, form the background to some other claim for relief".   Thus in both *White* v. *White* and *Cackett* v. *Cackett* it was held that the husband's refusal to permit his wife to bear a child whether by contraceptive measures or by *coitus interruptus* could amount to cruelty, if her health was affected, and it could now be the basis of a petition for divorce or judicial separation by virtue of sections 1 (2) (*b*) and section 17 of the Act of 1973, without the need for medical evidence of injury to health.

(iii) *That either party was at the time of the marriage of unsound mind or was then suffering from mental disorder within the meaning of the Mental Health Act 1959 of such a kind or to such an extent as to be unfitted for marriage and the procreation of children or was subject to recurrent attacks of insanity or epilepsy.*

Like the previous ground and the two which follow, this ground originates from the Matrimonial Causes Act 1937.[19]   It must be distinguished from unsoundness of mind which renders a marriage void for want of consent, in that the unsoundness of mind or mental disorder did not prevent the party in question, at the time of the ceremony, from understanding the nature of

---

[12] In *Morgan* v. *Morgan*, [1949] W.N. 250, the parties lived together for only four days.
[13] *S.* v. *S.*, *supra.*
[14] [1948] A.C. 274.
[15] [1948] P. 330.
[16] [1950] P. 253.
[17] [1948] P. 323.
[18] *Baxter* v. *Baxter, supra* at p. 290.
[19] See now Act of 1973, Sched. 1, Part II, para. 11 (1) (*b*).

marriage and the responsibilities which it involves. The wording was closely examined and strongly criticised by ORMROD, J., in *Bennett* v. *Bennett*,[20] particularly because "treatment for mental illness has changed and attitudes towards mental illness have changed, in consequence of which the terminology has become largely obsolete, which makes it extremely difficult". But since the ground has been considerably re-worded as regards marriages after July 31, 1971, and proceedings under the old wording are available only in respect of marriages before that date and must be commenced within one year of the date of the marriage,[1] it seems unnecessary to consider these difficulties in detail.

(iv) *That the respondent was at the time of the marriage suffering from venereal disease in a communicable form.*[2]

(v) *That the respondent was at the time of the marriage pregnant by some person other than the petitioner.*

This is a matter as to which the use of blood tests are of particular value. The use of such tests has been considered on p. 21.

In the case of the last three grounds, (iii), (iv) and (v) only, the petition had to be presented within one year after the date of the marriage[3] so that is unlikely, since no extension of that time limit is permissible, that a petition based upon them will still remain unheard today.

(c) Defences.

If the court is satisfied that the marriage is void for any reason other than lack of consent, there can be no defence (save for that of estoppel *per rem judicatam*, as to which see *ante*, p. 40) for it remains void whether or not a decree is granted. Collusion, which is no longer a bar to a suit for divorce or judicial separation, has no longer been a bar to a suit for nullity since section 6 (1) of the Nullity of Marriage Act 1971, whether the marriage took place or the proceedings were instituted before or after the Act. If the collusion took the form of an agreement to present a false case and came to the notice of the court the petition would fail, not because of the collusion, but because of failure to prove that there were grounds for a decree.

Where, however, the marriage is alleged to be void for lack of consent, whether due to duress, mistake or insanity, there survives from the canon law an illogical defence of ratification by a consent freely given subsequently.[4] There might be some justification for this in relation to duress, which makes contracts other than marriage voidable rather than void;[5] but it is difficult to see how a marriage which has never existed can be brought into existence by

---

[20] [1969] 1 W.L.R. 430, 435.
[1] Act of 1973, Sched. 1, Part II, para. 11 (3) (*b*).
[2] *Ibid.*, para. 11 (1) (*c*).
[3] *Ibid.*, para. 11 (3) (*c*).
[4] *Valier* v. *Valier (otherwise Davis)* (1925), 133 L.T. 830, and see Law Com. No. 33, paras. 11–13.
[5] And see *Parojcic (otherwise Ivetic)* v. *Parojcic*, [1959] 1 All E.R. 1, which suggests that duress only made a marriage voidable rather than void, a view which the Law Commission has not accepted.

ratification.   This difficulty will remain only in respect of marriages taking place before August 1, 1971, since, as regards subsequent marriages, lack of consent will make marriages voidable rather than void.

Where the marriage was alleged to be voidable there was formerly an additional defence, at one time called "lack of sincerity" but now generally called approbation of the marriage.

The principle was clearly stated in the House of Lords by Lord SELBORNE in *G.* v. *M.*[6]

> ". . . there may be conduct on the part of the person seeking this remedy which ought to estop that person from having it; as, for instance, any act from which the inference ought to be drawn that during the antecedent time the party has, with a knowledge of the facts and of the law, approbated the marriage which he or she afterwards seeks to get rid of, or has taken advantage and derived benefits from the matrimonial relation which it would be unfair and inequitable to permit him or her, after having received them, to treat as if no such a relation had ever existed".

Lord WATSON in the same case based the rule upon public policy[7]

> "In a suit for nullity there may be facts and circumstances proved which so plainly imply, on the part of the complaining spouse, a recognition of the existence and validity of the marriage, as to render it most inequitable and contrary to public policy that he or she should be permitted to go on to challenge it with effect."

The defence of approbation could succeed only if the petitioner at the relevant time was aware not only of the facts but also that the law enabled him to seek a decree of nullity in respect of them.   In *Slater* v. *Slater*,[8] at a time when she did not know that her husband's failure to consummate the marriage entitled her to petition for nullity, the wife underwent a course of artificial insemination and when this failed, joined with her husband in adopting a child.   Her ignorance prevented this conduct from amounting to approbation; whereas in *W.* v. *W.*[9] the nullity petition of a husband who had concurred in adoption proceedings with knowledge of his rights was dismissed.   Likewise, in *Tindall* v. *Tindall*[10] a wife who, with knowledge of her right to seek nullity, applied to a magistrates' court on grounds of desertion and persistent cruelty could not, having thus treated the marriage as valid, later seek to have it avoided.   Delay of itself was no bar to a decree, unless in the circumstances it showed an intention to approbate the marriage.

In any proceedings instituted after July 31, 1971, whether the marriage took place before or after that date, a statutory bar replaces approbation and is an absolute rather than a discretionary bar.[11]

---

[6] (1885), 10 App. Cas. 171, 186 (applied in *R. E. L.* (*otherwise R.*) v. *E. L.*, [1949] P. 211).
[7] *Ibid.*, at pp. 197–198.
[8] [1953] P. 235.
[9] [1952] P. 152.
[10] [1953] P. 63.
[11] It was not clear previously whether it was an absolute bar, as was held in *G.* v. *G.* (*otherwise H.*), [1961] P. 87 or a discretionary bar only, as was held in *Scott* v. *Scott* (*otherwise Fone*), [1959] P. 103 and *W.* v. *W.*, [1961] 2 All E.R. 56.

Section 13 of the Act of 1973 provides that in such proceedings the court shall not grant a decree of nullity on the ground that the marriage is voidable if the respondent satisfies the court on three points:—

(1) That the petitioner knew that it was open to him to have the marriage avoided. It seems clear that this requirement can be satisfied only by proof of actual knowledge of his legal right to seek a decree of nullity. It would be difficult in future to support the proposition in *W.* v. *W.*[12] that although there was no evidence that a husband know of his right to seek a decree on the ground of his wife's wilful refusal to consummate the marriage, it could be assumed that he knew his rights.

(2) That with that knowledge he so conducted himself in relation to the respondent as to lead the respondent reasonably to believe that he would not seek to do so. This must be a question of fact in each case. Clearly an agreement between the parties that the petitioner would not seek to have the marriage annulled would be an absolute bar to a petition.[13] So also would be the institution of other proceedings which would lie only on the basis that there was a valid marriage, such as those for adoption of a child[14] or a wife's application to a magistrates' court for a matrimonial order.[15] Presumably the view will still prevail that mere delay of itself after the petitioner's knowledge of his rights will not be a bar:[16] were it otherwise delays in the hope of overcoming a wilful refusal to consummate might be fatal. There might, however, be cases where a respondent had been led by long periods of delay into reasonably believing that the petitioner would not seek to have the marriage annulled, which would be fatal to his chance of success.

(3) That it would be unjust to the respondent to grant a decree. It will be noticed that considerations of public policy, to which Lord Watson referred in *G.* v. *M.*[17] are omitted. It was not clear whether a decree could be refused only if there was both injustice *and* conflict with public policy, or whether conflict with public policy alone would suffice. As the Law Commission observed[18] "Lawyers cannot advise their clients with any certainty if there is a risk of individual notions of public policy being involved". Presumably, as regards marriages celebrated before August 1, 1971, the defence of ratification could still be raised in answer to a petition based upon lack of consent, which will continue to make such marriages void rather than voidable.[19]

[12] [1952] P. 152, 162.
[13] *Aldridge* v. *Aldridge* (1888), 13 P.D. 210.
[14] *W.* v. *W.*, *supra.*
[15] *Tindall* v. *Tindall*, *supra.*
[16] *G.* v. *M.* (1885), 10 App. Cas. 171, 186.
[17] *Ante*, p. 76.
[18] Law Com. No. 33, para. 44.
[19] See *ante*, p. 75, and consider footnote 5.

Before leaving this matter it should be clear that what has been said on the subject of this defence does not affect the decision in *Pettit* v. *Pettit*,[20] which was in no way based upon the petitioner having led the respondent to believe that he would not petition, but upon the quite different point that when a petitioner seeks a decree on the ground of his own incapacity to consummate the marriage, it can be refused if in all the circumstances it would be unjust to allow him to petition.

3. Marriages on or after August 1, 1971.

When the marriage took place on or after this date both the grounds for and defences to proceedings for nullity are governed by the Act of 1973.

(a) Grounds rendering the marriage void.

The result of section 11 of the Act is that lack of consent ceases to be a ground rendering a marriage void and becomes instead (under section 12 (*c*)) a ground making it voidable. In other respects the grounds on which a marriage is void are unchanged, i.e. that it is not a valid marriage under the provisions of the Marriage Act 1949 (because the parties are within the prohibited degrees of relationship, or either party is under the age of sixteen or they have intermarried in disregard of certain requirements as the the formation of the marriage) that at the time of the marriage either party was already lawfully married, or that the parties are not respectively male and female. To these has been added (by section 11 (*d*)) the ground that, in the case of a polygamous marriage entered into outside England and Wales, either party was at the time of the marriage domiciled in England and Wales (and would thus have had no capacity to contract such a marriage: see *post*, p. 81).

The view of the Law Commission that the fact that the parties are of the same sex should not be a ground for nullity[1] was not accepted by Parliament and indeed the Commission observed that this was a question of social policy on which Parliament must be the judge. Had this ceased to be a ground for nullity and become the subject only of a declaration under R.S.C. Ord. 15, r. 16, the court would have been deprived of the powers to order ancillary relief which it has in a suit for nullity, and could not even have ordered maintenance pending suit.

(b) Grounds rendering the marriage voidable.

Here by virtue of section 12 of the Act of 1973, there are some changes. The grounds of incapacity and wilful refusal to consummate the marriage, venereal disease and pregnancy (i.e. grounds (b) (i), (ii), (iv) and (v) pp. 72 to 75) are unchanged. But the fact that either party to the marriage did not validly consent to it, whether in consequence of duress, mistake or unsoundness of mind or otherwise, has ceased to be a ground upon which a marriage is void and renders it voidable only. And there is some re-wording of ground (iii) on p. 74,

[20] [1963] P. 177, see *ante*, p. 73.
[1] Law Com. No. 33, paras. 30–32.

which had already met with criticism. By section 12 (*d*) this provision now reads—"*that at the time of the marriage either party, though capable of giving a valid consent, was suffering (whether continuously or intermittently) from mental disorder within the meaning of the Mental Health Act 1959 of such a kind or to such an extent as to be unfitted for marriage*". Thus the references to being unfitted for *both* marriage *and* the procreation of children have disappeared. As ORMROD, J. said in *Bennett* v. *Bennett*[2] "The question then is: what did Parliament mean by the use of the phrase 'unfitted for marriage *and* the procreation of children', because they are not disjunctive but conjunctive . . . I am unable to suggest any meaning that can be given to the phrase 'unfitted for the procreation of children' unless what is meant is unfitted to bring up children, which is not what is said." Also the reference to attacks of epilepsy is omitted because, as the Law Commission explained,[3]

"Whatever the medical position in 1937, today epilepsy responds to treatment and can be kept under control. There are valid reasons why unsoundness of mind and mental disorder should be grounds for nullity but epilepsy is not a mental illness and we think it is wrong that this one particular affliction should be singled out as a ground for nullity."

Finally, it is now clear that if the mental disorder renders the spouse unfitted for marriage, it is immaterial whether it is continuous or recurrent.

The law relating to divorce contains no express reference to unsoundness of mind, though it may be a ground for divorce, whether it existed at the date of the marriage or arose at a later date, if it leads to five years of life apart, when either spouse may petition, or if it leads to the respondent spouse behaving in such a way that the petitioner cannot reasonably be expected to live with the respondent. To be a ground for nullity the mental disorder must exist at the date of the marriage, must render the sufferer unfitted for marriage, and will enable either spouse to petition.

(c) Defences.

As is the case with marriages which took place before August 1, 1971, collusion is no longer a defence and if the marriage is void because one of the grounds in section 11 has been proved there is no defence.

But section 13 lays down at some length the bars to relief when the marriage is voidable.

The new statutory bar under subsection 13 (1), which has already been considered,[4] replaces the former bars of approbation, ratification or lack of sincerity. The requirement that proceedings based on mental disorder, venereal disease and pregnancy should be instituted within one year of the date of the marriage has been changed by extending the period from one year to three years and by making it applicable also to cases based upon lack of consent. The

---

[2] [1969] 1 W.L.R. 430, 434.
[3] Law Com. No. 33, para. 73.
[4] See *ante*, p. 77.

court has still no discretion to extend the period beyond three years, but it is unlikely to lead to the injustice which the shorter period of one year sometimes caused. On the other hand the chances of conduct within the three year period leading the respondent reasonably to believe that the petitioner would not seek to have the marriage avoided, which would also be a bar, are obviously greater.

By section 13 (3) the requirement that the petitioner must at the time of the marriage have been ignorant of the facts alleged is retained in relation to venereal disease and pregnancy by some person other than the petitioner. But it no longer applies to cases of mental disorder. The reasons which led to this change are first that the disorder must be such as to render the respondent "unfitted for marriage" and even if the petitioner knew of the disorder at the time of the marriage its gravity or possible results might not have been clear to him. Secondly he may have known that the respondent had previously suffered from mental disorder, but this may be quiescent at the time of the marriage and the medical prognosis may prove later to have been unduly optimistic. For these reasons the Law Commission recommended[5] that knowledge as such should not be a bar: it would not, however, be irrelevant, but its proper place should be within the framework of the statutory bar which replaces approbation under section 13 (1).

The further requirement, under the former law, that marital intercourse with the petitioner's consent should not have taken place after the petitioner discovered the existence of the grounds for a decree, which applied to cases of mental disorder, venereal disease and pregnancy in the cases of marriages before August 1, 1971, is altogether abolished. The reasons are various,[2] perhaps the strongest being that if the petitioner discovers the existence of a defect such as mental disorder or pregnancy by another man, he should not be placed in the position that if he attempts a reconciliation and fails to save the marriage he thereby loses all right to relief.

4. The foreign element in nullity.

The Act of 1973 codifies the English law relating to nullity of marriage, but does not attempt to deal with problems of the conflict of laws. Section 14 (1) provides that where, apart from this Act, any matter affecting the validity of a marriage would fall to be determined (in accordance with the rules of private international law) by reference to the law of a country outside England and Wales, nothing in sections 11 or 12 (which respectively govern the grounds on which a marriage celebrated after July 31, 1971, is void or voidable in English domestic law) or in section 13 (1) (which deals with one of the bars to relief in respect of a voidable marriage) shall:—

(a) preclude the determination of the matter as aforesaid (that is to say by reference to the law of a country outside England and Wales); or

(b) require the application to the marriage of the grounds or bar mentioned in these sections except in so far as it would be applicable in accordance with those rules.

---

[5] Law Com. No. 33, para. 79.
[2] See Law Com. No. 33, para. 81.

It is not possible to deal fully with these matters in a book of this nature,[3] but broadly the requirements of a valid marriage may be divided into formalities and capacity to marry.

Formalities cover all requirements concerning the actual celebration of the marriage; whether or not any formal ceremony is required[4] and if so the nature of that ceremony, whether religious or otherwise; whether or not a party to the ceremony can be represented by a proxy;[5] any requirements as to the giving of notices or obtaining of licences and of obtaining the consent of parents or guardians.[6] All such matters are generally governed by the law of the place where the marriage took place (the *lex loci celebrationis*),[7] and this is so even to the point of recognising the validity of a marriage formally void at the time when it was celebrated, but retrospectively validated by legislation in the country where it took place.[8] The exceptions to this rule as to formal validity are the subject of section 14 (2) of the Act, and are considered *post*, p. 82.

Capacity to marry covers matters which relate more personally to each of the parties, its essential rather than its formal validity. It includes such matters as the prohibited degrees of consanguinity or affinity,[9] the effect, if any, of duress or other matters which may have vitiated consent,[10] the earliest age at which a person is permitted to marry,[11] and the ability to contract a polygamous or potentially polygamous marriage.

It may well be that not all these matters of capacity to marry are governed by one and the same law and there is conflict, both between the text books on this subject and in the decided cases, as to the law which should govern them. Where the incapacity results from an express provision of an English statute which is intended to operate wherever the marriage takes place, the position is clear. If either party is domiciled in England and Wales at the date of the marriage, that marriage is void. Thus in *Pugh* v. *Pugh*[12] it was held that a person domiciled in England who was over the age of 16 had no capacity to marry anywhere a person under that age, even though the marriage was lawful by the law of the place where it was celebrated. Such a marriage in 1946 was prohibited by the Age of Marriage Act 1929 (now Marriage Act 1949, s. 2) and the express provision of the *lex domicilii* must prevail. A similar result would follow if a person domiciled in England and Wales entered into a polygamous or potentially polygamous marriage, after July 31, 1971, in some other country, since section 11 (*d*) of the Act of 1973 expressly includes such a marriage among the category of void marriages if either party was at the time of the marriage domiciled in England and Wales.

---

[3] See Dicey & Morris, 8th Edn.; Cheshire's Private International Law, 8th Edn.; Graveson's Conflict of Laws, 6th Edn.
[4] *Rooker* v. *Rooker* (1863), 3 Sw. & Tr. 526.
[5] *Apt* v. *Apt*, [1948] P. 83.
[6] *Simonin* v. *Mallac* (1860), 2 Sw. & Tr. 67; *Ogden* v. *Ogden*, [1908] P. 46, but see criticisms of the latter decision in Cheshire, *op. cit.* pp. 48–51.
[7] *Scrimshire* v. *Scrimshire* (1752), 2 Hag. Con. 395.
[8] *Starkowski* v. *A.-G.*, [1954] A.C. 155.
[9] *Mette* v. *Mette* (1859), 1 Sw. & Tr. 416.
[10] *H.* v. *H.*, [1954] P. 258.
[11] *Pugh* v. *Pugh*, [1951] P. 482.
[12] *Supra.*

But in the absence of express statutory provisions of this kind, which concern only persons domiciled in England and Wales, the position is less clear. Sir JOCELYN SIMON, P. (as he then was), unhesitatingly stated in *Padolecchia* v. *Padolecchia*[13] that "Each party must be capable of marrying by the law of his or her respective ante-nuptial domicile". CUMMING-BRUCE, J., in *Radwan* v. *Radwan (No. 2)*[14], took the contrary view that where the parties have different domiciles, their capacity to marry is governed by the law of their intended matrimonial home.[15] Accordingly he held to be valid a polygamous marriage abroad before August 1, 1971, between a woman domiciled in England and a man domiciled in Egypt, who intended to make their home in Egypt, notwithstanding that by the law of her English domicile she had no capacity to contract such a marriage.

The position in such cases must await judicial clarification, or elucidation by legislation based on some future consideration of the matter by the Law Commission.

To this general rule that each party must have capacity by the law of his or her domicile (or perhaps by the law of their intended matrimonial home) there are certain exceptions. First, if the marriage is celebrated in England, one of the parties is domiciled in England, and both parties would be regarded as having capacity by English law, the marriage is treated as valid despite the fact that the other party lacks capacity by the law of his or her domicile. This was established in *Sottomayor* v. *de Barros (No. 2)*,[16] where the wife's incapacity to marry her first cousin by the law of her Portuguese domicile was held not to invalidate the marriage, her husband being domiciled in England and the marriage having taken place there. Secondly an incapacity under the law of the domicile of either party which is unconscionable or repugnant to the policy of English law, such as a prohibition based on a colour bar, would not be recognised.[17]

The law of the domicile of each party apparently determines other matters of essential validity, such as the effect of duress,[18] or of inability or wilful refusal to consummate the marriage.[19] There would obviously be some difficulty if the law of the domicile of one party said that such matters made the marriage void, whereas the law of the domicile of the other made the marriage voidable only or even valid. But on principle if the law of the domicile of either party held that the marriage was void, then void the English courts must hold it to be.

Section 14 (2) of the Act of 1973 deals with a different case. It provides that where a marriage purports to have been celebrated under the Foreign Marriages Acts 1892 to 1947 or has taken place outside England and Wales and purports to be a marriage under common law, section 11 of the Act of 1973 is without prejudice to any ground on which the marriage may be void under those Acts or,

---

[13] [1968] P. 314, 336.
[14] [1973] Fam. 35, where the authorities are examined at length.
[15] A view also expressed by Lord GREENE, M.R., in *De Reneville* v. *De Reneville*, [1948] P. 100, 114.
[16] (1879), 5 P.D. 94.
[17] *Chetti* v. *Chetti*, [1909] P. 67; *Cheni (otherwise Rodriguez)* v. *Cheni*, [1965] P. 85.
[18] *Szechter (otherwise Karsov)* v. *Szechter*, [1971] 2 W.L.R. 170, 177–178.
[19] *De Reneville* v. *De Renevillv, supra.*

as the case may be, by virtue of the rules governing the celebration of marriage outside England and Wales under common law.

This provision covers the situation where a marriage celebrated abroad may sometimes be valid in English law although the formalities required by the law of the place where it was celebrated were not observed. The Foreign Marriages Acts deal with marriages abroad by an authorised officer, usually a British Ambassador or Consul, and with marriages of members of H.M. Forces serving abroad by a chaplain serving with those Forces. The scope of common law marriages has been extended not only to cases in which members of occupying forces, instead of submitting themselves to the local law, marry before a chaplain serving with their own forces,[20] but also to cases where persons in a displaced persons camp in former enemy territory were married by a Catholic priest without compliance with the local law.[1] It can even sanction marriage by mere exchange of consents where no minister in Holy Orders is available. The point of the subsection is that an English court must nevertheless be entitled, if the facts warrant this, to declare these marriages to be void if the provisions of the Foreign Marriages Acts, or the law concerning common law marriages, have not been complied with.

---

[20] As in *Taczanowska (otherwise Roth)* v. *Taczanowski*, [1957] P. 301.
[1] *Kochanski* v. *Kochanska*, [1958] P. 147.

CHAPTER 6

JURISDICTION AND RECOGNITION OF FOREIGN DECREES

1. Domicile.

Reference has been made already in the previous chapter to the possible submission of matters of the essential validity of a marriage to the law of the domicile of each party. Further reference to the significance of domicile will be made in considering the jurisdiction of the English courts and the circumstances in which those courts will recognise a foreign matrimonial decree. For this purpose some knowledge of the English law governing domicile is needed but it is not necessary here to embark upon exhaustive study of the subject.[1]

Precise definition of domicile is not possible. Roughly it is equivalent to the country in which a person has his permanent home, or where he is settled. "By domicile we mean home, the permanent home, and if you do not understand your permanent home I am afraid that no illustration drawn from foreign writers or foreign languages will very much help you to it."[2] But although domicile cannot be exhaustively defined, it can and must be distinguished from

(a) Mere presence—the fact of being in a country, which has little significance in Private International Law except in relation to service of process.

(b) Habitual residence, an expression used in several statutes, including the Domicile and Matrimonial Proceedings Act 1973. The precise meaning of this expression has not as yet been judicially decided. To quote from the Report of the Law Commission on Jurisdiction in Matrimonial Causes,[3]

> "The meaning of habitual residence seems to us to be similar to that of ordinary residence. To be habitual, a residence must be more than transient or casual; once established, however, it is not necessarily broken by a temporary absence. It has to be conceded that whatever term is used for the purpose of matrimonial jurisdiction, it will lack sharp definition and give rise to some difficult cases."

Dicey and Morris on Conflict[4] express doubts as to whether it does necessarily mean the same thing as ordinary residence. Assuming that it does, its meaning is well illustrated by the case of *Stransky* v. *Stransky*[5] where (for the purposes of the rules of jurisdiction in a suit for divorce as they then were), it was necessary

---

[1] See Dicey & Morris, 8th Edn.; Cheshire's Private International Law, 8th Edn.; Graveson's Conflict of Laws, 6th Edn.
[2] *Per* Lord CRANWORTH in *Whicker* v. *Hume* (1858), 7 H.L. Cas. 124, 160.
[3] Law Com. No. 48, para. 42.
[4] 8th Edn. at p. 598.
[5] [1954] P. 428.

to decide whether the wife had ordinarily resided in England for the previous three years. Her husband was domiciled in Czechoslovakia, and the wife had spent some fifteen months of the three years' period with him in Munich, where his business interests lay. But during the whole period of three years she had been the occupier of a flat in London to which she had returned after visits to her husband in Munich, which she kept ready for immediate occupation, and which was her "base" during the relevant period. Despite the periods of absence, amounting to so much as fifteen months, she had ordinarily resided in England for the whole three year period.

(c) Nationality—which depends generally upon place of birth or parentage and has nothing to do with home. Domicile must be in a State which is subject to a single system of law. A man may be a British subject, but there is no such thing as a British or even a United Kingdom domicile. A man may be domiciled in Scotland, or in Northern Ireland, or in England *and* Wales, but each of these areas has its own legal system, which the United Kingdom as a whole has not. He may be a subject of the U.S.A., but he must be domiciled in one of the states, in the State of New York, or of Virginia or as the case may be, but not in the United States of America as a whole. A man may have more than one nationality and more than one residence. He may have no nationality—there are many such persons as a result of war—and he may have no residence. But English law ensures that to every person there is attributed a domicile, and that no one can have more than one operative domicile at the same time. What is more, in proceedings before the English courts a person's domicile is determined according to English law, and our courts may hold that a person is domiciled in, for instance, France, when a French judge would say that the person was not domiciled in France at all.[6]

The rules which govern the question of domicile in English law may be divided into the cases in which the law attributes a domicile to a person independently of his own volition and the cases in which his domicile is a matter of his own choice.

(a) *Domicile by operation of law.*

Under this heading, which is in no way dependent upon the will of the person in question, come the topics of domicile of origin and the domicile of dependent persons.

(i) *Domicile of origin.*

At birth, in the eyes of English law, every child acquires a domicile of origin. In the case of a legitimate child, this is the domicile of his father at the date of the child's birth. In the case of an illegitimate or posthumous child, it is that of the mother when the child is born. If the child is subsequently legitimated, as by the subsequent marriage of its parents, it acquires the domicile of the father as from the moment of legitimation, but it is unsettled whether the mother's domicile at the child's birth remains its domicile of origin or whether the domicile of origin becomes retrospectively that of the father at the child's birth. The domicile of origin of a foundling, if the identity of the parents cannot be

---

[6] *Re Annesley, Davidson* v. *Annesley*, [1926] Ch. 692.

ascertained, is the place where the child was found. A domicile of origin may be in abeyance whilst a domicile of choice is operative, but it is never altogether lost, and will revive if one domicile of choice is abandoned without another being acquired.

(ii) *Domicile of married women and dependent persons*

The law which governs the domicile of a married woman and a minor has been changed by the Domicile and Matrimonial Proceedings Act 1973, which came into operation on January 1, 1974.

A married woman is no longer a dependent person, but before 1974 she took, on marriage, the domicile of her husband, and her domicile changed with his whilst the marriage lasted. Until it was ended by death or decree absolute of divorce or nullity, she could not have a different domicile from that of her husband, even if the marriage was voidable[7] or if the parties were judicially separated.[8] By section 1 of this Act, the domicile of a married woman as at any time after it came into force will, instead of being the same as her husband's by virtue only of marriage, be ascertained by reference to the same factors as in the case of any other individual capable of having an independent domicile— in other words she will be capable of acquiring a separate and different domicile. But where immediately before January 1, 1974, a woman was married and then had her husband's domicile by dependence, she is to be treated as retaining that domicile (as a domicile of choice, if it is not also her domicile of origin) unless and until it is changed by acquisition or revival of another domicile either on or after that date.

The changes effected by the Act in relation to the domicile of **a minor** are of a different kind. They deal with two points—the moment of time at which his domicile of dependence ceases and the position, whilst that domicile lasts, if his parents are alive but living apart.

Before the Act came into force a minor retained a domicile of dependence until reaching the age of eighteen. If she was a married female she took (as did any other wife) her husband's domicile. Subject to this a legitimate or legitimated minor, including a male minor who was married, followed the domicile of his father until reaching the age of majority. After the father's death the minor's domicile generally changed with that of the mother.[9] After the death of both parents he retained whatever domicile he then had until reaching full age. These rules could lead to ridiculous results. Suppose that a husband aged seventeen married a wife aged nineteen in England and both lived, as they always had, in England. If the husband's father emigrated to New Zealand and acquired a domicile there, both husband and wife would have been domiciled in New Zealand, a country they had never seen, until the husband reached the age of eighteen and was free to acquire a domicile of choice in England. This situation has been ended by the Act.

---

[7] *De Reneville* v. *De Reneville*, [1948] P. 100.
[8] *A.-G. for Alberta* v. *Cook*, [1926] A.C. 444.
[9] But see *Re Beaumont*, [1893] 3 Ch. 490, as to the mother's power to leave the child's domicile unchanged, and dicta in *Potinger* v. *Wightman* (1817), 3 Mer. 67, 79–80 as to changes with fraudulent intent.

By section 3, the time at which a person first becomes capable of having an independent domicile shall be when he attains the age of sixteen or marries under that age (as he may be permitted to do by the law of some countries, though not by English law). In the case of a person who immediately before January 1, 1974, was incapable of having a separate domicile but had attained the age of sixteen or been married, the domicile of dependence ceased on that date. He or she then became capable of acquiring a domicile of choice, and this, having regard to section 1, will also be so in the case of a female minor who is married.

Section 4 deals with a different situation, which arises when there is an unmarried child under the age of sixteen whose father and mother are alive but living apart. Formerly the child's domicile would have changed with that of his father whilst the father was alive. As from January 1, 1974, the child's domicile will be that of his mother if he then has his home with her and has no home with his father, or if he has at any time had her domicile by virtue of this provision, and has not since had a home with his father. In the case of an adopted child, references to his father and his mother are to be treated as references to his adoptive father or mother. As from January 1, 1974, the domicile of a child whose mother is dead will remain that which his mother last had before she died if at her death he had her domicile by virtue of this section and has not since had a home with his father. He will thus retain this domicile until he becomes capable of acquiring an independent domicile and will not revert to dependence upon the domicile of his father. On the other hand, the section preserves any existing rule of law as to cases in which a child's domicile is regarded as being, by dependence, that of his mother, so that after his father's death he will generally, as explained above, have his mother's domicile until he reaches the age of sixteen or marries.

A person of unsound mind is not a dependent person in the sense in which the words have been used above. He retains the last domicile he had before the disability commenced, not because of dependence upon any other person, but because a change of domicile requires a conscious intention, which he is incapable of forming. But it seems that if the disability commenced whilst he was unmarried and under the age of sixteen, he might perhaps continue to change domicile with that of his father or mother according to the rules described above, even after reaching full age.[10]

(b) *Domicile of choice.*

Every person other than a dependent person can acquire a domicile of choice by residence (and perhaps even by arrival) in the chosen country with the intention of settling permanently in that country. Thus if a minor, whose domicile of origin was in England has, at reaching the age of sixteen, a domicile of dependence in some other country because his father and mother lived together there and acquired a domicile there, he does not automatically revert to his domicile of origin, but his continued residence in England coupled with his continued intention that it shall be his permanent home would give him an English domicile of choice.

---

[10] Dictum in *Sharpe* v. *Crispin* (1869), L.R. 1 P. & D. 611, 618.

The practical difficulty in the concept of domicile is that of proving a person's intention.   The matter has unfortunately been complicated by decisions of the House of Lords in *Ramsay* v. *Liverpool Royal Infirmary*[11] and *Winans* v. *A.G.*[12] to the effect that much stronger evidence is required to prove a change from a domicile of origin to a domicile of choice than from one domicile of choice to another.   The result in the former case was that after 35 years' absence, and in the latter 37 years' absence, from the country of the domicile of origin, it was held that the domicile of origin was still operative.   Attempts to change this anomaly by legislation have proved abortive.   Subject to these decisions, almost any factor in a person's life may be relevant to his intention—the length of his residence, the purchase of a house, the establishment of children in business, naturalisation—all may be relevant, but no one factor is conclusive.

Just as the acquisition of a domicile of choice requires the coincidence at the same point of time of both residence and the intention that it shall be permanent, so also the abandonment of such a domicile requires that both residence and intention shall have ceased, so that an intention to leave a country and settle elsewhere may be ineffective to change a domicile of choice if it is defeated by illness which prevents actual departure.[13]   The intention required at the moment of departure in order to prove abandonment of a domicile of choice is not necessarily an intention to leave for ever: it is enough if, having departed, the person's intention of returning has merely withered away even though he has not formed any positive intention never to return to live in the country of the former domicile.[14]

If one domicile of choice is abandoned without another being acquired, the domicile of origin revives.[15]   But a domicile of origin cannot be thus abandoned, because it leaves the individual concerned with no operative domicile, and departure from the country of the domicile of origin will not result in a change of domicile until a fresh domicile of choice is acquired.[16]

2. Polygamy.

In *Hyde* v. *Hyde and Woodmansee*[17] Lord PENZANCE laid down the rule that the matrimonial jurisdiction of the English courts could be exercised only in respect of a marriage which was "the voluntary union for life of one man and one woman to the exclusion of all others".   The rule applied not only to marriages which were actually polygamous but also to those which were potentially polygamous, in the sense that although the husband had as yet married only one wife the relevant law permitted him to take further wives.[18]   The result was that the English courts could not entertain a petition for divorce, nullity or judicial separation in respect of such marriages.   Nor could the wife, or one of the wives, take proceedings in a divorce county court or in a magistrates'

[11] [1930] A.C. 588.
[12] [1904] A.C. 287.
[13] *In the goods of Raffenel* (1863), 3 Sw. & Tr. 49.
[14] *Re Flynn*, [1968] 1 All E.R. 49.
[15] *Udny* v. *Udny* (1869), L.R. 1 Sc. & Div. 441.
[16] *Bell* v. *Kennedy* (1868), L.R. 1 Sc. & Div. 307.
[17] (1886), L.R. 1 P. & D. 130.
[18] *Risk* v. *Risk*, [1951] P. 50.

court on the ground of her husband's wilful neglect to provide reasonable maintenance. This rule could cause considerable hardship. In *Sowa* v. *Sowa*[19] the parties had gone through a ceremony of marriage in Ghana, where both were domiciled, which was potentially polygamous, the husband having promised that he would go through a later ceremony which would render the marriage monogamous. The parties came to England, but he failed to keep his promise and deserted his wife with the result that she was denied the right to enforce a claim for maintenance against him. This hardship was to some extent alleviated by the fact that, if a wife and the children of a polygamous or potentially polygamous marriage are left destitute and claim or receive social security benefits, the Supplementary Benefits Commission can apply to a magistrates' court for an order that the cost be recovered from the husband.[20]

The subject of jurisdiction in matrimonial causes is now dealt with by the provisions of the Matrimonial Proceedings (Polygamous Marriages) Act 1972 which (so far as they relate to England and Wales) are now repealed and re-enacted in section 47 of the Act of 1973. But before considering the provisions of this Act it should be noted that for many other purposes such marriages are recognised as valid. This is so for the purposes of legitimacy of children.[21] It must be so for purposes of taxation. It is so for the purpose of freedom to marry. In *Baindail (otherwise Lawson)* v. *Baindail*[22] Lord GREENE, M.R., put the matter very simply. Despite the fact that by Indian law the marriage was potentially polygamous, the husband acquired by the law of his Indian domicile the status of a married man. A married man cannot marry in England, and the woman whom he has purported to marry here is entitled to a decree of nullity. It seems, however, that a prosecution for bigamy would not lie in such a case[23] though other criminal proceedings would doubtless be available in respect of any deception practised by the accused.

Reference has already been made[1] to the subject of capacity to contract a polygamous or potentially polygamous marriage, and in particular to the provisions of section 11 (d) of the Act of 1973 which renders void a polygamous marriage entered into outside England and Wales after July 31, 1971, if either party was at the time of the marriage domiciled in England and Wales. This is so even though the marriage was only potentially polygamous, in that at its inception neither spouse has any spouse additional to the other.

Assuming that the marriage is in other respects valid, section 47 of the Act of 1973 provides that a court in England and Wales is no longer to be precluded from granting matrimonial relief or making a declaration concerning the validity of a marriage by reason only that the marriage in question was entered into under a law which permits polygamy. This is so whether or not either party to that marriage has for the time being any spouse additional to the other party.[2]

---

[19] [1961] P. 70.
[20] *Iman Din* v. *National Assistance Board*, [1967] 2 Q.B. 213.
[21] *Bamgbose* v. *Daniel*, [1955] A.C. 107, P.C. *Sinha Peerage Claim*, [1946] 1 All E.R. 348, n. But query as to succession to entailed interests, at p. 349.
[22] [1946] P. 122, 127.
[23] *R.* v. *Sarwan Singh*, [1962] 3 All E.R. 612.
[1] *Ante*, p. 81.
[2] S. 47 (4). For the procedure in such cases see Rule 108.

The expression "matrimonial relief" is very widely defined. It includes decrees of divorce, nullity, judicial separation and decrees of presumption of death and dissolution, orders for financial provision under section 27 of the Act on the ground of wilful neglect to provide reasonable maintenance[3] and for alteration of a maintenance agreement,[4] and all powers exercisable by the High Court or a divorce county court in connection with such decrees or orders or proceedings for them. It includes also all orders under the Matrimonial Proceedings (Magistrates' Courts) Act 1960.[5] This change in the law has been rendered necessary in order that justice may be done in matrimonial causes involving the increasing number of immigrants to this country from other parts of the world where polygamy is permitted. There is as yet no judicial authority on the manner in which, for example, the powers as to financial provision and children of the family should be exercised when a husband with several wives and numerous children is divorced by one of his wives.

3. Jurisdiction of the English Courts

(i) *The basis of jurisdiction*

The rules which govern the jurisdiction of the English courts are contained in the Domicile and Matrimonial Proceedings Act 1973. It gives effect to recommendations made by the Law Commission,[6] and incidentally includes similar provisions as to the Law of Scotland in Part II and as to that of Northern Ireland in Part III. The provisions apply only to proceedings begun on or after January 1, 1974.[7] In considering their effect the changes effected by the Act in relation to the domicile of married women and married minors[8] must be borne in mind. The result of these changes is that it is no longer necessary to have different provisions as to jurisdiction according to whether the husband or the wife is the petitioner, as it was when a wife automatically had the same domicile as her husband whilst the marriage lasted and might have found herself unable to petition in England if he deserted her and obtained a domicile of choice in some other country.

In relation to the principal decrees jurisdiction may be based upon either domicile or habitual residence.[9]

(a) In proceedings for divorce or judicial separation it exists if (and only if) either of the parties to the marriage is domiciled in England and Wales when the proceedings are begun or was habitually resident there throughout the period of one year ending with that date.[10]

(b) In suits for nullity the basis of jurisdiction is the same with the additional alternative that if either party to the marriage has died before the date when the proceedings are begun there is jurisdiction if that party was at death

---

[3] See *post*, Chapter 10.
[4] See *post*, Chapter 12, p. 172.
[5] See *post*, Chapter 17.
[6] Report on Jurisdiction in Matrimonial Causes, Law Com. No. 48.
[7] Ss. 6 (4) and 17 (5).
[8] See *ante*, pp. 86, 87.
[9] As to the meaning of the latter expression, see *ante*, p. 84.
[10] S. 5 (2).

domiciled in England and Wales or had been habitually resident there throughout the period of one year ending with the date of death.[11] This alternative is
applicable only to cases in which the marriage is.alleged to be void, since it is
too late to bring proceedings for nullity in respect of a voidable marriage after
the death of either of the spouses. But in the case of a marriage alleged to be
void anyone with a sufficient interest can petition even after the death of one
or both of the parties to the marriage, though such cases are extremely rare.
If and when they arise the English court will have jurisdiction if either party
to the marriage was domiciled here at death or had been habitually resident
here throughout the year preceding the death, in addition to any jurisdiction
which can be founded on the domicile or habitual residence for one year of the
survivor.[12]

(c) It may sometimes happen that although the above requirements were
satisfied at the date when the original proceedings were begun, they have ceased
to exist at the time when the respondent wishes to claim cross-relief in the
answer, or by way of cross-petition, because, for example, the petitioner has
abandoned the English domicile or habitual residence on which jurisdiction was
founded. To meet this situation section 5 (5) provides that at any time when
proceedings are pending in respect of which the court has jurisdiction under the
provisions described in (a) and (b) above (or under section 5 (5) itself) it shall
also have jurisdiction to entertain other proceedings for divorce, judicial
separation or nullity in respect of the same marriage, although it would not be
exercisable under the provisions already described.

(d) In proceedings for death to be presumed and the marriage to be dissolved, the domicile and habitual residence of the party presumed to be dead
(if in fact he is still alive) are obviously unknown to the petitioner. Accordingly
there is jurisdiction if (and only if) *the petitioner* can satisfy the requirements
as to English domicile or one years' habitual residence.[13]

(ii) *Obligatory and discretionary stays of proceedings*

The Act contains a number of provisions aimed at preventing simultaneous
proceedings in respect of the same marriage in this country and elsewhere.

The first, which is contained in section 6 (3), is of transitory importance only.
No proceedings for *divorce* can be entertained by virtue of the Act[14] while proceedings for *divorce or nullity*, begun before January 1, 1974, are pending in
respect of the same marriage in Scotland, Northern Ireland, the Channel Isles
or the Isle of Man. It should be noted that this prohibition does not prevent the
institution in England of proceedings for judicial separation or nullity.

The remaining provisions, which are extremely detailed, are to be found in
Schedule 1. They do not require or authorise the stay of any proceedings
pending on January 1, 1974, or prejudice any other power which the court may

---

[11] S. 5 (3).
[12] See Law Com. No. 48, *supra*, paras. 50 and 61.
[13] S. 5 (4).
[14] I.e. under the provisions in paras. (a) and (c), *supra*.

have to stay proceedings.[15] But they provide for both obligatory and discretionary stays in proceedings commenced on or after that date.

The first essential is to ensure that the court is made aware that matrimonial proceedings are continuing in another jurisdiction in respect of the marriage or capable of affecting its validity or subsistence. Accordingly, while the trial of such proceedings which are pending in England has not yet begun, an obligation is placed upon the petitioner or a respondent who has included a prayer for relief in his answer to furnish the prescribed particulars of any other matrimonial proceedings of which he knows.[16] The expression "matrimonial proceedings" includes only proceedings (whether in a court or otherwise) for divorce, judicial separation, nullity, or a declaration as to the validity or subsistence of the petitioner's marriage.[17] The court may then have to consider the need for an obligatory or discretionary stay of the English proceedings.

(a) *Obligatory stays*

The necessity for this type of stay arises only if the English proceedings are for *divorce*, only upon the application of one of the parties to the marriage, and only if proceedings for *divorce or nullity* in respect of the same marriage are continuing in a "related jurisdiction", i.e. in Scotland, Northern Ireland, Jersey, Guernsey (including Alderney and Sark), or in the Isle of Man.[18]

If such an application is made before the beginning of the trial or first trial of the English divorce proceedings, it is the duty of the court to order them to be stayed[19] if it appears to the court that:—

(i) the parties have resided together since the date of the marriage; and

(ii) the place where they resided together when the proceedings in the English court were begun, or if they did not then reside together, where they last resided together before the proceedings were begun, was in the related jurisdiction; and

(iii) either of them was habitually resident there throughout the year during which they last resided together before the English proceedings were begun.

These somewhat complicated provisions cannot cause hardship, because by virtue of the Recognition of Divorces and Legal Separations Act 1971, s. 1,[20] a decree of divorce or nullity obtained elsewhere in the British Isles will be recognised as valid in England.

(b) *Discretionary stays*

The scope of these provisions is much wider.[1] They apply to all matrimonial proceedings (as defined above) in England and not only to proceedings for

---

[15] S. 5 (6).

[16] Domicile and Matrimonial Proceedings Act 1973, Sched. 1, para. 7 and Rules 9 (2) and 21 (4).

[17] *Ibid.*, Sched. 1, paras. 2 and 5.

[18] *Ibid.*, paras. 3 (2) and 8 (1).

[19] If the proceedings are for other forms of relief as well as divorce (e.g. for divorce or nullity in the alternative) only the divorce proceedings need by stayed. *Ibid.*, para. 8 (2).

[20] As amended by the Domicile and Matrimonial Proceedings Act 1973, s. 15 (2), see *post*, p. 94.

[1] Sched. 1, para. 9.

divorce, they are not dependent upon the application for a stay by one of the parties, and they apply when any proceedings in respect of the marriage, or capable of affecting its validity or subsistence, are continuing in *any country* outside England and Wales (including, of course, proceedings in a related jurisdiction). The court's discretion to order a stay must be exercised before the beginning of the trial or first trial, unless the court is satisfied that a person has failed to perform his duty to give particulars of proceedings elsewhere of which he knows,[2] when a stay may be ordered after the trial has begun, though no action lies in respect of the failure to perform that duty.[3] Subject to these conditions the court may exercise its discretion to order a stay of the English proceedings if it appears to the court that the balance of fairness (including convenience) as between the parties to the marriage is such that it is appropriate for the proceedings elsewhere to be disposed of before further steps are taken in the English proceedings, or part of them, having regard to all relevant factors, including the convenience of witnesses and any delay or expense which may result from the proceedings being stayed, or not being stayed.

(c) *Supplementary provisions*

When the court has granted an order for an obligatory or discretionary stay, it has a discretion, on the application of a party to the proceedings, to discharge the order if the proceedings elsewhere have been stayed or concluded or a party to those proceedings has delayed unreasonably in prosecuting them. Once it has discharged an order for an obligatory stay, it cannot grant an obligatory stay in respect of the same proceedings, though it could still grant a discretionary stay.[4]

There are complicated provisions[5] as to the position when proceedings for divorce, judicial separation or nullity are stayed by reference to proceedings for those forms of relief in a related jurisdiction, their object being to ensure that whilst the stay remains in force there shall not be inconsistent orders as to matters of financial provision and children pending the result of the suit in force simultaneously in England and in the related jurisdiction. They concern orders for maintenance pending suit, lump sum or periodical payments for children, for their custody, access to them and their education and training, and removal of them from England and Wales. Broadly the effect is that except in cases of urgency, the English court cannot make such orders whilst the stay remains in force and if such orders have already been made they will lapse after the expiration of three months from the date when the stay was imposed.

4. Recognition of foreign decrees.

(a) *Divorce and legal separation.*

The circumstances in which a divorce or legal separation obtained outside England and Wales will be recognised here are governed by the Recognition of

---

[2] See *ante*, p. 92.
[3] Sched. 1, para. 9 (4).
[4] *Ibid.*, para. 10.
[5] *Ibid.*, para. 11. They should be studied in detail in cases to which they may apply.

Divorces and Legal Separations Act 1971, the provisions of which are set out in Appendix 1 as amended by the Domicile and Matrimonial Proceedings Act 1973.

The Act follows the recommendations of the Law Commission (Law Com. No. 34) which was asked to advise upon the legislation which would be required to enable H.M. Government to ratify a Draft Convention on the subject adopted by the Hague Conference on Private International Law in October 1968, which forms Appendix A to the Commission's Report. But this is not the sole aim of the Act. For reasons stated in the Report its second aim, and perhaps an even more important one, is to restate and amend the whole law relating to the recognition of foreign decrees of divorce and legal separation, including those granted in countries for whose foreign relations the British Government is responsible. Accordingly it goes further than would be strictly necessary merely in order to ratify the Convention, and provides, for the first time, a code of the grounds of recognition which supersedes entirely the former judge-made law.[6] It must be particularly noticed that the provisions of the Act are made applicable to decrees granted in all countries and not only, as the Convention requires, to those granted in Contracting States which are parties to the Convention, and that its provisions came into force on January 1, 1972, although the Convention was not then in force.[7]

By section 1 (as amended) (subject to section 8, *infra*) the validity of a decree of divorce or judicial separation *granted after the commencement of the Act* shall, if granted under the law of any part of the British Isles, be recognised throughout the United Kingdom.[8] Such decrees would not come within the scope of the Hague Convention, but it would be absurd to recognise truly foreign decrees, as the Convention requires, more readily than those obtained in other parts of the British Isles.

Sections 3 to 6 in effect lay down an exclusive code for the recognition of overseas divorces and legal separations, that is to say those obtained in any country outside the British Isles. By section 10 (3) the word "country" includes a colony or other dependent territory of the United Kingdom, but for the purposes of the Act a person is to be treated as a national of such a territory only if it has a law of citizenship or nationality separate from that of the United Kingdom and he is a citizen or national of that territory under that law.

Whereas the provisions relating to recognition of decrees granted in the British Isles apply only to those granted on or after January 1, 1972, the provisions relating to overseas divorces and legal separations, by virtue of section 10 (4), have retrospective effect, and in relation to those obtained before the commencement of the Act require, or as the case may be, preclude, the recognition of their validity in relation to any time before the Act came into force as well as afterwards. This is unlikely to cause hardship in practice, because as the Law Commission observed[9]

---

[6] Law Com. No. 34, Cmd. 4542, Explanatory Note to draft bill at p. 33.
[7] By Article 27 it comes into force only on the sixtieth day after the deposit of the third instrument of ratification.
[8] S. 10 (2), defines "the British Isles" as meaning the United Kingdom, the Channel Islands and the Isle of Man.
[9] Law Com. No. 34, para. 48.

"We believe that given the wide grounds of recognition of foreign divorces approved in *Indyka* v. *Indyka*[10] the cases must be few in which the adoption of the Convention's grounds of recognition would in fact mean that a foreign divorce, hitherto unrecognised in our law, would in future fall to be recognised. Similarly we think that the cases must be few where a foreign divorce which is now recognised under the *Indyka* decision would not also be recognised under the Convention."

There is, however, a possibility that such retrospective recognition or non-recognition might affect property rights, as where an estate has been distributed on the basis that the marriage of the testator has not been validly dissolved by a foreign decree and the Act leads to retrospective recognition of the validity of the decree. Section 10 (4) (*b*) therefore provides that any property rights to which any person became entitled before the date of the commencement of the Act are not to be affected and also that any decision of a competent court in the British Isles before that date as to the validity of an overseas divorce or legal separation is to remain unaffected.

By section 2, the provisions of the Act are to govern the recognition in the United Kingdom of all overseas divorces and legal separations which are legally effective in the country where they were obtained, whether obtained there by means of judicial or other proceedings. Thus the Act is not limited to decrees granted by a court of law. This has been so before the Act, as is instanced by *Russ* v. *Russ*,[11] where a divorce by declaration of divorcement, or talaq, was recognised as validly terminating a monogamous marriage in England on the ground that it was valid by the law of Egypt, where the talaq was pronounced. A further example is to be found in *Lee* v. *Lau*,[12] where dissolution of a Chinese customary marriage in Hong Kong, where the parties were domiciled, by a "contract of divorce" in customary form was recognised in England. Any hardship which might have been caused if the circumstances had been different could be avoided by section 8 (2) (*b*), whereby recognition can be refused if it would be manifestly contrary to public policy. But the position would be different if the proceedings for divorce or separation were brought on or after January 1, 1974, in the United Kingdom, the Channel Isles or the Isle of Man, because by section 16 of the Domicile and Matrimonial Proceedings Act 1973, no such proceedings are to be regarded as validly dissolving a marriage unless instituted in the courts of law of one of those countries. Further (see *post*, p. 98) section 16 contains special provisions preventing a person domiciled outside that area but habitually resident within it from avoiding the effect of this section by going temporarily to some other country and obtaining a non-judicial divorce which would be regarded as valid by the law of his place of domicile. The provisions of section 16 are not, however, to affect the validity of any divorce obtained before that date and recognised as valid under the rules

---

[10] [1969] 1 A.C. 33. The House of Lords held that a decree should be recognised if there was a real and substantial connection between one of the parties and the country in which the decree was granted.

[11] [1964] P. 313.

[12] [1967] P. 14.

of law formerly applicable. They will not, therefore, affect such decisions as that in *Qureshi* v. *Qureshi*,[13] where in 1970 a monogamous marriage celebrated in England was held to have been validly dissolved by talaq pronounced in England on the ground that the divorce was effective by the law of Pakistan, where the parties were domiciled.

Section 3 lays down the basic principle that an overseas divorce or legal separation is to be recognised if, at the date of the institution of the proceedings in the country in which it was obtained

(i) either spouse was habitually resident in that country; or

(ii) either spouse was a national of that country.

Requirement (i) departs from the former principle whereby the recognition of such decrees depended primarily, though by no means exclusively, upon their being obtained in the country where the parties were domiciled. The reason is that the concept of domicile is overloaded with technicalities, is governed by different rules in different countries, and is by no means universally accepted. The expression "habitual residence" is devoid of these disadvantages though its meaning awaits judicial interpretation[14]. It is already used in other statutes implementing Conventions concluded at the Hague, such as the Wills Act 1963, s. 1, and the Adoption Act 1968, s. 11. But the concept of domicile does not altogether disappear, because section 3 (2) provides that in relation to a country the law of which uses this concept as a ground of jurisdiction in matters of divorce or legal separation, the reference to habitual residence is to *include* a reference to domicile as understood by the law of the country where the decree was obtained, which may well differ from the understanding of English law. In France and Luxembourg, for example, a person has his domicile at the place where he has his "principal establishment", in Germany, where he has a "permanent" (not necessarily "principal") establishment, in Belgium where he is entered on the official register of population.

In many overseas countries with a federal or quasi-federal constitution the systems of matrimonial law will differ as between different States and it would be impossible to say what the law of such a country as a whole provided. Provision is made for cases of this kind by section 3 (3) whereby in relation to a country comprising territories in which different systems of law are in force in matters of divorce and legal separation, the provisions of section 3 (except those relating to nationality) are to have effect as if each territory were a separate country.

The effect of section 4 (1) is somewhat complicated. It deals with cross-proceedings and provides that the validity of a divorce or separation obtained either in the original proceedings or in the cross-proceedings is to be recognised if the requirements of section 3 (1) (*a*) or (*b*) of the Act are satisfied in relation to the date of the institution either of the original proceedings or of the cross-proceedings, that is to say if at either date either spouse was habitually resident in the country where the decree was obtained or was a national of that country.

---

[13] [1972] Fam. 173.

[14] See *ante*, p. 84.

It is difficult to find better examples than those in the explanatory note to this clause of the Draft Bill in the Law Commission's Report.[15]

> "For example, if the wife applied for a divorce in a country where she was habitually resident and the husband, who was neither resident nor domiciled in, nor a national of, that country, brought cross-proceedings, we should have to recognise his resulting decree even though at the time that his proceedings commenced the wife had ceased to be resident in that country; and the same would apply if the wife had started proceedings when neither she nor her husband had any connection with the country, but he later became habitually resident there and instituted cross-proceedings, even though the decree was granted to her."

Evidently uniformity and codification are not synonomous with simplification! Fortunately such problems are likely to be uncommon in practice.

The situation envisaged in section 4 (2) is simple, and likely to be encountered more often. Where a legal separation, the validity of which is entitled to recognition under section 3 or section 4 (1), *supra* is converted, in the country in which it was obtained, into a divorce, the validity of the divorce is to be recognised whether or not it would be entitled to recognition under those provisions. In New Zealand, for example, if the petitioner and respondent are parties to a decree of separation made in New Zealand, and this decree has remained in full force for not less than two years, this constitutes a ground for divorce.[16] The conversion of such a decree into a decree of divorce, under provisions similar to those of the English Matrimonial Causes Act 1973, s. 4,[17] is entitled to recognition here if either party was habitually resident in, or was a national of New Zealand, when the original decree of separation was granted.

Section 5 deals with the extent to which, once an overseas court has based its assumption of jurisdiction upon a finding of fact, including a finding by implication and a finding that either spouse was habitually resident or domiciled in, or a national of, the country where the decree was granted, a court in Great Britain can go behind that finding. The result of the section is that, if both spouses took part in the proceedings (and a spouse who has appeared in judicial proceedings is treated as having taken part in them) these findings are conclusive evidence of the facts so found, but in any other case they are only sufficient proof of the facts unless the contrary is proved.

It must be noticed that this section is limited to findings which are relevant to jurisdiction. It must be contrasted with section 8 (3) whereby nothing in the Act is to be construed as requiring the recognition of any findings of fault made in any proceedings for divorce or separation, or of any maintenance, custody, or other ancillary order made in any such proceedings.

Thus far, since the provisions of the Act are in some respects wider than those of English judge-made law, they are in general unlikely to result in refusal to recognise an overseas decree which would previously have been recognised

---

[15] Law Com. No. 34, p. 39.
[16] Matrimonial Proceedings Act 1963, s. 21 (*n*) as amended by Matrimonial Proceedings Amendment Act 1968, s. 2 (*e*).
[17] See *ante*, p. 43 *et seq.*

in England.   But before the Act came into operation the English courts would
have recognised as valid a divorce or legal separation obtained in the country
in which both parties were domiciled at the date of institution of the proceedings
in accordance with the rules of English law, notwithstanding that the law of the
place where the decree was obtained took a different view of the domicile of the
parties.   The English courts would also have recognised as valid a divorce or
separation obtained in the courts of some other country which would be *recognised* as valid by the counts of the country in which (according to English law)
the parties were domiciled when the proceedings were instituted, as in *Armitage*
v. *A.-G.*[18] where a decree of divorce obtained by a wife in South Dakota on
grounds insufficient by English law or the law of New York, where the parties
were then domiciled, was valid here because it would have been recognised as
valid by the courts of New York.

Section 6 of the Act of 1971 (as substituted by section 2 of the Domicile and
Matrimonial Proceedings Act 1973) ensures that these common law rules are
preserved.   But since the latter Act enables a wife to have a separate domicile
from that of her husband, it has in effect extended the common law rules to
cover this possibility.   Recognition will be afforded to a divorce or legal separation obtained in a country outside the British Isles if at the time of the institution of the proceedings in the country in which the divorce or legal separation
was obtained either

(a) one of the spouses was domiciled[19] in that country and the divorce or
separation was recognised as valid under the law of the domicile of the other
spouse; or

(b) neither of the spouses having been domiciled in that country at the
material time, the divorce or separation was recognised as valid under the law
of the domicile of each of the spouses respectively.

Section 6 of the Act of 1971 also provides for the continued recognition of
divorces or legal separations obtained outside the British Isles by virtue of any
enactment other than that Act, such as the Colonial and Other Territories
(Divorce Jurisdiction) Acts 1926 to 1950 or the Matrimonial Causes (War Marriages) Act 1944, so far as these Acts are still in operation.

But at this point section 6 does, so to speak, close the list, by providing that
no divorce or legal separation obtained outside the British Isles shall be recognised as valid in the United Kingdom except as provided by sections 2 to 6 of
the Act.

Mention has already been made (see *ante,* p. 95) of the provisions of section
16 of the Domicile and Matrimonial Proceedings Act 1973 which precludes
recognition of a divorce obtained in the United Kingdom, the Channel Isles
or the Isle of Man by proceedings (such as a talaq, or declaration of divorcement)
which were not instituted in the courts of law of one of those countries.   Section
16 contains a further provision whereby, to a limited extent, a person habitually

---

[18] [1906] P. 135.
[19] The expression "domiciled" is in each case used as meaning domiciled according to
the rules of English law.

resident in that area but domiciled elsewhere is prevented from taking advantage of section 6 of the Act of 1971 by going temporarily to some other country and obtaining a "non-judicial" divorce valid by the law of the place where he had had domicile in the English sense of that word.

If recognition of the divorce was required by any of the provisions of sections 2 to 5 of the Act of 1971 (as, for example, if it was obtained in and was effective by the law of the country of which either spouse was a national at the date when the proceedings were instituted) the adherence of this country to the Convention on Recognition prevents any refusal to recognise its validity. But if those sections do not apply, and both parties to the marriage have been habitually resident in the United Kingdom during the period of one year immediately preceding the institution of the proceedings abroad, the "non-judicial" divorce is not to be regarded, by virtue of section 6 of the Act of 1971 only, as validly dissolving the marriage. This does not, however, affect the validity of any divorce obtained before January 1, 1974, and recognised as valid under rules of law formerly applicable.

The remainder of the Act consists of more general provisions. Section 7 provides that where the validity of a divorce is entitled to recognition under the Act, neither spouse shall be precluded from re-marrying in Great Britain on the ground that the validity of the divorce would not be recognised in any other country. This provision is designed to overrule the effect of such decisions as *R. v. Brentwood Superintendent Registrar of Marriages, Ex parte Arias*.[20] The parties were both domiciled in Switzerland, where they intended to make their matrimonial home, and where the husband had been divorced. But the husband was an Italian national, and since by Italian law the validity of the Swiss divorce was not recognised, he lacked capacity to marry by the law of his Swiss domicile. The refusal of the English registrar to issue a licence to marry was upheld by a Divisional Court. In comparable circumstances the parties may now contract a marriage in England which will be valid by English law, though it may lack validity elsewhere if the law of their nationality or domicile regards a marriage as indissoluble. In a sense this creates a sort of limping marriage rather than avoiding such a result, but the parties would regard it as a benefit rather than as a disadvantage.

Section 8 lays down the exceptions to the rules as to recognition contained in the earlier sections.

By subsection (1) the validity of a decree granted in any part of the British Isles, or of an overseas divorce or legal separation obtained elsewhere, is not to be recognised in any part of Great Britain if it was granted or obtained at a time when, according to the law of that part of Great Britain (including its rules of private international law and the provisions of the Act), there was no subsisting marriage between the parties. This situation can arise where, for example, a marriage has already been dissolved or annulled by an English decree, in which case a subsequent foreign divorce would not be recognised, or where a foreign court of the domicile had already annulled the marriage, in which case we should not recognise a subsequent divorce in the country of residence.

---

[20] [1968] 2 Q.B. 956.

These situations may not often arise. But section 8 (2) (which applies only to an overseas divorce or legal separation and not to a decree obtained in the British Isles) deals with situations of more frequent occurrence. It provides that subject to subsection (1), recognition by virtue of the Act or any rule preserved by section 6 thereof may be refused, if, *and only if*

(a) it was obtained by one spouse—

(i) without such steps having been taken for giving notice of the proceedings to the other spouse as, having regard to the nature of the proceedings and all the circumstances, should reasonably have been taken; or
(ii) without the other spouse having been given (for any reason other than lack of notice) such opportunity to take part in the proceedings as, having regard to the matters aforesaid, he should reasonably have been given; or

(b) its recognition would manifestly be contrary to public policy.

The court's discretion to refuse recognition in such cases is already well established in English law. Those under (a) correspond to insistence upon observance of the rules of natural justice, which require that both parties shall be afforded an equal opportunity to be heard. In *Macalpine* v. *Macalpine*[1] recognition was refused of a decree obtained by the husband in the State where he was domiciled because he had falsely sworn an affidavit that his wife's address was unknown to him, with the result that he obtained a decree without her receiving any notice of the proceedings. But the mere fact that the respondent has not received notice does not of itself justify the refusal of recognition. In England the Rules provide for substituted service or notice in lieu of service by advertisements, which may well not come to the respondent's notice, and even allow a registrar to dispense altogether with service on the respondent.[2] Recognition of a foreign divorce cannot be refused merely because rules on similar lines to those in force in England have proved ineffective to inform the respondent of the proceedings.[3] And whatever the circumstances in which notice was not given to the respondent, the divorce will still be recognised if no injustice will be caused, as in *Hornett* v. *Hornett*,[4] a strange case in which a husband in 1970 sought and obtained a declaration that a decree of divorce granted to his wife in France in 1924 was valid, despite the fact that he knew nothing of the decree until 1925, and thereafter resumed cohabitation with his former wife, notwithstanding that she had divorced him, and lived with her until 1937.

Ground (b) for the refusal of recognition involves a somewhat different and wider principle, that a decree granted by a competent court in circumstances which are procedurally regular can be refused recognition on the ground that it offends against English views of substantial justice.[5] A recent example is that

---

[1] [1958] P. 35.
[2] Rule 14 (10).
[3] *Boettcher* v. *Boettcher*, [1949] W.N. 83; *Igra* v. *Igra*, [1951] P. 404, 411–412.
[4] [1971] P. 255.
[5] See *Gray (otherwise Formosa)* v. *Formosa*, [1963] P. 259, a case of nullity.

of *In Re Meyer*,[6] where recognition was refused on grounds of duress.   The parties had been married in Germany in 1932, he being of Jewish and she of "Aryan" parentage.   In 1938 he escaped from Germany and came to England. She remained in Germany and as a result of extreme pressure was persuaded to divorce him there in 1939.   She came to England in 1949 and lived with him there until his death in 1965.   She sought a declaration that the German decree was invalid, in order to establish her right to a pension as his widow from the German Government.   BAGNALL, J., held that just as a marriage may be voidable on the ground of duress, so also a foreign decree of divorce will be declared invalid—

> "if the will of the party seeking the decree was overborne by a genuine and reasonably held fear caused by present and continuing danger to life, limb or liberty arising from external circumstances for which that party was not responsible.   I add that I think that 'danger to limb' means a serious danger to physical or mental health; and that 'danger' must include danger to at least a parent or child of that party."[7]

The Act covers all matters on which legislative changes were required in order to enable H.M. Government to ratify the Convention.   It does not deal with matters in which English law already satisfies the conditions which the Convention lays down.   Thus no action is required in respect of Article 6, whereby recognition is not to be refused because an English court would not have granted a decree upon the same facts, or would have applied a different law from that applicable under the rules of private international law of the State where the divorce or legal separation was obtained.   Subject to rules of natural justice and public policy, the English courts, in relation to divorce elsewhere, have always concerned themselves only with questions of jurisdiction rather than the grounds on which the decree was granted or the merits of the case.   As Sir GORELL BARNES said in relation to this principle in *Bater* v. *Bater*[8]

> "It is based upon the simple proposition that if this country recognises the right of a foreign tribunal to dissolve a marriage of two persons . . . it must also recognise that their marriage may be dissolved according to the law of that foreign country, even though that law would dissolve a marriage for a lesser cause than would dissolve it in this country."

Likewise, no legislation was necessary in respect of Article 12, whereby proceedings for divorce or legal separation may be suspended when proceedings relating to the matrimonial status of either party are pending in another contracting state.   The English courts already possess this power, though they are reluctant to exercise it if the English petitioner would derive advantages, for example as to maintenance, from the continuance of the English proceedings.[9]

---

[6] [1971] 2 W.L.R. 401.
[7] *Ibid.*, at p. 408.
[8] [1906] P. 209, 217.
[9] *Sealey (otherwise Callan)* v. *Callan*, [1953] P. 135.

(b) *Nullity of marriage.*

It is unfortunate that, whilst the recognition of foreign divorces and legal separations has been dealt with by statute, the recognition of foreign nullity decrees is, at all events for the time being, still dependent entirely upon case law. Anomalies seem bound to arise because some of the grounds for nullity in England are grounds for divorce in certain other countries. The New Zealand Matrimonial Proceedings Act 1963, for example, confines nullity to cases in which the marriage is void and deals with other grounds by a decree of "Dissolution of a Voidable Marriage". This is presumably a decree of divorce, and entitled to recognition as such under the Act of 1971.

The cases in which recognition will be afforded to a foreign decree of nullity are far from clear, but may perhaps be summarised as follows:—

(i) If the decree was obtained in the country or State in which both parties were then domiciled[10].

(ii) If the decree, though obtained elsewhere, would be recognised as valid by the courts of the country or State of domicile.[11]

(iii) If the decree was obtained in the country or State where both parties then resided. There is no specific authority for this proposition, but it seems to follow from the words of HODSON, L.J., in *Travers* v. *Holley and Holley*[12] where he said "... it would be contrary to principle and inconsistent with comity if the courts of this country were to refuse to recognise a jurisdiction which *mutatis mutandis* they claim for themselves".

(iv) Presumably, by virtue of this principle in *Travers* v. *Holley*, if in comparable circumstances the English courts would have assumed jurisdiction under the Domicile and Matrimonial Proceedings Act 1973, section 5 (3) e.g. if *either party* was domiciled in England or had habitually resided there for the year preceding the commencement of the proceedings.

(v) Presumably also in the much wider circumstances in which a decree of divorce would have been recognised by virtue of the decision of the House of Lords in *Indyka* v. *Indyka*[13] that is to say if the petitioner or the respondent[14] had a real and substantial connection with the country in which the decree was pronounced. Such a connection may arise from domicile, habitual residence, nationality or a combination of these and other facts. The principle leads to results very similar to those of the Act of 1971 in relation to divorce, and must be equally applicable to nullity.

The above grounds apply equally to cases in which the marriage was found to be void and those in which it was voidable. Since the English courts no longer accept jurisdiction to grant a decree of nullity in respect of a marriage

---

[10] *Salvesen (or von Lorang)* v. *Administrator of Austrian Property*, [1927] A.C. 641.
[11] *Abate* v. *Abate*, [1961] P. 29.
[12] [1953] P. 246, 256–57.
[13] [1969] 1 A.C. 33.
[14] See *Mayfield* v. *Mayfield*, [1969] P. 119.

alleged to be void because that marriage was celebrated in England, they will presumably no longer follow earlier decisions[15] whereby foreign nullity decrees in respect of marriages found to be void were recognised because they were obtained in the country where the marriage was celebrated.

What has been said in relation to divorce with regard to the requirements of natural justice and the discretion to refuse recognition because the decree offends against English views of substantial justice, applies equally to decrees of nullity. It was upon the latter ground, in *Gray (otherwise Formosa)* v. *Formosa*[16] and *Lepre* v. *Lepre*[17] that recognition was denied to decrees obtained in Malta by a husband on the ground that marriages which took place in an English register office were void because by the law of his Maltese domicile he had no capacity as a Roman Catholic to marry otherwise than in a Roman Catholic Church. Decrees of this nature, based on bars of colour, or race, or religion, manifestly offend against the policy of English law.

(c) *Declarations as to validity of a foreign decree.*

The High Court under its inherent jurisdiction has power to make declarations as to the validity or otherwise of foreign decrees of divorce or nullity. Its power to do so has hitherto depended upon R.S.C., Ord. 15, and 16, whereby no action or other proceedings is to be open to objection on the ground that a merely declaratory judgment or order is sought, and is now governed by Rule 109 of the Matrimonial Causes Rules 1973. A county court has no corresponding power.[18] The circumstances in which this jurisdiction can be exercised are far from clear, though it seems that the domicile or residence of the parties or one of them in England suffices.[19]

The whole question is the subject of Working Paper No. 48 published by the Law Commission, which provisionally recommends (*inter alia*) the continuance of power to make these particular declarations, the clarification of the jurisdictional requirements, that all such proceedings should be commenced in a divorce county court and should be subject to strict procedural safeguards.

---

[15] *Mitford* v. *Mitford*, [1923] P. 130 (where it is not, however, clear whether recognition was based on residence or place of celebration); *Corbett* v. *Corbett*, [1957] 1 All E.R. 621.
[16] [1963] P. 259.
[17] [1965] P. 52.
[18] See *Practice Direction*, [1970] 3 All E.R. 1024.
[19] *Garthwaite* v. *Garthwaite*, [1964] P. 356; *Qureshi* v. *Qureshi*, [1972] Fam. 173.

PART II

FINANCIAL PROVISION
AND PROPERTY RIGHTS

CHAPTER 7

ANCILLARY FINANCIAL PROVISION FOR A SPOUSE AND CHILDREN

This Chapter is concerned with the powers of the court to order financial provision for a spouse and children in proceedings ancillary to suits for divorce, nullity and judicial separation. The subject of financial provision in proceedings based only on wilful neglect to provide reasonable maintenance, which are not ancillary to a suit for some other form of relief, is covered separately in Chapter 10. The principles upon which the court is expected to exercise its powers are dealt with in Chapter 9 and the variation, discharge and enforcement of orders in Chapter 11. The greater powers which are now conferred upon the court assume particular importance in the view of the fact that a high proportion of cases remain undefended, and in others the conduct of the parties will not have been the subject of detailed investigation, so that the effective dispute between the parties will be as to matters of property and financial provision, rather than as to whether or not their marriage has irretrievably broken down.

1. Maintenance Pending Suit.[1]

The expression "maintenance pending suit" replaces that of "alimony pending suit" used in previous statutes. Section 22 provides simply that on a petition for divorce, nullity of marriage or judicial separation, the court may order either party to the marriage to make to the other such periodical payments for his or her maintenance and for such term, being a term beginning not earlier than the date of presentation of the petition and ending with the date of the determination of the suit, as the court thinks reasonable.

In contrast to the previous law no distinction is now drawn between husband and wife,[2] and orders may be made against, or in favour of, either spouse, whether that spouse be petitioner or respondent and whether or not the suit be defended. In contrast to the sections dealing with financial provision and property adjustment orders at the conclusion of the principal suit,[3] no direction is given (as it is by section 25) as to the matters which the court is to have in mind in deciding whether or not to order such maintenance, or in fixing the amount. All that is laid down is that this form of provision must consist of "periodical payments" and must be such "as the court thinks reasonable". It is, therefore, clear that there can be no question, pending the determination of

---

[1] See Law Com. No. 25, paras. 5–7.
[2] Compare Act of 1965, s. 15.
[3] Ss. 23 and 24.

the principal suit, of orders for payments to be secured, or for payment of a
lump sum, or of orders for a transfer of property by one spouse to the other. On
the other hand, as will be seen later,[4] once a decree of divorce, nullity or judicial
separation has been granted,[5] orders for periodical payments, secured or unsecured, can be dated back to the date of the making of the application for such
orders, thus enabling the court to rectify any deficiency in the maintenance
pending suit which was ordered,[6] and a lump sum payment can then be ordered
to enable a party to meet liabilities and expenses reasonably incurred before
making the application for an order for such a payment.[7]

Having regard to the discretion conferred by the words "as the court
thinks reasonable" it may be assumed that the court will in future ignore the
former practice whereby, as a rough guide only, a husband was usually ordered
to pay a sum sufficient to bring his wife's income (if any) up to one-fifth of their
joint incomes. Even before the Act the amount was entirely in the court's
discretion.[8] As the Law Commission has observed[9] the payments ordered
pending the outcome of the suit will be made prior to the court's adjudication
on conduct, and indeed, before there has been a full investigation of the
parties' means. In the light of the changed attitude of the court towards the
conduct of the parties, it is doubtful whether a prior judicial finding of adultery
by one party or the other should influence the order which the court would
make; even before the Act it has not necessarily been a bar to the making or
continuance of such an order.[10] Any suggestion that adultery as such was a bar
to an order may well have derived from the fact that under the Act of 1965,
(save in the case of a petition based on the husband's incurable insanity) alimony
pending suit was awarded only in favour of a wife and may have been influenced
by the common law doctrine of the wife's agency of necessity, which terminated
on proof of her adultery[11] unless her husband had condoned or connived at it.[12]
The abolition, by section 41 of the Matrimonial Proceedings and Property Act
1970 of this type of agency, and the emphasis placed upon irretrievable breakdown rather than upon a matrimonial offence as the ground for divorce, indicate
that, pending suit, the emphasis should be upon need and the ability to provide,
rather than any premature assessment of conduct.

It will not infrequently happen that, at the time when a petition for divorce
or nullity is presented, the petitioner will already have obtained a matrimonial order from a magistrates' court. This is often the first step taken
on behalf of a wife when matrimonial difficulties have resulted in her husband's
failure to provide reasonable maintenance for her and for her children. Should
these difficulties remain unresolved and lead to a petition for divorce, this does
not, of itself, affect the continuance of the magistrates' order which may

---

[4] Post, pp. 110, 111.
[5] See s. 23.
[6] See s. 28.
[7] See s. 23 (3)
[8] *Sherwood* v. *Sherwood*, [1929] P. 120; *Waller* v. *Waller*, [1956] P. 300.
[9] Law Com. No. 25, para. 6 (a).
[10] *Gordon* v. *Gordon*, [1969] 3 All E.R. 1254.
[11] *Govier* v. *Hancock* (1796), 6 Term. Rep. 603.
[12] *Wilson* v. *Glossop* (1888), 20 Q.B.D. 354.

indeed, in many cases, survive even the granting of a decree absolute of divorce.[13] In these circumstances there can usually be little point in applying for maintenance pending suit, since there is now no financial limit on the powers of the magistrates to order maintenance,[14] and the High Court or a divorce county court would be unlikely to order more. No doubt also these courts would follow the former practice of refusing to make an order whilst the magistrates' order remains in force.[15] To cover a situation of this kind, section 7 (3) of the Matrimonial Proceedings (Magistrates' Courts) Act 1960 provided that where, after the making by a magistrates' court of a matrimonial order or interim order, proceedings between the parties are begun in the High Court, the High Court may direct that the provisions in the magistrates' order for maintenance of either spouse or a child of the family shall cease to have effect on a date to be specified. When jurisdiction in undefended divorce suits was conferred upon divorce county courts by the Matrimonial Causes Act 1967, the fact that these courts would have no corresponding power was overlooked. This is remedied by section 33 of the Matrimonial Proceedings and Property Act 1970, so that either the High Court or a divorce county court can now, if it thinks fit, direct that the financial provisions in the magistrates' order shall terminate and substitute its own order as to maintenance.

The possible duration of maintenance pending suit is in no way different from that of alimony pending suit. By section 22 the term may begin not earlier than the date of presentation of the petition, and Rules made under section 26 provide that the application should be made in the petition or answer. The term must end "with the date of the determination of the suit", that is to say at the date of the final decree, whether it be a decree absolute of divorce or nullity, a decree of judicial separation, or a decision that the petition be dismissed. An appeal from the decision of the lower court has, however, been regarded as a continuation of the original *lis*, enabling the High Court or a divorce county court (but not the Court of Appeal) to order continuance of alimony pending suit pending the outcome of the appeal.[16] This will clearly also be so in respect of maintenance pending suit. The court is not necessarily obliged to order payments for the maximum possible term, since their duration (as well as their amount) is to be such "as the court thinks reasonable".

2. Ancillary financial provision for a spouse.[17]

The expression "ancillary" is used here in the sense that the powers are exercisable in proceedings which have led to the grant of a decree of divorce, nullity or judicial separation, in contrast to proceedings under section 27 of the Act[18] which are brought with the sole object of obtaining financial provision. The relevant section of the Act is section 23, supplemented by section 24, which deals with financial provision by way of property adjustments (as to which see Chapter 8).

---

[13] *Bragg* v. *Bragg*, [1925] P. 20; *Wood* v. *Wood*, [1957] P. 254.
[14] Maintenance Orders Act 1968, s. 1.
[15] *Kilford* v. *Kilford*, [1947] P. 100; *Pooley* v. *Pooley*, [1952] P. 65.
[16] *Schlesinger* v. *Schlesinger*, [1958] 3 All E.R. 20.
[17] See Law Com. No. 25, paras. 7–17 and 81–83.
[18] See *post*, Chapter 10.

The effect of section 23 is to sweep away the distinctions which formerly existed between maintenance in suits for divorce and nullity and permanent alimony in those for judicial separation, and to replace them by powers applicable to all three kinds of suit, and exercisable without distinction between husband and wife or between petitioner and respondent. On granting a decree of divorce, nullity or judicial separation, or at any time thereafter (and whether, in the case of divorce or nullity, before or after the decree is made absolute) the court may make any one or more of three orders, that is to say, an order that either party to the marriage

> (a) shall make to the other such periodical payments, for such term, as may be specified in the order;
>
> (b) shall secure to the other to the satisfaction of the court, such periodical payments, for such term, as may be so specified;
>
> (c) shall pay to the other such lump sum or sums as may be so specified.

By section 26 proceedings may be begun, subject to and in accordance with rules of court, at any time after the presentation of the petition but no order can be made until a decree has been granted[19] and, by section 23 (5), (subject to the court's power to order instruments to be settled by conveyancing counsel[20]), no order in proceedings for divorce or nullity, and no settlement made in pursuance of such an order, shall take effect unless the decree has been made absolute. It should also be noted that, although section 23 allows orders to be made on the granting of a decree "or at any time thereafter", section 26 (2) enables rules of court to be made whereby leave of the court may be required before making an application for ancillary relief which was not made in the petition or answer or within a prescribed period thereafter. This matter is now governed by Rule 68.

It might appear from section 23 (1) (*a*) or (*b*) that the Act places no limit on the possible duration of the term for which periodical payments, whether secured or not, may be ordered. Nevertheless both the commencement of that term and its maximum duration are strictly limited by section 28.

At first sight the requirement[21] that the term shall begin "not earlier than the date of the making of an application for the order in question" may seem puzzling. Applications for ancillary relief may be made in the petition or answer,[1] and the financial requirements of a spouse between the date of the presentation of the petition or the filing of the answer and the date of the final decree will usually be covered by maintenance pending suit. The intention is, however, as has already been pointed out,[2] to enable the court, after the facts concerning the breakdown of the marriage are fully known, to treat as inadequate the payments pending suit by back-dating the whole or some part of the eventual periodical payments to the date when application for them was first made. The importance of making such applications at the earliest permissible moment is self-evident.

---

[19] The decree must have been granted by an English court: *Torok* v. *Torok*, [1973] 3 All E.R. 101; [1973] 1 W.L.R. 1066.

[20] See s. 30.

[21] See s. 28 (1).

[1] S. 26 (2).

[2] See *ante*, p. 108.

If the circumstances of the parties permit, inadequacies in past financial provision, whether pending suit or before its commencement, may be more conveniently rectified by an order for payment of a lump sum or sums under section 23 (1) (*c*). It is expressly provided by section 23 (3) (*a*), without prejudice to the generality of the power to order lump sum payments, that they may be ordered for the purpose of enabling the other party to meet any liabilities or expenses reasonably incurred by him or her in maintaining himself or herself or any child of the family before making an application for an order under this section. Should it happen that the full amount required cannot be provided immediately, advantage can be taken of the further provision[3] whereby an order for a lump sum payment, whether in respect of past liabilities or expenses or not, may provide for the payment of that sum by specified instalments and may require them to be secured to the satisfaction of the court.

Section 28 also fixes the maximum term for which periodical payments or secured periodical payments in favour of a party to the marriage may be ordered. An order for unsecured payments cannot last beyond the joint lives of the spouses, whereas secured payments may continue for the life of the party in whose favour the order is made. But whereas the remarriage of the recipient of maintenance under the Act of 1965 was only a ground on which an application could be made to discharge, suspend or vary the order, under the Act of 1973 periodical payments, secured or unsecured, which were ordered in proceedings for divorce or nullity will always terminate on the remarriage of the recipient except in relation to arrears then due. For the avoidance of doubt section 52 (3) provides that references in the Act to remarriage include references to a marriage which is by law void or voidable. After remarriage that party is not permitted to apply, *by reference to the grant of that decree*, for a financial provision order (or for a property adjustment order under section 24) against the other party to that marriage. The effect of the words in italics is that if the remarriage was to the same person and a further decree of divorce nullity or judicial separation was made in respect of that marriage, the orders could again be made by reference to the later decree.

If the order for periodical payments was made in a suit for judicial separation, no immediate question of remarriage can arise and no reference to this possibility will be required in fixing the term for which payments are to continue. If, however, the marriage of the parties is subsequently dissolved or annulled but the order remains in force, it is provided by section 28 (2) that the order will, notwithstanding anything in it, cease to have effect on the remarriage of the party in whose favour it was made, except in relation to any arrears due under it on the date of the remarriage.

Practitioners will no doubt think it wise to draw the attention of clients to the effect of remarriage upon their financial position when explaining to them the effect of the order which the court has made in their favour. It should be noticed particularly that the provisions as to remarriage have no application to an existing order for payment of a lump sum under section 23 (1) (*c*), whether payable at once or by instalments. Such an order is made upon the basis that

---

[3] S. 23 (3) (*c*).

the payee is entitled to receive that sum, even though the instalments are spread over several years, and remarriage cannot affect that entitlement.

From the viewpoint of the recipient, an order to secure periodical payments has several advantages over an order to pay. Apart from the greater certainty that the payments will be forthcoming, the payments may be ordered to continue for the life of the payee, whereas unsecured periodical payments cannot last beyond joint lives. Further, whereas unsecured periodical payments are inalienable,[4] secured payments can be assigned or charged in order to raise a lump sum.[5] But this decision was given at a time when a secured provision could not be varied:[6] now that variation is possible even after the death of the person against whom the order was made[7] and the payments cease on remarriage, the value of such payments as security for raising money is highly questionable. The same is not true of an order for security for payment of a lump sum by instalments, which cannot be varied subsequently,[8] and is not affected by remarriage.

When the court orders security to be given, either for periodical payments or for payment of a lump sum by instalments, the person against whom the order is made will be required to transfer property or investments to trustees and to execute a deed of security. The security must take the form of specific assets: the court cannot order that it shall take the form of a general charge on all a party's assets, which would be oppressive and uncertain in operation, nor can the security take the form of a covenant to make the payments required.[9] The order will usually direct that unless the terms of the deed are agreed between the parties, the matter is to be referred to one of the conveyancing counsel of the court for him to settle a proper instrument under section 30 of the Act, which also empowers the court to defer the grant of the decree until the instrument has been duly executed. Should the party against whom the order was made refuse to execute the deed, application can be made to the High Court under section 47 of the Judicature Act 1925 to order that the deed be executed for him by some other person nominated by the court for that purpose.

The exact nature of the trusts will vary with the purpose for which the security was ordered. If, for example, a husband was ordered to secure some part of the periodical payments which he was directed to make to his wife, the trusts of the deed would usually provide that the income of the investments or other property held by the trustees by way of security should be paid to him so long as he made the payments required. Thus although he does not covenant to make the payments, he has the option to do so, and if he does the security held by the trustees will revert to him, or to his estate if he is dead, on his wife's death or remarriage. Should he fail to make any payment, the deed will require the trustees to make it out of the income of the investments with power, if necessary, to resort to capital should the income prove insufficient.

---

[4] *Smith* v. *Smith*, [1923] P. 191.
[5] *Harrison* v. *Harrison* (1888), 13 P.D. 180.
[6] Variation has been possible since the Law Reform (Miscellaneous Provisions) Act 1949.
[7] S. 31 (6), and see *post*, p. 161.
[8] See *post*, p. 158. The instalments can be varied.
[9] *Barker* v. *Barker*, [1952] P. 184.

The considerations to which the court must have regard in deciding whether, and if so in what manner, to exercise its powers under section 23 are dealt with separately in section 25, and are considered in detail in Chapter 9.

3. Ancillary financial provision for children.[10]

Before proceeding to consider the form or forms which an order of this kind can take, emphasis must be laid on the fact that this, and all other, powers in the Act can be exercised in respect of any "child of the family" as defined in section 52, that is to say (a) a child of both the parties to the marriage, including their illegitimate or adopted child[11] and (b) any other child who has been treated by both of those parties as a child of their family, other than a child who has been boarded out with them by a local authority or voluntary organisation.

This definition is in several respects wider than that applicable in matrimonial proceedings in a magistrates' court (see Chapter 17). It is not necessary that the child should be a child of either spouse, provided that both have treated it as a child of their family, as they might, for example, if they took into their household a child whose parents had died or been killed in an accident. Since the child need not be the natural child of either spouse the requirement that it should have been "accepted as one of the family by the other party" would be inappropriate and instead it must have been "treated by both of those parties as a child of their family". This wording will obviate decisions which turned upon the point that, for example, a husband could not be taken to have "accepted" his wife's child when he did not discover that he was not the father of that child until after his wife had left him.[12]

Irrelevant also may be decisions to the effect that "acceptance" involved not only a full knowledge of all material facts but a mutual agreement between the spouses;[13] it is arguable that both can independently regard the child as one of their family without any such agreement. It remains to be seen what effect the change will have on *Caller* v. *Caller*[14] where it was held that a husband who married his wife knowing that she was pregnant by another man and left her before the child was born could nevertheless be said to have "accepted" the unborn child as one of the family which came into existence at the moment of the marriage. It is by no means clear that a child could be "treated" as a child of the family before its birth. As the Law Commission has pointed out[15] the new wording would not be apt to include an au-pair girl, or nephews and nieces cared for during the school holidays because their parents were abroad. In effect it seems that the intention must be to treat the child *permanently* as one of the family. A useful guide may be provided by enquiring whether or not the child in question has been encouraged to refer to the parties to the marriage as mother and father or, for example, as aunt and uncle.[16]

---

[10] Law Com. No. 25, paras. 23–48.
[11] The detailed definition of "adopted" in s. 52 should also be noted.
[12] E.g. *B.* v. *B. and F.*, [1969] P. 37; and see *W. (R. J.)* v. *W. (S. J.)*, [1972] Fam. 152.
[13] E.g. *Dixon* v. *Dixon*, [1967] 3 All E.R. 659; *P. (R.)* v. *P. (P.)*, [1969] 3 All E.R. 777.
[14] [1968] P. 39.
[15] Law Com. No. 25, para. 31.
[16] Law Com. No. 25, para. 31 n. 65.

The powers of the court to order financial provision for children of the family in suits for divorce, nullity or judicial separation derive from section 23 (1) of the Act. Orders under the section can be made from time to time before or on granting any of these decrees, or at any time thereafter.[17] Further, where any such proceedings are dismissed after the beginning of the trial, orders may be made either forthwith or within a reasonable time after the dismissal,[18] and once such an order has been made in relation to a child, there is power to make a further order under the section in relation to him.[19] All these powers are, however, subject to the restrictions on the maximum duration of orders in favour of children laid down by section 29 of the Act.[20]

The orders which the court can make follow the general lines already considered in respect of ancillary cash provision for spouses[1] and, once again, orders can be made without distinction against husband or wife and against petitioner or respondent. Thus under section 23 (1) the court can make all or any of the following orders, i.e. that a party to the marriage

  (d) shall make to such person as may be specified in the order for the benefit of the child, or to the child, such periodical payments, for such term, as may be so specified;
  (e) shall secure to such person as may be so specified for the benefit of the child, or to the child, to the satisfaction of the court, such periodical payments, for such term, as may be so specified;
  (f) shall pay to such person as may be so specified for the benefit of the child, or to the child, such lump sum as may be so specified.

As in the case of cash payments to a spouse[2] the payments to, or for the benefit of, a child of the family, whether secured or unsecured, may be ordered to begin with the date of making an application for the order in question or any later date.[3] There is no corresponding rule that orders cannot be made until a decree has been granted or, in the case of suits for divorce or nullity, cannot come into operation until decree absolute. The reason is that all financial provision for children, whether pending suit or thereafter, is made under section 23, and there is no distinction drawn, as in the case of the parties to the marriage, between maintenance pending suit and financial provision thereafter. As in the case of financial provision for spouses under section 23, an order for payment of a lump sum may, without prejudice to the generality of the power to order such a payment, be made for the purpose of enabling any liabilities or expenses reasonably incurred by or for the benefit of that child before the making of an application for the order to be met.[4] And any order for payment of a lump sum under the section may provide for its payment by specified instalments and require these instalments to be secured to the satisfaction of the court.[5]

---

[17] Ss. 23 (1) and 23 (2) (a).
[18] S. 23 (2) (b).
[19] S. 23 (4).
[20] *infra.*
[1] See *ante*, p. 110.
[2] See *ante*, p. 110.
[3] S. 29 (2).
[4] S. 23 (3) (b).
[5] S. 23 (3) (c).

The maximum duration of orders under section 23 is limited by section 29. Subject to two qualifications, the court's powers are not to be exercised in favour of a child who has reached the age of eighteen and any periodical payments, whether ordered to be secured or not, are to cease at that age. Indeed they will in most cases end sooner, because section 29 (2) (*a*) provides that they should not in the first instance extend beyond the date of the birthday of the child next following his attaining the upper limit of the compulsory school age, *unless the court which makes the order thinks it right in the circumstances of the case to specify a later date.* The effect is that whilst the upper limit of the compulsory school age[6] remains at sixteen, orders will normally cease on the child's seventeenth birthday. If, however, it appeared to the court that the child's education or training would extend beyond the normal school leaving age, or if for some other reason the child would not become financially independent until a later age, the court could exercise its discretion to order the payments to continue until the age of eighteen.

The two qualifications to the rules set out above are contained in section 29 (3) whereby the court may make orders for periodical payments, secured or unsecured, in favour of a child who has reached the age of eighteen, and may include in an order relating to a child who has not yet reached that age a provision extending such payments beyond that age, if it appears to the court that—

(a) the child is, or will be, or if an order were made without provisions extending it beyond the age of eighteen, would be, receiving instruction at an educational establishment or undergoing training for a trade, profession or vocation, whether or not he is also, or will also be, in gainful employment; or

(b) there are special circumstances which justify the making of the order.

Thus the powers of the court in relation to extension of orders beyond the age of eighteen are much more strictly limited than the power to extend an order beyond school leaving age until eighteen, which can be done, as already noted, "if the court thinks it right in the circumstances".

A final distinction must be noted between orders to pay and orders to secure. In most respects there is no difference in their maximum duration. But by section 29 (4) an order to pay must end on the death of the person liable to make the payments, except in relation to arrears due at date of death. There is no such restriction upon an order that such payments be secured.

As in the case of orders for cash payments to spouses, the considerations which should govern the making of such payments to, or for the benefit of, children of the family are governed by section 25. They are discussed in detail in Chapter 9.

4. Provision out of the estate of a former spouse.

It is now necessary to consider the position after the death of one of the parties to a marriage which has been the subject of a decree absolute of divorce

---

[6] I.e., the limit for the time being under s. 35, Education Act 1944, together with any Order in Council made thereunder.

or nullity, or a decree of judicial separation. It is then too late to apply for financial provision in favour of the survivor[5] or in favour of a child of the family[6] under section 23 of the Act of 1973 and any application pending at date of the death could not be pursued. The same is true of applications for adjustment of property rights under section 24 of the Act[7]. If, however, an order had already been made before the death for periodical payments, or a lump sum payable by instalments, to be secured, although no agreement has been reached as to the property which is to constitute the security, the survivor will have an enforceable claim against the estate of the deceased, and his personal representatives can be ordered to execute the necessary deed.[8] Unless an order for security has already been made the survivor, more particularly if it is the wife who survives, is likely to be in financial difficulties, because unsecured periodical payments in favour of a spouse can last only for the joint lives of the parties to the marriage,[9] and unsecured periodical payments for the benefit of a child of the family cease on the death of the person liable to make the payments, except in relation to any arrears due at the date of the death.[10] Where an order for security is in existence in respect of payments to a wife, those payments will continue for the wife's life assuming that she does not re-marry.[11] But it is very rare for security to be ordered in respect of the whole of the payments to be made to a wife, and the cessation of the unsecured payments will leave her substantially worse off than she was before the death.

Where an order for secured periodical payments for the benefit of a spouse or child was in existence at the date of the death, the difficulty can in many cases be met by applying for variation of the existing order.[12] If the resources of the estate were sufficient, the periodical payments and the security could be increased. There would, however, be no power to vary an order in favour of a spouse by directing the payment of a lump sum,[13] though there is nothing in the Act to preclude such a variation in favour of a child. In all other cases, since neither a variation of an existing order nor an application for an order will be possible under the Act of 1973, the remedy, if there is one, must be to seek an order for provision out of the estate of the deceased.

Where such provision is sought on behalf of a wife who has obtained a decree of judicial separation, and who is therefore the widow of the deceased, or on behalf of a child, application must be made under the Inheritance (Family Provision) Act 1938,[14] which is outside the scope of this book. But the class of children who are "dependants" for the purposes of that Act is much narrower than the class of "children of the family" in whose favour orders can be made, or varied, under the Act of 1973 against a spouse who is still living. Dependent

[5] *Dipple* v. *Dipple*, [1942] P. 65.
[6] *Sugden* v. *Sugden*, [1957] P. 120.
[7] *D'Este* v. *D'Este*, [1973] Fam. 55, and see *post*, p. 122.
[8] *Mosey* v. *Mosey and Barker*, [1950] P. 26.
[9] S. 28 (1) (a).
[10] S. 29 (4).
[11] S. 28 (1) (b).
[12] S. 31 (6), see *post*, p. 161.
[13] S. 31 (5), see *post*, p. 159.
[14] As amended, particularly by the Intestates' Estate Act 1952 and the Family Provision Act 1966; the amended text is contained in Sched. 3 to the Act of 1966.

children must be children of the deceased, including his or her illegitimate children[15] and adopted children,[16] and cannot include a child of other parents who has been treated by the deceased as a member of the family.

Where the marriage has been ended by decree of divorce or nullity, no application under the Inheritance (Family Provision) Act 1938 is possible since the survivor is no longer the "wife or husband" of the deceased and thus not a dependant within the meaning of that Act. This situation was corrected by the Matrimonial Causes (Property and Maintenance) Act 1958, which enabled applications to be made by a *former* spouse. Such applications are now made under sections 26–28A of the Matrimonial Causes Act 1965, as amended.[17]

The prerequisites to an application under section 26 of that Act are first that the deceased should have died domiciled in England, secondly that he or she should have been survived by a former spouse (in that section called "the survivor") whose marriage was dissolved or annulled by a decree made in England, and thirdly that the survivor has not re-married. If these conditions are satisfied it is for the survivor to satisfy the court that it would have been reasonable for the deceased to make provision for the survivor's maintenance, and that the deceased has made no such provision, or has not made reasonable provision, and the court may then order that such reasonable provision be made out of the net estate of the deceased as it thinks fit. In determining an application the court must have regard to the past, present or future capital and any income of the survivor, to the survivor's conduct in relation to the deceased or otherwise, to any application for financial provision or adjustment of property rights made by the survivor in the deceased's life-time and the result of that application, and to any other matter which may be relevant in relation to the survivor or to persons interested in the estate.

The main considerations in these applications are the moral claim of the survivor to some provision out of the estate, and the claims of others, such as a second wife and children of the second marriage, which may well have been much happier than the first.[18] The position was well put by MORTON, J. in *Re Styler, Styler v. Griffith.*[19]

> "I do not think that a judge should interfere with a testator's dispositions merely because he thinks that he would have been inclined, if he had been in the position of the testator, to make provision for some particular person. I think the court has to find that it was unreasonable for the testator to make no provision for the person in question, or that it was unreasonable not to make a larger provision."

It might at first sight appear from this passage, which has been cited in many cases, that the test laid down in the section is a purely subjective one, whether the testator himself has acted reasonably or unreasonably, rather than whether,

---

[15] Family Law Reform Act 1969, s. 18 (1).
[16] Inheritance (Family Provision) Act 1938, ss. 1 (1) and 5 (1). Further, the circumstances in which provision can be ordered beyond the age of 21 are narrower than those under s. 29 (3) of the Act of 1973.
[17] See Appendix I for these sections in their amended form.
[18] *Roberts* v. *Roberts*, [1964] 3 All E. R. 503.
[19] [1942] Ch. 387, adopted by BAKER, J., in *Talbot* v. *Talbot*, [1962] 3 All E.R. 174.

in the outcome, the provision made is reasonable or not. This view received
some support from the decision of the Court of Appeal in *Re Howell, Howell* v.
Lloyds Bank, Ltd.[20] where a testator was held to have made reasonable provision
for his children in leaving all his property to his second wife, despite the fact of
her serious illness shortly after his death, as a result of which they had to return
to his first wife, who was their mother. A contrary view was taken by MEGARRY,
J., in *Re Goodwin*[1] where he said

> "The question is simply whether the will or disposition has made reason-
> able provision, and not whether it was unreasonable on the part of the
> deceased to have made no provision or no larger provision for the depen-
> dant. A testator may have acted entirely reasonably . . . yet through . . .
> some change of circumstance unknown to the testator in his lifetime, the
> provision in fact made may prove to be wholly unreasonable."

The latter view has the support of WINN, L.J., in *Re Gregory, Gregory* v. *Good-
enough*[2] who thought that the element of mistake enabled the view of MEGARRY,
J., to be distinguished from those of the Court of Appeal in *Re Howell*. The
objective approach has the further support of the decision of Lord SIMON OF
GLAISDALE in *Re Shanahan, De Winter* v. *Legal Personal Representatives of
Shanahan*,[3] who considered that the question was an open one, that the decision
in *Re Goodwin* was correct, and that both the language and the obvious policy
of the Act called for an objective construction, not upon whether the testator
had acted unreasonably, but upon whether on the facts the result was reasonable.
His Lordship also held that the result of an objective construction must be that
the value of the estate must be ascertained, not as at the date of death, but as
at the date when the matter was investigated by the court,[4] a matter of considerable importance in times of rapid increase of the value of house property
and diminution in the value of stocks and shares. The view that, in deciding
what sum it is reasonable to award, it is relevant to consider not only the value
of the estate at the date of death but also its value at the date when the award
is made, has the support of the decision of the Court of Appeal in *Lusternik* v.
Lusternik.[5]

Where the marriage has lasted for many years and ended in divorce resulting
from the adultery of the deceased, the first wife has a strong claim.[6] There is,
however, no rule that she should be accorded financial equality with a widow:
all the factors such as age, health, conduct and the needs of children of the
second marriage, must be considered.[7] The first wife's own unchastity after
the dissolution of the marriage is a relevant factor.[8] The fact that the first wife's
claim to maintenance has been dismissed on agreed terms does not prevent the
court from making an order under section 26, and the amount of secured

---

[20] [1953] 2 All E.R. 604.
[1] [1969] 1 Ch. 283, 287.
[2] [1970] 1 W.L.R. 1455, 1461.
[3] [1973] Fam. 1.
[4] *Ibid.*, at p. 8.
[5] [1972] Fam. 125.
[6] As in *Roberts* v. *Roberts*, supra and *Re Eyre*, [1968] 1 All E.R. 968.
[7] *Re Eyre*, supra.
[8] *Re Talbot*, [1962] 3 All E.R. 174.

maintenance awarded to a wife in the deceased's lifetime is not a pre-determination of what she should receive after his death;[9] there is no reason why she should not benefit from a substantial accretion of wealth to the estate which occurred after the divorce and before his death.

Application under the section should be made to the High Court unless the net estate of the deceased does not exceed £5,000, when it may be made to *any* county court and not only to a divorce county court.[10] It cannot be made without the leave of the court more than six months after the date when a grant to the deceased's estate was first taken out. The provision ordered may take the form of periodical payments or a lump sum payment. If periodical payments are ordered they may be of a specified amount, or payments equal to the whole or part of the income of the net estate, or of the income of any part of the estate set aside for that purpose, or may be determined in any way which the court thinks fit.[11] But such payments must terminate not later than the survivor's death or re-marriage,[12] and for this purpose re-marriage will include a marriage which is by law void or voidable.[13] In determining what order should be made the court is expressly required to have regard to the nature of the property representing the net estate and not to order a provision which would necessitate an imprudent realisation having regard to the interests of all persons concerned. Section 28A gives power to make an interim order when the applicant is in immediate need of financial assistance but it is not yet possible to determine what final order should be made and there is property which can be made available to meet that need.[14]

Where the court has made an order under these provisions of the Act of 1965, it has power to discharge or vary the original order or to suspend any provision of it temporarily and to revive the operation of any provision so suspended. Application can be made by the former spouse who obtained the order, any other former spouse, any dependant of the deceased, the trustees of any relevant property and any other person beneficially interested in the estate. But it is expressly provided that no variation or revival of a suspended provision shall affect any property except property the income of which, in accordance with the original order, is applicable wholly or in part for the maintenance of the former spouse who obtained the original order.[15] There can thus be no question of claiming back property to which other beneficiaries are entitled so as to increase the provision made for the former spouse.

The Law Commission has been considering the question of provision out of the estate of a former spouse as part of its general review of family property law.[16] There are obvious defects and inconsistencies in the present law. If the

---

[9] *Re S.*, [1965] P. 165; see also *Re Minter*, [1968] P. 174.

[10] Family Provision Act 1966, s. 7.

[11] *Ibid.*, s. 3 (2).

[12] Matrimonial Causes Act 1965, s. 26 (3).

[13] *Ibid.*, s. 26 (5A).

[14] *Ibid.*, ss. 28 (1) and 28A (4) protect the personal representatives from liability in respect of the possible results of these provisions. As to the possibility of backdating an order which is made see *Lusternik* v. *Lusternik*, [1972] Fam. 125.

[15] *Ibid.*, s. 27.

[16] Working Paper No. 42, pp. 159–203; First Report on Family Property, Law Com. No. 52, paras. 38–45.

marriage has ended in divorce, an application in the High Court by the former spouse must be made to the Family Division under the Act of 1965, whereas that on behalf of dependent children must be made to the Chancery Division under the Inheritance (Family Provision) Act 1938. The classes of children in respect of whom applications can be made under either of these Acts, and the ages up to which orders can continue, differ considerably from the position with regard to children of the family under the Matrimonial Causes Act 1973. But worst of all, it seems illogical that provision for a spouse or former spouse out of an estate should be restricted to "maintenance" by way of periodical payments or a lump sum, whereas in matrimonial proceedings, as is explained in detail in Chapter 9, the court proceeds on the basis of a fair division of the family assets of the spouses after considering (*inter alia*) the contribution made by each of the parties to the welfare of the family, including any contribution made by looking after the home or caring for the family. A further Report is promised aimed at ensuring that a surviving spouse can expect to be no less generously treated than a divorced spouse, and aimed at abolishing the other anomalies in the present law.

5. Maintenance for survivor of void marriage.

This is a matter which has no direct connection with matrimonial causes, since in effect it arises from the fact that no matrimonial proceedings have been taken in the lifetime of one of the parties involved. Section 6 of the Law Reform (Miscellaneous Provisions) Act 1970 deals with the situation where a person domiciled in England and Wales dies on or after January 1, 1971, and is survived by someone who had in good faith entered into a void marriage with the deceased. Such a person was, under the law as it was before that date, not a person who was a dependant for the purposes of the Inheritance (Family Provision) Act 1938 as amended, since there had never been a valid marriage. Nor could an application for provision out of the estate of the deceased be made under section 26 of the Matrimonial Causes Act 1965, since a void marriage was not dissolved or annulled by a decree under that Act.

The law is now changed so that if the marriage of the deceased and the survivor has not been dissolved or annulled during the deceased's lifetime by a decree recognised by the law of England and Wales, and the survivor has not, before the making of the order, entered into a later marriage, the survivor will be treated as a dependant entitled to apply for maintenance out of the estate of the deceased under the Inheritance (Family Provision) Act 1938. Such an order cannot, however, be made unless the court is satisfied that it would have been reasonable for the deceased to make provision for the survivor's mainten-ance, and if the order provides for periodical payments, they must terminate at the latest on the survivor's death or later marriage.

It is also provided that for the purpose of the section a "later marriage" includes references to a marriage which is by law void or voidable. The occasions when the section will operate at all are not likely to be numerous. The occasions when the survivor of a void marriage will be a party to a later marriage which is also void or voidable are likely to be even fewer. "Once bitten, twice shy"; but no doubt the proviso was inserted *ex abundante cautela*.

CHAPTER 8

PROPERTY ADJUSTMENTS ON THE BREAKDOWN OF MARRIAGE

Section 23 of the Act, which has already been considered, is aimed primarily at the provision of income for spouses and children of the family respectively, except in so far as the court may decide to order the payment of a lump sum. But when a marriage has broken down, more extensive powers are needed to ensure, if that be possible, that no injustice is done. These are conferred upon the court mainly by section 24, which deals with the transfer and settlement of property and with variation of settlements.

Before describing in more detail the nature and extent of these powers, certain points which are common to all of them should be noticed.

(i) All the orders under the section may be made by the court on granting a decree of divorce, nullity or judicial separation, or at any time thereafter, Parliament having accepted the view of the Law Commission that although judicial separation does not end the marriage, it does in practice almost invariably denote the death of it. It follows that orders under the section can only be made when the decree was granted by an English court and not when it was obtained abroad, though if this condition was satisfied the court would have power, for example, to vary a settlement made abroad in foreign form.[1]

(ii) As in the case of applications for financial provision, an application for an adjustment of property order may be made in the petition or answer or, subject to provisions in the Rules as to leave, at any time thereafter. But no order can be made until a decree nisi of divorce or nullity or a decree of judicial separation has been granted, and in the case of decrees of divorce or nullity no order, or settlement made in pursuance of an order, can take effect until the decree is made absolute.[2] This is without prejudice to section 30 of the Act, whereby if the court decides to make a property adjustment order, it may direct that the matter to be referred to one of the conveyancing counsel of the court for him to settle a proper instrument, and whereby the court may, if it thinks fit, defer the grant of a decree until the instrument settled by him has been executed.

(iii) It was held in *D'Este* v. *D'Este*[3] that "the whole of the matrimonial

---

[1] *Forsyth* v. *Forsyth*, [1891] P. 363.
[2] Ss. 24 (3) and 26; Rule 68.
[3] [1973] Fam. 55.

causes legislation ... is essentially a personal jurisdiction arising between the parties to the marriage or the children of the marriage". There is no "cause of action" which can survive the death of either party under the Law Reform (Miscellaneous Provisions) Act 1934. Accordingly, when a husband died after the date of his wife's application for variation of a settlement and before the application was heard, there was no longer any jurisdiction to entertain her application, though an application for variation for the benefit of children of the marriage might still be possible. The same principle applies to all orders under section 24, since it is "abundantly plain ... that the statute contemplates both parties to the marriage surviving ..."

(iv) By section 28 (3), if after a decree of divorce or nullity either party to the marriage re-marries, that party shall not be entitled to apply, *by reference to the grant of that decree,* for a property adjustment order against the other party to that marriage. The word "apply" has been held in *Jackson* v. *Jackson*[4] to refer to the initiation of the proceedings and not to the time when the application is to be heard. Such applications can be, and usually are, included in the prayer to the petition or answer, and the court has jurisdiction to entertain them, and to make an order, even after a decree of divorce has been made absolute and the applicant has re-married. In *Jackson* v. *Jackson* the application was for variation of settlements and the terms had been agreed between the parties. Had it not been for the agreement, although the court might have heard the application, the fact of remarriage might obviously have affected the order which would have been made. An application which was not included in the petition or answer can, with leave of the court, be made at a later date.[5] But in *Marsden* v. *Marsden*[6] the President not only refused an application for leave to apply for an order for transfer of property or variation of a settlement after the wife's remarriage, but indicated that even had he done so there would have been little prospect of an order being made.

The effect of the words "by reference to the grant of that decree" is that if the remarriage was to the same person, and a decree of divorce, nullity or judicial separation was made in respect of that later marriage, a property adjustment order could be made by reference to the later decree.

(v) Each of the orders under section 24 can be made, without any distinction, against, or in favour of, husband or wife, petitioner or respondent.

(vi) In so far as the orders are intended for the benefit of children, each can be made in favour of any child of the family. In the case of orders for the transfer of property, but *not* in the case of the court's power to order or vary settlements for the benefit of children, the

---

[4] [1973] Fam. 99.
[5] Rule 68 (2).
[6] [1973] 1 W.L.R. 641, 646.

court's discretion is limited by certain restrictions as to age laid down in section 29.[7]

(vii) The matters which the court is required to consider in deciding upon the exercise of any of its powers under section 24 are the same as those which are relevant to orders for periodical payments or payment of a lump sum. They are specified in section 25 of the Act and are considered hereafter.[8]

1. Orders for the transfer of property.

Section 24 (1) (*a*); from which this power derives, must be sharply distinguished from section 17 of the Married Women's Property Act 1882 (as amended) to which some reference will be made in Chapter 15.[9] The object of section 17 is to enable the court to determine summarily, either whilst the marriage still subsists or within three years after it is dissolved or annulled,[10] disputes between the spouses as to the title to, or right to possession of, individual items of property. Section 24 (1) (*a*) is designed to enable the court, where the marriage has irretrievably broken down, to adjust the property rights of the parties by ordering that property which unquestionably belongs to one of the spouses be transferred to the other or to, or for the benefit of, a child of the family. Such orders can be made in respect of any property to which either spouse is entitled, whether in possession or reversion, and whether the property was acquired before or after the celebration of the marriage, but not, of course, in such a way as to affect any rights which a third party may have in that property.

The considerations which will weigh with the court in deciding how to exercise this power are considered in Chapter 9. But it may not be uninteresting at this point to mention the ways in which the Law Commission envisaged that it would be exercised.[11] The intention was that an order for transfer of property would not normally be made except as an alternative to one for payment of a lump sum, since it would sometimes be more satisfactory to order the transfer of investments instead of their realisation and the payment of the proceeds of sale in cash. As between spouses, transfer might well be ordered for other purposes, such as a transfer of ownership of the matrimonial home, or the termination of a joint ownership of the home or of other property by the transfer of the interest of one spouse to the other. This has often been achieved in the past by regarding these forms of joint ownership, where the circumstances permitted this to be done, as a settlement capable of variation under section 17 (1) of the Matrimonial Causes Act 1965.[12] It will no longer be necessary to resort to this manœuvre, since the object can be achieved by an out-and-out transfer,

---

[7] See *post*, p. 124.
[8] *Post*, Chapter 9.
[9] See *post*, pp. 194 *et seq.*
[10] See Matrimonial Proceedings and Property Act 1970, s. 39.
[11] See Law Com. No. 25, paras. 68–70.
[12] As in e.g. *Brown* v. *Brown*, [1959] P. 86; *Cook* v. *Cook*, [1962] P. 235.

though since the rights of third parties cannot be affected, the existence of a mortgage on the property may preclude, or render difficult, such a transfer.[13]

Section 24 (1) (*a*) also provides a solution to decisions under section 17 (1) of the Act of 1965 to the effect that an absolute gift cannot be regarded as a settlement capable of variation.[14] It will now be possible, in appropriate cases, to order the gift in question, or the property which now represents the proceeds of sale of the gift, or was purchased with it, to be returned to the original donor, though it seems likely that such an order would be made only if the subject matter of the gift was of substantial rather than trivial value.

Although section 24 (1) (*a*) permits the court to order a transfer of property to a child of the family, or to such person as may be specified in the order for the benefit of such a child, it was not envisaged that this power would be exercised unless this would be a more businesslike method of providing for the child's education and maintenance than the payment of a lump sum. In other circumstances it is likely that the child's needs would be provided for by means of a settlement of property, or by secured periodical payments, rather than by an out-and-out transfer.[15] The duration of these types of provision can be fixed in relation to the purposes they are to serve. Property transferred to a child is gone for ever, and may even be thrown away be improvident realisation. These factors are further emphasised by the restrictions in relation to age which are placed upon this power by section 29 of the Act. No order for a transfer of property can be made in favour of a child who has attained the age of eighteen unless it appears to the court that the child is, or will be, or if such order were made would be, receiving instruction at an educational establishment or undergoing training for a trade, profession or vocation (whether or not he is also, or will also be, in gainful employment), or that there are special circumstances which justify the making of the order. Similar restrictions limit the power to order periodical payments or the payment of a lump sum,[16] but not the power to order a settlement or vary a settlement, in favour of a child.

2. Orders for a settlement of property.

This form of order is not new, though the effect of the Acts is greatly to extend the circumstances in which it can be made. Under the Matrimonial Causes Act 1965[17] it could be made only in suits for divorce, judicial separation and restitution of conjugal rights (which latter suit has been abolished[18]), and never in suits for nullity, only against a wife and never against a husband, and only in favour of the husband and children of the marriage. Section 24 (1) (*b*) enables the court to make an order against either spouse for the benefit of the other party to the marriage and of the children of the family or either or any of them, and to do so on granting a decree of divorce, nullity or judicial separation.

---

[13] See as to this *Practice Direction (Matrimonial Property: Transfer)*, [1971] 1 All E.R. 896, and Rules 74 (3) and 104 (3).
[14] *Prescott* v. *Fellowes*, [1958] P. 260.
[15] Consider Law Com. No. 25, para. 70.
[16] See *ante*, p. 115.
[17] Ss. 17 (2), 20 (2) and 21 (3) (*a*).
[18] See *ante*, p. 62.

Decisions under the Act of 1965, such as *Matheson* v. *Matheson*[19] show that the object of this form of provision was not to enable the court to punish a guilty wife, but to protect the husband and the children of the marriage from the financial consequences of the breaking away of the wife and her fortune from the matrimonial home. Certainly the wider power under section 24 (1) (*b*) of the Act of 1973 cannot in any way be intended to be punitive, the more so since the Divorce Reform Act 1969 abolished the doctrine of divorce for a matrimonial offence. In the earlier case of *March* v. *March*[20] it was said that "It would be of evil example if this court were to decide that the entire fortune of a wealthy married woman was reckoned as part of the prospects of an adulterer, or the resources of a second home for a guilty woman." These words may at first sight seem utterly out of tune with thinking today, but it is suggested that they may still have some force in view of the abolition, by the Law Reform (Miscellaneous Provisions) Act 1970, s. 4, of claims for damages for adultery. Such damages were not infrequently ordered to be settled for the benefit of children of the marriage.[21] Now that this source of financial provision is to be denied to them it may be argued that the case for ordering a settlement in their favour by a wealthy but "guilty" wife is much stronger. A similar consideration no doubt applies equally to a "guilty" husband, though the woman with whom he committed adultery could never have been ordered to pay damages.

The power of the court to order payment of a lump sum, or the transfer of property to, or for the benefit of, a spouse or a child of the family, has already been considered. One disadvantage of such orders is that the money or property has, so to speak, gone for ever. The recipient, whether spouse or child, could spend the money or sell the property and spend the proceeds. A wife might, for example, be persuaded to hand over the money or property, or leave it by her will, to a second husband, or the children of a second marriage, to the detriment of the children of the original family. Periodical payments to a spouse must end on re-marriage[22] and the duration of such payments for the benefit of children is strictly limited.[1] There is no way of ensuring that a lump sum payment or transfer of property, once made, is subject to any similar restrictions. A settlement can be so drafted as to cover matters of this kind. The trusts can be so worded that, if in favour of a spouse, the benefits cease on re-marriage or that, in the case of a child, they can continue only until the attainment of a certain age. What is more, the intervention of trustees guards against imprudent, or inappropriate, dealings with capital. It is true that these considerations apply only where substantial assets are involved, but this is equally true of many of the powers conferred upon the court by the Act.

3. Orders for variation of a settlement.

Just as section 24 (1) (*b*) has greatly widened the powers of the court to order a settlement of property, so also does section 24 (1) (*c*) extend the power to vary

---

[19] [1935] P. 171.
[20] (1867), 1 P. & D. 440, 443.
[21] Under powers contained in Matrimonial Causes Act 1965, s. 41, which is repealed.
[22] S. 28 and *ante*, p. 111.
[1] S. 29 and *ante*, p. 115.

an existing settlement. There is no radical extension of the definition of settlements which can be varied, except that the power is extended to cover settlements by will. But the court is now enabled to order variation in suits for judicial separation, as well as in those for divorce or nullity, and to do so in favour of any child of the family, instead of only in favour of a child of the marriage. The section permits variations "for the benefit of the parties to the marriage and of the children of the family or either or any of them". But for the avoidance of doubt it also provides that a variation may be ordered notwithstanding that there are no children of the family.

Variation can be ordered, as under section 17 (1) of the Matrimonial Causes Act 1965, in respect of "any ante-nuptial or post-nuptial settlement . . . made on the parties to the marriage", the Law Commission having admitted[2] that it found itself unable to suggest any clearer or better expression, the existing words being "hallowed by long usage and, in meaning, now reasonably definite".[3] The tendency of the courts has in the past been, as has already been mentioned, to regard as "settlements" transactions which would not ordinarily be so described. Thus when a house was purchased with money provided by both spouses, or by one alone, and conveyed to them both upon trust for sale and to hold the proceeds of sale on trust for themselves as joint tenants, the court regarded the transaction as a post-nuptial settlement and thus assumed the power to vary the trusts.[4] A similar course was taken when the purchase money was provided by both but the house conveyed into the name of the husband alone.[5] It is likely that in future cases of this kind will usually be dealt with by an order for transfer of the whole or part of the interest of one spouse in the property to the other, and that the power of variation will be reserved for settlements in the more usual sense of that term. Subject to this, the following are the main principles to be gathered from decisions under previous Acts.

(a) In *Melvill* v. *Melvill and Woodward*[6] the court declined, and will no doubt still decline, to fetter its discretion by any rigid definition of the word "settlement". As HILL, J. said in *Prinsep* v. *Prinsep*[7]

> "The particular form of it does not matter. It may be a settlement in the strictest sense of the term, it may be a covenant to pay by one spouse to the other, or by a third person to a spouse. What does matter is that it should provide for the financial benefit of one or other or both of the spouses as spouses and with reference to their married state."

Thus the court has regarded as a settlement an insurance policy, taken out by a husband on his own life for his wife's benefit under section 11 of the Married Women's Property Act 1882,[8] a single premium policy for her benefit contin-

---

[2] Law Com. No. 25, para. 66.
[3] The wording has remained virtually unchanged since the Matrimonial Causes Act 1859, s. 5.
[4] *Brown* v. *Brown*, [1959] P. 86.
[5] *Cook* v. *Cook*, [1962] P. 235.
[6] [1930] P. 159.
[7] [1929] P. 225 at first instance at p. 232.
[8] *Gunner* v. *Gunner and Stirling*, [1949] P. 77.

gently upon her surviving him,[9] and even a separation agreement not so drafted as to cease on divorce.[10]

(b) The expression "settlement" cannot, however, extend to an absolute assignment or gift of property. In *Prescott* v. *Fellowes*,[11] by deed expressed to be in consideration of their intended marriage, the wife had transferred to the husband as a gift securities valued at £15,000 and covenanted to lend to him later a further £20,000 to enable him, if he so wished, to become a member of Lloyds. When she later obtained a decree of divorce, it was held that she could not recover the £15,000 though, had there been periodical payments still to be made, there would still have been "property settled" so as to enable the court to relieve the wife of her obligation to make these payments. Under section 24 (1) (*b*) of the Act, the court could, of course, now order the husband in such a case to transfer to the wife the securities included in the gift, or other property into which they might have been converted, thus avoiding this difficulty.

(c) It follows from what was said in *Prinsep* v. *Prinsep* that the court's powers do not extend to all settlements, but only to those with a "nuptial element" as it was called in *Young* v. *Young*.[12] In that case a maintenance agreement entered into by a husband in favour of his wife between decree nisi and decree absolute of divorce failed to satisfy this test, being a provision made for her not because they were still married but separated, as in *Cooper* v. *Cooper*, but because they would shortly cease to be husband and wife. Many agreements entered into in cases of divorce by consent after two years of life apart will fall into this category. But although they are not post-nuptial "settlements", they would be variable as maintenance agreements under sections 34 to 36 of the Act.[13]

(d) It was held in *Burnett* v. *Burnett*[14] that there must be a marriage which is the subject of the court's decree and the settlement must have been made in contemplation of, and because of, *that* marriage, not marriage generally, so that a settlement made on the occasion of the husband's first marriage could not be varied on the dissolution of his second marriage to another woman. Likewise in *Hargreaves* v. *Hargreaves*,[15] where a man settled property on himself for life and thereafter on trusts for his children, with a power of appointment in favour of any wife whom he might marry, the settlement itself could not be varied, not having been made in contemplation of any particular marriage, though an appointment in favour of a wife whom he later married would itself have been a settlement capable of variation.

(e) The section refers to settlements "*on* the parties to the marriage", not necessarily *by* those parties, and it is clear from *Prinsep* v. *Prinsep*[16] and other cases that it is immaterial who made the settlement.

---

[9] *Bown* v. *Bown*, [1949] P. 91; contrast *Meldrum* v. *Meldrum*, [1970] 3 All E.R. 1084 —policy on husband's life as additional security for mortgage of house in joint names not intended for wife's benefit.

[10] *Cooper* v. *Cooper and Ford*, [1932] P. 75.

[11] [1958] P. 260.

[12] [1962] P. 27.

[13] *Post*, p. 172.

[14] [1936] P. 1.

[15] [1926] P. 42.

[16] *Supra.* See also *Nepean* v. *Nepean*, [1925] P. 97.

(f) The settlement must, as was held in *Jacobs* v. *Jacobs*,[17] be in existence at the date of the final decree.

Section 24 (1) (c) of the Act expressly provides that the expression "settlement" shall include a settlement made by will or codicil. This abrogates the decision in *Garratt* v. *Garratt*[18] where it was held that no variation was possible in respect of a settlement made by will, even if the will directed that property be held upon the trusts of an existing marriage settlement. The application of the decisions mentioned above to the provisions of a will or codicil may, however, present some problems.

Whereas in the case of a settlement inter vivos it is immaterial who made the settlement, section 24 (1) (c) clearly cannot apply to the will of either of the parties to the marriage, who will be living at the date of the decree. Having regard to *D'Este* v. *D'Este*,[19] it will be too late to apply after the death of the party who made the will, and it will not be operative until he (or she) dies. If it is considered that some additional provision should be made from the estate of a deceased spouse or former spouse, the appropriate remedy will be an application under the Inheritance (Family Provision) Act 1938 (as amended) or sections 26–28A of the Matrimonial Causes Act 1965.[20] With regard to dispositions by the will or codicil of some person other than a party to the marriage, it also seems plain that no variation is possible in the testator's lifetime, since the provisions will not be operative until he dies. What is not so clear is whether a variation would be possible in respect of the will of such a testator who died after, say, a decree absolute of divorce had been granted. It is true that section 24 (subject to rules of court)[1] allows an application to be made at any time after the grant of the decree, but it remains to be seen whether this will be permitted in relation to a settlement which was not operative when the decree was granted.

A further difficulty is that it may be less easy to identify the nuptial element in the case of a will than in the case of a settlement inter vivos, or to identify the connection of the dispositions with the marriage in question. No doubt, as in the case of dispositions inter vivos, an absolute devise or legacy to one of the spouses could not be regarded as a settlement, though it could be the subject of an order for transfer of the benefit under section 24 (1) (a). A disposition by a testator to his son for life and thereafter to the son's children in equal shares could not be identified with any particular marriage or the progeny of it, though no doubt the son's life interest might enable the amount of periodical payments under section 23 to be increased. The nuptial element in the case of a life interest given by a testator to his son's wife by name would be clear. The use of the word "widow" would show clearly that the testator had no particular marriage in mind, and certainly could not have had in

---

[17] [1943] P. 7.
[18] [1922] P. 230.
[19] [1973] Fam. 55, and see *ante*, p. 121.
[20] See *ante*, p. 115.
[1] See s. 26, *ante*, p. 121.

contemplation only his son's marriage to some person who, on the dissolution of a marriage, would have lost all prospect of surviving his son as his widow.

Practitioners will not doubt watch with interest the manner in which the court's power to vary the trusts of a will or codicil will be exercised, and have such decisions in mind in advising testators and in the choice of the words used in drafting the will. Not all testators would contemplate with equanimity the alteration by the court of the dispositions they had made, and this possibility, and possible means of avoiding it, may well require discussion when instructions to draft a will are received, especially if the stability of the marriage of intended beneficiaries is in doubt.

Thus the extension of the power of variation to settlements by will may prove less important in practice than might at first sight appear, and although the powers of the court have been widened in other respects, such as their extension to suits for judicial separation, it may well be that less use will in practice be made of these powers. In particular, as has already been noted, it will no longer be necessary for the court to stretch the definition of a settlement for the purpose of dealing with such matters as forms of joint ownership, since the power to order a transfer of the interest of one spouse to the other will more suitably meet such cases. Applications are likely, as the Law Commission envisaged, only where there is a settlement in the true sense.

Where, however, there is such a settlement, the extension of the class of children in whose favour variations are possible from children of the marriage to children of the family, and the wider definition of the latter class in the Act of 1973,[2] requires special notice. As regards orders against a party to the marriage, the court is required to have in mind special considerations laid down in section 25 (3)[3] in deciding whether to exercise its powers in favour of a child of the family who is not a child of that party, and this should prevent injustice in the variation of settlements made by either spouse. Subject to this, a spouse can hardly complain of variations in favour of a child whom he or she has treated as a child of their family. It may be quite otherwise where the settlor is a third party, whether the settlement be inter vivos or by will, and the Rules[4] now provide that the settlor, if still living, shall be served with notice of the application to enable him, as well as the trustees of the settlement, to be heard if they so wish.

As is the case in respect of orders for the settlement of property under section 24 (1) (*b*), the object of variation of a settlement has not been punitive but rather protect a spouse who is free from blame for the breakdown of the marriage, and the children of the family, from the financial consequences of the breakdown. It has not hitherto been the practice to interfere with the trusts of a settlement to any greater extent than is necessary to provide that protection,[5] though it may be that the philosophy of adjustment of property rights to do justice to the claims of both parties may lead in the future to some shift of emphasis. The emphasis today is against reliance upon the outmoded theory

[2] See *ante*, p. 113.
[3] See *post*, p. 147.
[4] Rule 74 (4).
[5] *Prinsep* v. *Prinsep*, [1930] P. 35, 47, C.A.

of a matrimonial offence and of "guilt" or "innocence". Even in the past, there was no reason why a variation should not be made in favour of a supposedly "guilty" party, and section 24 (1) (c) refers to variation "for the benefit of the parties to the marriage and of the children of the family *or either or any of them*". In *Garforth-Bles* v. *Garforth-Bles*[6] a husband who on the occasion of his marriage had behaved with special generosity in bringing into settlement virtually all that he possessed was allowed, when his wife obtained a decree of divorce against him, to withdraw some part of the funds which he had settled from the settlement. Had his request been refused, he might well have had a feeling of injustice which would have impaired his relationship with the child of the marriage, and thus not been in the interests of that child. It is unlikely, having regard to the extended definition of a child of the family under the Act of 1973, that the court will again be called upon to consider, as it was in *Purnell* v. *Purnell*[7] the possibility of variation in favour of a child, or indeed of any other person, who is not within the strict wording of the section. Such variation is possible only if there are compensating advantages to those whom the section is intended to benefit.

The nature and extent of the variation is entirely in the court's discretion. It may take the form of extinguishing the interest of one spouse altogether or reducing that interest, of depriving a party of a power of appointment or limiting the class of person in whose favour it may be exercised, of creating a fresh power of appointment, of relieving a spouse of obligations to make payments under covenant; these are but examples. The nature of the variation required must depend upon the facts of the case and upon the manner in which the court decides to exercise its many other powers to grant ancillary relief.

4. An order extinguishing or reducing an interest under a settlement.

Cases may arise in which the court would wish to extinguish or reduce the interest of one of the spouses under a settlement despite the fact that this will not benefit the other spouse or any child of the family. Suppose, to take the example given by the Law Commission,[8] property is settled on W for life, then on H for life, then for the children, and finally for W's next of kin, and that W divorces H whose adultery caused the breakdown of the marriage. If there are no children it is difficult to see what power the court had under the Act of 1965 to delete H's life interest, since this cannot benefit W or any child of the family. Section 24 (1) (d) therefore expressly enables the court to make such an order.

---

[6] [1951] P. 218.
[7] [1961] P. 141.
[8] Law Com. No. 25, para. 74.

CHAPTER 9

MATTERS AFFECTING FINANCIAL PROVISION AND ADJUSTMENT OF PROPERTY RIGHTS

Before the fundamental changes in the law introduced by the Divorce Reform Act 1969 and the Matrimonial Proceedings and Property Act 1970, which are now consolidated in the Act of 1973, there was little statutory guidance as to the way in which the court should exercise its powers to order financial provision for a spouse or child, or such limited powers as it had to adjust property rights. At the end of the last century a wife who had committed adultery was regarded as a "scarlet woman" who could at the most receive a small "compassionate allowance", generally limited *dum sola et casta vixerit*. By the year 1969 it was recognised that adultery is often a symptom of the breakdown of marriage rather than the cause of it, and that, to quote the favourite dictum of VAISEY, J., in ward of court cases, "it takes three to commit adultery".[1] As Lord Justice SACHS observed in *Porter* v. *Porter*[2] "it is now commonly accepted that a decree based upon a matrimonial offence, whilst of course establishing the factum of that offence, is often of little and sometimes of no importance in reaching conclusions as to whose conduct actually broke up the marriage". In the absence of statutory guidance the principles applicable immediately before the new legislation came into operation were based upon decisions of the courts which broadly laid down that the factors of the wife's fortune (if any), the husband's ability to pay and the conduct of the parties (which were laid down by statute only in relation to secured maintenance by a husband for his wife[3]) were the relevant factors in relation to all forms of order.[4]

Section 25 of the Act of 1973, re-enacting the provisions of section 5 of the Act of 1970, lays down in detail the matters which the court is required to consider in relation both to financial provision and property adjustment orders in favour of a spouse or child. Nevertheless the tendency initially was to follow the lines of earlier cases. As ORMROD, J., said in *Pheasant* v. *Pheasant*[5]

> "Whilst every effort has been made in section 5 of the Matrimonial Proceedings and Property Act 1970 to displace conduct of the parties from its hitherto pre-eminent position, it is still a factor, and a factor which is

---

[1] Quoted by ORMROD, J., in *Wachtel* v. *Wachtel*, [1973] 2 W.L.R. 84, 90.
[2] [1969] 1 W.L.R. 1155, at pp. 1159–60.
[3] Matrimonial Causes Act 1965, s. 16 (1) (a).
[4] *Kershaw* v. *Kershaw*, [1966] P. 13; *Sansom* v. *Sansom*, [1966] P. 52.
[5] [1972] Fam. 202, at p. 206.

likely to continue to influence decisions until the attitude of the public
and their advisers and of those who administer the law, changes."
That change has been brought about much sooner than might have been
expected by the decisions of the Court of Appeal in *Wachtel* v. *Wachtel*[6] and
Trippas v. *Trippas*,[7] which will later be considered in detail. For the moment
it suffices to quote from the latter case—

> "The Divorce Reform Act 1969 and the Matrimonial Proceedings and
> Property Act 1970 have revolutionised the law on all these matters.
> There is no point in going back to the cases on the earlier Acts. They are
> now out of date. The proper approach is to take the new Acts and the
> guidelines stated in *Wachtel* v. *Wachtel* . . . and build on those."[8]

and again, "In construing a reforming statute it is wrong, in my view, to pay
regard to cases that were decided before the Act was enacted."[9] That is not to
say that all the earlier decisions should be ignored but only that

> "the common sense principles embodied in the lettered sub-paragraphs,
> which found their origin in long standing judicial decisions, should con-
> tinue to be applied where appropriate in the new situation."

They should not be "slavishly followed against a different jurisdictional background."[10] Accordingly in discussing what Lord DENNING has called the
"guidelines" now laid down in section 25 of the Act of 1973, reference will only
be made to decisions before January 1, 1971, where they appear still to be
helpful, to cover matters not yet considered in subsequent cases, and to be in
no way inconsistent with the wording of the section or decisions directly based
upon its wording.

1. Orders in favour of a spouse.

By section 25 (1) of the Act, it is the duty of the court in deciding whether
to exercise its powers to make financial provision orders under section 23 or
adjustment of property orders under section 24 in relation to a party to the
marriage, and, if so, in what manner, to have regard to all the circumstances
of the case including the specific matters mentioned in the subsection. It is
therefore clear that although evidence of the specific matters (so far as they are
applicable) should always be before the court, they are in no way exclusive of
other matters, and that account may be taken of any circumstances which are
relevant to the decision in any particular case. In so far as there have been
appeals against orders which have been made they have, so far as is evident
from reported cases, been based upon allegations that insufficient regard has
been paid to the matters specified in the subsection. These are as follows.
(a) *The income, earning capacity, property and other financial resources which
each of the parties to the marriage has or is likely to have in the foreseeable future.*

---

[6] [1973] 1 Fam. 72.
[7] [1973] Fam. 134.
[8] *Ibid., per* Lord DENNING, M.R., at p. 140.
[9] *Ibid., per* SCARMAN, L.J., at p. 144.
[10] *Wachtel* v. *Wachtel*, [1973] Fam. 72, 91.

In *Wachtel* v. *Wachtel*,[11] Lord DENNING, M.R., in reading the judgment of the Court of Appeal, used the convenient expression "family assets" to refer to those things which are acquired by one or other or both of the parties with the intention that they should be continuing provision for them and their children during their joint lives, and used for the benefit of the family as a whole. They could be divided into two parts (i) those which are of a capital nature, such as the matrimonial home and the furniture in it and (ii) those which are of a revenue producing nature, such as the earning power of husband and wife. When the marriage comes to an end, the capital assets have to be divided; the earning power of each has to be allocated.

In assessing the earning capacity of each party, the court must have regard not only to their present income, but to their potential capacity to work and to earn. This is emphasised by a case such as *McEwan* v. *McEwan*,[12] where in considering the analogous question of a magistrates' order for maintenance of his wife, a Divisional Court upheld an order for payment of £6 a week, although the husband was unemployed and his police pension amounted only to £6 a week. He was in good health and as a retired detective constable aged 59 was well able to obtain employment should he choose to do so.

The position with regard to the wife's earning capacity has arisen in earlier cases which would be likely to be followed today. If she is earning an income, or if she has what should in all the circumstances be considered as a potential earning capacity, that must be taken into account in determining the resources of the parties. She will only be regarded as having a potential earning capacity if it is reasonable in the circumstances to expect her to work and to earn.[13] The wife of a very rich man would not, for example, be regarded as having a notional earning capacity behind the counter of a shop in which she had worked before the marriage.[14] If the wife is in fact earning, her income ought generally to be brought into account unless it would be reasonable to expect her to give up that source of income; but the whole of that income need not, and should not ordinarily, be brought into account so as to enure for the husband's benefit. This is particularly so when she has only taken up employment because her husband has disrupted the marriage, or where she would not reasonably be expected to be working if he had not done so.

The expression "family assets" in the sense used by Lord DENNING would not necessarily include all the property or financial resources which must be taken into account, not so much in the sense that they should be shared between the parties in the same way as family assets, but because they are relevant to the financial resources of the party who owns them. Account must be taken of prospects of benefit from the estate of a relative, or items such as valuable jewellery which belonged to the wife before marriage.[15] The expression "financial resources" will enable the court to have regard, as it always has had, to the realities of the case, and to take into account the current expenditure of the

---

[11] [1973] Fam. 72, 90.
[12] [1972] 2 All E.R. 708.
[13] *Attwood* v. *Attwood*, [1968] P. 591.
[14] *Rose* v. *Rose*, [1951] P. 29.
[15] *Lysaght* v. *Lysaght* (1928), 44 T.L.R. 723.

parties, rather than their income for purposes of taxation. Thus in *J.-P.C.* v. *J.-A.F.*[16] the husband's taxable income was £70 only, but maintenance was calculated upon the basis of expenditure for non-business purposes of £1,200 a year from capital gains made with the assistance of bank overdrafts. In *Ette* v. *Ette*[17] the court based its assessment on the husband's current expenditure resulting from a voluntary allowance made to him by his mistress, rather than upon the salary which was his as of right.

It was held by the Court of Appeal in *Barnes* v. *Barnes*[18] that a wife's right to social security benefit cannot be comprised in the expression "other financial resources which each of the parties to the marriage has or is likely to have in the foreseeable future". The court adopted the attitude which was taken in *Ashley* v. *Ashley*,[19] before the Acts, in relation to national assistance. In the first place, in seeking to arrive at what would be a proper order, the court should not have regard to social security benefits but, looking at all the matters set out in section 25, should seek to arrive at a fair figure. But if the total resources of both parties are so modest that an adjustment of that total would leave the husband with a sum quite inadequate to meet his own financial commitments, then the court may avoid making an order which would be financially crippling to him by having regard to the fact that in a proper case social security benefits will be available to his first wife and children.

(b) *The financial needs, obligations and responsibilities which each of the parties to the marriage has or is likely to have in the foreseeable future.*

"Needs" may obviously take various forms, of which those resulting from ill-health are separately listed in section 25 (1) (e). Needs might include, for example, the expenses of further education or training of a young husband or wife or the additional expenses of an older wife resulting from her custody of a child.[20] "Obligations" could cover unpaid debts or liabilities under hire-purchase agreements, or such matters as the requirements, educational or otherwise, of the children of either party by a previous marriage.[1] "Responsibilities" include those of a husband who has remarried after the dissolution of his first marriage; his legal responsibility to maintain his new wife "must be fully borne in mind and given the same degree and weight as his responsibility in any other financial respect".[2] The expression seems apt also to include what may be called "moral" obligations, such as those to a mistress with whom a husband whose wife has obtained a decree of judicial separation is living. Her claims, though no doubt of lesser weight than those of a wife, have hitherto been regarded as entitled to consideration.[3]

(c) *The standard of living enjoyed by the family before the breakdown of the marriage.*
This factor is doubtless deserving of consideration, but save where the parties

---

[16] [1955] P. 215.
[17] [1965] 1 All E.R. 341.
[18] [1972] 3 All E.R. 872.
[19] [1968] P. 582.
[20] *Kirke* v. *Kirke*, [1961] 3 All E.R. 1059.
[1] *Williams* v. *Williams*, [1965] P. 125; *P.* (*J. R.*) v. *P.* (*G. L.*), [1966] 1 All E.R. 439.
[2] *Barnes* v. *Barnes*, [1972] 1 W.L.R. 1381, C.A., at p. 1384.
[3] *Roberts* v. *Roberts*, [1970] P. 1.

are wealthy, little can be done to ensure that both spouses enjoy the same standard of living as they did before they parted. Reference will be made again to this point, which overlaps a consideration which is elaborated in the concluding words of the subsection.

(d) *The age of each party to the marriage and the duration of the marriage.*

Reference has already been made to this factor in considering cases of "grave financial hardship" under section 5 of the Act.[4] Just as it would be wrong not to dissolve a marriage which had irretrievably broken down when the parties are in the early thirties and the wife is able to work and has prospects of remarriage, so her age and earning capacity must be relevant in considering the way in which the powers of the court should be exercised. But although any periodical payments which are ordered to be made to a wife would cease on her remarriage,[5] her prospects of so doing should not reduce her share of any capital assets, and any periodical payments should be assessed without regard to prospects of remarriage.[6]

The duration of the marriage must always be important. If it ends whilst the parties are young, healthy and childless, both may be regarded as substantially able to fend for themselves. If a husband leaves his wife after many years of marriage, regard must be had to the contributions which he has made to the welfare of her husband and the family whilst the marriage lasted, in accordance with sub-paragraph (f) of the subsection.

The duration of a long period of marital separation may likewise be relevant. In *Krystman* v. *Krystman*[7] the parties married in Italy in 1946 when the husband, then aged 26, who was Polish, was serving with the British forces there. He lived with his Italian wife, then aged 37, for a fortnight only and then came to England and never saw her again, nor did she seek any maintenance from him. The Court of Appeal held that the de facto separation for 26 years and the duration of their separate lives, were such that when the husband obtained a divorce based upon five years' separation, it would be wrong to order him to make any financial provision for her.

(e) *Any physical or mental disability of either of the parties to the marriage.*

This factor seems to add little to that of "financial needs" mentioned in sub-paragraph (b) above. But doubtless the reminder is wise, since the enumeration of specific matters must always tend to divert attention from other matters.

It may happen that the court decides to make an order requiring payment (including a lump sum payment) to be made, or property to be transferred, to a party to a marriage and the court is satisfied that the person in whose favour the order is made is incapable, by reason of mental disorder within the meaing of the Mental Health Act 1959, of managing and administering his property and affairs. Section 40 provides that in such a case, subject to any order, direction or autority made or given in relation to that person under Part VIII

---

[4] See *Mathias* v. *Mathias*, [1972] Fam. 287 and *ante*, p. 56.
[5] S. 28 (1).
[6] *Wachtel* v. *Wachtel*, [1973] Fam. 72, 96.
[7] *Krystman* v. *Krystman*, [1973] 1 W.L.R. 927, C.A.

of the Act of 1959, the court may order the payment to be made, or the property to be transferred, to such persons having charge of that person as the court may direct.

(f) *The contributions made by each of the parties to the welfare of the family, including any contributions made by looking after the home or caring for the family.*

This was a factor to which little reference was made before the new legislation came into operation. The reference by Sachs, L.J., in *Porter* v. *Porter*[8] to "the extent to which the wife has rendered domestic services to the husband" covers but one aspect, and smacks somewhat of the thoughts of a bygone age. The point was put more clearly in 1965 in an extrajudicial address by Sir Jocelyn Simon when he said, "The cock bird can feather the nest because he does not have to spend most of his time sitting on it".[9]

Despite the disapproval shown by the House of Lords (before the new legislation) in *Pettitt* v. *Pettitt*[10] of the expression "family assets", the expression can now be regarded as part of the law, and the object of sub-paragraph (f) is to ensure that when the marriage breaks down the wife receives her share of them. As the Court of Appeal explained in *Wachtel* v. *Wachtel*,[11]

> "We may take it that Parliament recognised that the wife who looks after the home and family contributes as much to the family assets as the wife who goes out to work. The one contributes in kind, the other in money or money's worth. If the court considers that the home has been acquired and maintained by the joint efforts of both, then, when the marriage breaks down, it should be regarded as the joint property of both of them, no matter in whose name it stands. Just as a wife who makes substantial money contributions usually gets a share, so should the wife who looks after the home and cares for the family for twenty years or more."

(g) *In the case of proceedings for divorce or nullity of marriage, the value to either of the parties to the marriage of any benefit (for example, a pension) which, by reason of the dissolution or annulment of the marriage, that party will lose the chance of acquiring.*

This, the last of the specified matters, does not arise in suits for judicial separation since the marriage continues and the wife retains the chance of surviving the husband as his widow. In suits for divorce based upon five years' separation, under section 5 of the Act,[12] a husband's inability to compensate a respondent wife for loss of potential pension rights may result in his petition being dismissed by reason of her defence of grave hardship. In those based on two or five years' separation the court, in dealing with an application by the respondent for consideration of his or her financial position after the divorce

---

[8] [1969] 1 W.L.R. 1155, 1160.
[9] Quoted by Lord Hodson in *Pettitt* v. *Pettitt,* [1970] A.C. 777, 811,
[10] *Supra.*
[11] [1973] Fam. 72, 93.
[12] See *ante,* p. 54.

under section 10 (2),[13] is required, amongst other matters, to have regard to the financial position of the respondent as, having regard to the divorce, it is likely to be after the death of the petitioner should the petitioner die first, and the decree will not be made absolute unless the court is satisfied on the question of financial provision. In all suits for divorce or nullity, whatever the basis of the petition may be, this question of loss of potential benefits is important.

It does not arise only in relation to loss of a possible right to a widow's pension. In *Trippas* v. *Trippas*,[14] after the parties had separated and the wife was living with another man, the husband received a sum of £80,000 in cash and an allocation of £95,000 in shares on a "take-over" of his family business. On a subsequent divorce based upon two years' separation and an application by the wife under section 10 (2) to consider her financial position, she was awarded a lump sum of £10,000. Had the marriage continued and had she survived her husband, it was likely that he would have made some provision for her. This sum was not equivalent to capitalised maintenance: since her husband was not in pensionable employment it was in effect a substitute for a pension, for the benefit she might have expected under his will.

The subsection concludes with a direction to the court as to the manner in which, having considered all the circumstances, including the seven matters specifically mentioned, its powers are to be exercised. It is to place the parties so far as it is practicable and, having regard to their conduct, just so to do, in the financial position in which they would have been if the marriage had not broken down and each had properly discharged his or her financial obligations and responsibilities towards the other. There are thus two further matters to be considered, the conduct of the parties and the practicability of doing what the Act requires.

(1) The conduct of the parties.

Reference has already been made[15] to the extent to which the question of conduct has in the past influenced the orders which the court has made. This emphasis upon conduct continued for some considerable time after the Matrimonial Proceedings and Property Act 1970 came into operation. Rule 80 of the Matrimonial Causes Rules 1971 required that an application for ancillary relief pending in a divorce county court should, with some exceptions, be transferred to the High Court if there was a contested issue of conduct of a nature likely materially to affect the question whether any, or what, order should be made. In *O'Brien* v. *O'Brien*[16] the court had been asked to give directions for oral evidence of the parties to be given on the question of conduct notwithstanding that the husband's means were such that no payment could at that time be ordered. BAGNALL, J., declined to give such a direction on the ground that it was an "arid issue" and that the matter could be deferred until the financial position of the parties was such that some order could be made. But he recognised that there might be special circumstances in which the determination of

---

[13] See *ante*, p. 57.
[14] [1973] Fam. 134.
[15] See *ante*, p. 131.
[16] [1972] Fam. 20,

the issue of conduct could not be postponed because, for example, important witnesses were elderly and unlikely to survive, or were liable to go abroad. In *Ackerman* v. *Ackerman*[17] Sir GEORGE BAKER, P., whilst holding that "no woman can be a saint all the time" and that a wife's conduct was only relevant if it was of a serious nature and at least a contributory cause of the breakdown of the marriage, proposed that in such cases a "maximum discount figure" should be fixed when the first order was made and applied (unless subsequent conduct was relevant) when variation of the order was sought in the future. Some nine or ten pages of the report deal with charges and counter-charges as to conduct, based upon many affidavits.

It was at this point that the tide, so to speak, began to turn. The Court of Appeal[18] reversed the judgment in *Ackerman* v. *Ackerman*. It held that there was no power to give this form of "declaratory judgment" designed "to settle once and for all the question of past conduct", though a judge was entitled in his judgment to express his views as to the conduct of the parties for the guidance of the registrar in dealing with ancillary matters. What is more, there appeared a reference to the "one-third rule" as a starting point, subject to the comment that "it is not a rule".[19] This tendency towards arithmetical proportions, to award a "blameless" wife a sum sufficient to bring her own income up to one-third of the joint income of the spouses, had been condemned many times before the Act of 1970.[20] As will be seen later,[1] it has been re-incarnated in an altered form.

The present position results from the decision of the Court of Appeal in *Wachtel* v. *Wachtel*[2] in which the court responded to an invitation by counsel for both parties "to lay down some guidelines" for the purpose of avoiding divergencies of view and practice among judges and registrars and to assist parties and their legal advisers to come to agreement. The judgment of the court, read by Lord DENNING, M.R., deserves detailed study.

The court again condemned the idea of some "discount" or "reduction" in what a wife should receive because of her supposed misconduct, guilt or blame, whatever word is used. Divorce for irretrievable breakdown of a marriage carries no stigma, but only sympathy. When the Act says that the court must "have regard to their conduct",

> "Does this mean that the judge in chambers is to hear their mutual re-criminations and go into their petty squabbles for days on end, as he used to in the old days? Does it mean that, after a marriage has been dissolved, there is to be a post mortem to find out what killed it? We do not think so. In most cases both parties are to blame—or, as we would prefer to say—both parties have contributed to the breakdown."[3]

---

[17] [1972] Fam. 1.
[18] [1972] Fam. 225.
[19] *Ibid.*, at p. 234.
[20] E.g. in *Stibbe* v. *Stibbe*, [1931] P. 105; *Horniman* v. *Horniman*, [1933] P. 95; *Chichester* v. *Chichester*, [1936] P. 129.
[1] See *post*, p. 141.
[2] [1973] Fam. 72.
[3] *Ibid.*, at pp. 89, 90.

To continue further

"There will no doubt be a residue of cases where the conduct of one of the parties is . . . 'both obvious and gross', so much so that to order one party to support another whose conduct falls into this category is repugnant to anyone's sense of justice. In such a case the court remains free to decline to afford financial support or to reduce the support which it would otherwise have ordered. But, short of cases falling into this category, the court should not reduce its order for financial provision merely because of what was formerly regarded as guilt or blame. To do so would be to impose a fine for supposed misbehaviour in the course of an unhappy married life."

These words were further considered by BAGNALL, J., in *Harnett* v. *Harnett*[4]

"In this phrase I think that 'gross' describes the conduct; 'obvious' describes the clarity or certainty with which it is seen to be gross. If the conduct of one is substantially as bad as that of the other, then it matters not how gross that conduct is; they will weigh equally in the balance. In my view to satisfy the test the conduct must be obvious and gross in the sense that the party concerned must be plainly seen to have wilfully persisted in conduct, or a course of conduct, calculated to destroy the marriage in circumstances in which the other party is substantially blameless. I think there will be very few cases in which these conditions will be satisfied."

Perhaps the last word of advice on this matter of conduct should be that of SCARMAN, L.J., in *Trippas* v. *Trippas*[5]

"Where it is clear that conduct cannot play a significant part, it seems to me to be wrong to load the court with affidavits about ancient or modern discontents. A better use of the court's time, and of counsel's and solicitor's time, would be to concentrate on what really matters, namely, the financial position of the family."

(2) What is practicable.

It will be seldom that the court will in practice be able to achieve the ideal laid down in section 25 (1)—to place the parties in the financial position in which they would have been if the marriage had not broken down and each had properly discharged his or her financial obligations and responsibilities towards the other. Sometimes it might be possible to place one in that position at the expense of the other, but the section requires that if it be possible this should be done for both and also (see *post*, p. 146) for children of the family.

The truth of the matter lies in the oft-quoted passage from paragraph 210 of the Law Commission's Working Paper No. 9[6]—

"The bed rock of difficulty is simply that most men have neither the capital nor the income resources to provide adequately for the wife (or wives)

---

[4] [1973] Fam. 156, 165.
[5] [1973] Fam. 134, 146.
[6] Law Com. No. 25, App. II at p. 154.

they have deserted as well as for themselves and their new commitments. No amount of ingenuity by actuaries, lawyers or legislators can alter the facts, which may be summarised as follows:—

(a) wealthy men present the law with no problems;

(b) poor men present problems which can be solved only within the framework of national insurance, and Supplementary Benefit legislation;

(c) the man who is neither rich nor poor generally has available an earned income, a pension expectancy and a capital asset—a house which may be encumbered with a mortgage. He rarely has much else."

These factors are stressed in a Report of the Social Survey Division of the Office of Population Censures and Surveys[7]

"By knowing the facts about the matrimonial property of married couples, it is possible to put both the law and the couples into perspective. Our sample included married couples of all ages and ranges of financial circumstances. For many couples the law relating to property must seem very remote since they themselves own little property of great value; for example, 48% of couples were not owner occupiers, 47% of couples did not have a current bank account, and 23% of couples said that, excluding the house or current bank account if they had them, the total value of their other assets (small savings, investments, etc.) was less than £100."

What the Act of 1973 (re-enacting the provisions of the Matrimonial Proceedings and Property Act 1970) has done is to sweep away the old anomalies, to put the parties in an equal position and to recognise the wife's contribution to the family assets by looking after the home and caring for the family. It has given the court an armoury of powers for use when the financial position of the spouses makes it possible and just to do so. How then are these powers to be exercised?

(i) *Orders for transfer of property or payment of a lump sum.*

These are the powers which are mainly used to re-distribute the family assets, if assets there be. Neither is to be regarded as a capitalisation of periodical payments, though obviously if they diminish the needs of the recipient, as would the transfer of a home, the periodical payments required will be lessened. Whereas periodical payments cease on the remarriage of the payee, there is no question of re-adjusting an order for transfer, or of ordering re-payment of a lump sum because of re-marriage, and if the lump sum is payable by instalments, any instalments unpaid continue to be payable. Once made, the orders cannot be varied, and no property adjustment order in favour of a party to a marriage, or order for payment of a lump sum to a party, can be made on an application for variation of an order for periodical payments.[8] An order can be made on

---

[7] *Matrimonial Property*, by J. E. Todd and L. M. Jones, H.M. Stationery Office, 1972, at p. 105.

[8] See s. 31 and *post*, Chapter 15.

granting a decree of divorce, nullity or judicial separation or at any time thereafter.[9] But although section 23 (1) (c) enables the court to make "an order that either party to the marriage shall pay to the other such lump sum or sums" as may be specified, it was held in *Coleman* v. *Coleman*[10] that the words are intended only to enable the court to provide for more than one lump sum payment in one order. Since the section empowers the court only to make "an order" it is not permissible to make a series of orders, though no doubt if no order had been made on the original application, and the husband's wealth greatly increased, it is possible that the court could make "an order" for the wife to receive some of it as a lump sum, though even this is not entirely clear.[11]

The matrimonial home is usually the most important, and often the only, capital asset, and at first sight it might seem that a wife should have a half share in it. But most wives want in addition periodical payments to enable them to maintain their standard of living, and the husband has often also to provide for children of the family, whether they live with him or his wife. She cannot, as the Court of Appeal observed in *Wachtel* v. *Wachtel*, have both half the assets and half the earnings. Hence the resurrection, as a flexible starting point, of the so called "one-third rule", though it is not a rule and must never be so regarded. There may be cases when more is right and there are likely to be many others where less is the only practicable solution. It will serve in cases where the marriage has lasted for many years and the wife has been in the home bringing up the children. It may not be applicable when the marriage has lasted only a short time or where there are no children and she can go out to work. But it is convenient to begin with a transfer to the wife, in specie or as a lump sum payment, of one-third of the capital assets and to order periodical payments to bring her income, if any, up to one-third of their joint incomes.[12]

Suppose that the only capital asset is a matrimonial home, usually subject to a mortgage. Often it stands in the name of the husband alone. There are then three possible courses open to the court. If the husband is to remain in the home, the wife should be compensated for the loss of her share by a lump sum payment, if it is possible to raise such a sum by a further mortgage without crippling the husband financially. If the wife is to remain in the home, it may be appropriate to order the ownership to be transferred to her, or to be settled on her and the children of the family, perhaps subject to a deferred charge of an appropriate amount in her husband's favour.[13] If the home is mortgaged, as it generally will be, the terms of the mortgage will generally be such that the mortgagee's consent to the transfer will be required and if this is not forthcoming, or if the husband's financial position is such that he can no longer provide for the payments due under the mortgage, it may be inevitable that the house be sold and a lump sum payment made to the wife from the balance of the proceeds of the sale. This may even prove to be the solution in the case of parties whose means

---

[9] Ss. 23 (1) and 24 (1).
[10] [1973] Fam. 10.
[11] See *Powys* v. *Powys*, [1971] P. 340; *Jones* v. *Jones*, [1971] 3 All E.R. 1201; and *Coleman* v. *Coleman*, *supra*, at p. 18.
[12] [1973] Fam. 72 at pp. 94, 95; see also *Harnett* v. *Harnett*, [1973] Fam. 156, 165.
[13] See *Hector* v. *Hector*, [1973] 3 All E.R. 1070, C.A.

are very limited, as in *Hunter* v. *Hunter*.[14] The husband's income amounted to little more than £21 a week. The marriage had irretrievably broken down and each party had been granted a decree. The husband was unable to keep up the mortgage payments on the home, which was in his name only, the mortgagees had foreclosed and the house was in process of being sold. Although the wife would have been adjudged to have no interest in the home in proceedings under section 17 of the Married Women's Property Act 1882, the Court of Appeal ordered a transfer to her of one half of the husband's interest in the house, which interest was valued at some £3,000, and small payment of £1 a week for herself and £1·50 for each of the four children, which would have been larger but for the order for transfer.

There arises incidentally, from this case and other cases, and particularly from the judgments of the Court of Appeal in *Kowalczuk* v. *Kowalczuk*,[15] the view that after there has been a divorce, it is unnecessary to decide the exact property rights of the parties under section 17 of the Married Women's Property Act 1882, since their property rights can be adjusted under section 24 of the Act of 1973. The issue of whether a wife had made financial contributions which would entitle her to a share in the house is now of little importance once the marriage has ended, since the court has power under section 24 to adjust the rights of the parties according to all the circumstances: there are now hardly any cases in the Family Division under section 17.[16]

The question of a lump sum payment is not, of course, relevant only in relation to an existing matrimonial home. It is particularly relevant in the case of a wealthy man with substantial assets beyond that of the home. In *Davis* v. *Davis*[17] the parties had both been married before; their marriage had lasted some eleven years; their children were grown up. In the days before the new legislation, she obtained a decree of divorce on the ground of her husband's cruelty, discretion being exercised in respect of her own adultery with one man. She had no capital assets apart from her jewellery and furs. The husband's capital assets were worth some £400,000 and his income from investments and earnings was between £27,000 and £40,000 a year. He was ordered to make periodical payments at the rate of £8,500 a year less tax, of which £4,500 a year was to be secured, and to pay a lump sum of £25,000 to enable his wife to set herself up in a home commensurate with that to which she had been accustomed. Had similar facts arisen today, the lump sum would probably have been larger than £25,000, because the Court of Appeal specifically mentioned that they would have been disposed to award rather more had it not been for the wife's own misconduct, a factor which would now have little relevance in the light of the husband's cruelty.

The award of a lump sum to compensate for loss of pension rights has already been mentioned,[18] as has also an award to represent the provision which a husband might have been expected to make to his wife from the receipts from

---

[14] [1973] 1 W.L.R. 958, C.A.
[15] [1973] 1 W.L.R. 930, at p. 934; but see *Glenn* v. *Glenn*, [1973] 2 All E.R. 1187.
[16] *Wachtel* v. *Wachtel, supra,* at p. 92.
[17] [1967] P. 185.
[18] *Parker* v. *Parker*, [1972] Fam. 116.

a "take-over" of his business, had the marriage not ended in divorce.[19] The award of £25,000 out of a husband's assets of some £500,000 to a wife who, having been married at the age of 21, obtained leave to petition for divorce on the ground of her husband's exceptional depravity and obtained a decree absolute after only ten months of marriage, illustrates well the obligation to restore her to the position in which she should have been had her husband properly discharged his marital obligations. Such orders are not limited to some special purpose, such as the purchase of a house, of furniture or of a car.[20]

In the early days after the new legislation became operative, EDMUND DAVIES, L.J., said in *Millward* v. *Millward*[21] that "the making of lump sum orders . . . ought not in my judgment to become commonplace", and cited the comment of WILLMER, L.J., in *Davis* v. *Davis*[1] that

> "an order for a lump sum payment can only properly be made against a husband possessed of sufficient capital assets to justify it. It is not to be expected, therefore, that the question is likely to arise except in relatively rare cases."

It would be difficult to criticise the decision in that case that such a payment was not appropriate where a husband of very limited means had re-married, to enable his former wife to complete the mortgage payments of £400 on a house which she had purchased. Such payments are normally regarded as an income disbursement to be met from periodical payments, rather than as a capital liability. But some change in attitude to the question of lump sum payments is evident from the following words from the unanimous judgment of the Court of Appeal in *Wachtel* v. *Wachtel*.[2]

> "One thing is, however, obvious. No order should be made for a lump sum unless the husband has capital assets out of which to pay it—without crippling his earning power. Another thing is this: when the husband has available capital assets sufficient for the purpose, the court should not hesitate to order a lump sum. The wife will then be able to invest it and use the income to live on. This will reduce any periodical payments, or make them unnecessary. It will also help to remove the bitterness which is so often attendant on periodical payments. Once made, the parties can regard the book as closed. The third thing is that, if a lump sum is awarded, it should be made outright. It should not be made subject to conditions except where there are children. Then it may be desirable to let it be the subject of a settlement. In case she remarries, the children will be assured of some part of the family assets which were built up for them."

(ii) *Orders for a settlement of property.*

This reference to the interests of the children reflects the factors which have been regarded as relevant in the few cases of orders for a settlement of property

---

[19] *Trippas* v. *Trippas*, [1973] Fam. 134.
[20] *Brett* v. *Brett*, [1969] 1 All E.R. 1007.
[21] [1971] 1 W.L.R. 1432, 1437.
[1] *Supra*, at p. 192.
[2] [1973] Fam. 72, 95, 96.

reported since the new legislation became operative. It may not only be useful when the wife is likely to remarry and it is desirable to ensure that the benefit of the property transferred or the lump sum awarded enures to the children of the first marriage rather than to her second husband. Even though the means of the parties are small, a settlement may be useful when it is necessary to provide a home for a wife and for the children until they are of an age when this will no longer be required. A transfer of the ownership of the house to the wife might frequently give her more than her proper share in the re-distribution of the family assets: a settlement may avoid this difficulty.

An example can be found in *Mesher* v. *Mesher*[3] where the former home was owned beneficially by the parties in equal shares, their incomes were approximately equal, both intended to remarry and the wife intended to live in the home with their only child, a daughter. The Court of Appeal held that it would be wrong to deprive the husband of all interest in the home. It ordered that it should be held by the parties in equal shares on trust for sale with provisions designed to enable the wife to live in the house with the daughter until she reached the age of 17. The situation in *Harnett* v. *Harnett*[4] was somewhat more complicated. The wife's income was slightly larger than that of the husband. She had custody of the two daughters, aged eleven and nine. She had recently bought a house for £10,850, subject to mortgages of £9,650, and her income was insufficient to keep up the mortgage payments. The husband's only real capital asset was a house which, if it were sold and the mortgage paid off, would realise some £21,000. It was agreed that such a sale was inevitable. The court ordered the wife to convey her new house to two trustees (one to be selected by each party) and the husband to pay to her the sum of £12,500 and to pay £10 a week for each child, on condition that the liability of the husband to contribute towards the mortgage payments was thereby discharged and any remaining school expenses were paid by the wife. The house was to be held on trust for sale, and on beneficial trusts of income for the wife and each of the children during a trust period which should end on the death of the wife or earlier so soon as neither child should be under the age of 25 and unmarried: at the end of the trust period the capital would be held in trust for the husband and wife in equal shares. During the trust period the wife would be permitted to live in the house or any substituted house with directions as to the power of substitution, and for her liability for all outgoings. This case well illustrates the way in which the extended powers of the court enable difficulties to be overcome and injustice avoided.

(iii) *Variation of settlements.*

Few decisions have recently been reported on this type of order. Those on the effect of death or re-marriage on an application have already been noted.[5] Little reliance can be placed on the decision in March 1970 in *Meldrum* v.

---

[3] (1973), *Times*, February 13, mentioned by BAGNALL, J. in *Harnett* v. *Harnett*, [1973] Fam. 156, 163.

[4] *Supra.*

[5] *D'Este* v. *D'Este*, [1973] Fam. 55; *Jackson* v. *Jackson*, [1973] Fam. 99; *Marsden* v. *Marsden*, [1973] 2 All E.R. 851; *ante*, pp. 121, 122.

Meldrum[6] since STIRLING, J., in stating the principles applicable, used now outmoded phrases such as references to "mitigating any unfairness to the innocent spouse" and to ensuring "that the guilty spouse should not benefit under the existing trusts from his or her own wrong". The truth is that there are now few settlements in the strict sense of that term and that the court's power to order a transfer of property has rendered it unnecessary to regard as "settlements" situations where a house has been purchased and conveyed into the joint names of the spouses[7] or purchased with money provided by both but conveyed into the name of one alone.[8]

(iv) *Periodical payments.*

Little remains to be said under this heading. The one-third "rule" may provide a starting point and orders for adjustment of property rights or for lump sum payments, where these are possible, may reduce the periodical payments required. But the target of placing the parties in the financial position in which they would have been had the marriage not broken down is generally out of reach, save with the very rich. Usually both must be poorer, and since the husband's means must not be reduced below subsistence level, it may be inevitable that his first wife and children, and possibly also his wife and any children by the second marriage, may have to rely upon social security benefits.[9] In so many cases the fact that there can be no "rule" of one-third or any other proportion is self-evident.

There has been no recent authority on the subject of what proportion of the payments are to be paid and what secured. The advantages to the wife of security, and of the continuance of secured payments after the husband's death, are clear. The burden upon the husband of having a substantial part of his capital assets tied up in order to provide security is self-evident.

2. Provision for children.

The matters to which the court must have regard in relation to provision for children, whether by way of financial provision under section 23 or the adjustment of property rights under section 24, are laid down by section 25 (2) and (3). As in the case of spouses[10] the court, in deciding whether to exercise these powers and, if so, in what manner, is required to have regard to all the circumstances of the case including certain specified matters. These are as follows:—

(a) *The financial needs of the child.*

These will obviously vary according to the age of the child and are also affected by other matters specifically mentioned below, such as the child's health, education and training.

---

[6] [1970] 3 All E.R. 1084.
[7] As in *Brown* v. *Brown*, [1959] P. 86.
[8] As in *Cook* v. *Cook*, [1962] P. 235.
[9] *Barnes* v. *Barnes*, [1972] 3 All E.R. 872.
[10] See *ante*, p. 132.

(b) *The income, earning capacity (if any), property and other financial resources of the child.*

The reference to earning capacity is particularly relevant in cases in which the court decides to extend periodical payments for a child beyond the age of eighteen. It has power to do this[11] where the child's education or training still continues whether or not the child is, or will be, also in gainful employment, or where there are special circumstances. Thus the expression "earning capacity" must in such a case be interpreted as meaning earning capacity having regard to the continuance of the education or training, and not potential earning capacity were it to be discontinued, which would obviously be greater.

(c) *Any physical or mental disability of the child.*

This also would no doubt be one of the special circumstances justifying payments beyond the age of eighteen.

(d) *The standard of living enjoyed by the family before the breakdown of the marriage.*

Of necessity, if it be possible to maintain the previous standard of living of the spouse having custody of the child (which will seldom be the case), that of the child will likewise be maintained. The two must stand or fall together.

(e) *The manner in which he was being and in which the parties to the marriage expected him to be educated or trained.*

This is a factor of particular importance: a sudden change in the plans for a child's education or future career, removal from school and friends and the dashing of hopes, can have grave psychological effects. Where such changes may be involved, the judge may sometimes wish to see the child and discuss these matters with him.

The court is also required to have regard to the considerations mentioned in relation to the parties to the marriage in section 25 (1) (*a*) and (*b*) (see *ante*, pp. 132, 134), i.e. to the financial resources, needs and obligations of those parties. Little provision can be made for a child if neither spouse has the means to provide it; the needs of the spouses cannot be completely subordinated to those of the children.

Having considered all these matters the court is finally required so to exercise its powers as to place the child, so far as it is practicable and just so to do, in the financial position in which the child would have been if the marriage had not broken down and each of those parties had properly discharged his or her financial obligations and responsibilities towards him. What has already been said[12] as to the practical difficulties of so doing in relation to orders in favour of spouses has equal force in relation to orders for the benefit of the children.

Additional considerations arise when the court is being asked to exercise its powers against a party to a marriage in favour of a child of the family who

---

[11] S. 29 (3), see *ante*, p. 115.
[12] See *ante*, p. 139.

is not the child of that party and who (it will be remembered) may not even be a child of either of the spouses.[13] Section 25 (3) places a duty upon the court in such a case to have regard (amongst the circumstances of the case):—

(a) to whether that party had assumed any responsibility for the child's maintenance and, if so, to the extent to which, and the basis upon which, that party assumed such responsibility and the length of time for which that party discharged such responsibility;

(b) to whether in assuming and discharging such responsibility that party did so knowing that the child was not his or her own;

(c) to the liability of any other person to maintain the child.

Considerations (a) and (c) follow (with some elaboration) the general lines of section 34 (4) of the Matrimonial Causes Act 1965 (now repealed) in relation to a child of one party who was "accepted as one of the family by the other party". It was held under that section[14] that a husband could not be said to have "accepted" his wife's child as one of the family so long as he was ignorant of the fact that he was not the father of that child, since until he knew this the question of "acceptance" could never have entered his mind. This is still so in proceedings before a magistrates' court. Consideration (b) above takes account of the fact that despite this ignorance the child may nevertheless have been "treated by both those parties as a child of their family", which suffices under section 52 (1) of the Act of 1973. The husband's ignorance does not deprive the court of all its powers under the Act in relation to the child's welfare, as it would have done under the Act of 1965. It is, however, very relevant in relation to his liability to maintain the child.[15]

Consideration (c) will, in the case of an illegitimate child, include the liability of the putative father. Where a previous marriage has ended in divorce and the wife, who has custody of a child of that marriage, has remarried, the child may well have become a child of the new social unit, of the new family resulting from that second marriage.[16] Although the wife's remarriage will have ended the liability of the former husband to make periodical payments by way of maintenance for her, it will not have ended his liability to maintain his child, and regard must be had to it, just as when, if the child is the child of neither of the parties to the marriage, regard must be had to the liability of its natural parents. In all such cases, it is to the *liability* of such other persons that the court must have regard rather than to the extent to which they are in fact fulfilling that liability.[17]

Consideration will be given hereafter[18] to the duty laid upon the court by section 41 of the Act to be satisfied as to the arrangements made for the welfare of children of the family. It should, however, be noted that under that section "welfare" includes not only custody and education, but also financial provision,

---

[13] See *ante*, p. 113.
[14] E.g. in *R.* v. *R.*, [1968] P. 414 and *B.* v. *B. and F.*, [1969] P. 37.
[15] *W. (R. J.)* v. *W. (S. J.)*, [1972] Fam. 152.
[16] *Newman* v. *Newman*, [1970] 3 All E.R. 529.
[17] *Bowlas* v. *Bowlas*, [1965] P. 450.
[18] *Post*, Chapter 13.

so that the court cannot make absolute a decree of divorce or nullity, or make a decree of judicial separation, unless it is satisfied that the financial provision is satisfactory or the best that can be devised in the circumstances, or that it is impracticable for the party or parties appearing before the court to make any arrangements for such provision.

3. Agreements between the parties.

If the parties wish, or can be persuaded, to reach agreement on matters of financial provision and adjustment of property rights as between themselves and for the benefit of the children of the family, the advantages are plain. Not only the parties but also the children can hardly fail to benefit from the fact that some of the "heat" has, so to speak, been taken out of the breakdown of the marriage. A considerable proportion of the cases which were originally defended cease to be so before they come on for hearing because an agreement on these matters has been reached.

Mention has already been made[19] of the provisions of section 7 permitting Rules to be made enabling the parties to the marriage, or either of them, to refer to the court agreements or proposed agreements in relation to proceedings for divorce to enable the court, should it think it desirable to do so, to express an opinion as to whether the agreement is reasonable, and to give directions. This section applies also to proceedings for judicial separation,[20] but not to proceedings for nullity. Mention has also been made of the fact that the Matrimonial Causes Rules 1973 (unlike the Rules of 1971) make no provision for this matter. Even when (as in *Smallman* v. *Smallman*[1]) the parties have reached an agreement which deals with all essential matters "subject to the approval of the court", it remains a binding agreement from which neither can resile before the court has been asked to approve it particularly when one party has acted upon the agreed terms. The effect of the clause is only to suspend the duty to carry out the terms unless and until the court has approved them. Indeed the agreement in the *Smallman* case was reached in the year 1970, when collusion was a discretionary bar to divorce, and disclosure of the agreement to the court and approval of its terms was necessary, a situation which no longer exists today.

A *Practice Direction*[2] deals in detail with the procedure to be followed when, as is frequently the case, the parties wish the agreed provisions to be embodied in an order of the court. This has the advantage that, unlike the terms of a mere agreement, they will be enforceable without the necessity for an action and judgment in the applicant's favour and they will, like any other order, be subject to the usual provisions as to subsequent variation. The inclusion of the terms in an order will be justified only where they are in a form capable of subsequent variation or enforcement. Thus where it is intended (a)

---

[19] See *ante*, p. 60.
[20] S. 17 (3).
[1] [1972] Fam. 25, C.A.
[2] [1972] 3 All E.R. 704. See also *Practice Direction (Matrimonial Causes: Special Procedure)*, [1973] 3 All E.R. 182.

that a party should submit to an order which it is within the statutory power of the court to make, or (b) submit to an undertaking which, in the event of non-compliance, is to be enforceable by committal, the terms of the order or under-taking must be fully set out in the order and, in the case of an undertaking, the terms should be sufficiently precise to be enforceable. In such cases it will assist the court, the parties and their advisers, if an agreed draft, signed by the parties or their legal advisers, is handed in before the hearing of the application.

The reference to the "statutory powers" of the court no doubt rests upon the decision in *Mills* v. *Mills*[3] that the consent of the parties does not enable the court to make an order which is outside those powers. In view of the wide powers which the Act confers upon the court, this situation is now unlikely to occur. If, however, the parties do reach an agreement which the court has no power to make, such as an agreement whereby the periodical payments for a spouse are to extend beyond the period allowed by section 28, or continue despite remarriage, or those for a child of the family extend beyond the period allowed by section 29, the agreement, assuming that it is in writing, will usually constitute a maintenance agreement capable of alteration under sections 35 and 36 of the Act,[4] though an action will be necessary if the payments are not made and it is sought to enforce payment.

4. Taxation.

The Act in no way affects the tax implications involved in orders for period-ical payments, whether secured or unsecured, in favour of a spouse or a child of the family. Where there is no security the order should be to pay "less tax",[5] so that income tax at the full standard rate will be deducted when the payment is made.[6] Where security is ordered the proper wording is that the payment should be such as will after deduction of tax amount to the sum required. However, in the case of small maintenance payments not exceeding £12 a week or £52 a month for a spouse or child the payment must be made in full without deduction of tax.[7] The eventual result is the same. If the order is to pay "less tax" and a husband makes the payments out of taxed income he retains the tax which he deducts, and thus obtains tax relief on the amount of the income which he pays to his wife. She can then claim repayment from the Revenue up to the amount of any personal reliefs to which she may be entitled. If a small maintenance payment is made in full, the husband deducts the full amount paid from his income for purposes of tax; the wife suffers tax on the full amount she receives in so far as the personal reliefs to which she is entitled do not reduce the sum received below the limits upon which tax is payable.

The position as to lump sum payments and orders for adjustment of property rights is explained in the Law Commission's report[8] as follows:—

---

[3] [1940] P. 124.
[4] See *post*, Chapter 12.
[5] *Jefferson* v. *Jefferson*, [1956] P. 136; *Wallis* v. *Wallis*, [1941] P. 69.
[6] Income and Corporation Taxes Act 1970, ss. 52 and 53.
[7] *Ibid.*, s. 65; Income Tax (Small Maintenance Payments) Order 1972 (No. 436).
[8] Law Com. No. 25, para. 76.

"It is understood that the Revenue treat a lump sum payment made under an order of the court as being made for full consideration on the basis that it is the compounding of future maintenance liability, so that estate duty would not be payable even if the payer died within seven years. It is understood that they would take the same view of a disposition in favour of a spouse or children under a court order in matrimonial proceedings. Hence no problem should arise as regards estate duty. The main problem relates to liability for capital gains tax on a transfer or settlement of property. No such liability arises on disposals between spouses while the marriage subsists and they are living together;[9] a charge on any gain (or relief for any loss) is postponed until the property is disposed of outside the marital unit when the tax position is computed by reference to the original acquisition cost. But the powers recommended above[10] would be exercised when the spouses were living apart and, generally, when the marriage has ended. Moreover, there is no exemption from liability in connection with settlements on children. Hence the charge would not be postponed."

The Commission accordingly recommended[11] that there should be legislative changes whereby a lump sum payment, settlement or transfer under an order of the court should not be treated as a disposition for the purposes of capital gains tax. Some effect has been given to this view by a Revenue Concession contained in a Press Release dated October 22, 1973. Where as a result of the breakdown of a marriage one spouse ceases to occupy his or her matrimonial home and, subsequently as part of a financial settlement disposes of the home, or an interest in it, to the other spouse (or, if the transfer is after a divorce, ex-spouse) the home may be regarded for the purposes of section 29 of the Finance Act 1965 (exemption or relief from capital gains tax of an individual's main residence) as continuing to be a residence of the transferring spouse from the date his (or her) occupation ceases until the date of transfer, provided that it has throughout this period been the other spouse's only or main residence. Thus where a married couple separate and the husband leaves the matrimonial home while still owning it the usual capital gains tax exemption or relief for a tax-payer's only or main residence would be given in the subsequent transfer to the wife, provided she has continued to live in the house and the husband has not elected that some other house should be treated for capital gains tax purposes as his main residence for this period.

---

[9] Finance Act 1965, Sched. 7, para. 20.
[10] I.e. the powers to order a transfer or settlement of property.
[11] Law Com. No. 25, paras. 77 and 80(b).

CHAPTER 10

WILFUL NEGLECT TO MAINTAIN

Section 27 of the Act of 1973 re-enacts without substantial alteration the provisions of section 6 of the Matrimonial Proceedings and Property Act 1970, though an amendment has been made in relation to jurisdiction by the Domicile and Matrimonial Proceedings Act 1973. The section deals with provision for a spouse or child in proceedings brought solely with the object of obtaining financial provision and in no way ancillary to proceedings for any other form of relief.

As will be seen from Chapter 17, a magistrates' court has a similar power to make an order based solely upon wilful neglect to provide reasonable maintenance. The powers of the High Court and divorce county courts under section 27 are, however, wider in several respects than those of a magistrates' court. Unlike the magistrates, they have power to order periodical payments for a spouse or child to be secured and to order payment of a lump sum. The definition under the Act of 1973, of a child of the family is wider, in that in a magistrates' court it cannot include a child of some person other than one of the spouses, whereas under section 27 provision can be ordered for any child, no matter who the parents may be, who has been treated by both the spouses as a child of their family;[1] the possible duration of orders in favour of such a child may be longer, in that it may in certain circumstances extend beyond the age of 21, which is impossible in a magistrates' court. Nevertheless in practice very few applications are made under this section. In the year 1972 they numbered 266 only, as against 25,472 applications to the magistrates.[2] The reason was presumably the extra expense and delay involved in proceeding under what was then section 6 of the Act of 1970.

1. Jurisdiction.

In conformity with the changes in the law governing jurisdiction in other matrimonial causes, the Domicile and Matrimonial Proceedings Act 1973[3] now enables proceedings based on wilful neglect to maintain to be entertained if, and only if

(a) the applicant or the respondent is domiciled in England and Wales on the date of the application; or

---

[1] See *ante*, p. 113.
[2] Civil Judicial Statistics 1972, Cmnd. 5333, Tables M and 10 (ii) D.
[3] Amending s. 27 (2) of the Act of 1973.

(b) the applicant has been habitually resident there throughout the period of one year ending with that date; or

` (c) the respondent is resident there on that date.

It should be noticed that whereas requirement (b) uses the words "habitually resident", requirement (c) uses the word "resident" alone. This is presumably because a person can only be said to be habitually resident over a period of time and not on a given date. Whether, should the point arise, the courts may place some other significance on the difference in wording remains to be seen.

As in the case of other forms of matrimonial relief, a court in England and Wales is not to be precluded from granting a financial provision order under section 27 by reason only that the marriage was polygamous or potentially so.[4]

2. Grounds.

Under the Matrimonial Proceedings (Magistrates' Courts) Act 1960 those courts have power to make orders against either party to a marriage on the ground of wilful neglect to provide reasonable maintenance for the other party or a child of the family. Section 27 follows the precedent set by that Act. Accordingly, either party to the marriage may now apply for an order under the section.

A wife may make such an application on the ground that her husband has wilfully neglected to provide reasonable maintenance for her, or to provide, or to make a proper contribution towards, reasonable maintenance for any child of the family for whose maintenance it is reasonable in all the circumstances to expect him to provide, or towards whose maintenance it is reasonable to expect him to make a proper contribution.

As in the case of applications to a magistrates' court,[5] a husband can seek an order against his wife for his own maintenance only if, by reason of impairment of his earning capacity through age, illness or disability of mind or body, and having regard to the resources of the spouses respectively which are, or should properly be made, available for that purpose, it is reasonable in all the circumstances to expect her so to provide or contribute.[6] But as regards children of the family no such distinction is drawn between husband and wife. He need only prove that she has wilfully neglected to provide, or to make a proper contribution towards, reasonable maintenance for the child and that it is reasonable in all the circumstances to expect her to provide or contribute.[7] He is not required, when applying in respect of a child of the family, to prove in addition the impairment of his own earning capacity, as he is in a magistrates' court.

As has been explained in Chapter 7, it is possible under this Act (though not under the Matrimonial Proceedings (Magistrates' Courts) Act 1960) for a child to be a child of the family although it is not the child of either party to the

---

[4] S. 47.
[5] Matrimonial Proceedings (Magistrates' Courts) Act 1960, s. 1 (1) (i).
[6] S. 27 (1) (*b*) (i).
[7] S. 27 (1) (*b*) (ii) and 27 (3).

marriage. In that event by virtue of section 27 (4), the court is required not only to consider whether it would be reasonable in all the circumstances to require the respondent to provide for, or to make a proper contribution towards, its maintenance, but also to consider those additional circumstances mentioned in section 25 (3) of the Act, which have already been described on p. 147. These include a consideration of whether, in assuming and discharging any responsibility for the child's maintenance, the respondent was aware that the child was not his or her own.

Beyond the matters already mentioned, the Act gives no guidance as to the principles upon which the powers conferred by section 27 should be exercised: they will continue to be governed by cases decided before the Act came into operation. It will still be necessary to prove that the respondent was a "wrongdoer" though the wrongdoing may consist of the very fact of the failure to maintain.[8] This aspect of the matter was examined in detail by a Divisional Court in *Brannan* v. *Brannan*.[9] The husband was in most respects a normal person, save that he suffered from a fixed, irrational and unreasonable belief that his wife was going to kill or injure him, which persisted despite hospital treatment. He had left his wife and refused to return to her or maintain her, and a magistrates' court had found that he was not guilty of deserting her since his psychotic illness prevented him from forming the necessary intention. But as regards her complaint of wilful neglect to maintain the court said[10]

"... wilfulness in this context does not connote any malice or wickedness but that the misconduct, if it is appropriate to use that word, consists only in the failure to pay to the wife sums which, in the opinion of the court, are in all the circumstances sufficient for her reasonable maintenance and support. The wilfulness amounts to nothing more than this, that the husband knows what he is doing and intends to do what he is doing."

Thus the husband's delusions did not give rise to any legal justification for failing to maintain his wife, since he knew what he was doing and indeed his refusal was intentional. The state of mind which is an ingredient of "wilful" neglect to maintain is distinguishable from that required to establish a complaint of desertion.

A husband cannot, of course, be said to have done wrong—to have been guilty of what is still regarded as a matrimonial offence—unless he had the means with which to pay or contribute or was able to earn them.[11] A husband's wilful neglect to maintain his wife, and his wilful neglect to maintain or contribute towards the reasonable maintenance of a child of the family, are separate offences.[12] Thus it was held by the Court of Appeal in *Northrop* v. *Northrop*[13] that if a wife was precluded from alleging failure to maintain herself by reason of the husband's compliance with the terms of a consensual separation, but he

---

[8] *Lilley* v. *Lilley*, [1960] P. 158, 180.
[9] [1973] Fam. 120.
[10] Ibid., at p. 15.
[11] *Earnshaw* v. *Earnshaw*, [1896] P. 160.
[12] *Kinnane* v. *Kinnane*, [1954] P. 41; *Starkie* v. *Starkie* (*No. 2*), [1953] 2 All E.R. 1519.
[13] [1968] P. 74.

was guilty of neglect to maintain a child of the family, a magistrates' court would have power to order him to make payments for the maintenance of his wife as well as for the benefit of the child, if her earning capacity had been reduced by the necessity to look after the child. Cases such as *Northrop* v. *Northrop* were decided in relation to the powers of a magistrates' court in relation to wilful neglect to maintain at a time when, prior to the Maintenance Orders Act 1968, the maximum orders which those courts could make were limited to £7.50 a week for the wife and £2.50 a week for each child, and the object was to find ways of increasing the latter figure. The point is probably now academic. There is today no financial limit upon the powers of a magistrates' court or any other court to order provision for the maintenance of a child of the family, and the difficulties which arose in these earlier cases can be resolved by an increase in the payment to the wife for the child's benefit, rather than by argument as to whether some separate order can be made in her own favour. It must obviously be for the child's benefit that the wife should be in a position to care properly for the child.

In general it may be said that a husband's obligation to maintain his wife is co-terminous with his duty to cohabit with her, though this is not entirely true, as is evident from the case of *Brannan* v. *Brannan, supra*. The questions of "guilt" or "innocence" which have so little relevance in relation to financial provision after divorce, are fundamental under section 27. The same is true of her obligation to maintain him, or to contribute towards his maintenance, when his earning capacity is impaired. Thus a husband's liability to maintain his wife is suspended whilst she is guilty of deserting him, actually or constructively,[14] though if he were to refuse without good cause her bona fide offer to return his liability to maintain her would again arise.[15] He would be relieved of this obligation if she had committed adultery,[16] unless he had condoned that adultery,[17] when he could not longer rely upon it as a defence. Once condoned it is incapable of being revived, but any presumption of condonation which arises from the continuance or resumption of matrimonial intercourse may be rebutted by evidence sufficient to negative the necessary intent,[18] that is to say the intent to restore her to her former matrimonial position. If the wife's conduct leads him reasonably to believe, at the time of her application, that she had committed adultery, the application must be dismissed.[19] though he cannot be heard to say that his belief was reasonable unless he has given her a reasonable chance to explain the circumstances which aroused his suspicions.[20] If in these circumstances the court were to decide that his suspicions were unfounded, he could not again rely upon them as a defence to a later application by his wife founded upon the continuance of his refusal to provide maintenance for her.[1] It may be said that any behaviour such that one spouse cannot reasonably

---

[14] *Winnan* v. *Winnan*, [1949] P. 174.
[15] *Markovitch* v. *Markovitch* (1934), 151 L.T. 139.
[16] *West* v. *West*, [1954] P. 444.
[17] The question of condonation is more fully examined in relation to proceedings in a magistrates' court: see Chapter 17.
[18] S. 27 (8).
[19] *Chilton* v. *Chilton*, [1952] P. 196.
[20] *Marsden* v. *Marsden*, [1968] P. 544.
[1] *Allen* v. *Allen*, [1951] 1 All E.R. 724.

be expected to live with the other will completely bar an application based upon failure to maintain that spouse, but not an application based upon failure to maintain a child of the family.

An exception to the principle that where there is no obligation to cohabit there is no obligation to maintain arises in relation to separation agreements. If such an agreement provides for the payment of a fixed sum by way of maintenance and the husband has regularly paid to his wife the sum agreed, the court will not lightly go behind, or upset, an agreement into which the parties have freely entered by holding that the wife is entitled to more.[2] But if the agreed payments are not made, or if the circumstances in which they were negotiated have, to the husband's knowledge, fundamentally changed, the existence of the agreement, the fact that it relieves him of his obligation to cohabit with his wife, and the fact that he has strictly observed the terms agreed, provide no defence to his wife's allegation that he has wilfully neglected to provide her with reasonable maintenance. In *Tulip* v. *Tulip*,[3] by an agreement entered into in 1932, the husband agreed to pay to his wife the sum of £3 a week free of tax, and had regularly done so. By 1951 his income had greatly increased and, whereas in 1932 she had been able to earn her own living, her health had so deteriorated that she could no longer do so. Had her husband not known that this was so, it might well be that he could not be said to have *wilfully* neglected to provide reasonable maintenance for her. But he did know and an order was made against him. Where an agreement for separation is silent upon the question of maintenance, the proper inference is usually that the parties have agreed that each will be responsible for his or her own maintenance, so that the question of neglect to provide does not arise. But if, in such a case, some fresh need had arisen on the part of the wife of which the husband had notice, as where her health had broken down, the existence of the agreement and her acceptance of the fact that at that time she required no payments from her husband, would not preclude a successful application under section 27.[4]

Before leaving the subject of separation or maintenance agreements, mention must be made of sections 34 to 36 of the Act, which are considered in Chapter 12. These sections enable the court on the application of either party to vary or revoke the terms of a maintenance agreement as defined in section 34. This expression is limited to an agreement *in writing* which contains financial arrangements, or a separation agreement in writing which contains no such arrangements where none are included in any other agreement in writing between the same parties. If such an agreement exists there is a choice between an application to vary its terms under these sections, or an application for an order that despite its terms there has been a wilful neglect to provide reasonable maintenance. The decision as to which course to adopt may be influenced by the fact that breach of the agreement, as varied, will necessitate an action to enforce payment, whereas breach of an order already made under section 27 will be enforceable directly without the need for bringing such an action.

---

[2] *Morton* v. *Morton*, [1954] 2 All E.R. 248.
[3] [1951] P. 378.
[4] *Baker* v. *Baker* (1949), 66 T.L.R. (Pt 1) 81; *Pinnick* v. *Pinnick*, [1957] 1 All E.R. 873.

3. Interim Orders.

Where it appears to the court that the applicant or any child of the family to whom the application relates is in immediate need of financial assistance, but it is not yet possible to determine what order, if any, should be made on the application, the court may order the respondent to make to the applicant until the determination of the application such periodical payments as the court thinks reasonable.[5]

No restrictions are placed by this subsection upon the court's discretion to make such an order, nor is there (as in the case of an interim order made by a magistrates' court) any specified time limit to the maximum duration of such an order.[6] The court need only be satisfied that the applicant is a party to the marriage, or if application is made on behalf of a child, that the child is a child of the family, and that there is an immediate need of financial assistance.

4. Final Orders.

An order under section 27 does not necessarily indicate that the marriage has irretrievably broken down, as does a decree of divorce or nullity, and, in almost all cases. a decree of judicial separation. It is for this reason that on an application under this section the court cannot exercise the powers to adjust property rights between the parties which are conferred upon it by section 24 when it grants those decrees.[7] The powers are limited to ordering the *respondent* to make money payments: there is no power to order the applicant to make such payments, even in favour of a child of the family.[8]

It is unnecessary here to describe these powers in detail. Section 27 (6) enables the court to make precisely the same orders for periodical payments, whether secured or not, or for payment of a lump sum,[9] as it can under section 23 (1) in favour of a spouse, or in favour of a child of the family (see *ante*, pp. 110, 114). 23 (1). As is the case under that section, payment of a lump sum can be ordered for the purpose of enabling any liabilities or expenses reasonably incurred in maintaining the applicant, or any child of the family to whom the application relates, before the making of the application, to be met and orders may be made for the lump sum to be paid by instalments and for payment of the instalments to be secured.[10] This power is likely to be of particular value in cases of wilful neglect to maintain. The abolition of the wife's agency of necessity,[11] though it was probably not often used in practice, has deprived her in law of one method of maintaining herself and the children if her husband defaults in so doing. She will have often obtained credit from tradesmen, or overdraft facilities from a

---

[5] S. 27 (5).
[6] Cf. Matrimonial Proceedings (Magistrates' Courts) Act 1960, which usually fixes a maximum duration of three months.
[7] See *ante*, Chapter 8.
[8] Contrast Matrimonial Proceedings (Magistrates' Courts) Act 1960, s. 2 (1) (*h*) whereby either defendant or complainant may be ordered to pay maintenance for a child.
[9] There is one minor difference. Section 23 (1) (*c*) refers to "such lump sum or sums" and s. 27 (6) (*c*) only to "such lump sum".
[10] S. 27 (7).
[11] By the Matrimonial Proceedings and Property Act 1970, s. 41.

bank, or loans from relatives or friends, in her efforts to make ends meet. It is only right that her husband, if he has the means to do so, should be required to pay the sums needed to discharge liabilities of this kind.

In the case of payments to a party to the marriage, the possible duration is governed by section 28 of the Act, and is the same as the maximum term permitted in suits for divorce or judicial separation (see *ante*, p. 111), that is to say, if no security is ordered, the joint lives of the spouses, or if security is ordered, the life of the payee. The former rule laid down in *Pigott* v. *Pigott*[12] that even secured payments could not last beyond joint lives, has been abolished. There are the same rules as to the effect of remarriage should the marriage be subsequently dissolved or annulled whilst the order still remains in force.[13] It is probably unlikely that such an order in favour of a spouse would in practice survive the decree of divorce or nullity, instead of being replaced after a reconsideration of the altered circumstances by orders under section 23.

As regards children, the restrictions in relation to age laid down in section 29, which have already been examined in detail in relation to ancillary financial provision (see *ante*, p. 115) apply equally to non-ancillary provision under section 27. It follows that periodical payments will normally cease at the age of 17[14] but that orders for such payments could be made or continued up to the age of 18 and beyond that age in the circumstances laid down in section 29 (3).[15]

---

[12] [1958] P. 1.
[13] See *ante*, p. 111.
[14] S. 29 (2).
[15] S. 27 (6).

CHAPTER 11

VARIATION AND DISCHARGE OF ORDERS: ARREARS AND OVERPAYMENTS: BANKRUPTCY

1. Variation and discharge of orders.

These matters are governed by section 31 of the Act, which applies to the following orders:—

(a) Any order for maintenance pending suit or any interim order in proceedings based upon wilful neglect to provide, or contribute towards, reasonable maintenance.[1]

(b) Any periodical payments order in favour of a party to the marriage or a child of the family, whether made in proceedings for divorce, nullity or judicial separation or on the ground of wilful neglect to provide, or contribute towards, maintenance.[2]

(c) Any secured periodical payments order made in such proceedings in favour of a party to the marriage or a child of the family.[3]

(d) Any order for payment of a lump sum by instalments to a party to the marriage or to or for the benefit of a child of the family.[4]

(e) Any order for a settlement of property or variation of a settlement, being an order made on or after a decree of judicial separation,[5] and in each case only on an application made in proceedings for the recission of the decree of judicial separation by reference to which the the order was made, or for the dissolution of the marriage in question.[6]

A consideration of the list above, and particularly of the orders which are omitted from that list, will show that the policy of the Act is as follows:—

(a) All orders for periodical payments to a spouse, or to or for the benefit of a child, are variable, whether or not the payments were ordered to be secured.

(b) Once payment of a lump sum has been ordered, the amount of that sum can never be increased or reduced; it is made on the basis that

---

[1] Ss. 31 (2) (a) and 52 (2) (b).
[2] Ss. 31 (2) (b), 52 (2) (a) and 21 (1) (a).
[3] Ss. 31 (2) (c), 52 (2) (a) and 21 (1) (b).
[4] Ss. 31 (2) (d), 23 (3) (c) and 27 (7) (b).
[5] Ss. 31 (2) (e) and 24 (1) (b), (c) and (d).
[6] Ss. 31 (4).

the payee is entitled to it, even though actual payment is spread over a number of years. If the full amount has been paid, there can be no order for repayment. If the order was for payment by instalments, whether secured or not, there can be no order for repayment of any instalment, though variations will be possible by, for example, increasing or reducing the number of instalments, or reducing the amount of the security after some payments have been made.

(c) For similar reasons an order for transfer of property will not be variable. If, however, after a decree of judicial separation, the marriage should be terminated by a subsequent divorce, an order for re-transfer, or an order for payment back of a similar lump sum, would be possible. But this would in no sense be a variation of the original order, but a completely new order made on the occasion of a different decree.

(d) An order for a settlement of property, for variation of a settlement, or for reducing or extinguishing the interest of a spouse thereunder, can never be varied subsequently if the order was made on or after the grant of a decree of divorce or nullity. It is a property adjustment made upon the final breakdown of the marriage and neither changes in the means of the parties nor their subsequent conduct should affect it. If, however, the order was made on the grant of a decree of judicial separation, there are two occasions on which it should and will be possible for the court to reconsider the order, that is to say, if the parties become reconciled and the decree is rescinded, or if the marriage is ended by a subsequent decree of divorce, which may well result from the conduct of the very party who obtained the decree of judicial separation.

In pursuance of the policy outlined above, section 31 (5) imposes two further restrictions upon the powers of the court:—

(1) No property adjustment order (i.e. for a transfer or settlement of property, the variation of a settlement, or for extinguishing or reducing a spouse's interest thereunder[7]) can be made on an application to vary an order for periodical payments (secured or unsecured), in favour of a spouse or a child of the family. This preserves the principle that property adjustments are made on the occasion of the breakdown of the marriage, and should not normally be made, or varied, subsequently.

(2) A similar restriction is placed upon the power to order payment of a lump sum. No such order can be made upon application for variation of a periodical payments or secured periodical payments order in favour of a party to the marriage, whether that order was made in a suit for divorce, nullity or judicial separation, or in proceedings based upon wilful neglect to provide, or contribute towards, reasonable maintenance.[8]

---

[7] Ss. 52 (2) (*a*) and 21 (2).
[8] The effect is to abrogate the decision in *H. v. H.*, [1966] 3 All E.R. 560, to the effect that such variations were permissible.

It should be observed that no mention is made in the second restriction of orders for periodical payments (secured or unsecured) to be made to, or for the benefit of, a child of the family, so that on an application to vary these orders it will be possible to make an order for payment of a lump sum. It is not easy to see the reason for this distinction. Possibly the object is to preserve the decision in *Freeman-Thomas* v. *Freeman-Thomas*[9] where it was held that the court could order payment by a father to a mother of a lump sum to meet school fees which he had undertaken to meet but had not in fact paid. A default of this kind could not be cured easily by a mere increase in periodical payments, even if that increase were back-dated.

Section 31 (5) is limited to applications to *vary* an order which has already been made. It says nothing of original applications. Reference has already been made to *Coleman* v. *Coleman*[10] where it was held that although the Act[11] allowed the court to order either party to pay to the other "such lump sum or sums" as may be specified, this only enabled the court to provide for more than one lump sum payment in one order. Having once ordered payment of a lump sum, it could not subsequently order a second lump sum payment. But suppose that when the original order for periodical payments by a husband to his wife was made he had little or no capital assets so that no order for a lump sum payment or property adjustment order could be made, but subsequently he acquired a considerable fortune. His wife could obviously seek an increase in the payments, but could she also obtain an order for a lump sum payment or for a transfer of property to her? Applications for such orders may be made on granting a decree of divorce, nullity or judicial separation *"or at any time thereafter"* and in the case of divorce or nullity *"before or after the decree is made absolute"*.[12] This is subject to section 26 (2), whereby rules of court have been made which provide that applications for such orders which are not made in the petition or answer can be made subsequently only with the leave of the court.[13] The point has only arisen for consideration in cases in which the divorce proceedings took place under the Act of 1965 and it was sought to obtain an order after January 1, 1971. The point did not directly arise in *Williams* v. *Williams*,[14] where it was held that although the wife's petition contained only a claim for maintenance and the decree was made absolute in July 1970, the Act of 1970 operated retrospectively to enable her to seek and be granted an order for transfer of the matrimonial home after the Act came into force on January 1, 1971. It arose more directly in *Powys* v. *Powys*.[15] The divorce took place in 1961, and in 1962 the wife obtained orders for maintenance and a secured provision. No order for a lump sum payment was made. Subsequently, in 1971, the wife obtained leave to apply for such an order. BRANDON, J., held

---

[9] [1963] P. 157.
[10] [1973] Fam. 10, see *ante*, p. 141.
[11] Then Matrimonial Proceedings and Property Act 1970, s. 2 (1) (*c*); now Act of 1973, s. 23 (1) (*c*).
[12] Ss. 23 (1) and 24 (1).
[13] See Rule 68.
[14] [1971] P. 271.
[15] [1971] P. 340.

that he had power to make the order, but declined to do so. There might be cases in which such an order would be proper, but it is a question of fact and degree in any particular case whether the application is in substance, though not in form, an application for variation of a periodical payments or secured periodical payments order. If it is, the policy of the Act could not be outflanked by making, on an original application many years after the decree, and many years after the making of the original order for secured and unsecured periodical payments, an order which could not be made on an application to vary.

The Act of 1970 abrogated the former rule that no variation of a secured provision was possible after the death of the spouse who was ordered to provide it. The reason for this change cannot be better expressed than in the words of the Law Commission[16] as follows—"During the life of the person liable he may have acquired other responsibilities, for example, to a second wife or to children of the second marriage and their position may be dramatically changed by the cessation of his earnings on his death. Alternatively the cessation on his death of unsecured financial provision and the payment of large capital sums under his assurance policies may make it reasonable to increase the secured provision or the security." Accordingly section 31 (6) provides that when the person liable to make the payments under an order for ancillary or non-ancillary secured provision for a spouse or child[17] has died, an application for variation may be made by the person entitled to payments under the order or by the personal representatives of the deceased person.

By analogy to the provisions of the Inheritance (Family Provision) Act 1938 and the Matrimonial Causes Act 1965, s. 26 (as amended by the Family Provision Act 1966, s. 5), no such application can, except with the permission of the court, be made after the end of the period of six months from the date on which representation in regard to the estate of the person liable to make the payments was first taken out.[18] The personal representatives of that person are protected from liability for having distributed any part of his estate after the expiration of this period of six months without considering the possibility of an application for variation of the secured provision, but this is without prejudice to any power to recover any part of the estate so distributed arising by virtue of any order for variation.[19]

In all cases to which section 31 applies the court is given power to vary or discharge the order or to suspend any provision thereof temporarily or to revive the operation of any provision so suspended.[20] These powers are exercisable not only in relation to the order itself but also in relation to any instrument executed in pursuance of the order,[1] such as an instrument securing periodical payments or the payment of a lump sum by instalments. In exercising these powers the court is required to have regard to all the circumstances of the case, including any change in any of the matters to which it was required to have

---

[16] Law Com. No. 25, para. 91.
[17] I.e. an order under s. 23 (1) (*b*) or (*e*), or s. 27 (6) (*b*) or (*e*).
[18] S. 31 (6). As to limited grants see s. 31 (9).
[19] S. 31 (8).
[20] S. 31 (1).
[1] S. 31 (3).

regard when making the original order and, where the party against whom that order was made has died, the changed circumstances resulting from his or her death.[2] Thus the matters detailed in section 25 of the Act, which have already been examined in detail in Chapter 9, will be as relevant in relation to the variation of an order as they are to the making of the order in the first instance. They will include not only increases or decreases in the means or earning capacity of either party, but also changes in their needs and any physical or mental disabilities which may have supervened.

The question of remarriage of either spouse after their marriage has been dissolved or annulled merits special mention. If a former husband who is making periodical payments should remarry, the requirements of his second wife and any children of the second marriage will be "obligations and responsibilities" within the meaning of section 25 (1) (b) which will require consideration. But if his former wife should remarry any order for payments to her made under the Act will have been so worded as to cease automatically without the need for an application to discharge it,[3] and this will be so even if the remarriage is in law void or voidable.[4] If the order was made under the Matrimonial Causes Act 1965, the same result will follow by virtue of the Act of 1973, Sched. 1, para. 15, though in each case without prejudice to the right to recover any arrears due at the date of the remarriage. Orders for maintenance, secured or unsecured, made before January 1, 1971, in suits for divorce or nullity will cease automatically on the remarriage on or after that date of the party in whose favour the order was made. If the order was for permanent alimony in a suit for judicial separation or restitution of conjugal rights, or for periodical payments (secured or unsecured) in a suit for restitution of conjugal rights or in proceedings under section 22 of the Act of 1965 on the ground of wilful neglect to maintain, there is of course no question of remarriage unless the marriage of the parties is subsequently dissolved or annulled. But if this has occurred and the order nevertheless continues in force, any remarriage on or after January 1, 1971, of the party entitled to payments under the order will result in it ceasing automatically to have effect.

2. Arrears and Overpayments.

It has for a long time been clear that arrears due under orders for the maintenance of a wife or child in matrimonial proceedings are not enforceable as of right. They are not a "debt" recoverable by action in the Queen's Bench Division[5] nor, in view of the court's discretion as to their enforcement, are they provable in bankruptcy[6] since owing to the discretion of the court they are incapable of being fairly estimated.[7] A practice has grown up of refusing to enforce payment of more than one year's arrears except in special circum-

---

[2] S. 31 (7).
[3] See s. 28 (1) and *ante*, p. 111.
[4] S. 52 (3).
[5] *Robins* v. *Robins*, [1907] 2 K.B. 13.
[6] *Kerr* v. *Kerr*, [1897] 2 Q.B. 439; and see *Re Hedderwick, Morten* v. *Brinsley*, [1933] Ch. 669.
[7] *James* v. *James*, [1964] P. 303.

stances.[8] This practice has now statutory force by virtue of section 32 of the Act of 1973.

As regards orders made in suits for divorce, nullity or judicial separation, section 32 applies to maintenance pending suit, to interim orders for maintenance made on applications based upon wilful neglect to maintain, or to contribute rewards, the maintenance of a spouse or child of the family, and to any order for secured or an unsecured periodical payments or payment of a lump sum in favour of a spouse or child of the family. It provides that a person shall not be entitled to enforce through the High Court or *any* county court the payment of any arrears under these orders without leave of that court if those arrears became due more than twelve months before proceedings to enforce the payment of them are begun. Obviously, a client in whose favour such orders have been made should be warned of this provision and advised to inform his or her solicitor in good time if default is made in punctual payment.

It will be noticed that the powers under section 32 are exercisable by the High Court or any county court. They are not limited to divorce county courts since proceedings for recovery of arrears might be taken in other courts.[9]

The court which hears an application for leave under section 32 may refuse it, or may grant leave subject to such restrictions or conditions (including conditions as to the allowing of time for payment or the making of payment by instalments) as that court thinks proper. It is also expressly given power, when hearing such an application, to remit the payment of the arrears or any part thereof. This was a power which the High Court and a county court did not previously possess,[10] though it could achieve the same result by back-dating an order for variation of the sums payable, or an order for discharge of the original order.[11] Even under the Act of 1973 the power to remit payment of arrears is exercisable only on an application for leave to enforce payment of arrears which became due more than twelve months previously, so that unless an application for such leave is made a husband who is in arrears with his payments cannot apply under section 32, or under any other section, for an order remitting the payment of them. As was the case before the Act of 1970, he will have to seek variation of the original order and such back-dating of the variation as the court may order in his favour.

In relation to repayment of sums already paid the Act distinguishes between two possible situations. The first arises when the original order has ceased to operate because of the remarriage of the person entitled to receive payments under it, as will be the case not only in respect of orders made under that Act but also, as has already been noticed[12] in respect of orders made before the Act comes into operation. A husband whose wife has divorced him may well continue to make periodical payments to her in ignorance of the fact that she has remarried, either because she has deliberately concealed this from him or because

---

[8] *Luscombe* v. *Luscombe*, [1962] 1 All E.R. 668.
[9] Corresponding amendments are made to s. 2 (3) of the Matrimonial Causes Act 1967 by Sched. 2, para. 6 (1) (*b*) of the Act of 1973.
[10] *W.* v. *W.* (*No. 3*), [1962] P. 131.
[11] *MacDonald* v. *MacDonald*, [1964] P. 1.
[12] See *ante, p.* 162.

she was not aware of its effect upon his liability. This situation is covered by section 38 of the Act.

The other type of case in which questions of repayment may arise is where payments have been made which, in the light of changes in circumstances, were excessive, although those circumstances did not of themselves operate, as does remarriage, to terminate the liability to pay altogether. A wife who was in receipt of periodical payments might perhaps deliberately conceal from her former husband the fact that she had inherited, or in some other way acquired, a large capital sum; or a husband who had suffered heavy financial losses in business, or whose earning capacity had been reduced by an accident, might continue to make the full payments for some time without taking legal advice, and without realising that he might apply to have those payments reduced. This situation is covered by section 33.

Section 33 applies to all orders for periodical payments, secured or unsecured, in favour of a spouse or a child of the family, and also to maintenance pending suit and to interim orders made on applications based on wilful neglect to maintain or provide for them. An application under the section can be made only where there has been a change in the circumstances of the person entitled to, or liable to make, payments under the order since the order was made, or where changed circumstances have resulted from the death of the person so liable. If it then appears to the court that the amount received by the person entitled to payments under the order in respect of a period after the circumstances changed, or after the death of the person liable to make the payments, exceeds the amount which that person or his or her personal representatives should have been required to pay, the court may order the respondent to the application to pay to the applicant such sum, not exceeding the amount of the excess, as the court thinks just. There is no absolute right to any repayment, the matter being entirely in the court's discretion. Often the sums overpaid will have been spent and the recipient will not have the means to repay them. In other cases difficulties as to repayment can be met by exercising the power to order it to be made by specified instalments.[13] No doubt also the court would be influenced by the question of whether or not the changed circumstances had been deliberately concealed from the applicant.

Section 33 (3) provides that an application under the section may be made by the person liable to make payments under the order or his or her personal representatives and may be made against the person entitled to payments under the order or his or her personal representatives.

There is nothing in the section to limit an application by the personal representatives of the person who was liable to make the payments to changes of circumstances resulting from his death. Indeed it must be borne in mind that the only orders within the scope of section 33 under which payments will have been made in respect of a period after the death of the person liable to pay will be orders which required the deceased to make secured periodical payments in favour of a spouse or a child of the family. All other orders for periodical payments will have ceased to operate at the date of the death.[14]

---

[13] S. 33 (6).
[14] See ss. 28 (1) and 29 (4), *ante*, pp. 111, 115.

If no action to recover overpayments has been taken in the lifetime of the recipient, the effect of the section is to enable proceedings to be taken to recover payment from his or her estate. No time limit is provided in respect of such an application, but the court would be unlikely to look favourably at a stale claim.

Applications under the section may be made[15] in proceedings in the High Court or a county court for the variation or discharge of the order in question or for leave to enforce, or the enforcement of, payment of arrears under that order. As in the case of applications under section 32 (see *ante*, p. 163) applications under this section may be made to any county court, and not only to a divorce county court. Clearly, if any such proceedings are pending, it will be convenient for applications for an order for repayment to be made at the same time. But there is no requirement that applications must be made in such proceedings, and if they are not (as in the case of an application for repayment simpliciter) they must be made to a county court.

Section 38 deals with the question of repayment of sums paid to a party to a marriage under a periodical payments or secured periodical payments order after the order has ceased to have effect by reason of the remarriage of that party. If in such a case the person liable to make payments under the order or his or her personal representatives made payments in accordance with it in respect of a period after the date of the remarriage in the mistaken belief that the order was still subsisting, they are deprived by this section of any right to bring an action to recover the money paid as money paid under a mistake of fact. Instead they must make application under the section and in place of a common law right to recover overpayments in full the matter will be in the discretion of the court. It has power[16] to order the respondent to repay the amount wrongly paid in full or, if it considers that this would be unjust, it may either order payment of a lesser sum or dismiss the application.

There are similar provisions to those in section 33 dealing with the persons by and against whom application may be made,[17] the proceedings and the court in which it is to be made,[18] and the power to order repayment by specified instalments.[19] Section 38 also protects the clerk of a magistrates' court and the collecting officer under an attachment of earnings order from liability for acts done in relation to orders which have ceased to have effect by reason of remarriage, unless at the time the act was done they had received notice in writing of the remarriage.

A county court may exercise jurisdiction under both sections 33 and 38 irrespective of the amount involved,[20] and proceedings under both sections are added to the list of proceedings specified in the County Courts Act 1959, s. 109 (2) in which appeals lie as of right on a question of fact.[1]

---

[15] S. 33 (4).
[16] S. 38 (2).
[17] S. 38 (1).
[18] S. 38 (3).
[19] S. 38 (5).
[20] Ss. 33 (5) and 38 (4).
[1] Sched. 2, para. 4.

3. Transitional Provisions.

In view of the fact that the relevant parts of the law now embodied in the Act of 1973 have been in operation since January 1, 1971, it seems unnecessary to consider provisions as to petitions filed before that date.[2] It is unlikely that they will not have been disposed of by now. But mention must be made of the provisions of Part III of the First Schedule to the Act, which covers the position of orders, for example for financial provision, made under the Matrimonial Causes Act 1965, many of which will remain in force for years to come. The main points may be briefly summarized as follows:—

(a) Orders for payment of maintenance, secured or unsecured, in suits for divorce or nullity will cease to have effect on the remarriage of the recipient on or after January 1, 1971, except in relation to arrears due on the date of the remarriage.[3] There are similar provisions as to orders for alimony in suits for judicial separation, for periodical payments in those for restitution of conjugal rights or proceedings based upon wilful neglect to maintain, applicable in each case if the marriage of the parties is subsequently dissolved or annulled but the order remains in force: it will cease to do so on subsequent remarriage.[4] Application can be made under section 38 for repayment of sums paid after the remarriage, and in ignorance of it.[5]

(b) Section 31 will govern the variation, discharge, suspension and revival of orders for alimony pending suit, permanent alimony, maintenance of a spouse or child or a settlement of the wife's property.[6] In general the court will have power to vary these orders in any way in which it would have power to vary an order made under the corresponding provision of the Act of 1973.[7]

However, as is also the case under section 31:—

(i) There can be no variation of an order for payment of a lump sum.[8]

(ii) On an application to vary an order for maintenance of a spouse or child, or for permanent alimony, there is no power to order payment of a lump sum, or to make a property adjustment order under any of the provisions of section 24 of the Act.[9]

(iii) An order for variation of a settlement cannot be subsequently varied and an order for settlement of a wife's property can be varied only if it was made in proceedings for judicial separation and the application is made in proceedings for recision of that decree or for dissolution of the marriage in question.[10]

(iv) It will be possible to apply, after the death of the person liable to make the payments, for variation of an order requiring that person to

---

[2] Sched. 1, Pt. I, paras. 3 and 4.
[3] Sched. 1, Part III, para. 15 (1).
[4] *Ibid.*, para. 15 (2).
[5] *Ibid.*, para. 16.
[6] *Ibid.*, para. 17 (1). There are certain reservations as to orders made in proceedings for restitution of conjugal rights, see para. 17 (1) (a) and 18.
[7] *Ibid.*, para. 17 (2).
[8] *Ibid.*, para. 17 (1).
[9] *Ibid.*, para. 17 (3).   [10] *Ibid.*, para. 17 (1) (c) and 17 (3).

secure an annual sum or periodical payments (but not a lump sum) to any other person. The application may be made by the person entitled to payments under the order or by the personal representatives of the deceased person. But no application can be made, without the leave of the court, more than six months after representation in regard to the estate of the deceased is first taken out.[11]

(c) The court may exercise its power to make an order for financial provision for a child from time to time under the Act of 1973 notwithstanding that a previous order has been made under the Act of 1965.[12]

(d) Section 32 (which deals with leave to enforce payment of arrears and the power to remit payment of arrears) applies to proceedings to enforce orders for payment made under the Act of 1965 which are begun on or after January 1, 1971.[13]

(e) Where there has been a change in the circumstances of the person entitled to, or liable to make, payments in respect of orders (other than an order for payment of a lump sum) made under the Act of 1965, or there has been a change in circumstances resulting from the death of the person so liable, an application can be made under section 33 for an order for repayment of sums in excess of what the person liable or his person representatives should have been required to pay.[14]

(f) Where an order has been obtained under the Act of 1965 the court can exercise its powers under section 37 of the Act of 1973, to avoid transactions intended to frustrate or impede the enforcement of that order.[15]

4. Arrears and Overpayments in magistrates' courts.

In the light of the policy under the Matrimonial Proceedings and Property Act 1970 with regard to arrears and overpayments under orders made by the High Court or a divorce county court, it would clearly be wrong to permit a different policy to apply to orders made by magistrates' courts. Were this to be done the order of a magistrates' court, which can now be made without financial limit, would have obvious attractions in comparison with the order of other courts having matrimonial jurisdiction. It is for this reason that sections 30–32 (which have not been repealed or re-enacted in the Act of 1973) were included in the Act of 1970.

It has not been considered necessary to make any alteration in the powers of a magistrates' court as to enforcement of arrears. These courts have followed the practice of the High Court in not enforcing payment of arrears which become due more than twelve months before the date of the application, except in special circumstances.[16] Further, since an order for payment of money made under the Matrimonial Proceedings (Magistrates' Courts) Act 1960 is (by virtue

---

[11] *Ibid.*, para. 17 (3).
[12] *Ibid.*, para. 20.
[13] *Ibid.*, para. 22.
[14] *Ibid.*, para. 23.
[15] *Ibid.*, para. 24 (2).
[16] See *Pilcher* v. *Pilcher* (*No. 2*), [1956] 1 W.L.R. 298.

of section 13 (1) of that Act) enforceable in the same way as an affiliation order, a magistrates' court has already, under the Magistrates' Courts Act 1952, s. 76, power to remit payment of the whole or any part of the arrears which are due and unpaid on any application to enforce, revoke, revive, vary or discharge the order. This power extends also to an order of the High Court or a county court which is registered in a magistrates' court under the Maintenance Orders Act 1958.[17] However, section 32 of the Act of 1970 makes provision for the converse case in which it is sought to enforce payment in the High Court or any county court of arrears due under the order of a magistrates' court.[18] Three further subsections are added to section 13 of the Matrimonial Proceedings (Magistrates' Courts) Act 1960. These require leave to be obtained in such cases to enforce payment of arrears which became due more than twelve months before proceedings to enforce payment of them are begun, and give to the court hearing the application for the grant of leave the same powers, including the power to remit payment of arrears or any part thereof, as the court would have had in respect of orders which that court itself had made.[19]

No provisions are contained in, or inserted in, the Matrimonial Proceedings (Magistrates' Courts) Act 1960 enabling that court, or any other court, to order repayment of sums already paid, by reason of changes in the circumstances of either party other than the remarriage of the recipient.[20] As has hitherto been the case, there is not even power to remit payments of sums already paid to, but not collected from, a collecting officer.[1]

Provision is, however, made by section 30 for the case in which a recipient of payments has remarried. If the magistrates' order consisted of or contained a provision for payments for the maintenance of either spouse, and that order continued in force despite the dissolution or annulment of the marriage, the order, or the provision for payments, as the case may be, will terminate on the remarriage of the spouse in whose favour it was made (and will not be capable of being revived) unless the remarriage took place before January 1, 1971. As in other parts of the Act, a remarriage for this purpose includes a marriage which is void or voidable. Termination does not, of course, affect any arrears due at the date of the remarriage.

Similar provision is made[2] for termination on remarriage of orders made by a magistrates' court in England or Wales against a person resident in a part of Her Majesty's Dominions outside the United Kingdom and confirmed by a competent court in that part in accordance with the Maintenance Orders (Facilities for Enforcement) Act 1920, s. 3.

Section 31 of the Act of 1970 inserts a new section 13A in the Matrimonial Proceedings (Magistrates' Courts) Act 1960, dealing with repayment of sums paid after a magistrates' order (including such an order as is mentioned in the

---

[17] Maintenance Orders Act 1958, s. 3(2).
[18] As where the magistrates' order is registered in the High Court under Maintenance Orders Act 1958, s. 1.
[19] I.e. under s. 32 of the Act of 1973, see *ante,* p. 163.
[20] Contrast s. 33 of the Act of 1973, *ante,* p. 164.
[1] *Fildes* v. *Simkin,* [1960] P. 70, though since that was a case of remarriage, repayment could now be ordered on those facts under s. 31 of the Act of 1970.
[2] Act of 1970, s. 30 (2).

preceding paragraph) has ceased on remarriage. This section follows the lines of section 38 of the Act of 1973 which have already been considered. The only points which require notice appear to be as follows:—

(a) If the person against whom the order was made has died, his personal representatives can seek to recover payments made by him in his lifetime. But section 13A of the Act of 1960 (unlike section 38 of the Act of 1973) makes no reference to payments made by the personal representatives themselves after his death, because his death ends all liability to make further payments under the order.[3] On the other hand both sections enable recovery to be made from the personal representatives of the recipient of payments.[4]

(b) As under section 38, no action lies for recovery of any payments made after the order has ceased on remarriage as money paid under a mistake of fact: the only remedy is an application under the section. But this application cannot be made to a magistrates' court. It must, by virtue of section 13A (4), be made to the High Court or a county court in proceedings for leave to enforce, or for the enforcement of, payment of arrears under the order, but otherwise must be made to a county court—though not necessarily to a divorce county court. Payment of any sums directed to be repaid are not enforceable in the same way as an affiliation order,[5] but by the normal means of enforcement in the High Court or a county court. As under section 38, there are no financial limits on the power of a county court to order repayment,[6] and an appeal will lie upon a question of fact without leave.[7]

5. Maintenance Orders Acts 1950 and 1958.

By virtue of amendments made by the Act of 1973, an order for periodical or other payments made under Part II of that Act[8]

(1) are to be included among the orders to which section 16 of the Maintenance Orders Act 1950 applies, so that they will be registrable for enforcement in other parts of the United Kingdom under Part II of that Act;[9] and

(2) are to be maintenance orders within the meaning of the Maintenance Orders Act 1958, so that they will be registrable for enforcement in magistrates' courts under Part I.[10] The provisions as to attachment of earnings in Part II of that Act are, however, now replaced by the Attachment of Earnings Act 1971, which is considered in Chapter 16 in relation to enforcement of judgements.

---

[3] Compare s. 13A (1) (*b*) with s. 38 (1) (*b*).
[4] S. 13A (3) and s. 38 (1).
[5] See s. 13A (7).
[6] See s. 13A (6).
[7] Act of 1973, Sched. 2, para. 4.
[8] I.e. orders under ss. 22, 23 (1), (2) and (4) and 27 (but not, of course property adjustment orders).
[9] Sched. 2, para. 3 (1) (a).
[10] *Ibid.*, para. 10 (2), amending Sched. 8 to the Administration of Justice Act 1970 (see also s. 27 (3) of the latter Act.)

6. Bankruptcy.

It has already been pointed out that, owing to the court's discretion as to enforcement of arrears, they do not constitute a debt provable in the bankruptcy of the spouse who has failed to make payments in accordance with the order of the court.[11] It follows that discharge in bankruptcy does not release the debtor from his obligation to make payments due under that order.[12] Nevertheless, if an application is made for leave to enforce payment of arrears which became due more than twelve months before the date of the application, the bankruptcy of the respondent to that application is clearly a factor for consideration in deciding whether or not to exercise the power to remit payment of arrears under section 32 (2) of the Act. No doubt the bankruptcy will have led to accumulation of arrears; what is relevant is whether that bankruptcy was due to fault or misfortune, and the present financial circumstances of the spouses.

The power of the court, under section 24 of the Act of 1973, to order transfers of property, or a settlement of a property by husband or wife, creates special problems: if bankruptcy supervenes, should the claims of a spouse be subordinate to those of creditors? The Law Commission favoured the view which has been approved by Parliament in the Matrimonial Homes Act 1967, s. 2 (5), whereby when a spouse's rights of occupation are a charge on the estate or interest of the other spouse in a dwelling house, that charge is void against the trustee in bankruptcy of the other spouse or the personal representatives of a deceased spouse who dies insolvent. Marriage, said the Law Commission, is a form of partnership, and neither partner should compete with the partners' creditors. It follows that a transfer of the property of one spouse to the other, or to a child of the family, or the settlement of the property of one spouse for the benefit of the other or such a child, although made under the order of the court, should not prevent that settlement or transfer from being a "voluntary" settlement of property to which section 42 (1) of the Bankruptcy Act 1914 applies, and section 39 of the Act of 1973 so provides. As a result such settlements or transfers will only be unimpeachable if made at least ten years before the commencement of the bankruptcy. If less than ten but more than two years have elapsed, it will be for the beneficiaries to show that the person against whom the order was made was solvent at the date of the transfer or settlement without the aid of the property comprised in it. If it took place within two years of the commencement of the bankruptcy it will in any event be void against the trustee in bankruptcy. The expression "void" has been interpreted as meaning "voidable", so that the trustee in bankruptcy cannot recover property which has again been transferred by the recipient to a bona fide purchaser for value without notice of an act of bankruptcy on the part of the spouse against whom the order for transfer or settlement of the property was made.[13]

No corresponding provision is made in respect of instruments executed under the order of the court for the purpose of securing periodical payments for

---

[11] See *ante*, p. 162.
[12] *Kerr* v. *Kerr*, [1897] 2 Q.B. 439.
[13] *Re Hart, Ex parte Green*, [1912] 3 K.B. 6.

a spouse or a child of the family.[14] Illogically, it seems that the transfer of investments to trustees under an order of the court upon trusts to secure the payments still cannot be regarded as a "voluntary" settlement, and since the payment of arrears will not be enforced through the machinery of the court, but under the trusts of the deed of security, no leave of the court will be required under section 32 of the Act, and the court cannot preserve the settled property by remitting arrears under that section. This has always been the case, and the Act has not altered the position. Security for periodical payments thus protects a wife and children from the consequences of a husband's bankruptcy whereas an order for a settlement in their favour does not. This can no doubt be provided for in the wording of the trusts of the instrument of security. It might have been better had it been dealt with by the Act.

If the person required to make payments for a spouse or child has died, the question of voluntary settlements does not arise since section 42 of the Bankruptcy Act 1914 does not apply to the administration of an insolvent estate. Arrears of payments cannot be enforced against the estate, whether solvent or insolvent,[15] though since secured payments can be ordered to last beyond the date of the death of the person against whom the order was made, the security will continue and will not, of course, be affected by the fact that the estate was insolvent.

---

[14] See *ante*, p. 112.
[15] *Re Hedderwick*, [1933] Ch. 669; *Re Woolgar*, [1942] Ch. 318; *Re Bidie*, [1949] Ch. 121.

CHAPTER 12

ALTERATION OF MAINTENANCE AGREEMENTS AND THE AVOIDANCE OF TRANSACTIONS

This short chapter covers proceedings which may affect transactions entered into by the parties to the marriage themselves, as distinguished from the variation or discharge of orders which were made by the court itself. The power to alter maintenance agreements derived originally from the Maintenance Agreements Act 1957 and the power to set aside dispositions made for the purpose of defeating claims for financial relief from the Matrimonial Causes (Property and Maintenance) Act 1958. Both Acts had, so to speak, a common ancestry, since they were based upon recommendations in the Report of the Morton Commission.[1] The relevant provisions, with modifications, are now embodied in sections 34 to 37 of the Act of 1973.

1. Alteration of maintenance agreements.

Little advantage is taken in practice of the court's powers to alter maintenance agreements. In the year 1972, in the High Court and divorce county courts together, there were only 111 applications to alter agreements in the lifetime of the parties and 14 to do so after one of the parties to the agreement had died.[2] It seems likely that this is not to be explained by the defects in the statutory powers of the court, but rather by the fact that few such agreements are entered into in practice.

Perhaps the main reasons for this are as follows:—

    (a) From the husband's viewpoint it is difficult to advise him to reach a compromise which will avoid the expense and publicity of litigation when it is clear that the terms of the compromise will not be binding on his wife. This is the position with regard to the financial provisions of a maintenance agreement, since any provision which seeks to restrict the wife's right to apply to the court for maintenance in excess of the agreed amount has been held to be void by the House of Lords in *Hyman* v. *Hyman*.[3] Indeed it was held in *Bennett* v. *Bennett*[4]

---

[1] Cmnd. 9678 paras. 726–733 and 531–534.
[2] Civil Judicial Statistics for 1972, Cmnd. 5333, Table 10 (ii) (D).
[3] [1929] A.C. 601.
[4] [1952] 1 K.B. 249.

that unless severance was possible the presence of a covenant by a wife not to apply to the court for maintenance for herself and her son would invalidate the whole agreement. The effect of the latter decision is mitigated, from the wife's viewpoint, by section 34 (1) of the Act of 1973 whereby, as regards agreements to which the section applies, the fact that the restriction on the right to apply to the court is void is not of itself to render any other financial arrangements in the agreement void or unenforceable. From the husband's view-point this is even worse. He remains bound by the financial obliga-tions he has undertaken: she is free to go back on her agreement not to ask for more whenever she chooses to do so.

(b) The fact that the husband has regularly complied with his obligations under the agreement does not necessarily protect him from proceed-ings by his wife alleging his wilful neglect to provide reasonable maintenance for her.[5] No doubt it has strong evidential value as to what is reasonable,[6] but it is in no way conclusive if some fresh need on the part of his wife has arisen of which he has notice.[7]

(c) From the wife's viewpoint, her only remedy should the husband fail to honour his obligations under the agreement is to commence an action seeking judgment against him for the sums he has failed to pay. If, instead of reaching an agreement, she has already obtained an order from the court, it will be enforceable by the appropriate means of execution without the delay occasioned by bringing an action.

(d) The very fact that the court has power to alter the terms of the agreement gives extra force to those objections. One might cynically ask the riddle "When is an agreement not worth the paper on which it is written?", and answer "When the court has an unrestricted power to vary it."

What has been said above is intended only to suggest reasons for the comparatively small number of maintenance agreements which are entered into today and not to suggest that the parties to matrimonial discord should be kept at arm's length and dissuaded from agreement on matters upon which they may be disposed to agree. The value of agreement on matters of financial provision since the Divorce Reform Act 1969 came into operation has already been emphasised,[8] as has also the evident advantages of reaching an agree-ment in terms which fall within the statutory powers of the court and which can therefore be incorporated in an order of the court, rather than an agree-ment outside the powers of the court enforceable only by action and variable only as a maintenance agreement under sections 34 to 36 of the Act.

Be that as it may, one result of the Act of 1969 has been that parties have been encouraged to reach agreement upon matters of financial provision and property rights, particularly when it is sought to obtain the respondent's consent

---

[5] *Tulip* v. *Tulip*, [1951] P .378.
[6] *Morton* v. *Morton*, [1954] 2 All E.R. 248.
[7] *Pinnick* v. *Pinnick*, [1957] 1 All E.R. 873.
[8] See *ante*, pp. 60, 148.

to the grant of a decree of divorce after two years of life apart. The fact that the court has sanctioned an agreement whereby the wife undertakes to make no further claim to maintenance does not absolutely preclude a subsequent application by her for an award of financial provision though no doubt it is unlikely that she would succeed in the absence of some radical change in circumstances.[9] Nor does the fact that an order was made by consent prevent a later application to vary it if, for example, the husband had given his consent under a mistake as to his financial position such that but for that mistake the order would have been substantially different.[10] Since both parties must face the possibility of variation, or of some further award, whether or not the terms of their agreement are embodied in the order of the court, it is important that the statutory provisions as to variation of an agreement which has not been embodied in an order of the court should be clearly understood.

By section 34 of the Act the power to alter a maintenance agreement applies to any agreement in writing, whenever made, between the parties to a marriage, being an agreement containing financial arrangements (whether made during the continuance or after the dissolution or annulment of the marriage) or being a separation agreement which contains no financial arrangements where no other agreement in writing between the same parties contains such arrangements. For this purpose "financial arrangements" are defined as meaning provisions governing the rights and liabilities towards one another, when living separately, of the parties to a marriage (including a marriage which has been dissolved or annulled) in respect of the making or securing of payments or the disposition or use of any property, including such rights and liabilities with respect to the maintenance or education of any child, whether or not a child of the family. It will be seen that such an agreement need not be made "for the purposes of their living separately". The definition would include also an agreement made with a view to reconciliation, which could lawfully contain financial arrangements covering the position if the attempt at reconciliation should fail.[11] It was, however, held in *Young* v. *Young*[12] that since the definition required that the agreement should be "between the parties to a marriage" it could not include an agreement to which a third person was a party. The agreement in question contained provisions whereby the husband and his brother were to allow the wife to occupy a house which they jointly owned and she covenanted with both to keep the house in good repair. Such an agreement might constitute a post-nuptial settlement variable under section 24 of the Act in the event of divorce or judicial separation: but it is outside the terms of section 34.

Section 35 of the Act of 1973 deals with applications during the lifetime of the parties. If each of the parties is for the time being either domiciled or resident in England and Wales, either may apply to a divorce county court[13] for an

---

[9] *Wright* v. *Wright*, [1970] 3 All E.R. 209—a decision on s. 5 (2) of the Matrimonial Causes Act 1965.
[10] *Brister* v. *Brister*, [1970] 1 W.L.R. 664.
[11] *Harrison* v. *Harrison*, [1910] 1 K.B. 35.
[12] (1973), 117 Sol. Jo. 204.
[13] Matrimonial Causes Act 1967, s. 2 (1), as amended by the Act of 1973, Sched. 2, para. 6.

order under this section. The onus lies upon the applicant to prove one or other of two grounds. First, he may satisfy the court that by reason of a change in the circumstances in the light of which any financial arrangements contained in the agreement were made or, as the case may be, omitted from it, the agreement should be altered so as to make different or, as the case may be, so as to contain, financial arrangements. The test of what those financial circumstances were is normally an objective one, so that they include factors which reasonable spouses would have taken into account at the time when they made the agreement, though this would not exclude evidence that the parties did in fact rely upon other circumstances.[14] The section expressly provides that a change in circumstances may include a change foreseen by the parties when making the agreement, so that the case of *K.* v. *K.*[15] where it was held that this was not so, is no longer law. The alternative ground on which an application is possible is that the agreement does not contain any proper financial arrangements for any child of the family, in which case it is not necessary to prove that there has been any change in circumstances.

If satisfied as to one of these grounds, the court has power to alter the agreement by varying or revoking any financial arrangements contained in it, or by inserting in it financial arrangements for the benefit of one of the parties to the agreement or of a child of the family. But it should do so only if this would be just in all the circumstances.[16] Even if, as in *Gorman* v. *Gorman*[17] the husband's means have greatly increased and the wife's health has broken down, it might nevertheless be unjust, having regard to the nature of the provision made for the wife, including a voluntary allowance made to assist her, to alter the provision that she should not claim maintenance, which was the whole basis on which the agreement was made. Further, in deciding to make alterations for the benefit of a child of the family who is not the child of the party against whom the order is made, the court is expressly required to have regard to the matters laid down in section 25 (3) in relation to financial provision for such a child.[18]

A magistrates' court has also jurisdiction to alter maintenance agreements if both parties to the agreement are resident in England and Wales and at least one is resident in the petty sessions area for which the court acts. But its powers are limited to the insertion, increase, reduction or termination of provisions for periodical payments, and it cannot make alterations of any other kind.[19]

Subsections (4) and (5) of section 35 ensure that when the court alters an agreement by inserting a provision for the making or securing of periodical payments for a spouse or child, the term for which these payments, or the increase in these payments, can continue cannot exceed the maximum term laid

---

[14] *Gorman* v. *Gorman*, [1964] 3 All E.R. 739.
[15] *K.* v. *K.*, [1961] 2 All E.R. 266.
[16] S. 35 (2); *Ratcliffe* v. *Ratcliffe*, [1962] 3 All E.R. 993.
[17] *Supra.*
[18] See *ante*, p. 147.
[19] S. 35 (3).
[20] See *ante*, p. 111.

down by section 28 (1) in respect of a spouse 20,, or by section 29 (2) and (3) in respect of a child.[1] Thus, if, for example, the original agreement provided for unsecured payments by the husband to his wife for her life, and the court decided to increase these payments, the *increase* in the payments (unlike those originally agreed) could not last beyond joint lives if unsecured (or the wife's life if secured) and would in any event terminate on her remarriage. Likewise payments, or increased payments, to a child, could only last beyond the age of 18 in the special circumstances mentioned in section 29 (3). It should also be noticed that although, since the Maintenance Orders Act 1968, there has been no financial limit on the powers of a magistrates' court in relation to the alteration of a maintenance agreement, the maximum term of any payments, or any increase in the payments, ordered by such a court will be governed by subsections (4) and (5) of section 35 as above.

If the agreement continues despite the death of one of the parties to it and that party died domiciled in England and Wales, section 36 (1) now enables an application to alter the agreement to be made by the personal representatives of the deceased party, as well as by the surviving party. This follows the pattern of section 31 (6) in relation to secured periodical payments, which has already been noticed,[2] and enables the payments to be increased or decreased according to the resources of the deceased's estate. An application cannot be made under section 36, except with the permission of the High Court or a county court, after the end of six months from the date on which representation in regard to the estate of the deceased is first taken out.

A magistrates' court has no power to order an alteration after the death of a party. A county court (not necessarily a divorce county court) has no jurisdiction to entertain such an application, or an application for permission to make an application, unless it would have jurisdiction by virtue of section 7 of the Family Provision Act 1966 to entertain an application for provision out of the estate of a former spouse, i.e. it can deal only with cases in which the value of the deceased's net estate does not exceed £5,000 or such larger sum as may be fixed by the Lord Chancellor.[3]

Whereas it is clear from section 31 (5) that the court cannot vary an *order* for periodical payments to a spouse by inserting an order for payment of a lump sum,[4] there appears to be nothing in sections 34 to 36 to prevent the High Court or a county court from altering a maintenance agreement by inserting an order for a lump sum payment. Indeed section 35 (2) expressly provides that the agreement may be altered "by inserting in it financial arrangements for the benefit of one of the parties to the agreement or of a child of the family". By contrast section 35 (3) limits the powers of a magistrates' court to periodical payments.

---

[1] See *ante*, p. 115.
[2] See *ante*, p. 161.
[3] S. 36 (3). S. 7 (3) of the Act of 1966, as to transfer of applications from the High Court to a county court, is also made applicable by s. 36 (7) and by Sched. 2, para. 4 an appeal from the decision of the county court judge on a question of fact lies without leave.
[4] See *ante*, p. 159.

2. Avoidance of transactions.

The object of section 37 of the Act is to prevent either spouse from disposing of property with the intention of defeating the claim of the other spouse for financial relief for himself or herself, or for the benefit of any child of the family. For this purpose financial relief includes:—

(a) Maintenance pending suit under section 22.

(b) Periodical or lump sum payments for a spouse or for the benefit of a child in suits for divorce, nullity or judicial separation under section 23, or under section 27 in cases of wilful neglect to maintain.

(c) Adjustment of property rights under section 24.

(d) Variation of orders in the lifetime of both spouses under section 31, but not variations after the death of either under section 31 (6).

(e) Alteration of maintenance agreements during the lifetime of both spouses under section 35, but not after the death of either under section 36.

The intention to defeat the applicant's claim for financial relief may take various forms. The disposition may have been intended to prevent financial relief being granted to the applicant, or to the applicant for the benefit of a child of the family, or to reduce the amount of the relief which might be granted, or to frustrate the enforcement of any order which might be or has been made.[5]

An application under section 37 may be made by either husband or wife, but cannot be made by a child of the family or some third party on the child's behalf. It can be made in respect of any disposition other than a provision in a will or codicil and other than a disposition made before January 1, 1968. But no order can be made in respect of a disposition made for valuable consideration (other than marriage) to a person who, at the time of the disposition, acted in good faith and without notice of any intention to defeat the applicant's claim. The section envisages three situations:—

(1) Where proceedings are brought for any of the forms of financial relief mentioned above, and an application is made in these proceedings. If the court is then satisfied that the other party has, with the intention of defeating that claim, made a disposition of any property and that if that disposition were set aside, financial relief, or different financial relief, would be granted to the applicant, it may make an order setting aside the disposition and give consequential directions. Thus if a husband had disposed of capital assets by way, for example, of a gift to his mistress, so that he was left only with his earnings and without capital with which to give security for periodical payments to his wife, or to her for the benefit of a child of the family, the court could set aside the gift and give directions, if necessary, for some payment by the mistress or disposal by her of property and thus enable a different provision—secured instead of unsecured—to be made.

---

[5] S. 37 (1).

(2) Where the applicant has already obtained an order for financial relief, and the disposition is intended to prevent the enforcement of that order, or to deprive the other party of the means of complying with it. Here the court can take the same action as in (1) above.

(3) Where no disposition has yet been made, but the applicant can satisfy the court that the other party is, with the intention of defeating the claim for financial relief, about to make any disposition or transfer property out of the jurisdiction, or otherwise deal with it. Here the court can make such order as it thinks fit restraining the other party from so doing or otherwise for protecting the claim.

Subsection (5) deals with the onus of proof. In cases (1) and (2), if the disposition took place three years or more before the date of the application, the onus is upon the applicant to satisfy the court of the existence of the necessary intention to defeat the claim. In all other cases (that is to say if the disposition took place less than three years before the date of the application or if the application relates to a disposition which is about to take place), then if the court is satisfied in cases (1) and (3) that it would have the consequence of defeating the claim, or in case (2) above that it has had that consequence, it is to be presumed that the other party had or has that intention, and the onus is on him to prove the contrary.

CHAPTER 13

PROTECTION AND WELFARE OF CHILDREN

When a marriage has broken down it is generally the children who are likely to suffer most, both from the discord in the family prior to the final breakdown and the psychological effects of the disturbance in their lives. In many cases questions concerning their custody and upbringing are foremost in the minds of parties to the marriage and are hotly disputed; in other case the parties may be indifferent to the welfare of the children. But in all cases these matters cannot be left entirely to the wishes of the parties, and the Act gives the court extensive powers to ensure, so far as this is practicable, that the arrangements which are made are satisfactory. These powers apply not only to children of the parties themselves, including their illegitimate and adopted children, but to all children of the family, the definition of whom has already been considered.[1] The statutory provisions concerning ancillary and non-ancillary financial provision for children, and adjustment of property rights for their benefit, have been described in Chapters 7 to 10. It is now necessary to consider other matters.

1. Custody and education of children.

Among the results of the reduction of the age of majority from twenty-one to eighteen by the Family Law Reform Act 1969 is the fact that, although the court's powers in relation to financial provision and property adjustments may in certain circumstances extend beyond the age of eighteen, the powers in relation to custody and education cannot in any circumstances extend beyond that age.

Section 42 enables the court to make such orders as it thinks fit for the custody and education of any child of the family who is under the age of eighteen, in any proceedings for divorce, nullity or judicial separation, before or on granting a decree or at any time thereafter (whether, in the case of divorce or nullity, before or after the decree is made absolute), and also where such proceedings are dismissed after the beginning of the trial,[2] either forthwith or within a reasonable time thereafter. For this purpose "custody" of a child includes access to the child and "education" includes training.[3] These powers may be

---

[1] See *ante*, p. 113.
[2] As to the meaning of this expression see *P. (L. E.)* v. *P. (J. M.)*, [1971] P. 318.
[3] S. 52 (1).

exercised from time to time, and when an order is made on the dismissal of a suit, a further order may be made from time to time until the child attains the age of eighteen.[4] The court is also expressly empowered to discharge or vary an order, or to suspend any provision in the order temporarily, and to revive the operation of any provision so suspended.[5]

Although the powers of the court in relation to custody continue until the age of eighteen, it is not the practice of the court to make or enforce an order against the wishes of a child who has reached years of discretion which, for this purpose, means beyond the age of sixteen, unless there are exceptional circumstances.[6] The reason is that there is no order against the child personally, so that if the child reaches years of discretion when an order is already in force and of its own accord returns to the parent who has been deprived of custody, the court will not order the parent to return the child; this would be pointless since there would be nothing to prevent the child returning to the parent against whom the order was made.[7]

The principle upon which these matters of custody and upbringing are to be determined is laid down by the Guardianship of Minors Act 1971, s. 1, as amended by the Guardianship Act 1973, whereby the court is to regard the welfare of the minor as the first and paramount consideration and not to take into consideration whether from any other point of view the claim of the father, is superior to that of the mother, or the claim of the mother superior to that of the father. Further, by section 1 (1) of the latter Act, in relation to the custody and upbringing of a minor, a mother has the same rights and authority as the law allows to a father, and the rights and authority of mother and father are equal and exercisable by either without the other. This principle prevails even over a contrary order by a competent foreign court;[8] the English court will pay regard to that order but can make a different order if it considers that the child would otherwise suffer serious harm.[9] Regard for the child's welfare may even prevail over the principle of estoppel *per rem judicatam*. It was held in *Hull* v. *Hull*[10] that if an issue had been decided in a divorce suit between the father and the mother, upon which the judge either decided to grant a decree or reject it, then both the father and the mother were bound by that decision even in the custody proceedings, and could not be heard to give any evidence to show that the decision was wrong. But in *F.* v. *F.*[11] both SALMON and SACHS, L.JJ., without deciding the point, expressed doubts whether this decision was correct if the result might be contrary to the interests of the child. There is, of course, no estoppel as to matters which were not decided at the hearing of the suit.[12]

---

[4] S. 42 (6).
[5] S. 42 (7).
[6] *Hall* v. *Hall* (1945), 62 T.L.R. 151.
[7] *Stark* v. *Stark and Hitchins*, [1910] P. 190.
[8] *McKee* v. *McKee*, [1951] A.C. 352, P.C.
[9] *Re E. (D) (an infant)*, [1967] Ch. 761—a wardship case.
[10] [1960] P. 118.
[11] [1968] 2 All E.R. 946. These dicta were not apparently cited to BRANDON, J. in *Gower* v. *Gower*, [1970] 1 W.L.R. 1556, where he held that the principle of estoppel applied to findings both of cruelty and as to the paternity of a child in custody proceedings following an undefended divorce suit.
[12] *Tumath* v. *Tumath*, [1970] P. 78; and see *ante*, p. 50.

Where the conduct of one of the spouses has been entirely or mainly responsible for the breakdown of the marriage it may well be that the welfare of the child will be better served by giving custody of the other spouse. But there is no rule of thumb in these matters. It was at one time considered that a mother who had committed adultery (the "scarlet" woman of the Victorian era) could never be allowed custody of or access to a child.[13] There is no such rule today, and if the child's happiness depends upon being with her mother, for whom she has great affection, and this will not lead to contact with undesirable influences, the mother, against whom the decree was obtained, may be awarded custody.[14] In many cases it may be right to say that the welfare of a young child requires that it should be in the care of its mother. In such cases, if the breakdown is due to the fault of the mother the court sometimes orders that the child should remain in the care and control of the mother until further order, but that custody shall be given to the father, thus giving him a greater say in matters such as the child's education and upbringing than he would otherwise have had. But once again there is no rule to the effect that a young child must remain with the mother: the welfare of the child may be the first and paramount consideration but it is not the only consideration. In *Re L. (an infant)*,[15] where the father was blameless and well able to provide for the care of the children, and the breakdown of the marriage was entirely due to the mother's adultery, it was held that in view of her conduct the father should have both custody and care and control. In recent years, the practice has grown up in some cases of making a joint order for both parents to have custody, with care and control to one parent only, thus preserving the right of both to have an equal voice in decisions as to the child's future. Such an order is appropriate only where there is a reasonable prospect that they will co-operate sensibly over the welfare of the children and give affection and wise guidance to them.[16] The parties to a marriage which has ceased to exist as a marriage may yet remain on terms of friendship.

What has been said above applies in the main to orders made after the hearing of the suit. Pending the hearing the usual practice is not to attempt to pre-judge the case but to preserve the *status quo*, unless the welfare of the children otherwise requires.[17] Once the petition has been filed, although it has not yet been served, the petitioner may apply ex parte for an injunction restraining the respondent from taking the children out of the jurisdiction or, if this has already occurred, for a mandatory injunction requiring them to be returned.[18]

When the court gives custody to one party it will usually allow the other party reasonable access to the child. The Court of Appeal has said that this is the basic right of every parent and should not be refused except in most unusual circumstances. As WILLMER, L.J. put it, merely to say of a woman that she is a bad wife or mother, while it may be an excellent reason for not giving her care

---

[13] *Clout* v. *Clout* (1861), 2 Sw. & Tr. 391.
[14] *Allen* v. *Allen*, [1948] 2 All E.R. 413; *Willoughby* v. *Willoughby*, [1951] P. 184.
[15] [1962] 3 All E.R. 1; see also *Re F. (an infant) F.* v. *F.*, [1969] 2 Ch. 238.
[16] *Jussa* v. *Jussa*, [1972] 2 All E.R. 600, D.C.
[17] *Boyt* v. *Boyt*, [1948] 2 All E.R. 436.
[18] *Fabbri* v. *Fabbri*, [1962] 1 All E.R. 35.

and control, is not sufficient ground for depriving her of any kind of access.[19] In such a case, where the spouse who has been granted access has committed adultery, the order may, in the child's interests, be made subject to the condition that the child shall not be brought into contact with the person with whom the adultery is committed. Whether the principle that access should be granted almost as of right is wise does seem to be open to question. It often exposes a child to continual competition by the parents for the child's affection, which might better be avoided by insistence upon a complete break. This point is emphasised by the decision in *M*. v. *M*.,[20] which in a sense departs from the principle laid down by the Court of Appeal that access is the basic right of every parent in favour of the principle that it is the basic right of the child, and not the parent. If contact with a parent leads to emotional and psychological disturbance, the welfare of the child demands that access be discontinued, at all events for the time being. A similar decision was reached by the Court of Appeal in *B*. v. *B*.,[1] where a father who was in no way unfit to have access was denied it because his son was determined not to resume contact with his father.

The position when the proceedings are not for one of the principal decrees, but for wilful neglect to provide reasonable maintenance, is governed by section 42 (2). If the court makes an order under section 27 of the Act, whether it is made on the ground of wilful neglect to maintain the applicant, or wilful neglect to maintain or contribute towards the maintenance of a child of the family, the court is given power from time to time to make orders for custody of any child of the family who is for the time being under the age of eighteen. But this power and any order made in pursuance of it can continue only whilst the order under section 27 remains in force and the child is under that age. The threat posed to a husband who is failing to maintain his wife is evident: should he fail to do so the custody of his children may be taken from him.

Whether the order is sought in proceedings for divorce, nullity, or judicial separation, or in proceedings relating to wilful neglect to maintain, provision has been made for the fact that a child may be a child of the family if it has been treated by both the spouses as such, although they have not adopted it and it is the child of some other person or persons. In such a case the Act[2] preserves the rights of the natural parents by providing that an order under the section shall not affect the rights over or with respect to the child of any person, other than a party to the marriage in question, unless the child is the child of one or both of the parties to that marriage and that person was a party to the proceedings on the application for an order under the section. Thus if the child is the child of neither spouse, but they have cared for it as one of the family without adopting it, the rights of the natural parents are in no way affected by any order which the court may have made. If the child is the child of one of the spouses only and has not been adopted by them or either of them (as in the case of a child of one spouse by a previous marriage which has been

---

[19] *S*. v. *S and P*., [1962] 2 All E.R. 1.
[20] [1973] 2 All E.R. 81, D.C.
[1] [1971] 3 All E.R. 682, C.A.
[2] S. 42 (5).

dissolved or the illegitimate child of one spouse by some third person) the other parent is in no way bound by the order unless he or she has been made a party to the proceedings.

2. Additional powers in special cases.

Cases arise from time to time in which the powers outlined above are insufficient to ensure adequate protection of the interests of a child. In such cases there are a number of further steps which the court may take.

(a) Instead of making an order in a suit for divorce, nullity or judicial separation, it may instead if it thinks fit direct that proceedings be taken for making the child a ward of court.[3] This wardship will continue until the age of eighteen, though by the Family Law Reform Act 1969, s. 6, either parent may be ordered to continue payments for the maintenance and education of the ward up to the age of twenty-one. Whilst the wardship continues the consent of the court will be required to the marriage of the ward and decisions as to such matters as custody and education of the ward must be sanctioned by the court. The conflict which has sometimes appeared in the past between the wardship jurisdiction of the Chancery Division and the custody jurisdiction of the Probate Divorce and Admiralty Division[4] have been ended since, by virtue of the Administration of Justice Act 1970, s. 1, both the matrimonial and the wardship jurisdiction of the High Court are now vested in the Family Division.

(b) When the court makes, or makes absolute, a decree of divorce or makes a decree of judicial separation it may include in the decree a declaration that either party to the marriage is unfit to have the custody of the children of the family. The result will be that, if the person to whom the declaration relates is a parent of any child of the family that person will not, on the death of the other parent, be entitled as of right to the custody or the guardianship of that child.[5]

(c) If there are exceptional circumstances making it impracticable or undesirable for the child to be entrusted to either of the parties to the marriage or to any other individual, the court may make an order committing the child to the care of the local authority for the area in which the child was resident before the order was made. Such an order cannot be made without first hearing representations from the local authority including any representations as to the making of a financial provision order in favour of the child; it cannot be made after the child has reached the age of seventeen and will cease at the age of eighteen.[6]

(d) Where it appears to the court that there are exceptional circumstances

---

[3] S. 42 (1).
[4] See *Re Andrews, Sullivan* v. *Andrews*, [1958] Ch. 665; *Hall* v. *Hall*, [1963] P. 378.
[5] S. 42 (3) and (4).
[6] S. 43. As to s. 43 (2) see Law Com. No. 51 (Cmnd. 5167). Representations can now include those for an order for a lump sum payment or secured periodical payment.

making it desirable that the child should be under the supervision of an independent person the court may order that, as respects any period during which the child is committed to the custody of any person, it be under the supervision of a court welfare officer or a local authority.[7]

3. Restrictions on decrees.

It remains to consider section 41 of the Act, the object of which is to ensure that the marriage shall not be ended, or a decree of judicial separation granted, unless the court is satisfied that proper arrangements have been made, so far as this is possible, for the welfare of the children of the family.

The section applies to every minor child of the family who is under the age of sixteen or is receiving instruction at an educational establishment or undergoing training for any trade, profession or vocation, whether or not he is also in gainful employment. Further, the court is given power to direct that it shall apply to any other child of the family, whether of full age or not, if it considers that there are special circumstances making this desirable in the interest of the child,[8] as might be the case if, for example, the child suffered from some severe mental or physical disability. The court is precluded from making absolute a decree of divorce or nullity, or from granting a decree of judicial separation, unless it has by order declared that it is satisfied that at the date of the order there are no children of the family to whom the section applies or that the only children who are or may be children of the family to whom the section applies are the children named in the order and either arrangements have been made for the welfare of each such child which are satisfactory or the best that can be devised in the circumstances, or that it is impracticable for the party or parties appearing before the court to make any such arrangements.[9] Where, however, there are circumstances making it desirable that the decree should be made absolute (or granted, as the case may be) without delay although the court is unable to declare that it is satisfied as to these matters, it may instead make an order stating that this is so provided that it has first obtained a satisfactory undertaking from either or both of the parties to bring the question of the arrangements for the children named in the order before the court within a specified time.[10]

The expression "welfare" in the section is widely defined. It includes both custody of and access to the child, the education and training of the child and financial provision for him or her.[11] The order can only be made by the judge and in an undefended case the consideration of these matters will usually occupy considerably more time than will the question of whether or not a decree shall be granted. If a decree of divorce or nullity is made absolute, or a decree of judicial separation is granted without the requisite order under the section

---

[7] S. 44.
[8] S. 41 (5).
[9] S. 41 (41) (a) and (b).
[10] S. 41 (1) (c) and 41 (2).
[11] Ss. 41 (6) and 52 (1).

having been made, the decree is void: but if such an order was made, no-one is entitled to challenge the validity of the decree on the ground that conditions prescribed by the section were not satisfied.[12]

Certain points on this section require notice:—

(a) It was held in *P. v. P.*[13] under the Matrimonial Causes Act 1965, s. 33, that failure to comply with the requirements as to declarations concerning the care and upbringing of children rendered the marriage voidable rather than void, a situation which arose owing to the failure to disclose to the court the birth of a child of the marriage between decree nisi and decree absolute of divorce. At first sight the provisions of section 41 that the decree shall be void, rather than voidable, if the decree is made absolute without the requisite order having been made, appear likely to have more serious consequences. But in fact the section contains safeguards to ensure that they will not arise.

(b) The court is required *by order* to declare that it is satisfied, either that for the purposes of the section there are no children of the family to whom the section applies, or that the only children who are *or may be* such children of the family are the children named in the order.[14] If such an order has been made, no person is entitled to challenge the validity of the decree on the ground that the conditions have not been satisfied. Thus the existence, unknown to the court, of another child of the family, or the birth of such a child after the order was made, but before decree absolute, would not invalidate the order or the decree. Further, if at the time when the court was asked to consider the matter there was an unresolved dispute as to the paternity of a child born to the wife, and consequently as to whether or not it was a child of the family, it would not be necessary to delay the making of the order, or the decree absolute, until that dispute was resolved. The order could state that the child "may be" a child of the family and that, whether or not this is so, the court is satisfied as to its welfare.

(c) The order of the court must also declare that it is satisfied that arrangements have been made for the welfare of every child so named which are satisfactory or are the best that can be devised in the circumstances or that it is impracticable for the party or parties appearing before the court to make any such arrangements. If the court refuses to make that order it is bound, on the application of either party, to make an order declaring that it is not so satisfied.[15] Thus, in whichever way the court may decide any question concerning the children to whom the section applies or the arrangements made for them, there will be an order against which either party will be able to appeal.

---

[12] S. 41 (3).
[13] [1971] P. 217.
[14] S. 14 (1).
[15] S. 41 (4).

A Report from Mr. John Hall, of St. John's College, Cambridge, published by the Law Commission as Working Paper No. 15, revealed weaknesses in the operation of these statutory provisions in force before the Act of 1970. It was not so much that the arrangements approved by judges were unsatisfactory (though some judges did not often avail themselves of the power to seek the assistance of a welfare officer), but that the arrangements which they did approve were often not carried out. In a sample of thirty-seven cases in which the decree nisi had been pronounced about twelve months previously, six of the persons who should have had the custody of a child refused to be visited, four could not be traced, and in one case the address at which the children were said in the petition to be living did not even exist. Of the remaining twenty-six cases, in only sixteen were the actual arrangements exactly as approved by the court. These seem to be difficulties which can only be solved by greater use of the power to order supervision by a welfare officer, though it will no doubt be helpful that the Rules now require much fuller information to be supplied to the court when the arrangements for the children are being considered.

CHAPTER 14

COSTS

The grant or refusal of costs is always in the court's discretion. As regards proceedings in the Supreme Court the matter is governed by the Supreme Court of Judicature (Consolidation) Act 1925, s. 50 (1) whereby "Subject . . . to rules of court and to the express provisions of any other Act, the costs of and incidental to all proceedings in the Supreme Court . . . shall be in the discretion of the court or a judge, and the court or judge shall have full power to determine by whom and to what extent the costs are to be paid." As regards proceedings in a county court, a similar principle is applied by Order 47, r. 1 of the County Court Rules 1936, whereby "Subject to the provisions of any Act or Rule, the cost of proceedings in a county court shall be in the discretion of the court."

Emphasis upon the court's discretion was focussed by the decision in *Gooday* v. *Gooday*[1] where the Court of Appeal shared the views of Lord Dip-lock when he said, "I do not accept that in the 1960's there should be any settled practice peculiar to the Divorce Division from which judges are not entitled to depart." Nevertheless the Court of Appeal in that case did draw a distinction between the general discretion referred to above and the particular question of quantum where the party in question is in receipt of legal aid.

Where an appeal relates to the question of whether any, and if so which, of the parties should be ordered to pay costs and (if the party in question is not legally aided, the amount for which he should be made liable) the right of an appellate court to interfere with the decision of the court below is governed by the decision of the House of Lords in *Donald Campbell & Co.* v. *Pollak*.[2] In that case Viscount Cave, L.C.[3] emphasised that an appellate court was entitled to interfere, whether or not leave to appeal was required, if the judge had exercised his discretion for some reason unconnected with the nature of the case. But he continued—

> "Where a judge, deliberately intending to exercise his discretionary powers, has acted on facts connected with or leading up to the litigation which had been proved before him or which he has himself observed during the progress of the case, a Court of Appeal, although it may deem his reasons insufficient and may disagree with his conclusion, is prohibited by the statute from entertaining an appeal from it."

---

[1] [1969] P. 1, 6.
[2] [1927] A.C. 732. In relation to the High Court, but not (it seems) a county court there is a statutory prohibition of appeals for an order as to costs only without leave (Judicature Act 1925, s. 31 (1) (*h*)).
[3] At pp. 811–812.

Where the party against whom the court proposes to make an order as to costs is legally aided, a further factor becomes relevant, in that the Legal Aid and Advice Act 1949, s. 2 (2) (e) provides that—

"Where a person receives legal aid in connection with any proceedings . . . (e) his liability by virtue of an order for costs made against him with respect to the proceedings shall not exceed the amount (if any) which is a reasonable one for him to pay having regard to all the circumstances, including the means of all the parties and their conduct in connection with the dispute."

The Court of Appeal in *Gooday* v. *Gooday* accordingly felt able to vary the amount of the costs for which an unsuccessful wife petitioner who was legally aided should be held liable, although the court was unable to question (and indeed did not wish to question) the decision, in the judge's discretion, that she should pay costs.

The reasoning in *Gooday* v. *Gooday* is obviously relevant in relation to the decision in *Nowotnik* v. *Nowotnik*.[4] The Court of Appeal was called upon in the latter case to consider whether the costs of an unassisted husband who successfully defended divorce proceedings brought against him by his legally aided wife should be paid out of public funds under the Legal Aid Act 1964. The husband satisfied three of the four conditions laid down in that Act. The proceedings were instituted against him, it would have been just and equitable that his costs should have been paid from public funds, and he would have suffered severe financial hardship if an order that this should be done was not made. Nevertheless the Court of Appeal refused to order that his costs should be so paid on the ground that he had failed to prove the fourth requirement because, apart from the Act, no order would normally be made for an unsuccessful wife petitioner to pay her husband's costs in defending the suit. The Court of Appeal in *Hanning* v. *Maitland (No. 2)*[5] regarded such matrimonial proceedings as a special case, and for that reason only saw no reason to criticize the decision in *Nowotnik* v. *Nowotnik*. This difficulty has since been considered by the Divisional Court in *Povey* v. *Povey*[6] where Sir JOCELYN SIMON, P. suggested that the cases might be reconciled because

"although there is now no special practice in matrimonial causes that an impecunious, or nearly impecunious, wife, should not have an order for costs made against her, there is equally no general practice in matrimonial causes that costs should follow the event, because there are many cases in which such an order would be inappropriate . . ."

(a) *Costs as between husband and wife.*

Historically there is no doubt that there "has been a settled practice of the Divorce Court, going back for many years well into the last century, not to

---

[4] [1967] P. 83.
[5] [1970] 1 Q.B. 580.
[6] [1972] Fam. 40, at p. 52.

make an order for costs against an impecunious wife and in favour of a husband who has means".[7] The reasons for the end of that practice are clearly stated by WIDGERY, L.J.:—

> "But I respectfully agree with DIPLOCK, L.J., that, if that ever was more than a simple rule of practice, it has no place in the twentieth century. In these days, when wives are frequently skilled women who can earn as much, if not more than, their husbands, there is no reason at all why one should start with any kind of presumption in favour of one against the other when these matters arise."[8]

It is the same reasoning which has led to the abolition by section 41 of the Matrimonial Proceedings and Property Act 1970, of the wife's agency of necessity, as distinguished from any presumption of agency arising from cohabitation or from the fact that the husband had held out his wife as having authority to pledge his credit. With it, by section 41 (2), has perished the rule whereby if, in a case of judicial separation, alimony has been ordered but has not been paid by the husband, he is liable to for necessaries supplied for the use of his wife.[9] The wife's agency of necessity enabled her to pledge her husband's credit in respect of the costs of matrimonial proceedings brought against him, unless she had sufficant means of her own or had been guilty herself of adultery which had not been condoned or connived at by her husband. But as STABLE, J., said in *Nabarro & Sons* v. *Kennedy*,[10] which was a case concerned with the question of such costs:—

> "This right of a wife, her right at common law, goes back in our social history to the time when a woman was, for practical purposes, a chattel, and, when the husband took the wife, he took, not only the woman, but everything which she had, with the result that, if he did not provide for her, she had no means of providing for herself."

What is more, as the Law Commission observed,[11] the continued existence of the right could have deprived a legally aided husband of the protection afforded by section 2 (2) (*e*) of the Legal Aid and Advice Act 1949.[12] The court, under that section, might order him to pay to his wife only such part of her costs as it was reasonable for him to pay. But she could have pledged his credit, and her solicitors could have held him liable in contract, for the whole of their solicitor-and-own-client costs.

The result of what has been said above is that the law is not quite as the Morton Commission said it should be[13]—"We recommend that in respect of liability for costs of matrimonial proceedings husband and wife should now be

---

[7] *Per* WILLMER, L.J. in *Gooday* v. *Gooday, supra,* at p. 11.

[8] *Ibid.,* at p. 9.

[9] These changes, including the repeal of Matrimonial Causes Act 1965, s. 20 (4), took effect on August 1, 1970.

[10] [1954] 2 All E.R. 605, 606.

[11] Working Paper No. 9, para. 108, reprinted in Law Com. No. 25, Appendix II, at p. 132.

[12] See *ante,* p. 188.

[13] Comd. 9678, paras. 438, 460.

treated on exactly the same footing." The reason is best explained in the words of Sir JOCELYN SIMON in *Povey* v. *Povey*:—[14]

> "But this is not to say that any practice in matrimonial causes that in the absence of special circumstances an unsuccessful litigant wife should have her costs against her husband, or at least that no order for costs should be made against her, are to be replaced by a general practice that costs should follow the event. This will often be inappropriate because unjust: the wife may be entirely dependent on the husband; because with the functional division of labour between husband and wife, she may have sacrificed her own financial or economic prospects in order to free him to pursue his: . . . Social developments, in nullifying much of the rationale underlying the former special practice in matrimonial causes, have left the judge's discretion . . . entirely untrammelled."

Thus far what has been said applies equally to all matrimonial causes, whether the proceedings are for divorce, nullity, or judicial separation. There remains the question of the attitude which the court will take, in the exercise of its discretion as to costs, now that the irretrievable breakdown of the marriage is the only ground for divorce. Where the petition is dismissed it is likely that the court will, in the absence of special circumstances, lean towards an award of costs to the successful party, whether that party be husband or wife. But where the petition succeeds much will depend upon which of the facts enumerated in section 1 (2) of the Act of 1973 was relied upon and proved by the petitioner in support of the allegation of irretrievable breakdown.

Taking first cases where reliance is placed, under section 1 (2) (*d*), on two years' separation and the respondent's consent to the grant of a decree, Sir George BAKER, P. in *Hymns* v. *Hymns* [15] laid down the principle that it does not follow that, because in such cases no fault is attributable to either party, nobody, and in particular a respondent husband, should pay any costs. On the facts of that case he ordered that each party should pay half the costs of the petition.

This decision can lead to difficulties in cases involving legal aid, and there may be some 13,000 legal aid certificates granted in "consent" cases in a single year.[16] Where the wife is the petitioner and her means are such that she can obtain legal aid, her husband, though financially well able to pay costs, is likely to refuse his consent except upon terms that the petition contains no prayer for costs, in which case the court will have no power to award them. Indeed, in a case of this kind, there is an obvious temptation for the parties, both of whom want a divorce, to agree that the wife shall petition and the husband give his consent subject to the condition that the wife shall refrain from claiming costs, thus throwing the whole cost of the proceedings onto the Legal Aid Fund. This situation was examined in detail by Sir George BAKER in *Beales* v. *Beales*.[17]

---

[14] [1972] Fam. 40, at p. 51.
[15] [1971] 3 All E.R. 596.
[16] See *Beales* v. *Beales*, [1972] Fam. 210, at p. 216.
[17] [1972] Fam. 210.

The President did not resile from the view he expressed in *Hymns* v. *Hymns* that in consent cases each party should pay half the costs. It was a sound general principle which could continue to apply where the husband, or wife, respondent is able to pay. There is no objection to including a prayer for "half the costs" in the petition. But if legal aid were to be refused to an impecunious wife merely because her husband would give his consent only if he was freed from liability for costs, she would be compelled to rely upon proof of adultery, unreasonable conduct, or desertion, which might lead to a contested suit, or to wait until the separation had lasted for five years. Legal aid could not be refused on the ground that it appeared unreasonable that she should receive it,[18] for she has done nothing unreasonable, save perhaps in an exceptional case in which the agreement as to costs has been reached at the wife's instigation in order to leave her husband with more money to make financial provision for her. In the result the President reached the following conclusions:—

(1) Nothing should be done to discourage consent cases or to force the parties to make accusations against each other merely to decide a question of costs.

(2) The court has no right to intervene on the question of costs except in very special circumstances, as where improper pressure has been put by one spouse upon the other.

(3) Costs are questions inter partes, and now that collusion is no longer a bar to proceedings for divorce, there is no need to submit an agreement about costs for the approval of the court.

(4) The fact that the petitioner is legally aided can make no difference in view of the express provision in section 7 (1) of the Legal Aid and Advice Act 1949, whereby this fact is not to affect the rights or liabilities of other parties to the proceedings or the principles on which the court's discretion is normally exercised.

(5) A respondent cannot be forced to give an unconditional consent to a decree being granted and cannot be prevented from withdrawing his consent up to the moment when a decree nisi is granted.

(6) If, after such persuasion as is administratively possible, a respondent will consent only on condition that he pays no costs, this will generally have to be accepted.

His Lordship added that no effective or acceptable means of protecting the Legal Aid Fund had yet been discovered, with the result that the costs of such a consensual divorce will, subject to any contribution by the petitioner, have to be borne by the fund and not by the affluent respondent who is well able to pay them. The burden on the fund in such cases has, however, been considerably reduced by the new Rules whereby undefended divorce cases based upon consent where there are no children of the family to whom section 41 of the Act applies are dealt with by a registrar upon affidavit evidence.[19]

---

[18] See Legal Aid (General) Regulations 1971, reg. 7 (*f*).
[19] See *ante*, pp. 40, 41 and Rule 48.

The position as to costs in cases in which reliance is placed upon five years' separation under section 1 (2) (*e*) is dealt with by the decision of the Court of Appeal in *Chapman* v. *Chapman*.[20] The court held that in such cases the petition should not contain any allegation of fault against the respondent and the court should not inquire into whose fault it was that the marriage had broken down. This would lead to mutual recriminations in open court and often to an answer containing counter allegations, so that the case would become a defended case to be tried in the High Court solely to decide, at much expense, the question of who should pay the costs. Having held that in a five-year case fault should not be made the basis of any order as to costs, Lord DENNING, in giving the judgment of the court, continued[1]

> "This being so, is there any other basis on which an order should be made for costs? Take the ... case when a husband is the petitioner in a five-year case, wishing to marry another woman. No-one would suggest that the wife should pay his costs. He is the one who wants the divorce. He should pay the costs of it ... I see no reason whatever for differentiating between a wife and a husband in this regard. If a wife seeks a divorce on the five-year ground, she should pay her own costs of it. I go further. In all ordinary cases I do not think the petition should contain a prayer for costs: because that would only mean that the husband would have to come to court to resist it: and his resistance will usually be successful. It would mean more costs with no good to either party."

If reliance is placed on section 1 (2) (*b*) or (*c*)—that the respondent has behaved in such a way that the petitioner cannot reasonably be expected to live with the respondent, or that the respondent has deserted the petitioner for at least two years—it seems likely that (subject to what was said in *Povey* v. *Povey* as to the position of a wife) costs will normally follow the event. The decree may not be based upon the commission of a matrimonial offence, but the facts proved do reveal such an offence. The position in relation to adultery under section 1 (2) (*a*) is discussed below, since it involves a third person.

(b) *Costs where a third party is involved.*

Other considerations arise when the petitioner relies upon section 1 (2) (*a*) and alleges only that the respondent has committed adultery and that the petitioner finds it intolerable to live with the respondent. This may also be the case when reliance is placed upon section 1 (2) (*b*), and the respondent's behaviour involves some improper association with a third person, when the court may have directed, under Rule 13 (3), that the third person shall be made a respondent in the cause. The abolition of the husband's right to claim damages from a co-respondent does not exclude his liability for costs. Indeed the same is true of a woman with whom the husband has committed adultery, who is now also referred to as a co-respondent.[2] Much must here depend upon the extent

---

[20] [1972] 3 All E.R. 1089.
[1] *Ibid.*, at p. 1547.
[2] Rule 13.

to which the change in the attitude towards matrimonial offences, and in particular towards adultery, is accepted by the courts—upon whether the adulterer or adulteress (for there is no logical reason for distinctions between the sexes) is always to be regarded as the instigator and author of the breakdown of the marriage. If this attitude is to persist he, or she, should be condemned in costs. If not, the decision as to costs may turn upon whether the court regards the adultery as the cause of the breakdown, or only the symptom of a breakdown which has in fact already occurred.

Section 49 (1) of the Act provides that where in a petition for divorce or judicial separation, or in any other pleading praying for either form of relief, one party to a marriage alleges that the other has committed adultery, he or she shall make the person alleged to have committed adultery with the other spouse a party to the proceedings unless excused by the court on special grounds from so doing.[3] Most cases, even when adultery is alleged, are undefended, and the real dispute between the parties arises in proceedings after the decree nisi has been granted concerning financial provision, property adjustments and the welfare of children. In this connection, particular regard must be paid to the Rule[4] whereby in proceedings after a decree nisi of divorce no order shall be made the effect of which would be to make a person, against whom adultery with one of the spouses is alleged, liable for costs which are not directly referable to the decree unless that person is a party to those proceedings or has been given notice of the intention to apply for such an order.

(c) *Suits for judicial separation*

What has been said as to costs in suits for divorce appears to be equally applicable to those for judicial separation, despite the fact that the facts available to prove the irretrievable breakdown of marriage in a divorce suit are themselves the actual grounds for judicial separation. There appears to be as yet no actual decision to this effect, but equally there appears to be no reason why the principles should be different.

---

[3] See s. 49 (2) and Rule 13.
[4] Rule 49 (4) and consider *B. v. B. & E. (No. 2)*, [1970] 1 All E.R. 732.

CHAPTER 15

PROPERTY RIGHTS

The subject of the property rights of husband and wife is in one sense no part of the law relating to matrimonial causes, except in so far as the courts, when making a decree of divorce, nullity or judicial separation, have power to modify existing rights, a matter which has already been considered. Disputes as to property can arise when there is as yet no question of proceedings concerning the marriage itself and not infrequently arise after the death of one or other of the spouses. Nevertheless this is a question which most married couples do not even consider whilst they are living happily together and the fact that the marriage has broken down or is likely to do so will always be likely to precipitate disputes of this nature. It seems inappropriate in this book to examine the decided cases at great length because the subject belongs more properly to the law of property and its relation to family law than to the much more limited subject of matrimonial causes. But it would be unrealistic to ignore it altogether. It can be considered under two main headings—the power of the court to determine disputes summarily under section 17 of the Married Women's Property Act 1882, and the provisions of the Matrimonial Homes Act 1967.

1. The Married Women's Property Act 1882, s. 17.

Section 17 of the Married Women's Property Act 1882 provides a convenient method of determining summarily "any question between husband and wife as to the title to or possession of property" and enables a judge to "make such order with respect to the property in dispute . . . as he thinks fit". Applications under the section may be made to the judge of any county court (not only a divorce county court) in the district in which either party resides, irrespective of the value of the property in question. Alternatively, they may be made to the Family Division of the High Court, to which such proceedings are now assigned.[1] Where proceedings for divorce, nullity or judicial separation have been commenced, the court which is to exercise the powers to order financial provision or adjustment of property rights in those proceedings cannot always effectively do so until disputes as to the ownership of property have been decided. If, for example, a wife obtains a decree of divorce and is already the owner of the matrimonial home she may need less by way of periodical payments. If she does not own it or any share in it provision must be made for a home for her, particularly

---

[1] Administration of Justice Act 1970, s. 1 (2) and Sched. 1, as amended by Matrimonial Causes Act 1973, Sched. 2, para. 10 (and s. 50 (1)).

if she is to have custody of children of the family and is unable to earn her own living. This may be done by transferring the ownership of the home to her, ordering it to be settled for her benefit and that of the children, granting her rights of occupation,[2] ordering her husband to pay her a lump sum to enable her to purchase a house, or by ordering him to make periodical payments to enable her to pay rent under a lease. Thus if it is necessary to decide the question of ownership it should be dealt with by the court which is seised of the matrimonial proceedings, the divorce county court rather than any other county court if they are undefended, the High Court Division to which they are assigned if they are defended, and by the same person, judge or registrar as the case may be.[3] The hope was, however, expressed by Lord DENNING in *Kowalczuk* v. *Kowalczuk* [4] that in future, after there has been a divorce, the property rights of the spouses may be adjusted by means of an application under what is now section 24 of the Act of 1973, since it is unncessary to decide the exact property rights under section 17 of the Act of 1882 when all appropriate orders can be made under the Act of 1973.

Since section 17 refers to questions "between husband and wife" it was held before the Matrimonial Proceedings and Property Act 1970 came into operation that proceedings could not be commenced after the marriage had been ended by decree absolute of divorce or nullity, though proceedings started before decree absolute could be continued thereafter.[5] Section 39 of that Act now provides that proceedings can be commenced by either party although the marriage has been dissolved or annulled, so long as the application is made within three years of the decree absolute. Thus if the inter-related questions of title to property and adjustment of property rights cannot be finally determined before the marriage is ended, the summary procedure for determination of the former question will remain available for a reasonable time after the final decree. Incidentally, section 17 has also been applied by the Law Reform (Miscellaneous Provisions) Act 1970, s. 2 to property disputes between the parties to broken engagements to marry, provided the application is made within three years of the termination of the agreement.

Amongst the matters to which the court is required to have regard in exercising its powers to grant ancillary relief are "the property and other financial resources" of the parties.[6] It must not be supposed, from the mention above of the matrimonial home, that the procedure under section 17 of the Act of 1882 is limited to real property. It can apply to property of any kind, to wedding presents,[7] stock and shares, furniture or the credit balance in a banking account, or even the benefit of a hire-purchase agreement.[8] Prior to the Matrimonial Causes (Property and Maintenance) Act 1958, s. 7 there was no way in

---

[2] See Matrimonial Homes Act 1967, s. 2 (2), *post*, p. [206].
[3] See *Practice Note (Matrimonial Property: Related Applications)*, [1971] 1 W.L.R. 260 and *G.* v. *G.*, [1973] 2 All E.R. 1187.
[4] [1973] 1 W.L.R. 930, at p. 934; BUCKLEY and STEPHENSON, L.JJ. agreed.
[5] *Fribance* v. *Fribance*, [1956] P. 99.
[6] Act of 1973, s. 25 (1) (*a*)—see *ante*, p. 132.
[7] As to which the answer may well be that those from the husband's family and relations belong to him, and those from hers to her. *Samson* v. *Samson*, [1960] 1 All E.R. 653.
[8] *Spellman* v. *Spellman*, [1961] 2 All E.R. 498.

which the court, in proceedings under section 17 of the Act of 1882, could give a judgment ordering the payment of money. Whilst one spouse remained in possession of property in respect of which the title was disputed the section could enable the court to determine the question of title. If that spouse had disposed of the property, and expended the proceeds of sale on the acquisition of other assets, or simply spent them, the summary procedure under the section was not available.[9] The court has now power to make orders as to the ownership of property which represents the proceeds of sale or to order the payment by one spouse to the other of such sum as is appropriate.[10]

(a) *Questions of title.*

Until the matter came before the House of Lords in *Pettitt* v. *Pettitt*[11] and *Gissing* v. *Gissing*[12] the decisions of the Court of Appeal showed acute differences of opinion as to the way in which the powers of the court under section 17 of the Married Women's Property Act 1882 should be exercised. These arose from the words in the section whereby the judge is to make such order "as he thinks fit". The extent of these differences is evident from the following quotations:—

> "I know of no power that the court has under section 17 to vary agreed or established titles to property. It has power to ascertain the respective rights of husband and wife to disputed property, and frequently has to do so on very little material: but where, as here, the original rights to property are established by the evidence, and those rights have not been varied by subsequent agreement, the court cannot in my opinion under section 17 vary those rights merely because it thinks that in the light of subsequent events the original agreement was unfair." (*Per* ROMER, L.J. in *Cobb* v. *Cobb*[13]).

> "It seems to me that the jurisdiction of the court over family assets under section 17 is entirely discretionary. Its discretion transcends all rights, legal or equitable, and enables the court to make such order as it thinks fit. This means, as I understand it, that the court is entitled to make such orders as appears to be fair and just in all the circumstances of the case." (*Per* Lord DENNING, M.R. in *Hine* v. *Hine*[14]).

> "In these circumstances, it is not correct to look and see whether there was any bargain in the past, or any expressed intention. A judge can only do what is fair and reasonable in the circumstances. Sometimes the test has been put in these cases: what term is to be implied? What would the parties have stipulated had they thought about it? That is one way of putting it. But as they never did think about it at all, I prefer to take the simple test: what is reasonable and fair in the circumstances as they have developed, seeing that they are circumstances which no-one

---

[9] *Tunstall* v. *Tunstall*, [1953] 2 All E.R. 310.
[10] Matrimonial Causes (Property and Maintenance) Act 1958, s. 7 (3) and (4).
[11] [1970] A.C. 777.
[12] [1971] A.C. 886.
[13] [1955] 1 W.L.R. 731, 736, 737.
[14] [1962] 1 W.L.R. 1124, 1127, 1128.

contemplated before?" (*Per* Lord DENNING, M.R. in *Appleton* v. *Appleton*[15]).

As a result of the decisions in *Pettitt* v. *Pettitt* and *Gissing* v. *Gissing* it is now clear that the view expressed by ROMER, L.J. was right, and the two ways in which the matter was put by Lord DENNING were wrong. Section 17 is a purely procedural section devised as a means of resolving a dispute or question as to title rather than as a means of giving some title not previously existing. In a question of the title to property the question for the court is "whose is this" and not "to whom shall this be given"[16]

"When an application is made under section 17 there is no power in the court to make a contract for the parties which they have not themselves made. Nor is there power to decide what the court thinks the parties would have agreed had they discussed the possible breakdown or ending of their relationship. Nor is there power to decide on some general principle of what seems fair and reasonable how property rights are to be re-allocated".[17]

Thus far then, the matter is clear; questions of title are to be determined on the same principles, and the decision must be the same, whether they arise in proceedings under section 17, or in an action in contract or tort between the spouses or between one of them and, say, the trustee in bankruptcy of the other. The court must not, to use the words of Coke,[18] "substitute the uncertain and crooked cord of discretion for the golden and straight metwand of the law". The expression "family assets" which was used by Lord DENNING in *Hine* v. *Hine* and by Lord DIPLOCK in *Ulrich* v. *Ulrich*[19] may be, as it is in relation to adjustment of property rights consequent upon the breakdown of a marriage,[20] a convenient one to describe property acquired by either spouse and intended for the common use or enjoyment of both spouses or their children, such as the matrimonial home and its furniture; but it has no connotation as to the ownership of such assets.

Before turning to the way in which these matters must be approached in practice, some further points which have been made by the House of Lords must be noticed. There is no merit in suggestions that property rights may be different before and after the breakdown of a marriage. This is irrelevent in determining where the ownership lay before the breakdown: the breakdown will merely have caused the need for a decision but will not of itself have altered whatever was the pre-existing position as to ownership.[1] The presumption of advancement, whereby if a husband transferred property into, or made financial contribution towards property in, his wife's name it was presumed that

15 [1965] 1 W.L.R. 25, 28.
16 *Pettitt* v. *Pettitt supra, per* Lord MORRIS OF BORTH-Y-GEST at p. 798.
17 *Ibid., per* Lord MORRIS OF BORTH-Y-GEST at pp. 804, 805.
18 Fourth Institute, p. 41, "Metwand" or "Metewand" = measuring stick or rod.
19 [1968] 1 W.L.R. 180, 189.
20 *Wachtel* v. *Wachtel*, [1973] Fam. 72, see *ante*, p. 133.
1 *Pettitt* v. *Pettitt, supra*, at pp. 793, 803, 816.

his intention was that it should be a gift to her, has no place, or at any rate very little place, in the law today.[2] It would be wrong "to apply to transactions between the post-war generation of married couples presumptions which are based upon inferences of fact which an earlier generation of judges drew as the most likely intentions of earlier generations of spouses belonging to the propertied classes of a different social era".[3]

The excessive application of the equitable maxim "Equality is equity" has also been condemned. It may be reasonable to apply it where there have been very substantial contributions by one spouse to the purchase of property in the name of the other spouse, and the proportions are difficult to fix. But if it is plain that the contributing spouse has contributed about one quarter, the court should not feel obliged to award a one-half share or nothing.[4] The principle of equality is, however, preserved by statute in relation to savings from a housekeeping allowance. Before the Married Women's Property Act 1964, if a husband made such an allowance to his wife, any savings which she contrived to make, and any property which she bought or acquired by means of such savings, belonged to the husband alone. In *Hoddinott* v. *Hoddinott*[5] this principle was applied, no doubt to the indignation of the wife, to money won by "investment" of such savings in a football pool, and furniture purchased with the winnings. The Act now provides that if any question arises as to the right of a husband or wife to money derived from any allowance made by the husband for the expenses of the matrimonial home, or for similar purposes, or to any property acquired out of such money, the money or property shall, in the absence of any agreement to the contrary, be treated as belonging to them in equal shares. The Act does not apply to money provided by the husband for purposes other than the expenses of the home,[5a] and would presumably not apply to a separate dress allowance made to the wife, or the clothes which she bought with it. Nor is the principle of equality completely preserved, since the Act does not apply to an allowance made by the wife to the husband—an unlikely event, though there are cases where the wife alone is engaged in a business or profession and the husband runs the home.

Now that so much has been held to be wrong, with what has it been replaced? Since the majority of cases have concerned the matrimonial home, or other real or leasehold property, certain principles with regard to those forms of property are clear:—

(i) If the conveyance or lease declares not merely in whom the legal title is to vest but also in whom the beneficial title is to vest, that concludes the question between the spouses for all time in the absence of fraud or mistake.[6] Thus, in the absence of all other evidence, if the property is conveyed into the joint names of husband

---

[2] *Ibid.*, at pp. 793, 811, 824. *Falconer* v. *Falconer*, [1970] 3 All E.R. 449. Contrast *Tinker* v. *Tinker*, [1970] P. 136.
[3] *Pettitt* v. *Pettitt*, supra, *per* Lord DIPLOCK at p. 824.
[4] *Gissing* v. *Gissing, supra*, at pp. 897, 903, 908.
[5] [1949] 2 K.B. 406.
[5a] See *Tymoszczuk* v. *Tymoszczuk* (1964), 108 Sol. Jo. 676.
[6] *Per* Lord UPJOHN in *Pettitt* v. *Pettitt*, at p. 813.

and wife as joint tenants upon trust for sale and to hold the proceeds of sale for themselves as joint tenants, as in *Bedson* v. *Bedson*,[7] they have equal shares.

(ii) If the conveyance is to the husband or to the wife alone, prima facie the other spouse has no interest unless there is evidence which establishes the existence of a resulting trust in favour of that other spouse.[8]

(iii) Such a trust is most easily established by proving that the other spouse made direct contributions to the cost of the purchase, either by paying part of the purchase money, the deposit or legal charges, or mortgage instalments. The inference in such cases is that there is a common intention that the spouse contributing should acquire a beneficial interest in the property proportionate to the amount of the contributions. Thus in *Falconer* v. *Falconer*[9] the wife, with the assistance of her mother, purchased a plot of land. On this a house was built with money raised on mortgage and, without entering into exact figures, the husband contributed about half the mortgage instalments. The Court of Appeal, applying the principles laid down in *Gissing's* case, held that the land belonged to the wife alone, but that there was a resulting trust in the husband's favour as regards a half interest in the house itself.

There remains the more difficult problem of indirect contributions, which may take the form of contributions by one spouse towards the improvement of property which belongs to the other, or of notional assistance resulting from the application of the earnings of one towards the acquisition of property in the name of the other alone.

It is convenient to consider first the question of improvements, since the doubts which arise from the decision of the House of Lords in *Pettit* v. *Pettit* are now largely dispelled by section 37 of the Matrimonial Proceedings and Property Act 1970. The case arose from an application by a husband under section 17 of the Married Women's Property Act 1882, in which he claimed that work done by him in redecoration and improvement of a house purchased by his wife entitled him to a beneficial interest in the proceeds of the sale of that house. On the facts of the case the House unanimously decided that he had no such interest. Their Lordships approved of the decision in *Button* v. *Button*[10] that where the work done by either spouse upon their home is no more than "the do-it-yourself jobs which husbands often do", or where the wife "cleans the walls or works in the garden or helps her husband with the painting and decorating"[11] they do not thereby acquire any interest in the house. This of itself would have sufficed to decide the husband's application in the *Pettitt* case. But their Lordships went further in their consideration of cases where the improvements were of a more

---

[7] [1965] 2 Q.B. 666.
[8] *Pettitt* v. *Pettitt*, *per* Lord UPJOHN at p. 815. *Gissing* v. *Gissing*, *per* Viscount DILHORNE at p. 900, and Lord DIPLOCK at p. 904.
[9] [1970] 3 All E.R. 349.
[10] [1968] 1 W.L.R. 457.
[11] *Ibid.*, *per* Lord DENNING, M.R. at pp. 461, 462.

substantial nature, as in *Jansen* v. *Jansen*[12] where the husband gave up other work and converted the first and second floors of a house owned by his wife into two self-contained flats.   Lords REID and DIPLOCK[13] considered that the decision in that case giving the husband a beneficial interest in the house was right.   Lords HODSON and UPJOHN[14] took the view that it was wrong.

It is this question of improvements alone (and not the many other questions arising from alleged contributions towards the purchase of a home) that is dealt with by section 37.   Since it may be that it will leave unsolved problems, the wording requires examination in detail.

(i)   It purports to *declare* the law—not the law as it has hitherto been, since that has been in doubt, but the law as it is now to be presumed to have been—whether the work of improvement took place before or after the Act came into operation.[15]

(ii)   It applies only "where a husband or wife contributes in money or money's worth to the improvement of real or personal property in which or in the proceeds of sale of which either or both of them has or have a beneficial interest".   It is clear, therefore, that it is not limited to work upon the matrimonial home, but extends to any property, and that the contribution may take the form of the payment of money or of work and labour.   What may be much more difficult is the meaning of the word "improvement".   An attempt in the Commons to extend the section to cover maintenance as well as improvement was unsuccessful.[16]   But the line may be hard to draw.   No doubt the "do-it-yourself work" on redecorating a house referred to in *Button* v. *Button, supra* is mere maintenance.   But suppose that a wife, with her own money, buys a house which is in serious decorative disrepair.   The same "do-it-yourself" work by a husband might well be regarded as an improvement making habitable a house which otherwise would not have been so.   Indeed Lord REID, in the opening words of his opinion in *Pettitt* v. *Pettitt, supra*, referred to "a number of improvements, largely redecorating".[17] The solution might be that work which makes the condition of a house better than it was when it was purchased is "improvement" whereas work which merely keeps it in the condition it was in at the time of the purchase is "maintenance".

(iii)   The contribution made by a husband or wife is to give to him or her a share or enlarged share in the beneficial interest only if it is of "a substantial nature".   No doubt these words will serve to exclude claims based on such work as was mentioned in *Button* v. *Button*.

---

[12] [1965] P. 478.
[13] [1970] A.C. 777, at pp. 796 and 826.
[14] *Ibid.*, at pp. 809 and 818.
[15] *Per* Lord DENNING, M.R. in *Davis* v. *Vale*, [1971] 1 W.L.R. 1022, at p. 1026.
[16] Hansard May 27, 1970, cols. 1965–1969.
[17] [1970] A.C. 777, 792.

But the word "substantial" is described in Stroud's *Judicial Dictionary*[18] as "A word of no fixed meaning. It is an unsatisfactory medium for carrying the idea of some ascertainable proportion of the whole." It is, of course, a question of degree in each case, but may well lead to inconsistent decisions by different courts.

(iv) The section is subject to any "agreement to the contrary express or implied". Although such a proviso is no doubt necessary, express contrary agreements on such a matter are likely to be infrequent in practice, and it is not easy to imagine cases when an agreement to the contrary would be implied.

(v) The extent of the beneficial interest is to be such as the parties "have then agreed or, in default of such agreement, as may seem in all the circumstances just . . .". It is unlikely in most cases that the spouses will even have considered this matter, much less reached agreement upon it. Nor is the court then required to determine what agreement they would have reached had the matter entered their minds, or to award a share commensurate with or proportional to the cost or value of the improvements.[19] The danger would seem to be that the court, in determining what is just, may rely overmuch on the principle that "equality is equity". The excessive application of this principle has been criticised by the House of Lords in *Gissing* v. *Gissing*.[20]

(vi) The decision as to the extent of the share or enlarged share of the beneficial interest of a husband or wife resulting from section 37 is to be determined by any court before which this question arises, whether in proceedings between them or in any other proceedings. Accordingly the section is in no way limited to proceedings under section 17 of the Married Women's Property Act 1882.

Unfortunately, in *Gissing* v. *Gissing*, the Law Lords expressed conflicting opinions on the subject of indirect contributions other than those made in money or money's worth for the purpose of improvements to property. There is little difficulty where the parties engage in a common venture. Thus in *Nixon* v. *Nixon*[1] where the wife worked in her husband's business without wages and the prosperity of the business enabled him to buy the matrimonial home, she was held to be entitled to a half share. Likewise in *Muetzel* v. *Muetzel*[2] the wife paid the deposit on the purchase of a house as a direct contribution and contributed indirectly to the cost by taking in paying guests and helping the husband in his business, she was held to be entitled to a beneficial interest to the extent of a one-third share. Similar results would no doubt follow from direct arrangements where the wife agreed to pay the whole of the housekeeping expenses to enable her husband to meet the mortgage instalments. But what of the more nebulous

---

[18] Quoting from the Australian case of *Terry's Motors Ltd.* v. *Rinder*, [1948] S.A.S.R 167, 180.
[19] Reasons for this are given in Law Com. No. 25, Appendix I, at p. 103.
[20] [1971] A.C. 886 and *ante*, p. 192.
[1] [1969] 3 All E.R. 1133.
[2] [1970] 1 All E.R. 443.

situation where her efforts in fact enabled the payments to be made although there had been no actual agreement on the matter, as where her earnings enabled her to accept a reduced housekeeping allowance or otherwise contribute to the general expenses of the household?

The Court of Appeal has consistently accepted the view expressed in the opinion of Lord REID in *Gissing* v. *Gissing*, that if a wife by her efforts or contributions has relieved her husband of other expenses which he would otherwise have had to bear, so that he would have been unable to meet mortgage instalments or a loan without her help, she makes an indirect contribution which entitles her to a share. In several cases[3] the Court of Appeal has unanimously accepted Lord DENNING's summary of the position in the following words:

"It may be indirect, as where both go out to work, and one pays the housekeeping and the other the mortgage instalments. It does not matter which way round it is. It does not matter who pays what. So long as there is a substantial financial contribution towards the family expenses, it raises the inference of a trust."

The situation is, however, different, in a case like *Kowalczuk* v. *Kowalczuk*,[4] where the matrimonial home had been bought by, and belonged exclusively to, the husband some years before the date of the marriage. In those circumstances the wife obtains no share in the house by reason of subsequent contributions unless they are *directly* referable to the making of substantial improvements to the house or to the payment of the mortgage instalments.

This does not, however, mean that the contributions which a wife has made to the welfare of the family, including her contributions by looking after the home or caring for the family, are to be ignored if the marriage breaks down. Such contributions of themselves give her no legal or equitable entitlement to a share in the matrimonial home or other "family assets". But they are among the very factors which the court is required (as already explained in Chapter 9) to take into account in exercising its powers to order financial provision or adjustment of property rights in her favour. The "cold legal question" (as Lord DENNING called it in the Court of Appeal in *Gissing* v. *Gissing*[5]) of whether she already owns a share in the matrimonial home or other property (and if so, how large or small the share is) matters little when, if the court grants a decree of divorce, nullity or judicial separation, it can order a transfer of property of one spouse to the other or a settlement of property for the other's benefit. Repetition is boring, but it is surely not in vain to emphasize again that in matrimonial causes it will generally suffice to rely upon the powers of the court under the Matrimonial Causes Act 1973 rather than upon the difficulties resulting from section 17 of the Act of 1882. BAGNALL, J., put the point so well in *Cowcher* v. *Cowcher*[6] when he said:—

"But I cannot escape the thought that Parliament evinced an intention that in the vast majority of cases justice would be done by exercising the

[3] *Falconer* v. *Falconer*, [1970] 1 W.L.R. 1333, 1336; *Hargrave* v. *Newton*, [1971] 1 W.L.R. 1611, 1613; *Hazell* v. *Hazell*, [1972] 1 W.L.R. 301, 304.
[4] [1973] 1 W.L.R. 930, C.A.
[5] [1969] 2 Ch. 83, 93.
[6] [1972] 1 W.L.R. 425, 437.

statutory discretion in relation to all the capital and income resources of the parties rather than by isolating one asset—the matrimonial home— and by inferring a dubious consensus from equivocal facts fitting that particular asset uncomfortably into the framework of a resulting trust."

(b) *Questions of possession.*

What has been said above relates to the application of section 17 of the Act of 1882 to disputes as to title. But this section refers also to disputes as to possession. It is here that the court has greater freedom to exercise its discretion. The difference was explained by Lord DIPLOCK[7] when he said:—

"The power conferred upon the judge 'to make such order with respect to the property in dispute . . . as he shall think fit' gives him a wide discretion as to the enforcement of the proprietary or possessory rights of one spouse in any property against the other, but confers on him no jurisdiction to transfer any proprietary interest in property from one spouse to the other or to create new proprietary rights in either spouse."

Thus it was held in *Lee* v. *Lee*[8] in 1952 that the court could protect the wife's right to possession of the matrimonial home by directing the husband to permit his wife and children to reside in the home, which belonged to him, until he had provided them with suitable alternative accommodation and prohibit him from selling or otherwise dealing with the house in such a way as to interfere with their right to reside there.

From that time onwards there was a long series of cases, beginning with *Bendall* v. *McWhirter*,[9] in which the Court of Appeal sought to establish that a deserted wife had a right of occupation in the matrimonial home, although it belonged to her husband, which was in the nature of an equity enforceable not only against him but against all other persons other than a bona fide purchaser for value without notice of this right. These cases can now be disregarded and the so-called equity treated as an equity which never existed. The House of Lords finally disposed of the matter in *National Provincial Bank, Ltd.* v. *Ainsworth*,[10] holding that the rights of a deserted wife were purely personal rights enforceable against her husband and that these rights could not as a matter of law affect third parties. This decision led to the enactment of the Matrimonial Homes Act 1967.

2. The Matrimonial Homes Act 1967.

This Act is intended not only to give to each spouse rights of occupation in the matrimonial home enforceable against the other spouse in whom the legal estate is vested, but also to provide means of protecting those rights against the claims of third parties.

---

[7] *Pettitt* v. *Pettitt*, at p. 820.
[8] [1952] Q.B. 489; see also *Halden v. Halden*, [1966] 3 All E.R. 412.
[9] [1952] 2 Q.B. 466.
[10] [1965] A.C. 1175.

It provides[11] that where one spouse is entitled to occupy a dwelling house by virtue of any estate or interest or contract, or by virtue of any enactment giving him or her the right to remain in occupation, *and the other spouse is not so entitled*, the spouse not so entitled is to have certain "rights of occupation". If already in occupation, he or she is to have a right not to be evicted from the dwelling house, or any part thereof, by the other spouse except with the leave of the court given by order under the section. If not in occupation there is instead a right, with the leave of the court so given, to enter and occupy the dwelling house. The expression "dwelling house" includes any building or part thereof which is occupied as a dwelling, and any yard, garden, garage or out-house belonging to the dwelling house and occupied with it.[12] But the Act does not apply to a dwelling house which has at no time been a matrimonial home of the spouses in question.[13]

By section 2, where during the subsistence of the marriage one spouse is entitled to occupy a dwelling house by virtue of an estate or interest, the rights of occupation of the other spouse under the Act are to be a charge on that estate or interest which is registrable as a Land Charge Class F under the Land Charges Act 1925, or in the case of registered land, as a notice or caution under the Land Registration Act 1925. Where the spouses have two or more dwelling houses which can properly be regarded as matrimonial homes, perhaps a flat in London and a cottage by the sea, there is no reason why, if the husband is the owner of both, the wife should not have rights of occupation as against her husband under the Act in respect of both. But she cannot take advantage of the protection which the Act affords against third parties in respect of both, but must make her choice, because where she is entitled under the Act to a charge on her husband's estate or interest in two or more dwelling houses, only one of these charges may be registered at any one time, and if she attempts to register a second charge when one charge is already registered, the first registration must be cancelled.[14] The importance of registration of such a charge is that in practice it ensures that thereafter there will be no sale or mortgage of the dwelling house by the spouse in whom the legal estate is vested unless the registration is discharged or the other spouse consents.[15] This will be of particular importance as preserving the power of the court to deal, should it think fit to do so, with the matrimonial home, unsold and unmortgaged, in the exercise of its powers of adjustment of property rights on the breakdown of the marriage under section 24 of the Act of 1973, though it will be of no assistance in relation to a mortgage already in existence when the charge was registered, which will take priority over the charge.

Section 1 is so worded that it has no application when the home is owned by both spouses jointly. It only protects a wife who has *no* proprietary, contractual or statutory right to remain in the matrimonial home—a "bare',

---

[11] S. 1 (1).
[12] S. 1 (7).
[13] S. 1 (8).
[14] S. 3.
[15] See s. 4

wife as Lord DENNING M.R. has called her.[16] Nevertheless in a case in which the home is owned by both spouses jointly, each has a common law right to occupy the home, so that the court would have jurisdiction to order the husband, who was in occupation and whose conduct had been such that his wife could not reasonably be expected to live with him, to vacate the home and to allow her to re-enter and live there unmolested.[17]

Where the legal estate is vested in both spouses, the protection of the Matrimonial Homes Act 1967 is not required, for both have rights of occupation and neither can dispose of the dwelling house without the concurrence of the other. If the marriage ends in divorce, the court can, if it thinks fit, order the transfer of the interest of one spouse to the other under section 24 of the Act of 1973. Where, however, the legal estate is vested in one spouse alone and the interest of the other is equitable only, as where it results from contributions to the acquisition or improvement of the house, a purchaser from the legal owner would take free from the equitable interest of the other spouse unless he had notice of it. The fact that a purchaser or mortgagee knows of the presence of the wife of the legal owner in the house does not amount to constructive notice of the fact that she may have some equitable interest, or put him upon enquiry as to this possibility.[18] It follows that in such cases registration of a charge resulting from rights of occupation is necessary for protection of the equitable interest.

But the Court of Appeal took the view[19] that a spouse who had merely an equitable interest had already a right of occupation by virtue of that interest, so that the test laid down in section 1 (1) of the Act was not satisfied and no charge registrable under that Act could arise. Suggestions had even been made that registration of a Land Charge Class F in these circumstances might later estop a spouse from claiming such an interest.

Section 38 of the Matrimonial Proceedings and Property Act 1970, put an end to these speculations. It adds a new subsection (9) to section 1 of the Matrimonial Homes Act 1967 declaring that a spouse who has an equitable interest in a dwelling house or in the proceeds of sale thereof, not being a spouse in whom is vested (whether solely or as a joint tenant) a legal estate in fee simple or a legal term of years absolute in the dwelling house, is to be treated for the purpose only of determining whether he or she has rights of occupation under that section as not being entitled to occupy the dwelling house by virtue of that interest. He or she will have rights of occupation under section 1, and the resulting charge will be registrable.

So long as one of the spouses has rights of occupation, either of the spouses (and not only the spouse on whom the Act confers those rights) may apply to the court under section 1 (2) of the Act for an order declaring, enforcing, restricting or terminating those rights, or regulating the exercise by either spouse of the right to occupy the dwelling house. It has, however, been held by the

[16] *Gurasz* v. *Gurasz*, [1970] P. 11.
[17] *Ibid.*
[18] *Caunce* v. *Caunce*, [1969] 1 All E.R. 722.
[19] See Law Com. No. 25, para. 59, and *Bull* v. *Bull*, [1955] 1 Q.B. 234.

House of Lords in *Tarr* v. *Tarr*[1] that the word "regulations" is not apt to include a power to prohibit, so that there is no power under this Act to prohibit, even temporarily, a husband who owns the matrimonial home from exercising to his right to occupy it.   Orders under the section may be made by the High Court or any county court, irrespective of the value of the property.[2]   In deciding what order to make the court must have regard to the conduct of the spouses in relation to each other and otherwise, to their respective needs and financial resources, to the needs of any children and all the circumstances of the case.   The court has power to except part of the dwelling house from a spouse's rights of occupation (such as a part used in connection with a trade, business or profession), to order a spouse occupying the dwelling house or part of it to make periodical payments to the other spouse and to impose on either spouse obligations as to repair and maintenance or the discharge of other liabilities.   Any order which is made may be limited to a specified period or to continue until further order.[3]

Although a spouse's right of occupation are a charge on an estate or interest in the dwelling house, the rights come to an end on the death of either spouse or on the termination of the marriage otherwise than by death unless in the event of a matrimonial dispute or estrangement the court sees fit to direct otherwise by an order made under section 1 whilst the marriage still subsists.[4] Just as it is vitally important to protect a wife's rights of occupation by registration of a charge in respect of the matrimonial home if the husband owns the legal estate and there are signs of matrimonial discord, so also it is essential in her interests when proceedings for divorce or nullity are pending to seek an order from the court before the decree is made absolute that her rights of occupation shall continue when the marriage is ended.   If such an order is made she may, if her charge has already been registered, renew the registration or, if not, register the charge.[5]   In all cases it is essential that a charge under the Act shall be correctly registered.   In *Miles* v. *Bull (No. 2)*[6] the wife lost the protection which she should have obtained against a purchaser from her husband because her solicitor had registered a Land Charge Class F under the Land Charges Act 1925 when, because the title to the land was registered under the Land Registration Act 1925, a notice or caution should have been registered under that Act.

In *Watts* v. *Waller*[7] the Court of Appeal considered the question of whether a spouse who is out of occupation and therefore entitled to enter into and occupy the house only with the leave of the court under section 1 of the Act, has a right capable of registration as a charge before that leave had been obtained.   If she has no such right, her husband could defeat the object of the Act by locking her out of the house before any charge has been protected by registration and

---

[1] [1973] A.C. 254.
[2] S. 1 (6).
[3] S. 1 (3) and (4).
[4] S. 2 (2).
[5] S. 5 (3).
[6] [1969] 3 All E.R. 1585.
[7] [1973] 1 Q.B. 153, over-ruling *Rutherford* v. *Rutherford*, [1970] 3 All E.R. 422.

entering into a binding contract to sell the house before she is able to obtain the court's leave to re-enter. Accordingly it was held that she has a conditional right of occupation which, although it cannot be enforced without the leave of the court, is capable of registration as a charge. But each member of the Court of Appeal drew attention to the desirability of some provision for the notification of the registration of a charge to be given to the spouse who owns the house, a plea which has fallen on ears which thus far remain deaf. As the Morton Commission on Marriage and Divorce observed,[8]

> "Wives may be selfish and grasping as well as husbands; it is necessary to guard against the risk that substantial injustice may be done to husbands as a result of measures designed to alleviate the hardship which some wives may suffer."

Suppose that a wife has deserted her husband and is living in adultery with another man. Being unable to maintain his life in the home unaided, he enters into a binding contract to sell it, only to find that, on the day after the contracts have been exchanged, his wife has registered her conditional right of occupation as a charge. True, he may apply to the court under section 1 (2) to terminate her right, but the financial disaster which may befall him (though in circumstances very different from those imagined above) is all too clearly illustrated by the recent case of *Wroth* v. *Tyler*.[9] At least it is to be hoped that in appropriate cases conduct of this kind will, should the marriage end in divorce, fall within the class of conduct which is "both obvious and gross' and seriously affect the wife's prospects of financial provision or orders for property adjustment in her favour.

This account must suffice for the purposes of matrimonial causes, though the Act of course contains many other provisions with regard for example to the effect of the payment or tender of rent, rates, or mortgage instalments[10] and as to the position where the matrimonial home is subject to the Rent Act 1968.[11]

3. Position when proceedings for a matrimonial decree are pending.

The court has jurisdiction to grant an injunction in any pending cause or matter in which it appears to the court to be just so to do, and this jurisdiction exists not only when proceedings for divorce, nullity or judicial separation are pending, but also when there is a pending application for leave to petition for divorce within three years of the date of the marriage.[12] A party has a right to pursue his or her remedies in court free from pressure or threats of pressure to abandon or modify the proceedings, and free from intimidation in any form. Generally such injunctions take the form of an order that one party shall not

---

[8] Cmnd. 9678, para. 648.
[9] [1973] 1 All E.R. 897.
[10] S. 1 (5).
[11] S. 7.
[12] *McGibbon* v. *McGibbon*, [1973] Fam. 170.

molest the other, but sometimes it is necessary to go further and grant an injunction in relation to occupancy of the matrimonial home.[13]

The court has power to restrain a husband from entering the matrimonial home pending the hearing of a petition, although he is the owner of the premises,[14] or the tenant.[15] But where the parties are living in a large house with their children, an order that one spouse should leave the matrimonial home pending the determination of a petition should not be made unless it is necessary for the protection of the other spouse or the children; mere tension is not enough; it must be proved that it is impossible for them to live together in peace in the same house.[16] An injunction will, however, be granted where the court considers it necessary for the protection of the children of the family,[17] and injunctions are readily granted requiring a husband to remove his mistress from the matrimonial home whilst the proceedings are pending.[18]

An injunction granted before decree absolute of divorce can be ordered to continue after the decree,[19] but it is only in the most exceptional cases, as where the wife and child of the marriage would otherwise become psychiatric invalids, that an order will be made after decree absolute for a husband to leave a house of which he and his wife are joint tenants, or of which he is the owner.[20] In view of the wide powers of the court to make orders for the adjustment of property rights under the Act of 1973, these questions of the situation with regard to the matrimonial home after the termination of the marriage can often be best dealt with by orders for the transfer or settlement of the home on appropriate terms.

4. Family Property Law: The Law Commission's First Report (Law Com. No. 52)

As a result of consultation upon a Working Paper on Family Property Law,[1] the Law Commission has published its first Report in April 1973. The Working Paper covered five main topics, that of the matrimonial home, the household goods, family provision out of the estate of a deceased person, fixed legal rights of inheritance, and some form of community of property. The Report concludes that, as at present advised, no action is required on the last two topics, but that legislation is necessary on the first three, and may well be in draft during the course of 1973.

Briefly, the main proposals may be summarized as follows:—

(a) The introduction of a general principle of co-ownership of the matrimonial home (which is generally the principal and often the only

---

[13] It is not clear whether this is possible in proceedings for leave to petition; see *McGibbon* v. *McGibbon, supra.*
[14] *Silverstone* v. *Silverstone*, [1953] P. 174.
[15] *Jones* v. *Jones*, [1971] 2 All E.R. 737, C.A.
[16] *Hall* v. *Hall*, [1971] 1 All E.R. 762, C.A.
[17] *Robinson* v. *Robinson*, [1965] P. 39.
[18] *Jones* v. *Jones, supra; Pinckney* v. *Pinckney*, [1966] 1 All E.R. 121n.
[19] *Robinson* v. *Robinson, supra.*
[20] *Phillips* v. *Phillips*, [1973] 2 All E.R. 423, C.A.; *Stewart* v. *Stewart*, [1973] Fam. 21.
[1] Working Paper No. 42.

substantial asset of the spouses), subject to any agreement to the contrary.

(b) Amendments designed to extend and strengthen a spouse's rights of occupation under the Matrimonial Homes Act 1967.

(c) Recommendations for protecting the right of a spouse who is in occupation of the matrimonial home to the continued use and enjoyment of the household goods until that right is terminated by order of the court.

(d) That so far as is practicable in the differing circumstances, the claim of a surviving spouse upon the family assets should be at least equal to that of a divorced spouse, and the court's powers to order family provision for a surviving spouse should be as wide as its powers to order financial provisions on a divorce.

PART III

PROCEDURE

CHAPTER 16

AN OUTLINE OF PROCEDURE

Procedure in Matrimonial Causes is governed by the Matrimonial Causes Rules 1973, and a reference to a Rule, unless otherwise stated, is to these Rules and a reference to a Form is to that Form in the Appendix to these Rules. Where there is no other provision for any particular matter, Rule 3 provides that it is governed by the County Court Rules 1936 (C.C.R.) or by the Rules of the Supreme Court (R.S.C.). The way in which the Rules operate in practice is much easier to understand if they are read in conjunction with the appropriate Forms, and a selection of those most frequently used in practice will be found in Part 1 of Appendix II to this book. Part 2 of that Appendix contains Precedents, with an explanation of the way in which they are drafted.

1. The Courts having jurisdiction.

Since the Matrimonial Causes Act 1967 came into operation on April 11, 1968, every matrimonial cause has been required to be commenced in a divorce county court designated as such by the Lord Chancellor. If the cause remains undefended it may be tried in any divorce county court which has also been designated as a court of trial, but if it ceases to be undefended it must be transferred to the High Court.[1] For the purposes of the Act of 1967 and the Rules, the principal registry of the Family Division of the High Court, which is known as the Divorce Registry[2] is treated as a divorce county court, so that proceedings may be commenced in that registry, and, if so, will usually be tried by a county court judge sitting in the Royal Courts of Justice.[3]

For the purposes of the Act of 1967, matrimonial causes mean proceedings for divorce, nullity or judicial separation, and applications for leave to petition for divorce within three years of the date of the marriage.[4] The expression does not include proceedings in which the *only* relief sought is a declaration as to matrimonial status, which must be begun in the divorce registry and must, unless otherwise directed, proceed in London.[5] It sometimes happens that a decree of divorce or nullity in respect of the marriage has already been obtained abroad. The petitioner, who wishes to be free to re-marry, is uncertain as to whether the foreign decree will be recognised as valid in England. In such a case it is wrong to file a petition in a divorce county court claiming in the alternative a declaration as to the validity of the decree or a dissolution of the marriage,

---

[1] Matrimonial Causes Act 1967, s. 1.
[2] Administration of Justice Act 1970, s. 1 and Sched. 2.
[3] Matrimonial Causes Act 1967, s. 4, Rule 4.
[4] *Ibid.*, s. 10 (1), as amended by Act of 1973, Sched. 2, para. 6 (3).
[5] Rules 109 and 111.

since the county court has no jurisdiction to entertain the proceedings for the declaration. The petition should pray only for divorce when, if the suit is undefended, the county court judge will have jurisdiction to determine the validity of the marriage as a necessary preliminary to deciding upon the prayer for dissolution. He cannot dissolve a marriage without determining first whether there is an existing marriage to dissolve.[6]

A divorce county court has also jurisdiction to exercise the various powers under Part II (financial relief) and Part III (protection, custody etc. of children) of the Act of 1973, including the powers under section 27 (wilful neglect to maintain) and section 35 (alteration of maintenance agreements in the lifetime of the parties).[7] There are, moreover, certain powers which are not conferred upon divorce county courts as such but upon all county courts.[8] These are as follows:

(a) Applications under section 32 for leave to enforce payment of arrears which became due more than twelve months before the date of the application, which are made to the court through which it is sought to enforce payment, which may be the High Court or any county court.

(b) Applications under section 33 or 38 for an order for repayment of sums already paid irrespective of what the amount claimed may be.[9] These may be made in proceedings in the High Court or a county court for variation or discharge of the order under which the payments were made, or for leave to enforce, or the enforcement of, payment of arrears under that order, but must otherwise be made to "a county court".[10]

(c) Applications under section 26 and 27 of the Matrimonial Causes Act 1965 for provision out of the estate of a former spouse or for variation or discharge of an order for such provision. These may be made to any county court if, and only if, the value of the deceased's net estate does not exceed £5,000 or such larger sum as may be fixed by order of the Lord Chancellor.[11]

(d) Applications under section 36 of the Act of 1973 for alteration of a maintenance agreement after the death of one of the parties to that agreement. These may be made to any county court if it would have had jurisdiction under section 26 to order provision out of the estate, i.e. if the net value of the estate does not exceed £5,000 or such larger sum as may be fixed.[12]

---

[6] *Practice Direction*, [1970] 3 All E.R. 1024. Proposals for alteration of this procedure are contained in the Law Commission's Working Paper No. 48—Family Law, Declarations in Family Matters.
[7] Matrimonial Causes Act 1967, s. 2 (1), as amended by Act of 1973, Sched. 2, para. 6 (1) (a).
[8] Act of 1973, Sched. 2, para. 6 (1) (b).
[9] Act of 1973, ss. 33 (5) and 38 (4).
[10] Act of 1973, ss. 33 (4) and 38 (3).
[11] Family Provision Act 1966, s. 7.
[12] Act of 1973, s. 36 (3).

2. Application in the course of the proceedings.

For those who are not familiar with the every-day working of the courts, it may be convenient at this stage to say something of the methods of making such applications as may be required in the course of the proceedings.

Except where the Rules otherwise provide, such applications are made to a registrar.[13] So long as the cause remains undefended and no order for transfer to the High Court has been made, the application will be to the registrar of the divorce county court in which the cause is pending or, if it is pending in the divorce registry in London, to a registrar of the Family Division. Some applications can be made ex parte (i.e. without notice to the other parties to the proceedings). Examples are such matters as applications for leave to dispense with joining a person with whom adultery is alleged as a co-respondent,[14] or for leave to omit the residence of the petitioner from the petition. Otherwise the application is by notice in writing served on the opposite party; as will be seen from the Form on p. 414, it simply states the date and time for hearing and the nature and grounds of application. Copies of this Form (and of most other Forms in Appendix II) can be obtained from the court office. The notice must be served on opposite parties not less than two clear days before the hearing.[15] Service is effected, if a solicitor is acting for the person to be served, by leaving the notice at, or sending it by post to, the solicitor's address. If the person to be served is acting in person the notice is served by delivering it to him, or leaving it at, or sending it by post to, his address for service or, if none, his last known address.[16]

If, by reason of the fact that the cause has become defended, or for some other reason, it is ordered to be transferred to the High Court, it will usually proceed in the registry nearest to the divorce county court from which it is transferred.[17] Applications thereafter will be made, if transfer was to a district registry, to the district registrar, or if transfer was to the divorce registry, to a registrar of the Family Division. Where the cause is to proceed in a district registry in the same town as the divorce county court from which it was transferred, the county court office and that of the district registry will usually be housed in the same building and the same person will hold the offices of county court registrar and district registrar. The application is made by summons, instead of by notice of application, the rules as to service being the same.[18]

In the case of applications which are required to be made to a judge, such as those relating to custody or education of a child, the method of application is the same—by notice of application in a divorce county court and by summons in the High Court.

---

[13] Rule 122 (1) (a). The expression "the court" is defined in Rule 2 as meaning "a judge or the registrar" and when it is used in a Rule it gives the registrar jurisdiction.
[14] See Rule 13 (4).
[15] Rule 122 (2) and C.C.R. Ord. 13, r. 1.
[16] Rule 119.
[17] Rule 129 (3).
[18] Rule 122 (1) (b).

What has been said above does not apply to applications which are made when there is as yet no cause pending, or to applications for ancillary relief. These will be dealt with later, as appropriate.

3. Acting for the petitioner.

(a) *Leave to petition for divorce.*

The procedure on an application for leave to petition for divorce within three years of the date of the marriage is governed by Rule 5. The application must be made by originating application filed in the divorce county court to which it is proposed to present the petition. With the application must be filed an affidavit by the applicant exhibiting a copy of the proposed petition and stating the grounds of the application, the hardship or depravity alleged, whether there has been any previous application for leave, whether any, and if so what, attempts at reconciliation have been made, particulars of any circumstances which may assist the court in deciding whether there is a reasonable probability of reconciliation, and the date of birth of each of the parties or, if this be the case, that he or she has attained 18. The applicant must also file a copy of the application and supporting affidavit for service on the respondent spouse, and, unless otherwise directed, a marriage certificate.

The registrar will annex to the copy of the originating application which is to be served on the respondent a copy of the supporting affidavit and a notice in Form 1 with Form 6 attached. As will be seen from the copy of Form 1 at p. 395 it explains to the respondent that if the application is undefended it will be heard at the time and place stated on the Form and that he should complete and detach Form 6, the Acknowledgement of Service[1] and return it to reach the court within eight days of service, inclusive of the day of service. Should he wish to resist the application he should answer "Yes" to question 4 on that Form, when the application will be transferred to the High Court and a fresh time and place for hearing will be notified to him. The copy application, with the two Forms annexed, will be served on the respondent in the same way as a petition.[2] The application is heard by a judge and, unless otherwise directed, will be heard in chambers.

(b) *Contents of the petition.*

Proceedings for divorce, nullity or judicial separation, are begun by petition and Rule 9 (1) requires that unless otherwise directed, every petition shall contain the information required by Form 2, as nearly as may be in the order there set out and, in certain cases only, some additional information required by other paragraphs of the Rule.

Form 2 will be found on p. 396, and should be carefully studied. The object of the requirement that the information should follow the order of the

---

[1] See Form at p. 401.
[2] See *post*, p. 221.

Form is to ensure that, so far as possible, there is uniformity in the way in which it is placed before the court and that, in opening the case, the advocate will usually follow the same order. A *Practice Direction*[3] makes it clear that there is no objection to the use of printed forms sold by law stationers, provided that they are satisfactory in other respects, and that there may be advantages in their use, since the detailed information required is less likely to be overlooked. It will be seen that the petition begins[4] with details of the marriage, the places, if any, in which the parties have cohabited in England and Wales, of the domicile or habitual residence of either or both (according to the basis of jurisdiction alleged—see ante pp. 90, 91) and of their respective occupations. If for good reason, such as fear of molestation, the petitioner does not wish his, or her, address to be disclosed, it should be omitted from the petition when it is filed and, before it is served, application should be made ex parte to the registrar to dispense with its inclusion.[5] There follow five paragraphs[6] giving details concerning the children of the family, their full names (including surnames), ages and, if over the age of 16, whether they are continuing their education or undergoing training. Any dispute as to whether a child is a child of the family must be pleaded, details must be given of any proceedings under the Children Act 1948, ss. 1 or 2, and, if the petitioner seeks an order for support of a child of whom the respondent is not a parent, there must be details as to the extent to which the respondent assumed responsibility for the child's maintenance and the liability of any other person to maintain the child.

The details concerning the marriage and children of the family being now clear, the petition begins to turn to matters relating to the breakdown. Details are required[7] of any previous proceedings in England and Wales or elsewhere with regard to the marriage or children of the family, also of whether there are any proceedings continuing outside England and Wales which are in respect of the marriage or are capable of affecting its validity, and if so, with particulars of them[8] and as to whether or not any agreement or arrangement has been made or is proposed to be made between the parties for the support of the respondent and children.[9] Finally comes the allegation, in the case of a petition for divorce, that the marriage has broken down irretrievably, and upon which the facts specified in section 1 (2) of the Act of 1973 the petitioner relies,[10] with particulars of the facts relied upon, but not of the evidence by which it is intended to prove them. To this there is one exception, that if the petitioner intends to rely upon section 11 or 12 of the Civil Evidence Act 1968[11] and adduce evidence of previous convictions or findings of adultery or paternity, he must include a statement to this effect in his petition with particulars of the conviction or finding and of the issue to which he says that the evidence is relevant.[12]

---

[3] [1971] 3 All E.R. 288.
[4] Paras. (1)–(3).
[5] *Practice Direction*, [1968] 2 All E.R. 88.
[6] Paras (4)–(8).
[7] Para. (9).
[8] Para. (10); Rule 9 (2).
[9] Para. (11).
[10] Paras. (13)–(14).
[11] See *ante*, pp. 47 and 48.
[12] Rule 9 (5).

Where the reliance is placed only, under section 1 (2) (*e*) of the Act of 1973, on the fact that the parties have lived apart for a continuous period of at least five years the petitioner is also required[13] to set out the proposals which he makes for financial provision for the respondent should a decree nisi be granted or to state that he makes no such proposals, and if a proposal is made which has not been agreed between the parties the petition must be accompanied by an affidavit by the petitioner giving brief particulars of his means and commitments.[14] The reason for this requirement is that in many such cases the period of five years' separation has been entirely, or mainly, the fault of the petitioner and the respondent ought to be able to know what the financial position is likely to be in order to consider whether to put forward a defence of grave financial or other hardship under section 5 of the Act of 1973.

There are special provisions as to suits for nullity and presumption of death and dissolution.[15]

(c) *The prayer to the petition.*

The petition ends with a prayer for the relief claimed, i.e. that the marriage may be dissolved, or as the case may be. But it is important to note that there are a number of other claims which, if the petitioner wishes to put them forward, should be included in the prayer since, if they are omitted, it will be necessary either to seek leave to amend the petition,[16] or in the case of claims for ancillary relief, to seek leave to make them subsequently.[17] These comprise claims for:—

    (i) custody of any child of the family,
    (ii) an order for costs,
    (iii) an order for maintenance pending suit,
    (iv) a financial provision order,
    (v) a property adjustment order.

It will be noticed that (iii) to (v) above include all possible forms of ancillary relief except an avoidance of disposition order and an order for variation of some order already made.[1]

(d) *Address for service and signature of the petition.*

The petition ends by giving the names and addresses of the persons on whom it is to be served and the petitioner's address for service. This, if a solicitor is acting for him, will consist of the solicitor's name or firm and address, or if he is acting in person, an address in England or Wales at or to which documents for him may be delivered or sent.

The petitioner is not required to sign the petition unless he or she is acting in person. Otherwise it must be signed by counsel if settled by him or, if it was not settled by counsel, by the petitioner's solicitor in his own name or that of

---

[13] Para. (12).
[14] Rule 8 (3).
[15] Rule 9 (3) and (4).
[16] See *post*, p. 223.
[17] See Rule 68 – *post*, p. 249.
[1] See definition in Rule 2.

his firm.[2] The solicitor or counsel need not sign the copy petition which is filed. It suffices if he signs the draft, provided that the signature is reproduced on the copy which is filed.

Some Precedents of various kinds of petition will be found in Appendix II, Part 2 of this Book.

(e) *Arrangements for children.*

The information contained in the petition itself suffices to identify the children who are children of the family. But the actual details of the arrangements proposed for the welfare of each child as to whom the court must declare itself satisfied before the decree of divorce or nullity can be made absolute, or the decree of judicial separation made[3] are contained, not in the petition, but in a separate Form 4. This must be filed with any petition which discloses that there is a minor child of the family who is under 16 or who is over that age and is receiving instruction at an educational establishment or undergoing training for a trade or profession.[4]

Again, this Form, which will be found on p. 398, must be studied. It sets out, as regards each such child as above, where the child is living, particulars of the accommodation, what other persons (naming them) live there and who looks after the child; it also gives details of the present arrangements as to education or training, financial provision and access. It then indicates under each of these headings, how the grant of the decree will affect the present arrangements and if possible indicates any long term proposals for education or training. If any such child suffers from any serious disability or chronic illness this must be stated and a copy of any up-to-date medical report must be attached. The object of this Form is to ensure that the court may have before it very much more detailed information than it at one time had to enable a decision under section 41 of the Act of 1973 to be reached.

A Precedent will be found on p. 422.

(f) *Reconciliation.*

As directed by section 6 (1) of the Act of 1973, Rule 12 (3) requires that where a solicitor is acting for a petitioner for divorce or judicial separation, a certificate in Form 3 shall be filed with the petition, unless otherwise directed on an application made ex parte. This form will be found on p. 398.

It consists of a certificate that the petitioner's solicitor has, or has not, discussed with the petitioner the possibility of a reconciliation and has, or has not, given him the names and addresses of persons qualified to help to effect a reconciliation. The Form as printed appears to require signature by an individual solicitor, being couched in the first person singular. But the wording, "We, the solicitors acting for the petitioner . . . do hereby certify . . .", and a signature of the firm name by a partner will be accepted since otherwise an individual

---

[2] Rule 11.
[3] Act of 1973, s. 41, see *ante*, p. 184.
[4] Rule 8 (2).

partner in the firm would have to discuss this matter personally with each client.

A *Practice Direction*[5] makes it clear that it is not necessary for the names of individuals to be given to the petitioner and that the following organisations and persons will be regarded as persons qualified to help effect a reconciliation for the purposes of the section: any marriage guidance council affiliated to the National Marriage Guidance Council, any centre of the Catholic Marriage Advisory Council, the Jewish Marriage Education Council, any probation officer and certain clergymen of the Church of England and ministers of Free Church denominations. This list is not exclusive, and in the particular circumstances of any case there may be others who should be regarded as qualified.

The Direction emphasises that the object of the section and the Rule is to ensure that parties know where to seek guidance when there is a sincere desire for reconciliation and that reference to a marriage guidance counsellor should not be regarded as a formal step which must be taken in all cases irrespective of whether or not there is any prospect of reconciliation.

The description of the counselling process which a solicitor should try to convey to his client when discussing reconciliation has been summarised by the Chief Officer of the National Marriage Guidance Council as follows:[6]

> "Reference to a reconciliation agency does not mean 'go to see if a counsellor can save your marriage before proceeding to divorce'. Rather it means 'go to discuss with a counsellor, without any prejudice to future action, whether in seeking divorce you are making a decision which you feel to be the best in the circumstances, to see whether these circumstances can be adjusted and to help you at an emotional level to an understanding of what the decision implies'. A message of this sort could be explored with many people making the first approach for a divorce, though it would be fruitless in cases where both parties were long past the point of no return."

A *Practice Note*[7] emphasises that even if complete reconciliation cannot be achieved, expert help will often enable the parties to resolve, with the minimum possible anxiety and harm to themselves and their children, many of the issues liable to be ancillary to the breakdown of a marriage. Short of this, it should at least identify the issues on which they are seriously at variance and on which adjudication is required. Accordingly it provides for machinery to be available in the High Court and divorce county courts whereby if the court considers that there is a reasonable possibility of reconciliation or that there are ancillary proceedings in which conciliation might serve a useful purpose, the court may refer the case, or any particular matter in dispute, to the court welfare officer. If he decides, after discussion with the parties, that there is no such reasonable prospect, he will so report. If not, he may continue to deal with the matter himself or refer it to some other person duly qualified, and the welfare officer will report to the court, this report being limited to a statement of whether or not

---

[5] [1972] 3 All E.R. 768.
[6] Law Society's Gazette, January 1971, at pp. 37, 39.
[7] [1971] 1 W.L.R. 223.

reconciliation has been effective or to what extent, if at all, the parties have been assisted to resolve their disputes by agreement.

(g) *Parties to a petition.*

This is a problem which arises only when the conduct of which the petitioner complains involves not only the respondent spouse but also some other person.

Section 49 of the Act imposes a general requirement that if in proceedings for divorce or judicial separation one spouse alleges that the other has committed adultery, the person with whom the adultery is alleged must be made a party to the proceedings unless this is excused on special grounds. But the section gives power to relax this requirement by rules of court and Rule 13, which deals with this matter, has abolished the distinction which formerly existed according to whether the petitioner was the husband or the wife. The difference between a "co-respondent" and "a woman named who is made a respondent" has vanished; both are now "co-respondents" and the word "respondent" is used throughout the Rules in place of the words "respondent spouse".

Where the petition alleges that the respondent has committed adultery, the person with whom the adultery is alleged must be made a co-respondent, unless he or she is not named in the petition and, if reliance is placed upon section 2 (1) (*a*) of the Act, the petition contains a statement that his or her identity is not known to the petitioner, or the court otherwise directs. Where the petition charges the respondent with an improper association (other than adultery) with a person named, that person need not be joined as a party in the first instance but the petitioner must as soon as is practicable after the time limited for the respondent to give notice of intention to defend has expired, apply for directions as to whether that person shall be made a co-respondent. This situation is most likely to arise when reliance is placed upon section 1 (2) (*b*) of the Act and a husband is alleged to have been engaged in a homosexual relation, or a wife in a lesbian relation, with a named person, or either is charged with indecent familiarities, falling short of adultery, with a person named. None of these provisions, however, applies when the person named has died before the petition is filed,[8] and in cases where directions are required the application may be made ex parte if no notice of intention to defend has been given.[9]

Special provision is made for cases in which a husband is accused of rape upon a person named. Notwithstanding that this is an accusation of adultery against him, she is not thereby accused of adultery, and should not be made a co-respondent unless the court so directs.[10]

The position where the petition relates to a marriage entered into under a law which permits polygamy is covered by Rule 108. The petition must state that the marriage in question is polygamous and whether or not there is, to the petitioner's knowledge, any living spouse of the petitioner additional to the respondent. If so, the petition must state the full name and address of that spouse and the date and place of their marriage or, if it be so, that this infor-

---

[8] Rule 13 (1), (3) and (5).
[9] Rule 13 (4).
[10] Rule 13 (2).

mation is unknown to the petitioner. The court has power to order that any additional spouse shall be added as a party to the proceedings or be given notice of the proceedings, and may do so at any stage of the proceedings on the application of any party or of its own motion. Where an additional spouse is mentioned in a petition or an acknowledgement of service of a petition, the petitioner must, on making any application in the proceedings or, if no previous application has been made, on making a request for directions for trial, ask for directions as to whether the additional spouse should be added as a party to, or given notice of, the proceedings. It is not easy to see why such a spouse should wish to resist an application for dissolution of the marriage between the petitioner and the respondent, though the position might often be otherwise in relation to resulting applications for financial relief and adjustment of property rights.

(h) *Filing the petition.*

A petition may be presented to any divorce county court or to the divorce registry in London, there being no rules requiring the proceedings to be started in any particular court, as there are in relation to other county court proceedings.[11] It is presented by filing it, together with:—

   (i) a marriage certificate;

  (ii) a certificate as to reconciliation in Form 3, if a solicitor is acting for the petitioner;[12]

 (iii) a statement in Form 4 as to arrangements for children with any medical report attached as required by Rule 8 (2);[13]

 (iv) where a petitioner who relies only upon section 1 (2) (*e*) of the Act of 1973 has included in his petition proposals for financial provision for the respondent spouse which have not been agreed, an affidavit giving brief particulars of his means and commitments;[14]

  (v) as many copies of the petition as there are persons to be served and a copy of the statement, report and affidavit mentioned in (iii) and (iv) above for service on the respondent.[15]

Requirements (i) and (ii) above may be dispensed with on application made ex parte.[16]

On the filing of all these documents the registrar will enter the cause in the books of the court and annex to every copy for service a Notice of Proceedings in Form 5 (see p. 400) with Form 6, an Acknowledgement of Service attached (see p. 401). He will also annex to the copy for service on the respondent the additional copy documents mentioned in (v) above.

---

[11] Rule 12 (1).
[12] See *ante*, p. 217.
[13] See *ante*, p. 217.
[14] See *ante*, p. 216.
[15] Rule 12 (5).
[16] Rule 12 (2) and (3).

(i) *Service of the petition.*

Unless an order dispensing with such service is obtained, a copy of the petition must be served on every respondent and co-respondent.[17] Each copy for service is accompanied by a copy of Form 5 which explains to the recipient the courses which are open to him and of Form 6, whereby he can acknowledge receipt of the petition and indicate his intentions. These Forms are discussed more fully on p. 224. The copy for service on the respondent must also be accompanied by copies of Form 4 with any medical report attached and of the affidavit of means and commitments where appropriate.[18] It should be noted that although Form 3 (the certificate as to reconciliation) is filed with the petition, no copy of it is served on any other person.

Special rules govern the methods of service on a person under disability.[19] In all other cases service may be effected through the court or, if the petitioner so requests, through the petitioner. In the majority of cases service is through the court and is effected by ordinary pre-paid post. If the petitioner's solicitor elects to effect service he may do so either by post or by personal service, but the costs of personal service will be disallowed on taxation unless there was good reason for not adopting the less costly method of using the post. Whichever method is adopted, the petition is deemed to have been duly served if an Acknowledgement of Service in Form 6, signed by the party to be served or his solicitor on his behalf, is returned to the court office and, where this Form purports to be signed by the respondent, his signature is proved at the hearing.[20] The petitioner's solicitor will be informed that an Acknowledgement of Service has been received at the court office, because a photographic copy will be sent to him,[21] and he will thus know not only that service has been effected, but also what answers have been given to the various questions in the Form, and in particular to Question 4—"Do you intend to defend the Case?" Where service was effected through the court he will also be informed if it has proved unsuccessful, because notice will be given to him if no Acknowledgement of Service is received in the court office within fifteen days of posting of the papers.

If service by post is impossible because, for example, the address of the person to be served is not known, or it proves ineffectual, the next step is usually to attempt to effect personal service on the respondent or co-respondent by handing to him a copy of the petition and accompanying documents. Should he refuse to accept them he should be told what they are and they should be left in his possession as nearly as may be, usually by throwing them down at his feet. Service is not permitted on a Sunday, Christmas Day or Good Friday[1] and may not be effected by the petitioner himself,[2] no doubt for fear of a breach of the peace. As in the case of service by post, due service is presumed if an Acknowledgedment of Service is received at the court office,

---

[17] Rule 14 (1).
[18] See (v) *supra.*
[19] Rule 113, see *post,* p. 233.
[20] Rule 14 (5).
[21] Rule 14 (8).
[1] C.C.R. Ord. 6, r. 3; R.S.C. Ord. 65, r. 10.
[2] Rule 14 (3).

subject in the case of a respondent to proof of the signature at the hearing. But in the absence of any such acknowledgement, service must be proved by filing an affidavit by the process server showing, in the case of a respondent, his means of knowledge of the identity of the person served. Instructions on this matter must be given to the process server. The most convenient method of identification is usually by means of a photograph exhibited to the affidavit and proved at the hearing to be that of the respondent. Failing this it may be either by the personal knowledge of the process server, the petitioner or some other person present that the person served is the spouse of the petitioner (who cannot, of course, himself effect the service) or by the admission of the person served that he is the spouse of the petitioner. In the latter two cases the full circumstances and means of knowledge and such corroborative evidence as is available must be set out in the affidavit. Where there is no identification by a photograph or signature, or by the presence of some person to be called at the hearing, the case must be referred to the registrar for a decision as to proof of identity.[3]

In some cases when service is by post, despite the absence of an Acknowledgement of Service, it may not be necessary to attempt personal service. It there is some good reason for believing that the party in question received the petition the registrar, on being satisfied by affidavit or otherwise that this is so, may direct that the petition shall be deemed to have been duly served on him.[4] It is not often that advantage can be taken of this Rule. It was applied, for example, in *Heath* v. *Heath*,[5] where two registered letters containing the papers had been sent by the English wife to her American husband at the last address from which he had written to her, and neither had been returned.

More usually if service by post and personal service are ineffective or impossible, application should be made to the registrar to order substituted service, as by serving an agent or manager employed by the party to be served, or, more usually, to order advertisements in lieu of service. The application is made ex parte by lodging an affidavit showing the grounds for the application, which must show clearly what enquiries have been made in an effort to trace the person concerned.[6] Where an order for notice by advertisement is sought, a draft of the proposed advertisement must accompany the application and the registrar will give directions as to the newspapers in which it is to be inserted. To save expense, arrangements for bulk advertisements, covering a number of cases, are made by the court office.

If all else fails, application may be made for an order dispensing with service altogether, which may be made "where it appears necessary or expedient to do so".[7] The Rule formerly provided that only a judge could dispense with service on a respondent spouse. But a registrar has always been able to grant leave to substitute notice of proceedings by advertisement and obviously

---

[3] Rule 14 (7) and *Practice Direction* (Petition: Personal Service), [1972] 2 All E.R. 623.
[4] Rule 14 (6).
[5] [1950] P. 193.
[6] Rule 14 (9).
[7] Rule 14 (10).

such a notice will frequently not reach the respondent. Accordingly Rule
14 (10) now enables a registrar to dispense with service of a copy of the
petition on the respondent or on any other person, and reliance should no
longer be placed upon cases[8] which suggest that such leave should not be
given unless it is clear that the respondent is at least aware that proceedings
are contemplated.[9] An application for an order in respect of the respondent or
any other person may, if no notice of intention to defend has been given, be
made ex parte by lodging an affidavit setting out the grounds of the application[10] though presumably the former practice, of granting leave only upon
terms that any claim for costs against the person named will be waived, will
continue.

Finally it should be mentioned that although leave is needed to serve a writ
or notice of a writ out of the jurisdiction (i.e. outside England and Wales) no
such leave is needed to serve any document in matrimonial proceedings. The
details are given in Rule 117 but it is worth mentioning that the time for
returning the Acknowledgement of Service and giving notice of intention to
defend is enlarged according to the air mail facilities available, and Form 5
must be amended accordingly.[11]

(j) *Amendment and supplemental petitions.*

If it becomes necessary to alter details already given in the petition, such
as dates or places, or to strike out charges, perhaps by reason of some agreement
reached by the parties, or to add claims, such as claims for ancillary relief or
costs not already included in the prayer, the appropriate course is to seek to
amend the petition. But when it is desired to add further charges based upon
facts which are not alleged in the petition, the procedure varies according to
when those facts occurred. If they took place before the date of the petition,
amendment to include them is still possible. If they occurred subsequently, a
supplemental petition is required. Even this may not always be possible,
particularly in the case of desertion. Section 1 (2) (c) of the Act of 1973 requires
a period of two years' desertion "immediately preceding the presentation of the
petition", and if that period is not completed until after presentation of a
petition in which reliance is placed upon, say, adultery, has been filed, neither
amendment nor a supplemental petition is permissible in respect of it, because a
supplemental petition can only allege a period of desertion immediately preceding the main petition.[12] In such a case, if the petition has not yet been
served, the petitioner could file a notice of discontinuance, whereupon the

---

[8] E.g., *Paolantonio* v. *Paolantonio*, [1950] 2 All E.R. 404; *Luccioni* v. *Luccioni*, [1943] P.
49; *Spalenkova* v. *Spalenkova*, [1954] P. 141.
[9] As to suits for a decree of presumption of death and dissolution, see *N.* v. *N.; L.* v. *L.;
C.* v. *C.*, [1957] P. 385.
[10] Rule 14 (10).
[11] Rule 117 (4) (a).
[12] *Spawforth* v. *Spawforth*, [1946] P. 131.

petition would stand dismissed and he could start afresh.[13]   Otherwise he would
have to seek leave to file a second petition because where there is before the
court a petition which has not been dismissed or otherwise disposed of by a
final order, another petition by the same petitioner in respect of the same
marriage may not be presented without such leave.[14]

A petition may be amended without leave before it is served: thereafter
leave is required.   Leave is always required to file a supplemental petition.[15]
If all opposite parties consent in writing leave can in either case be obtained ex
parte by lodging in the court office the supplemental petition, or a copy of the
petition as proposed to be amended.   In all other cases the application is on
notice, or in the High Court by summons, to be served, unless otherwise directed,
on every opposite party.   The registrar may require the application to be supported by an affidavit.[16]   Unless otherwise directed, a copy of the amended or
supplemental petition, and of the order made, must be served on every respondent and co-respondent named in the original, supplemental, or amended petition.[17]   Since the object of matrimonial proceedings is to ensure that justice
is done, an amendment may even be allowed by the judge at the hearing
of the case, subject to such conditions as to costs or otherwise as may be
appropriate.

4. Acting for a respondent, co-respondent or party cited.

(a) *The Notice of Proceedings and Acknowledgement of Service.*

As has already been explained, every copy of the petition which is served
will have annexed to it a copy of Form 5, the Notice of Proceedings, with Form
6, the Acknowledgement of Service, attached.   These Forms will be found on
pp. 400 and 401.   It will be seen that Form 5 explains to the respondent the
various courses which are open to him or her and the consequences.   Form 6
serves the functions of acknowledging that the petition has been duly served on
the respondent or co-respondent, giving his address for service and indicating
the intentions of the party in question.   Both Forms indicate that a party who
intends to instruct a solicitor to act for him should give him the Forms, with all
documents which accompany them, immediately.   Form 5 requires the
respondent or his solicitor on his behalf to complete and detach the Acknowledgement of Service and send it so as to reach the court office within eight
days after receiving it, inclusive of the day of receipt,[18] and warns him that
delay in returning the Form may add to the costs.   In view of the much greater

---

[13] Rule 7.
[14] Rule 12 (4).   There is an exception where a petition for judicial separation has been
presented within three years of the marriage and it is proposed after the three years to
petition for divorce on the same facts.
[15] Rule 17 (1) and (2).
[16] Rule 17 (3) and (4).
[17] Rule 17 (8).
[18] Extra time is allowed when service is effected out of the jurisdiction—see Rayden
11th Edn. at p. 415 for the times,

number of courses open to a respondent these are considered first, and the position of a co-respondent is dealt with later (*post*, p. 231).

(b) *Notice of intention to defend.*

The first important decision is whether or not the respondent should defend the case, a matter which has already been discussed.[19] If it is decided to do so the answer "Yes" should be given to the question "Do you intend to defend the case?" in Form 6, and for the purposes of the Rules this answer constitutes notice of intention to defend.[20] This answer should be given by a respondent who wishes

   (i) to defend the petition or to dispute any of the facts alleged in it; or

  (ii) to make in the proceedings any charge against the petitioner in respect of which the respondent wishes to pray for relief; or

 (iii) where the petitioner relies upon five years' separation under section 1 (2) (*e*) of the Act of 1973, to oppose the grant of a decree on the ground of grave financial or other hardship under section 5 of that Act.

In case (iii) the respondent should also answer in the affirmative to question 6 in Form 6 to indicate that it is his intention to oppose the grant of a decree on that ground.

In each of these three cases the respondent spouse should also, within 29 days of receipt of the petition inclusive of the day of receipt, file an answer to the petition with a copy for service on every opposite party.[21] The case then becomes a defended case and the registrar must order it to be transferred to the High Court[22] and will give notice of the transfer to all parties. The mere fact that notice of intention to defend has been given does not make the case a defended case or necessitate such a transfer: this occurs only when an answer is filed. Even if no notice of intention to defend was given when the Acknowledgement of Service was returned to the court office, it may be given subsequently at any time before directions for trial have been given,[23] and an answer may be filed even though the time for so doing has expired and even though no notice of intention to defend has been given, at any time before the giving of such directions.[1] Nothing said above is intended to suggest that delays of the kind mentioned are desirable: they are likely, as Form 5 gives warning, to result in costs for which the party responsible may be held liable.

Once directions for trial have been given, no pleading can be filed without leave because directions will already have been given for trial of the case as an undefended case, and fresh directions will be needed if it becomes defended.[2]

---

[19] See *ante*, Chapter 3 and p. 50.
[20] Rule 15.
[21] Rules 18 (1) and 23.
[22] Rule 18 (5). An exception occurs in a case of nullity based on mental disorder where the answer contains only a simple denial of the facts.
[23] Rule 15.
[1] Rule 18 (2).
[2] Rule 20.

In *Huxford* v. *Huxford*[3] the husband had petitioned for divorce on the basis of his wife's adultery and she did not discover that he was committing adultery until after the expiration of the time for filing without leave an answer containing a cross-prayer for divorce. Her application for leave to do so was granted on the ground that adultery still involves some moral stigma and she should be entitled to have the true facts established by public decree even though her position as to financial provision would be unaffected. Leave was, however, refused in *Collins* v. *Collins*[4] where a wife, whose husband's petition was based on five years' separation, wished to file an answer praying for a decree on the ground of his desertion, since no question of stigma or of financial advantage arose. And in *Spill* v. *Spill*[5] it was held that where a party seeks a discretionary indulgence from the court, such as leave to file an answer out of time, because of a change of mind he should file an affidavit of merits explaining on oath his change of mind so as to show that it was genuine and not a mere tactical device.

(c) *The answer.*

An answer may take various forms. It may consist of a bare denial of the facts alleged, such as a denial that the adultery charged was committed or that the conduct complained of in a petition based upon section 1 (2) (*b*) of the 1973 Act ever occurred. But since the object of pleadings is to ensure that each party has notice of the case which the other intends to raise, and is not taken by surprise at the hearing, a bare denial is sometimes insufficient. This would seem to be so where, for example, in a case founded upon adultery, the respondent alleges that the petitioner does not find it intolerable to live with the respondent, or where it is alleged that the conduct complained of under section 1 (2) (*b*) was prompted by provocation, or that the petitioner had consented to it.[6] In these cases it is advisable, whether or not it is strictly necessary, to set out the facts relied upon, though not the evidence by which they are to be proved.[7] This is certainly necessary where, whether the facts alleged in the petition are admitted or denied, it is sought also to raise some defence, such as the fact that in any event the marriage has not irretrievably broken down[8] or, in a case based on five years' separation, that to grant a decree would cause grave financial or other hardship.[9] These are defences, and the facts which are said to support them must be specifically pleaded (see Precedent, *post*, p. 427). Where it is considered that the details in the petition are too vague to enable an answer to be framed, application may be made first for further and better particulars.[10]

Whether the facts alleged in the petition are admitted or denied, and whether

---

[3] [1972] 1 All E.R. 330.
[4] [1972] 2 All E.R. 658, C.A.
[5] [1972] 3 All E.R. 9, C.A.
[6] See *Porr* v. *Porr*, [1963] 1 All E.R. 213.
[7] Rule 21 (1).
[8] Act of 1973, s. 1 (4).
[9] *Ibid.*, s. 5.
[10] *Post*, p. 232.

or not some other defence is raised, the answer may also make charges and pray for relief in respect of them.[11] Thus if the petition prayed for dissolution, the answer could also pray for dissolution or for judicial separation, the facts relied upon under section 1 (2) being set out with sufficient particularity. There will often be little point in a cross-prayer for dissolution, as has already been explained,[12] but if the petitioner relied upon five years' separation and for financial or other reasons the respondent did not wish the marriage to be ended, there is no reason why the answer should not pray for judicial separation on the basis of the same five years of life apart. One exception must be noted. If the petition prays for nullity the answer cannot pray for dissolution or for judicial separation, since this is not an answer to the allegation that the marriage is void or voidable. This difficulty can, however, be avoided by repeating the allegation in the answer that the marriage is valid and subsisting, and adding the words "by way of cross-petition" before the prayer for dissolution or judicial separation.[13]

Whether or not the answer consists only of a simple denial of the facts, it must also, if there is any dispute as to the paragraphs in the petition concerning who are or are not children of the family,[14] contain full particulars of the facts relied upon unless otherwise directed.[15] It must also, if application is made for support by the petitioner of a child of whom he is not a parent, contain a statement of the extent to which the petitioner assumed responsibility for the child's maintenance and of the liability of any other person to maintain the child.[16] If the answer is more than a simple denial but alleges other facts it must also state whether or not any agreement has been made, or is proposed to be made, for the support of the petitioner and children of the family and, if cross-relief is sought by way of divorce on the basis of five years' separation, details are required as to proposals for financial support of the petitioner.[17]

The answer concludes with a prayer giving details of the relief claimed which, with appropriate modifications, is the same as that which can be claimed in the prayer to a petition,[18] except that it is not necessary in an answer to include a claim for costs against the petitioner.[19] But if the respondent does not wish to defend the case it is not necessary to file an answer merely with the object of raising other claims. Rule 49 provides that a respondent, without filing an answer, may be heard on any question of custody of, or access to, any child of the family, any question of ancillary relief and any question of whether a child should be committed to the care of a local authority under section 43, or a supervision order should be made in respect of a child under section 44, of the Act of 1973. It also provides that any respondent, co-respondent or party cited

---

[11] Act of 1973, s. 20; Rule 18 (1) (*b*).
[12] See *ante*, p. 50.
[13] *Pickett* v. *Pickett*, [1951] P. 267.
[14] Form 2, paras. (4), (5) and (6)—*post*, p. 396.
[15] Rule 21 (2).
[16] Form 2, para. (8), and see *ante*, p. 147.
[17] *Ibid.*, paras. (11) and (12), and see *ante*, p. 216. See also Rules 21 (5) and 9 (5) as to Civil Evidence Act 1968, ss. 11 and 12.
[18] See *ante*, p. 216.
[19] Rule 21 (3).

may, without filing an answer, be heard on any question as to costs, but in this case no allegation can be made against the party who is claiming costs unless the party making the allegation has filed an answer. There is no such requirement in respect, for example, of questions of custody and of access to children or ancillary relief in respect of which, as will be explained later,[20] serious questions of conduct may arise later although the suit was undefended and no answer was filed.

The rules as to signature of an answer are the same as those for a petition[1] as also are the rules as to joinder of third parties against whom the respondent alleges adultery and as to the position when charges of other improper association or of rape are made. But in this case, whether the third party is a man or a woman, he or she is referred to in the title of the proceedings and for other purposes as a "party cited" and not as a co-respondent.[2] The registrar will annex to every copy answer for service on a party cited the usual notice in Form 5 with Form 6 annexed, and the copy answer must be served on each party cited as if it were a petition.[3] He will also send a copy to the address for service of the petitioner.

(d) *Consent to decree after two years' separation.*

Form 5 contains an explanation to the respondent, in a case in which the petitioner relies upon section 1 (2) (*d*) of the Act of 1973, of the consequences of consenting to the grant of a decree, particularly as to rights should the petitioner die intestate and as to pension rights. Form 6 requires an answer in such a case to the question "Do you consent to a decree being granted?" An affirmative answer to this question does not, however, prevent a subsequent change of mind. Rule 16 provides that where, before the hearing, the respondent wishes to indicate to the court that he consents to the grant of a decree, this must be done by giving to the registrar a notice to that effect signed by the respondent personally. For this purpose an Acknowledgement of Service containing an affirmative answer to the question "Do you consent to a decree being granted?" is a sufficient notice provided that the Acknowledgement is signed in the case of a respondent acting in person, by the respondent, and in the case of a respondent represented by a solicitor, by the respondent as well as by the solicitor. The Rule also enables the respondent in such a case to give notice to the court that he does not consent to a decree being granted or that he withdraws any consent which he has already given. In that event, if the petition does not also allege any of the other facts specified in section 1 (2) of the Act of 1973, the proceedings on the petition must be stayed and the registrar will give notice of the stay to all parties. The wisdom of relying also, if that be possible, on some one or more of the other facts in section 1 (2) such as two years' desertion, and not only upon section 1 (2)(*d*), is evident because, if consent under section 1 (2) (*d*) was given

---

[20] *Post*, p. 254.
[1] Rules 21 (7) and 11, see *ante*, p. 216.
[2] Rule 22.
[3] Rules 22 (1) and 23.

and then withdrawn, the petition could still proceed upon the basis of the other facts alleged.

It is presumably too late to withdraw a consent under Rule 16 after the decree nisi has been granted. But even then, at any time before the decree is made absolute, the respondent may apply under section 10 (1) of the Act of 1973 to have the decree nisi rescinded on the ground that the petitioner misled the respondent about any matter which the respondent took into account in deciding to consent.[4] The procedure is governed by Rule 56. The application must be made to a judge and must be made in open court. It is made in the High Court by notice to attend before the judge on a day specified in the notice and in a divorce county court on notice of application.[5] These notices, must, unless otherwise directed, be served on the petitioner not less than fourteen days before the date fixed for hearing. The application must be supported by an affidavit setting out the allegations relied upon, a copy of which must be served on the petitioner.

(e) *Applications under section* 10 (2) *of the Act of* 1973.

As has already been explained, where the court has granted a decree nisi on the basis of a finding that the petitioner was entitled to rely in support of his petition on the fact of two years' or five years' separation (as the case may be) and has made no such finding as to any other fact mentioned in section 1 (2) of the Act of 1973, the respondent can apply to the court to consider his or her financial position after the divorce.[6] It is not, however, necessary to await the decree nisi before taking steps to enable such an application to be made. Form 5 particularly warns the respondent spouse of the need to consider carefully such financial proposals as are contained in a petition based upon five years' separation and explains the effects of section 10 (2). Form 6 contains a question as to whether or not the respondent intends to apply to the court under the section. If so, the subsequent procedure will be governed by Rule 57.

The application to consider the respondent's position after the divorce must be made by notice in Form 12, which will be found on p. 406. The notice must be filed, if the case is pending in a divorce county court, in that court, or if it is pending in the High Court, in the registry in which it is proceeding, and within four days after filing the notice the applicant must serve a copy of the notice on the respondent to the application.[7] Both parties are required, unless they have already done so, to file affidavits giving full particulars of their property and income.[8] The former requirement that these applications must be heard by a judge has been abolished, and the powers of the court on the hearing of the application may be exercised by the registrar who, once a decree nisi containing the necessary findings has been granted, will fix an appointment for hearing.[9]

---

[4] See *ante*, p. 59.
[5] See C.C.R. Ord. 13, r. 1, and *ante*, p. 213.
[6] See *ante*, pp. 57, 58.
[7] Rule 70.
[8] Rule 57 (2) and (3).
[9] Rule 57 (4) and (5).

The procedure is the same as that on an application for ancillary relief[10] and Rule 80 (which deals with transfer to the High Court in cases of contested issues of conduct)[11] and Rule 81 (which allows such transfer for purposes of expedition)[12] will apply. At any time before the hearing by the registrar is concluded (and without prejudice to any right of appeal) the registrar may refer the application, or any question arising thereon, to a judge, and he *must* do this if either party so requests.[13] A statement that the requirements of section 10 (3) or (4) have been satisfied[14] must be entered in the court minutes, and until this has been done the decree cannot be made absolute.[15]

In cases based upon five years' separation, a respondent will often be well advised to take advantage of both section 5 and section 10 (2) of the Act of 1973. If, for example, the breakdown of the marriage is wholly or mainly due to the conduct of the petitioner, who has left his wife to live with another woman and now seeks to take advantage of his own wrong, his wife, unless suitable financial proposals have been made or agreed, should in appropriate cases raise a defence of grave financial or other hardship under section 5 and also, in case that defence should fail because the hardship was not sufficiently grave, give notice of intention to apply for consideration of whether the financial provision is reasonable and fair or the best which can be made in the circumstances, under section 10 (2). This situation is less likely to arise after two years of life apart because the respondent's consent to the grant of a decree is unlikely to have been given unless he or she was satisfied as to the financial arrangements consequent upon that decree. But if the petitioner's financial position should substantially improve after the consent had been given, or even after decree nisi, an application under section 10 (2) would be the appropriate course to take, since the respondent was in no way misled into giving consent, and an application under section 10 (1) to rescind the decree nisi would not be possible. Such things can occur; the petitioner might have a big win in the football pools or his rich aunt might die and leave everything to her favourite nephew. If they occur before decree nisi the consent can be withdrawn: if they occur later the decree absolute can be delayed until the financial proposals have been re-adjusted.

(f) *Arrangements for children.*

Whether or not the case is defended, the respondent may not be happy about the contents of Form 4 in relation to the present or proposed arrangements for the children of the family. In such cases Rule 50 allows the respondent at any time before the judge makes an order under section 41 of the Act of 1973[16] to file in the court office a written statement of his or her views on the

---

[10] Rule 77 (3) to (7), and see *post*, p. 252.
[11] See *post*, p. 253.
[12] See *post*, p. 254.
[13] Rule 57 (6).
[14] See *ante*, pp. 58, 59.
[15] Rules 57 (7) and 65 (2) (g). But see *Practice Direction (Divorce: Financial Application Withdrawn)*, [1972] 3 All E.R. 623.
[16] See *ante*, p. 184.

present and proposed arrangements for the children, and on receipt of such a statement the registrar will send a copy to the petitioner. Form 5 explains to the respondent that if this is done a copy of the statement will be placed before the judge dealing with the arrangements for children. It must be borne in mind that in an undefended case the judge will generally deal with the question of the arrangements for the children when he pronounces the decree nisi and that it is important to have the statement of any objections to these arrangements before him at that moment.

(g) *The co-respondent.*

When acting for a co-respondent there are far fewer matters to be considered. Whether he or she was made a party to the proceedings by reason of a charge of adultery, or directed to be made a co-respondent by reason of some allegation or improper association or of rape, it is only necessary to decide whether or not the case should be defended in order to deny the charges in the petition because of the stigma which they may otherwise involve or because of the potential liability for costs. The claim for damages which in the past often led a male adulterer to contest the case can no longer be made. The decision whether or not to defend must be for the client, who must in reaching his decision have in mind that whatever the outcome may be, defended proceedings will always be more likely to attract publicity than those which are undefended, and that the costs of a defended case, should they be awarded against the party concerned, will inevitably be very much higher than those of an undefended suit. These points may seem cynical, but they are undeniable.

(h) *Pleadings subsequent to answer.*

If the case is undefended no question of any pleading other than the petition arises. But in a defended case a petitioner may, without leave, file a reply to the answer within fourteen days after receipt of a copy of the answer.[17] If the answer does not contain a prayer for a decree the petitioner is deemed, on making a request for directions for trial, to have denied every material allegation of fact contained in the answer;[18] there is thus little point in that case in filing a reply unless the petitioner desires to introduce additional facts to counter the allegations made in the answer. But where the answer prays for a decree, the petitioner's failure to file a reply will result in the cross-prayer being undefended. No pleading subsequent to reply can be filed without leave.[19] Such a pleading, known as a rejoinder, is very rare.

A party cited who wishes to defend the answer or dispute any facts alleged in it may himself give notice in his Acknowledgement of Service of his intention to defend and may file an answer (often referred to as a reply) within 29 days of service of the answer on him, inclusive of the day of service.[20] Whether he

---

[17] Rule 19 (1).
[18] Rule 19 (2).
[19] Rule 19 (3).
[20] Rules 22 (2) and 18.

wishes to do so will be determined by the same factors which will influence a co-respondent.

When a reply or an answer by a party cited is filed, additional copies must be filed for every opposite party and the registrar will send these copies to them at their addresses for service.[21]

These subsequent pleadings may be filed out of time up to the moment when directions for trial have been given, but thereafter can be filed only with leave.[22]

(i) *Particulars*.

A party who is served with a pleading, whether it be a petition, an answer or a reply, may sometimes feel that the allegations in his opponent's pleading are so vague, or couched in such general terms, that he cannot be certain of the case which is being put forward against him. In that event he may in writing request the party whose pleading it is to give particulars of the allegation or other matter pleaded, and will usually make this request before drafting and filing his own pleading. If that party fails to give the particulars within a reasonable time, or they are insufficient, the party requiring them may apply to the registrar for an order that the particulars be given.[23] If an application for an order was made without first making a request in writing, the costs of application to the registrar would usually be disallowed.

The party giving the particulars must incorporate in them the request or order, each item following immediately after the corresponding item in the request or order, so that they can be readily identified.[1] Whether the particulars are given in pursuance of a request or an order, a copy of them must be filed at the same time.[2] When given, they form part of the pleading and the party giving them cannot give evidence of matters which are not contained in the original pleading or the particulars unless he first gets leave to amend the pleading.

5. **Persons under disability.**

Special provisions are contained in Rules 112 and 113 as to persons under disability, that is to say a minor or a patient, defined as a person who by reason of mental disorder within the meaning of the Mental Health Act 1959, is incapable of managing and administering his property and affairs.

Such a person may begin and prosecute any matrimonial proceedings by his next friend. Where a petitioner is a minor who is not also a patient any person may act as his next friend, but a parent or other relative will usually act. No order is needed, but the written consent of the next friend to act must be filed, together with a certificate by the minor's solicitor that he is a proper person to act and has no interest adverse to that of the minor. Where the petitioner is a patient and some person is authorised under Part VIII of the Mental Health Act 1959 to conduct legal proceedings on his behalf that person will act

---

[21] Rule 23.
[22] Rule 20.
[23] Rule 26.
[1] Rule 26 (2).
[2] Rule 26 (3).

as next friend, and his written consent to act with an office copy of the order or other authorisation under Part VIII must be filed. If there is no such person, the Official Solicitor may consent to act, but otherwise the written consent of the next friend must be filed with the solicitor's certificate mentioned above, which must also state his grounds for knowing or believing that the petitioner is a patient and that no person has been authorised under Part VIII of the Act.

A person under disability may defend matrimonial proceedings by his guardian *ad litem*. The minor or patient is named as a respondent or co-respondent to the petition in the same way as any other party, but service cannot be effected through the court.[3] If the person to be served is a minor who is not also a patient, the petition must be served on his father or guardian or, if he has neither, on the person with whom he resides or in whose care he is.[4] If a patient is to be served, the petition must be served on the person authorised under Part VIII of the Mental Health Act 1959, or if there is no such person, on the Official Solicitor if he has consented to act as guardian *ad litem*, or otherwise on the person with whom the patient resides or in whose care he is. It may sometimes happen that the petitioner is not aware that the person with whom adultery is alleged was a person under disability, and that service by post was effected on that person through the court. If this matter comes to light before a decree nisi is granted, the court has power if the circumstances justify this to order that the service be deemed to be good service.[5] If the matter comes to light after decree nisi, the result is that, by virtue of R.S.C. Ord. 70, r. 1, the decree nisi is voidable rather than void, and the court may if it thinks fit allow it to be made absolute.[6] A petition (or other document) served on a person under disability in accordance with this Rule must be served with a notice that the contents are to be communicated to him if he is over the age of 16, or the recipient is satisfied, after consultation with his medical officer or attendant, that this would be detrimental to his mental condition.[7]

When service has been effected on a person under disability, the proceedings must be defended on his behalf by a guardian *ad litem*, and no notice of intention to defend can be given, or answer filed, by or on behalf of that person unless there is a guardian *ad litem* and the appropriate documents have been filed.[8] If the person in question is a minor who is not also a patient, no order is required and any person may act as guardian *ad litem*; the consent and certificate required to be filed are the same as those required in the case of a next friend. If a person has been authorised to defend proceedings for a patient under Part VIII of the Act of 1959 he will act as guardian *ad litem*, and again the same consent and office copy order are required as for a next friend. If there is no such person, the Official Solicitor will act, if he consents, but otherwise an application may be made on behalf of the patient for the appointment of a guardian.[9]

---

[3] Rule 14 (2).
[4] Rule 113 (1) (*a*)
[5] Rule 113 (1).
[6] *John* v. *John and Goff*, [1965] P. 289.
[7] Rule 113 (2); Form 25.
[8] Rule 112 (7).
[9] Rule 112 (5).

If the petition or other document is served on a person whom there is reasonable ground for believing to be a person under disability and no notice of intention to defend has been given or answer filed on his behalf, the petitioner must, before taking any further step in the proceedings, apply to a registrar for directions as to whether a guardian *ad litem* should be appointed to act for him and the registrar may, if he thinks this necessary in order to protect his interests, order that some proper person be appointed to act as his guardian *ad litem*. In a nullity suit based on mental disorder, whether or not notice of intention to defend has been given, the petitioner cannot proceed with the case without leave, and the registrar may make it a condition of granting leave that a guardian *ad litem* should first be appointed.[10]

These rules apply, with appropriate modifications, to parties cited in an answer and to persons who may be made parties to other proceedings, such as those based upon wilful neglect to maintain, or for alteration of a maintenance agreement or for provision out of the estate of a former spouse.

6. Preparation for trial.

(a) *Discovery of documents in a defended cause.*

The rules as to discovery and inspection of documents which apply to an action begun by writ[11] apply also, with some modification, to a defended matrimonial cause begun by petition.[12] Accordingly, if the cause is defended, the parties between whom pleadings are closed must, within 14 days after the pleadings are deemed to be closed between them, exchange lists of the documents which are or have been in their possession, custody or power relating to matters in question in the proceedings. At this stage these lists will presumably be confined to documents relating to the question of whether or not the decree which is sought should be granted, since separate provision is made by Rule 77 (4)[13] for lists of documents relating to applications for ancillary relief. For the purposes of the rule, pleadings are deemed to be closed after the expiration of fourteen days after service of the reply, or if there is no reply, after service of the answer. Where in addition to the spouses there are other parties to the proceedings, such as a co-respondent or party cited, whose answer may be served at different times, it follows that the pleadings as between the spouses and as between the petitioner and some other party may not be deemed to close on the same day.

The form which each list should take is prescribed.[14] There are annexed to it two Schedules. The First Schedule lists the documents in the possession, custody or power of the party in question, and is divided into Part I, those documents which he does not object to produce, and Part II, those which he objects to produce, the grounds for objection being stated in the body of the list rather than the Schedule. The Second Schedule lists those documents which were formerly in his possession, custody or power, but with which he has now

---

[10] Rules 112 (6) and 114.
[11] R.S.C. Ord. 24.
[12] Rule 28.
[13] See *post*, p. 252.
[14] R.S.C. Ord. 25, r. 5, Appendix A, Form 26.

parted, and in the body of the list he states what has become of them. Thus the originals of letters written by that party will appear in the Second Schedule, with a statement that they were despatched on the dates which they respectively bear to the persons to whom they were respectively addressed, and any copies which the party retains will be listed in the First Schedule. Amongst the grounds for objection to produce are that the document is covered by legal professional privilege, or was prepared with a view to anticipated litigation, or that production would be injurious to the public interest. It is no longer, however, a valid objection that the document would tend to show that he has been guilty of adultery, so that incriminating letters in a person's possession must be disclosed and produced.[15] The petitioner or any party to the proceedings who has filed an answer is to be supplied on request, free of charge with a copy of any list served on any other party.[16] At any time before directions for trial have been given any party can by notice in writing require that a list served on him be verified by affidavit, and this must be done within fourteen days of service of the notice. Should a party fail to serve a list of documents as required by these rules, or to verify it by affidavit when requested to do so, application may be made by summons to the registrar for an order that he shall do so. Alternatively an application may be made to the registrar, supported by an affidavit that a party has, or has had, a specific document in his possession, custody or power, and the registrar may order him to answer by affidavit whether he has it, or has had it, and in the latter event what has become of it.[17]

This process of discovery enables each party to ascertain what documents, if any, are in the hands of other parties which may assist him to prove his own case or to destroy that of his opponent. But knowing that such documents exist will not help him unless he inspects them. Accordingly each party, when he serves his list on any other party, must also serve a notice giving a time and place at which they may be inspected and copies taken within the next seven days. If a party fails to give this notice, or objects to produce any document, the registrar may make an order for production of the documents for inspection, and in this way will determine the validity of any objection to production of documents in the Second Part of the First Schedule to a list. Disobedience to an order for disovery or production of documents is punishable by committal.

(b) *Interrogatories in a defended case.*

The object of interrogatories is to obtain from an opposite party admissions of fact and to discover more exactly what his case is, though not how he proposes to prove it. The interrogatories consist of a list of questions which he is required to answer by affidavit. Unlike further and better particulars, the answers do not form part of the pleadings, but may be given in evidence at the trial of the case.

As in the case of discovery of documents the rules governing discovery of

---

[15] *Skone* v. *Skone*, [1971] 2 All E.R. 582, H.L.; Civil Evidence Act 1968, s. 16 (5).
[16] Rule 28(3).
[17] R.S.C. Ord. 24, r. 7.

of facts by interrogatories in an action begun by writ[18] apply also, with modifications, to a defended matrimonial cause.[19] Application for leave to administer interrogatories is made by summons to the registrar, a copy of the proposed interrogatories being filed when the summons is issued, and served with the summons. Leave will be given only in respect of such interrogatories as the registrar thinks necessary for disposing fairly of the cause or for saving costs. In *Nast* v. *Nast*[20] where the husband had petitioned for divorce on the basis of his wife's adultery with one co-respondent, and both she and the co-respondent had filed answers, a direct question to the wife as to whether or not she had committed adultery with the co-respondent was allowed by the Court of Appeal. Any privilege which might formerly have excused her from answering such a question was abolished by section 16 (5) of the Civil Evidence Act 1968. But in *C.* v. *C.*[21] the position was very different. The husband's petition had charged his wife with adultery with three co-respondents. Two of them had filed answers denying the adultery, although the wife had not. Mr. Justice Latey refused to allow interrogatories to be administered to the wife as to whether or not she had committed adultery with them. The words "fairly disposing of the cause" included fairness to the co-respondents as well as to the wife. If she admitted the adultery in sworn answers, that sworn evidence would presumably be evidence against them as well as against her, but they would be unable to cross-examine her unless she were called to give evidence. Further, as she was not contesting the suit and if required to answer would need legal aid, it was questionable whether an order that she should do so would save costs. It must not, however, be supposed that interrogatories are limited to matters of adultery. They may well be aimed, for example, at questions of unreasonable behaviour under section 1 (2) (*b*) of the Act of 1973, or obtaining details of a husband's means and commitments in support of a defence of grave financial or other hardship under section 5 of that Act.[22] Since the case is defended, they will normally be drafted by counsel.

The registrar's order will require such interrogatories as he may allow to be answered by affidavit within a fixed time, objections to answer being taken in the affidavit. If an answer is insufficient, the registrar may order a further answer by affidavit or oral examination. If the order to file an affidavit, or further affidavit, is disobeyed, the disobedience is punishable with committal.

(c) *Allegations under section* 1 (2) (*b*) *of the Act of* 1973.

Where in a defended case the petitioner alleges that the respondent has behaved in such a way that the petitioner cannot reasonably be expected to live with the respondent, the conduct complained of may often consist of a number of incidents, perhaps differing in kind and spread over some considerable period of time.[23] The defence might consist, as regards some of these incidents, of a denial that they ever occurred, as regards others, that the respondent's conduct resulted from some provocation on the part of the petitioner, and as

---

[18] R.S.C. Ord. 26.   [19] Rule 29.
[20] [1972] Fam. 142, C.A.
[21] [1973] 3 All E.R. 770.
[22] Separate provision is made by Rule 77 (4) for discovery in relation to ancillary relief.
[23] See Precedent, *post*, p. 425.

regards yet others, that what was done was done with the petitioner's consent. The task of unravelling this tangled web at the trial might be formidable.

Accordingly Rule 35 provides that in cases where reliance is placed upon section 1 (2) (*b*) the registrar may, of his own motion on giving directions for trial or on the application of any party made at any time before the trial, order or authorise the party who made the request for or obtained such directions to file a Schedule of the allegations and counter-allegations made in the pleadings or particulars. Where such an order is made the allegations or counter-allegations must, unless otherwise directed, be listed concisely in chronological order, each counter-allegation being set against the allegation to which it relates, and the party filing the Schedule must serve a copy on any other party to the cause who has filed a pleading. Since the case is defended, counsel who is instructed to act for the party in question will normally be instructed to draft the Schedule.

(d) *Medical examination in nullity suits.*

Where a decree of nullity is sought on the basis that the marriage has not been consummated, the success or failure of the petition must often depend upon the medical evidence. In proceedings for nullity on the ground of inability to consummate the marriage the petitioner must, subject to the exceptions mentioned below, apply to the registrar to determine whether medical inspectors should be appointed to examine the parties. The petitioner is not, however, required to do this in an undefended cause:—

(i) if the husband is the petitioner; or

(ii) if the wife is the petitioner and it appears that she has previously been married or has borne a child, or a statement by her that she is not a virgin has been filed

unless, in either case, the petitioner is alleging his or her own incapacity.[1] With these exceptions, the petitioner should apply, where the respondent has not given notice of intention to defend, after the time limited for giving the notice has expired.[2] If this notice has been given, the application should be made after the expiration of the time allowed for filing an answer,[3] or if an answer has been filed, after it has been filed.[4] If the petitioner fails to apply within a reasonable time, the respondent may do so.

Where the petition is based upon wilful refusal to consummate the marriage, either party may apply to the registrar for the appointment of medical inspectors, but neither is compelled to do so.[5] In all cases in which no notice of intention to defend has been given the application to the registrar may be made ex parte.

If the registrar hearing the application thinks it expedient to do so, he may appoint a medical inspector, or if he thinks it necessary, two medical inspectors

---

[1] Rule 30 (1) and (2).

[2] I.e., usually after 8 days from receipt of the petition, inclusive of the day of receipt. See *ante*, p. 225.

[3] I.e. 29 days after receipt of the petition, inclusive of the day of receipt. See *ante*, p. 225.

[4] Rule 30 (4).

[5] Rule 30 (6).

to examine the parties and report to the court, and the party who made the application must serve on the other party notice of the time and place for the examination.[6] The occasion for appointment of two medical inspectors will usually arise if the wife prefers to be examined by a woman doctor, who will not also be appointed to examine the husband, and sometimes if they reside at places a long distance apart. Examination will usually take place at the doctor's consulting room, unless the registrar orders it to be held at the court office or some other convenient place.[7] In order to avoid impersonation by some other more (or less) capable party, a spouse attending for examination is required to sign in the doctor's presence a statement that he or she is the person referred to as petitioner or respondent, and the doctor must certify in the statement that this was done. The inspector's report is filed and either party is entitled to a copy on payment of the prescribed fee.[8]

(e) *Transfer of a cause.*

All matrimonial causes are commenced in a divorce county court. The necessity for transfer to the High Court of an application for leave to petition for divorce within three years of the date of the marriage if notice of intention to defend that application is given has already been explained.[9] So also has the requirement that a suit for divorce, nullity or judicial separation must be transferred to the High Court if an answer is filed.[10] Rule 32 (1) gives a much more general discretion to the court[11] to order a cause pending in a divorce county court to be transferred to the High Court where, having regard to all the circumstances, including the difficulty or importance of the cause or any issue arising therein, the court thinks it desirable that the case (although undefended) should be heard in the High Court. Such transfers have been rare. A case which is likely to arise more often occurs when, by reason of a contested issue of conduct, an order is made for an application for ancillary relief in an undefended case to be transferred to the High Court under Rule 80. If a decree nisi has already been pronounced, it may then be more convenient to transfer the whole cause to the High Court.[12] This matter is considered more fully on p. 254.

It may sometimes happen that a defended case which has been transferred to the High Court becomes undefended, probably because the parties have been able to reach some agreement as to questions of financial provision and property rights. In such a case the court must order it to be re-transferred to a divorce county court unless, because of the proximity of the probable date of trial or otherwise, the court thinks it desirable for it to be heard in the High Court.[13]

Finally there are cases in which, for reasons of convenience or otherwise, a case ought to be transferred from one divorce county court to another[14] or,

---

[6] Rule 30 (8) and (10).
[7] Rule 31 (1).
[8] Rule 31 (2) and (3).
[9] See *ante*, p. 213.
[10] See *ante*, p. 225.
[11] I.e. to a judge or the registrar—see Rule 2.
[12] Rule 80 (6).
[13] Rule 27.
[14] Rule 32 (2).

when it has already been transferred to the High Court, from the registry in which it is proceeding to another registry.[15] The court (i.e. a judge or the registrar) may order that this be done.

In all these cases the judge or registrar may make the order for transfer of his own motion or on the application of a party. But before doing so of his own motion he must give the parties an opportunity of being heard.[16]

(f) *Stay of Proceedings under Domicile and Matrimonial Proceedings Act* 1973.

The requirements of Schedule 1 of this Act as to obligatory and discretionary stays of proceedings on the ground that matrimonial proceedings are pending in another jurisdiction have already been explained (see *ante*, pp. 91–93). In accordance with paragraph 7 of that Schedule every petition for divorce, nullity or judicial separation, and every answer to any such petition which contains a prayer for relief, must state whether or not there are to the knowledge of the petitioner (or the respondent, as the case may be) any proceedings continuing in any country outside England and Wales which are in respect of the marriage or capable of affecting its validity or subsistence.[17] If there are such proceedings, particulars must be given of the court, tribunal or authority before which they were begun, the date when they were begun, the names of the parties, the date, or expected date, of the trial and any other factors which may be relevant to the question of whether the proceedings here should be stayed.[18]

An application by the petitioner or respondent in proceedings for divorce for an obligatory stay[19] on the ground that proceedings for divorce or nullity are continuing in a "related jurisdiction",[20] or for the discharge of an order already made for an obligatory or a discretionary stay,[21] must be made to the registrar, who may determine it himself or refer it, or any question arising on it, to a judge for his decision as if it were an application for ancillary relief.[22] A registrar has, however, no power to deal with an application for a discretionary stay,[23] which must always be made to a judge.[24] Any party who makes a request for directions for trial must, if there has been any change in the information as to proceedings elsewhere given in the petition or answer, file a statement giving particulars of the change[25] and if, on giving directions for trial, the registrar considers that the question of whether there should be a discretionary stay ought to be determined by the court, he will fix a time and date for the consideration of that question by a judge and give notice of it to all parties.[26]

---

[15] Rule 32 (3).
[16] Rule 32 (4).
[17] Rules 9 (2) (a) and 21 (4). And see Form 2, para. (10), *post*, p. 397.
[18] Rule 9 (2) (b). Note also its provisions as to proceedings not instituted in a court of law.
[19] Under Sched. 1, para. 8.
[20] I.e. in Scotland, Northern Ireland, Jersey, Guernsey, (including Alderney and Sark) or the Isle of Man; Sched. 1, para. 3 (2).
[21] Sched. 1, para. 10, and Rule 36 (5).
[22] Rule 36 (1).
[23] Under Sched. 1, para. 9.
[24] Rule 36 (2).
[25] Rule 36 (4).
[26] Rule 36 (3).

(g) *Directions for trial.*

When the case is ready for trial, the petitioner, or any party who is defending, can make a written request to the registrar for directions for trial. Before giving these directions the registrar must satisfy himself that a number of steps which have already been considered have been taken,[27] i e.

(i) That where a charge of improper association with, a person named has been made, application has been made for directions as to whether that person should be made a co-respondent.[28]

(ii) That a copy of the petition and any subsequent pleading has been duly served on every party required to be served.[29]

(iii) If no notice of intention to defend has been given by any party entitled to give it, that the time for giving that notice has expired.[30]

(iv) If notice of intention to defend has been given by any party, that the time for filing an answer has expired.[1]

(v) If an answer has been filed, that the time for filing any subsequent pleading has expired.[2]

(vi) In proceedings for nullity, that the rules as to medical inspection[3] have been complied with and that if inspection was ordered the report of the inspector or inspectors has been filed.

If the case is undefended, the request for directions, on a Form which is obtainable from the court office, must state the place of trial desired, where the witnesses whom it is proposed to call reside, an estimate of the probable length of the trial, and any other fact which may be relevant for determining the place of trial.[4] In some cases the registrar may be in a position to fix the arrangements for the trial immediately. This may be so when the case is pending in a divorce county court which is also a court of trial and the registrar directs trial at that court. In that event he gives directions by fixing the date, place and as nearly as may be, the time of the trial and gives notice to all parties.[5] If, although trial is to be at that divorce county court, it is not possible to determine the date of trial at this stage, or if trial is to be in some other court, or if the case is pending in the divorce registry in London, the registrar instead gives directions for trial by setting the cause down for trial and giving notice that he has done so to all parties. If trial is to be in another divorce county court, the registrar of the court in which it is pending will send the file to the registrar of the court of trial, who will fix the date, time and place and give notice to the parties.[6]

To these general rules as to directions for trial, there is now a somewhat

---

[27] Rule 33.
[28] Rule 13, *ante*, p. 219.
[29] See *ante*, p. 221. Where that party is under disability, Rule 113 (2) (*ante*, p. 233) must also have been complied with.
[30] See *ante*, p. 225.
[1] See *ante*, p. 225.
[2] See *ante*, p. 231.
[3] See *ante*, p. 237.
[4] Rule 34 (2).
[5] Rule 33 (2).
[6] Rule 44 (1) and (2).

debatable exception, which has already been mentioned briefly on pages 40 and 41. Despite the unanimous view of the Court of Appeal in *Santos* v. *Santos*[7] that the issues inherent in petitions based upon two years' separation need careful judicial scrutiny and ought not to be determined on affidavit evidence or otherwise than by a judge, the Rules provide that in certain circumstances these cases can be determined upon affidavit evidence by a registrar. To those who feel that the bonds of matrimony, even though they be flimsy, should not too lightly be severed, this may be regarded as the thin edge of what may later grow to be a very thick wedge; to others it may seem to be a recognition of the realities of the situation and a sensible saving of costs.

The relevant provisions as to what is to be known as "the Special Procedure List" are to be found in Rule 33 (3).[8] It applies only to petitions for divorce or judicial separation pending in a divorce county court in which the only fact relied upon by the petitioner is two years' separation, there are no children of the family as to whose welfare the court must be satisfied under section 41 of the Act of 1973, and the respondent has returned to the court office an acknowledge-ment of service containing a statement to the effect that he consents to a decree being granted or a statement to that effect signed by him has been lodged in the court office. In these circumstances, unless otherwise directed, there must be filed with the request for directions for trial an affidavit by the petitioner con-taining the information required by Form 7 (see *post*, p. 403) as nearly as may be in the order there set out, together with any corroborative evidence on which the petitioner intends to rely. The essential points appear to be the date on which the spouses separated, the reason or main reason and when and in what circumstances the petitioner came to the conclusion that the marriage was in fact at an end (because it is only at that moment that the period of two years commenced to run and there will not infrequently be a temptation, on the part of both spouses, to ante-date it). It is only when these requirements are satis-fied that the registrar will enter the cause in the Special Procedure List.

Once the case is entered in this list, the registrar is required by Rule 48 to consider as soon as is practicable the evidence filed by the petitioner, though neither party is required to attend before him personally or by solicitor or counsel. If he is satisfied that the case is proved, that the petitioner is entitled to a decree and to any costs prayed for, and that section 41 of the Act does not apply, he will make and file a certificate to that effect and a day will be fixed for the pronouncement of a decree nisi (or no doubt a number of such decrees) by a judge in open court and at a court of trial. The parties are given notice of the day and placed so fixed, but neither need appear.

If the registrar is not satisfied he may either give the petitioner an oppor-tunity to file further evidence or remove the cause from the Special Procedure List, in which case the registrar will give directions for trial in the same manner as in other cases.[9]

---

[7] [1972] Fam. 247, at pp. 263, 264.
[8] See generally on this subject, *Practice Direction*, (*Matrimonial Causes; Special Pro-cedure*), [1973] 3 All E.R. 182, which deals also with agreements as to financial provisions in such cases.
[9] Rules 48 (1) (*b*) and 33.

In a defended case the procedure is more complicated because all parties must be given an opportunity to put forward their views as to where the case should be tried. Assuming that it is the petitioner who intends to make a request for directions he must, not less than eight days before so doing, give notice of the place of trial desired to every other party who has given notice of intention to defend, stating the number of witnesses he intends to call and where he and his witnesses reside.[10] If a party served with such a notice objects to the place of trial suggested it is for him, within the next eight days, to apply to the registrar to direct trial at some other place. If he consents, he must within the same time instead send to the petitioner a statement signed by his solicitor (or by him if he is acting in person) indicating that he has received the notice and giving the number of his witnesses and where he and his witnesses reside.[11] The petitioner will then make a written request for directions stating the place of trial desired, the number of witnesses he intends to call, the places where he and his witnesses reside, and an estimate of the probable length of the trial. If he has received a statement from any other party, this will be filed with the request: if no such statement has been received from any particular party, the request must so state.[12] The registrar will then fix the place of trial having regard to all the circumstances, including the convenience of the parties and their witnesses, the costs likely to be incurred, the date when the trial can take place, the estimated length of the trial and the respective facilities for trial at the Royal Courts of Justice or elsewhere.[13] Cases which are not directed to be tried at the Royal Courts of Justice may be tried at any Divorce Town.[14] The registrar gives directions by setting the cause down for trial and gives notice that he has done so to all parties and, if necessary, sends the file of the cause to the divorce registry or the appropriate district registry.

Unless otherwise directed, the case will be heard by a judge without a jury.[15] Trial by jury is very rarely ordered in practice.

7. Evidence.

The general rules of evidence applicable in matrimonial causes, whether defended or undefended, are the same as those in any other proceedings, and it is only necessary to mention a few matters which apply specially to such causes. Some of these matters, such as the onus and standard of proof,[16] blood tests,[17] and certain provisions of the Civil Evidence Act 1968,[18] have already been considered.

The evidence of witnesses is generally given orally and in open court.[19] The attendance of a witness in a cause pending in a divorce county court is

[10] Rule 34 (3).
[11] Rule 34 (4).
[12] Rule 34 (5).
[13] Rule 34 (7).
[14] See definition of such Towns in Rule 2.
[15] Rule 43 (1).
[16] See *ante*, p. 15.
[17] See *ante*, p. 21.
[18] See *ante*, pp. 47–49.
[19] Rule 37.

compelled by witness summons issued in that court, or in the court of trial in which the cause is to be tried.[20] If the cause is pending in the High Court it is compelled by subpoena issued out of the registry in which the cause is proceeding or, if the case is to be tried in London, the divorce registry or, if it is to be tried at a divorce town, the registry for that town. A witness who is required to produce a document should be served with a witness summons to do so if the case is proceeding in a divorce county court or a subpoena *duces tecum* if the cause is pending in the High Court.[21]

The requirement of oral evidence is subject to the Civil Evidence Act 1968. Section 2 of that Act, subject to numerous safeguards,[22] renders admissible in any civil proceedings a statement made, whether orally or in a document or otherwise by any person, whether called as a witness in those proceedings or not, as evidence of any fact therein stated of which oral evidence by him would be admissible. Unless otherwise directed, in an undefended cause no notice of intention to adduce such evidence is required to be served on any other party,[23] so that a petitioner could theoretically present the whole of his case by means of such hearsay evidence, and since other parties would not know of his intention, they would have no opportunity to exercise their right to object. But in a matrimonial cause the judge is required to be satisfied that the facts upon which reliance is placed have been proved, and it is unlikely that he would express his satisfaction, even in an undefended case, if reliance were placed solely upon this section.

Rule 39 contains provisions enabling an order to be made that the affidavit of any witness be read at the trial on such conditions as the court thinks reasonable, or that evidence of any particular fact may be given by statement on oath of information or belief, or the production of a document or copy of a document, or in cases of matters of common knowledge, by production of a specified newspaper. It also enables the court to make an order that no more than specified numbers of expert witnesses shall be called. In undefended divorce cases, leave for medical evidence to be given by affidavit is usually given if the evidence is purely factual. Provision is made for dispensing with the attendance of medical inspectors at the trial of proceedings for nullity on the ground of incapacity or wilful refusal to consummate the marriage.[24]

The existence and validity of a marriage celebrated outside England and Wales may, in any case where this is not disputed, be proved by the evidence of one of the parties and production of a document purporting to be a marriage certificate or similar document issued, or a certified copy of an entry in a marriage register kept, in the foreign country in question. If in a foreign language, it should normally be accompanied by a translation certified by a notary public or authenticated by affidavit.[25]

---

[20] Rule 41 (1); C.C.R. Ord. 20, r. 8.
[21] Rule 41 (2).
[22] R.S.C. Ord. 38, rr. 20–33 as modified by Rule 42.
[23] Rule 42 (2).
[24] Rule 31 (4) to (6).
[25] Rule 40.

8. The hearing.

The manner in which cases in the Special Procedure list are dealt with has already been considered. Subject to this, little need be said of the hearing of an undefended cause, which is usually brief. Normally the petitioner is called as a witness and taken briefly through the facts alleged in the petition by means of leading questions, except in relation to the facts alleged in support of the allegation of irretrievable breakdown. The witness should at this point be allowed to tell his or her story. Leading questions on such matters are wrong, and detract greatly from the value of any answers given.[1] Other witnesses, or other evidence, in support of that story should be available if possible in case the judge is not satisfied with the evidence of the petitioner alone. It is important, where the return of an acknowledgement of service to the court office is relied upon as proof of service, to ask the petitioner to identify the signature of the respondent on the acknowledgement.[2] The judge will usually be asked to make the order as to the welfare of the children of the family as required by section 41 of the Act of 1973 at the same time as he makes the decree, and the petitioner should be ready to answer questions as to the contents of the statement in Form 4,[3] and any statement of the views of the respondent which may have been submitted.[4]

If the case is defended it will be conducted by counsel, who will have advised upon the evidence required. Normally counsel for the petitioner has the right to begin, opens his case and calls his witnesses in any order which he pleases.[5] At the conclusion of the evidence for the petitioner, counsel for a respondent or co-respondent may submit that there is no case to answer in which case the court, before giving a decision on the submission, may require counsel to elect to call no evidence if the submission fails. The court has a discretion not to put counsel to his election, but this will be exercised only in exceptional circumstances.[6] Section 49 (3) of the Act of 1973 expressly enables the court to dismiss a co-respondent or party cited, who is charged with adultery, from the suit if after the close of the evidence on the part of the person alleging adultery it is of opinion that there is not sufficient evidence against him or her. This discretion has the result that the court tends to be less ready to put counsel for third parties to their election.[7]

Where no such submission is made, or if counsel was not put to his election and the submission was overruled, counsel for other parties open their cases and call their evidence in such order as they may agree. It is usual for counsel for the respondent to begin, followed by counsel for a co-respondent, or party cited, counsel making their closing speeches in the reverse order. Finally counsel for the petitioner may reply.

The fundamental principle of English law that proceedings should be heard in open court, unless the judge orders a hearing in camera because justice

---

[1] *Perry* v. *Perry*, [1952] P. 203, 209; *Moor* v. *Moor*, [1954] 2 All E.R. 458.
[2] Rule 14 (5) and *ante*, p. 221.
[3] See *ante*, p. 217.
[4] Rule 50 and *ante*, p. 230.
[5] *Briscoe* v. *Briscoe*, [1968] P. 501.
[6] *Wilson* v. *Wilson*, [1958] 3 All E.R. 195.
[7] *Lance* v. *Lance and Gardiner*, [1958] P. 134n.

cannot otherwise be done, applies to matrimonial causes in the same way as to other proceedings.[8] An exception occurs in nullity proceedings where evidence on the question of sexual capacity must be heard in camera unless in any case the judge is satisfied that in the interests of justice the evidence ought to be heard in open court.[9] If some part of the hearing takes place in camera without sufficient justification, as where the judge retires to his room and gives his decision there, the decision is voidable and may be set aside.[10]

But although, subject to what is said above, the public are entitled to be present at the hearing, there are statutory provisions regulating the reporting of matrimonial proceedings otherwise than in a bona fide series of law reports or in technical legal or medical publications. The Judicial Proceedings (Regulation of Reports) Act 1926 makes it illegal to publish in relation to any judicial proceedings any indecent matter or matter the publication of which would be calculated to injure public morals. In relation to proceedings for divorce, nullity and judicial separation, the Act in addition prohibits the publication of any particulars except (i) the names, addresses and occupations of the parties and witnesses; (ii) a concise statement of the charges, defences and counter-charges in support of which evidence has been given; (iii) submissions on any point of law arising in the course of the proceedings, and the decision of the court thereon; (iv) the summing up of the judge and the finding of the jury (if any) and the judgment of the court and observations made by the judge in giving judgment.

Contravention of the Act is punishable on summary conviction by imprisonment not exceeding four months or a fine not exceeding £500, or both. But no person other than a proprietor, editor, master printer or publisher, is liable to conviction, and a prosecution must be sanctioned by the Attorney-General.[11]

9. The decree and intervention to show cause.

In suits for judicial separation there is a single decree, but in divorce and nullity the decree is in the first instance a decree nisi. All decrees are drawn up by the registrar and he sends a copy of the decree to every party to the cause,[12] whether or not it was defended. Where a case pending in one divorce county court was set down for trial in another divorce county court, the registrar of the latter court will, so soon as is practicable after the case has been tried, return the file to the registrar from whom he received it, and subsequent proceedings will take place in the divorce county court in which it was pending before the trial.[13]

Should the Queen's Proctor wish to show cause against a decree nisi being made absolute, he must give notice to that effect to the registrar and to the party in whose favour the decree was pronounced, and if the cause is pending in a

---

[8] *Scott* v. *Scott*, [1913] A.C. 417.
[9] Act of 1973, s. 48 (2).
[10] *Stone* v. *Stone*, [1949] P. 165.
[11] There are similar restrictions as to newspaper reports of proceedings in a magistrates' domestic court (Magistrates' Courts Act 1952, s. 58). See also Domestic and Appellate Proceedings (Restriction of Publicity) Act 1968, *post*, p. 297.
[12] Rules 55 and 58.
[13] Rule 55 (3).

divorce county court, the registrar must order it to be transferred to the High Court.[14] Within the next 21 days the Queen's Proctor must file his plea setting out the grounds for his intervention with a copy for service on the party in whose favour the decree was pronounced and every other party affected by it, and these copies will be served by the registrar.[15] Subsequent procedure is the same as that on a petition except that if no answer to the plea is filed within 29 days of service inclusive of the day of service, or if the answer is struck out or is not proceeded with, the Queen's Proctor may forthwith apply by motion for an order rescinding the decree nisi and dismissing the petition.[16] Directions for trial must be applied for by the Queen's Proctor if all the charges in his plea are denied in the answer, otherwise by the party who obtained the decree.[17]

Section 9 of the Act of 1973 also enables any other person who is not a party to the proceedings to show cause why the decree should not be made absolute. In that event the procedure is different, and is governed by Rule 62. An affidavit stating the facts on which reliance is placed must be filed by that person and a copy served on the person who obtained the decree, who may, within 14 days after service, file an affidavit in answer, a copy of which is served on the person showing cause, who is allowed to file and serve an affidavit in reply. Service is in each case effected by the court. The person showing cause then applies to the judge for directions and if he fails to apply the person who obtained the decree may do so. If directions are given for trial of an intervention in a cause pending in a divorce county court, the registrar must order the cause to be transferred to the High Court.

All interventions to show cause, whether by the Queen's Proctor or any other person, must be tried in London at the Royal Courts of Justice unless the President otherwise orders.[18] The court may make the decree absolute, rescind the decree nisi, require further inquiry or otherwise deal with the case as it thinks fit.[19]

10. Decree absolute.

The Act of 1973 provides that a decree nisi of divorce or nullity cannot be made absolute before the expiration of six months from the date on which it was granted unless the court by general or special order fixes a shorter time.[20] The general order at present in force has reduced this period to six weeks.[21] If no application for it to be made absolute has been made by the party to whom it was granted then, at any time after the expiration of three months from the earliest date upon which the party who obtained the decree could have applied the party against it was obtained may apply, and the court may make the decree absolute, rescind the decree nisi, require further inquiry or otherwise deal with the case as it thinks fit.[1]

---

[14] Rule 61 (1), and see *ante*, p. 61.
[15] Rule 61 (2) and (3).
[16] Rule 61 (4) and (5).
[17] Rule 61 (6).
[18] Rule 63.
[19] Act of 1973, s. 9 (1).
[20] Act of 1973, ss. 1 (5) and 15.
[21] Matrimonial Causes (Decree absolute) General Order 1972.
[1] Act of 1973, ss. 9 (2) and 15.

The usual procedure is for the party who obtained the decree, after the period of six weeks has elapsed, to lodge in the registry a Notice of Application in Form 8 signed by his solicitor.[2] There are a number of points on which the registrar must first satisfy himself by searching the court minutes before the decree can be made absolute, i.e.

(a) that no appeal or application for re-hearing or for rescission of the decree is pending;

(b) that the time for appealing or for applying for a re-hearing has not been extended, or if extended has expired;

(c) that no application for an order extending the time for appealing or for applying for a re-hearing is pending;

(d) that no intervention by the Queen's Proctor or any other person is pending;

(e) that the judge has made an order as to the welfare of children of the family under section 41 (1) of the Act of 1973;

(f) where a certificate has been granted under the Administration of Justice Act 1969, s. 12, for "leapfrogging" an appeal from the High Court direct to the House of Lords,[3] that no application for leave to appeal directly to the House of Lords is pending, that the time for applying for such leave has not been extended or if extended has expired, and that the time for any appeal to the Court of Appeal has also expired;

(g) that the provisions of section 10 (2) to (4) of the Act of 1973 as to application for consideration of the respondent's financial position in the event of divorce do not apply or have been complied with.

If the registrar is thus satisfied he will make the decree absolute and send to the petitioner and the respondent spouse a certificate to this effect.

Provision is made for cases in which the party who obtained the decree nisi delays making application to have it made absolute. If his Notice of Application is lodged more than twelve months after the decree nisi, the registrar may require him to file an affidavit explaining the delay, and may make such order on the application as he thinks fit or refer the application to the judge.[4] It is not easy to appreciate why this provision has been retained now that unreasonable delay in prosecuting the petition is no longer a bar to divorce. The inference may be that such delay may indicate that the breakdown of the marriage is not irretrievable. A further consequence of delay on the part of the party who obtained the decree is, as has already been noticed, that the party against whom it was obtained is given the opportunity to apply to have it made absolute. Assuming that three months have elapsed from the earliest date on which the person who obtained the decree could have applied, the party against whom it was obtained may apply to a judge or the registrar by summons, if the case is proceeding in the High Court, or by notice of application

---

[2] Rule 65 and see Form on p. 405.
[3] See *post*, p. 296.
[4] Rule 65 (2).

...oceedings in a divorce county court, which in either case must be served ...other spouse not less than four days before the hearing.[5]

...ases sometimes arise in which it is desired to obtain a decree absolute in a ...orter time than the period of six weeks mentioned above. The reason may be that, for example, the wife is expecting a child by another man whom she wishes to marry before the child is born, or the husband is about to be posted overseas in the armed forces and wishes to remarry before his departure. This matter is governed by *Practice Directions*.[6] They point out that now that the general order has reduced the period to six weeks, a special order further reducing the period may result in the respondent losing the statutory protection afforded by section 10 of the Act of 1973, or of an appeal (which lies within six weeks) resulting in the recission of the decree, which might invalidate any re-marriage. A special order reducing the period to less than six weeks should therefore rarely be required or desirable. Wherever possible an application should be made to expedite the hearing in preference to an application at or after the trial to expedite the decree absolute. In the rare cases in which some matter arises after the hearing, the application may be made to a judge in chambers after notice to all parties. Only the party who obtained the decree can apply, the other party having no standing except as provided by section 9 (2) of the Act of 1973. Once again, it is not easy to see why, once the court has found that a marriage has irretrievably broken down and now that the doctrine of a matrimonial offence as the basis of a decree has gone, the rights of the spouses in relation to the making absolute of the decree, assuming the regis-trar is satisfied as to all the matters mentioned above, should be different. It is not necessary for such cases to be referred to the Queen's Proctor, unless the judge specially so directs.

11. Ancillary relief.

The expression "ancillary relief" is defined in Rule 2 as including

(*a*) an avoidance of disposition order,
(*b*) a financial provision order,
(*c*) an order for maintenance pending suit,
(*d*) a property adjustment order, or
(*e*) a variation order.

It thus includes under all forms of financial provision or adjustment or property rights which can be ordered for the benefit of a spouse or child of the family in proceedings for divorce, nullity or judicial separation. The nature of these orders and the principles on which they are granted have been described in Chapters 7 to 9. The expression does not include orders for financial provision in proceedings based on wilful neglect to maintain, which are in no way ancillary to other proceedings.[7]

---

[5] Rule 66 (2) and (3).
[6] [1972] 3 All E.R. 416 and [1964] 3 All E.R. 775.
[7] As to procedure in these cases see *post*, p. 256.

(a) *Methods of application.*

The way in which a petitioner or respondent should apply for ancillary relief is dealt with by Rule 68.

An application by a petitioner, or a respondent who files an answer claiming relief, for any order under (*b*) (*c*) or (*d*) above should be made in the prayer to the petition or answer, as the case may be. If a claim which should have been included in the petition or answer is omitted from it this may be remedied at any time up to the hearing of the cause by applying for leave to amend the petition or answer; re-service will normally be ordered, so that the other spouse may have notice of the claim which is made.[8] Thereafter such applications may be made with leave of a judge or the registrar either by Notice in Form 11 or at the trial, unless the parties are agreed upon the terms of the proposed order, when they may be made by Notice in Form 11 without leave. Sections 23 and 24 of the Act of 1973 expressly provide that orders for financial provision or property adjustment in favour of a spouse or child of the family can be made on granting a decree of divorce, nullity or judicial separation or at any time thereafter, and section 23 (4) further provides that orders for financial provision in favour of a child of the family can be made "from time to time". There is no reason, therefore, why leave should not be given to apply by Notice in Form 11 even several years after the final decree, though a satisfactory explanation of the delay would be required.

There remain applications for ancillary relief which could not have been included in the petition or answer, i.e. applications for orders under (*b*), (*c*) or (*d*) above by a respondent who did not file an answer or whose answer did not claim relief, applications for an order for avoidance of a disposition and applications for variation of some order already made. These may be made by notice in Form 11 without leave.[9]

In addition to Form 11, there are two other Forms of Notice used in connection with these applications. Where a petitioner or respondent who has applied for ancillary relief in his petition or answer intends to proceed with the application before a registrar, he files notice of his intention to do so in Form 13.[10] Forms 11 and 13 should be studied (see pp. 405, 406). It will be seen that they indicate the nature of the ancillary relief which is claimed and indicate the position with regard to the hearing by the registrar and as to filing evidence. It should particularly be noticed that the applicant must not only file these notices but must also serve a copy on the respondent to the application. Service is *not* effected through the court. Instead of giving notice in Form 13, where at or after a decree nisi of divorce or nullity an order for maintenance pending suit is in force, the party in whose favour the order was made may, if he has included an application for periodical payments in the petition or answer, request the registrar in writing to make what is called a "corresponding order" for periodical payments at the same rate as the maintenance pending suit. But in practice orders for maintenance pending suit are likely to be at a lower rate than the eventual payments made after decree absolute, and this must be kept

---

[8] *Practice Note*, [1957] 1 All E.R. 290.
[9] Rule 68 (3).
[10] Rule 73.

in mind before making such a request. If it is made, the registrar will serve on the other spouse a notice in Form 15[11] giving him an opportunity to object, and if he fails to object may make the order requested and serve copies on both spouses.[12]

(b) *Affidavit evidence.*

On all applications for ancillary relief evidence by affidavit is required. But the question of which party is to file the first affidavit varies with the nature of the application.

Where an application is made for a property adjustment order or an avoidance of disposition order, the application, whether it be contained in the petition or answer or in the notice in Form 11, must state briefly the nature of the adjustment proposed or the disposition to be set aside, and the notice in Form 11 or 13 as the case may be must, unless otherwise directed, be supported by affidavit stating the grounds relied upon. Rule 74 sets out in detail the particulars which must be contained in the affidavit, and the persons who are to be served with a copy of Form 11 or Form 13, as the case may be, together with a copy of the supporting affidavit. Any such person *may* (but is not bound to) serve an affidavit in answer within 14 days after service. The particulars required, in the case of an application relating to land, now include details of any mortgage (so far as they are known to the applicant) of the land or any interest in it, and the mortgagee is among the persons who must be served.[13] An application for an order for variation under section 31 of the Act of 1973 must be supported by an affidavit by the applicant giving full particulars of his property and income and the grounds for the application, a copy being served with Form 11, and again an affidavit in answer *may* be filed within fourteen days.[14]

In all other cases (that is to say on any application for maintenance pending suit or financial provision) the party making the application is not required to support it by affidavit, but the notice in Form 11 or 13, as the case may be will, unless the terms of the proposed order are agreed, require the respondent or petitioner who is served with the notice, within fourteen days after service, to file an affidavit in answer to the application giving full particulars of his property and income, and if he does not, the registrar may order him to do so. A copy of this affidavit must be served on the applicant, who is now obliged to file an affidavit in reply within fourteen days after service or within such time as the court may fix.[15]

There is appended to a *Practice Direction*[16] a suggested form of affidavit of means including a questionnaire designed to provide the information likely to be required on the hearing of most applications for ancillary relief (see Form on p. 415). It cannot include every relevant question and may require alterations

---

[11] See *post*, p. 407.
[12] Rule 83.
[13] Rule 74 (3) and (4).
[14] Rule 75.
[15] Rule 73.
[16] [1973] 1 All E.R. 192.

and additions in particular cases, but the hope is expressed that practitioners will find it convenient to use it, with such modifications as are necessary, in most cases. This will ensure a uniform presentation of the facts in ordinary cases, and where, instead of using the form, an affidavit is drawn in the conventional narrative style, the information should be presented in the order in which the questions appear in the form.

(c) *Parties to applications for ancillary relief.*

Since the Divorce Reform Act 1969 came into operation, many more petitions remain undefended and contested issues of conduct may arise for the first time in relation to applications for ancillary relief. It follows that an affidavit filed by either party under the Rules considered above may contain allegations concerning some person who is not as yet a party to the proceedings. Rule 76 accordingly requires that where such an affidavit contains an allegation of adultery or of an improper association with a named person it must, unless otherwise directed, be endorsed with a notice in Form 14 and a copy of the affidavit, or of such part thereof as the court may direct, endorsed with that notice, must be served *by the person who filed the affidavit* on the person against whom the allegation is made. As will be seen from Form 14 on p. 407 it informs the person named that if he or she wishes to be heard on the matters alleged, an application for leave to intervene may be made by applying to the court, within eight days of receipt of the notice, for directions as to the filing and service of pleadings and as to the further conduct of the proceedings. As is the case with a co-respondent or party cited, a person served with such a notice cannot be made liable for the costs of the proceedings for ancillary relief, since they are not directly referable to the decree, unless he is a party to those proceedings (as he would be were he to intervene) or he has been given notice of an intention to apply for an order for costs against him.[17]

Normally applications for the benefit of children of the family will be made by one of the spouses. But Rule 69 enables a number of other persons specified in that Rule to apply for any order for ancillary relief as respects such a child by notice in Form 11. Such persons include (inter alia) the child's guardian, the person who has custody or care and control of the child under an order of the High Court or a divorce county court, or a local authority to whom the care of the child has been committed by such a court.

On an application for variation of a settlement, both the trustees of the settlement and the settlor, if still living, must be made parties, as must the person in whose favour a disposition is alleged to have been made when there is an application for avoidance of that disposition and any mortgagee in the case of applications relating to land. Clearly a mortgagee should have notice of the application and an opportunity to be heard, since if a transfer is effected, or a disposition is avoided, without his consent he may in some cases have a right to foreclose and in others his interests may be affected.[18] Rule 74 requires that such a person must be served with a copy of Form 11 or 13 as the case may be and a copy of the supporting affidavit, which enables him to file an affidavit in

---

[17] Rules 76 (2) and 49 (4).
[18] Rule 74 (3) and (4), superseding *Practice Direction*, [1971] 1 All E.R. 896.

answer. Difficulties which may be insuperable unless the mortgagee will co-operate obviously arise when an application is made for an order for transfer of property such as the matrimonial home which is subject to a mortgage.

(d) *The hearing of the application.*

Whatever the nature of the application for ancillary relief may be, the first appointment for the hearing of the application will be before the registrar and notice of it will be included in Form 11 or 13 or notified subsequently to the parties by the registrar.[19] Before the registrar can complete his investigation there are several matters on which it may be necessary for him to give directions, and where a party intends at the hearing to apply only for such directions, he must file and serve on every other party a notice to that effect.[20] Thus:

(i) Before the hearing any of the parties to the application may by letter require any other party to give further information concerning any matter in any affidavit filed by the other party or any other relevant matter or to furnish a list of relevant documents or allow inspection of any such documents. This is an important provision and can be most useful in discovering precisely what means another party possesses. In default of compliance, application may be made to the registrar for directions.[21]

(ii) It may be desirable to require the attendance of some person for the purpose of being examined or cross-examined and the registrar may order this.[1]

(iii) He may also at any stage order the discovery and production of any document or require further affidavits.[2]

(iv) At any stage the registrar may give directions as to the filing and service of pleadings.[3] This is particularly likely to be required when there are contested issues as to conduct, in order that these issues may be clearly defined and each party may have notice of what the other party alleges.

(v) Finally, if the case is undefended, the registrar must before investigating the application consider whether the application should be transferred to the High Court under Rule 80, as to which see *post*, p. 253.

It is obviously desirable that the various applications which can be made should be dealt with by one person, since they are of necessity interrelated, and the Rules ensure that this shall be so. Where there is an application for avoidance of a disposition, this application, and any related application for financial provision, must if practicable be heard at the same time and unless the parties are agreed as to the terms of the order to be made the registrar, after

---

[19] Rule 77 (1) and (3).
[20] Rule 77 (7).
[21] Rule 77 (4).
[1] Rule 77 (5).
[2] *Ibid.*
[3] Rule 77 (6).

completing his investigation, is required by Rule 79 to report the result in writing to a judge and adjourn the application to him, when the judge may confirm or vary the registrar's report or make such other order as he thinks just. In all other cases the registrar himself is empowered by Rule 78 to make an order, though he may at any time refer the application to a judge and pending the final determination, may make an interim order. A *Practice Direction*[4] deals in detail with the problems which may arise in relation to inter-related applications under section 17 of the Married Women's Property Act 1882, applications for ancillary relief and applications under the Matrimonial Homes Act 1967. It ensures that so far as is possible the applications and, in the event of appeals, the appeals shall be heard by the same tribunal, i.e. by a judge at first instance with appeal to the Court of Appeal.

(e) *Transfer of applications to the High Court.*

Although the great majority of divorce cases are undefended there may still, having regard to the decision in *Tumath* v. *Tumath*,[5] be serious differences between the parties as to ancillary relief. Since the decision of the Court of Appeal in *Wachtel* v. *Wachtel*,[6] the order to be made in such matters will not generally be affected by disputes as to conduct unless it is "both obvious and gross"; but since the basic principle of the Matrimonial Causes Act 1967 is that defended causes should be tried in the High Court and undefended cases in a divorce county court, Rule 80 provides for the transfer in certain circumstances of contested applications for ancillary relief to the High Court. This Rule provides for three situations:

(i) If a judge or the registrar considers that an application for ancillary relief pending in a divorce county court gives rise to a contested issue of conduct of a nature which is likely materially to affect the question whether any, or what, order should be made and for that reason the application should be transferred to the High Court, he must make an order for transfer, and in this case the application will be heard by a High Court judge,[7] and will unless otherwise directed be heard in chambers.[8]

(ii) If the parties to the application consent to an order for transfer, they may apply to a judge or the registrar, who must order the transfer unless he is of the opinion that it would not be justified.[9]

(iii) Without prejudice to (i) and (ii) above, the judge or registrar may order a transfer from a divorce county court to the High Court, or from the High Court to a divorce county court, if it appears to him to be desirable.[10]

---

[4] [1971] 1 W.L.R. 260.
[5] [1970] P. 78; see *ante*, p. 450.
[6] See *ante*, pp. 138, 139.
[7] Rule 80 (1); and see *Practice Direction (Matrimonial Causes)* R.C.J., [1973] 2 All E.R. 288
[8] Rule 82 (2).
[9] Rule 80 (2).
[10] Rule 80 (3).

The judge before hearing, and the registrar before investigating, an application for ancillary relief pending in a divorce county court, is required to consider whether he should exercise his powers under (i) or (iii) above. If a transfer is ordered, he may give directions for the conduct of the proceedings. He may do so on the application of any party or of his own motion, but in the latter event he must first give the parties an opportunity to be heard.[11] In reaching his decision he must have regard to all relevant considerations, including the nature and value of the property involved, the relief sought and the financial limits for the time being relating to the jurisdiction of county courts in other matters. This final point is far from clear; does it, for example, refer to the limit of £750 applicable to actions of contract or tort, or the limit of £500 in equity matters.[12] And how far is the number of years for which the payment is likely to be made relevant to the amount involved?

Transfers of applications for maintenance pending suit are unlikely to be frequent, and in suits for divorce or nullity orders for transfer will not usually be likely until after a decree nisi has been granted. Emphasis has already been laid upon the fact that applications for ancillary relief are inter-connected, that if property is ordered to be transferred, smaller periodical payments may be needed, and that greater provision for a spouse may mean that less is left for the children, and vice-versa. It is for this reason that, when a decree nisi has been pronounced, the judge or registrar is required to consider whether, instead of transferring the application in question, it would not be more convenient to transfer the whole cause to the High Court, so that all these matters may be dealt with together.[13]

Rule 81 deals with a different situation. It enables a judge or the registrar, on the application of a party or of his own motion, to order the transfer to the High Court of an application for ancillary relief pending in a divorce county court if he thinks this desirable for the purpose of expediting the hearing. Such a situation may arise from time to time in London but may be less likely elsewhere. Further, whereas when a transfer is ordered under Rule 80, either of the individual application or of the whole cause, the costs thereafter are on the High Court scale, the costs of an application transferred under Rule 81 for purposes of expedition are on the county court scale unless the judge or registrar who hears the application in the High Court considers that a transfer would have been justified otherwise than for the purpose of expediting the hearing.

(f) *Applications relating to children.*

Whereas questions of financial provision or adjustment of property rights for the benefit of children are normally dealt with by the registrar under the general heading of ancillary relief, questions of custody and education of children, whether the cause is defended or not, must be dealt with by a judge, who must also deal with questions of access to a child, except if the other party consents to give access, and the only question is the extent to which it should be given, when the question may be determined by the registrar.[14]

---

[11] Rule 80 (4), (7) and (10).
[12] Administration of Justice Act 1969, ss. 1 and 5.
[13] Rule 80 (6).
[14] Rule 92 (1) and (2).

A petitioner should include any claim for custody (which includes access[15]) in the prayer to his petition,[16] and a respondent in the prayer to the answer,[17] but a respondent who does not intend to contest the case and does not file an answer will indicate his intentions in the Acknowledgement of Service. The proposals made by the petitioner will be evident from Form 4, and those of the respondent from any statement by him in writing under Rule 50.[18] Pending the hearing, any application to the judge must be on notice of application[19] in a divorce county court, or on summons in the High Court, and the probability is that the judge will endeavour to preserve the status quo. In the absence of any dispute, the judge will generally deal further with these matters and make the order required by section 41 of the Act of 1973 when he pronounces the decree nisi or the decree of judicial separation. But should there be disagreement, or if the judge is not satisfied as to the arrangements proposed, he will generally adjourn the matter for hearing in chambers.

The Court of Appeal in *H.* v. *H. and C.*[20] held that in considering the future of a small child the personality and character of the parents are often decisive matters, which cannot properly be determined without the judge seeing the parents himself. Accordingly the Rules now provide that on any application to a judge relating to the custody, care and control of, or access to, a child neither the applicant nor the respondent shall be entitled to be heard in support of, or in opposition to, the application unless he is available at the hearing to give oral evidence or the judge otherwise directs. The judge is also empowered to refuse to admit any affidavit by any other person who is or is proposed to be responsible for the child's care and upbringing, or with whom the child is living or is proposed to live, unless that person is available at the hearing to give oral evidence.[1] There are no such strict requirements as to affidavit evidence by persons less closely concerned, such as schoolmasters or neighbours. The judge or a registrar may also at any time refer to a court welfare officer for investigation and report any matter which concerns a child's welfare. Without prejudice to this power any party to any application concerning a child may, before the application is heard, request the registrar to call for such a report, and if the other parties consent the registrar may refer the matter to the court welfare officer for report before the hearing. The welfare officer's report will be filed and the parties may inspect it and bespeak copies.[2]

There are detailed provisions enabling the guardian of the child, or any person who has the custody or control or care of the child under an order of the court, to seek orders concerning the child's custody and education,[3] and as to the rights of a local authority in relation to orders under sections 43 and 44 of the

---

[15] Act of 1973, s. 52 (1).
[16] Rule 9 (1) and Form 2.
[17] Rule 21 (3).
[18] See *ante*, p. 230.
[19] See *ante*, p. 213 and *post*, p. 414.
[20] [1969] 1 All E.R. 262.
[1] Rule 92 (4).
[2] Rule 95.
[3] Rule 92 (3).

Act of 1973.[4] There are rules similar to those already considered[5] enabling a person who is accused in an affidavit of adultery or improper association to intervene in the proceedings.[6]

Rules 80 and 81, which deal with the transfer of applications for ancillary relief to the High Court, are made applicable with some modifications to questions of custody, education, care and control, and supervision of children. Such transfer is mandatory in the case of contested applications for leave to remove a child permanently from the jurisdiction, or to commit a child to the care of a local authority, and in all cases in which the child is a ward of court.[7]

12. Other applications.

Under this heading are included a number of applications which are not made in relation to a pending cause, but stand by themselves.

(a) *Applications based on wilful neglect to maintain.*

Proceedings under section 27 of the Act of 1973 must be commenced in a divorce county court by originating application. A special Form (Form 19, *post*, p. 408) is prescribed for this purpose and the application must, unless otherwise directed, contain the information required by that Form. It will be seen that in addition to details of the marriage, children of the family and previous proceedings in England or elsewhere, details are required of the wilful neglect to provide or contribute towards reasonable maintenance which is alleged, the means of the applicant, and so far as they are known to the applicant the means of the respondent, the provision which is asked for and the basis on which the court is said to have jurisdiction.

The application may be made to any divorce county court accompanied by an affidavit verifying the statements in the application and a copy of the application and of the affidavit for service on the respondent.[8] The registrar annexes to the copy of the originating application for service on the respondent a Notice of Application in Form 20 (see *post*, p. 410) with a Form of Acknowledgement of Service (Form 6, suitably modified, see *post*, p. 401) annexed. Service is effected in the same way as service of a petition.[9] The registrar may, if practicable, fix the date and place for the hearing and include it in the Notice in Form 20, or he may fix it subsequently and give notice to all parties.[10] Form 20 requires the respondent to return the Acknowledgement of Service to the court office within eight days of service, inclusive of the day of service. If he intends to contest the application he will give notice of intention to defend by his answer to the question in the Acknowledgement and must, within the next fourteen days, file an answer setting out the grounds on which he relies, including any allegations which he makes against the applicant. Whether or not he

---

[4] I.e. orders committing the child to the care of a local authority or for supervision. See *ante* pp. 183, 184 and Rule 93.

[5] See *ante*, p. 251.

[6] Rule 92 (5).

[7] Rule 97; as to uncontested applications, or those for temporary removal, see Rule 94.

[8] Rule 98 (1) and (2).

[9] See *ante*, p. 221.

[10] Rules 98 (4) and 99 (7).

intends to contest the application, he is also required, within the same time, to file an affidavit giving full particulars of his property and income, and the registrar sends a copy of the answer (if any) and the affidavit to the applicant's address for service. Should the respondent fail to file an affidavit, the registrar may order him to do so.[11] If the answer alleges adultery, the alleged adulterer must, unless otherwise directed, be made a party cited and must be served with a copy of the answer as if it were a petition; he has 29 days from service, inclusive of the day of service, in which to file an answer.[12] Within fourteen days after service of the respondent's answer, the applicant may file a reply; quite independently of this right he may also, within fourteen days after being served with a copy of the respondent's affidavit, file a further affidavit as to means and as to any fact in the respondent's affidavit which he wishes to dispute. No further affidavits can be filed without leave.[13]

The Rules as to transfer of applications under section 27 to the High Court are somewhat complicated. Such a transfer *must* be ordered if it appears to the court that the respondent intends to contest the application on the ground that by reason of the applicant's conduct or otherwise he is not liable to maintain the applicant or that no court in England or Wales has jurisdiction to entertain the application.[14] Thus transfer is obligatory if the respondent denies his liability on the ground that, for example, the applicant has committed adultery or has deserted him or alleges that the English courts would have no jurisdiction to entertain proceedings by the applicant under the Act of 1973.[15] But in addition Rules 80 and 81[16] are made to apply with the necessary modifications.[17] Thus even though transfer is not obligatory because the respondent does not completely deny his liability to maintain the applicant, it must be ordered if there is a contested issue of conduct which is likely materially to affect the order which should be made, or if both parties consent, unless the court considers that transfer would not be justified, or if for any other reason the court thinks it desirable.

Whether the application is heard in a divorce county court or in the High Court, it must be heard by a judge in open court. If the judge decides that the allegation of wilful neglect to maintain is made out, or that under section 27 (5) of the Act of 1973 it is not yet possible to determine what order should be made but the applicant or any child of the family is in immediate need of financial assistance, he may himself make an order, or may refer the application to the registrar for him to investigate the means of the parties.[18] If the judge has already made a finding of wilful neglect to maintain or that an interim order should be made, the registrar can make an order himself. But in all other cases he must report in writing to the judge who will make such order as he

---

[11] Rule 98 (5) and (8).
[12] Rule 98 (6) and (7).
[13] Rule 98 (9) and (10).
[14] Rule 99 (1).
[15] See *ante*, Chapter 10.
[16] See *ante*, pp. 253, 254.
[17] Rule 99 (2). Paragraphs (5) and (7) of Rule 80 do not apply.
[18] Rule 99 (4).

thinks fit.[19] When an order under section 27 is made, the power under section 42 (2) of the Act of 1973 to make orders as to the custody of any child of the family can be exercised only by the judge.

(b) *Applications for alteration of a maintenance agreement.*

An application under section 35 of the Act of 1973 for the alteration of a maintenance agreement in the lifetime of the parties is governed by Rule 100. The proceedings are started by originating application which may be filed in any divorce county court, the application containing the information required by Form 21 (see *post*, p. 411). With the application must be filed an affidavit by the applicant exhibiting a copy of the agreement and verifying the statements in Form 21, with a copy of the application and affidavit for service on the respondent. The registrar annexes to the application Form 20 (see *post*, p. 410) with Form 6 attached, and service on the respondent is effected in the same way as service of a petition. If the respondent wishes to defend the application he will so indicate in the Acknowledgement of Service, which he should return to the court office within eight days of service, inclusive of the day of service and, within the next fourteen days, file an affidavit in answer giving full particulars of his property and income, failing which the court may order him to do so. Unlike proceedings under section 27 of the Act of 1973, in which pleadings are filed and the application is heard by a judge in open court, proceedings under section 35 follow the procedure already described in relation to ancillary relief. Notice of allegations of adultery must be given to any person named, the registrar investigates the application and may himself make an order, and the Rules as to transfer to the High Court apply.[20]

An application under section 36 of the Act of 1973 to alter a maintenance agreement after the death of one of the parties must usually be made in the High Court, though *any* county court has jurisdiction if the net estate does not exceed £5,000. Procedure is governed by Rules 101 and 102.

Assuming that application is made to the High Court, it must be made by originating summons in Form 22 (see *post*, p. 412). It will be seen that this Form gives an appointment for hearing before the registrar, and explains to the respondent the steps which he should take. The summons may be issued out of the divorce registry or any district registry and must be supported by an affidavit. This exhibits a copy of the agreement and gives details showing that the court has jurisdiction, of the marriage and children of the family, of previous proceedings, the applicant's means and the facts justifying the application and, if application is made for leave to apply more than six months after the first grant of representation to the deceased's estate, the grounds for applying. Additional copies of the documents for service on the respondent must also be lodged. Respondents are required to return the Acknowledgement of Service attached to the summons to the registry within eight days of service, inclusive of the day of service. A respondent who is a personal representative is also required, within the next fourteen days, to file an affidavit in answer giving par-

---

[19] Rule 99 (5).
[20] I.e. Rules 76, 77 (4) to (7), 78, and 80 to 82 apply.

ticulars of the deceased's estate and of the beneficiaries: any other respondent may, within the same time, file an affidavit in answer if he wishes to do so. Procedure thereafter is the same as upon an application for ancillary relief,[1] except that (unless the parties reach an agreement as to the terms of the order to be made), the registrar is not empowered to make an order but must instead, after completing his investigation, report in writing to the judge, who will confirm or vary the report and make such other order as he thinks fit.

If application is made to a county court instead of to the High Court, the procedure is similar, except that proceedings are started by originating application instead of originating summons.[2]

(c) *Applications for provision from a deceased's estate.*

These applications are governed by Rule 103. Again they must normally be made in the High Court, except that *any* county court has jurisdiction if the net estate does not exceed £5,000. The application in the High Court is by Originating Summons in Form 23 (see *post*, p. 413). If the decree dissolving or annulling the marriage was made in a cause proceeding in the divorce registry the summons must be filed there, otherwise it may be filed in the divorce registry or in any district registry. Apart from the fact that details required in the affidavit in support are different, the procedure is otherwise the same as that in applications for alteration of a maintenance agreement after the death of one of the parties.

13. Enforcement of orders.

(a) *Orders for payment of money.*

Orders for payment of money can be enforced by the usual methods of execution, that is to say, in the High Court by writ of fieri facias, garnishee proceedings, a charging order, the appointment of a receiver by way of equitable execution or by writ of sequestration,[3] and in a county court by warrant of execution and by any of the methods indicated above except sequestration, which is available only in the High Court.[4] Attention has already been drawn to section 32 of the Act of 1973, whereby payment of arrears under orders for ancillary relief cannot be enforced through the High Court or any county court without leave if they became due more than twelve months before proceedings to enforce payment are begun.[5] Before any process is issued for the enforcement of an order for payment of money made in matrimonial proceedings an affidavit must be filed showing the amount due and how it is arrived at. [6]

Enforcement is also possible by means of a judgment summons under the Debtors Act 1869, whereby the debtor is required to appear for examination as to his means and, should it appear that he has had the means to pay since the

---

[1] I.e. Rules 76, 77 (4) to (7), 79 (3) and (4), 80 (9) and (10) and 82 (1) and (2) apply.
[2] C.C.R. Ord. 6, r. 4.
[3] R.S.C. Ord. 45, r. 1.
[4] C.C.R. Ord. 24.
[5] See *ante*, p. 163.
[6] Rule 86 (1).

date of the order, he may be committed to prison for not more than six weeks, not for debt, but for disobedience to the order to pay, although in practice an order is usually made in the first instance for payment by instalments, and imprisonment only follows if that order is disobeyed. Procedure is regulated by Rules 87 to 89, and is available in the High Court and in a divorce county court, the latter court having jurisdiction even as regards default on an order made by the High Court. By section 11 of the Administration of Justice Act 1970[7] this procedure will remain available in respect of orders for periodical or other payments made under Part II of the Matrimonial Causes Act 1973,[7] or similar orders made under statutes replaced by that Act,[8] though the general abolition of the procedure except in relation (inter alia) to maintenance orders will prevent its use in respect of orders as to costs.

Enforcement is also possible by means of an attachment of earnings order under the Attachment of Earnings Act 1971. By section 1 of that Act, the High Court may make such an order to secure payments under a High Court maintenance order and a county court (not necessarily a divorce county court) in respect of payments under a High Court or county court maintenance order. The application may be made by the debtor himself or the person entitled to the payment, but in the latter event it cannot be made unless fifteen days have elapsed since the maintenance order was made and until the debtor has failed to make one or more payments under the order. Except upon the application of the debtor, the order cannot be made if it appears to the court that the failure to pay is not due to his wilful refusal or culpable neglect.[9] The order is directed to the employer and requires him to make periodical deductions from the debtor's earnings and pay them to the collecting officer of the court. It specifies the normal deduction rate, being such as the court thinks reasonable, and the protected earnings rate below which his earnings are not to be reduced.[10] An attachment of earnings order may be made as an alternative to committal on a judgment summons, and when an attachment of earnings order has been made no committal is permitted in consequence of any proceedings for enforcement of the maintenance order begun before the making of the attachment of earnings order.[11] The procedure appears at first sight to be attractive. It remains to be seen whether it will be stultified in practice by the debtor changing his employment to avoid the consequences, as has been so often the case with the procedure previously in force. Section 21 of the Act goes some way towards avoiding this difficulty by requiring the debtor to notify the court in writing within seven days of every occasion when he changes his employment and every new employer who knows that such an order is in force likewise to notify the court; non-compliance by the debtor is punishable on summary conviction by imprisonment for not more

---

[7] Such orders have been added to the list of "maintenance orders" in Schedule 8 of the Administration of Justice Act 1970 by Sched. 2, para. 10 (2) of the Act of 1973.

[8] I.e. the Matrimonial Causes Act of 1965 and the Matrimonial Proceedings (Property and Maintenance) Act 1970 (see Sched. 3 para. 5 of the latter Act).

[9] Attachment of Earnings Act 1971, s. 3.

[10] *Ibid.*, s. 6.

[11] *Ibid.*, ss. 3 (4) and 8 (1).

than fourteen days or a fine of not more than £25, and such a fine may also be imposed by a High Court or county court judge.[12]

A further method of enforcing maintenance orders made by the High Court or a county court is as provided by Part I of the Maintenance Orders Act 1958, which enables these orders[13] to be registered in a magistrates' court, when they are enforceable by that court in the same way as an affiliation order,[14] and are no longer enforceable in the High Court or in a divorce county court.[15] This has the advantage that payment may be required to be made to the clerk of the court and the person entitled will have his assistance in recovery of arrears.[16] The application for registration may be made at the time of the making of the maintenance order or an order varying it, and if not by lodging a certified copy of the maintenance order and an affidavit in the form specified in R.S.C. Ord. 104, r. 8, and C.C.R. Ord, 46, r. 17, which govern the procedure. Whilst the order is registered in a magistrates' court that court may vary the payments under the order, there being now no limit on the amounts which the magistrates' court may order,[17] and in so doing that court must have regard to the same considerations as those which the court which made the order must observe.[18] If it appears to the magistrates' court that it is for any reason appropriate to remit the application for variation to the court which originally made the order, it has power to do so, and should do so where the facts are complicated and an appeal against such order as the magistrates may make is likely.[19] Apart from this the original court has usually no jurisdiction to vary the order.[20]

Provision is made by Part II of the Maintenance Orders Act 1950 for the enforcement by registration of an order made in one part of the United Kingdom in another part, and by the Maintenance Orders (Facilities for Enforcement) Act 1920 for reciprocal enforcement of maintenance orders in other parts of Her Majesty's territories abroad. The latter Act will in due course be replaced by the Matrimonial Orders (Reciprocal Enforcement) Act 1972, which will come into operation on a day or days to be appointed. It will deal not only with the enforcement of maintenance orders made in the United Kingdom but also enable the United Kingdom to accede to the United Nations Convention on the Recovery Abroad of Maintenance done at New York on June 20, 1956.

(b) *Orders other than those for payment of money.*

Disobedience to an order to do some act other than the payment of money, or to an injunction, can be enforced in proceedings in the High Court by a

---

[12] *Ibid.*, ss. 15 and 23.
[13] Including an order for costs incurred in relation to the maintenance order before it was registered. Maintenance Orders Act 1958, s. 1.
[14] See *post*, p. 286.
[15] Maintenance Orders Act 1958, s. 3.
[16] Magistrates' Courts Act 1952, s. 52.
[17] Maintenance Orders Act 1958, s. 4, as amended by Administration of Justice Act 1970, s. 48.
[18] *Miller* v. *Miller*, [1961] P. 1.
[19] *Gsell* v. *Gsell*, [1971] 1 All E.R. 559.
[20] But see Act of 1958, supra, s. 4 (5).

summons for an order of committal[1] and in a divorce county court by application on notice for a warrant of attachment.[2]   In either case a copy of the order,
endorsed with a penal notice giving warning of the consequences of disregarding
the order, must first be served personally on the person who is required to do
or abstain from doing the act in question or delivered to his solicitor.[3]

Taxation of costs.

The costs which one party to a matrimonial cause is ordered to pay to another
are, unless otherwise directed, taxed on a party and party basis, and on a
taxation on that basis there will be allowed "all such costs as were necessary or
proper for the attainment of justice or for enforcing or defending the rights of
the party whose costs are being taxed".[4]   Where a party is legally aided, the
costs ordered to be paid to him by any other party will also be taxed on that
basis.   The costs which the assisted party's solicitor will receive from the Legal
Aid Fund are taxed on the common fund basis, i.e. "according to the ordinary
rules applicable as between solicitor and client where the costs are to be paid
out of a common fund in which the client and others are interested".[5]   This
basis is somewhat more generous, both as to the items which may be included
and the amounts which may be allowed in respect of them, than the party and
party basis.

The scales of costs are governed by R.S.C. Ord. 62, Appendix 2, in respect
of proceedings in the High Court and by the divorce scale for proceedings in a
divorce county court.[6]   But in relation to undefended causes for divorce or
judicial separation in a county court in which the petitioner is granted a decree
with costs, his solicitor may elect to accept fixed costs instead of the costs being
taxed; in a legally aided case in which counsel has acted, he cannot do this
unless counsel also so elects.[7]   These fixed costs do not, however, cover the costs
of any ancillary application unless a consent order has been made and the
solicitor so requests: otherwise the costs relating to such an application will be
taxed in the usual way.[8]

The costs will be taxed in the registry in which the cause is proceeding at the
time of the taxation.   Thus if a cause has been transferred from a divorce county
court to the High Court, either because it has become defended or for any other
reason, taxation will take place in the High Court, the costs of the proceedings
prior to the transfer being allowed on the county court scale and those of
subsequent proceedings on the High Court scale.   Wherever the taxation is
proceeding, the party entitled to require the costs to be taxed must begin
proceedings for such taxation not later than three months after the final decree

---

[1] Rule 90.
[2] C.C.R. Ord. 25. rr. 67 and 68.
[3] Rule 60.
[4] R.S.C. Ord. 62, r. 28 (2) and (3).
[5] Legal Aid and Advice Act 1949, Sched. 3, para. 4 (1).   And see post Chapter 19.
[6] Matrimonial Causes (Costs) Rules 1971, r. 5; Matrimonial Causes Costs (Amendment)
Rules 1973, dealing with value added tax.
[7] *Ibid.*, r. 7, which lays down the amounts to be allowed, and Matrimonial Causes (Amendment No. 2) Rules 1973 providing a new item of fixed costs for cases in the Special Procedure
List.
[8] *Ibid.*, r. 7 (6).

or order in the cause. But this does not apply when a notice of application for ancillary relief in Form 11 or 13 has been filed within this period of three months, in which case the time is extended to three months after the making of any order on the application for ancillary relief.[9] Within the time allowed, the solicitor must lodge his bill of costs in the divorce registry, a district registry or the divorce county court, as the case may be.

When taxation is complete, the taxing officer endorses his certificate on the completed bill and the order to pay will usually direct payment within seven days after it is made.[10] At any time before the final certificate is signed, any party who is dissatisfied with the taxing officer's decision as to any item may apply to him to review his decision. The procedure and times within which the application may be made differ somewhat in the High Court and divorce county courts.[11] If still dissatisfied, either party may seek a review by the judge.

---

[9] *Ibid.*, r. 3.
[10] *Ibid.*, r. 8.
[11] Compare R.S.C. Ord. 62, rr. 33-35 with C.C.R. Ord. 47, r. 42.

PART IV

MAGISTRATES' COURTS

CHAPTER 17

PROCEEDINGS IN MAGISTRATES' COURTS[1]

The Matrimonial Proceedings (Magistrates' Courts) Act 1960 (as amended) empowers a magistrates' court to make matrimonial orders for the separation and maintenance of the parties to a marriage and for custody and maintenance of, and access to, children of the family. Since the Maintenance Orders Act 1968 there has been no financial limit on the powers of these courts to order maintenance. The use made of these proceedings is evident from the fact that in the year 1972 there were 25,472 applications for maintenance under this Act by married women, of which 16,592 were granted.[2] The Act has not, however, been subjected to amendments on the lines of those introduced by the Divorce Reform Act 1969 and the Matrimonial Proceedings and Property Act 1970, with the result that the grounds for and defences to proceedings before magistrates differ considerably from those applicable in proceedings for judicial separation. Differences there always have been, but they are much greater than they were. This is unfortunate and inconvenient. It means that great care must be taken in deciding upon the choice of court; there will be cases which would have little hope of success before magistrates which would be almost certain to succeed in a suit for judicial separation in a divorce county court. It means also that whereas in other courts an advocate must base his case upon the new law, in a magistrates' court he must still proceed on the basis of law which in other courts has been abolished as unsatisfactory and outmoded. These difficulties have been referred by the Home Secretary to the Law Commission for consideration and report. They are further considered at the end of this Chapter.

1. Definitions.

It is first necessary to consider some of the definitions contained in section 16.

Child, in relation to one or both of the parties to a marriage includes (as it does also under the Matrimonial Causes Act 1973, s. 52 (1)) an illegitimate or adopted child of that party, or, as the case may be, of both parties.[3]

Child of the family is less widely defined than in the Act of 1973; it includes only a child of both parties and any other child of either party who has been

---

[1] In this Chapter unless otherwise stated the expression "the Act" or "the Act of 1960" refers to the Matrimonial Proceedings (Magistrates' Courts) Act 1960 and a reference to a section (e.g. s. 1 or s. 2) is to that section in the Act.

[2] Civil Judicial Statistics 1972, Cmnd. 5333, Table M.

[3] The word "adopted" is more widely defined in s. 52 of the Act of 1973, to include e.g. overseas adoption under the Adoption Act 1968.

accepted as one of the family by the other party. By section 52 of the Act of 1973 it could include another child, no matter who the parents might be, who had been treated by both those parties as a child of their family. This matter is explained more fully in Chapter 7 at p. 113.

Dependant means a person under the age of sixteen years or who, having attained that age but not the age of twenty-one, is either receiving full-time instruction at an educational establishment or undergoing whole time training for a trade, profession or vocation for at least two years or has his earning capacity impaired through illness or disability of mind or body.

This definition is important in considering the maximum possible duration of maintenance for the benefit of a child of the family.

2. Grounds.

The grounds upon which complaint can be made are set out in section 1 (1) of the Act, and are broadly the same whether the complainant is the wife or the husband. The subsection provides that the complaint may be made by "a married woman or a married man", so that jurisdiction depends on the subsistence of the marriage and not upon cohabitation of the parties.[4] By section 47 of the Matrimonial Causes Act 1973, a court is not to be precluded from granting matrimonial relief by reason only that the marriage in question was entered into under a law which permits polygamy and such relief includes orders under the Matrimonial Proceedings (Magistrates' Courts) Act 1960. This matter has already been considered in more detail in Chapter 5.[5]

Complaint can be made on any of the following grounds arising during the subsistence of the marriage.

(a) *That the defendant has deserted the complainant.*

Now that the remedy of restitution of conjugal rights has been abolished,[6] proceedings before a magistrates' court provide the only remedy immediately available in cases of actual desertion. No petition for divorce or judicial separation can be filed until the desertion has lasted for two years, but a matrimonial order of a magistrates' court enables a wife to obtain maintenance from her husband in the meanwhile. But in cases of constructive desertion, as has already been explained.[7] a petition for divorce or judicial separation can be filed immediately on the basis that the conduct which drove the petitioner away has been such that he or she cannot reasonably be expected to live with the respondent.

(b) *That the defendant has been guilty of persistent cruelty to the complainant, or an infant child of the complainant, or an infant child of the defendant who, at the time of the cruelty, was a child of the family.*

Conduct of this kind would also, in almost all cases, satisfy the requirements of section 1 (2) (b) of the Matrimonial Causes Act 1973. But if the complainant elects to proceed in a magistrates' court, the burden of proof will be much

---

[4] *Waters* v. *Waters*, [1968] P. 401.
[5] See *ante*, pp. 88-90,
[6] Matrimonial Proceedings and Property Act 1970, s. 20.
[7] See *ante*, pp. 25, 28-29, 32.

heavier than if a petition had been filed in a divorce county court. This is so for two reasons.

First, it will be necessary to prove cruelty in the legal sense of the word. Some examples of cruelty have already been considered [8] in relation to section 1 (2) (*b*). The courts have deliberately refrained from a precise definition, but by way of reminder it must be emphasised that the conduct complained of must be sufficiently grave—such that the complainant ought not to be called upon to endure it—that an intention to hurt, though relevant, is not essential,[9] and that the whole history of the marriage must be considered.[10] The difficulty does not, however, arise from these points but from the decision of the House of Lords, so long ago as 1897, in *Russell* v. *Russell*,[11] that it is essential to a charge of cruelty to prove injury, or a reasonable apprehension of injury, to life, limb or health, bodily or mental. In that case a wife had falsely accused her husband or unnatural offences with another man, and persisted in these charges although she knew them to be untrue; yet as his health had not been affected a charge of cruelty failed. Yet in *Jeapes* v. *Jeapes*[12] a husband who had falsely spread reports that he was not the father of a child born to his wife was held to have been cruel, her health having been affected. From this viewpoint the test of cruelty is subjective—what affect has the conduct in question upon the health of the complainant in question. It is not possible to state that some particular conduct must in all the circumstances be cruel: it is a question of fact in each case.

The second factor which increases the burden of proof is the use in the section of the word "persistent". An isolated act, however, grave, cannot suffice; there must usually be conduct persisted in over a period of time,[13] though in *Broad* v. *Broad*[14] it was stated (obiter) that a number of acts all committed on the same day might be sufficient.

These difficulties may at first sight seem troublesome. It must, however, be remembered that if the conduct complained of led the complainant to leave the defendant, it would amount to constructive desertion. The point was clearly explained by DENNING, L.J. in *Timmins* v. *Timmins*[15] when he said:

> "Conduct which is of a grave and weighty character may sometimes fall short of cruelty because it lacks the element of injury to health . . .; but nevertheless it may give good cause for leaving. On the other hand, conduct which is not of a grave and weighty character and is for that reason not cruelty, does not give good cause for leaving."

It is quite possible for a single isolated act to be sufficiently grave to drive the complainant from the home, and reliance upon constructive desertion instead of cruelty can avoid difficulties both as to persistence and as to injury to health.

---

[8] See *ante*, pp. 28, 29.
[9] *Gollins* v. *Gollins*, [1964] A.C. 644; *Williams* v. *Williams*, [1964] A.C. 698.
[10] *King* v. *King*, [1953] A.C. 124.
[11] [1897] A.C. 395.
[12] (1903), 89 L.T. 74.
[13] *Rigby* v. *Rigby*, [1944] P. 33. Persistent dishonesty can suffice, *Stanwick* v. *Stanwick*, [1971] P. 124, C.A.
[14] (1898), 78 L.T. 687.
[15] [1953] 2 All E.R. 187.

(c) *That the defendant has been found guilty of certain specified assaults.*

If the conviction was on indictment it is sufficient if it was "for any offence which involved an assault upon the complainant". It is not necessary that the charge should have been one of assault: it might for example have been one of attempted murder. Where the conviction was by a magistrates' court, however, it must have been for an offence of wounding or inflicting grievous bodily harm, of aggravated assault, of assault occasioning actual bodily harm or of common assault, upon the complainant.[16] and in the case of common assault only, the defendant must have been sentenced to imprisonment or some other form of detention for at least one month: in the case of the other convictions the sentence is immaterial.

In addition to convictions for assaults upon the complainant, it is also a ground for an order that the defendant has been convicted by any court of an offence, or of an attempt to commit an offence, under sections 1 to 29 of the Sexual Offences Act 1956 or under section 1 of the Indecency with Children Act 1960 against an infant child of the complainant, or against an infant child of the defendant who was, at the time of the offence or attempt, a child of the family.

(d) *That the defendant has committed adultery.*

It is unnecessary to add anything to what has been said about this offence, except that in a magistrates' court it is not necessary to prove in addition (as it is under the Matrimonial Causes Act 1973, s. 1 (2) (*a*) that the complainant finds it intolerable to live with the defendant.

(e) *That the defendant, while knowingly suffering from a venereal disease, has insisted on, or has without the complainant being aware of that disease permitted, sexual intercourse between the complainant and the defendant.*

The word "insisted" here must be contrasted with the word "compelled" used in section 1 (1) (*g*) below; something short of actual compulsion will suffice.[17]

(f) *That the defendant is for the time being an habitual drunkard or a drug addict.*

Both these expressions are defined in section 16 (1) of the Act in such a way as to ensure that the complaint can be made only in really serious cases of drunkenness or addiction. The defendant must be a person (not being a mentally disordered person within the meaning of the Mental Health Act 1959) who by reason of habitual intemperate drinking of intoxicating liquor or by reason of habitual taking or using, otherwise than on medical advice, of any controlled drug within the meaning of the Misuse of Drugs Act 1971[18]

    (i) is at times dangerous to himself or to others, or incapable of managing himself or his affairs; or

---

[16] I.e. an offence under ss. 20, 42, 43 or 47 of the Offences Against the Person Act 1861.
[17] *Rigby* v. *Rigby*, [1944] P. 33, 36.
[18] Misuse of Drugs Act 1971, s. 34.

(ii) so conducts himself that it would not be reasonable to expect a spouse of ordinary sensibilities to continue to cohabit with him.

(g) *That a husband has compelled his wife to submit herself to prostitution, or has been guilty of such conduct as was likely to result and has resulted in her so doing.*

(h) *That a husband has wilfully neglected to provide reasonable maintenance for his wife or for any child of the family who is, or but for that neglect would have been, a dependant.*

The meaning of "wilful neglect to maintain" has already been explained in Chapter 10 in relation to section 27 of the Matrimonial Causes Act 1973. Under both Acts there are two distinct grounds for complaint,[19] the failure to maintain a spouse and the failure to maintain a child of the family. It follows that if a husband has a defence to his wife's claim for maintenance for herself because, for example, of her own adultery, she is not thereby precluded from complaining of his wilful neglect to maintain the children.[20]

(i) *That a wife has wilfully neglected to provide, or to make a proper contribution towards, reasonable maintenance for the husband or for any child of the family who is, or would but for that neglect have been, a dependant, in a case where, by reason of the impairment of the husband's earning capacity through age, illness or disability of mind or body, and having regard to any resources of the husband and the wife respectively which are, or should properly be made, available for the purpose, it is reasonable in all the circumstances to expect the wife so to provide or contribute.*

Under this heading there is a difference between the provisions of the Matrimonial Causes Act 1973, s. 27 (1) (*b*), and the law applicable in a magistrates' court. Under both statutes a husband cannot complain of his wife's neglect to maintain him or contribute towards his maintenance unless his own earning capacity is impaired. In a magistrates' court he must also prove this if he complains of her failure to maintain or contribute towards the maintenance of a child of the family. Under section 27 of the Act of 1973 he is not required to prove impairment of his own earning capacity when he complains only in respect of maintenance of children.[21]

3. Jurisdiction.

There are really two problems here, whether there will be some magistrates' court in England which will have jurisdiction to consider a complaint, and, if so, to which magistrates' court application should be made.

The provisions of the Domicile and Matrimonial Proceedings Act 1973 as to jurisdiction in suits for divorce and judicial separation[22], and in proceedings

---

[19] See *Northrop* v. *Northrop*, [1968] P. 74, and *ante*, p. 152.
[20] *Cooke* v. *Cooke*, [1961] P. 16.
[21] See *ante*, p. 152.
[22] See *ante*, p. 90.

based upon wilful neglect to provide reasonable maintenance,[23] must be carefully contrasted with those governing proceedings before a magistrates' court. In the High Court or a divorce county court the domicile of either spouse in England and Wales suffices to found jurisdiction. In a magistrates' court it is irrelevant, and section 14 (3) of the Act of 1960 so provides. In suits for divorce or judicial separation it is also sufficient if either spouse has habitually resided in England or Wales during the preceding year and in those based on wilful neglect to maintain it suffices if the applicant has so resided or if the respondent resides there at the date of the application. With one exception there will be no magistrates' court entitled to exercise jurisdiction under the Act of 1960 unless the defendant is ordinarily resident in England or Wales at the date when the summons is issued.[1] The exception arises under section 1 (3) whereby a court can exercise jurisdiction notwithstanding that the defendant resides in Scotland or Northern Ireland if the complainant resides in England or Wales and the parties last ordinarily resided together there as man and wife.[2] In this exceptional case, however, any order made by the court cannot contain a provision that the complainant is no longer bound to cohabit with the defendant—the order must be a maintenance rather than a separation order.

Assuming that the above tests are satisfied, in which magistrates' court should proceedings be started? This matter is dealt with by section 2 (2) whereby such a court can hear a complaint.:

> (a) if at the date of making the complaint either the complainant or the defendant ordinarily resides within the petty sessions area for which the court acts; or
>
> (b) except in the case of complaints based upon convictions for assault under section 2 (1) (c) above, if the cause of complaint arose wholly or partly within that petty sessions area; or
>
> (c) in the case of complaints based upon such convictions, if the offence or attempt to which the complaint relates occurred within that area.

These provisions may offer a wide choice of court. In case of persistent cruelty, for example, proceedings could be started in the court for the petty sessions area where either husband or wife resided or where any of the acts which went to establish the cruelty took place.[3]

4. Contents of a matrimonial order.

By section 2 (1) of the Act the court hearing a complaint may make a matrimonial order containing any one or more of the following provisions:—

(a) A provision that the complainant be no longer bound to cohabit with the defendant. Subject to the Matrimonial Causes Act 1973, s. 18 with regard to intestate succession,[4] such a provision whilst in force has effect in all other

---

[23] See *ante*, pp. 151, 152.

[1] *Macrae* v. *Macrae*, [1949] P. 397.

[2] S. 2 (3) also declares that if the defendant resides in England the fact that the complainant resides in Scotland or Northern Ireland is immaterial.

[3] *Hudson* v. *Hudson* (1947), 176 L.T. 335.

[4] See *ante*, p. 65.

respects as a decree of judicial separation. This provision cannot be included where the defendant resides in Scotland or Northern Ireland [5] and there is no power to include a provision that the *defendant* is no longer bound to cohabit with the *complainant*.[6]

The inclusion of a non-cohabitation clause is in the court's discretion but in exercising this discretion the court should consider whether the clause is reasonably necessary for the complainant's protection, whether the case is more than ordinarily serious, and whether there is a reasonable prospect of the parties becoming reconciled.[7] If there is such a prospect it should not be included, because it is obviously a hindrance to reconciliation, nor should it be included in cases of simple desertion (which it will terminate) or of wilful neglect to maintain.[8]

(b) A provision that the husband shall pay to the wife such weekly sum as the court considers reasonable in the circumstances of the case. The financial limits on this and other provisions were removed by the Maintenance Orders Act 1968, s. 1. The considerations which the court should have in mind in exercising its power to order financial provision by one spouse for the other were held, in cases decided before the coming into operation of the Matrimonial Proceedings and Property Act 1970[9] to be the same as those applicable in the High Court or in a divorce county court. It seems likely that many of the statutory provisions (which are now embodied in the Matrimonial Causes Act 1973, s. 25 (1)) governing the matters to be considered in these courts in a suit for divorce or judicial separation [10] will be regarded in the future to be equally applicable to magistrates' courts.

(c) Where by reason of the impairment of the husband's earning capacity through age, illness or disability of mind or body, it appears to the court to be reasonable in all the circumstances so to order, a provision that the wife shall pay to the husband such weekly sum as the court considers reasonable in the circumstances of the case. This wording is similar to that in section 27 of the Act of 1973. But it must be observed that under section 2 (1) (b) and (c) the powers of the magistrates are limited to ordering payment of a weekly sum, and they have no power to order such payments to be secured, or to order payment of a lump sum. The same is true of provision for children under section 2 (1) (h) below.

(d) A provision for legal custody of any child of the family who is under the age of sixteen years. The powers of the High Court or a divorce county court in relation to custody extend until the age of eighteen, but as has been explained already,[11] it is not the practice of these courts to make orders for custody against the wishes of a child who has reached the age of sixteen. Whereas the High

---

[5] S. 1 (3).
[6] *Wall* v. *Wall*, [1967] 3 All E.R. 408, where a husband defendant wished the clause to be included because immigration into Canada would otherwise be forbidden.
[7] *Corton* v. *Corton*, [1965] P. 1.
[8] *Jolliffe* v. *Jolliffe*, [1965] P. 6.
[9] See e.g. *Kershaw* v. *Kershaw*, [1966] P. 13; *Attwood* v. *Attwood*, [1968] P. 591.
[10] See *ante*, Chapter 9.
[11] See *ante*, p. 180.

Court or a divorce county court can make a "split order" awarding custody to one spouse and care and control to the other,[12] a magistrates' court has no power under the Matrimonial Proceedings (Magistrates' Courts) Act to do this.[13] Such a court has, however, this power upon a summons under the Guardianship of Minors Act 1971,[14] and if the complainant particularly wishes to obtain such an order he should issue a summons under the latter Act returnable immediately after the proceedings under the Act of 1960 are concluded.

(e) If it appears to the court that there are exceptional circumstances making it impracticable or undesirable for a child of the family to be entrusted to either of the parties or to any other individual, a provision committing the care of the child to a specified local authority, being the local social services authority for the area[15] in which the child was, in the opinion of the court, resident immediately before being so committed. Before so doing the court must inform the local authority of the proposal and hear any representations which the authority wishes to make.[16] The provision will cease to have effect when the child reaches the age of eighteen.[17]

(f) If any child is committed to the legal custody of any person and it appears to the court that there are exceptional circumstances making this desirable, a provision that the child shall be under the supervision of a probation officer or a specified local social services authority. Such a provision will cease to have effect when the child reaches the age of sixteen.[18]

(g) A provision for access to any child of the family by either of the parties or by any other person who is a parent of that child in a case where the child is committed to the custody of a person other than that party or parent. There is no power to make an order for access by the person who is given custody.[19]

(h) A provision for the payment of maintenance for any child of the family by the complainant or the defendant, or by both of them. The payments can be ordered to be made to any person who has the legal custody of the child for the time being,[20] or to the local authority in whose care the child is, so long as the child is under the age of sixteen. If it appears to the court that the child is, or will be, or if such payment were made would be, a dependant[21] though over the age of sixteen years, and the court thinks this expedient, it may order the payments to be made, or to continue, whilst the child remains a dependant either directly to the child, or to some other person for the child's benefit, or to the local authority having care of the child. But unlike the powers of the High Court or a divorce county court,[1] payments can in no circumstances be ordered

---

[12] See *ante*, p. 181.
[13] *Wild* v. *Wild*, [1969] P. 33.
[14] *Re. W (an infant)*, [1964] Ch. 202.
[15] Defined as the council of a non metropolitan county or a metropolitan district or London Borough, or the Common Council of the City of London, Local Government Act 1972 Sched. 3, para. 10.
[16] S. 3 (1).
[17] S. 3 (4).
[18] S. 3 (9).
[19] See *Wild* v. *Wild*, *supra*.
[20] But not by any such person—*Wild* v. *Wild*, *supra*.
[21] For definition of a dependant see *ante*, p. 268.
[1] Matrimonial Causes Act 1973, s. 29.

to continue beyond the age of twenty-one. In considering whether either party should be ordered to make payments for the maintenance of a child of the family who is not a child of that party, the court must have regard to the extent, if any, to which that party had, on or after the acceptance of the child as one of the family, assumed responsibility for the child's maintenance, and to the liability of any other person to maintain the child.[2]

In most cases the complainant cannot be ordered to make any payments for the maintenance of the defendant, although either party may be ordered to pay maintenance for a child of the family. The only exception occurs when an order is made on the ground of the defendant's habitual drunkenness or addiction to drugs, and that order contains a non-cohabitation clause. In that case the court has power, after giving each party an opportunity to be heard, to order the complainant to make such payments as are mentioned in (b) or (c) above for the defendant's maintenance.[3] In many such cases the defendant's behaviour will amount to constructive desertion, so that this provision can be avoided by making the complaint on the ground of desertion instead of drunkenness or addiction to drugs.

In all cases the court has power to order either party to pay the costs of the other party.

5. Bars to an order.

Just as the grounds for an order under the Act, unlike those now applicable in suits for divorce or judicial separation, are still based upon the commission of a matrimonial offence, so also the defences which have been abolished in suits for divorce or judicial separation are still available in proceedings before magistrates.

By section 2 (3) of the Act, the court is prohibited from making a matrimonial order containing a non-cohabitation clause, or for payments by either spouse for the maintenance of the other (though it can still make all the orders relating to children of the family), in two cases.

(a) *Complaints based on adultery.*

Such an order cannot be made on the ground of the defendant's adultery unless the court is satisfied that the complainant has not condoned or connived at or by wilful neglect or misconduct conduced to that act of adultery.

Condonation involves the conditional forgiveness of the adultery, with full knowledge of the material facts concerning the act of adultery in question, coupled with a restoration of the offender to his or her former position. Mere suspicion does not amount to knowledge, so that in *Burch* v. *Burch*[4] a husband who suspected his wife of adultery with an American soldier was not precluded

---

[2] Contrast this provision with ss. 25 (3) (and 27 (4)) of the Act of 1973 (see *ante*, pp. 147 and 153), the differences being accounted for by the wider definition of a child of the family for the purposes of the Act of 1973.

[3] S. 2 (2).

[4] [1958] 1 All E.R. 848.

from relying upon adultery with a Canadian airman which he subsequently discovered. It is knowledge of the adultery upon which reliance is placed which is essential, and a husband who knew of, and forgave, adultery to which his wife confessed would not be precluded from relying upon earlier adultery with the same man of which he was ignorant, unless he had chosen to waive enquiry.[5] There can be no condonation without restoration of the offending spouse to his or her former position,[6] though a resumption of sexual intercourse it not essential. It was at one time held that if a husband had intercourse with his wife with knowledge of her offence, condonation must be conclusively presumed against him,[7] unless he was induced to do so by her false statement of some material fact, such as her denial that she was pregnant as a result of the adultery.[8] In contrast, proof of such intercourse by a wife was prima facie evidence of adultery only, and not conclusive.[9] The rule which formerly applied to the wife now applies to the husband also, because the Matrimonial Causes Act 1965, s. 42 (1),[10] provides that, for the purposes of the Matrimonial Proceedings (Magistrates' Courts) Act 1960, any presumption of condonation which arises from the continuance or resumption of marital intercourse can be rebutted by evidence sufficient to negative the necessary intent. The existence of this intent may be rebutted upon a balance of probability.[11]

The law as to condonation may obviously deter the complainant from attempts to affect a reconciliation, since should these attempts fail the possibility of proceedings may be lost. In an attempt to avoid this difficulty the Matrimonial Causes Act 1963, s. 2 (now embodied in the Matrimonial Causes Act 1965, s. 42 (2)) provided that for the purposes of the Act of 1960 adultery or cruelty shall not be deemed to have been condoned by reason only of a continuance or resumption of cohabitation between the parties for any one period not exceeding three months, or of anything done during such cohabitation, if it is proved that the cohabitation was continued or resumed, as the case may be, with a view to effecting a reconciliation. The effect of this provision was largely nullified by the decision in *Brown* v. *Brown*[12] that this provision did not provide a probationary period of three months or apply where cohabitation was resumed or continued because the parties had become reconciled, but only where it took place *with a view to effecting a reconciliation*. This is still the position in a magistrates' court, though the defence of condonation is no longer available in proceedings for divorce or judicial separation, and one or more periods of life together, not amounting in all to more than six months, are permitted without interrupting periods of desertion, or of life apart, no matter what the circumstances in which cohabitation was resumed or continued may have been.[13]

Once adultery has been condoned it ceases for all time to be available as a

---

[5] *Inglis* v. *Inglis and Baxter*, [1968] P. 639.
[6] *Mackrell* v. *Mackrell*, [1948] 2 All E.R. 858; *Cook* v. *Cook*, [1949] 1 All E.R. 384.
[7] *Cramp* v. *Cramp and Freeman*, [1920] P. 158; *Henderson* v. *Henderson and Crellin*, [1944] A.C. 49.
[8] *Roberts* v. *Roberts* (1917), 117 L.T. 157.
[9] *Morley* v. *Morley*, [1961] 1 All E.R. 428.
[10] As amended by the Matrimonial Causes Act 1973, Sched. 2, para. 5 (2).
[11] *Blyth* v. *Blyth*, [1966] A.C. 643.
[12] [1967] P. 105.
[13] Matrimonial Causes Act 1973, s. 2.

ground for an order by a magistrates' court and cannot be revived.[14] though it might still be available in support of a petition for divorce or judicial separation if the petitioner for that, or some other, reason found it intolerable to live with the respondent.[15] But although the Act of 1960 makes no express mention of condonation as a bar to a complaint based on persistent cruelty, in practice it is regarded as a principle of general application and indeed is expressly referred to in the Matrimonial Causes Act 1965, s. 42 (2), in relation to cruelty in proceedings in such courts. For that purpose, condoned cruelty, unlike condoned adultery, is capable of being revived. The forgiveness is in law conditional upon the condoned offence not being repeated and upon the offender not being guilty of other behaviour which, although not of itself a specific ground for an order under the Act of 1960, would make married life together impossible.[16] In view of the gravity of this offence, however, a complainant would not often wish to proceed in a magistrates' court on the ground of persistent cruelty which had been condoned and was said to have been revived, when the very conduct which was alleged to have resulted in revival would, without any reliance upon any allegation of cruelty, have sufficed as a basis for a petition for divorce or judicial separation under section 1 (2) (*b*) of the Matrimonial Causes Act 1973.

Connivance is the intentional concurrence in the act of adultery of which complaint is made. It is based on the maxim *volenti non fit injuria*, so that in *Peters* v. *Peters*[17] a wife whose mental condition resulting from epilepsy was such that she could not give a willing consent was held for that reason not to have been guilty of connivance. It may be active (as in the case of a "wife-swapping" expedition in a caravan in *Richmond* v. *Richmond*[18]), or passive (as by taking no action despite knowledge of the probability of adultery[19]). Something more than mere negligence, inattention or indifference is required.[20] Connivance will generally precede the inception of the adultery, being in effect a prior consent unlike the subsequent forgiveness involved in condonation. But there may be connivance by encouraging or tolerating an adulterous association which has already commenced.[21] In some cases a husband who has suspected that his wife is committing adultery has lulled her into a false sense of security by pretending, for example, that he would be away from home for some days, and thus obtained evidence of her adultery. In such cases the question for the court is whether or not he was in reality consenting to the adultery—whether he hoped that he would obtain such evidence[22]—or whether he was distressed by what he feared was likely to happen and in no sense intended to encourage it.[1]

Difficulties which arose in relation to divorce as to whether connivance

---

[14] Matrimonial Causes Act 1965, s. 42 (3).
[15] As to intolerability, see *ante*, p. 23.
[16] *Richardson* v. *Richardson*, [1950] P. 16; *Cundy* v. *Cundy*, [1956] 1 All E.R. 245.
[17] [1963] 3 All E.R. 67.
[18] [1952] 1 All E.R. 838.
[19] *Lloyd* v. *Lloyd and Leggeri*, [1938] P. 174.
[20] *Rogers* v. *Rogers* (1830), 3 Hag. Ecc. 57, 59.
[21] *Rumbelow* v. *Rumbelow*, [1965] P. 207.
[22] *Manning* v. *Manning*, [1950] 1 All E.R. 602.
[1] *Douglas* v. *Douglas*, [1951] P. 85.

at adultery with one person would preclude reliance upon adultery with another —as to whether a petitioner could be permitted to say *"non omnibus dormio"*, "I do not shut my eyes to everyone"—do not arise in a magistrates' court, since section 2 (3) of the Act of 1960 specifically refers to connivance at "that act of adultery" rather than other such acts. The question of whether earlier connivance has spent its force, so that it no longer remains a bar in relation to subsequent adultery with the same person, was considered by the House of Lords in *Godfrey* v. *Godfrey*.[2] The main question is whether there remains any causal connection between the original connivance and the subsequent adultery. Where the original consent (in that case the words—"If you two want to go to bed together, why the hell don't you?") was to adultery with the same person, it is likely to be very difficult to prove that the later adultery in no way results from the original invitation or permission, though this might be possible if a complete reconciliation between the spouses had intervened.

Wilful neglect or misconduct conducing to the act of adultery in question differs from connivance in that it is only necessary to prove that the adultery resulted from the complainant's behaviour and not that he in any way consented to the adultery or intended that it should occur. The conduct complained of must have occurred during the marriage and not before it,[3] and must be in a marital capacity, so that the fact that the complainant had been sentenced to a long term of imprisonment would not suffice.[4] Beyond this it is difficult to lay down principles, the question being one of fact and degree in each case. Desertion of itself is not conduct conducing to adultery[5] though in special circumstances the likelihood that it would result in adultery would make it so.[6] Refusal of sexual intercourse may suffice,[7] as might the complainant's improper association with some other person, provided the defendant knew of it,[8] or placing the defendant wife in circumstances in which adultery is particularly likely to occur, a case of "voluntary blindness".[9]

(b) *Complaints based on any ground.*

The same absolute prohibition against the making of an order containing a non-cohabitation clause, or for the maintenance of one spouse by the other, applies to complaints based on any ground if the complainant is proved to have committed adultery during the subsistence of the marriage. In that case, by section 2 (3) (*b*) of the Act, such an order cannot be made unless the court is satisfied that the defendant has condoned or connived at or by wilful neglect or misconduct conduced to, that act of adultery.

6. Special powers and duties with respect to children.

Section 4 of the Act confers on the court a number of additional powers in relation to children of the family. Whenever it has begun to hear a complaint

---

    [2] [1965] A.C. 444.
    [3] *Allen* v. *Allen and D'Arcy* (1859), 28 L.J.P. & M. 81.
    [4] *Cunnington* v. *Cunnington and Noble* (1859), 1 Sw. & Tr. 475.
    [5] *Richards* v. *Richards*, [1952] P. 307.   [6] *Jenkins* v. *Jenkins*, [1956] P. 458.
    [7] *Callister* v. *Callister* (1947), 63 T.L.R. 503.   [8] *Brown* v. *Brown*, [1956] P. 438.
    [9] *Robinson* v. *Robinson and Dearden*, [1903] P. 155.

(a) on any of the grounds available under section 1; or
(b) for the variation of a matrimonial order by the revocation, addition or alteration of provision for the legal custody of a child or for the revocation of a provision committing a child to the care of a local authority or directing that the child be under supervision; or
(c) a complaint for the revocation of the whole of the matrimonial order containing such provisions with regard to such a child,

then whether or not the court makes the order for which the complaint is made, it may make a matrimonial order containing, or as the case may be, vary the matrimonial order so that it contains, any of the provisions relating to children which can be made under section 2 (1) (*d*) to (*h*), which are set out on pp. 273 and 274. But before so doing it must give each party to the proceedings the opportunity to be heard. This follows the general principle that if the spouses are in dispute the court must have the power to concern itself with the welfare of the children. Indeed it is bound to do so, because section 4 provides that the court shall not dismiss or make its final order on any complaint in which its powers under the section are or may be exercisable until it has decided whether or not, and if so how, these powers shall be exercised.

The section also contains a number of very detailed provisions whereby if the court feels that it has not sufficient information to enable it to reach a decision on these matters it may call for a report of a probation officer or an officer of a local authority.[10]

7. Refusal of order in cases more suitable for the High Court.

At the time when the Act of 1960 was passed proceedings for divorce or judicial separation could be commenced only in the High Court, and situations could arise in which one spouse commenced proceedings under the Act in a magistrates' court and the other spouse, at about the same time, proceedings in the High Court. Such a situation could lead to confusion and conflicting orders as to such matters as maintenance and welfare of children. Accordingly, for this and other reasons, section 5 of the Act of 1960 provides that where on hearing a complaint under section 1 of the Act of 1960 the magistrates' court is of opinion that the matters in issue could be more conveniently dealt with by the High Court, it may refuse to make a matrimonial order. There is no appeal from such a refusal, but the High Court may order a re-hearing by a magistrates' court.

When jurisdiction in undefended matrimonial causes was transferred to divorce county courts by the Matrimonial Causes Act 1967, no amendment was made to section 5 of the Act of 1960. The situation can thus arise today in which divorce proceedings are started in a county court whilst proceedings by the other spouse in a magistrates' court are still pending. This does not in law deprive the magistrates' court of jurisdiction and section 5 makes no mention of refusal to make an order on the ground that the matter could more conveniently be dealt with by a divorce county court, as would usually be the case

---

[10] See Guardianship Act 1973, s. 8, and Magistrates' Courts (Matrimonial Proceedings) Rules 1960, rr. 1–4.

as regards questions of ancillary relief and children. However, it seems clear from cases decided before the transfer of divorce jurisdiction to county courts that in such cases the magistrates should decline to make an order and leave all questions to be decided in the divorce proceedings[11] unless the divorce proceedings are a tactical device for securing delay.[11a]

8. Interim orders.

It frequently happens that a wife who is applying for a matrimonial order is in need of immediate financial assistance and that the court is not in a position to make a final order without time for further investigation. Section 6 enables a magistrates' court to make an interim order where at any time before making its final order it adjourns the complaint for more than one week and also when it refuses to make any order on the ground that the matter could more conveniently be dealt with by the High Court.[12] The High Court itself is empowered to do this when, after such refusal by a magistrates' court, or on an appeal from the decision of such a court, the High Court orders a re-hearing by a magistrates' court.[13] The interim order may contain a provision for the maintenance of one spouse by the other, and a provision that either shall pay maintenance for a child of the family.[14] In special circumstances it may also provide for custody of or access to such a child.[15] The maximum duration of an interim order is three months or, if two or more interim orders are made on the same complaint, three months from the making of the first such order.[16]

9. Termination and variation of orders.

(a) *Effect of cohabitation.*

There is nothing in the Act to prevent a complaint being made whilst the parties are still living together in one household, and indeed there are cases where a wife may have good reason for leaving her husband and taking the children with her but is unable to do so because she would be without money. Section 7 of the Act deals with two situations.

(i) If the parties are cohabiting at the date when a matrimonial order or an interim order is made, it is not enforceable and no liability accrues under it until they cease to cohabit, and if in the case of a matrimonial order they continue to do so for three months,[17] the order ceases to have effect.

(ii) If they resume cohabitation after the date of a matrimonial order or interim order, it ceases to have effect immediately,[18] and the court must on complaint being made revoke the order.[19]

---

[11] *Higgs* v. *Higgs*, [1935] P. 28; *Knott* v. *Knott*, [1935] P. 158.
[11a] *Lanitis* v. *Lanitis*, [1970] 1 All E.R. 466.
[12] S. 6 (1) (a) and (b).
[13] S. 6 (1) (c).
[14] I.e. orders under s. 2 (1) (b), (c) or (h)—see *ante*, pp. 273, 274.
[15] I.e. orders under s. 2 (1) (d) or (g).
[16] S. 6 (3).
[17] By virtue of s. 6, an interim order cannot last for more than three months.
[18] S. 7 (2).
[19] S. 8 (2).

In both cases, unless the court in making the order otherwise directs, the above provisions do not apply to certain provisions concerning children, i.e.

(i) a provision committing a child to the legal custody of a person other than one of the parties, or for access to that child by either party or any other person who is the child's parent;

(ii) a provision committing a child to the care of a local authority or for supervision by a probation officer or local authority;

(iii) a provision requiring either party to make payments for a child's maintenance to a person other than one of those parties.

(b) *Effect of adultery.*

By section 8 (2) the court is bound, at the request of the person who was defendant when the order was made, to revoke a matrimonial order on proof that the party on whose complaint the order was made has been guilty of adultery during the subsistence of the marriage, not necessarily after the order was made. If however it is of opinion that the party who is seeking variation has condoned or connived at, or by wilful neglect or misconduct conduced to, that act of adultery, the section provides that it shall not revoke the order on that ground. In neither case is the court given any discretion. If there was no condonation, connivance or wilful neglect or misconduct, it must revoke the order: if there was, it cannot do so. The obligation to revoke the order relates only to any non-cohabitation clause and any requirement that either spouse should pay maintenance to the other. Proof of adultery does not oblige the court to revoke any of the provisions concerning children of the family.[20]

(c) *Effect of divorce.*

A matrimonial or interim order made by a magistrates' court is not automatically terminated by a decree of divorce, whichever party obtained the decree[1] and this is so whether the decree was obtained in England or elsewhere.[2] The fact that the marriage has ended does, however, give the magistrates a discretion to revoke or vary their order, and in the case of a foreign decree the circumstances, so far as they concern maintenance, are matters for consideration.[2] If the findings on which the magistrates based their order were inconsistent with the basis on which the divorce was granted, as where they had held that the husband had deserted his wife and a divorce was granted on the ground that she had deserted him, the magistrates have no discretion and must discharge their order.[3]

Where the decree was granted on the ground of adultery, the magistrates' court has again no discretion. It must, by reason of the provisions mentioned above, revoke the order on complaint being made unless the party against whom the order was made had been guilty of condonation, connivance or wilful neglect or misconduct in respect of the adultery in question, when the court

---

[20] I.e. those under s. 2 (1) (*d*) to (*h*).
[1] *Bragg* v. *Bragg*, [1925] P. 20.
[2] *Wood* v. *Wood*, [1957] P. 254.
[3] *Sternberg* v. *Sternberg*, [1963] 3 All E.R. 319.

would have no power to revoke the order by reason of that adultery. Now that these matters are no bar to a decree of divorce there may be cases where decrees have been obtained despite, for example, condonation. But presumably although the magistrates' court could not then revoke its order because of the condoned adultery, it would still retain its discretion to do so because of the decree of divorce.

When proceedings for divorce are pending, and particularly, in view of the matters mentioned above, when reliance is placed upon the respondent's adultery, the petitioner may be well advised, if there is a matrimonial order of a magistrates' court subsisting against him, to apply to the High Court[4] or to a divorce county court,[5] to direct that the provisions in the matrimonial order for maintenance of the respondent spouse and any child of the family shall cease to have effect, thus enabling the court in which the divorce proceedings are pending to make such other provision as it thinks appropriate.

A magistrates' court is not compelled to revoke an order by reason of adultery committed after the subsistence of the marriage has been terminated by divorce, nor by reason of intercourse by the person in whose favour the order was made which did not amount to adultery, since both participants were unmarried. The court then has a discretion in the matter.

(d) *Effect of re-marriage.*

Reference has already been made[6] to the Matrimonial Proceedings and Property Act 1970, s. 30, whereby in pursuance of the policy of that Act, where a matrimonial order consists of or contains a provision for payment by one spouse for the maintenance of the other, and that order continues in force, as it may do, despite the dissolution or annulment of the marriage the order, or the provision for payments, as the case may be, will terminate on the re-marriage on or after January 1, 1971, of the spouse in whose favour it was made, and will not be capable of being revived. Any remaining provisions of the order in relation to children will not be affected.

The Rules[7] require that where the clerk of a magistrates' court to whom payments are made under an order is notified in writing of the re-marriage of the person entitled to the payments, he must notify the clerk or other appropriate officer of any other court which has made the order or is concerned with its enforcement.

Termination will not affect any arrears due at the date of the re-marriage. As to repayment of sums paid after the order has ceased, see *ante*, p. 169.

(e) *Variation of orders generally.*

A magistrates' court may, on complaint being made, revoke, revive or vary a matrimonial order or interim order[8] and may add to such an order any

---

[4] S. 7 (3).
[5] Matrimonial Proceedings and Property Act 1970, s. 33; see *ante*, p. 109.
[6] *Ante*, p. 168.
[7] Magistrates' Court (Amendment) (No. 2) Rules 1970, inserting a new Rule 37A in the Rules of 1968.
[8] S. 8 (1) applying Magistrates' Courts Act 1952, s. 53, and proviso to s. 55 (1) as to costs, to such orders.

provision which is authorised by the Act to be included in these orders.[9] There is no express requirement that fresh evidence must be adduced before these powers can be exercised, that is to say evidence of matters which have occurred since the order was made or could not with reasonable diligence have been made available at the original hearing. But the court would be unlikely to exercise its powers unless evidence of some valid reason for so doing was given. The Act does however make the exercise of these powers subject to section 4 of the Act, which confers on the court special powers and duties in relation to children[10] and also provides[11] that no complaint can be made—

(i) for the variation of an order by the addition of a provision committing a child to the care of a local authority or providing for a child to be under the supervision of a probation officer or local authority; or

(ii) for the revival of any such provision which has ceased to be in force; or

(iii) for the variation of a provision committing a child to the care of a local authority.[12]

The powers of revocation, revival and variation can be exercised although the proceedings are brought by or against a person residing outside England, though a non-cohabitation clause cannot be added if the defendant so resides. Detailed provisions as to these cases are contained in section 9. Provisions as to who is entitled to seek revocation, revival or variation of an order are contained in section 10 and as to who should be made defendants in the Magistrates' Courts (Matrimonial Proceedings) Rules 1960, r. 7.

10. Procedure.

(a) *The Complaint.*

Proceedings under the Act are commenced by complaint to a justice of the peace, who may issue a summons directed to the party against whom the complaint is made requiring him to appear before the court to answer the complaint.[13] The complaint may be made by the complainant in person, or by his counsel or solicitor or other person authorised: the complaint need not be made in writing or on oath.[14]

In general complaint must be made within six months of the cause of complaint.[15] But:—

(i) A complaint on the ground of adultery may be made within six

---

[9] S. 8 (1).
[10] See *ante*, p. 278.
[11] S. 8 (1), proviso.
[12] As to complaints for the revocation of such a provision see s. 10 (1) (*e*).
[13] Magistrates' Courts Act 1952, s. 43.
[14] Magistrates' Courts Rules 1968, r. 1. As to complaints for variation etc., see Rule 34 and for variations of a maintenance agreement Rule 87.
[15] Magistrates' Courts Act 1952, s. 104.

months of the date when that act of adultery first became known to the complainant.[16]

(ii) If the complaint is based upon persistent cruelty there must have been a specific act of cruelty within the six months' period, but evidence of earlier acts may then be given in order to prove that the cruelty was persistent.[17]

(iii) The time limit does not apply to complaints based upon desertion or wilful neglect to maintain, which are continuing offences, though complaint must be made whilst the cause of complaint exists and it must still be in existence at the date of the hearing.[18] Nor does the time limit apply to applications to revoke, vary or revive an order[19] or to recovery of arrears.[20]

(b) *The Domestic Court.*

Proceedings under the Act of 1960, other than proceedings for enforcement of an order, are "domestic proceedings" for the purposes of section 56 of the Magistrates' Courts Act 1952, except that proceedings for variation of a provision for payment of money contained in a matrimonial order or interim order are not to be treated as domestic proceedings unless the court in its discretion so orders.[21]

A magistrates' court when hearing domestic proceedings must be composed of not more than three justices, including, so far as is practicable, both a man and a woman.[1] The business of such a court must, so far as is consistent with the due dispatch of business, be so arranged as to separate the hearing from other business of the court.[2] The object of these provisions is that the hearing shall be conducted in an atmosphere which shall, so far as possible, give opportunities for reconciliation, which would hardly be encouraged by an intermixture of criminal and domestic cases. In furtherance of this purpose, only certain persons may be present at the hearing,[3] and although such persons include representatives of the press and news agencies (though not members of the general public), newspaper reports are restricted to details of the parties and witnesses, the charges, defences and counter-charges, submissions and decisions on points of law, the court's decision and any observations by the court in giving it.[4] Further the court may, if it thinks it necessary in the interest of the administration of justice or of public decency, direct that any persons, except the officers of the court, the parties and their solicitors or counsel and

---

[16] Matrimonial Proceedings (Magistrates' Courts) Act 1960, s. 12, which also allows extra time in certain circumstances for members of the armed forces serving abroad or of the crew of a British ship.

[17] *Donkin* v. *Donkin*, [1933] P. 17.

[18] *Irvin* v. *Irvin*, [1968] 1 All E.R. 271.

[19] Act of 1960, s. 8 (1).

[20] Magistrates' Courts Act 1952, s. 74 (2). As to leave to enforce payment of arrears more than 12 months old through the High Court or any county court, see *ante*, p. 168.

[21] Act of 1960, s. 8 (3).

[1] Magistrates' Courts Act 1952, s. 56.

[2] *Ibid.*, s. 57 (1).

[3] *Ibid.*, s. 57 (2).

[4] *Ibid.*, s. 58.

other persons directly concerned in the case, shall be excluded during the taking of any evidence of an indecent character.[5]

The Magistrates' Courts Act 1952[6] also makes provision to enable the domestic court to seek the assistance of a probation officer or other person to attempt to effect a reconciliation; it must in selecting that officer or person, have regard to the religious persuasion of the parties. If the person selected is unsuccessful and he thinks fit to do so, he may furnish to the court a report in a prescribed form containing the allegations made by each party and such other information as may be prescribed.[7] No allegation made by either party can be included in such a report without the consent in writing of the party who made the allegation, and the report cannot be put in evidence, though the court may use it for the purpose of questioning witnesses. Thus even though the attempt at reconciliation may fail, this procedure may enable the court to understand the viewpoint of parties who might otherwise be silent or incoherent in the atmosphere of a court of law, and may assist the court to arrive at the truth of the matter.

Section 60 of the Act of 1952 enables the court to obtain the assistance of a probation officer for another purpose, that of investigating the means of the parties for the purpose of deciding what order for periodical payments shall be made, or upon problems of variation or enforcement of such orders. No direction to report to the court under this section can be given to a probation officer until the court has determined all the issues arising in the proceedings other than that of the amount which should be directed to be paid.[8] The probation officer's report may be given by reading a statement in writing aloud in court in the presence of the parties or by an oral statement, but either party can require that he shall give evidence on oath.

(c) *The hearing*.

The order of evidence and speeches at the hearing is governed by Rule 14 of the Magistrates' Courts Rules 1968. The complainant begins by calling his evidence, and before so doing may address the court. When the evidence for the complainant is concluded, the defendant may address the court, whether or not he afterwards calls evidence, but if he chooses to address the court at this stage, he cannot do so a second time without leave.

He may at this stage choose to make a submission that there is no case to answer. A distinction must be drawn between two possible forms of submission. It may be a submission that, accepting the complainant's evidence at its face value, no case has been established in law, or a submission that the evidence for the complainant is so unsatisfactory and unreliable that the burden of proof has not been discharged.[9] The magistrates have a discretion if a submission is made to require the advocate to elect to call no evidence if the

---

[5] *Ibid.*, s. 57 (3).
[6] *Ibid.*, ss. 59 and 62.
[7] See Magistrates' Courts (Forms) Rules 1968, Form 101.
[8] But note the exception under s. 4 (8) of the Act of 1960 in relation to special powers concerning children.
[9] *Storey* v. *Storey*, [1961] P. 63, 68; *Disher* v. *Disher*, [1965] P. 31.

submission fails. But if the submission is of the former type, a submission of law does not debar the advocate, if it is rejected, from addressing the bench on the facts. Until he has done so he has not exhausted his rights.[10] It is also open to the magistrates of their own accord to dismiss the case, but they cannot do this before the close of the case for the complainant, and should they do so a re-hearing must be ordered.[11] It will rarely be satisfactory for them to come to a conclusion in a matrimonial case without hearing both sides.[12] Although magistrates have the power to dismiss a complaint at the conclusion of a complainant's case, the power should be exercised only in exceptional cases, as where no credence can be given to the complainant's evidence, or where it is crystal clear that the complainant has no case in law.[13]

Assuming that the case proceeds, the evidence for the defence is called, and the advocate may (as may the complainant) call his evidence in any order he pleases.[14] The complainant may then if he wishes call evidence in rebuttal, and at the conclusion of the evidence for the defence and evidence in rebuttal, if any, the defendant may address the court, if he has not already done so.

Neither party has any right to address the court a second time, but the court may give leave to do so, and if it gives leave to one party cannot refuse it to the other. If the defendant, having addressed the court before calling his evidence, is given leave to do so for a second time, his second address must be made before the second address of the complainant, thus giving the complainant the last word.

11. Enforcement of orders.

The payment of any sum of money directed to be paid under the Act may be enforced in the same way as payment of money is enforced under an affiliation order,[15] i.e.

(a) by warrant of distress directing a levy upon and sale of the debtor's property;[16] or

(b) by an attachment of earnings order;[17] or

(c) by committal to prison for not more than six weeks in default of sufficient distress.[18]

The subject of attachment of earnings orders has already been considered in relation to the enforcement of orders made by the High Court or a divorce county court.[19] In particular it must be remembered that, except upon the application of the person liable to make the payments, such an order cannot be

---

[10] *Disher* v. *Disher, supra.*
[11] *Vye* v. *Vye*, [1969] 2 All E.R. 29.
[12] *Storey* v. *Storey*, [1961] P. 63.
[13] *Bond* v. *Bond*, [1967] P. 39, 47.
[14] *Briscoe* v. *Briscoe*, [1968] P. 501.
[15] Matrimonial Proceedings (Magistrates' Courts) Act 1960, s. 13.
[16] Magistrates' Courts Act 1952, s. 64.
[17] Attachment of Earnings Act 1971, s. 1 (3).
[18] Magistrates' Courts Act 1952, s. 64 and 74, as amended by Maintenance Orders Act 1958, s. 16. And see Administration of Justice Act 1970, s. 12.
[19] See *ante*, p. 260.

made if it appears that his failure to pay is not due to his wilful refusal or culpable neglect.[20]

None of these remedies is available except by an order made upon complaint.[1] A magistrates' court cannot impose imprisonment without first enquiring, in the defendant's presence, whether the default was due to his wilful refusal or culpable neglect, and must not impose imprisonment if of opinion that it was not so due. And without prejudice to this provision imprisonment is not to be imposed in any case in which the court has power to make an attachment of earnings order, unless of opinion that such an order would be inappropriate or, in any case, in the defendant's absence.[2] Imprisonment does not discharge the defendant from his liability to pay the sums due,[3] but unless otherwise directed no arrears accrue whilst he is in custody.[4]

The above are the only methods by which payment can be enforced. The arrears are not provable in bankruptcy and there is no way of enforcing them against the estate of a deceased husband. There is no statutory provision requiring the leave of the court to be obtained before payment of arrears which became due more than twelve months previously can be enforced, as there is in the High Court or a county court.[5] The reason is that in any event enforcement in a magistrates' court is only possible by order made on complaint,[6] and upon hearing a complaint for the enforcement, revocation, revival, variation or discharge of an order the court has power to remit the whole or any part of the arrears.[7]

One of the advantages of the order of a magistrates' court is that the order will, unless otherwise requested, usually order the periodical payments to be made to the clerk of the court[8] and if any sums due are in arrear for four weeks, the clerk must usually give notice to the person entitled to those payments[9] and must on the request of that person in writing, unless this appears to the clerk to be unreasonable, proceed in his own name for the recovery of the sums due, but at the expense of that person as to any liability for costs.[10]

Part I of the Maintenance Orders Act 1958, makes provision for the registration of maintenance orders made by the High Court or a county court in a magistrates' court, and of orders made by a magistrates' court in the High Court. Whilst so registered they are enforceable in the same way as an order made by the court of registration.[11] If such an order is registered in a magistrates' court, that court will also have power to vary the order, though it may

---

[20] Attachment of Earnings Act 1971, s. 3 (5). For procedure see Magistrates' Courts (Attachment of Earnings) Rules 1971.
[1] Magistrates' Courts Act 1952, s. 74 (1).
[2] Magistrates' Courts Act 1952, s. 74 (6), as substituted by Maintenance Orders Act 1958, s. 16.
[3] *Ibid.*, s. 74 (8), as so substituted.
[4] *Ibid.*, s. 75.
[5] See *ante*, p. 163.
[6] Magistrates' Courts Act 1952, s. 74 (1). For procedure see Magistrates' Courts Rules 1968, r. 49.
[7] Act of 1952, s. 76.
[8] Magistrates' Courts Act 1952, s. 52, Matrimonial Proceedings (Magistrates' Courts) Act 1960, s. 13 (2).
[9] Magistrates' Courts Rules 1968, r. 33.
[10] Act of 1952, s. 52 (3) as amended by Maintenance Orders Act 1958, s. 20.
[11] Maintenance Orders Act 1958, s. 1.

alternatively remit the matter to the court which originally made the order.[12]

12. Some disadvantages of proceeding in a magistrates' court.

In Appendix B to a Working Paper (No. 9) entitled "Matrimonial & Related Proceedings—Financial Relief" published in April 1967, the Law Commission drew attention to the anomalies which would arise if the law relating to proceedings in the High Court and in a divorce county court were to be changed and that governing proceedings in a magistrates' court left unaltered. In December 1970, the Home Secretary invited the Law Commission to consider this matter and a Working Paper (No. 53) containing provisional conclusions was circulated for comment and criticism in September 1973. Some considerable time must, however, elapse before the Commission can consider the views expressed upon the Working Paper and prepare its Report, and no doubt still further time will pass before the recommendations in that Report can be given legislative effect.

Meanwhile, practitioners must still face the many differences which at present exist between the law applicable in a suit for divorce or judicial separation and that applicable in a magistrates' court. Most of them will be apparent from what has already been said in this Chapter, but it may be useful to highlight some of the main inconsistencies in tabular form.

Magistrates' Courts	High Court and Divorce County Courts
1. Grounds still based upon proof of a matrimonial offence. Even cruelty insufficient unless it is persistent.	1. Relief available without proof of an offence.
2. Connivance at adultery an absolute bar.	2. No such bar.
3. Condonation of adultery or cruelty an absolute bar.	3. No such bar.
4. Complainant's adultery usually bars the making of an order and necessitates revocation of case already made.	4. Petitioner's adultery no bar.
5. Six months' period of limitation in many cases.	5. Delay no bar.
6. Definition of a child of the family can include only a child of one or both of the spouses.	6. Definition may include child of other parents.
7. Court cannot order payment of a lump sum or secured maintenance.	7. Can do so.
8. No order possible for maintenance of a child who has reached the age of 21.	8. Such order is possible in certain circumstances.
9. Relief available immediately desertion commences.	9. No divorce or judicial separation for actual desertion (as opposed to unreasonable behaviour amounting to constructive desertion) until it has lasted for two years.

[12] *Ibid.*, s. 4, as amended. As to the desirability of so doing in cases of difficulty, see *Gsell* v. *Gsell*, [1971] 1 All E.R. 559.

The differences are less marked when the application is based only upon wilful neglect to provide reasonable maintenance, and in such cases there is usually very little advantage in applying to a divorce county court rather than a magistrates' court.

It would be premature to describe in detail the 45 provisional conclusions put forward in the Working Paper. Briefly they would allocate to the magistrates' courts the role of dealing with family relations during a period of breakdown which is not necessarily irretrievable, and of preserving the existence of the marriage where this is possible. Thus the outmoded matrimonial offences and bars would disappear and orders could be made without distinction in favour of or against either spouse on three grounds only—failure to provide reasonable maintenance for the applicant or children, behaviour such that the applicant cannot reasonably be expected to live with the respondent, and desertion. The definition of a child of the family would be brought into line with that applicable in divorce proceedings, and the law as to age limits adjusted. The magistrates would be given power to order a lump sum payment, though not to order secured payments or adjustment of property rights. Thus virtually all the anomalies listed above would disappear. There is much more in the Working Paper—as to the effect of conduct, as to reconciliation and as to procedural improvements. Most of the conclusions seem likely to meet with general approval.

PART V

MISCELLANEOUS

CHAPTER 18

APPEALS AND RE-HEARING

1. Appeals from the High Court and Divorce County Courts.

(a) *Appeals from a registrar.*

Appeals from the order of a registrar lie generally to a judge in chambers, in a divorce county court to a judge of the appropriate court of trial, in a case in the divorce registry which is treated as a pending in a divorce county court to a county court or circuit judge sitting in the Royal Courts of Justice, in cases pending in the High Court to a High Court or circuit judge. In either case the appeal is on notice, though the time within which it must be issued varies according to whether the case is pending in the High Court or a divorce county court.[1] An exception occurs in relation to High Court (though not county court) decisions under section 17 of the Married Women's Property Act 1882, and in interpleader and garnishee proceedings, when appeals from the final decision of the registrar lie direct to the Court of Appeal.[2] The judge is in no way fettered by the manner in which the registrar has exercised his discretion, but must consider the matter afresh.

(b) *Appeals from a judge in chambers.*

Appeal from the judge in chambers, whether in the High Court or in a divorce county court, lies direct to the Court of Appeal. No leave is required in cases in which the liberty of the subject or the custody of infants is concerned, or where an injunction or the appointment of a receiver is granted or refused.[3] But otherwise the leave of the judge or of the Court of Appeal is required unless, in the High Court only, an application has first been made to the judge sitting in open court to set aside the order or decision, and has been refused.[4] If the judge does not wish to have the matter argued further in open court, he should be asked so to certify, and for leave to appeal.

The appeal, whether from a High Court or county court judge, is on notice of motion, called a "notice of appeal",[5] which must be served within fourteen days on all parties to the proceedings who are directly affected by the appeal, and must specify the grounds of appeal and the precise order which the Court of Appeal is asked to make.[6] Once the time limit has expired only the Court of

---

[1] R.S.C. Ord. 58, rr. 1 and 4. Matrimonial Causes Rules 1973, r. 124.
[2] R.S.C. Ord. 58, rr. 2 and 4.
[3] Judicature Act 1925, s. 31 (i).
[4] R.S.C. Ord. 58, r. 7 (2).
[5] R.S.C. Ord. 59, r. 3 (1).
[6] R.S.C. Ord. 59, rr. 3 (2), (5), and 4 (1) (a).

Appeal has power to extend it.[7]   The appellant must also, within seven days after service of the notice of appeal or such further time as may be allowed, leave two copies of the notice of appeal and certain other documents with the proper officer in order that the appeal may be set down for hearing.[8]

(c) *Final judgments and orders—appeals and re-hearing.*

A distinction must be drawn here between an appeal, which is an application to reverse the judgment, and an application for re-hearing, which seeks to set aside the decision and order the cause to be tried again.

In both the High Court and a divorce county court, if the case was tried by a judge alone (as it almost invariably is) and no error of the court at the hearing is alleged, the application for re-hearing is made to a judge.   Unless otherwise directed it must be made to the same judge who heard the case, and must be heard in open court.[9]   In both cases the application is on notice, which must be issued within six weeks after the judgment and served on every other party not less than fourteen days before the hearing.   This procedure is particularly appropriate where a case has remained undefended because the respondent spouse was not served with, and had no notice of, the petition,[10] or where the case remained undefended because of the negligence of the respondent's solicitor.[11]   In such cases the trial judge will have no means of knowing of these irregularities, and there can have been no "error" on his part.

All appeals, and all applications for re-hearing not covered by the above Rules, lie direct to the Court of Appeal without leave on questions of both fact and law.   The restriction on appeals upon question of fact from the decision of a county court judge contained in the County Courts Act 1959, s. 109, do not apply to proceedings in divorce county courts,[12] or to proceedings in any county court for the repayment of sums overpaid under orders for ancillary relief by reason of re-marriage or other cause or for alteration of a maintenance agreement after the death of one of the parties.[13]   But except with the leave of the judge who made the order no appeal lies from the decision of a High Court judge from an order made with the consent of the parties, or as to costs only which are left in the judge's discretion.[14]   There is no similar restriction on appeals from a county court judge.

As in the case of appeals from a judge in chambers, the appeal is by notice of appeal which, in the case of decrees, and of orders based on wilful neglect to maintain, must be served within six weeks of the decree or order unless the time is extended by the Court of Appeal.[15]   This period runs, in the case of petitions for divorce or nullity in which a decree nisi is pronounced, from the date when the decree nisi is pronounced or refused, and no appeal lies from decree absolute

---

[7] R.S.C. Ord. 59, r. 15.
[8] See R.S.C. Ord. 59, r. 5.
[9] Matrimonial Causes Rules 1973, r. 54.
[10] *Manners* v. *Manners and Fortescue*, [1936] P. 117.
[11] *D.* v. *D.*, [1963] 1 All E.R. 602.
[12] Matrimonial Causes Act 1967, s. 6.
[13] Matrimonial Causes Act 1973, Sched. 2, para. 4.
[14] Judicature Act 1925, s. 31 (1) (*h*).   As to the effect of this provision see *ante*, p. 187.
[15] R.S.C. Ord. 59, r. 4 (1).   As to time for leaving documents with the proper officer see Ord. 59, r. 16;   if this is not done the appeal is not competent.

by a party who had the time and opportunity to appeal from decree nisi and did not do so.[16] This rule only applies to appeals against the decree itself, and not to appeals against orders as to costs.[17]

The Court of Appeal has power to receive fresh evidence, to draw inferences of fact and to give any judgment or make any order which ought to have been given or made.[18] But it will not interfere with the exercise of the judge's discretion, whether exercised at the trial of the cause or in chambers, unless it is clear that the discretion has been exercised on wrong principles or that it is plainly wrong.[19]

2. Appeals from a magistrates' court.

In three cases there is no appeal from the decision of a magistrates' court—

(a) From the court's refusal to make a matrimonial order on the ground that the matter could be more conveniently dealt with by the High Court (though the High Court may order a re-hearing by a magistrates' court);[20]

(b) From an interim order if the appeal relates only to maintenance of a spouse or child;[1]

(c) From a decision that proceedings for the variation of a provision for payment of money in a matrimonial or interim order shall, or shall not, be treated as domestic proceedings.[2]

Subject to these three exceptions, an appeal lies without leave to a Divisional Court of the Family Division (which consists normally of three judges) from the making of, or refusal to make, a matrimonial or interim order or the revocation of, or refusal to revoke, such an order.[3]

The appeal is entered by lodging in the Divorce Registry in London, within six weeks of the order appealed against, two copies of the notice of motion, together with the other documents specified in R.S.C. Ord. 112, rule 6 (4). These include two copies of the justices' clerk's notes of the evidence and of the justices' reasons for their decision, and a certificate that the notice of motion has been duly served on the clerk and every other party affected by the appeal.

The justices' clerk's note is, normally, the best evidence of what occurred in the court below, and only in exceptional circumstances will the Divisional Court allow any other evidence.[4] The justices must themselves supply their reasons and it is most improper for the clerk to the court to request the advocate who has appeared for the successful party to draw up, or assist in the

---

[16] Judicature Act 1925, s. 31 (1) (*e*).
[17] *Kingston* v. *Kingston*, [1958] P. 122.
[18] R.S.C. Ord. 59, r. 10.
[19] *Evans* v. *Bartlam*, [1937] A.C. 473; *Ward* v. *James*, [1966] 1 Q.B. 273.
[20] Matrimonial Proceedings (Magistrates' Courts) Act 1960, s. 5.
[1] *Ibid.*, s. 6 (2).
[2] *Ibid.*, s. 8 (3).
[3] *Ibid.*, s. 11.
[4] As to the manner in which it may be supplemented if it is imperfect. see *Bond* v. *Bond*, [1967] P. 39.

drawing-up, of these reasons.[5] At the hearing the court may draw any inferences of fact which might have been drawn in the magistrates' court, and give any judgment or decision or make any order which ought to have been given or made by that court;[6] but not infrequently the only way in which justice can be done is by ordering a re-hearing before a different magistrates' court.[7] A further appeal lies from the Divisional Court to the Court of Appeal, but only with the leave of the Divisional Court or the Court of Appeal.[8]

There is one exception to the rules set out above. Appeals from any order or determination by a magistrates' court with regard to the enforcement of orders for payment of money under a matrimonial or interim order, or under an order of the High Court or a divorce county court which has been registered in a magistrates' court under the Maintenance Orders Act 1958, are by case stated to a Divisional Court of the Family Division.[9]

3. Appeals from Court of Appeal to House of Lords.

From the Court of Appeal a further appeal lies to the House of Lords only:—

    (a) from the grant or refusal of a decree of divorce or nullity or a declaration of legitimacy; or

    (b) on a question of law.[10]

In case (a) leave to appeal must first be obtained from the Court of Appeal or from the House of Lords.[11] In case (b) only the Court of Appeal can give leave to appeal.[12] The appeal must be brought within one month of the decision of the Court of Appeal if the House is then sitting, or if not, within fourteen days after it next sits.[13] If the leave of the House of Lords is required a petition for leave to appeal must be lodged in the Parliament Office within one month.

4. Appeals from High Court to House of Lords.

Part II of the Administration of Justice Act 1969 provides a procedure whereby, in certain circumstances, an appeal from a High Court judge or a Divisional Court on a point of law may be "leap-frogged" direct to the House of Lords, instead of going first to the Court of Appeal.

In the case of an appeal from the trial judge this is permissible only upon the judge's certificate, which he cannot grant unless he is satisfied:—

    (a) that a point of law of general public importance is involved which either relates wholly or mainly to the construction of an enactment or of a statutory instrument and has been fully argued in the proceedings and fully considered in the judge's judgment or is one in respect of which he is bound by a decision of the Court of Appeal or of the

[5] *Johnson* v. *Johnson*, [1961] 1 All E.R. 153.
[6] R.S.C. Ord. 55, r. 7 (3) and (5).
[7] As to the difficulties see *Marsden* v. *Marsden*, [1968] P. 544, 548.
[8] Judicature Act 1925, s. 31 (1) (*f*).
[9] R.S.C. Ord. 56, r. 5.
[10] Judicature Act 1925, s. 27 (2).
[11] Administration of Justice (Appeals) Act 1934, s. 1.
[12] Judicature Act 1925, s. 27 (2); *B.* v. *B.* (*No.* 2), [1955] 1 W.L.R. 557.
[13] Judicature Act 1881, s. 9.

House of Lords in previous proceedings, and was fully considered in in the judgments given by the Court of Appeal or the House of Lords (as the case may be) in those previous proceedings;[14]

(b) that there is a sufficient case for an appeal to the House of Lords to justify an application to the House of Lords for leave to bring such an appeal:[15]

(c) that all parties to the proceedings consent to the grant of a certificate;[16] and

(d) that the case is one in which an appeal would lie from the judge's decision to the Court of Appeal with or without leave and, if such leave is needed, the case would be a proper one for granting such leave.[17]

The application for the certificate must be made to the judge immediately after he gives judgment, though he may entertain it within fourteen days from the date when the judgment was given. No appeal lies from the grant or refusal of the certificate.[18] In cases before a Divisional Court, the requirements are the same, and the certificate must be granted by that court.[19]

Within one month after the certificate has been granted, or such further time as the House of Lords may allow, any party to the application may apply to the House of Lords for leave to appeal directly to the House.[20] If this leave is granted, no appeal from the decision to which the certificate relates lies to the Court of Appeal, and once a certificate has been granted by the judge or the Divisional Court no appeal lies to the Court of Appeal until the time for applying to the House of Lords for leave has expired or, if an application for such leave has been made, it has been determined.[1]

5. Restrictions on publicity.

The Domestic and Appellate Proceedings (Restriction of Publicity) Act 1968, s. 1, contains provisions enabling the courts hearing certain appeals and applications to sit in private. Where an appeal is brought against a decision of the Court of Appeal, the High Court, a county court or a magistrates' court and that court had power to sit in private during the whole or any part of the proceedings in which the decision was given, the court hearing the appeal or application has the same power to sit in private during the whole or any part of the appeal or application. These provisions would apply to matters dealt with in chambers in the High Court or a divorce county court such as, for example, the grant of leave to petition for divorce within three years from the date of the marriage, or as to custody of or access to children, or indeed any matter dealt

---

[14] Administration of Justice Act 1969, s. 12 (3).
[15] *Ibid.*, s. 12 (1) (*b*).
[16] *Ibid.*, s. 12 (1) (*c*).
[17] *Ibid.*, s. 15 (1) and (3). Leave would be needed, e.g. in the case of a decision as to costs only—see *ante*, p. 187.
[18] *Ibid.*, s. 12 (4) and (5).
[19] *Ibid.*, s. 12 (8).
[20] *Ibid.*, s. 13 (1). For procedure see *Practice Direction*, [1970] 1 W.L.R. 97.
[1] *Ibid.*, s. 13.

with in chambers, and to the taking of evidence of sexual capacity in nullity suits[2] or evidence of an indecent character in the magistrates' domestic court.[3]

An application to the appellate court to sit in private must also be heard in private unless the court otherwise orders. But the court hearing the appeal or application must give its decision and the reasons for it in public unless there are good and sufficient grounds for giving them in private, and in that case the court must state those grounds in public.

---

[2] Matrimonial Causes Act 1973, s. 48 (2).
[3] Magistrates' Courts Act 1952, s. 57 (3).

CHAPTER 19

LEGAL AID

For some years past the number of petitioners in matrimonial causes who have been legally aided has consistently averaged over sixty per cent. This, and the fact that the provisions of Part I of the Legal Advice and Assistance Act 1972 are now in operation, means that although a fully detailed description of this topic would be beyond the scope of this book, it would be incomplete if the subject were not examined in outline. It can be divided into two parts—legal advice and assistance under the Act of 1972, and legal aid in civil proceedings under the Legal Aid and Advice Act 1949, and the Legal Aid Acts 1960 and 1964. The general administration is in the hands of the Law Society in consultation with the General Council of the Bar, under the general guidance of the Lord Chancellor, in accordance with the Legal Aid Scheme 1973 made by the Law Society with his approval.[1] In this Chapter, unless otherwise stated,

    (a) references to "the Act of 1949", "the Act of 1960", "the Act of 1964" and "the Act of 1972" are to the Acts mentioned above;

    (b) references to "the Scheme" are to the Legal Aid Scheme 1973.

The Scheme divides England and Wales into fifteen areas, each with an Area Committee appointed by the Council of the Law Society, comprising both practising solicitors and barristers. Each Area Committee appoints Local Committees in the places within its area set out in the Scheme, again comprising practising solicitors and barristers.[2] The functions of the Law Society also include the establishment and administration of the Legal Aid Fund and all receipts and expenses of the Society under the Acts are paid into and out of that fund, the sums required to meet payments being paid out of moneys provided by Parliament.[3]

Panels are maintained containing the names and addresses and firm names of solicitors willing to act for persons who seek legal advice or assistance under the Act of 1972 or are given legal aid under the Act of 1949, separate panels being maintained in respect of different types of proceedings. Similar panels are maintained of the names and addresses of barristers who are willing to act.[4] Provision is made whereby the Area Committee can bring matters concerning a member of a panel to the notice of the Council of the Law Society or

---

[1] Act of 1949, s. 8; Act of 1972, s. 6 (1) (a).
[2] Paras. 2–10 and Scheds. 1 and 2 of the Scheme.
[3] Act of 1949, s. 9; Act of 1972, s. 12.
[4] Act of 1949, s. 6; Act of 1972, s. 6 (1) (a). Paras. 20–26.

the Bar Council, and if they consider that there may be good reason for excluding a solicitor or barrister from a panel the Council of the Law Society or the Bar Council, as the case may be, may refer the matter to a Panel (Complaints) Tribunal.[5] Appeal from a decision excluding a solicitor or barrister from the panels lies to the High Court, whose decision is final.[6]

1. Legal Advice and Assistance.

The former statutory and voluntary legal aid schemes, and the provisions of section 5 of the Act of 1949[7] concerning legal aid in matters not involving litigation, have been replaced by the comprehensive provisions as to legal advice and assistance contained in Part I of the Act of 1972. These are supplemented by the Legal Advice and Assistance Regulations 1973[8] (to which any reference to a regulation in this part of this Chapter relates).

The Act of 1972[9] covers oral or written advice by a solicitor, or, if necessary, by counsel, on the application of English law to any particular circumstances which have arisen in relation to the applicant for advice and to any steps which that person might appropriately take in those circumstances. It applies also to assistance given to the client (for client he is in every sense of the word[10]) by a solicitor, or, if necessary, by counsel, in taking those steps, either by taking them on his behalf, or by assisting him to take them himself. There are, however, two important restrictions. Assistance cannot be given by taking on the client's behalf any step in the institution or conduct of any proceedings before a court,[11] for which purpose a legal aid certificate is required, and advice and assistance under the Act of 1972 cannot be given to a person in connection with any proceedings before a court at a time when such a certificate issued to him in connection with those proceedings is in force.[12]

Assuming that the applicant is eligible for advice and assistance under the Act of 1972, it is clear that, so far as matrimonial proceedings are concerned, the help required in the early stages before proceedings are commenced will usually be given under the Act. The client can be advised as to the form of relief appropriate to his case, be it divorce, nullity, judicial separation or proceedings in a magistrates' court, and of the consequences of seeking that relief. If divorce or judicial separation is to be sought on the ground of two years' separation, negotiations can be conducted with a view to obtaining the consent of the other spouse and reaching an agreement as to the terms on which the consent will be given. Whatever proceedings are contemplated, steps can be taken to obtain the necessary evidence, and the client can be assisted in his application for a legal aid certificate in respect of those proceedings. These are but examples; short of taking steps in the institution or conduct of proceedings,

[5] Paras. 27–32 of the Scheme.
[6] Act of 1949, s. 6 (3); Act of 1972, s. 6 (1) (a); R.S.C. Ord. 94 r. 6.
[7] Repealed by the Act of 1972, Sched. 3.
[8] As amended by the Legal Advice and Assistance (Amendment) Regulations 1973.
[9] See s. 2.
[10] See Reg. 1 (2).
[11] Act of 1972, s. 2 (3).
[12] *Ibid.*, s. 2 (2) (a).

the solicitor can take any action which he would take on behalf of any other client. There is, however, by virtue of section 3 of the Act, a financial limit. Where it appears to the solicitor that the cost of giving the advice and assistance (including, if necessary, the cost of instructing counsel) is likely to exceed £25 (or such larger sum as may be prescribed), he must not exceed that limit without the prior authority of the Area Committee;[13] there is no power to give this authority retrospectively.

The eligibility of an applicant is determined by his financial resources. The limit of his disposable capital is £250[14] and, unless he is in receipt of Supplementary Benefit or Family Income Supplement, his disposable income must not exceed £24·50 a week.[15] Both disposable capital and income are assessed in accordance with detailed provisions contained in the Schedule to the Regulations. The assessment is made by the solicitor obtaining the necessary information from the client and inserting it on a green form, authenticated by the client's signature.[16]. Where help is sought in relation to matrimonial causes, it will be the resources of the applicant alone which are relevant. Those of the other spouse will not be aggregated, since this is not required where they have a contrary interest in the matter, or where they are living separate and apart.[17] The allowances and deductions permitted by the Schedule are generous, so that the figures for disposable capital and income are considerably less than the gross figures.

In computing disposable capital, the applicant's household furniture and effects, clothing and tools of trade are to be ignored, as is also the value of the applicant's home (less the amount of any outstanding encumbrance) if this does not exceed £6,000. Should it do so, one half of the excess must be taken into account, unless it appears to the solicitor to be inequitable or impracticable to do so, which will usually be so. Where the applicant has living with him one or more dependent children or a dependent relative wholly or substantially maintained by him, a deduction is made of £125 in respect of the first person, £80 in respect of the second and £40 in respect of each further person. No allowance is made in respect of a spouse, since their means will not be aggregated.[18]

Disposable income is assessed on a weekly basis, usually, but not necessarily, in respect of the preceding seven days. Deductions are made from the gross weekly income in respect of income tax, and of National Health, National Insurance and Industrial Injuries contributions. Further deductions are made in respect of dependants on a scale which varies annually,[19] and also for

---

[13] Reg. 5 (5).

[14] Legal Advice and Assistance (Financial Conditions) Regulations 1973, which double the figure of £125 in s. 1 of the Act.

[15] Act of 1972, s. 1; Legal Advice and Assistance (Financial Conditions) (No. 2) Regulations 1973.

[16] Regs. 4 and 5 (2)–(4).

[17] Sched. to Regs., para. 6.

[18] *Ibid.*, para. 7.

[19] *Ibid.*, para. 8 (*b*) as substituted by Legal Advice and Assistance (Amendment) Regulations 1973. A "Schedule of Dependants Allowances" at the current rate is obtainable from the Law Society.

maintenance bona fide paid for a spouse who is living apart, a former spouse, or a child or relative who is not a member of the household.[20].

If the client is not receiving Supplementary Benefit or Family Income Supplement, he may be required to pay a contribution towards the cost, which is also assessed by the solicitor on the green form. This ranges from a maximum of £1 if the disposable income exceeds £12·50 but does not exceed £13·50 a week, to a maximum of £15 for a person where disposable income reaches the maximum of £24·50 a week.[1] It is for the solicitor himself to collect this contribution from the client, though he may do so in instalments agreed with the client. If the cost is likely to be less than the maximum contribution, he will only require payment of the expected costs.[2] Even if authority is given to exceed the normal maximum cost of £25, no further contribution is payable by the client.

A solicitor may, for reasonable cause, refuse an application for advice and assistance or, having accepted it, decline to give advice and assistance, and is not required to disclose his reasons to the applicant. He must, however, supply information to the Area Committee if requested,[3] and has a general duty to give them such information as they require.[4] Subject to this, the fact that the services of a solicitor or counsel are given under the Act does not affect the relationship between or rights of counsel, solicitor or client or any privilege arising out of that relationship.[5]

It remains to consider the solicitor's remuneration. By section 5 (3) of the Act, any charges or fees in respect of advice or assistance, in so far as they are not covered by any contribution payable by the client, constitute a first charge for the benefit of the solicitor or any money or property recovered or preserved for the client in connection with the matter, including his rights under any compromise or settlement arrived at to avoid or bring to an end any proceedings. But this is subject to a long list of exceptions contained in Regulation 6, which include moneys payable, whether by way of arrears or otherwise, under an agreement in writing or order for payment of maintenance, and any dwelling, household furniture, or tools of trade which may be recovered or preserved, so that such a charge will seldom arise in relation to advice or assistance in respect of matrimonial causes. In so far as the client's contribution and any such charge are insufficient to meet the solicitor's charges and fees, they are payable out of the Legal Aid Fund,[6] and the solicitor will submit a bill to the Area Committee.[7] He will do this by completing the report and claim form on the back of each green form, and normally submit monthly a composite sheet with the green forms attached.

Provision is made by Part II of the Act of 1972 for the employment by the

---

[20] Sched., para. 9.
   [1] Act of 1972, s. 4 and Sched. 1 ; Legal Aid and Advice (Financial Provisions) (No. 3) Regulations 1973.
   [2] Reg. 5 (6).
   [3] Reg. 5 (1).
   [4] Reg. 5 (2).
   [5] Act of 1949, s. 1 (7) ; Act of 1972, s. 6 (1) (a).
   [6] Act of 1972, s. 5 (4).
   [7] Reg. 5 (7).

Law Society of solicitors to perform the services under the Act; but this Part of the Act is not, as yet, in operation.

2. Legal Aid in Civil Proceedings.

Mention has already been made of the fact that assistance under the Act of 1972 cannot include the taking of any step in the institution or conduct of any proceedings before a court. This form of aid is available only under a legal aid certificate granted under the provisions of the Act of 1949. Procedure is governed by the Legal Aid (General) Regulations 1971, as amended.

Legal Aid is available in respect of proceedings in the Supreme Court, in the House of Lords and in any county court; it is also available in respect of proceedings in a magistrates' court under the Matrimonial Proceedings (Magistrates' Court) Act 1960 and under section 22 of the Maintenance Orders Act 1950 or section 4 of the Maintenance Orders Act 1958 (which deal with variations of orders registered in a magistrates' court). It cannot be granted to any person whose "disposable income" exceeds £1175 a year[8] and may be refused to a person whose "disposable capital" exceeds £1200 if it appears that he can afford to proceed without it.[9] An assisted person may be required to make a contribution to the legal aid fund in respect of the sums paid from the fund on his account; this contribution cannot exceed one third of the amount (if any) by which his disposable income exceeds £375[10] plus the amount (if any) by which his disposable capital exceeds £250.[11] The disposable income and disposable capital of an applicant for legal aid are determined by the Supplementary Benefits Commission in accordance with the Legal Aid (Assessment of Resources) Regulations 1960, as amended. The "disposable" income and capital of an applicant are calculated in accordance with detailed provisions contained in the First and Second Schedules to these Regulations respectively. In both cases generous allowances are made. Thus a person's disposable income is much less than his gross income, deductions being allowed, for example, for the maintenance of dependants, repayment of loans, hire-purchase, the full income tax payable, the net rent of a householder, rates, expenses involved in relation to his employment and regular payments for the maintenance of a spouse who is living apart. Likewise, in relation to disposable capital, such items as household furniture, personal clothing, tools of trade and the first £6000 of the unencumbered value of the applicant's dwellinghouse are excluded.[12] The result, although the figures may at first sight appear different, is that the financial conditions for eligibility of legal advice and assistance, and those for legal aid, are virtually the same.

An applicant for legal aid may apply for a certificate to any local committee unless he is resident outside the United Kingdom and the Republic of Ireland, when he must apply to a local committee in London. If, however, legal aid is desired in respect of an appeal (other than interlocutory appeal from a court

---

[8] Legal Aid (Financial Conditions) Regulations 1973.
[9] Legal Aid (Financial Conditions) Regulations 1972.
[10] Legal Aid (Financial Conditions) Regulations 1973.
[11] Act of 1960, s. 1 (2); Legal Aid (Financial Conditions) Regulations 1972.
[12] Legal Aid (Assessment of Resources) (Amendment) Regulations 1972.

below), application is instead made to the appropriate area committee.[13] The application must be in writing on a form approved by the Law Society, copies being obtainable from Legal Aid Offices. In cases of urgency application may be made for an emergency certificate. This will remain in force for such period as the appropriate committee may allow (which will not usually exceed three months) and this period may be extended by the secretary.[14] An emergency certificate cannot be issued in respect of proceedings in a magistrates' court, but the applicant may, with a view to expediting the issue to him of a certificate, lodge with the secretary an undertaking to pay any contribution which may be assessed.[15]

In certain cases the application will be considered by the secretary of the appropriate committee. He can approve an application in respect of proceedings by a petitioner for divorce, judicial separation, or for nullity on the grounds of incapacity or wilful refusal to consummate a marriage, by a respondent who applies under section 10 (2) of the Matrimonial Causes Act 1973 to resist the making absolute of a decree nisi, and by either party in respect of summary proceedings before magistrates.[16] Should he not approve it he must refer it to the committee, but in the case of summary proceedings no appeal lies from refusal by the committee.[17] If a local committee refuses a certificate for proceedings other than summary proceedings (as it may do if, for example, the applicant has not shown that he has reasonable grounds for taking, defending, or being a party to the proceedings, or if it is unreasonable that he should receive it in the circumstances[18]) an appeal lies to the Area Committee, whose decision is final.[19] If the application is approved in a case where no contribution will be payable, or in relation to summary proceedings where the undertaking mentioned in the preceding paragraph has been lodged, the appropriate committee will issue a legal aid certificate. In all other cases the applicant will be notified of the amount of his contribution and of the terms on which a certificate will be issued, and will then have 28 days (or such further time as the committee may allow) in which to signify his acceptance and to lodge with the Law Society an undertaking in respect of his contribution. Except in the case of summary proceedings, he is also notified of his position should an order for costs be made against him.[20]

Once a certificate has been granted, legal aid will consist of representation by the solicitor whose name the client has selected from the appropriate panel, and so far as is necessary, by counsel (including all such assistance as is usually given by solicitor or counsel in steps preliminary or incidental to the proceedings or in arriving at or giving effect to a compromise to avoid or bring the proceedings to an end).[21] Except as otherwise provided by the Act of 1949 or by regulations,

---

[13] Reg. 3.
[14] Reg. 11 (1), (8) and (9).
[15] Regs. 11 (12) and 3 (4).
[16] Reg. 5 (1); Legal Aid (General) (Amendment) Regulations 1971 and 1972.
[17] Reg. 10 (1).
[18] Act of 1949, s. 1 (6); Reg. 7.
[19] Reg. 10 (6).
[20] Reg. 6 (5), (8) and (9).
[21] Act of 1949, s. 1 (5).

the fact that the services of counsel or a solicitor are given by way of legal aid is not to affect the relationship between or the rights of counsel, solicitor or client or any privilege arising out of such relationship and the rights conferred upon the assisted person are not to affect the rights or liabilities of other parties to the proceedings or the principles on which the court's discretion is exercised.[1] It follows that in general the proceedings will be conducted throughout in precisely the same way as if neither party was in receipt of assistance and that solicitors and counsel should take such steps in the proceedings, no less and no more, as they would have taken on behalf of an unassisted litigant. In the same way, the decisions of the courts (save in relation to costs—see *post*, pp. 307–310) will be in no way influenced by the existence of legal aid. But these generalities are subject to certain restrictions resulting from the Regulations.

Some such restrictions may result from the wording of the legal aid certificate. It may be issued in respect of the whole or part of the proceedings in a court of first instance or proceedings in an appellate court, though it cannot relate to proceedings (other than interlocutory appeals) both in a court of first instance and in an appellate court, or to proceedings in more than one appellate court.[2] Thus if the local committee had issued a certificate in respect of proceedings for divorce, a further certificate from the area committee would be required in respect of an appeal to the Court of Appeal against the decree nisi which had been granted and a further certificate again in respect of an appeal to the House of Lords. The certificate in relation to proceedings might be limited to certain steps only. There may be cases in which the certificate should be limited to taking counsel's opinion.[3] In any event, unless a certificate otherwise provides, it does not extend to lodging an interlocutory appeal without prior authority from the area committee.[4]

Regulation 15, which deals with the duties of solicitors, requires careful study. Unless prior authority has been included in the certificate, the authority of the area committee is required to instruct more than one counsel or to instruct counsel in summary proceedings. Where an assisted person's solicitor considers it necessary for the proper conduct of the proceedings to take certain steps not expressly authorised by the certificate, including (inter alia) the obtaining of an expert's report or opinion (in relation, for example, to the effect of certain matters upon the health of the petitioner) or to tender expert evidence or bespeak shorthand notes,[5] he may apply to the area committee for authority.[6] Perhaps most important of all, where he considers it necessary to do something which is unusual or involves unusually large expenditure, such as the bringing of a witness from a distant country to give evidence,[7] he may seek the area

---

[1] Act of 1949, s. 1 (7).
[2] Reg. 6 (1).
[3] *Law Society* v. *Elder*, [1956] 2 Q.B. 93.
[4] Regs. 6 (2) and 15 (1).
[5] No general authority as to these matters exists in relation to matrimonial causes. If the judge requires a transcript, no special authority is needed. *Theocharides* v. *Joannou*, [1955] 1 All E.R. 615.
[6] Reg. 15 (6) and (8).
[7] *Ammar* v. *Ammar*, [1954] P. 468.

committee's authority beforehand.[8] In any case where such authority has been given, no question of the propriety of the act can be raised on a legal aid taxation, but failure to obtain prior authority does not necessarily preclude the allowance of the payment on taxation.[9] Regulation 15 (9) now specifically forbids the solicitor or counsel of an assisted person to take any payment for work done during the currency of a legal aid certificate, whether within the scope of the certificate or not, except such payments as may be made to him out of the legal aid fund.

Without prejudice to the right of a solicitor or counsel to give up a case for any good reason, he may do so if in his opinion the assisted person has required it to be conducted unreasonably so as to incur an unjustifiable expense to the fund or has required unreasonably that the case be continued or has wilfully failed to comply with any regulation as to information required from him or knowingly made a false statement in representation. In such cases the solicitor must report to the area committee.[10] The powers of the area committee to discharge a certificate (in which case it operates up to the date of discharge) or to revoke it (when it has effect as if it had never been granted) are contained in Regulations 12 and 13. Generally speaking revocation is appropriate only in cases of wilful falsehood or non-disclosure or wilful failure to comply with the Regulations, and other unreasonable conduct will lead only to discharge of the certificate. In considering whether an assisted person is acting unreasonably in persisting in his desire to defend a case it was held in *Iverson* v. *Iverson*[11] that his solicitor must bear in mind, as must also the area committee, that his client may properly be influenced by matters other than material ancillary consequences which could be dealt with although the case remained undefended, such as the regard in which he is held in his circle of family and friends, and the desire to show that it is not his fault that the marriage was destroyed. How far these considerations have the same weight now that an irretrievable breakdown is the sole ground for divorce is a matter of some difficulty: much may depend upon the facts upon which the petitioner relies in support of that allegation. Neither revocation nor discharge of a certificate affects the entitlement of solicitor or counsel to payment from the legal aid fund for work already done. On the other hand, except in summary proceedings (where the costs are not taxed), any costs wasted by failure to conduct the proceedings with reasonable competence and expedition may be disallowed on taxation.[12] Provision is also made for amendment of certificates by extending them or limiting them or adjustment of the contribution payable. An assisted person is required to inform the area committee if his disposable income has increased by more than £52, or his disposable capital by more than £75, and may seek a decrease in his contribution if his disposable income has been reduced by more than £26.[13]

By Regulation 17 a solicitor who receives from the appropriate committee a

---

[8] Reg. 15 (6) (*d*).
[9] Reg. 15 (7) and (8).
[10] Reg. 16 (1) and (2).
[11] [1967] P. 134.
[12] Reg. 23 (1).
[13] Reg. 9.

certificate relating to proceedings is required, if proceedings have begun, or otherwise upon their commencement or thereafter, to send it by prepaid post to the appropriate court office or registry; he must also do this in respect of any notice of revocation or discharge or amendment of the certificate. Notice of the fact that a party is an assisted person must also be served on all other parties in accordance with this Regulation.

As has already been mentioned, the fact that one or both of the parties are legally aided makes little difference to the conduct of the proceedings except in relation to costs. It is here that there are real differences. The liability of the assisted person for his own costs is limited to the maximum contribution which he has undertaken to pay, and where the area committee approves an application for proceedings (other than interlocutory proceedings) in an appellate court in which the applicant was an assisted person in the court below, or proceedings by way of new trial ordered by a court before which the applicant was an assisted person, the committee will not require the Supplementary Benefits Commission to re-assess his disposable income and capital, unless his circumstances have altered, but if his maximum contribution was not required in respect of the previous proceedings may increase it up to the maximum contribution, but no further.[14] His solicitor or counsel are forbidden to take any payment except from the legal aid fund.[15] In certain cases the sum payable to solicitor or counsel from the fund will be assessed by the area committee. These include (inter alia) summary proceedings,[16] cases where the retainer of the solicitor or counsel is determined before proceedings are actually begun (as in divorce cases where the parties are reconciled before the petition is filed)[17] and cases which are settled after their commencement on terms including a provision for an agreed sum in respect of costs to be paid to the assisted person which the solicitor and counsel are willing to accept in full satisfaction for work done.[18] In other cases the court which makes the final decree or order in the proceedings must (in addition to any other directions as to taxation) include a direction that the costs of an assisted person be taxed in accordance with Schedule 3 of the Act of 1949. This requires taxation "according to the ordinary rules applicable on a taxation between solicitor and client where the costs are to be paid out of a common fund in which the client and others are interested". This common fund basis is somewhat more generous, both as to items which may be allowed and the amounts which may be allowed, than is the usual party and party basis. In connection with proceedings in the House of Lords and in the Supreme Court the sums allowed to counsel are 90 per cent of the amount allowed on taxation and to a solicitor the full amount allowed on taxation on account of disbursements and 90 per cent of the amount allowed on account of profit costs.[19] The sums allowed to counsel and solicitor in connection with proceedings in a county court are the full amounts allowed on

---

[14] Reg. 6 (10)
[15] Reg. 15 (9).
[16] Reg. 21. Detailed provisions are contained in Schedule 4 to the Regulations.
[17] Reg. 22 (1) (*a*).
[18] Reg. 22 (2) (*b*).
[19] Act of 1949, Sched. 3, paras. 1 and 2, as amended by Act of 1960, s. 2. Reg. 22 (10) and (11).

taxation.[20]   By the Matrimonial Causes (Costs) Rules 1971, rule 7, however, the costs of an undefended cause for divorce or judicial separation or nullity in which the petitioner is granted a decree with costs shall, if his solicitor so elects, be fixed in accordance with that Rule[1] instead of being taxed, save that if the petitioner is an assisted person for whom counsel has acted, the costs cannot be fixed unless counsel also so elects.   These fixed costs cover the costs of the proceedings and also, if the solicitor so requests, include a further sum of £6.50 in respect of any ancillary application on which a consent order for maintenance has been made.   With this exception, however, the fixed costs do not include the costs of any ancillary application, which must be taxed in the usual way.

What has been said thus far applies only to the position as to costs incurred on behalf of the assisted person.   Should he be unsuccessful, he can be ordered to pay the costs of any opposite party.   But section 2 (2) of the Act of 1949 provides that his liability by virtue of an order for costs made against him shall not exceed the amount (if any)which is a reasonable one for him to pay having regard to all the circumstances, including the means of all the parties and their conduct in connection with the dispute.   It is also provided by this section and by Regulation 20 that in determining the amount of his liability his dwelling-house and household furniture and the tools and implements of his trade are to be left out of account to the same extent that they are left out in determining his disposable income and capital.   The court may direct that payment under the order for costs shall be limited to such amount, payable in instalments or otherwise as the court thinks reasonable, and the court has power to suspend the order until such date as it may determine or *sine die*.   The party in whose favour the order was made may, within six years, apply for it to be varied if material information as to the assisted person's means, which could not previously have been obtained with reasonable diligence, becomes available, or if there is a change in the circumstances of the assisted person.   Subject to this, the order is final.

If one party to the proceedings is assisted and the other is not, these rules could produce injustice; the result of them is that if the assisted party is successful and the case is one in which costs are claimed and would usually be awarded,[2] his opponent will be ordered to pay the costs of the assisted party on a party and party basis and these will be paid into the legal aid fund.   If, on the other hand, the unassisted party is successful and the assisted party has little or no means, the unassisted party will receive little, if anything, in respect of any order for costs which he may obtain.   He stands to lose financially in either event.   This situation is to some extent mitigated by the Act of 1964.

Section 1 of this Act provides that where one party to the proceedings is legally aided and the other is not, and the proceedings are finally decided in favour of the unassisted party, the court which so decided may make an order for payment to the unassisted party out of the legal aid fund of the whole or

---

[20] Act of 1949, Sched. 3, paras. 1 (2) and 2 (2).
   [1] See also Matrimonial Causes (Costs) (Amendment) and (Amendment) (No. 2) Rules 1973.   As to the position when the parties have agreed upon the amount, see Reg. 22 (7) and *Practice Direction* (*Family Division : Legal Aid Costs*), [1972] 3 All E.R. 911 [1972] 1 W.L.R. 1472.
   [2] As to which see *ante*, Chapter 14.

any part of the costs incurred by him in these proceedings. This, however, is subject to a number of provisoes.

As regards all proceedings, whether at first instance or appellate, an order can be made only if the court is satisfied that it is just and equitable in all the circumstances that payment should be made out of public funds; and before making an order the court must in every case (whether or not an application is made) consider what orders should be made for costs against the assisted party and for determining his liability in respect of costs. Further, no order is to be made by any court in respect of costs incurred by an unassisted party in any proceedings in which, apart from the Act, no order would be made for payment of his costs. The decision in *Nowotnik* v. *Nowotnik*,³ where an unassisted husband was refused an order for costs on this last ground against his assisted wife, has already been considered on p. 188. In *addition to the above provisions*, the Act places further restrictions upon an order in respect of costs incurred in a court of first instance. No order can be made in respect of such costs unless the proceedings were instituted by the party receiving legal aid and the court is satisfied that the unassisted party will suffer severe financial hardship unless an order is made. The expression "severe financial hardship" should not be too narrowly construed. It does not mean "serious impoverishment", but only that the costs will be "hard to bear".⁴

The requirements that the proceedings should have been instituted by the legally aided party and that the unassisted party would suffer severe financial hardship have no application in relation to appeals, where the only question is whether it is just and equitable to order payment out of the Legal Aid Fund. Such an order can be made to the Court of Appeal even though the appellant was the unassisted party⁵ and the House of Lords has jurisdiction to order payment out of the Fund of the appellant's costs, not only in the House of Lords, but also in the Court of Appeal.⁶

Finally it must be noted that in order that the legal aid fund may be reimbursed, so far as is possible, for the sums expended it will not only receive the contributions (if any) required from the assisted person and any party and party costs ordered or agreed to be paid by any opposite party, but is also given a first charge on any property recovered or preserved for the assisted person. This may often benefit the fund in a common law action for damages, but will produce little benefit in matrimonial causes. The reason is that, by virtue of Regulation 18 (10), this charge does not apply (inter alia):—

(a) to virtually any form of payment, or arrears of payment, of financial provision for a spouse (including a deceased former spouse) or child, whether ordered by the High Court, a divorce county court, or a magistrates' court, or due under a separation agreement in writing ; or

(b) to property which is the subject of an order for transfer or settlement, or for avoidance of a disposition, made by the High Court or a divorce county court.

---

³ [1967] P. 83.
⁴ See *Hanning* v. *Maitland*, [1970] 1 Q.B. 580.
⁵ *Clifford* v. *Walker*, [1972] 2 All E.R. 806, C.A.
⁶ *Shiloh Spinners, Ltd.* v. *Harding (No. 2)*, [1973] 1 All E.R. 966, H.L.

There is little left in respect of which a charge could operate, save perhaps money payable under an order for repayment resulting from a change in circumstances under section 33, or from cessation of an order by reason of re-marriage under section 38, of the Matrimonial Causes Act 1973, though it is not easy to see why these particular payments should have been singled out for discrimination. But the result as a whole is that a high proportion of matrimonial causes are litigated almost entirely at the expense of public funds.

APPENDIX I
STATUTES

THE MATRIMONIAL CAUSES ACT 1965
(1965 c. 72)

[This appendix contains the few provisions of the Matrimonial Causes Act 1965 which will remain operative when the Matrimonial Causes Act 1973 is in operation.]

An Act to consolidate certain enactments relating to matrimonial causes, maintenance and declarations of legitimacy and British nationality, with corrections and improvements made under the Consolidation of Enactments (Procedure) Act 1949. [8th November 1965]

*   *   *   *   *

8. Remarriage of divorced persons

(2) No clergyman of the Church of England or the Church in Wales shall be compelled—

    (*a*) to solemnise the marriage of any person whose former marriage has been dissolved and whose former spouse is still living; or

    (*b*) to permit the marriage of such a person to be solemnised in the church or chapel of which he is the minister.

*   *   *   *   *

25. Alteration of agreements by court after death of one party

(1)–(3) . . .

(4) In considering for the purposes of subsection (1) of this section the question when representation was first taken out, a grant limited to settled land or to trust property shall be left out of account, and a grant limited to real estate or to personal property shall be left out of account unless a grant limited to the remainder of the estate has previously been made or is made at the same time.

(5) For the purposes of section 162 (1) of the Supreme Court of Judicature (Consolidation) Act 1925 (which relates to the discretion of the court as to the persons to whom administration is to be granted) a person by whom an application is proposed to be made by virtue of this section shall be deemed to be a person interested in the deceased's estate.

NOTE
    Sections 25 (4) and (5) are preserved by Sch. 3 of the Matrimonial Causes Act 1973 insofar as they are applied by section 28 (2).

Maintenance from estate of deceased former spouse

26. Orders for maintenance from deceased's estate

(1) Where after 31st December 1958 a person dies domiciled in England and is survived by a former spouse of his or hers (hereafter in this section referred to as "the survivor") who has not remarried, the survivor may . . . apply to the court for an order under this section on the ground that the deceased has not made reasonable provision for the survivor's maintenance after the deceased's death.

[An application under this section shall not, except with the permission of the court, be made after the end of the period of six months from the date on which representation in regard to the estate of the deceased is first taken out.]

(2) If on an application under this section the court is satisfied—

    (*a*) that it would have been reasonable for the deceased to make provision for the survivor's maintenance; and

    (*b*) that the deceased has made no provision, or has not made reasonable provision, for the survivor's maintenance,

the court may order that such reasonable provision for the survivor's maintenance as the court thinks fit shall be made out of the net estate of the deceased, subject to such conditions or restrictions (if any) as the court may impose.

(3) Where the court makes an order under this section requiring provision to be made for the maintenance of the survivor, the order shall require that provision to be made by way of periodical payments terminating not later than the survivor's death and, if the survivor remarries, not later than the remarriage, so however that [if the court sees fit] the order may require that provision to be made wholly or in part by way of a lump sum payment.

(4) On an application under this section the court shall have regard—

    (*a*) to the past, present or future capital of the survivor and to any income of the survivor from any source;

    (*b*) to the survivor's conduct in relation to the deceased and otherwise;

    (*c*) to any application made or deemed to be made by the survivor during the lifetime of the deceased—

        (i) where the survivor is a former wife of the deceased, for such an order as is mentioned in section 16 (1) of this Act or that subsection as applied by section 19 of this Act;

        (ii) where the survivor is a former husband of the deceased, for such an order as could be made either under the said section 16 (1) as applied by subsection (3) of that section or under section 17 (2) of this Act,

        [(iii) where the survivor is a former wife or a former husband of the deceased, for an order under section 2 or 4 of the Matrimonial Proceedings & Property Act 1970 [or under section 23 (1) (*a*) (*b*) or (*c*) or 24 of the Matrimonial Causes Act 1973]

and to the order (if any) made on any such application, or (if no such application was made by the survivor, or such an application was made by the survivor and no order was made on the application) to the circumstances appearing to the court to be the reasons why no such application was made, or no such order was made, as the case may be; and

(d) to any other matter or thing which, in the circumstances of the case, the court may consider relevant or material in relation to the survivor, to persons interested in the estate of the deceased, or otherwise.

(5) In determining whether, and in what way, and as from what date, provision for maintenance ought to be made by an order under this section, the court shall have regard to the nature of the property representing the net estate of the deceased and shall not order any such provision to be made as would necessitate a realisation that would be imprudent having regard to the interests of the dependants of the deceased, of the survivor, and of the persons who apart from the order would be entitled to that property.

[(5A) For the avoidance of doubt it is hereby declared that references in this section to remarriage include references to a marriage which is by law void or voidable.]

(6) In this and [the three next following sections]—

["court" [means the High Court and] includes a county court in relation to cases in which a county court has jurisdiction];

"former spouse", in relation to a deceased person, means a person whose marriage with the deceased was during the deceased's lifetime dissolved or annulled by a decree made or deemed to be made under [the Matrimonial Causes Act 1973], and "former wife" and "former husband" shall be construed accordingly;

"net estate" and "dependant" have the same meanings as in the Inheritance (Family Provision) Act 1938 [as amended by the Family Provision Act 1966] [and the Family Law Reform Act 1969]; and

"property" means any real or personal property, any estate or interest in real or personal property, any money, any negotiable instrument, debt or other chose in action, or any other right or interest whether in possession or not.

GENERAL NOTE

The words omitted from sub-s. (1) were repealed by the Family Provision Act 1966, ss. 5 (3), 10 (2) and Sch. 2, and the words in square brackets in that subsection were inserted by s. 5 (3) of that Act, subject to the savings in s. 5 (4) of that Act.

The words in square brackets in sub-s. (3) were substituted by s. 4 (1) (b) of the said Act of 1966, subject to the saving in s. 4 (2) thereof.

The words in square brackets in sub-s. (4) were inserted by the Matrimonial Causes Act 1973, Sch. 2, para. 5 (1) (a). Sub-s. (5A) was added by s. 36 of the Matrimonial Proceedings and Property Act 1970.

The words in square brackets in the first place in sub-s. (6) were substituted by s. 6 (2) of the Act of 1966, those in the second place were inserted by s. 7 (4) of that Act, those in the third place were inserted by s. 8 (2) thereof, the words in square brackets within the words in square brackets in the third place remain in force despite the repeal of the Divorce Reform Act 1969 (Act of 1973, Sch. 2, para. 5 (1) (b)). The words in square brackets in the fourth place were substituted by the Act of 1973, Sch. 2, para. 5 (1) (c), and those in the fifth place are inserted, as from 1st January, 1970, by the Family Law Reform Act 1969, s. 18 (2), though by s. 18 (3) of that Act, this amendment does not apply in relation to persons dying before that date.

27. Discharge and variation of orders under s. 26

(1) Subject to the following provisions of this section, where an order (in this section referred to as "the original order") has been made under the last foregoing section, the court, on an application under this section, shall have power by order to discharge or vary the original order or to suspend any provision of it temporarily and to revive the operation of any provision so suspended.

(2) An application under this section may be made by any of the following persons, that is to say,—

    (a)   the former spouse on whose application the original order was made;
    (b)   any other former spouse of the deceased;
    (c)   any dependant of the deceased;
    (d)   the trustees of any relevant property;
    (e)   any person who, under the will or codicil of the deceased or under the law relating to intestacy, is beneficially interested in any relevant property.

(3) An order under this section varying the original order, or reviving any suspended provision of it, shall not be made so as to affect any property which, at the time of the application for the order under this section, is not relevant property.

(4) In exercising the powers conferred by this section, the court shall have regard to all the circumstances of the case, including any change in the circumstances to which the court was required to have regard in determining the application for the original order.

(5) In this section "relevant property" means property the income of which, in accordance with the original order or any consequential directions given by the court in connection with it, is applicable wholly or in part for the maintenance of the former spouse on whose application the original order was made.

---

28. Additional provisions as to orders under ss. 26 and 27

(1) The provisions of the last two foregoing sections shall not render the personal representatives of a deceased person liable for having distributed any part of the estate of the deceased after the end of the period mentioned in subsection (1) of section 26 of this Act on the ground that they ought to have taken into account the possibility that the court might permit an application under that section after the end of that period, or that an order under that section might be varied under section 27 of this Act; but this subsection shall not prejudice any power to recover any part of the estate so distributed arising by virtue of the making of an order under section 26 or section 27 of this Act.

(2) Section 25 (4) of this Act shall apply for the purposes of section 26 (1) of this Act as it applies for the purposes of subsection (1) of the said section 25; and section 25 (5) of this Act shall apply in relation to an application

under section 26 or section 27 of this Act as it applies in relation to an application in pursuance in the said section 25.

(3) Section 3 of the Inheritance (Family Provision) Act 1938 [as amended by the Family Provision Act 1966] (which relates to the effect and form of orders under that Act) shall have effect in relation to orders under sections 26 and 27 of this Act as it has effect in relation to orders under that Act.

AMENDMENT
The words in square brackets were added by the Family Provision Act 1966, s. 3 (2).

[28A. Interim orders

(1) Where on an application for maintenance under section 26 of this Act it appears to the court—

(a) that the applicant is in immediate need of financial assistance, but it is not yet possible to determine what order (if any) should be made on the application for the provision of maintenance for the applicant; and

(b) that property forming part of the net estate of the deceased is or can be made available to meet the need of the applicant;

the court may order that, subject to such conditions or restrictions, if any, as the court may impose and to any further order of the court, there shall be paid to or for the benefit of the applicant out of the deceased's net estate such sum or sums and (if more than one) at such intervals as the court thinks reasonable.

(2) In determining what order, if any, should be made under this section the court shall, so far as the urgency of the case admits, take account of the same considerations as would be relevant in determining what order should be made on the application for the provision of maintenance for the applicant; and any subsequent order for the provision of maintenance may provide that sums paid to or for the benefit of the applicant by virtue of this section shall be treated to such extent, if any, and in such manner as may be provided by that order as having been paid on account of the maintenance provided for by that order.

(3) Subject to subsection (2) above, section 3 of the Inheritance (Family Provision) Act 1938 as applied by section 28 of this Act shall apply in relation to an order under this section as it applies in relation to an order providing for maintenance.

(4) Where the deceased's personal representative pays any sum directed by an order under this section to be paid out of the deceased's net estate, he shall not be under any liability by reason of that estate not being sufficient to make the payment, unless at the time of making the payment he has reasonable cause to believe that the estate is not sufficient.]

GENERAL NOTE
This section was added by the Family Provision Act 1966, s. 6 (2).

---

*   *   *   *   *

42. Condonation

(1) [For the purposes of the Matrimonial Proceedings (Magistrates' Courts) Act 1960] any presumption of condonation which arises from the continuance or resumption of marital intercourse may be rebutted by evidence sufficient to negative the necessary intent.

(2) For the purposes of ... the Matrimonial Proceedings (Magistrates' Courts) Act 1960, adultery or cruelty shall not be deemed to have been condoned by reason only of a continuation or resumption of cohabitation between the parties for one period not exceeding three months, or of anything done during such cohabitation, if it is proved that cohabitation was continued or resumed, as the case may be, with a view to effecting a reconciliation.

(3) [For the purposes of the Matrimonial Proceedings (Magistrates' Courts) Act 1960] adultery which has been condoned shall not be capable of being revived.

AMENDMENT
> Subsections (1) and (3) were repealed so far as they apply in relation to proceedings for divorce or judicial separation by the Divorce Reform Act 1969, s. 9 (2), Sch. 2. The words omitted were repealed by the Divorce Reform Act 1969, s. 9 (2), Sch. 2.
> The words in square brackets in sub-s. (1) and (3) were inserted by the Matrimonial Causes Act 1973, Sch. 2, para. 5 (2)).

43. Evidence

(1) The evidence of a husband or wife shall be admissible in any proceedings to prove that marital intercourse did or did not take place between them during any period; *but a husband or wife shall not be compellable in any proceedings to give evidence of the matters aforesaid.*

(2) The parties to any proceedings instituted in consequence of adultery and the husbands and wives of the parties shall be competent to give evidence in the proceedings ...

(3) In any proceedings for nullity of marriage, evidence on the question of sexual capacity shall be heard in camera unless in any case the judge is satisfied that in the interests of justice any such evidence ought to be heard in open court.

AMENDMENT
> The words in italics were preserved in relation to criminal proceedings only by the Civil Evidence Act 1968, s. 16 (4) and the Matrimonial Causes Act 1973, Sch. 3. The words omitted at the end of sub-s. (2) were repealed by s. 16 (5) of the Civil Evidence Act 1968.

*   *   *   *   *

46. Short title, interpretation, commencement and extent

(1) This Act may be cited as the Matrimonial Causes Act 1965.

(2) (3) ...

(4) This Act does not extend to Scotland or Northern Ireland.

AMENDMENT
> Nothing more remains of this section since the Matrimonial Causes Act 1973, Sch. 3.

THE MATRIMONIAL PROCEEDINGS AND PROPERTY ACT 1970

(1970 c. 45)

An Act to make fresh provision for empowering the court in matrimonial proceedings to make orders ordering either spouse to make financial provision for, or transfer property to, the other spouse or a child of the family, orders for the variation of ante-nuptial and post-nuptial settlements, orders for the custody and education of children and orders varying, discharging or suspending orders made in such proceedings; to make other amendments of the law relating to matrimonial proceedings; to abolish the right to claim restitution of conjugal rights; to declare what interest in property is acquired by a spouse who contributes to its improvement; to make provision as to a spouse's rights of occupation under section 1 of the Matrimonial Homes Act 1967 in certain cases; to extend section 17 of the Married Women's Property Act 1882 and section 7 of the Matrimonial Causes (Property and Maintenance) Act 1958; to amend the law about the property of a person whose marriage is the subject of a decree of judicial separation dying intestate; to abolish the agency of necessity of a wife; and for purposes connected with the matters aforesaid [29th May 1970]

PART I

PROVISIONS WITH RESPECT TO ANCILLARY AND OTHER RELIEF IN MATRIMONIAL CAUSES AND TO CERTAIN OTHER MATRIMONIAL PROCEEDINGS

*   *   *   *

1–29. *Repealed.*

REPEAL
The whole of Part I of this Act is repealed by the Matrimonial Causes Act 1973.

PART II

MISCELLANEOUS PROVISIONS

Provisions relating to orders made by magistrates' courts in matrimonial proceedings

30. Order for maintenance of party to marriage made by magistrates' court to cease to have effect on remarriage of that party

(1) At the end of section 7 of the Matrimonial Proceedings (Magistrates' Courts) Act 1960 there shall be added the following subsections—

"(4) Where after the making by a magistrates' court of a matrimonial order consisting of or including a provision such as is mentioned in paragraph (b) or (c) of section 2 (1) of this Act the marriage of the parties to the proceedings in which that order was made is dissolved or annulled but the order continues in force, then, subject to subsection (5) of this section, that order or, as the case may be, that provision thereof shall cease to have effect on the remarriage of the party in whose favour it was made, except in relation to any arrears due under it on the date of such remarriage and shall not be capable of being revived.

(5) Subsection (4) of this section shall not apply where the party in whose favour such an order as is therein mentioned was made remarried before the commencement of the Matrimonial Proceedings and Property Act 1970.

(6) For the avoidance of doubt it is hereby declared that references in this section to remarriage include references to a marriage which is by law void or voidable."

(2) Subsections (4), (5) and (6) of section 7 of the Matrimonial Proceedings (Magistrates' Courts) Act 1960 shall apply in relation to an order consisting of or including a provision such as is mentioned in section 2 (1) (b) or (c) of that Act made by a magistrates' court and confirmed in accordance with section 3 of the Maintenance Orders (Facilities for Enforcement) Act 1920 (which enables a magistrates' court to make a maintenance order against a person resident in a part of Her Majesty's dominions outside the United Kingdom but provides that the order shall have no effect unless and until confirmed by a competent court in that part) as they apply in relation to such an order as is referred to in the said subsection (4), but with the modification that for the reference to the making of such an order as is referred to in that subsection there shall be substituted a reference to the confirmation in accordance with the said section 3 of the order referred to in this subsection.

31. Sums paid after cessation of order of magistrates' court by reason of remarriage may be ordered to be repaid in certain cases
After section 13 of the Matrimonial Proceedings (Magistrates' Courts) Act 1960 there shall be inserted the following section—

13A. Orders for repayment in certain cases of sum paid after cessation of order by reason of remarriage
(1) Where—
  (a) an order to which this section applies or a provision thereof has ceased to have effect by reason of the remarriage of the person entitled to payments under the order, and
  (b) the person liable to make payments under the order made payments in accordance with it in respect of a period after the date of such remarriage in the mistaken belief that the order or provision was still subsisting,

no proceedings in respect of a cause of action arising out of the circumstances mentioned in paragraphs (*a*) and (*b*) above shall be maintainable by the person so liable or his or her personal representatives against the person so entitled or her or his personal representatives, but on an application made under this section the court may exercise the powers conferred on it by the following subsection.

This section applies to an order in relation to which subsection (4) of section 7 of this Act, as amended by the Matrimonial Proceedings and Property Act 1970, applies.

(2) The court may order the respondent to an application made under this section to pay to the applicant a sum equal to the amount of the payments made in respect of the period mentioned in subsection (1) (*b*) of this section or, if it appears to the court that it would be unjust to make that order, if may either order the respondent to pay to the applicant such lesser sum as it thinks fit or dismiss the application.

(3) An application under this section may be made by the person liable to make payments under an order to which this section applies or his or her personal representatives and may be made against the person entitled to payments under the order or her or his personal representatives.

(4) An application under this section may be made in proceedings in the High Court or a county court for leave to enforce, or the enforcement of, the payment of arrears under an order to which this section applies, but except as aforesaid such an application shall be made to a county court, and accordingly references in this section to the court are references to the High Court or a county court, as the circumstances require.

(5) An order under this section for the payment of any sum may provide for the payment of that sum by instalments of such amount as may be specified in the order.

(6) The jurisdiction conferred on a county court by this section shall be exercisable by a county court notwithstanding that by reason of the amount claimed in an application under this section the jurisdiction would not but for this subsection be exercisable by a county court.

(7) Section 13 (1) and (2) of this Act shall not apply to an order under this section.

(8) The clerk of a magistrates' court to whom any payments under an order to which this section applies are required to be made, and the collecting officer under an attachment of earnings order made to secure payments under the first mentioned order, shall not be liable—

(*a*) in the case of that clerk, for any act done by him in pursuance of the first mentioned order after the date on which that order or a provision thereof ceased to have effect by reason of the remarriage of the person entitled to payments under it, and

(*b*) in the case of the collecting officer, for any act done by him after that date in accordance with any enactment or rule of court specifying how payments made to him in compliance with the attachment of earnings order are to be dealt with, if, but only if, the act was one which he would have been under a duty to do had the first mentioned order or a provision thereof not ceased to have effect as aforesaid and the act was done before notice in writing of the fact that the person so entitled had remarried was given to him by or on behalf of that person, the person liable to make payments under the first mentioned order or the personal representatives of either of those persons.

(9) In this section "collecting officer", in relation to an attachment of earnings order, means the officer of the High Court, the registrar of a county court or the clerk of a magistrates' court to whom a person makes payments in compliance with the order.

32. Restriction on enforcement in High Court or county court of certain orders of magistrates' courts

At the end of section 13 of the Matrimonial Proceedings (Magistrates' Courts) Act 1960 there shall be added the following subsections:—

"(5) A person shall not be entitled to enforce through the High Court or any county court the payment of any arrears due under an order made by virtue of this Act without the leave of that court if those arrears became due more than twelve months before proceedings to enforce the payment of them are begun.

(6) The court hearing an application for the grant of leave under subsection (5) of this section may refuse leave, or may grant leave subject to such restrictions and conditions (including conditions as to the allowing of time for payment or the making of payment by instalments) as that court thinks proper, or may remit the payment of such arrears or any part thereof.

(7) An application for the grant of leave under the said subsection (5) shall be made in such manner as may be prescribed by rules of court."

33. Minor corrections of Matrimonial Proceedings (Magistrates' Courts) Act 1960, s. 7 (3)

Section 7 (3) of the Matrimonial Proceedings (Magistrates' Courts) Act 1960 (which provides that where after the making by a magistrates' court of a matrimonial or interim order proceedings between, and relating to the marriage of, the parties to the proceedings in which the order was made have been begun in the High Court, the High Court may direct that the order shall cease to have effect on a date specified by that court) shall be amended as follows:—

(a) after the words "the High Court", where first occurring, there shall be inserted the words "or a county court";
(b) for the words "the High Court", where next occurring, there shall be substituted the words "the court in which the proceedings or any application made therein are or is pending"; and
(c) for the words "the High Court may specify" there shall be substituted the words "may be specified in the direction".

Provisions relating to certain proceedings in county courts

34. Jurisdiction of, and appeal on question of fact from, county courts. *Repealed.*

Amendments of the Matrimonial Causes Act 1965

35. Amendment of reference to child in 1965 c. 72, s. 2. *Repealed.*

36. Construction of references to remarriage in 1965 c. 72, s. 26

Section 26 of the Matrimonial Causes Act 1965 (which authorises the making of orders for maintenance out of a deceased's estate for a former spouse who has not remarried and provides that maintenance by way of periodical payments out of the estate shall terminate not later than his or her death or remarriage) shall have effect, and be deemed always to have had effect, as if after subsection (5) there were inserted the following subsection:—

"(5A) For the avoidance of doubt it is hereby declared that references in this section to remarriage include references to a marriage which is by law void or voidable."

Provisions relating to property of married persons

37. Contributions by spouse in money or money's worth to the improvement of property

It is hereby declared that where a husband or wife contributes in money or money's worth to the improvement of real or personal property in which or in the proceeds of sale of which either or both of them has or have a beneficial interest, the husband or wife so contributing shall, if the contribution is of a substantial nature and subject to any agreement between them to the contrary express or implied, be treated as having then acquired by virtue of his or her contribution a share or an enlarged share, as the case may be, in that beneficial interest of such an extent as may have been then agreed or, in default of such agreement, as may seem in all the circumstances just to any court before which the question of the existence or extent of the beneficial interest of the husband or wife arises (whether in proceedings between them or in any other proceedings).

38. Rights of occupation under Matrimonial Homes Act 1967 of spouse with equitable interest in home, etc.

There shall be inserted in section 1 of the Matrimonial Homes Act 1967 (which protects against eviction from the home the spouse not entitled by virtue of any estate or interest, etc., to occupy it) a new subsection—

"(9) It is hereby declared that a spouse who has an equitable interest in a dwelling house or in the proceeds of sale thereof, not being a spouse in whom is vested (whether solely or as a joint tenant) a legal estate in fee simple or a legal term of years absolute in the dwelling house, is to be treated for the purpose only of determining whether he or she has rights of occupation under this section as not being entitled to occupy the dwelling house by virtue of that interest".

39. Extension of s. 17 of Married Women's Property Act 1882

An application may be made to the High Court or a county court under section 17 of the Married Women's Property Act 1882 (powers of the court in disputes between husband and wife about property) (including that section as extended by section 7 of the Matrimonial Causes (Property and Maintenance) Act 1958) by either of the parties to a marriage notwithstanding that their marriage has been dissolved or annulled so long as the application is made within the period of three years beginning with the date on which the marriage was dissolved or annulled; and references in the said section 17 and the said section 7 to a husband or a wife shall be construed accordingly.

40. Judicially separated spouses not entitled to claim in intestacy of each other. (*Repealed.*)

GENERAL NOTE
The whole of this section was repealed by the Matrimonial Causes Act 1973, Sch. 3.

Abolition of wife's agency of necessity
41. Abolition of wife's agency of necessity. (*Repealed.*)

GENERAL NOTE
The whole of this section was repealed by the Matrimonial Causes Act 1973, Sch. 3.

PART III
SUPPLEMENTARY

42. Minor and consequential amendments and repeals. (*Repealed.*)

GENERAL NOTE
The whole of this section was repealed by the Matrimonial Causes Act 1973, Sch. 3.

43. Citation, commencement and extent

(1) This Act may be cited as the Matrimonial Proceedings and Property Act 1970.

(3) Any reference in any provision of this Act, or in any enactment amended by a provision of this Act, to the commencement of this Act shall be construed as a reference to the date on which that provision comes into force.

(4) This Act does not extend to Scotland or Northern Ireland.

AMENDMENT
This section is printed as amended by the Matrimonial Causes Act 1973, Sch. 3.

THE RECOGNITION OF DIVORCES AND LEGAL SEPARATIONS ACT 1971

An Act to amend the law relating to the recognition of divorces and legal separations.
[27th July 1971]

Decrees of divorce and judicial separation granted in British Isles

1. Recognition in Great Britain of divorces and judicial separations granted in the British Isles

Subject to section 8 of this Act, the validity of a decree of divorce or judicial separation granted after the commencement of this section shall [if it was granted under the law of any part of the British Isles, be recognised throughout the United Kingdom]

AMENDMENT
   The words in square brackets were substituted for the former wording by the Domicile and Matrimonial Proceedings Act 1973, s. 15 (2).

Overseas divorces and legal separations

2. Recognition in Great Britain of overseas divorces and legal separations

Sections 3 to 5 of this Act shall have effect, subject to section 8 of this Act, as respects the recognition in [the United Kingdom] of the validity of overseas divorces and legal separations, that is to say, divorces and legal separations which—

(*a*) have been obtained by means of judicial or other proceedings in any country outside the British Isles; and

(*b*) are effective under the law of that country.

AMENDMENT
   The words [the United Kingdom] were substituted for the words "Great Britain" by the Domicile and Matrimonial Proceedings Act 1973, s. 15 (2).

---

3. Grounds for recognition

(1) The validity of an overseas divorce or legal separation shall be recognised if, at the date of the institution of the proceedings in the country in which it was obtained—

(*a*) either spouse was habitually resident in that country; or

(*b*) either spouse was a national of that country.

(2) In relation to a country the law of which uses the concept of domicile as a ground of jurisdiction in matters of divorce or legal separation, subsection (1) (*a*) of this section shall have effect as if the reference to habitual residence included a reference to domicile within the meaning of that law.

(3) In relation to a country comprising territories in which different systems of law are in force in matters of divorce or legal separation, the foregoing provisions of this section (except those relating to nationality) shall have effect as if each territory were a separate country.

4. Cross-proceedings and divorces following legal separations

(1) Where there have been cross-proceedings, the validity of an overseas divorce or legal separation obtained either in the original proceedings or in the cross-proceedings shall be recognised if the requirements of paragraph (*a*) or (*b*) of section 3 (1) of this Act are satisfied in relation to the date of the institution either of the original proceedings or of the cross-proceedings.

(2) Where a legal separation the validity of which is entitled to recognition by virtue of the provisions of section 3 of this Act or of subsection (1) of this section is converted, in the country in which it was obtained, into a divorce, the validity of the divorce shall be recognised whether or not it would itself be entitled to recognition by virtue of those provisions.

5. Proof of facts relevant to recognition

(1) For the purpose of deciding whether an overseas divorce or legal separation is entitled to recognition by virtue of the foregoing provisions of this Act, any finding of fact made (whether expressly or by implication) in the proceedings by means of which the divorce or legal separation was obtained and on the basis of which jurisdiction was assumed in those proceedings shall—

(*a*) if both spouses took part in the proceedings, be conclusive evidence of the fact found; and

(*b*) in any other case, be sufficient proof of that fact unless the contrary is shown.

(2) In this section "finding of fact" includes a finding that either spouse was habitually resident or domiciled in, or a national of, the country in which the divorce or legal separation was obtained; and for the purposes of subsection (1) (*a*) of this section, a spouse, who has appeared in judicial proceedings shall be treated as having taken part in them.

General provisions

6. Existing common law and statutory rules

(1) In this section "the common law rules" means the rules of law relating to the recognition of divorces or legal separations obtained in the country of the spouses' domicile or obtained elsewhere and recognised as valid in that country.

(2) In any circumstances in which the validity of a divorce or legal separation obtained in a country outside the British Isles would be recognised by virtue only of common law rules if either—

(*a*) the spouses had at the material time both been domiciled in that country; or

(*b*) the divorce or separation were recognised as valid under the law of the spouses' domicile,

its validity shall also be recognised if subsection (3) below is satisfied in relation to it.

(3) This subsection is satisfied in relation to a divorce or legal separation obtained in a country outside the British Isles if either—

(*a*) one of the spouses was at the material time domiciled in that country and the divorce or separation was recognised as valid under the law of the domicile of the other spouse; or

(*b*) neither of the spouses having been domiciled in that country at the material time, the divorce or separation was recognised as valid under the law of the domicile of each of the spouses respectively.

(4) For any purpose of subsection (2) or (3) above "the material time", in relation to a divorce or legal separation, means the time of the institution of proceedings in the country in which it was obtained.

(5) Sections 2 to 5 of this Act are without prejudice to the recognition of the validity of divorces and legal separations obtained outside the British Isles by virtue of the common law rules (as extended by this section), or of any enactment other than this Act; but, subject to this section, no divorce or legal separation so obtained shall be recognised as valid in the United Kingdom except as provided by those sections.

AMENDMENT
> By virtue of the Domicile and Matrimonial Proceedings Act 1973, s. 2, this section is substituted for s. 6 of the original Act.

---

7. Non-recognition of divorce by third country no bar to re-marriage

Where the validity of a divorce obtained in any country is entitled to recognition by virtue of [sections 1 to 5 or section 6 (2) of this Act or by virtue of any rule or enactment preserved by section 6 (5) of this Act], neither spouse shall be precluded from re-marrying in [the United Kingdom] on the ground that the validity of the divorce would not be recognised in any other country.

AMENDMENT
> The first words in square brackets are printed as amended by the Domicile and Matrimonial Proceedings Act 1973, s. 2 (3). By s. 15 (2) the words "the United Kingdom" are substituted for the words "Great Britain".

8. Exceptions from recognition

(1) The validity of—

   (*a*) a decree of divorce or judicial separation granted under the law of any part of the British Isles; or

   (*b*) a divorce or legal separation obtained outside the British Isles,

shall not be recognised in any part of [the United Kingdom] if it was granted or obtained at a time when, according to the law of that part of [the United Kingdom] (including its rules of private international law and the provisions of this Act), there was no subsisting marriage between the parties.

(2) Subject to subsection (1) of this section, [recognition by virtue of sections 2 to 5 or section 6 (2) of this Act or any rule preserved by section 6 (5) thereof] of the validity of a divorce or legal separation obtained outside the British Isles, may be refused if, and only if—

   (*a*) it was obtained by one spouse—

   (i) without such steps having been taken for giving notice of the proceedings to the other spouse as, having regard to the nature of the proceedings and all the circumstances, should reasonably have been taken; or

   (ii) without the other spouse having been given (for any reason other than lack of notice) such opportunity to take part in the proceedings as, having regard to the matters aforesaid, he should reasonably have been given; or

   (*b*) its recognition would manifestly be contrary to public policy.

(3) Nothing in this Act shall be construed as requiring the recognition of any findings of fault made in any proceedings for divorce or separation or of any maintenance, custody or other ancillary order made in any such proceedings.

AMENDMENT
   In sub-s. (1) the words [the United Kingdom] were substituted for the words "Great Britain" by the Divorce and Matrimonial Proceedings Act 1973, s. 15 (2).
   The words in square brackets in sub-s. (2) are printed as amended by s. 2 (4) of that Act.

---

9. Powers of Parliament of Northern Ireland

Notwithstanding anything in the Government of Ireland Act 1920, the Parliament of Northern Ireland shall have power to make laws for purposes similar to the purposes of this Act.

GENERAL NOTE
   By the Domicile and Matrimonial Proceedings Act 1973, s. 15, this Act now extends to Northern Ireland.

---

10. Short title, interpretation, transitional provisions and commencement

(1) This Act may be cited as the Recognition of Divorces and Legal Separations Act 1971.

(2) In this Act "the British Isles" means the United Kingdom, the Channel Islands and the Isle of Man.

(3) In this Act "country" includes a colony or other dependent territory of the United Kingdom but for the purposes of this Act a person shall be treated as a national of such a territory only if it has a law of citizenship or nationality separate from that of the United Kingdom and he is a citizen or national of that territory under that law.

(4) The provisions of this Act relating to overseas divorces and legal separations and other divorces and legal separations obtained outside the British Isles apply to a divorce or legal separation obtained before the date of the commencement of those provisions as well as to one obtained on or after that date and, in the case of a divorce or legal separation obtained before that date—

(*a*) require, or, as the case may be, preclude, the recognition of its validity in relation to any time before that date as well as in relation to any subsequent time; but

(*b*) do not affect any property rights to which any person became entitled before that date or apply where the question of the validity of the divorce or legal separation has been decided by any competent court in the British Isles before that date.

(5) Section 9 of this Act shall come into operation on the passing of this Act and the remainder on 1st January 1972.

MATRIMONIAL CAUSES ACT 1973

(1973 c. 18)

An Act to consolidate certain enactments relating to matrimonial proceedings, maintenance agreements, and declarations of legitimacy, validity of marriage and British nationality, with amendments to give effect to recommendations of the Law Commission. [23rd May 1973]

PART I

DIVORCE, NULLITY AND OTHER MATRIMONIAL SUITS

Divorce

1. Divorce on breakdown of marriage

(1) Subject to section 3 below, a petition for divorce may be presented to the court by either party to a marriage on the ground that the marriage has broken down irretrievably.

(2) The court hearing a petition for divorce shall not hold the marriage to have broken down irretrievably unless the petitioner satisfies the court of one or more of the following facts, that is to say—

(a) that the respondent has committed adultery and the petitioner finds it intolerable to live with the respondent;

(b) that the respondent has behaved in such a way that the petitioner cannot reasonably be expected to live with the respondent;

(c) that the respondent has deserted the petitioner for a continuous period of at least two years immediately preceding the presentation of the petition;

(d) that the parties to the marriage have lived apart for a continuous period of at least two years immediately preceding the presentation of the petition (hereafter in this Act referred to as "two years' separation") and the respondent consents to a decree being granted;

(e) that the parties to the marriage have lived apart for a continuous period of at least five years immediately preceding the presentation of the petition (hereafter in this Act referred to as "five years' separation").

(3) On a petition for divorce it shall be the duty of the court to inquire, so far as it reasonably can, into the facts alleged by the petitioner and into any facts alleged by the respondent.

(4) If the court is satisfied on the evidence of any such fact as is mentioned in subsection (2) above, then, unless it is satisfied on all the evidence that the marriage has not broken down irretrievably, it shall, subject to sections 3 (3) and 5 below, grant a decree of divorce.

(5) Every decree of divorce shall in the first instance be a decree nisi and shall not be made absolute before the expiration of six months from its grant unless the High Court by general order from time to time fixes a shorter period, or unless in any particular case the court in which the proceedings are for the time being pending from time to time by special order fixes a shorter period than the period otherwise applicable for the time being by virtue of this subsection.

2. Supplemental provisions as to facts raising presumption of breakdown

(1) One party to a marriage shall not be entitled to rely for the purposes of section 1 (2) (*a*) above on adultery committed by the other if, after it became known to him that the other had committed that adultery, the parties have lived with each other for a period exceeding, or periods together exceeding, six months.

(2) Where the parties to a marriage have lived with each other after it became known to one party that the other had committed adultery, but subsection (1) above does not apply, in any proceedings for divorce in which the petitioner relies on that adultery the fact that the parties have lived with each other after that time shall be disregarded in determining for the purposes of section 1 (2) (*a*) above whether the petitioner finds it intolerable to live with the respondent.

(3) Where in any proceedings for divorce the petitioner alleges that the respondent has behaved in such a way that the petitioner cannot reasonably be expected to live with him, but the parties to the marriage have lived with each other for a period or periods after the date of the occurrence of the final incident relied on by the petitioner and held by the court to support his allegation, that fact shall be disregarded in determining for the purposes of section 1 (2) (*b*) above whether the petitioner cannot reasonably be expected to live with the respondent if the length of that period or of those periods together was six months or less.

(4) For the purposes of section 1 (2) (*c*) above the court may treat a period of desertion as having continued at a time when the deserting party was incapable of continuing the necessary intention if the evidence before the court is such that, had that party not been so incapable, the court would have inferred that his desertion continued at that time.

(5) In considering for the purposes of section 1 (2) above whether the period for which the respondent has deserted the petitioner or the period for which the parties to a marriage have lived apart has been continuous, no account shall be taken of any one period (not exceeding six months) or of any two or more periods (not exceeding six months in all) during which the parties resumed living with each other, but no period during which the parties lived with each other shall count as part of the period of desertion or of the period for which the parties to the marriage lived apart, as the case may be.

(6) For the purposes of section 1 (2) (*d*) and (*e*) above and this section a husband and wife shall be treated as living apart unless they are living with each other in the same household, and references in this section to the parties to a marriage living with each other shall be construed as references to their living with each other in the same household.

(7) Provision shall be made by rules of court for the purpose of ensuring that where in pursuance of section 1 (2) (*d*) above the petitioner alleges that the respondent consents to a decree being granted the respondent has been given such information as will enable him to understand the consequences to him of his consenting to a decree being granted and the steps which he must take to indicate that he consents to the grant of a decree.

3. Restriction on petitions for divorce within three years of marriage

(1) Subject to subsection (2) below, no petition for divorce shall be presented to the court before the expiration of the period of three years from the date of the marriage (hereafter in this section referred to as "the specified period").

(2) A judge of the court may, on an application made to him, allow the presentation of a petition for divorce within the specified period on the ground that the case is one of exceptional hardship suffered by the petitioner or of exceptional depravity on the part of the respondent; but in determining the application the judge shall have regard to the interests of any child of the family and to question whether there is reasonable probability of a reconciliation between the parties during the specified period.

(3) If it appears to the court, at the hearing of a petition for divorce presented in pursuance of leave granted under subsection (2) above, that the leave was obtained by the petitioner by any misrepresentation or concealment of the nature of the case, the court may—

    (*a*) dismiss the petition, without prejudice to any petition which may be brought after the expiration of the specified period upon the same facts, or substantially the same facts, as those proved in support of the dismissed petition; or

    (*b*) if it grants a decree, direct that no application to make the decree absolute shall be made during the specified period.

(4) Nothing in this section shall be deemed to prohibit the presentation of a petition based upon matters which occurred before the expiration of the specified period.

4. Divorce not precluded by previous judicial separation

(1) A person shall not be prevented from presenting a petition for divorce, or the court from granting a decree of divorce, by reason only that the petitioner or respondent has at any time, on the same facts or substantially the same facts as those proved in support of the petition, been granted a decree of judicial separation or an order under, or having effect as if made under, the Matrimonial Proceedings (Magistrates' Courts) Act 1960 or any corresponding enactments in force in Northern Ireland, the Isle of Man or any of the Channel Islands.

(2) On a petition for divorce in such a case as is mentioned in subsection (1) above, the court may treat the decree or order as sufficient proof of any adultery, desertion or other fact by reference to which it was granted, but shall not grant a decree of divorce without receiving evidence from the petitioner.

(3) Where a petition for divorce in such a case follows a decree of judicial separation or an order containing a provision exempting one party to the marriage from the obligation to cohabit with the other, for the purposes of that petition a period of desertion immediately preceding the institution of the proceedings for the decree or order shall, if the parties have not resumed cohabitation and the decree or order has been continuously in force since it was granted, be deemed immediately to precede the presentation of the petition.

5. Refusal of decree in five year separation cases on grounds of grave hardship to respondent

(1) The respondent to a petition for divorce in which the petitioner alleges five years' separation may oppose the grant of a decree on the ground that the dissolution of the marriage will result in grave financial or other hardship to him and that it would in all the circumstances be wrong to dissolve the marriage.

(2) Where the grant of a decree is opposed by virtue of this section, then—

    (a) if the court finds that the petitioner is entitled to rely in support of his petition on the fact of five years' separation and makes no such finding as to any other fact mentioned in section 1 (2) above, and

    (b) if apart from this section the court would grant a decree on the petition,

the court shall consider all the circumstances, including the conduct of the parties to the marriage and the interests of those parties and of any children or other persons concerned, and if of opinion that the dissolution of the marriage will result in grave financial or other hardship to the respondent and that it would in all the circumstances be wrong to dissolve the marriage it shall dismiss the petition.

(3) For the purposes of this section hardship shall include the loss of the chance of acquiring any benefit which the respondent might acquire if the marriage were not dissolved.

6. Attempts at reconciliation of parties to marriage

(1) Provision shall be made by rules of court for requiring the solicitor acting for a petitioner for divorce to certify whether he had discussed with the petitioner the possibility of a reconciliation and given him the names and addresses of persons qualified to help effect a reconciliation between parties to a marriage who have become estranged.

(2) If at any stage of proceedings for divorce it appears to the court that there is a reasonable possibility of a reconciliation between the parties to the marriage, the court may adjourn the proceedings for such period as it thinks fit to enable attempts to be made to effect such a reconciliation.

The power conferred by the foregoing provision is additional to any other power of the court to adjourn proceedings.

7. Consideration by the court of certain agreements or arrangements

Provision may be made by rules of court for enabling the parties to a marriage, or either of them, on application made either before or after the presentation of a petition for divorce, to refer to the court any agreement or arrangement made or proposed to be made between them, being an agreement or arrangement which relates to, arises out of, or is connected with, the proceedings for divorce which are contemplated or, as the case may be, have begun, and for enabling the court to express an opinion, should it think it desirable to do so, as to the reasonableness of the agreement or arrangement and to give such directions, if any, in the matter as it thinks fit.

8. Intervention of Queen's Proctor

(1) In the case of a petition for divorce—

    (*a*) the court may, if it thinks fit, direct all necessary papers in the matter to be sent to the Queen's Proctor, who shall under the directions of the Attorney-General instruct counsel to argue before the court any question in relation to the matter which the court considers it necessary or expedient to have fully argued;

    (*b*) any person may at any time during the progress of the proceedings or before the decree nisi is made absolute give information to the Queen's Proctor on any matter material to the due decision of the case, and the Queen's Proctor may thereupon take such steps as the Attorney-General considers necessary or expedient.

(2) Where the Queen's Proctor intervenes or shows cause against a decree nisi in any proceedings for divorce, the court may make such order as may be just as to the payment by other parties to the proceedings of the costs incurred by him in so doing or as to the payment by him of any costs incurred by any of those parties by reason of his so doing.

(3) The Queen's Proctor shall be entitled to charge as part of the expenses of his office—

    (*a*) the costs of any proceedings under subsection (1) (*a*) above;

    (*b*) where his reasonable costs of intervening or showing cause as mentioned in subsection (2) above are not fully satisfied by any order under that subsection, the amount of the difference;

    (*c*) if the Treasury so directs, any costs which he pays to any parties under an order made under subsection (2).

9. Proceedings after decree nisi: general powers of court

(1) Where a decree of divorce has been granted but not made absolute, then, without prejudice to section 8 above, any person (excluding a party to the proceedings other than the Queen's Proctor) may show why the decree should not be made absolute by reason of material facts not having been brought before the court; and in such a case the court may—

(*a*) notwithstanding anything in section 1 (5) above (but subject to sections 10 (2) to (4) and 41 below) make the decree absolute; or

(*b*) rescind the decree; or

(*c*) require further inquiry; or

(*d*) otherwise deal with the case as it thinks fit.

(2) Where a decree of divorce has been granted and no application for it to be made absolute has been made by the party to whom it was granted, then, at any time after the expiration of three months from the earliest date on which that party could have made such an application, the party against whom it was granted may make an application to the court, and on that application the court may exercise any of the powers mentioned in paragraphs (*a*) to (*d*) of subsection (1) above.

10. Proceedings after decree nisi: special protection for respondent in separation cases

(1) Where in any case the court has granted a decree of divorce on the basis of a finding that the petitioner was entitled to rely in support of this petition on the fact of two years' separation coupled with the respondent's consent to a decree being granted and has made no such finding as to any other fact mentioned in section 1 (2) above, the court may, on an application made by the respondent at any time before the decree is made absolute, rescind the decree if it is satisfied that the petitioner misled the respondent (whether intentionally or unintentionally) about any matter which the respondent took into account in deciding to give his consent.

(2) The following provisions of this section apply where—

(*a*) the respondent to a petition for divorce in which the petitioner alleged two years' or five years' separation coupled, in the former case, with the respondent's consent to a decree being granted, has applied to the court for consideration under subsection (3) below of his financial position after the divorce; and

(*b*) the court has granted a decree on the petition on the basis of a finding that the petitioner was entitled to rely in support of his petition on the fact of two years' or five years' separation (as the case may be) and has made no such finding as to any other fact mentioned in section 1 (2) above.

(3) The court hearing an application by the respondent under subsection (2) above shall consider all the circumstances, including the age, health, conduct, earning capacity, financial resources and financial obligations of each of the parties, and the financial position of the respondent as, having regard to the divorce, it is likely to be after the death of the petitioner should the petitioner die first; and, subject to subsection (4) below, the court shall not make the decree absolute unless it is satisfied—

(*a*) that the petitioner should not be required to make any financial provision for the respondent, or

(*b*) that the financial provision made by the petitioner for the respondent is reasonable and fair or the best that can be made in the circumstances.

(4) The court may if it thinks fit make the decree absolute notwithstanding the requirements of subsection (3) above if—

(*a*) it appears that there are circumstances making it desirable that the decree should be made absolute without delay, and

(*b*) the court has obtained a satisfactory undertaking from the petitioner that he will make such financial provision for the respondent as the court may approve.

Nullity

11. Grounds on which a marriage is void

A marriage celebrated after 31st July 1971 shall be void on the following grounds only, that is to say—

(*a*) that it is not a valid marriage under the provisions of the Marriages Acts 1949 to 1970 (that is to say where—

(i) the parties are within the prohibited degrees of relationship;

(ii) either party is under the age of sixteen; or

(iii) the parties have intermarried in disregard of certain requirements as to the formation of marriage);

(*b*) that at the time of the marriage either party was already lawfully married;

(*c*) that the parties are not respectively male and female;

(*d*) in the case of a polygamous marriage entered into outside England and Wales, that either party was at the time of the marriage domiciled in England and Wales.

For the purposes of paragraph (*d*) of this subsection a marriage may be polygamous although at its inception neither party has any spouse additional to the other.

12. Grounds on which a marriage is voidable

A marriage celebrated after 31st July 1971 shall be voidable on the following grounds only, that is to say—

(*a*) that the marriage has not been consummated owing to the incapacity of either party to consummate it;

(*b*) that the marriage has not been consummated owing to the wilful refusal of the respondent to consummate it;

(*c*) that either party to the marriage did not validly consent to it, whether in consequence of duress, mistake, unsoundness of mind or otherwise;

(*d*) that at the time of the marriage either party, though capable of giving a valid consent, was suffering (whether continuously or intermittently) from mental disorder within the meaning of the Mental Health Act 1959 of such a kind or to such an extent as to be unfitted for marriage;

(*e*) that at the time of the marriage the respondent was suffering from venereal disease in a communicable form;

(*f*) that at the time of the marriage the respondent was pregnant by some person other than the petitioner.

13. Bars to relief where marriage is voidable

(1) The court shall not, in proceedings instituted after 31st July 1971, grant a decree of nullity on the ground that a marriage is voidable if the respondent satisfies the court—

    (a) that the petitioner, with knowledge that it was open to him to have the marriage avoided, so conducted himself in relation to the respondent as to lead the respondent reasonably to believe that he would not seek to do so; and

    (b) that it would be unjust to the respondent to grant the decree.

(2) Without prejudice to subsection (1) above, the court shall not grant a decree of nullity by virtue of section 12 above on the grounds mentioned in paragraph (c), (d), (e) or (f) of that section unless it is satisfied that proceedings were instituted within three years from the date of the marriage.

(3) Without prejudice to subsections (1) and (2) above, the court shall not grant a decree of nullity by virtue of section 12 above on the grounds mentioned in paragraph (e) or (f) of that section unless it is satisfied that the petitioner was at the time of the marriage ignorant of the facts alleged.

14. Marriages governed by foreign law or celebrated abroad under English law

(1) Where, apart from this Act, any matter affecting the validity of a marriage would fall to be determined (in accordance with the rules of private international law) by reference to the law of a country outside England and Wales, nothing in section 11, 12 or 13 (1) above shall—

    (a) preclude the determination of that matter as aforesaid; or

    (b) require the application to the marriage of the grounds or bar there mentioned except so far as applicable in accordance with those rules.

(2) In the case of a marriage which purports to have been celebrated under the Foreign Marriage Acts 1892 to 1947 or has taken place outside England and Wales and purports to be a marriage under common law, section 11 above is without prejudice to any ground on which the marriage may be void under those Acts or, as the case may be, by virtue of the rules governing the celebration of marriages outside England and Wales under common law.

15. Application of ss. 1 (5), 8 and 9 to nullity proceedings

Sections 1 (5), 8 and 9 above shall apply in relation to proceedings for nullity of marriage as if for any reference in those provisions to divorce there were substituted a reference to nullity of marriage.

16. Effect of decree of nullity in case of voidable marriage

A decree of nullity granted after 31st July 1971 in respect of a voidable marriage shall operate to annul the marriage only as respects any time after the decree has been made absolute, and the marriage shall, notwithstanding the decree, be treated as if it had existed up to that time.

Other matrimonial suits

17. Judicial separation

(1) A petition for judicial separation may be presente[d]
party to a marriage on the ground that any such fact a[s]
1 (2) above exists, and the provisions of section 2 above
for the purposes of a petition for judicial separation al[l]
they apply in relation to a petition for divorce alleging

(2) On a petition for judicial separation it shall be tne duty of the court to inquire, so far as it reasonably can, into the facts alleged by the petitioner and into any facts alleged by the respondent, but the court shall not be concerned to consider whether the marriage has broken down irretrievably, and if it is satisfied on the evidence of any such fact as is mentioned in section 1 (2) above it shall, subject to section 41 below, grant a decree of judicial separation.

(3) Sections 6 and 7 above shall apply for the purpose of encouraging the reconciliation of parties to proceedings for judical separation and of enabling the parties to a marriage to refer to the court for its opinion an agreement or arrangement relevant to actual or contemplated proceedings for judicial separation, as they apply in relation to proceedings for divorce.

18. Effects of judicial separation

(1) Where the court grants a decree of judicial separation it shall no longer be obligatory for the petitioner to cohabit with the respondent.

(2) If while a decree of judicial separation is in force and the separation is continuing either of the parties to the marriage dies intestate as respects all or any of his or her real or personal property, the property as respects which he or she died intestate shall devolve as if the other party to the marriage had then been dead.

(3) Notwithstanding anything in section 2 (1) (a) of the Matrimonial Proceedings (Magistrates' Courts) Act 1960, a provision in force under an order made, or having effect as if made, under that section exempting one party to a marriage from the obligation to cohabit with the other shall not have effect as a decree of judicial separation for the purposes of subsection (2) above.

19. Presumption of death and dissolution of marriage

(1) Any married person who alleges that reasonable grounds exist for supposing that the other party to the marriage is dead may, . . . present a petition to the court to have it presumed that the other party is dead and to have the marriage dissolved, and the court may, if satisfied that such reasonable grounds exist, grant a decree of presumption of death and dissolution of the marriage.

(2) . . .

(3) In any proceedings under this section the fact that for a period of seven years or more the other party to the marriage has been continually absent from the petitioner and the petitioner has no reason to believe that the other party has been living within that time shall be evidence that the other party is dead until the contrary is proved.

Sections 1 (5), 8 and 9 above shall apply to a petition and a decree under section as they apply to a petition for divorce and a decree of divorce respectively.

(5) . . .

(6) It is hereby declared that neither collusion nor any other conduct on the part of the petitioner which has at any time been a bar to relief in matrimonial proceedings constitutes a bar to the grant of a decree under this section.

GENERAL NOTE

The words in sub-s. (1) and sub-ss. (2) and (5) are repealed by the Domicile and Matrimonial Proceedings Act 1973, s. 17 and Sched. 6.

General
20. Relief for respondent in divorce proceedings
If in any proceedings for divorce the respondent alleges and proves any such fact as is mentioned in subsection (2) of section 1 above (treating the respondent as the petitioner and the petitioner as the respondent for the purposes of that subsection) the court may give to the respondent the relief to which he would have been entitled if he had presented a petition seeking that relief.

PART II
FINANCIAL RELIEF FOR PARTIES TO MARRIAGE AND
CHILDREN OF FAMILY
Financial provision and property adjustment orders
21. Financial provision and property adjustment orders
(1) The financial provision orders for the purposes of this Act are the orders for periodical or lump sum provision available (subject to the provisions of this Act) under section 23 below for the purpose of adjusting the financial position of the parties to a marriage and any children of the family in connection with proceedings for divorce, nullity of marriage or judicial separation and under section 27 (6) below on proof of neglect by one party to a marriage to provide, or to make a proper contribution towards, reasonable maintenance for the other or a child of the family, that is to say—

(a) any order for periodical payments in favour of a party to a marriage under section 23 (1) (a) or 27 (6) (a) or in favour of a child of the family under section 23 (1) (d), (2) or (4) or 27 (6) (d);

(b) any order for secured periodical payments in favour of a party to a marriage under section 23 (1) (b) or 27 (6) (b) or in favour of a child of the family under section 23 (1) (e), (2) or (4) or 27 (6) (e); and

(c) any order for lump sum provision in favour of a party to a marriage under section 23 (1) (c) or 27 (6) (c) or in favour of a child of the family under section 23 (1) (f), (2) or (4) or 27 (6) (f);

and references in this Act (except in paragraphs 17 (1) and 23 of Schedule 1 below) to periodical payments orders, secured periodical payments orders, and orders for the payment of a lump sum are references to all or some of the financial provision orders requiring the sort of financial provision in question according as the context of each reference may require.

(2) The property adjustment orders for the purposes of this Act are the orders dealing with property rights available (subject to the provisions of this Act) under section 24 below for the purpose of adjusting the financial position of the parties to a marriage and any children of the family on or after the grant of a decree of divorce, nullity of marriage or judicial separation, that is to say—

(*a*) any order under subsection (1) (*a*) of that section for a transfer of property;

(*b*) any order under subsection (1) (*b*) of that section for a settlement of property; and

(*c*) any order under subsection (1) (*c*) or (*d*) of that section for a variation of settlement.

Ancillary relief in connection with divorce proceedings, etc.

22. Maintenance pending suit

On a petition for divorce, nullity of marriage or judicial separation, the court may make an order for maintenance pending suit, that is to say, an order requiring either party to the marriage to make to the other such periodical payments for his or her maintenance and for such term, being a term beginning not earlier than the date of the presentation of the petition and ending with the date of the determination of the suit, as the court thinks reasonable.

23. Financial provision orders in connection with divorce proceedings, etc.

(1) On granting a decree of divorce, a decree of nullity of marriage or a decree of judicial separation or at any time thereafter (whether, in the case of a decree of divorce or of nullity of marriage, before or after the decree is made absolute), the court may make any one or more of the following orders, that is to say—

(*a*) an order that either party to the marriage shall make to the other such periodical payments, for such term, as may be specified in the order;

(*b*) an order that either party to the marriage shall secure to the other to the satisfaction of the court such periodical payments, for such term, as may be so specified;

(*c*) an order that either party to the marriage shall pay to the other such lump sum or sums as may be so specified;

(*d*) an order that a party to the marriage shall make to such person as may be specified in the order for the benefit of a child of the family, or to such a child, such periodical payments, for such term, as may be so specified;

(*e*) an order that a party to the marriage shall secure to such person as may be so specified for the benefit of such a child, or to such a child, to the satisfaction of the court, such periodical payments, for such term, as may be so specified;

(*f*) an order that a party to the marriage shall pay to such person as may be so specified for the benefit of such a child, or to such a child, such lump sum as may be so specified;

subject, however, in the case of an order under paragraph (*d*), (*e*) or (*f*) above, to the restrictions imposed by section 29 (1) and (3) below on the making of financial provision orders in favour of children who have attained the age of eighteen.

(2) The court may also, subject to those restrictions, make any one or more of the orders mentioned in subsection (1) (*d*), (*e*) and (*f*) above—

(*a*) in any proceedings for divorce, nullity of marriage or judicial separation, before granting a decree; and

(*b*) where any such proceedings are dismissed after the beginning of the trial, either forthwith or within a reasonable period after the dismissal.

(3) Without prejudice to the generality of subsection (1) (*c*) or (*f*) above—

(*a*) an order under this section that a party to a marriage shall pay a lump sum to the other party may be made for the purposes of enabling that other party to meet any liabilities or expenses reasonably incurred by him or her in maintaining himself or herself or any child of the family before making an application for an order under this section in his or her favour;

(*b*) an order under this section for the payment of a lump sum to or for the benefit of a child of the family may be made for the purpose of enabling any liabilities or expenses reasonably incurred by or for the benefit of that child before the making of an application for an order under this section in his favour to be met; and

(*c*) an order under this section for the payment of a lump sum may provide for the payment of that sum by instalments of such amount as may be specified in the order and may require the payment of the instalments to be secured to the satisfaction of the court.

(4) The power of the court under subsection (1) or (2) (*a*) above to make an order in favour of a child of the family shall be exercisable from time to time; and where the court makes an order in favour of a child under subsection (2) (*b*) above, it may from time to time, subject to the restrictions mentioned in subsection (1) above, make a further order in his favour of any of the kinds mentioned in subsection (1) (*d*), (*e*) or (*f*) above.

(5) Without prejudice to the power to give a direction under section 30 below for the settlement of an instrument by conveyancing counsel, where an order is made under subsection (1) (*a*), (*b*) or (*c*) above on or after granting a decree of divorce or nullity of marriage, neither the order nor any settlement made in pursuance of the order shall take effect unless the decree has been made absolute.

24. Property adjustment orders in connection with divorce proceedings, etc.

(1) On granting a decree of divorce, a decree of nullity of marriage or a decree of judicial separation or at any time thereafter (whether, in the case of a decree of divorce or of nullity of marriage, before or after the decree is made absolute), the court may make any one or more of the following orders, that is to say—

(*a*) an order that a party to the marriage shall transfer to the other party, to any child of the family or to such person as may be specified in the order for the benefit of such a child such property as may be so specified, being property to which the first-mentioned party is entitled, either in possession or reversion;

(b) an order that a settlement of such property as may be so specified, being property to which a party to the marriage is so entitled, be made to the satisfaction of the court for the benefit of the other party to the marriage and of the children of the family or either or any of them;

(c) an order varying for the benefit of the parties to the marriage and of the children of the family or either or any of them any ante-nuptial or post-nuptial settlement (including such a settlement made by will or codicil) made on the parties to the marriage;

(d) an order extinguishing or reducing the interest of either of the parties to the marriage under any such settlement;

subject, however, in the case of an order under paragraph (a) above, to the restrictions imposed by section 29 (1) and (3) below on the making of orders for a transfer of property in favour of children who have attained the age of eighteen.

(2) The court may make an order under subsection (1) (c) above notwithstanding that there are no children of the family.

(3) Without prejudice to the power to give a direction under section 30 below for the settlement of an instrument by conveyancing counsel, where an order is made under this section on or after granting a decree of divorce or nullity of marriage, neither the order nor any settlement made in pursuance of the order shall take effect unless the decree has been made absolute.

25. Matters to which court is to have regard in deciding how to exercise its powers under sections 23 and 24

(1) It shall be the duty of the court in deciding whether to exercise its powers under section 23 (1) (a), (b) or (c) or 24 above in relation to a party to the marriage and, if so, in what manner, to have regard to all the circumstances of the case including the following matters, that is to say—

(a) the income, earning capacity, property and other financial resources which each of the parties to the marriage has or is likely to have in the foreseeable future;

(b) the financial needs, obligations and responsibilities which each of the parties to the marriage has or is likely to have in the foreseeable future;

(c) the standard of living enjoyed by the family before the breakdown of the marriage;

(d) the age of each party to the marriage and the duration of the marriage;

(e) any physical or mental disability of either of the parties to the marriage;

(f) the contributions made by each of the parties to the welfare of the family, including any contribution made by looking after the home or caring for the family;

(g) in the case of proceedings for divorce or nullity of marriage, the value to either of the parties to the marriage of any benefit (for example, a pension) which, by reason of the dissolution or annulment of the marriage, that party will lose the chance of acquiring;

and so to exercise those powers as to place the parties, so far as it is practicable and, having regard to their conduct, just to do so, in the financial position in which they would have been if the marriage had not broken down and each had properly discharged his or her financial obligations and responsibilities towards the other.

(2) Without prejudice to subsection (3) below, it shall be the duty of the court in deciding whether to exercise its powers under section 23 (1) (*d*), (*e*) or (*f*), (2) or (4) or 24 above in relation to a child of the family and, if so, in what manner, to have regard to all the circumstances of the case including the following matters, that is to say—

(*a*) the financial needs of the child;
(*b*) the income, earning capacity (if any), property and other financial resources of the child;
(*c*) any physical or mental disability of the child;
(*d*) the standard of living enjoyed by the family before the breakdown of the marriage;
(*e*) the manner in which he was being and in which the parties to the marriage expected him to be educated or trained;

and so to exercise those powers as to place the child, so far as it is practicable and, having regard to the considerations mentioned in relation to the parties to the marriage in paragraph (*a*) and (*b*) of subsection (1) above, just to do so, in the financial position in which the child would have been if the marriage had not broken down and each of those parties had properly discharged his or her financial obligations and responsibilities towards him.

(3) It shall be the duty of the court in deciding whether to exercise its powers under section 23 (1) (*d*), (*e*) or (*f*), (2) or (4) or 24 above against a party to a marriage in favour of a child of the family who is not the child of that party and, if so, in what manner, to have regard (among the circumstances of the case)—

(*a*) to whether that party had assumed any responsibility for the child's maintenance and, if so, to the extent to which, and the basis upon which, that party assumed such responsibility and to the length of time for which that party discharged such responsibility;
(*b*) to whether in assuming and discharging such responsibility that party did so knowing that the child was not his or her own;
(*c*) to the liability of any other person to maintain the child.

26. Commencement of proceedings for ancillary relief, etc.

(1) Where a petition for divorce, nullity of marriage or judicial separation has been presented, then, subject to subsection (2) below, proceedings for maintenance pending suit under section 22 above, for a financial provision order under section 23 above, or for a property adjustment order may be begun, subject to and in accordance with rules of court, at any time after the presentation of the petition.

(2) Rules of court may provide, in such cases as may be prescribed by the rules—

(*a*) that applications for any such relief as is mentioned in subsection (1) above shall be made in the petition or answer; and

(*b*) that applications for any such relief which are not so made, or are not made until after the expiration of such period following the presentation of the petition or filing of the answer as may be so prescribed, shall be made only with the leave of the court.

Financial provision in case of neglect to maintain

27. Financial provision orders, etc., in case of neglect by party to marriage to maintain other party or child of the family

(1) Either party to a marriage may apply to the court for an order under this section on the ground that the other party to the marriage (in this section referred to as the respondent)—

(*a*) being the husband, has wilfully neglected—

(i) to provide reasonable maintenance for the applicant, or

(ii) to provide, or to make a proper contribution towards, reasonable maintenance for any child of the family to whom this section applies;

(*b*) being the wife, has wilfully neglected to provide, or to make a proper contribution towards, reasonable maintenance—

(i) for the applicant in a case where, by reason of the impairment of the applicant's earning capacity through age, illness or disability of mind or body, and having regard to any resources of the applicant and the respondent respectively which are, or should properly be made, available for the purpose, it is reasonable in all the circumstances to expect the respondent so to provide or contribute, or

(ii) for any child of the family to whom this section applies.

(2) The court shall not entertain an application under this section unless—

(*a*) the applicant or the respondent is domiciled in England and Wales on the date of the application; or

(*b*) the applicant has been habitually resident there throughout the period of one year ending with that date; or

(*c*) the respondent is resident there on that date.

(3) This section applies to any child of the family for whose maintenance it is reasonable in all the circumstances to expect the respondent to provide or towards whose maintenance it is reasonable in all the circumstances to expect the respondent to make a proper contribution.

(4) Where the child of the family to whom the application under this section relates is not the child of the respondent, then, in deciding—

(*a*) whether the respondent has been guilty of wilful neglect to provide, or to make a proper contribution towards, reasonable maintenance for the child, and

(b) what order, if any, to make under this section in favour of the child, the court shall have regard to the matters mentioned in section 25 (3) above.

(5) Where on an application under this section it appears to the court that the applicant or any child of the family to whom the application relates is in immediate need of financial assistance, but it is not yet possible to determine what order, if any, should be made on the application, the court may make an interim order for maintenance, that is to say, an order requiring the respondent to make to the applicant until the determination of the application such periodical payments as the court thinks reasonable.

(6) Where on an application under this section the applicant satisfies the court of any ground mentioned in subsection (1) above, the court may make such one or more of the following orders as it thinks just, that is to say—

(a) an order that the respondent shall make to the applicant such periodical payments, for such terms, as may be specified in the order;

(b) an order that the respondent shall secure to the applicant, to the satisfaction of the court, such periodical payments, for such term, as may be so specified;

(c) an order that the respondent shall pay to the applicant such lump sum as may be so specified;

(d) an order that the respondent shall make to such person as may be specified in the order for the benefit of the child to whom the application relates, or to that child, such periodical payments, for such term, as may be so specified;

(e) an order that the respondent shall secure to such person as may be so specified for the benefit of that child, or to that child, to the satisfaction of the court, such periodical payments, for such term, as may be so specified;

(f) an order that the respondent shall pay to such person as may be so specified for the benefit of that child, or to that child, such lump sum as may be so specified;

subject, however, in the case of an order under paragraph (d), (e) or (f) above, to the restrictions imposed by section 29 (1) and (3) below on the making of financial provision orders in favour of children who have attained the age of eighteen.

(7) Without prejudice to the generality of subsection (6) (c) or (f) above, an order under this section for the payment of a lump sum—

(a) may be made for the purpose of enabling any liabilities or expenses reasonably incurred in maintaining the applicant or any child of the family to whom the application relates before the making of the application to be met;

(b) may provide for the payment of that sum by instalments of such amount as may be specified in the order and may require the payment of the instalments to be secured to the satisfaction of the court.

(8) For the purpose of proceedings on an application under this section adultery which has been condoned shall not be capable of being revived, and any presumption of condonation which arises from the continuance or resump-

tion of marital intercourse may be rebutted by evidence sufficient to negative the necessary intent.

NOTE

Section 27 (2) is printed as amended by the Domicile and Matrimonial Proceedings Act 1973, s. 6 (1).

Additional provisions with respect to financial provision and property adjustment orders

28. Duration of continuing financial provision orders in favour of party to marriage, and effect of remarriage

(1) The term to be specified in a periodical payments or secured periodical payments order in favour of a party to a marriage shall be such term as the court thinks fit, subject to the following limits, that is to say—

(a) in the case of a periodical payments order, the term shall begin not earlier than the date of the making of an application for the order, and shall be so defined as not to extend beyond the death of either of the parties to the marriage or, where the order is made on or after the grant of a decree of divorce or nullity of marriage, the remarriage of the party in whose favour the order is made; and

(b) in the case of a secured periodical payments order, the term shall begin not earlier than the date of the making of an application for the order, and shall be so defined as not to extend beyond the death or, where the order is made on or after the grant of such a decree, the remarriage of the party in whose favour the order is made.

(2) Where a periodical payments or secured periodical payments order in favour of a party to a marriage is made otherwise than on or after the grant of a decree of divorce or nullity of marriage, and the marriage in question is subsequently dissolved or annulled but the order continues in force, the order shall, notwithstanding anything in it, cease to have effect on the remarriage of that party, except in relation to any arrears due under it on the date of the remarriage.

(3) If after the grant of a decree dissolving or annulling a marriage either party to that marriage remarries, that party shall not be entitled to apply, by reference to the grant of that decree, for a financial provision order in his or her favour, or for a property adjustment order, against the other party to that marriage.

29. Duration of continuing financial provision orders in favour of children, and age limit on making certain orders in their favour

(1) Subject to subsection (3) below, no financial provision order and no order for a transfer of property under section 24 (1) (a) above shall be made in favour of a child who has attained the age of eighteen.

(2) The term to be specified in a periodical payments or secured periodical payments order in favour of a child may begin with the date of the making of an application for the order in question or any later date but—

(a) shall not in the first instance extend beyond the date of the birthday of the child next following his attaining the upper limit of the compulsory school age (that is to say, the age that is for the time being that limit by virtue of section 35 of the Education Act 1944 together with any Order in Council made under that section) unless the court thinks it right in the circumstances of the case to specify a later date; and

(b) shall not in any event, subject to subsection (3) below, extend beyond the date of the child's eighteenth birthday.

(3) Subsection (1) above, and paragraph (b) of subsection (2), shall not apply in the case of a child, if it appears to the court that—

(a) the child is, or will be, or if an order were made without complying with either or both of those provisions would be, receiving instruction at an educational establishment or undergoing training for a trade, profession or vocation, whether or not he is also, or will also be, in gainful employment; or

(b) there are special circumstances which justify the making of an order without complying with either or both of those provisions.

(4) Any periodical payments order in favour of a child shall, notwithstanding anything in the order, cease to have effect on the death of the person liable to make payments under the order, except in relation to any arrears due under the order on the date of the death.

30. Direction for settlement of instrument for securing payments or effecting property adjustment

Where the court decides to make a financial provision order requiring any payments to be secured or a property adjustment order—

(a) it may direct that the matter be referred to one of the conveyancing counsel of the court for him to settle a proper instrument to be executed by all necessary parties; and

(b) where the order is to be made in proceedings for divorce, nullity of marriage or judicial separation it may, if it thinks fit, defer the grant of the decree in question until the instrument has been duly executed.

*Variation, dicharge and enforcement of
cetain orders, etc.*

31. Variation, discharge, etc., of certain orders for financial relief

(1) Where the court has made an order to which this section applies, then, subject to the provisions of this section, the court shall have power to vary or discharge the order or to suspend any provision thereof temporarily and to revive the operation of any provision so suspended.

(2) This section applies to the following orders, that is to say—

(a) any order for maintenance pending suit and any interim order for maintenance;

(b) any periodical payments order;

(c) any secured periodical payments order;

(d) any order made by virtue of section 23 (3) (c) or 27 (7) (b) above (provision for payment of a lump sum by instalments);

(e) any order for a settlement of property under section 24 (1) (b) or for a variation of settlement under section 24 (1) (c) or (d) above, being an order made on or after the grant of a decree of judicial separation.

(3) The powers exercisable by the court under this section in relation to an order shall be exercisable also in relation to any instrument executed in pursuance of the order.

(4) The court shall not exercise the powers conferred by this section in relation to an order for a settlement under section 24 (1) (b) or for a variation of settlement under section 24 (1) (c) or (d) above except on an application made in proceedings—

(a) for the rescission of the decree of judicial separation by reference to which the order was made, or

(b) for the dissolution of the marriage in question.

(5) No property adjustment order shall be made on an application for the variation of a periodical payments or secured periodical payments order made (whether in favour of a party to a marriage or in favour of a child of the family) under section 23 above, and no order for the payment of a lump sum shall be made on an application for the variation of a periodical payments or secured periodical payments order in favour of a party to a marriage (whether made under section 23 or under section 27 above).

(6) Where the person liable to make payments under a secured periodical payments order has died, an application under this section relating to that order may be made by the person entitled to payments under the order or by the personal representatives of the deceased person, but no such application shall, except with the permission of the court, be made after the end of the period of six months from the date on which representation in regard to the estate of that person is first taken out.

(7) In exercising the powers conferred by this section the court shall have regard to all the circumstances of the case, including any change in any of the matters to which the court was required to have regard when making the order to which the application relates and, where the party against whom that order was made has died, the changed circumstances resulting from his or her death.

(8) The personal representatives of a deceased person against whom a secured periodical payments order was made shall not be liable for having distributed any part of the estate of the deceased after the expiration of the period of six months referred to in subsection (6) above on the ground that they ought to have taken into account the possibility that the court might permit an application under this section to be made after that period by the person entitled to payments under the order; but this subsection shall not prejudice any power to recover any part of the estate so distributed arising by virtue of the making of an order in pursuance of this section.

(9) In considering for the purposes of subsection (6) above the question when representation was first taken out, a grant limited to settled land or to trust property shall be left out of account and a grant limited to real estate or to personal estate shall be left out of account unless a grant limited to the remainder of the estate has previously been made or is made at the same time.

32. Payment of certain arrears unenforceable without the leave of the court

(1) A person shall not be entitled to enforce through the High Court or any county court the payment of any arrears due under an order for maintenance pending suit, an interim order for maintenance or any financial provision order without the leave of that court if those arrears became due more than twelve months before proceedings to enforce the payment of them are begun.

(2) The court hearing an application for the grant of leave under this section may refuse leave, or may grant leave subject to such restrictions and conditions (including conditions as to the allowing of time for payment or the making of payment by instalments) as that court thinks proper, or may remit the payment of the arrears or of any part thereof.

(3) An application for the grant of leave under this section shall be made in such manner as may be prescribed by rules of court.

33. Orders for repayment in certain cases of sums paid under certain orders

(1) Where on an application made under this section in relation to an order to which this section applies it appears to the court that by reason of—

    (a) a change in the circumstances of the person entitled to, or liable to make, payments under the order since the order was made, or

    (b) the changed circumstances resulting from the death of the person so liable,

the amount received by the person entitled to payments under the order in respect of a period after those circumstances changed or after the death of the person liable to make payments under the order, as the case may be, exceeds the amount which the person so liable or his or her personal representatives should have been required to pay, the court may order the respondent to the application to pay to the applicant such sum, not exceeding the amount of the excess, as the court thinks just.

(2) This section applies to the following orders, that is to say—

    (a) any order for maintenance pending suit and any interim order for maintenance;

    (b) any periodical payments order; and

    (c) any secured periodical payments order.

(3) An application under this section may be made by the person liable to make payments under an order to which this section applies or his or her personal representatives and may be made against the person entitled to payments under the order or her or his personal representatives.

(4) An application under this section may be made in proceedings in the High Court or a county court for—

(*a*) the variation or discharge of the order to which this section applies, or

(*b*) leave to enforce, or the enforcement of, the payment of arrears under that order;

but when not made in such proceedings shall be made to a county court, and accordingly references in this section to the court are references to the High Court or a county court, as the circumstances require.

(5) The jurisdiction conferred on a county court by this section shall be exercisable notwithstanding that by reason of the amount claimed in the application the jurisdiction would not but for this subsection be exercisable by a county court.

(6) An order under this section for the payment of any sum may provide for the payment of that sum by instalments of such amount as may be specified in the order.

Maintenance agreements

34. Validity of maintenance agreements

(1) If a maintenance agreement includes a provision purporting to restrict any right to apply to a court for an order containing financial arrangements, then—

(*a*) that provision shall be void; but

(*b*) any other financial arrangements contained in the agreement shall not thereby be rendered void or unenforceable and shall, unless they are void or unenforceable for any other reason (and subject to sections 35 and 36 below), be binding on the parties to the agreement.

(2) In this section and in section 35 below—

"maintenance agreement" means any agreement in writing made, whether before or after the commencement of this Act, between the parties to a marriage, being—

(*a*) an agreement containing financial arrangements, whether made during the continuance or after the dissolution or annulment of the marriage; or

(*b*) a separation agreement which contains no financial arrangements in a case where no other agreement in writing between the same parties contains such arrangements;

"financial arrangements" means provisions governing the rights and liabilities towards one another when living separately of the parties to a marriage (including a marriage which has been dissolved or annulled) in respect of the making or securing of payments or the disposition or use of any property, including such rights and liabilities with respect to the maintenance or education of any child, whether or not a child of the family.

35. Alteration of agreements by court during lives of parties

(1) Where a maintenance agreement is for the time being subsisting and each of the parties to the agreement is for the time being either domiciled or resident in England and Wales, then, subject to subsection (3) below, either party may apply to the court or to a magistrates' court for an order under this section.

(2) If the court to which the application is made is satisfied either—

    (a) that by reason of a change in the circumstances in the light of which any financial arrangements contained in the agreement were made or, as the case may be, financial arrangements were omitted from it (including a change foreseen by the parties when making the agreement), the agreement should be altered so as to make different, or, as the case may be, so as to contain, financial arrangements, or

    (b) that the agreement does not contain proper financial arrangements with respect to any child of the family,

then subject to subsections (3), (4) and (5) below, that court may by order make such alterations in the agreement—

    (i) by varying or revoking any financial arrangements contained in it, or

    (ii) by inserting in it financial arrangements for the benefit of one of the parties to the agreement or of a child of the family,

as may appear to that court to be just having regard to all the circumstances, including, if relevant, the matters mentioned in section 25 (3) above; and the agreement shall have effect thereafter as if any alteration made by the order had been made by agreement between the parties and for valuable consideration.

(3) A magistrates' court shall not entertain an application under subsection (1) above unless both the parties to the agreement are resident in England and Wales and at least one of the parties is resident in the petty sessions area (within the meaning of the Magistrates' Courts Act 1952) for which the court acts, and shall not have power to make any order on such an application except—

    (a) in a case where the agreement includes no provision for periodical payments by either of the parties, an order inserting provision for the making by one of the parties of periodical payments for the maintenance of the other party or for the maintenance of any child of the family;

    (b) in a case where the agreement includes provision for the making by one of the parties of periodical payments, an order increasing or reducing the rate of, or terminating, any of those payments.

(4) Where a court decides to alter, by order under this section, an agreement by inserting provision for the making or securing by one of the parties to the agreement of periodical payments for the maintenance of the other party or by increasing the rate of the periodical payments which the agreement provides shall be made by one of the parties for the maintenance of the other, the term for which the payments or, as the case may be, the additional payments attributable to the increase are to be made under the agreement as altered by the order shall be such term as the court may specify, subject to the following limits, that is to say—

(*a*) where the payments will not be secured, the term shall be so defined as not to extend beyond the death of either of the parties to the agreement or the remarriage of the party to whom the payments are to be made;

(*b*) where the payments will be secured, the term shall be so defined as not to extend beyond the death or remarriage of that party.

(5) Where a court decides to alter, by order under this section, an agreement by inserting provision for the making or securing by one of the parties to the agreement of periodical payments for the maintenance of a child of the family or by increasing the rate of the periodical payments which the agreement provides shall be made or secured by one of the parties for the maintenance of such a child, then, in deciding the term for which under the agreement as altered by the order the payments, or as the case may be, the additional payments attributable to the increase are to be made or secured for the benefit of the child, the court shall apply the provisions of section 29 (2) and (3) above as to age limits as if the order in question were a periodical payments or secured periodical payments order in favour of the child.

(6) For the avoidance of doubt it is hereby declared that nothing in this section or in section 34 above affects any power of a court before which any proceedings between the parties to a maintenance agreement are brought under any other enactment (including a provision of this Act) to make an order containing financial arrangements or any right of either party to apply for such an order in such proceedings.

36. Alteration of agreements by court after death of one party

(1) Where a maintenance agreement within the meaning of section 34 above provides for the continuation of payments under the agreement after the death of one of the parties and that party dies domiciled in England and Wales, the surviving party or the personal representatives of the deceased party may, subject to subsections (2) and (3) below, apply to the High Court or a county court for an order under section 35 above.

(2) An application under this section shall not, except with the permission of the High Court or a county court, be made after the end of the period of six months from the date on which representation in regard to the estate of the deceased is first taken out.

(3) A county court shall not entertain an application under this section, or an application for permission to make an application under this section, unless it would have jurisdiction by virtue of section 7 of the Family Provision Act 1966 (which confers jurisdiction on county courts in proceedings under the Inheritance (Family Provision) Act 1938 or section 26 of the Matrimonial Causes Act 1965 if the value of the deceased's net estate does not exceed £5,000 or such larger sum as may be fixed by order of the Lord Chancellor) to hear and determine proceedings for an order under section 26 of the Matrimonial Causes Act 1965 (application for maintenance out of deceased's estate by former spouse) in relation to the deceased's estate.

(4) If a maintenance agreement is altered by a court on an application made in pursuance of subsection (1) above, the like consequences shall ensue as if the alteration had been made immediately before the death by agreement between the parties and for valuable consideration.

(5) The provisions of this section shall not render the personal representatives of the deceased liable for having distributed any part of the estate of the deceased after the expiration of the period of six months referred to in sub-section (2) above on the ground that they ought to have taken into account the possibility that a court might permit an application by virtue of this section to be made by the surviving party after that period; but this subsection shall not prejudice any power to recover any part of the estate so distributed arising by virtue of the making of an order in pursuance of this section.

(6) Section 31 (9) above shall apply for the purposes of subsection (2) above as it applies for the purposes of subsection (6) of section 31.

(7) Subsection (3) of section 7 of the Family Provision Act 1966 (transfer to county court of proceedings commenced in the High Court) and paragraphs (*a*) and (*b*) of subsection (5) of that section (provisions relating to proceedings commenced in county court before coming into force of order of the Lord Chancellor under that section) shall apply in relation to proceedings consisting of any such application as is referred to in subsection (3) above as they apply in relation to any such proceedings as are referred to in subsection (1) of that section.

Miscellaneous and supplemental

37. Avoidance of transactions intended to prevent or reduce financial relief

(1) For the purposes of this section "financial relief" means relief under any of the provisions of sections 22, 23, 24, 27, 31 (except subsection (6)) and 35 above, and any reference in this section to defeating a person's claim for financial relief is a reference to preventing financial relief from being granted to that person, or to that person for the benefit of a child of the family, or reducing the amount of any financial relief which might be so granted, or frustrating or impeding the enforcement of any order which might be or has been made at his instance under any of those provisions.

(2) Where proceedings for financial relief are brought by one person against another, the court may, on the application of the first-mentioned person—

    (*a*) if it is satisfied that the other party to the proceedings is, with the intention of defeating the claim for financial relief, about to make any disposition or to transfer out of the jurisdiction or otherwise deal with any property, make such order as it thinks fit for restraining the other party from so doing or otherwise for protecting the claim;

    (*b*) if it is satisfied that the other party has, with that intention, made a reviewable disposition and that if the disposition were set aside financial relief or different financial relief would be granted to the applicant, make an order setting aside the disposition;

(c) if it is satisfied, in a case where an order has been obtained under any of the provisions mentioned in subsection (1) above by the applicant against the other party, that the other party has, with that intention, made a reviewable disposition, make an order setting aside the disposition;

and an application for the purposes of paragraph (b) above shall be made in the proceedings for the financial relief in question.

(3) Where the court makes an order under subsection (2) (b) or (c) above setting aside a disposition it shall give such consequential directions as it thinks fit for giving effect to the order (including directions requiring the making of any payments or the disposal of any property).

(4) Any disposition made by the other party to the proceedings for financial relief in question (whether before or after the commencement of those proceedings) is a reviewable disposition for the purposes of subsection (2) (b) and (c) above unless it was made for valuable consideration (other than marriage) to a person who, at the time of the disposition, acted in relation to it in good faith and without notice of any intention on the part of the other party to defeat the applicant's claim for financial relief.

(5) Where an application is made under this section with respect to a disposition which took less than three years before the date of the application or with respect to a disposition or other dealing with property which is about to take place and the court is satisfied—

(a) in a case falling within subsection (2) (a) or (b) above, that the disposition or other dealing would (apart from this section) have the consequence, or

(b) in a case falling within subsection (2) (c) above, that the disposition has had the consequence,

of defeating the applicant's claim for financial relief, it shall be presumed, unless the contrary is shown, that the person who disposed of or is about to dispose of or deal with the property did so or, as the case may be, is about to do so, with the intention of defeating the applicant's claim for financial relief.

(6) In this section "disposition" does not include any provision contained in a will or codicil but, with that exception, includes any conveyance, assurance or gift or property of any description, whether made by an instrument or otherwise.

(7) This section does not apply to a disposition made before 1st January 1968.

38. Orders for repayment in certain cases of sums paid after cessation of order by reason of remarriage

(1) Where—

(a) a periodical payments or secured periodical payments order in favour of a party to a marriage (hereafter in this section referred to as "a payments order") has ceased to have effect by reason of the remarriage of that party, and

(b) the person liable to make payments under the order or his or her personal representatives made payments in accordance with it in respect of a period after the date of the remarriage in the mistaken belief that the order was still subsisting.

the person so liable or his or her personal representatives shall not be entitled to bring proceedings in respect of a cause of action arising out of the circumstances mentioned in paragraphs (a) and (b) above against the person entitled to payments under the order or her or his personal representatives, but may instead make an application against that person or her or his personal representatives under this section.

(2) On an application under this section the court may order the respondent to pay to the applicant a sum equal to the amount of the payments made in respect of the period mentioned in subsection (1) (b) above or, if it appears to the court that it would be unjust to make that order, it may either order the respondent to pay to the applicant such lesser sum as it thinks fit or dismiss the application.

(3) An application under this section may be made in proceedings in the High Court or a county court for leave to enforce, or the enforcement of, payment of arrears under the order in question, but when not made in such proceedings shall be made to a county court; and accordingly references in this section to the court are references to the High Court or a county court, as the circumstances require.

(4) The jurisdiction conferred on a county court by this section shall be exercisable notwithstanding that by reason of the amount claimed in the application the jurisdiction would not but for this subsection be exercisable by a county court.

(5) An order under this section for the payment of any sum may provide for the payment of that sum by instalments of such amount as may be specified in the order.

(6) The clerk of a magistrates' court to whom any payments under a payments order are required to be made, and the collecting officer under an attachment of earnings order made to secure payments under a payments order, shall not be liable—

(a) in the case of the clerk, for any act done by him in pursuance of the payments order after the date on which that order ceased to have effect by reason of the remarriage of the person entitled to payments under it, and

(b) in the case of the collecting officer, for any act done by him after that date in accordance with any enactment or rule of court specifying how payments made to him in compliance with the attachment of earnings order are to be dealt with.

if, but only if, the act was one which he would have been under a duty to do had the payments order not so ceased to have effect and the act was done before notice in writing of the fact that the person so entitled had remarried was given to him by or on behalf of that person, the person liable to make payments under the payments order or the personal representatives of either of those persons.

(7) In this section "collecting officer", in relation to an attachment of earnings order, means the officer of the High Court, the registrar of a county court or the clerk of a magistrates' court to whom a person makes payments in compliance with the order.

39. Settlement, etc., made in compliance with a property adjustment order may be avoided on bankruptcy of settlor

The fact that a settlement or transfer of property had to be made in order to comply with a property adjustment order shall not prevent that settlement or transfer from being a settlement of property to which section 42 (1) of the Bankruptcy Act 1914 (avoidance of certain settlements) applies.

40. Payments, etc., under order made in favour of person suffering from mental disorder

Where the court makes an order under this Part of this Act requiring payments (including a lump sum payment) to be made, or property to be transferred, to a party to a marriage and the court is satisfied that the person in whose favour the order is made is incapable, by reason of mental disorder within the meaning of the Mental Health Act 1959, of managing and administering his or her property and affairs then, subject to any order, direction or authority made or given in relation to that person under Part VIII of that Act, the court may order the payments to be made, or as the case may be, the property to be transferred, to such persons having charge of that person as the court may direct.

PART III
PROTECTION, CUSTODY, ETC., OF CHILDREN

41. Restrictions on decrees for dissolution, annulment or separation affecting children

(1) The Court shall not make absolute a decree of divorce or of nullity of marriage, or grant a decree of judicial separation, unless the court, by order, has declared that it is satisfied—

(a) that for the purposes of this section there are no children of the family to whom this section applies; or—

(b) that the only children who are or may be children of the family to whom this section applies are the children named in the order and that—

(i) arrangements for the welfare of every child so named have been made and are satisfactory or are the best that can be devised in the circumstances; or

(ii) it is impracticable for the party or parties appearing before the court to make any such arrangements; or

(c) that there are circumstances making it desirable that the decree should be made absolute or should be granted, as the case may be, without delay notwithstanding that there are or may be children of the family to whom this section applies and that the court is unable to make a declaration in accordance with paragraph (b) above.

(2) The court shall not make an order declaring that it is satisfied as mentioned in subsection (1) (c) above unless it has obtained a satisfactory undertaking from either or both of the parties to bring the question of the arrangements for the children named in the order before the court within a specified time.

(3) If the court makes absolute a decree of divorce or of nullity of marriage, or grants a decree of judicial separation, without having made an order under subsection (1) above the decree shall be void but, if such an order was made, no person shall be entitled to challenge the validity of the decree on the ground that the conditions prescribed by subsections (1) and (2) above were not fulfilled.

(4) If the court refuses to make an order under subsection (1) above in any proceedings for divorce, nullity of marriage or judicial separation, it shall, on an application by either party to the proceedings, make an order declaring that it is not satisfied as mentioned in that subsection.

(5) This section applies to the following children of the family, that is to say—

(a) any minor child of the family who at the date of the order under subsection (1) above is—
    (i) under the age of sixteen, or
    (ii) receiving instruction at an educational establishment or undergoing training for a trade, profession or vocation, whether or not he is also in gainful employment; and

(b) any other child of the family to whom the court by an order under that subsection directs that this section shall apply;

and the court may give such a direction if it is of opinion that there are special circumstances which make it desirable in the interest of the child that this section should apply to him.

(6) In this section "welfare", in relation to a child, includes the custody and education of the child and financial provision for him.

42. Orders for custody and education of children in cases of divorce, etc., and for custody in cases of neglect

(1) The court may make such order as it thinks fit for the custody and education of any child of the family who is under the age of eighteen—

(a) in any proceedings for divorce, nullity of marriage or judicial separation, before or on granting a decree or at any time thereafter (whether, in the case of a decree of divorce or nullity of marriage, before or after the decree is made absolute);

(b) where any such proceedings are dismissed after the beginning of the trial, either forthwith or within a reasonable period after the dismissal;

and in any case in which the court has power by virtue of this subsection to make an order in respect of a child it may instead, if it thinks fit, direct that proper proceedings be taken for making the child a ward of court.

(2) Where the court makes an order under section 27 above, the court shall also have power to make such order as it thinks fit with respect to the custody of any child of the family who is for the time being under the age of eighteen; but the power conferred by this subsection and any order made in exercise of that power shall have effect only as respects any period when an order is in force under that section and the child is under that age.

(3) Where the court grants or makes absolute a decree of divorce or grants a decree of judicial separation, it may include in the decree a declaration that either party to the marriage in question is unfit to have the custody of the children of the family.

(4) Where a decree of divorce or of judicial separation contains such a declaration as is mentioned in subsection (3) above, then, if the party to whom the declaration relates is a parent of any child of the family, that party shall not, on the death of the other parent, be entitled as of right to the custody or the guardianship of that child.

(5) Where an order in respect of a child is made under this section, the order shall not affect the rights over or with respect to the child of any person, other than a party to the marriage in question, unless the child is the child of one or both of the parties to that marriage and that person was a party to the proceedings on the application for an order under this section.

(6) The power of the court under subsection (1) (*a*) or (2) above to make an order with respect to a child shall be exercisable from time to time; and where the court makes an order under subsection (1) (*b*) above with respect to a child it may from time to time until that child attains the age of eighteen make a further order with respect to his custody and education.

(7) The court shall have power to vary or discharge an order made under this section or to suspend any provision thereof temporarily and to revive the operation of any provision so suspended.

43. Power to commit children to care of local authority

(1) Where the court has jurisdiction by virtue of this Part of this Act to make an order for the custody of a child and it appears to the court that there are exceptional circumstances making it impracticable or undesirable for the child to be entrusted to either of the parties to the marriage or to any other individual, the court may if it thinks fit make an order committing the care of the child to the council of a county other than a metropolitan county, or of a metropolitan district or London borough or the Common Council of the City of London (hereafter in this section referred to as "the local authority"); and thereupon Part II of the Children Act 1948 (which relates to the treatment of children in the care of a local authority) shall, subject to the provisions of this section, apply as if the child had been received by the local authority into their care under section 1 of that Act.

(2) The authority specified in an order under this section shall be the local authority for the area in which the child was, in the opinion of the court,

resident before the order was made to commit the child to the care of a local authority, and the court shall before making an order under this section hear any representations from the local authority, including any representations as to the making of a financial provision order in favour of the child.

(3) While an order made by virtue of this section is in force with respect to a child, the child shall continue in the care of the local authority notwithstanding any claim by a parent or other person.

(4) An order made by virtue of this section shall cease to have effect as respects any child when he becomes eighteen, and the court shall not make an order committing a child to the care of a local authority under this section after he has become seventeen.

(5) In the application of Part II of the Children Act 1948 by virtue of this section—

(a) the exercise by the local authority of their powers under sections 12 to 14 of that Act (which among other things relate to the accommodation and welfare of a child in the care of a local authority) shall be subject to any directions given by the court; and

(b) section 17 of that Act (which relates to arrangements for the emigration of such a child) shall not apply.

(6) It shall be the duty of any parent or guardian of a child committed to the care of a local authority under this section to secure that the local authority are informed of his address for the time being, and a person who knowingly fails to comply with this subsection shall be liable on summary conviction to a fine not exceeding ten pounds.

(7) The court shall have power from time to time by an order under this section to vary or discharge any provision made in pursuance of this section.

(8) So long as by virtue of paragraph 13 of Schedule 4 to the Children and Young Persons Act 1969 sections 15 and 16 of the Children Act 1948 continue to apply in relation to a local authority, subsection (5) (a) above shall have effect in relation to that authority as if for the reference to sections 12 to 14 of the last-mentioned Act there were substituted a reference to sections 12 to 16 of that Act.

(9) Subject to the following provisions of this subsection, until 1st April 1974 subsection (1) above shall have effect as if for the words "other than a metropolitan county, or of a metropolitan district" there were substituted the words "county borough".

An order (or orders) made under section 273 (2) of the Local Government Act 1972 (orders bringing provisions of that Act into force before 1st April 1974) may appoint an earlier date (or, as the case may be, different dates for different different purposes or areas) on which subsection (1) above shall cease to have effect as mentioned above.

44. Power to provide for supervision of children

(1) Where the court has jurisdiction by virtue of this Part of this Act to make an order for the custody of a child and it appears to the court that there are

exceptional circumstances making it desirable that the child should be under the supervision of an independent person, the court may, as respects any period during which the child is, in exercise of that jurisdiction, committed to the custody of any person, order that the child be under the supervision of an officer appointed under this section as a welfare officer or under the supervision of a local authority.

(2) Where the court makes an order under this section for supervision by a welfare officer, the officer responsible for carrying out the order shall be such probation officer as may be selected under arrangements made by the Secretary of State; and where the order is for supervision by a local authority, that authority shall be the council of a county other than a metropolitan county, or of a metropolitan district or London borough selected by the court and specified in the order or, if the Common Council of the City of London is so selected and specified, that Council.

(3) The court shall not have power to make an order under this section as respects a child who in pursuance of an order under section 43 above is in the care of a local authority.

(4) Where a child is under the supervision of any person in pursuance of this section the jurisdiction possessed by a court to vary any financial provision order in the child's favour or any order made with respect to his custody or education under this Part of this Act shall, subject to any rules of court, be exercisable at the instance of that court itself.

(5) The court shall have power from time to time by an order under this section to vary or discharge any provision made in pursuance of this section.

(6) Subject to the following provisions of this subsection, until 1st April 1974 subsection (2) above shall have effect as if for the words "other than a metropolitan district" there were substituted the words "county borough".

An order (or orders) made under section 273 (2) of the Local Government Act 1972 may appoint an earlier date (or, as the case may be, different dates for different purposes or areas) on which subsection (2) above shall cease to have effect as mentioned above.

PART IV

MISCELLANEOUS AND SUPPLEMENTAL

45. Declarations of legitimacy, etc.

(1) Any person who is a British subject, or whose right to be deemed a British subject depends wholly or in part on his legitimacy or on the validity of any marriage, may, if he is domiciled in England and Wales or in Northern Ireland or claims any real or personal estate situate in England and Wales, apply by petition to the High Court for a decree declaring that he is the legitimate child of his parents, or that the marriage of his father and mother or of his grandfather and grandmother was a valid marriage or that his own marriage was a valid marriage.

(2) Any person claiming that he or his parent or any remoter ancestor became or has become a legitimated person may apply by petition to the High Court, or may apply to a county court in the manner prescribed by county court rules, for a decree declaring that he or his parent or remoter ancestor, as the case may be, became or has become a legitimated person.

In this subsection "legitimated person" means a person legitimated by the Legitimacy Act 1926, and includes a person recognised under section 8 of that Act as legitimated.

(3) Where an application under subsection (2) above is made to a county court, the county court, if it considers that the case is one which owing to the value of the property involved or otherwise ought to be dealt with by the High Court, may, and if so ordered by the High Court shall, transfer the matter to the High Court; and on such a transfer the proceeding shall be continued in the High Court as if it had been originally commenced by petition to the court.

(4) Any person who is domiciled in England and Wales or in Northern Ireland or claims any real or personal estate situate in England and Wales may apply to the High Court for a decree declaring his right to be deemed a British subject.

(5) Applications to the High Court under the preceding provisions of this section may be included in the same petition, and on any application under the preceding provisions of this section the High Court or, as the case may be, the county court shall make such decree as it thinks just, and the decree shall be binding on Her Majesty and all other persons whatsoever, so however that the decree shall not prejudice any person—

(a) if it is subsequently proved to have been obtained by fraud or collusion; or

(b) unless that person has been given notice of the application in the manner prescribed by rules of court or made a party to the proceedings or claims through a person so given notice or made a party.

(6) A copy of every application under this section and of any affidavit accompanying it shall be delivered to the Attorney-General at least one month before the application is made, and the Attorney-General shall be a respondent on the hearing of the application and on any subsequent proceedings relating thereto.

(7) Where any application is made under this section, such persons as the court hearing the application thinks fit shall, subject to rules of court, be given notice of the application in the manner prescribed by rules of court, and any such persons may be permitted to become parties to the proceedings and to oppose the application.

(8) No proceedings under this section shall affect any final judgment or decree already pronounced or made by any court of competent jurisdiction.

(9) The court hearing an application under this section may direct that the whole or any part of the proceedings shall be heard in camera, and an application for a direction under this subsection shall be heard in camera unless the court otherwise directs.

46.—[Repealed]

47. Matrimonial relief and declarations of validity in respect of polygamous marriages

(1) A court in England and Wales shall not be precluded from granting matrimonial relief or making a declaration concerning the validity of a marriage by reason only that the marriage in question was entered into under a law which permits polygamy.

(2) In this section "matrimonial relief" means—

(a) any decree under Part I of this Act;

(b) a financial provision order under section 27 above;

(c) an order under section 35 above altering a maintenance agreement;

(d) an order under any provision of this Act which confers a power exercisable in connection with, or in connection with proceedings for, any such decree or order as is mentioned in paragraphs (a) to (c) above;

(e) an order under the Matrimonial Proceedings (Magistrates' Courts) Act 1960.

(3) In this section "a declaration concerning the validity of a marriage" means—

(a) a declaration that a marriage is valid or invalid; and

(b) any other declaration involving a determination as to the validity of a marriage;

being a declaration in a decree granted under section 45 above or a declaration made in the exercise by the High Court of its jurisdiction to grant declaratory relief in any proceedings notwithstanding that a declaration is the only substantive relief sought in those proceedings.

(4) This section has effect whether or not either party to the marriage in question has for the time being any spouse additional to the other party; and provision may be made by rules of court—

(a) for requiring notice of proceedings brought by virtue of this section to be served on any such other spouse; and

(b) for conferring on any such other spouse the right to be heard in any such proceedings.

in such cases as may be prescribed by the rules.

48. Evidence

(1) The evidence of a husband or wife shall be admissible in any proceedings to prove that marital intercourse did or did not take place between them during any period.

(2) In any proceedings for nullity of marriage, evidence on the question of sexual capacity shall be heard in camera unless in any case the judge is satisfied that in the interests of justice any such evidence ought to be heard in open court.

49. Parties to proceedings under this Act

(1) Where in a petition for divorce or judicial separation, or in any other pleading praying for either form of relief, one party to a marriage alleges that the other has committed adultery, he or she shall make the person alleged to have committed adultery with the other party to the marriage a party to the proceedings unless excused by the court on special grounds from doing so.

(2) Rules of court may, either generally or in such cases as may be prescribed by the rules, exclude the application of subsection (1) above where the person alleged to have committed adultery with the other party to the marriage is not named in the petition or other pleading.

(3) Where in pursuance of subsection (1) above a person is made a party to proceedings for divorce or judicial separation, the court may, if after the close of the evidence on the part of the person making the allegation of adultery it is of opinion that there is not sufficient evidence against the person so made a party, dismiss him or her from the suit.

(4) Rules of court make provision, in cases not falling within subsection (1) above, with respect to the joinder as parties to proceedings under this Act of persons involved in allegations of adultery or other improper conduct made in those proceedings, and with respect to the dismissal from such proceedings of any parties so joined; and rules of court made by virtue of this subsection may make different provision for different cases.

(5) In every case in which adultery with any party to a suit is alleged against any person not made a party to the suit or in which the court considers, in the interest of any person not already a party to the suit, that that person should be made a party to the suit, the court may if it thinks fit allow that person to intervene upon such terms, if any, as the court thinks just.

50. Matrimonial causes rules

(1) The authority having power to make rules of court for the purposes of—
  (a) this Act, the Matrimonial Causes Act 1967 (which confers jurisdiction on county courts in certain matrimonial proceedings), section 45 of the Courts Act 1971 (transfer of matrimonial proceedings between High Court and county court, etc.) and sections 26 to 28A of the Matrimonial Causes Act 1965 (maintenance of survivor from estate of deceased former spouse);
  (b) proceedings in the High Court or a divorce county court for an order under section 7 of the Matrimonial Homes Act 1967 (transfer of protected or statutory tenancy under Rent Act 1968 on dissolution or annulment of marriage);
  (c) certain other proceedings in the High Court, that is to say—
    (i) proceedings in the High Court under section 17 of the Married

Women's Property Act 1882, not being proceedings in the divorce registry treated by virtue of rules made under this section for the purposes of section 45 of the Courts Act 1971 as pending in a county court;

(ii) proceedings in the High Court under section 1 of the Matrimonial Homes Act 1967 (rights of occupation of matrimonial home for spouse not otherwise entitled);

(iii) proceedings in which the only substantive relief sought is a declaration with respect to a person's matrimonial status;

(*d*) any enactment passed after this Act which relates to any matter dealt with in this Act, the Matrimonial Causes Act 1967 or sections 26 to 28A of the Matrimonial Causes Act 1965; or

(*e*) any enactment contained in Part II or of Schedule 1 to the Domicile and Matrimonial Proceedings Act 1973 which does not fall within paragraph (*d*) above.

shall, subject to the exceptions listed in subsection (2) below, be the Lord Chancellor together with any four or more of the following persons, namely, the President of the Family Division, one puisne judge attached to that division, one registrar of the divorce registry, two Circuit judges, one registrar appointed under the County Courts Act 1959, two practising barristers being members of the General Council of the Bar and two practising solicitors of whom one shall be a member of the Council of the Law Society and the other a member of the Law Society and also of a local law society.

All the members of the authority, other than the Lord Chancellor himself and the President of the Family Division, shall be appointed by the Lord Chancellor for such time as he may think fit.

(2) The following shall be excepted from the purposes mentioned in subsection (1) above—

(*a*) proceedings in a county court in the exercise of a jurisdiction exercisable by any county court whether or not it is a divorce county court, that is to say, proceedings in a county court under section 32, 33, 36, 38 or 45 above or under section 26 or 27 of the Matrimonial Causes Act 1965;

(*b*) section 47 above, in so far as it relates to proceedings in a county court under section 45 above or to proceedings for an order under the Matrimonial Proceedings (Magistrates' Courts) Act 1960;

(*c*) any enactment passed after this Act in so far as it relates to proceedings in a county court in the exercise of any such jurisdiction as is mentioned in paragraph (*a*) above or to any aspect of section 47 above which is excepted by paragraph (*b*) above.

(3) Rules of court made under this section may apply, with or without modification, any rules of court made under the Supreme Court of Judicature (Consolidation) Act 1925, the County Courts Act 1959 or any other enactment and—

(*a*) may modify or exclude the application of any such rules or of any provision of the County Courts Act 1959;

(*b*) may provide for the enforcement in the High Court of orders made in
a divorce county court;

and, without prejudice to the generality of the preceding provisions, may make
with respect to proceedings in a divorce county court any provision regarding
the Official Solicitor or any solicitor of the Supreme Court which could be made
by rules of court with respect to proceedings in the High Court.

(4) The power to make rules of court by virtue of subsection (1) above shall
be exercisable by statutory instrument, which shall be subject to annulment in
pursuance of a resolution of either House of Parliament.

(5) In this section "divorce county court" means a county court designated
under section 1 of the Matrimonial Causes Act 1967 and "divorce registry"
means the principal registry of the Family Division of the High Court.

NOTE
    Sub. s. 1 (*e*) was added by the Domicile and Matrimonial Proceedings Act 1973, s. 6 (2).

---

51. Fees in matrimonial proceedings

The fees to be taken in any proceedings to which rules under section 50 above
apply shall be such as the Lord Chancellor with the concurrence of the Treasury
may from time to time by order made by statutory instrument prescribe.

52. Interpretation

(1) In this Act—

    "adopted" means adopted in pursuance of—

        (*a*) an adoption order made under the Adoption Act 1958, any
previous enactment relating to the adoption of children, the Adoption
Act 1968 or any corresponding enactment of the Parliament of
Northern Ireland: or

        (*b*) an adoption order made in the Isle of Man or any of the Channel
Islands; or

        (*c*) subject to sections 5 and 6 of the Adoption Act 1968, an over-
seas adoption within the meaning of section 4 of that Act;

    "child", in relation to one or both of the parties to a marriage, includes an
illegitimate or adopted child of that party or, as the case may be, of
both parties;

    "child of the family", in relation to the parties to a marriage, means—

        (*a*) a child of both of those parties; and

        (*b*) any other child, not being a child who has been boarded-out
with those parties by a local authority or voluntary organisation, who
has been treated by both of those parties as a child of their family;

    "the court" (except where the context otherwise requires) means the High
Court or, where a county court has jurisdiction by virtue of the Matrimonial Causes Act 1967, a county court;

    "custody", in relation to a child, includes access to the child;

    "education" includes training.

(2) In this Act—

    (*a*) references to financial provision orders, periodical payments and secured periodical payments orders and orders for the payment of a lump sum, and references to property adjustment orders, shall be construed in accordance with section 21 above; and

    (*b*) references to orders for maintenance pending suit and to interim orders for maintenance shall be construed respectively in accordance with section 22 and section 27 (5) above.

(3) For the avoidance of doubt it is hereby declared that references in this Act to remarriage include references to a marriage which is by law void or voidable.

(4) Except where the contrary intention is indicated, references in this Act to any enactment include references to that enactment as amended, extended or applied by or under any subsequent enactment, including this Act.

53. Transitional provisions and savings

Schedule 1 to this Act shall have effect for the purpose of—

    (*a*) the transition to the provisions of this Act from the law in force before the commencement of this Act;

    (*b*) the preservation for limited purposes of certain provisions superseded by provisions of this Act or by enactments repealed and replaced by this Act; and

    (*c*) the assimilation in certain respects to orders under this Act of orders made, or deemed to have been made, under the Matrimonial Causes Act 1965.

54. Consequential amendments and repeals

(1) Subject to the provisions of Schedule 1 to this Act—

    (*a*) the enactments specified in Schedule 2 to this Act shall have effect subject to the amendments specified in that Schedule, being amendments consequential on the provisions of this Act or on enactments repealed by this Act; and

    (*b*) the enactments specfied in Schedule 3 to this Act are hereby repealed to the extent specified in the third column of that Schedule.

(2) The amendment of any enactment by Schedule 2 to this Act shall not be taken as prejudicing the operation of section 38 of the Interpretation Act 1889 (which relates to the effect of repeals).

55. Citation, commencement and extent

(1) This Act may be cited as the Matrimonial Causes Act 1973.

(2) This Act shall come into force on such day as the Lord Chancellor may appoint by order made by statutory instrument.

(3) Subject to the provisions of paragraphs 3 (2) and 7 (3) of Schedule 2 below, this Act does not extend to Scotland or Northern Ireland.

SCHEDULES

SCHEDULE I

TRANSITIONAL PROVISIONS AND SAVINGS

PART I

MISCELLANEOUS AND GENERAL

General transitional provisions and savings

1. Without prejudice to the provisions of section 38 of the Interpretation Act 1889 (which relates to the effect of repeals)—

    (*a*) nothing in any repeal made by this Act shall affect any order or rule made, direction given or thing done, or deemed to have been made, given or done, under any enactment repealed by this Act, and every such order, rule, direction or thing shall, if in force at the commencement of this Act, continue in force, so far as it could have been made, given or done under this Act, be deemed to have been made, given or done under the corresponding provisions of this Act; and

    (*b*) any reference in any document (including an enactment) to any enactment repealed by this Act, whether a specific reference or a reference to provisions of a description which includes, or apart from any repeal made by this Act includes, the enactment so repealed, shall be construed as a reference to the corresponding enactment in this Act.

2. Without prejudice to paragraph 1 above, but subject to paragraph 3 below, any application made or proceeding begun, or deemed to have been made or begun, under any enactment repealed by this Act, being an application or proceeding which is pending at the commencement of this Act, shall be deemed to have been made or begun under the corresponding provision of this Act.

3. Nothing in Part I of this Act shall apply in relation to any petition for divorce or judicial separation presented before 1st January 1971 and notwithstanding any repeal or amendment made by this Act the Matrimonial Causes Act 1965 (hereafter in this Schedule referred to as the Act of 1965) and any rules of court made for the purposes of that Act shall continue to have effect in relation to proceedings on any such petition which are pending at the commencement of this Act as they had effect immediately before the commencement of this Act.

4. Notwithstanding any repeal or amendment made by this Act the Act of 1965 and any rules of court made for the purposes of that Act shall continue to have effect in relation to—

    (*a*) any proceedings on a petition for damages for adultery or for restitution of conjugal rights presented before 1st January 1971 which are pending at the commencement of this Act, and

    (*b*) any proceedings for relief under section 21 or 34 (1) (*c*) of the Act of 1965 brought in connection with proceedings on a petition for restitution of conjugal rights so presented, being proceedings for relief which are themselves pending at the commencement of this Act,

as they had effect immediately before the commencement of this Act; and nothing in Schedule 2 below shall affect the operation of any other enactment in relation to any such proceedings.

5. Nothing in any repeal made by this Act shall affect any order made, or deemed to have been made, under the Act of 1965 which was continued in force by paragraph 1 of Schedule 1 to the Matrimonial Proceedings and Property Act 1970 notwithstanding the repeal by the last-mentioned Act of the provision of the Act of 1965 under which the order had effect, and every such order shall, if in force at the commencement of this Act, continue in force subject to the provisions of this Act.

6. Nothing in sections 11 to 14 or 16 of this Act affects any law or custom relating to the marriage of members of the Royal Family.

7. Nothing in section 50 (1) (*a*) or (*c*) above affects—

(*a*) any rules of court made under the Supreme Court of Judicature (Consolidation) Act 1925 for the purposes of proceedings under section 39 of the Act of 1965 and having effect by virtue of paragraph 1 (*b*) above iñ relation to proceedings under section 45 above;

(*b*) any rules of court so made for the purposes of proceedings under section 17 of the Married Women's Property Act 1882 or under section 1 of the Matrimonial Homes Act 1967; or

(*c*) any rules of court so made for the purposes of the exercise by the High Court of its jurisdiction to grant declaratory relief in proceedings in which the only substantive relief sought is a declaration with respect to a person's matrimonial status;

but rules of court made under section 50 may revoke any rules of court made under the said Act of 1925 in so far as they apply for any such purposes.

Transitional provisions derived from the Act of 1965

8. Any agreement between the petitioner and the respondent to live separate and apart, whether or not made in writing, shall be disregarded for the purposes of section 1 (2) (*c*) above (including that paragraph as it applies, by virtue of section 17 above, to proceedings for judicial separation) if the agreement was entered into before 1st January 1938 and either—

(*a*) at the time when the agreement was made the respondent had deserted the petitioner without cause; or

(*b*) the court is satisfied that the circumstances in which the agreement was made and the parties proceeded to live separate and apart were such as, but for the agreement, to amount to desertion of the petitioner by the respondent.

9. Where the party chargeable under a maintenance agreement within the meaning of section 24 above died before 17th August 1957, then—

(*a*) subsection (1) of that section shall not apply to the agreement unless there remained undistributed on that date assets of that party's estate (apart from any property in which he had only a life interest) representing not less than four-fifths of the value of that estate for probate after providing for the discharge of the funeral, testamentary and administrative expenses, debts and liabilities payable thereout (other than any liability arising by virtue of that subsection); and

(*b*) nothing in that subsection shall render liable to recovery, or impose any liability upon the personal representatives of that party in respect of, any part of that party's estate which had been distributed before that date.

10. No right or liability shall attach by virtue of section 34 (1) above in respect of any sum payable under a maintenance agreement within the meaning of that section in respect of a period before 17th August 1957.

PART II
PRESERVATION FOR LIMITED PURPOSES OF CERTAIN PROVISIONS OF PREVIOUS ENACTMENTS
Nullity

11.—(1) Subject to sub-paragraphs (2) and (3) below, a marriage celebrated before 1st August 1971 shall (without prejudice to any other grounds on which a marriage celebrated before that date is by law void or voidable) be voidable on the ground—

(a) that the marriage has not been consummated owing to the wilful refusal of the respondent to consummate it; or

(b) that at the time of the marriage either party to the marriage—

    (i) was of unsound mind, or

    (ii) was suffering from mental disorder within the meaning of the Mental Health Act 1959 of such a kind or to such an extent as to be unfitted for marriage and the procreation of children, or

    (iii) was subject to recurrent attacks of insanity or epilepsy; or

(c) that the respondent was at the time of the marriage suffering from venereal disease in a communicable form; or

(d) that the respondent was at the time of the marriage pregnant by some person other than the petitioner.

(2) In relation to a marriage celebrated before 1st November 1960, for heads (ii) and (iii) of sub-paragraph (1) (b) above there shall be substituted the following heads—

"(ii) was a mental defective within the meaning of the Mental Deficiency Acts 1913 to 1938, or

(iii) was subject to recurrent fits of insanity or epilepsy; or".

(3) The court shall not grant a decree of nullity in a case falling within sub-paragraph (1) (b), (c) or (d) above unless it is satisfied that—

(a) the petitioner was at the time of the marriage ignorant of the facts alleged; and

(b) proceedings were instituted within a year from the date of the marriage; and

(c) marital intercourse with the consent of the petitioner has not taken place since the petitioner discovered the existence of the grounds for a decree;

and where the proceedings with respect to the marriage are instituted after 31st July 1971 the application of section 13 (1) above in relation to the marriage shall be without prejudice to the preceding provisions of this sub-paragraph.

(4) Nothing in this paragraph shall be construed as validating a marriage which is by law void but with respect to which a decree of nullity has not been granted.

12. Where a decree of nullity was granted on or before 31st July 1971 in respect of a voidable marriage, any child who would have been the legitimate child of the parties to the marriage if at the date of the decree it had been dissolved instead of being annulled shall be deemed to be their legitimate child.

Succession on intestacy in case of judicial separation

13. Section 18 (2) above shall not apply in a case where the death occurred before 1st August 1970, but section 20 (3) of the Act of 1965 (which provides that certain property of a wife judicially separated from her husband shall devolve, on her death intestate, as if her husband had then been dead) shall continue to apply in any such case.

Validation of certain void or voidable decrees

14. Any decree of divorce, nullity of marriage or judicial separation which, apart from this paragraph, would be void or voidable on the ground only that the provisions of section 33 of the Act of 1965 (restriction on the making of decrees of dissolution or separation where children are affected) or of section 2 of the Matrimonial Proceedings (Children) Act 1958 (corresponding provision replaced by section 33) had not been complied with when the decree was made absolute or granted, as the case may be, shall be deemed always to have been valid unless—

(*a*) the court declared the decree to be void before 1st January 1971, or

(*b*) in proceedings for the annulment of the decree pending at that date the court has before the commencement of this Act declared or after that commencement declares the decree to be void.

PART III

ASSIMILATION IN CERTAIN RESPECTS TO ORDERS UNDER THIS ACT OF ORDERS MADE, ETC., UNDER THE ACT OF 1965, ETC.

Cesser on remarriage of orders made, etc., under the Act of 1965 and recovery of sums mistakenly paid thereafter

15.—(1) An order made, or deemed to have been made, under section 16 (1) (*a*) or (*b*) of the Act of 1965 (including either of those paragraphs as applied by section 16 (3) or by section 19) shall, notwithstanding anything in the order, cease to have effect on the remarriage after the commencement of this Act of the person in whose favour the order was made, except in relation to any arrears due under it on the date of the remarriage.

(2) An order for the payment of alimony made, or deemed to have been made, under section 20 of the Act of 1965, and an order made, or deemed to have been made, under section 21 or 22 of that Act shall, if the marriage of the parties to the proceedings in which the order was made was or is subsequently dissolved or annulled but the order continues in force, cease to have effect on the remarriage after the commencement of this Act of the party in whose favour the order was made, except in relation to any arrears due under it on the date of the remarriage.

16. Section 38 above shall apply in relation to an order made or deemed to have been made under section 16 (1) (including that subsection as applied by section 16 (3) and by section 19), 20 (1), 21 or 22 of the Act of 1965 as it applies in relation to a periodical payments or secured periodical payments order in favour of a party to a marriage.

Variation, etc., of certain orders made, etc., under the Act of 1965

17.—(1) Subject to the provisions of this paragraph, section 31 above shall apply, as it applies to the orders mentioned in subsection (2) thereof, to an order (other than an order for the payment of a lump sum) made or deemed to have been made under any of the following provisions of the Act of 1965, that is to say—

(*a*) section 15 (except in its application to proceedings for restitution of conjugal rights);

(*b*) section 16 (1) (including that subsection as applied by section 16 (3) and by section 19);

(*c*) section 20 (1) and section 17 (2) as applied by section 20 (2);

(*d*) section 22;

(*e*) section 34 (1) (*a*) or (*b*), in so far as it relates to the maintenance of a child, and section 34 (3).

(2) Subject to the provisions of this paragraph, the court hearing an application for the variation of an order made or deemed to have been made under any of the provisions of the Act of 1965 mentioned in sub-paragraph (1) above shall have power to vary that order in any way in which it would have power to vary it had the order been made under the corresponding provision of Part II of this Act.

(3) Section 31, as it applies by virtue of sub-paragraph (1) above, shall have effect as if for subsections (4), (5) and (6) there were substituted the following subsections—

"(4) The court shall not exercise the powers conferred by this section in relation to an order made or deemed to have been made under section 17 (2) of the Act of 1965, as applied by section 20 (2) of that Act, in connection with the grant of a decree of judicial separation except on an application made in proceedings—

>   (*a*) for the rescission of that decree, or
>   (*b*) for the dissolution of the marriage in question.

(5) No order for the payment of a lump sum and no property adjustment order shall be made on an application for the variation of any order made or deemed to have been made under section 16 (1) (including that subsection as applied by section 16 (3) or by section 19), 20 (1), 22, 34 (1) (*a*) or (*b*) or 34 (3) of the Act of 1965.

(6) In the case of an order made or deemed to have been made under section 16 (1) (including that subsection as applied by section 16 (3) or by section 19), 22 or 34 (3) of the Act of 1965 and requiring a party to a marriage to secure an annual sum or periodical payments to any other person, an application under this section relating to that order may be made after the death of the person liable to make payments under the order by the person entitled to the payments or by the personal representatives of the deceased person, but no such application shall, except with the permission of the court, be made after the end of the period of six months from the date on which representation in regard to the estate of that person is first taken out'';

and in that section, as it so applies, the reference in subsection (8) to a secured periodical payments order shall be construed as a reference to any such order as is mentioned in subsection (6).

(4) In relation to an order made before 16th December 1949 on or after granting a decree of divorce or nullity of marriage and deemed, by virtue of paragraph 1 of Schedule 1 to the Act of 1965, to have been made under section 16 (1) (*a*) of that Act (secured provision), the powers conferred by this paragraph shall not be exercised unless the court is satisfied that the case is one of exceptional hardship which cannot be met by discharge, variation or suspension of any other order made by reference to that decree, being an order made, or deemed by virtue of that paragraph to have been made, under section 16 (1) (*b*) of that Act (unsecured periodical payments).

18.—(1) Subsections (1) and (3) of section 31 above shall apply to an order made or deemed to have been made under section 15 of the Act of 1965 in its application to proceedings for restitution of conjugal rights, or under section 21 or 34 (1) (*c*) of that Act, as they apply to the orders mentioned in subsection (2) of section 31.

(2) In exercising the powers conferred by virtue of this paragraph the court shall have regard to all the circumstances of the case, including any change in any of the matters to which the court was required to have regard when making the order to which the application relates.

19. Section 42 (7) above shall apply in relation to an order for the custody or education of a child made or deemed to have been made under section 34 of the Act of 1965, and in relation to an order for the custody of a child made or deemed to have been made under section 35 of that Act, as it applies in relation to an order made under section 42.

Orders made under the Act of 1965 to count as orders under this Act for certain purposes

20. The power of the court under section 23 (1) or 2 (*a*) or 42 (1) (*a*) above to make from time to time a financial provision order or, as the case may be, an order for custody or education in relation to a child of the family shall be exercisable notwithstanding the making of a previous order or orders in relation to the child

under section 34 (1) (*a*) of the Act of 1965; and where the court has made an order in relation to a child under section 34 (1) (*b*) of that Act sections 23 (4) and 42 (6) above shall apply respectively in relation to that child as if the order were an order made under section 23 (2) (*b*) or section 42 (1) (*b*), as the case may be.

21. Where the court has made an order under section 22 of the Act of 1965 the court shall have the like power to make orders under section 42 above with respect to the custody of any child of the family as it has where it makes an order under section 27 above.

Applications of provisions of this Act with respect to enforcement of arrears and recovery of excessive payments to certain orders made, etc., under the Act of 1965

22. Section 32 above shall apply in relation to the enforcement, by proceedings begun after 1st January 1971 (whether before or after the commencement of this Act), of the payment of arrears due under an order made, or deemed to have been made, under any of the following provisions of the Act of 1965, that is to say—

(*a*) section 15;
(*b*) section 16 (1) (including that subscription as applied by section 16 (3) **and** by section 19);
(*c*) section 20 (1);
(*d*) section 21;
(*e*) section 22;
(*f*) section 34 (1), in so far as it relates to the maintenance of a child, and section 34 (3);

as it applies in relation to the enforcement of the payment of arrears due under any such order as is mentioned in that section.

23. Section 33 above shall apply to an order (other than an order for the payment of a lump sum) made or deemed to have been made under any of the provisions of the Act of 1965 mentioned in paragraph 22 above as it applies to the orders mentioned in section 33 (2).

Avoidance under this Act of transactions intended to defeat claims for relief and relief granted under the Act of 1965

24.—(1) Section 37 above shall apply in relation to proceedings for relief under section 21 or 34 (1) (*c*) of the Act of 1965 continuing by virtue of paragraph 4 (*b*) above as it applies in relation to proceedings for relief under any of the provisions of this Act specified in section 37 (1).

(2) Without prejudice to sub-paragraph (1) above, section 37 shall also apply where an order has been obtained under any of the following provisions of the Act of 1965, that is to say—

(*a*) section 16 (1) (including that subsection as applied by section 16 (3) and by section 19);
(*b*) section 17 (2) (including that subsection as applied by section 20 (2));
(*c*) section 20 (1);
(*d*) section 21;
(*e*) section 22;
(*f*) section 24;
(*g*) section 31;
(*h*) section 34 (1), in so far as it relates to the maintenance of a child, and section 34 (3);
(*i*) section 35;

as it applies where an order has been obtained under any of the provisions of this Act specified in section 37 (1).

Care and supervision of children

25. —(1) Sections 43 and 44 above shall apply where the court has jurisdiction by virtue of paragraph 4 (*b*) above to make an order for the custody of a child under section 34 (1) (*c*) of the Act of 1965 as they apply where the court has jurisdiction to make an order for custody under Part III of this Act, but as if the reference in section 43 (2) to a financial provision order in favour of the child were a reference to an order for payments for the maintenance and education of the child.

(2) Without prejudice to the effect of paragraph 1 (*a*) of this Schedule in relation to an order made under section 36 or 37 of the Act of 1965 which could have been made under section 43 or, as the case may be, section 44 above, any order made under section 36 or 37 of that Act by virtue of the jurisdiction of the court to make an order for the custody of a child under section 34 (1) (*c*) of that Act shall be deemed to have been made under section 43 or 44 above, as the case may require.

26. Section 44 (4) above shall apply in relation to the jurisdiction possessed by a court to vary an order made or deemed to have been made with respect to a child's custody, maintenance or education under Part III of the Act of 1965 as it applies in relation to the jurisdiction possessed by a court to vary any financial provision order in a child's favour and any order made with respect to a child's custody or education under Part III of this Act.

SCHEDULE 2

Consequential Amendments

1. In section 225 of the Supreme Court of Judicature (Consolidation) Act 1925 (interpretation), in the definition of "matrimonial cause", for the words from "jactitation" to "rights" there shall be substituted the words "or jactitation of marriage".

2. In section 2 (1) of the Limitation (Enemies and War Prisoners) Act 1945, in the definition of "statute of limitation" for the words "subsection (1) of section seven of the Matrimonial Cuases Act 1937" there shall be substituted the words "section 13 (2) of the Matrimonial Causes Act 1973 and paragraph 11 (3) of Schedule 1 to that Act".

3.—(1) In section 16 of the Maintenance Orders Act 1950 (orders enforceable under Part II of that Act)—

    (*a*) in subsection (2) (*a*), for sub-paragraph (i) there shall be substituted the following sub-paragraph:—

        "(i) sections 15 to 17, 19 to 22, 30, 34 and 35 of the Matrimonial Causes Act 1965 and sections 22, 23 (1), (2) and (4) and 27 of the Matrimonial Causes Act 1973"; and

    (*b*) in subsection (2) (*c*), for sub-paragraph (v) there shall be substituted the following sub-paragraph:—

        "(v) any enactment of the Parliament of Northern Ireland containing provisions corresponding with section 22 (1), 34 or 35 of the Matrimonial Causes Act 1965, with section 22, 23 (1), (2) or (4) or 27 of the Matrimonial Causes Act 1973, or with section 12 (2) of the Guardianship of Minors Act 1971".

(2) Sub-paragraph (1) above extends to Scotland and Northern Ireland, and the references to section 16 (2) (*c*) of the Maintenance Orders Act 1950 in paragraph 8 of Schedule 8 to the Administration of Justice Act 1970 and paragraph 9 of Schedule 1 to the Attachment of Earnings Act 1971 shall be construed as references to section 16 (2) (*c*) as amended by sub-paragraph (1) (*b*) above.

4. In section 109 (2) of the County Courts Act 1959 (proceedings in which appeals on questions of fact are to lie) the following paragraph shall be inserted after paragraph (*f*) (in place of the paragraph inserted by section 34 (2) of the Matrimonial Proceedings and Property Act 1970):—

"(*g*) any proceedings on an application under section 13A of the Matrimonial Proceedings (Magistrates' Courts) Act 1960 or under section 33, 36 or 38 of the Matrimonial Causes Act 1973".

5.—(1) In section 26 of the Matrimonial Causes Act 1965 (orders for maintenance of survivor from estate of deceased former spouse)—

(*a*) in subsection (4) (matters to which the court is to have regard on an application under the section), in paragraph (*c*) the following sub-paragraph shall be inserted after sub-paragraph (ii) (in place of the sub-paragraph inserted by paragraph 1 (1) of Schedule 2 to the Matrimonial Proceedings and Property Act 1970):—

"(iii) where the survivor is a former wife or a former husband of the deceased, for an order under section 2 or 4 of the Matrimonial Proceedings and Property Act 1970 or under section 23 (1) (*a*), (*b*) or (*c*) or 24 of the Matrimonial Causes Act 1973";

(*b*) in subsection (6), the words "means the High Court and" inserted by paragraph 8 of Schedule 1 to the Divorce Reform Act 1969 (after the word "court" where first occurring in the definition of "court" inserted in that subsection by section 7 (4) of the Family Provision Act 1966) shall continue to have effect notwithstanding the repeal by this Act of the Divorce Reform Act 1969;

(*c*) in subsection (6), in the definition of "former spouse", for the words "this Act" there shall be substituted the words "the Matrimonial Causes Act 1973".

(2) In section 42 of that Act (provisions as to condonation), at the beginning of subsections (1) and (3) there shall be inserted the words "For the purposes of the Matrimonial Proceedings (Magistrates' Courts) Act 1960".

6.—(1) In section 2 of the Matrimonial Causes Act 1967 (jurisdiction of divorce county court with respect to ancillary relief and the protection of children)—

(*a*) in subsection (1), for the words "Part II or Part III of the Matrimonial Causes Act 1965" there shall be substituted the words "Part II or Part III of the Matrimonial Causes Act 1973", and for the words "section 22 or section 24 of that Act" in the subsection as originally enacted there shall be substituted the words "section 27 or 35 of that Act" (in place of the words substituted for the words originally enacted by paragraph 2 (1) (*a*) of Schedule 2 to the Matrimonial Proceedings and Property Act 1970);

(*b*) for subsection (3) as originally enacted there shall be substituted the following subsection (in place of that substituted by paragraph 2 (1) (*b*) of Schedule 2 to the Matrimonial Proceedings and Property Act 1970):—

"(3) A divorce county court shall not by virtue of this section have jurisdiction to exercise any power under section 32, 33, 36 or 38 of the Matrimonial Causes Act 1973; but nothing in this section shall prejudice the exercise by a county court of any jurisdiction conferred on county courts by any of those sections"; and

(*c*) in subsection (4) as originally enacted, for the words from "section 24" to the end of the subsection there shall be substituted the words "section 35 of the Matrimonial Causes Act 1973" (in place of the words substituted for the words originally enacted by paragraph 2 (1) (*c*) of Schedule 2 to the Matrimonial Proceedings and Property Act 1970).

(2) In section 3 of that Act (consideration of agreements or arrangements by divorce county courts) for the words "section 5 (2) of the Matrimonial Causes Act 1965" there shall be substituted the words "section 7 of the Matrimonial Causes Act 1973".

(3) In section 10 of that Act (interpretation), in the definition of "matrimonial cause" in subsection (1), for the words from "section 2 of the Matrimonial Causes Act 1965" to "that Act" there shall be substituted the words "section 3 of the Matrimonial Causes Act 1973".

7.—(1) In subsection (1) of section 2 of the Domestic and Appellate Proceedings (Restriction of Publicity) Act 1968 (restriction of publicity for certain proceedings) for the words in paragraph (*a*) "section 39 of the Matrimonial Causes Act 1965" there shall be substituted the words "section 45 of the Matrimonial Causes Act 1973", the following paragraph shall be substituted for the paragraph (*c*) inserted in the subsection by paragraph 3 of Schedule 2 to the Matrimonial Proceedings and Property Act 1970:—

> "(*c*) proceedings under section 27 of the Matrimonial Causes Act 1973 (which relates to proceedings by a wife against her husband, or by a husband against his wife, for financial provision) and any proceedings for the discharge or variation of an order made under that section or for the temporary suspension of any provision of any such order or the revival of the operation of any provision so suspended";

subsection (2) of that section shall be omitted, and the references in subsection (3) of that section to subsection (1) and to subsection (1) (*a*) thereof shall be construed as references to subsection (1) and to subsection (1) (*a*) as they respectively have effect by virtue of this sub-paragraph.

(2) In section 4 (3) of that Act, for the words "or 2 (2) of this Act" there shall be substituted the words "of this Act or to section 45 (9) of the Matrimonial Causes Act 1973".

(3) Sub-paragraph (2) above extends to Northern Ireland.

8. In section 7 of the Family Law Reform Act 1969 (commital of wards of court to care of local authority and supervision of wards of court)—

> (*a*) in subsection (3), for the words "section 36 of the Matrimonial Causes Act 1965" there shall be substituted the words "section 43 of the Matrimonial Causes Act 1973";
> (*b*) in subsection (4), for the words from "subsections (2)" to "1965" there shall be substituted the words "section 44 (2) of the Matrimonial Causes Act 1973".

9. In section 63 (6) of the Children and Young Persons Act 1969 (local authority functions to be the subject of reports to Parliament by the Secretary of State), in paragraph (*g*), for the words "section 37 of the Matrimonial Causes Act 1965" there shall be substituted the words "section 44 of the Matrimonial Causes Act 1973".

10.—(1) In Schedule 1 to the Administration of Justice Act 1970 (High Court business assigned to the Family Division)—

> (*a*) for the words (in the first paragraph) "section 7 (1) of the Matrimonial Causes Act 1967" there shall be substituted the words "section 50 (1) of the Matrimonial Causes Act 1973";
> (*b*) the paragraphs relating respectively to proceedings for a declaration, to proceedings under section 17 of the Married Women's Property Act 1882, and to proceedings under section 1 of the Matrimonial Homes Act 1967 shall be omitted; and
> (*c*) for the words (in the last paragraph) "section 24 of the Matrimonial Causes Act 1965" there shall be substituted the words "section 35 of the Matrimonial Causes Act 1973".

(2) In Schedule 8 to that Act (as it applies to define maintenance orders for both the purposes of Part II of that Act and for the purposes of the Maintenance Orders Act 1958) the following paragraph shall be inserted after paragraph 2:—

"2A. An order for periodical or other payments made, or having effect as if made, under Part II of the Matrimonial Causes Act 1973".

11. In Schedule 1 to the Local Authority Social Services Act 1970 the entry relating to section 37 of the Matrimonial Causes Act 1965 shall be omitted, and the following entry shall be added at the end of the Schedule—

"Matrimonial Causes Act 1973   Supervision of child subject to court
    Section 44   order in matrimonial proceedings".

12. In section 45 of the Courts Act 1971 (transfer of matrimonial proceedings between High Court and county court, etc.)—

(a) in subsection (1), for paragraphs (a) and (b) there shall be substituted the following paragraphs:—

"(a) sections 26 to 28A of the Matrimonial Causes Act 1965;
(b) Part II or Part III of the Matrimonial Causes Act 1973";

(b) in subsection (6), after the word "under" there shall be inserted the words "section 50 of the Matrimonial Causes Act 1973 for the purposes of"; and

(c) subsection (7) shall be omitted.

13. In Schedule 1 to the Attachment of Earnings Act 1971 (maintenance orders to which the Act applies) for paragraph 3 there shall be substituted the following paragraph—

"3. An order for periodical or other payments made, or having effect as if made, under Part II of the Matrimonial Causes Act 1973".

SCHEDULE 3

ENACTMENTS REPEALED

Chapter	Short Title	Extent of Repeal
1965 c. 72.	The Matrimonial Causes Act 1965.	The whole Act, except: section 8 (2); sections 26 to 28A and section 25 (4) and (5) as applied by section 28 (2); section 42; in section 43 (1) the words from "but a husband" to the end of the subsection; in section 46, subsection (1) and in subsection (4) the words from "this Act does not" to the end of the subsection.
1967 c. 56.	The Matrimonial Causes Act 1967.	Sections 7 and 8.
1967 c. 80.	The Criminal Justice Act 1967.	In Part I of Schedule 3, the entry relating to section 36 (6) of the Matrimonial Causes Act 1965.
1968 c. 63.	The Domestic and Appellate Proceedings (Restriction of Publicity) Act 1968.	Sections 2 (2) and 3 (4).

Chapter	Short Title	Extent of Repeal
1969 c. 55.	The Divorce Reform Act 1969.	The whole Act.
1970 c. 31.	The Administration of Justice Act 1970.	In Schedule 1, the paragraphs relating respectively to proceedings for a declaration, to proceedings under section 17 of the Married Women's Property Act 1882, and to proceedings under section 1 of the Matrimonial Homes Act 1967. In Schedule 2, paragraph 27.
1970 c. 33.	The Law Reform (Miscellaneous Provisions) Act 1970.	Section 4.
1972 c. 42.	The Local Authority Social Services Act 1970.	In Schedule 1, the entry relating to section 37 of the Matrimonial Causes Act 1965.
1970 c. 45.	The Matrimonial Proceedings and Property Act 1970.	The whole of Part I. Sections 34, 35, 40, 41 and 42. In section 43, subsection (2) and, in subsection (4), the words from the beginning to "of this Act". The Schedules.
1971 c. 3.	The Guardianship of Minors Act 1971.	In Schedule 1, in the entry relating to section 16 (2) of the Maintenance Orders Act 1950, the words from "and" to "1971'".
1971 c. 23.	The Courts Act 1971.	Section 45 (7). In Schedule 8, paragraph 47.
1971 c. 44.	The Nullity of Marriage Act 1971.	The whole Act.
1972 c. 38.	The Matrimonial Proceedings (Polygamous Marriages) Act 1972.	Sections 1 and 4.
1972 c. 70.	The Local Government Act 1972.	In Schedule 23, paragraph 13.

TABLE OF DERIVATIONS

Showing the Derivations of the Provisions of the Act.

Note:—The following abbreviations are used in this Table—

1965 = The Matrimonial Causes Act 1965
    (1965 c. 72)

1967 = The Matrimonial Causes Act 1967
    (1967 c. 56)

1969 = The Divorce Reform Act 1969
    (1969 c. 55)

1970 = The Matrimonial Proceedings and Property Act 1970
    (1970 c. 45)

1971 = The Nullity of Marriage Act 1971
    (1971 c. 44)

1972 = The Matrimonial Proceedings (Polygamous Marriages) Act 1972
    (1972 c. 38)

R (followed by = The recommendation set out in the paragraph of that number in
a number)   the Appendix to the Report of the Law Commission
    (Cmnd. 5167)

Section of Act	Derivation	Page References
1 (1)	1969, s. 1	15 to 18
(2)	1969, s. 2 (1)	18 to 43
(3)	1969, s. 2 (2)	15
(4)	1969, s. 2 (3)	15
(5)	1965, s. 5 (7)	246
2 (1)	1969, s. 3 (3) (*b*)	24, 26
(2)	1969, s. 3 (3) (*a*)	24
(3)	1969, s. 3 (4)	26
(4)	1969, s. 2 (4)	34
(5)	1969, s. 3 (5)	37, 41, 43
(6)	1969, ss. 2 (5), 3 (6)	39, 40
(7)	1969, s. 2 (6)	228
3 (1)	1965, s. 2 (1)	⎫
(2)	1965, s. 2 (2); 1970, s. 35	⎪
(3)	1965, s. 5 (5)	⎬ 13 to 15, 214
(4)	1965, s. 2 (3)	⎭
4	1965, s. 3; 1969, s. 9 (1), Sch. 1, para. 1	43 to 45
5	1969, s. 4; R. 1	54 to 57
6	1969, s. 3 (1), (2)	17, 217
7	1969, s. 7 (1)	59, 60, 148, 149
8	1965, s. 6	61
9	1965, s. 7	61
10 (1)	1969, s. 5: R. 1	59
(2)–(4)	1969, s. 6; R. 1	57 to 59, 229, 230
11 (*a*)–(*c*)	1971, s. 1	⎫
(*d*)	1972, s. 4	⎬ 78
12	1971, s. 2	78, 79
13	1971, s. 3	79, 80
14	1971, s. 4	80 to 83
15	1965, s. 10	61
16	1971, s. 5	67

Section of Act	Derivation	Page References
17 (1)	1965, s. 12 (1) ; 1969, s. 8 (1), (2)	⎫
(2)	1965, s. 12 (1) ; 1969, s. 8 (2), (3) ;	⎬ 62, 63
	1970, s. 42 (1), Sch. 2, para. 4	⎭
(3)	1965, s. 12 (1) ; 1969, s. 8 (2)	⎫
18 (1)	1965, s. 12 (2)	
(2)	1970, s. 40 (1)	⎬ 64, 65
(3)	1970, s. 40 (2)	⎭
19 (1)–(5)	1965, s. 14	⎫ 51, 52, 91
(6)	1971, s. 6 (2)	⎭
20	1965, s. 5 (6); 1969, s. 9 (1), Sch. 1, para. 3	227
21	—	Chapters 7 and 8
22	1970, s. 1	107 to 109
23 (1)	1970, ss. 2 (1), 3 (1) (*a*), (2)	109 to 119
(2)	1970, s. 3 (1)	114
(3)	1970, ss. 2 (2), 3 (3), (4)	111, 114
(4)	1970, s. 3 (5)	114
(5)	1970, s. 24 (1) (*b*)	110
24 (1), (2)	1970, s. 4	121 to 130
(3)	1970, s. 24 (1) (*b*)	121
25	1970, s. 5	131 to 150
26	1970, s. 24	110, 121, 249
27 (1)–(7)	1970, s. 6	151 to 157
(8)	1965, s. 42, (1), (3)	154
28	1970, s. 7	111, 157
29	1970, s. 8	115, 157
30	1970, s. 25	110, 121
31	1970, s. 9	158 to 162
32	1970, s. 10	163, 212
33 (1)–(4)	1970, s. 11	⎫
(5)	1970, s. 34 (1)	⎬ 164, 165, 212
(6)	1970, s. 11	⎭
34	1970, s. 13	172 to 174
35	1970, s. 14	174 to 176
36	1970, s. 15	176, 212
37 (1)	1970, s. 16 (4)	⎫
(2), (3)	1970, s. 16 (1)	
(4)	1970, s. 16 (2)	
(5)	1970, s. 16 (3)	⎬ 177, 178
(6)	1970, s. 16 (4)	
(7)	1970, s. 16 (5)	
38 (1)–(3)	1970, s. 22	⎭
(4)	1970, s. 34 (1)	⎬ 165, 249
(5)–(7)	1970, s. 22	⎭
39	1970, s. 23	170
40	1970, s. 26	135, 136
41	1970, s. 17	184 to 186
42 (1)	1970, s. 18 (1)	179 to 183
(2)	1970, s 19 (1)	182
(3)	1970, s. 18 (3)	⎫
(4)	1970, s. 18 (4)	⎬ 183
(5)	1970, ss. 18 (2), 19 (2)	—
(6)	1970, ss. 18 (5), 19 (1)	⎫
(7)	1970, ss. 18 (6), 19 (2)	⎬ 179, 180
43 (1)–(7)	1965, s. 36 ; Criminal Justice Act 1967, c. 80, s. 92,	⎫
(8)	Sch. 3, Part I ; 1970, s. 42 (1), Sch. 2, para. 1 (2) ;	⎬ 183
(9)	Local Government Act, 1972, c. 70, s. 273, Sch. 23,	⎭
	para. 13 (1) : R. 2.	
	—	

Section of Act	Derivation	Page References
44	1965, s. 37; 1970, s. 42 (1), Sch. 2, para. 1 (2), (3); Local Government Act, 1972, c. 70, s. 273, Sch. 23, para. 13 (2)	} 183, 184
45 (1)–(8)	1965, s. 39	—
(9)	Domestic and Appellate Proceedings (Restriction of Publicity) Act, 1968, c. 63, s. 2 (2)	
46	1965, s. 40; 1971, s. 7 (2)	Repealed: Domicile and Matrimonial Proceedings Act 1973, Sched. 6. See pp. 90, 91
47	1972, s. 1.	89, 90
48	1965, s. 43	245
49	1965, ss. 4, 44; 1969, s. 9 (1), Sch. 1, para. 2; R. 3	219
50	Act of 1967, s. 7 (Power to make Rules) as amended	—
51	1967, s. 8	
52 (1)	1970, s. 27 (1)	113, 179
(2)	—	
(3)	1970, s. 27 (2)	111
(4)	1970, s. 27 (3); 1972, s. 4 (2)	—
53	[Transitional provisions and savings]	—
54	[Consequential amendments and repeals]	—
55	[Citation, commencement and extent]	—
Sched. 1		
Part I	Proceedings before January 1, 1971	—
Part II	Preservation for Limited Purposes of Certain Provisions in Previous Enactments	
para. 11 (1)	1965, s. 9 (1)	} 73 to 75
(2)	1965, Sch. 1, para. 4	
(3)	1965, s. 9 (2); 1971, s. 3 (4)	
(4)	1965, s. 9 (3)	
12	1965, s. 11	67
13	1970, s. 40 (1), (3)	65
14	1970, s. 29	—
Part III	Assimilation in Certain Respects to Orders under this Act of Orders made etc. under the Act of 1965, etc.	
para. 15	1970, s. 21	166
16	1970, s. 22 (1)	166
17	1970, Sch. 1, para. 3 (1)–(4)	166, 167
18	1970, Sch. 1, para. 3 (5)	—
19	1970, Sch. 1, para. 6	—
20	1970, Sch. 1, para. 11; R. 6	167
21	1970, Sch. 1, para. 12	—
22	1970, Sch. 1, para. 4	167
23	1970, s. 34 (1), Sch. 1, para. 5	167
24	1970, Sch. 1, para. 9; R. 5	167
25	1965, ss. 36, 37; R. 5	—
26	1965, s. 37 (5)	—
Sched. 2	Consequent Amendments	The amendments have been incorporated in the text of the relevant statutes in Appendix 1 to this Book
Sched. 3	Enactments Repealed; R. 8, 9, 10	

DOMICILE AND MATRIMONIAL PROCEEDINGS ACT 1973

(1973 c. 45)

An Act to amend the law relating to the domicile of married women and persons not of full age, to matters connected with domicile and to jurisdiction in matrimonial proceedings including actions for reduction of consistorial decrees; to make further provision about the recognition of divorces and legal separations; and for purposes connected therewith. [25th July 1973]

PART I

DOMICILE

Husband and wife

1. Abolition of wife's dependent domicile

(1) Subject to subsection (2) below, the domicile of a married woman as at any time after the coming into force of this section shall, instead of being the same as her husband's by virtue only of marriage, be ascertained by reference to the same factors as in the case of any other individual capable of having an independent domicile.

(2) Where immediately before this section came into force a woman was married and then had her husband's domicile by dependence, she is to be treated as retaining that domicile (as a domicile of choice, if it is not also her domicile of origin) unless and until it is changed by acquisition or revival of another domicile either on or after the coming into force of this section.

(3) This section extends to England and Wales, Scotland and Northern Ireland.

2. Amendments of Recognition Act consequent on s. 1

(1) The Recognition of Divorces and Legal Separations Act 1971 shall be amended in accordance with this section.

(2) For section 6 of the Act saving for common law rules, and previous enactments, as to recognition) there shall be substituted—

"6. Existing common law and statutory rules

(1). In this section "the common law rules" means the rules of law relating to the recognition of divorces or legal separations obtained in the country of the spouses' domicile or obtained elsewhere and recognised as valid in that country.

(2) In any circumstances in which the validity of a divorce or legal separation obtained in a country outside the British Isles would be recognised by virtue only of the common law rules if either—

(*a*) the spouses had at the material time both been domiciled in that country; or

(*b*) the divorce or separation were recognised as valid under the law of the spouses' domicile,

its validity shall also be recognised if subsection (3) below is satisfied in relation to it.

(3) This subsection is satisfied in relation to a divorce or legal separation obtained in a country outside the British Isles if either—

(*a*) one of the spouses was at the material time domiciled in that country and the divorce or separation was recognised as valid under the law of the domicile of the other spouse; or

(*b*) neither of the spouses having been domiciled in that country at the material time, the divorce or separation was recognised as valid under the law of the domicile of each of the spouses respectively.

(4) For any purpose of subsection (2) or (3) above "the material time", in relation to a divorce or legal separation, means the time of the institution of proceedings in the country in which it was obtained.

(5) Sections 2 to 5 of this Act are without prejudice to the recognition of the validity of divorces and legal separations obtained outside the British Isles by virtue of the common law rules (as extended by this section), or of any enactment other than this Act; but, subject to this section, no divorce or legal separation so obtained shall be recognised as valid in the United Kingdom except as provided by those sections."

(3) In section 7 of the Act (non-recognition of divorce by third country no bar to re-marriage)—

(*a*) for "the foregoing provisions" there shall be substituted "sections 1 to 5 or section 6 (2)"; and

(*b*) for "section 6" there shall be substituted "section 6 (5)".

(4) In section 8 (2) of the Act (particular circumstances in which recognition may be refused)—

(*a*) after "by virtue of" there shall be inserted "sections 2 to 5 or section 6 (2) of"; and

(*b*) for "section 6" there shall be substituted "section 6 (5)".

(5) This section extends to England and Wales, Scotland and Northern Ireland.

Minors and pupils

3. Age at which independent domicile can be aquired

(1) The time at which a person first becomes capable of having an independent domicile shall be when he attains the age of sixteen or marries under that age;

and in the case of a person who immediately before 1st January 1974 was incapable of having an independent domicile, but had then attained the age of sixteen or been married, it shall be that date.

(2) This section extends to England and Wales and Northern Ireland (but not to Scotland).

4. Dependent domicile of child not living with his father

(1) Subsection (2) of this section shall have effect with respect to the dependent domicile of a child as at any time after the coming into force of this section when his father and mother are alive but living apart.

(2) The child's domicile as at that time shall be that of his mother if—

> (a) he then has his home with her and has no home with his father; or
> (b) he has at any time had her domicile by virtue of paragraph (a) above and has not since had a home with his father.

(3) As at any time after the coming into force of this section, the domicile of a child whose mother is dead shall be that which she last had before she died if at her death he had her domicile by virtue of subsection (2) above and he has not since had a home with his father.

(4) Nothing in this section prejudices any existing rule of law as to the cases in which a child's domicile is regarded as being, by dependence, that of his mother.

(5) In this section, "child" means a person incapable of having an independent domicile; and in its application to a child who has been adopted, references to his father and his mother shall be construed as references to his adoptive father and mother.

(6) This section extends to England and Wales, Scotland and Northern Ireland.

PART II

JURISDICTION IN MATRIMONIAL PROCEEDINGS

(ENGLAND AND WALES)

5. Jurisdiction of High Court and county courts

(1) Subsections (2) to (5) below shall have effect, subject to section 6 (3) and (4) of this Act, with respect to the jurisdiction of the court to entertain—

> (a) proceedings for divorce, judicial separation or nullity of marriage; and
> (b) proceedings for death to be presumed and a marriage to be dissolved in pursuance of section 19 of the Matrimonial Causes Act 1973;

and in this Part of this Act "the court" means the High Court and a divorce county court within the meaning of the Matrimonial Causes Act 1967.

(2) The court shall have jurisdiction to entertain proceedings for divorce or judicial separation if (and only if) either of the parties to the marriage—

(*a*) is domiciled in England and Wales on the date when the proceedings are begun; or

(*b*) was habitually resident in England and Wales throughout the period of one year ending with that date.

(3) The court shall have jurisdiction to entertain proceedings for nullity of marriage if (and only if) either of the parties to the marriage—

(*a*) is domiciled in England and Wales on the date when the proceedings are begun; or

(*b*) was habitually resident in England and Wales throughout the period of one year ending with that date; or

(*c*) died before that date and either—

(i) was at death domiciled in England and Wales, or

(ii) had been habitually resident in England and Wales throughout the period of one year ending with the date of death.

(4) The court shall have jurisdiction to entertain proceedings for death to be presumed and a marriage to be dissolved if (and only if) the petitioner—

(*a*) is domiciled in England and Wales on the date when the proceedings are begun; or

(*b*) was habitually resident in England and Wales throughout the period of one year ending with that date.

(5) The court shall, at any time when proceedings are pending in respect of which it has jurisdiction by virtue of subsection (2) or (3) above (or of this subsection), also have jurisdiction to entertain other proceedings, in respect of the same marriage, for divorce, judicial separation or nullity of marriage, notwithstanding that jurisdiction would not be exercisable under subsection (2) or (3).

(6) Schedule 1 to this Act shall have effect as to the cases in which matrimonial proceedings in England and Wales are to be, or may be, stayed by the court where there are concurrent proceedings elsewhere in respect of the same marriage, and as to the other matters dealt with in that Schedule; but nothing in the Schedule—

(*a*) requires or authorises a stay of proceedings which are pending when this section comes into force; or

(*b*) prejudices any power to stay proceedings which is exercisable by the court apart from the Schedule.

6. Miscellaneous amendments, transitional provision and savings

(1) In section 27 (2) of the Matrimonial Causes Act 1973 (which excludes the court's jurisdiction on a maintenance application unless it would have jurisdiction to decree judicial separation), for the words from "unless" onwards there shall be substituted the words "unless—

(*a*) the applicant or the respondent is domiciled in England and Wales on the date of the application; or (*b*) the application has been habitually resident there throughout the period of one year ending with that date; or

(*c*) the respondent is resident there on that date."

(2) In subsection (1) of section 50 of the Matrimonial Causes Act 1973 (scope of the Matrimonial Causes Rules), the word "or" at the end of paragraph (*c*) shall be omitted and after paragraph (*d*) there shall be inserted the following words

"or

(*e*) any enactment contained in Part II of or Schedule 1 to the Domicile and Matrimonial Proceedings Act 1973 which does not fall within paragraph (*d*) above".

(3) No proceedings for divorce shall be entertained by the court by virtue of section 5 (2) or (5) of this Act while proceedings for divorce or nullity of marriage, begun before the commencement of this Act, are pending (in respect of the same marriage) in Scotland, Northern Ireland, the Channel Islands or the Isle of Man; and provision may be made by rules of court as to when for the purposes of this subsection proceedings are to be treated as begun or pending in any of those places.

(4) Nothing in this Part of this Act—

(*a*) shall be construed to remove any limitation imposed on the jurisdiction of a county court by section 1 of the Matrimonial Causes Act 1967;

(*b*) affects the court's jurisdiction to entertain any proceedings begun before the commencement of this Act.

*   *   *   *   *

PART V

MISCELLANEOUS AND GENERAL

15. Extension of Recognition Act to Northern Ireland

(1) The Recognition of Divorces and Legal Separations Act 1971 (as amended by this Act) shall extend to Northern Ireland.

(2) In section 1 of that Act (recognition of divorces etc. as between territories forming part of the British Isles) the following shall be substituted for paragraphs (*a*) and (*b*)—

"if it was granted under the law of any part of the British Isles, be recognised throughout the United Kingdom";

and in each of sections 2, 7 and 8 of that Act for "Great Britain" there shall be substituted "the United Kingdom".

(3) In so far as section 1 of that Act operates as part of the law of Northern Ireland, it shall do so only in relation to a decree of divorce or judicial separation granted after the coming into force of this section; and as respects the recognition in Northern Ireland of any such divorce or separation as is referred to in

section 10 (4) of the Act (transitional provisions) that subsection shall have effect as if any reference in it to the date of the commencement of the provisions of the Act there referred to were a reference to the date of the coming into force of this section.

(4) This section shall be deemed for the purposes of section 6 of the Government of Ireland Act 1920 to have been passed before the day referred to in that section as the appointed day.

16. Non-judicial divorces

(1) No proceeding in the United Kingdom, the Channel Islands or the Isle of Man shall be regarded as validly dissolving a marriage unless instituted in the courts of law of one of those countries.

(2) Notwithstanding anything in section 6 of the Recognition of Divorces and Legal Separations Act 1971 (as substituted by section 2 of this Act), a divorce which—

> (a) has been obtained elsewhere than in the United Kingdom, the Channel Islands and the Isle of Man; and
> (b) has been so obtained by means of a proceeding other than a proceeding instituted in a court of law; and
> (c) is not required by any of the provisions of sections 2 to 5 of that Act to be recognised as valid.

shall not be regarded as validly dissolving a marriage if both parties to the marriage have throughout the period of one year immediately preceding the institution of the proceeding been habitually resident in the United Kingdom.

(3) This section does not affect the validity of any divorce obtained before its coming into force and recognised as valid under rules of law formerly applicable.

17. Citation, etc.

(1) This Act may be cited as the Domicile and Matrimonial Proceedings Act 1973.

(2) Subject to sections 6 (4), 12 (6) and 14 (3) of this Act, the enactments specified in Schedule 6 to this Act (including certain enactments of the Parliament of Northern Ireland) are hereby repealed to the extent specified in the third column of that Schedule.

(3) So long as section 2 of the Southern Rhodesia Act 1965 remains in force, this Act shall have effect subject to such provision as may (before or after this Act comes into force) be made by Order in Council under and for the purposes of that section.

(4) Part II of this Act extends to England and Wales only; Part III extends to Scotland only; Part IV extends to Northern Ireland only; and this Part extends to the whole of the United Kingdom.

(5) This Act shall come into force on 1st January 1974.

SCHEDULES

SCHEDULE 1

Interpretation

1. The following five paragraphs have effect for the interpretation of this Schedule.

2. "Matrimonial proceedings" means any proceedings so far as they are one or more of the five following kinds, namely, proceedings for—

divorce,
judicial separation,
nullity of marriage,
a declaration as to the validity of a marriage of the petitioner, and
a declaration as to the subsistence of such a marriage.

3.—(1) "Another jurisdiction" means any country outside England and Wales.

(2) "Related jurisdiction" means any of the following countries, namely, Scotland, Northern Ireland, Jersey, Guernsey and the Isle of Man (the reference to Guernsey being treated as including Alderney and Sark).

4.—(1) References to the trial or first trial in any proceedings do not include references to the separate trial of an issue as to jurisdiction only.

(2) For purposes of this Schedule, proceedings in the court are continuing if they are pending and not stayed.

5. Any reference in this Schedule to proceedings in another jurisdiction is to proceedings in a court of that jurisdiction, and to any other proceedings in that jurisdiction, which are of a description prescribed for the purposes of this paragraph; and provision may be made by rules of court as to when proceedings of any description in another jurisdiction are continuing for the purposes of this Schedule.

6. "Prescribed" means prescribed by rules of court.

Duty to furnish particulars of concurrent proceedings in another jurisdiction

7. While matrimonial proceedings are pending in the court in respect of a marriage and the trial or first trial in those proceedings has not begun, it shall be the duty of any person who is a petitioner in the proceedings, or is a respondent and has in his answer included a prayer for relief, to furnish, in such manner and to such persons and on such occasions as may be prescribed, such particulars as may be prescribed of any proceedings which—

(*a*) he knows to be continuing in another jurisdiction; and
(*b*) are in respect of that marriage or capable of affecting its validity or subsistence.

Obligatory stays

8.—(1) Where before the beginning of the trial or first trial in any proceedings for divorce which are continuing in the court it appears to the court on the application of a party to the marriage—

(*a*) that in respect of the same marriage proceedings for divorce or nullity of marriage are continuing in a related jurisdiction; and
(*b*) that the parties to the marriage have resided together after its celebration; and
(*c*) that the place where they resided together when the proceedings in the court were begun or, if they did not then reside together, where they last resided together before those proceedings were begun, is in that jurisdiction; and

(*d*) that either of the said parties was habitually resident in that jurisdiction throughout the year ending with the date on which they last resided together before the date on which the proceedings in the court were begun,

it shall be the duty of the court, subject to paragraph 10 (2) below, to order that the proceedings in the court be stayed.

(2) References in sub-paragraph (1) above to the proceedings in the court are, in the case of proceedings which are not only proceedings for divorce, to the proceedings so far as they are proceedings for divorce.

Discretionary stays

1.—(1) Where before the beginning of the trial or first trial in any matrimonial proceedings which are continuing in the court it appears to the court—

(*a*) that any proceedings in respect of the marriage in question, or capable of affecting its validity or subsistence, are continuing in another jurisdiction; and

(*b*) that the balance of fairness (including convenience) as between the parties to the marriage is such that it is appropriate for the proceedings in that jurisdiction to be disposed of before further steps are taken in the proceedings in the court or in those proceedings so far as they consist of a particular kind of matrimonial proceedings,

the court may then, if it thinks fit, order that the proceedings in the court be stayed or, as the case may be, that those proceedings be stayed so far as they consist of proceedings of that kind.

(2) In considering the balance of fairness and convenience for the purposes of sub-paragraph (1) (*b*) above, the court shall have regard to all factors appearing to be relevant, including the convenience of witnesses and any delay or expense which may result from the proceedings being stayed, or not being stayed.

(3) In the case of any proceedings so far as they are proceedings for divorce, the court shall not exercise the power conferred on it by sub-paragraph (1) above while an application under paragraph 8 above in respect of the proceedings is pending.

(4) If, at any time after the beginning of the trial or first trial in any matrimonial proceedings which are pending in the court, the court declares by order that it is satisfied that a person has failed to perform the duty imposed on him in respect of the proceedings by paragraph 7 above, sub-paragraph (1) above shall have effect in relation to those proceedings and, to the other proceedings by reference to which the declaration is made, as if the words "before the beginning of the trial or first trial" were omitted; but no action shall lie in respect of the failure of a person to perform such a duty.

Supplementary

10.—(1) Where an order staying any proceedings is in force in pursuance of paragraph 8 or 9 above, the court may, if it thinks fit, on the application of a party to the proceedings, discharge the order if it appears to the court that the other proceedings by reference to which the order was made are stayed or concluded, or that a party to those other proceedings has delayed unreasonably in prosecuting them.

(2) If the court discharges an order staying any proceedings and made in pursuance of paragraph 8 above, the court shall not again stay those proceedings in pursuance of that paragraph.

11.—(1) The provisions of sub-paragraphs (2) and (3) below shall apply (subject to sub-paragraph (4)) where proceedings for divorce, judicial separation or nullity of marriage are stayed by reference to proceedings in a related jurisdiction for divorce, judicial separation or nullity of marriage; and in this paragraph—

"custody" includes access to the child in question;

"education" includes training;

"lump sum order" means such an order as is mentioned in paragraph (*f*) of section 23 (1) of the Matrimonial Causes Act 1973 (lump sum payment for children), being an order made under section 23 (1) or (2) (*a*);

"the other proceedings", in relation to any stayed proceedings, means the proceedings in another jurisdiction by reference to which the stay was imposed;

"relevant order" means—

(*a*) an order under section 22 of the Matrimonial Causes Act 1973 (maintenance for spouse pending suit),

(*b*) such an order as is mentioned in paragraph (*d*) or (*e*) of section 23 (1) of that Act (periodical payments for children) being an order made under section 23 (1) or (2) (*a*),

(*c*) an order under section 42 (1) (*a*) of that Act (orders for the custody and education of children), and

(*d*) except for the purposes of sub-paragraph (3) below, any order restraining a person from removing a child out of England and Wales or out of the custody, care or control of another person; and

"stayed" means stayed in pursuance of this Schedule.

(2) Where any proceedings are stayed, then, without prejudice to the effect of the stay apart from this paragraph—

(*a*) the court shall not have power to make a relevant order or a lump sum order in connection with the stayed proceedings except in pursuance of paragraph (*c*) below; and

(*b*) subject to paragraph (*c*) below, any relevant order made in connection with the stayed proceedings shall, unless the stay is previously removed or the order previously discharged, cease to have effect on the expiration of the period of three months beginning with the date on which the stay was imposed; but

(*c*) if the court considers that, for the purpose of dealing with circumstances needing to be dealt with urgently, it is necessary during or after that period to make a relevant order or a lump sum order in connection with the stayed proceedings or to extend or further extend the duration of a relevant order made in connection with the stayed proceedings, the court may do so and the order shall not cease to have effect by virtue of paragraph (*b*) above.

(3) Where any proceedings are stayed and at the time when the stay is imposed an order is in force, or at a subsequent time an order comes into force, which was made in connection with the other proceedings and provides for any of the four following matters, namely, periodical payments for a spouse of the marriage in question, periodical payments for a child, the custody of a child and the education of a child then, on the imposition of the stay in a case where the order is in force when the stay is imposed and on the coming into force of the order in any other case—

(*a*) any relevant order made in connection with the stayed proceedings shall cease to have effect in so far as it makes for a spouse or child any provision for any of those matters as respects which the same or different provision for that spouse or child is made by the other order;

(*b*) the court shall not have power in connection with the stayed proceedings to make a relevant order containing for a spouse or child provision for any of those matters as respects which any provision for that spouse or child is made by the other order; and

(*c*) if the other order contains provision for periodical payments for a child, the court shall not have power in connection with the stayed proceedings to make a lump sum order for that child.

(4) If any proceedings are stayed so far as they consist of matrimonial proceedings of a particular kind but are not stayed so far as they consist of matrimonial proceedings of a different kind, sub-paragraphs (2) and (3) above shall not apply to the proceedings but, without prejudice to the effect of the stay apart from this paragraph, the court shall not have power to make a relevant order or a lump sum order in connection with the proceedings so far as they are stayed; and in this sub-paragraph references to matrimonial proceedings do not include proceedings for a declaration.

(5) Nothing in this paragraph affects any power of the court—

    (a) to vary or discharge a relevant order so far as the order is for the time being in force; or

    (b) to enforce a relevant order as respects any period when it is or was in force; or

    (c) to make a relevant order or a lump sum order in connection with proceedings which were but are no longer stayed.

*   *   *   *   *

SCHEDULE 6
REPEALS

Chapter	Short Title	Extent of Repeal
2 & 3 Geo. 6. c. 13. (N.I.)	The Matrimonial Cuases Act (Northern Ireland) 1939.	Section 26.
7 & 8 Geo. 6 c. 43.	The Matrimonial Causes (War Marriages) Act 1944.	Section 3.
1946 c. 16. (N.I.)	The Marriage and Matrimonial Causes Act (Northern Ireland) 1946.	Section 3.
12, 13 & 14 Geo. 6. c. 100	The Law Reform (Miscellaneous Provisions) Act 1949.	In section 2, subsections (1), (2) and (3).
14 Geo. 6. c. 37.	The Maintenance Orders Act 1950.	In section 6 (2), the words "an action of separation and aliment".
1951 c. 7. (N.I.)	The Law Reform (Miscellaneous Provisions) Act (Northern Ireland) 1951.	Section 1.
10 & 11 Eliz. 2. c. 21.	The Commonwealth Immigrants Act 1962.	Section 20.
1937 c. 18.	The Matrimonial Causes Act 1973.	In section 19, in subsection (1) the words "subject to subsection (2) below", subsections (2) and (5). Section 46.

APPENDIX II

PRESCRIBED FORMS AND PRECEDENTS

PART 1

PRESCRIBED FORMS

MATRIMONIAL CAUSES RULES 1973

Rule 5 (3)

Form 1

Notice of Application under Rule 5

In the   County Court
[Divorce Registry]
No. of
Matter

(Seal)

In the Matter of a proposed petition for dissolution
of marriage

Between   Applicant
and   Respondent

TAKE NOTICE that an application has been made by the above-named Applicant for leave to present a petition for dissolution of his [her] marriage with you before the expiration of the period of three years from the date of the said marriage. If the application is undefended, it will be heard at

County Court [*insert address of court-house*] on the   day of
19 , at   o'clock, and if you do not attend at that time and place, such order will be made as the court thinks just.

A sealed copy of the application and of the affidavit to be used in support of the application is delivered with this notice.

You must complete and detach the acknowledgment of service and send it so as to reach the Court within 8 days after you receive this notice, inclusive of the day of receipt. Delay in returning the form may add to the costs. If the reply to Question 4 in the acknowledgment is Yes, the application will be transferred to the High Court and will not be heard at the place and time above-mentioned. If you intend to instruct a solicitor to act for you, you should at once give him all the documents which have been served on you, so that he may send the acknowledgment to the Court on your behalf.

Dated this   day of   19 .

Registrar

To the Respondent

. . . .
[*Here set out Form* 6]

395

Form 2

General Form of Petition

In the   County Court
[Divorce Registry]
No. of
Matter

THE PETITION OF   SHOWS THAT—

(1) On the   day of   19   the petitioner
was lawfully married to   (hereinafter called the respondent) at

(2) The petitioner and the respondent have cohabited at [*state the last address at which they have cohabited in England or Wales*] [*or* The petitioner and the respondent have not cohabited in England or Wales*].

(3) [*In the case of a petition for divorce, nullity, judicial separation or presumption of death and dissolution of marriage where it is alleged that the court has jurisdiction based on domicile.*] The petitioner is domiciled in England and Wales [*or* The petitioner is domiciled in   and the respondent is domiciled in England and Wales] [*or, where it is alleged that the court has jurisdiction based on habitual residence*] The petitioner has [*or* The respondent has] [*or,* The petitioner and the respondent have] been habitually resident in England and Wales throughout the period of one year ending with the date of presentation of the petition [*or as the case may be*] [*give details of the habitual residence relied on including the addresses of places of residence during the one year period and the length of residence at each place*] ; the petitioner is a [*state occupation*] [and resides at   ], and the respondent is a [*state occupation*] [and resides at   ].

(4) There is [are] [no [or *state number*] children of the family now living] [namely [*state the full names (including surname) of each child and his date of birth or, if it be the case, that he is over 18 and, in the case of each minor child over the age of 16, whether he is receiving instruction at an educational establishment or undergoing training for a trade, profession or vocation*]].

(5) [*In the case of a husband's petition*] No other child now living has been born to the respondent during the marriage so far as is known to the petitioner [*or in the case of a wife's petition*] No other child now living has been born to the petitioner during the marriage [except [*state the name of any such child and his date of birth, or if be the case, that he is over* 18]].

(6) [*Where there is a dispute whether a child is a child of the family*] The petitioner alleges that   is [not] a child of the family because [*give full particulars of the facts relied on by the petitioner in support of his or her allegation that the child is or, as the case may be, is not, a child of the family*].

(7) [*Where appropriate in the case of a child who is under* 18] The said   was, on the   day of   19 , received into the care of [*or* is a child with respect to whom a resolution was, on the day of   19 , passed by] [*name of local authority*] under section 1 [*or* 2] of the Children Act 1948.

(8) [*Where an application is made in the petition for an order for the support*

of a child of whom the respondent is not a parent] The respondent assumed responsibility for the maintenance of the said   to the following extent and for the following time namely [*give details*]. There is no other person liable to maintain the said child [except   ].

(9) There have been no previous proceedings in any court in England and Wales or elsewhere with reference to the marriage [or to any children of the family] [or between the petitioner or the respondent with reference to any property of either or both of them] [except [*state the nature of the proceedings, the date and effect of any decree or order and, in the case of proceedings with reference to the marriage, whether there has been any resumption of cohabitation since the making of the decree or order*]].

(10) There are no proceedings continuing in any country outside England and Wales which are in respect of the marriage or are capable of affecting its validity or subsistence [except [*give particulars of the proceedings, including the court in or tribunal or authority before which they were begun, the date when they were begun, the names of the parties, the date or expected date of any trial in the proceedings and such other facts as may be relevant to the question whether the proceedings on the petition should be stayed under Schedule 1 to the Domicile and Matrimonial Proceedings Act* 1973]].

(11) The following [*or* No] agreement or arrangement has been made or is proposed to be made between the parties for the support of the respondent [*or* the petitioner]
[and the said children] [namely [*state details*]].

(12) [*In the case of a petition for divorce alleging five years' separation*] The petitioner proposes, if a decree nisi is granted, to make the following financial provision for the respondent [*give details of any proposal not mentioned in paragraph* (11)] [*or* The petitioner makes no proposals for financial provision for the respondent in the event of a decree nisi being granted].

(13) [*In the case of a petition for divorce*] The said marriage has broken down irretrievably.

(14) The respondent has committed adultery with   and the petitioner finds it intolerable to live with the respondent [*or* The respondent has behaved in such a way that the petitioner cannot reasonably be expected to live with the respondent] [*or* The respondent has deserted the petitioner for a continuous period of at least two years immediately preceding the presentation of this petition] [*or* The parties to the marriage have lived apart for a continuous period of at least two years immediately preceding the presentation of this petition and the respondent consents to a decree being granted] [*or* The parties to the marriage have lived apart for a continuous period of at least five years immediately preceding the presentation of the petition] [*or, where the petition is not for divorce or judicial separation, set out the grounds on which relief is sought, and in any case with sufficient particularity the facts relied on but not the evidence by which they are to be proved*].

The petitioner therefore prays—

(1) That the said marriage may be dissolved [*or* declared void] [*or* annulled] [*or as the case may be*].

(2) That he [she] may be granted the custody of [*state name[s] of the child[ren]* *and add any application for a declaration under section 42 (3) of the Matrimonial Causes Act* 1973].

(3) [*Where appropriate*] That   may be ordered to pay the costs of this suit.

(4) That he [she] may be granted the following ancillary relief, namely [*state particulars of any application for ancillary relief which it is intended to claim*].

The names and addresses of the persons who are to be served with this petition are [*give particulars, stating if any of them is a person under disability*].

The petitioner's address for service is [*Where the petitioner sues by a solicitor, state the solicitor's name or firm and address, or, where the petitioner sues in person, state his place of residence as given in paragraph* 3 *of the petition or, if no place of residence in England or Wales is given, the address of a place in England or Wales at or to which documents for him may be delivered or sent*].

Dated this   day of   19 .

Note: Under the Matrimonial Causes Rules 1973 *further information is required in certain cases.*

Rule 12 (3)

Form 3

Certificate with Regard to Reconciliation

[*Heading as in Form* 5]

I   the solicitor acting for the petitioner in the above cause do hereby certify that I have [*or* have not] discussed with the petitioner the possibility of a reconciliation and that I have [*or* have not] given to the petitioner the names and addresses of persons qualified to help effect a reconciliation

Dated this   day of   19 .

Signed
Solicitor for the Petitioner

Rule 8 (2)

Form 4

Statements as to Arrangements for Children

[*Heading as in Form* 5]

The present arrangements for the minor children of the family under 16 and those over 16 who are receiving instruction at an educational establishment or undergoing training for a trade profession or vocation are as follows:—

[*State in respect of each child*]

(i) residence [*state where the child is living, particulars of the accommodation, what other persons (naming them) live there and who looks after the child*]

(ii) education etc. [*state the school or other educational establishment which the child is attending or, if he is working, his place of employment, the nature of his work and details of any training he is receiving*]

(iii) financial provision [*state who is supporting the child or contributing to his support and the extent thereof*]

(iv) access [*state any arrangements which have been agreed for access by either of the parties and the extent to which access is and has been afforded*]

The arrangements proposed for the children in the event of a decree being granted are as follow:

(i) residence   (iii) financial provision

(ii) education, etc.   (iv) access.

[*In each of these paragraphs state whether the grant of a decree will affect the present arrangements set out above, whether it is proposed that those arrangements should continue, and if not, and to the extent that they are likely to alter, state what alteration is anticipated and what proposals in substitution are proposed. In the case of residence, where it is proposed that for any period a child should be in the immediate care of a person other than the petitioner, give details of that person's willingness and ability to care for the child. In the case of education state if possible, any long-term proposals for further education or training. In the case of financial provision give details of any application which will be made for ancillary relief in respect of the children and, where applicable, state the object of any application which is other than for the day-to-day support of the child*].

The said child[ren] is [are] [not] suffering from [any] serious disability or chronic illness or from the effects of [any] serious illness [namely [*state, in respect of each child so suffering the nature of the disability or illness and attach a copy of any up-to-date medical report which is available*]].

The said child[ren] is [are] [not] under the care or supervision of a welfare officer or officer appointed by a local authority or other person or organisation [namely [*state the date of any order for care or supervision and the circumstances which gave rise to its being made*]].

Dated this   day of   19 .

Signed

[Solicitor for the] Petitioner.

Rule 12 (6)

Form 5

Notice of Proceedings

In the	County Court[1]
[Divorce Registry]	
No. of	
Matter	
	(Seal)
Between	Petitioner
and	Respondent
[and	Co-Respondent]

TAKE NOTICE that a petition [for divorce][2] has been presented to this Court. A sealed copy of it [and a copy of the petitioner's proposals regarding the children] [is] [are] delivered with this notice.

1. You must complete and detach the acknowledgment of service and send it so as to reach the Court within 8 days after you receive this notice, inclusive of the day of receipt. Delay in returning the form may add to the costs.

2.[3] If you wish to do so, you may send to the Court a statement setting out your views on the proposals regarding the children. If you send a statement it will be placed before the Judge dealing with the arrangements for the child[ren] and a copy of your statement will be sent to the petitioner.

3. If the reply to Question 4 [or 6][3] in the acknowledgment is Yes, you must, within 29 days after you receive this notice, inclusive of the day of receipt, file in the Court office an answer to the petition,[2] together with a copy for every other party to the proceedings. The case will then be transferred to the High Court.[4]

4.[3] If the reply to Question 5 in the acknowledgement is YES the consequences to you are that—

(a) provided the petitioner establishes the fact that the parties to the marriage have lived apart for two years immediately preceding the presentation of the petition and that you consent, a decree will be granted unless, in the case of a petition for divorce, the Court is satisfied that the marriage has not broken down irretrievably;

(b) your right to inherit from the petitioner if he or she dies without having made a will ceases on the grant of a decree of judicial separation or on a decree nisi of divorce being made absolute;

(c) in the case of divorce the making absolute of the decree will end the marriage thereby affecting any right to a pension which depends upon the marriage continuing or upon your being a left a widow; the State widow's pension will not be payable to you when the petitioner dies and any rights of occupation you may have in the matrimonial home under the Matrimonial Homes Act 1967 will cease unless the Court directs otherwise during the subsistence of the marriage;

(*d*) apart from the consequences listed above there may be others applicable to you depending on your particular circumstances. About these you should obtain legal advice from a solicitor.

5.³ If after consenting you wish to withdraw your consent you must immediately inform the Court and give notice to the petitioner.

6.³ The petitioner relies in support of the petition on the fact that the parties to the marriage have lived apart for at least five years. Section 10 of the Matrimonial Causes Act 1973 provides that if in such a case the respondent applies to the Court for it to consider the respondent's financial position after the divorce, a decree nisi based on five years' separation only cannot be made absolute unless the Court is satisfied that the petitioner has made or will make proper financial provision for the respondent, or else that the petitioner should not be required to make any financial provision for the respondent. Paragraph (12) of the petition will tell you whether the petitioner proposes to make any financial provision for you. It is important that you should consider this information carefully before answering Question 7 in the acknowledgement.

7.³ If the reply to Question 7 in the acknowledgment is YES you must, before the decree is made absolute, make application to the Court by filing and serving on the petitioner a notice in Form 12 which may be obtained from the Court.

8. If you intend to instruct a solicitor to act for you, you should at once give him all the documents which have been served on you, so that he may send the acknowledgment to the Court on your behalf. If you do not intend to instruct a solicitor you should nevertheless give an address for service in the acknowledgment so that any documents affecting your interests which are sent to you will in fact reach you. Change of address should be notified to the Court.

Dated this   day of   19 .

To   Registrar.

¹ Amend if the proceedings are pending in High Court.
² Or as the case may be.
³ Delete if inapplicable.
⁴ Delete if case has already been transferred to High Court.

. . . .

[*Here set out Form* 6]

Rule 14 (5)

Form 6

Acknowledgment of Service

If you intend to instruct a solicitor to act for you, give him this form immediately

[*Heading as in Form* 5]

1. Have you received the originating application [*or* summons] [and copy of the supporting affidavit] [*or* the petition for divorce][2] delivered with this form?

2. On what date and at what address did you receive it?

3. Are you the person named as the Respondent in the application [*or* as   in the petition][2]?

4. Do you intend to defend the case?

5.[3] [*In the case of a petition alleging two years' separation coupled with the respondent's consent to a decree being granted*] : Do you consent to a decree being granted?

6.[3] [*In the case of a petition asking for divorce and alleging five years' separation*]. Do you intend to oppose the grant of a decree on the ground that the divorce will result in grave financial or other hardship to you and that in all the circumstances it would be wrong to dissolve the marriage?

7.[3] In the event of a decree nisi being granted on the basis of two years' separation coupled with the respondent's consent, or five years' separation, do you intend to apply to the court for it to consider your financial position as it will be after the divorce?

8.[4] Even if you do not intend to defend the case do you wish to be heard on the claim[s] in the petition for—[5]

    (*a*) costs ...
    (*b*) custody of the children ...
    (*c*) maintenance pending suit ...
    (*d*) periodical payments ...
    (*e*) secured periodical payments ...
    (*f*) lump sum provision ...
    (*g*) settlement or transfer of property ...
    (*h*) variation of a settlement ...

9.[6] Do you wish to make any application on your own account for—

    (*a*) access to the children ...
    (*b*) custody of the children ...
    (*c*) periodical payments or secured periodical payments for the children ...
    (*d*) maintenance pending suit ...
    (*e*) periodical payments or secured periodical payments for yourself ...
    (*f*) lump sum provision ...
    (*g*) settlement of transfer of property ...
    (*h*) variation of a settlement ...

(If possible answer YES or NO against each item in Question[s] 8 [and 9]. If you are uncertain leave a blank).

10.[3] [*In the case of proceedings relating to a polygamous marriage*] If you have any wife [*or* husband] in addition to the petitioner [*or* applicant] who is not mentioned in the petition [*or* originating application] [*or* summons]], what is the name and address of each such wife [*or* husband] and the date and place of your marriage to her [*or* him?]

Dated this   day of   19 .

[*If a solicitor is instructed, he will sign below on your behalf [but if the answer to question 5 is Yes, you must also sign here]].*

Signed

Address for service [Unless you intend to instruct a solicitor, give your place of residence, or if you do not reside in England or Wales, the address of a place in England or Wales to which documents may be sent to you. If you subsequently wish to change your address for service, you must notify the court.]

I am [We are] acting for the Respondent [*or* the above-named   ] in this matter.

Signed

Address for service:]

² Or as the case may be.
³ Delete if inapplicable.
⁴ Delete Question 8 except in the case of a petition.
⁵ Insert whichever of the following items is applicable.
⁶ Delete Question 9 (except in the case of a respondent in proceedings begun by petition).

Rule 33 (3)

Form 7

Affidavit by petitioner in Support of Petition under Section 1 (2) (*d*) of Matrimonial Causes Act 1973

[*Heading as in Form* 5]

Question	Answer
1. Have you read your petition dated ?	
2. Do you wish to alter or add to any statement in the petition?	
If so, state the alterations or additions.	
3. Subject to these alterations and additions (if any), is everything stated in your petition true?	
Indicate which statements are true to your own knowledge and which to the best of your information and belief.	

Question	Answer
4. State the date on which you and the respondent separated.	
5. State briefly the reason or main reason for the separation.	
6. When and in what circumstances did you come to the conclusion that the marriage was in fact at an end?	

7. State as far as you know the various addresses at which you and the respondent have respectively lived since the date given in the answer to Question 4, and the periods of residence at each address :

Petitioner's Address		*Respondent's Address*	
From		From	
to		to	

8. Since the date given in the answer to Question 6, have you ever lived with the respondent in the same household? If so, state for which period or periods, giving dates.	

I,   (*full name*)

of   (*full residential address*)
                                            (*occupation*)

make oath and say as follows:—

    1. I am the petitioner in this cause.

    2. The answers to Questions 1 to 8 above are true.

    3. I identify the signature
appearing on the copy acknowledgement of service now produced to me and marked "A" as the signature of my husband [wife], the respondent in this cause.

    4. [*Exhibit any other documents on which the petitioner wishes to rely.*]

    5. I ask the Court to grant a decree dissolving my marriage with [*or* a decree that I be judicially separated from] the respondent on the grounds stated in my petition [and to order the respondent to pay the costs of this suit *or as the case may be*].

Sworn at

in the County of

this   day of   , 19   .

A Commissioner for Oaths
[*or as the case may be*]

Rule 65 (1)

Form 8

Notice of Application for Decree Nisi to be Made Absolute

[*Heading as in Form* 5]

TAKE NOTICE that the petitioner [*or* respondent] applies for the decree nisi pronounced in his [her] favour on the   day of   19 , to be made absolute.

Dated this   day of   19 .

Signed
[Solicitor for the] Petitioner
[*or* Respondent]

Rule 68 (2)
and (3)

Form 11

Notice of Application for Ancillary Relief

[*Heading as in Form* 5]

TAKE NOTICE that the petitioner [*or* respondent] intends to apply to the Court for [*here set out the ancillary relief claimed, stating the terms of any agreement as to the order which the court is to be asked to make and, in the case of an application for a property adjustment order or an avoidance of disposition order, stating briefly the nature of the adjustment proposed or the disposition to be set aside*].

Notice will be given to you of the place and time fixed for the hearing of the application [*or* The application will be heard by the registrar in chambers at   on   day, the   day of   19 , at   o'clock].

[*Unless the parties are agreed upon the terms of the proposed order, add in the case of an application for an order for maintenance pending suit or a financial provision order:* TAKE NOTICE ALSO that you must send to the registrar, so as to reach him within 14 days after you receive this notice, an affidavit giving full particulars of your property and income. You must at the same time send a copy of your affidavit to the [solicitor for] the applicant.

If you wish to allege that the petitioner has property or income, you should say so in your affidavit.]

Dated this   day of   19 .

            Signed
            [Solicitor for the] Respondent
            [*or* Petitioner]

Rule 57

Form 12

Notice of Application under Rule 57

[Heading as in Form 5]

TAKE NOTICE that the respondent applies to the Court under section 10 (2) of the Matrimonial Causes Act 1973 for the Court to consider the financial position of the respondent after the divorce.

The application will be heard on a date to be fixed [*or if, in the case of an application made after a decree nisi, a date has been fixed* by the registrar in chambers at   on   day, the   day of 19 , at   o'clock].

[*Unless the petitioner has already filed an affidavit with his petition under Rule 8 (3), or in connection with an application for ancillary relief under Rule 73 (2):*

TAKE NOTICE ALSO that you must send to the registrar, so as to reach him within 14 days after you receive this notice, an affidavit giving full particulars of your property and income. You must at the same time send a copy of your affidavit to the [solicitor for the] respondent.

If you wish to allege that the respondent has property or income, you should say so in your affidavit]

Dated this   day of   19 .

            Signed
            [Solicitor for the] Respondent

Rule 73 (1)

Form 13

Notice of Intention to Proceed with Application for Ancillary Relief made in Petition or Answer

[Heading as in Form 5]

The petitioner [*or* respondent] having applied in his [her] petition [*or answer*] for [*here set out the ancillary relief claimed and intended to be proceeded with, stating the terms of any agreement as to the order which the court is to be asked to make*].

[*Add where applicable* TAKE NOTICE that the application will be heard by the registrar in chambers at   on   day, the
day of   19 , at   o'clock].
  [TAKE NOTICE [ALSO] that [*continue as in third paragraph of Form* 11]]
  Dated this   day of   19 .

Signed
[Solicitor for the] Petitioner [*or* Respondent]

Rules 76 and
92 (5)

Form 14

Notice of Allegation in Proceedings for Ancillary Relief

[*Heading as in Form* 5]

  TAKE NOTICE that this affidavit has been filed in proceedings for [*state nature of application*] and that if you wish to be heard on any matter affecting you in the proceedings you may intervene by applying to the Court, within 8 days after you receive this notice, inclusive of the day of receipt, for directions as to the filing and service of pleadings and as to the further conduct of the proceedings.
  Dated this   day of   19 .
  Issued by
  [Solicitor for the] Petitioner [*or* Respondent]

Rule 83 (2)

Form 15

Notice of Request for Periodical Payments Order at Same Rate as Order for Maintenance Pending Suit

[*Heading as in Form* 5]

To   of   .

  The petitioner [*or* respondent] having on the   day of   19
obtained an order for payment by you of maintenance pending suit at the rate
of   .

  AND the petitioner [*or* respondent] having applied in his [her] petition [*or* answer] for a periodical payments order for himself [*or* herself].

  TAKE NOTICE that the petitioner [*or* respondent] has requested the Court to make a periodical payments order for himself [*or* herself] providing for payments by you at the same rate as those mentioned above.

AND TAKE NOTICE that if you object to the making of such a periodical payments order, you must give notice to that effect to the registrar and the petitioner [*or* respondent] within 14 days after service of this notice on you, and if you do not do so, the registrar may make such a periodical payments order without further notice to you.

Dated this   day of   19 .

Registrar

Rule 98 (1)

Form 19

Originating Application on Ground of Wilful Neglect to Maintain

In the   County Court
[Divorce Registry]
No. of
Matter

(Seal)

In the Matter of an Application under section 27 of the Matrimonial Causes Act
1973

Between   Applicant
and   Respondent

1. I,   , of   , the wife [husband] of   of (hereinafter called the respondent) say that the respondent [*in the case of a wife's application* has wilfully neglected to provide reasonable maintenance for me *or in the case of a husband's application* has wilfully neglected to provide [*or* make a proper contribution towards*] reasonable maintenance [for me] [and] the child[ren] of our family]].

2. On the   day of   19 , I [*in the case of an application by a wife* being then [*state full name and status before the marriage*]] was lawfully married to the respondent [*in the case of an application by a husband* who was then [*state respondent's full name and status before marriage*]] at

3. There is [are] [no [*or state number*] children of the family now living] [namely [*state the name (including surname) of each child and his date of birth or, if it be the case, that he is over 18 and, in the case of each minor child over the age of 16, whether he is, or will be, or if an order or provision were made would be, receiving instruction at an educational establishment or undergoing training for a trade, profession or vocation*] who is now residing at [*state the place*] with [*state the person*]].

4. There have been no previous proceedings in any court in England and Wales or elsewhere with reference to the marriage [or the children of the

family] [except *state the nature of the proceedings, the date and effect of any decree or order and, in the case of proceedings with reference to the marriage, whether there has been any resumption of cohabitation since the making of the decree or order*].

5. [*Where appropriate in the case of a child who is under* 18] The said
, was, on the   day of   19   , received into the care of [*or* is a child with respect to whom a resolution was, on the   day of
19   , passed by] [*name of local authority*] under section 1 [*or* 2] of the Children Act 1948.

6. The following are particulars of the wilful neglect [*give particulars adding the name[s] of the child[ren] concerned and in the case of a husband's application in respect of himself the matters set out in section* 27 (1) (*b*) (i) *of the Act of* 1973 *on which he relies*].

7. The respondent has not made any payments to me by way of maintenance for myself [or the said child[ren]] [except [*give particulars*]].

8. My means are as follows:—

9. To the best of my knowledge and belief the respondent's means are as follows:—

10. I apply for an order that the respondent do make provision by way of [periodical payments, secured periodical payments, a lump sum *delete as appropriate*] for me [and [*such of the said provisions as may be claimed*] for [*state name[s] of child[ren] in respect of whom such claim is made*]].

11. I ask that I may be granted the custody of the said [*state name[s] of the child[ren]*].

12. This Court has jurisdiction to entertain these proceedings by reason of the fact that [*in the case of an application based on domicile* I am [*or* the respondent is] [*or* the respondent and I are] domiciled in England and Wales] [*or in the case of an application based on residence* I have been habitually resident in England and Wales throughout the period of one year ending with the date of this application [*or* the respondent is now resident in England and Wales].

My address for service is [*Where the applicant sues by a solicitor, state the solicitor's name or firm and address or, where the applicant sues in person, state her place of residence as given in paragraph* 1 *or, if no place or residence in England or Wales is given, the address of a place in England or Wales at or to which documents for her may be delivered or sent*].

Dated this   day of   19

Form 20

Notice of Application under Rule 98 or 100

[Heading as in Form 19 or 21]

TAKE NOTICE that this application will be heard at   County Court *[insert address of court-house]* on the   day of   19 , at   o'clock *[or on a day to be fixed]*, and if you do not attend at that place and time, such order will be made as the court thinks just.

A sealed copy of the application [and of the affidavit in verification] is delivered with this notice.

You must complete and detach the acknowledgment of service and send it so as to reach the Court within 8 days after you receive this notice inclusive of the day of receipt. Delay in returning the form may add to the costs.

[Where the application is under rule 98] If you intend to contest the application, you must file an answer setting out the grounds on which you rely (including any allegation which you wish to make against the applicant), and in any case, unless otherwise directed, you must file an affidavit containing full particulars of your property and income. The affidavit and any answer you wish to file must be sent, together with a copy for the applicant, so as to reach the Court within 14 days after the time allowed for sending the acknowledgment of service. If you file an answer alleging adultery it must be accompanied by a copy for the alleged adulterer.

[Where the application is under rule 100] You must also swear an affidavit in answer to the application, setting out any grounds on which you intend to contest the application and containing full particulars of your property and income, and send the affidavit, together with a copy for the applicant, so as to reach the Court within 14 days after the time allowed for sending the acknowledgment of service.

If you intend to instruct a solicitor to act for you, you should at once give him all the documents which have been served on you, so that he may take the necessary steps on your behalf.

Dated this   day of   19 .

To the Respondent

                                          Registrar

[Here set out Form 6]

Rule 100 (1)

Form 21

Originating Application for Alteration of Maintenance Agreement during Parties' Lifetime

In the   County Court
[Divorce Registry]
No. of
Matter

(Seal)

In the Matter of an Application under section 35 *of the Matrimonial Causes Act* 1973

Between   Applicant
and   Respondent

1. I   , the wife [*or* husband] of
(hereinafter called "the respondent"), apply for an order altering the maintenance agreement made between me and the respondent on the   day of   19 .

2. I reside at   , and the respondent resides at

[*Add, unless both parties are resident in England or Wales* We are both domiciled in England and Wales [*or as the case may be*]].

3. On the   day of   19 , I was lawfully married to the respondent at
I [*or, in the case of an application by the husband* The respondent] was then [*state full name and status of wife before marriage*].

4. There is [are] [no [*or state number*] child[ren] of the family [namely [*state the name (including surname) of each child now living and his date of birth or, if it be the case, that he is over* 18 *and, in the case of each minor child over the age of* 16, *whether he is, or will be, or if an order or provision were made would be, receiving instruction at an educational establishment or undergoing training for a trade, profession or vocation*] who is now residing at [*state the place*] with [*state the person*] [and [*state name of any child who has died since the date of the agreement*] who died on the   day of   19]. [The agreement also makes financial arrangements for [*give similar particulars of any other child for whom the agreement makes such arrangements*]].

5. There have been no previous proceedings in any court with reference to the agreement or to the marriage [or to the child[ren] of the family] [or to the other child[ren] for whom the agreement makes financial arrangements] or between the applicant and the respondent with reference to any property of either or both of them [except *state the nature of the proceedings and the date and effect of any order or decree*].

6. My means are as follows:—

7. I ask for the following alteration[s] to be made in the agreement:—

8. The facts on which I rely to justify the alteration[s] are:—

My address for service is [*Where the applicant sues by a solicitor, state the solicitor's name or firm and address, or, where the applicant sues in person, state his or her place of residence as given in paragraph 2 or, if no place of residence in England or Wales is given, the address of a place in England or Wales at or to which documents for him or her may be delivered or sent*].

Dated this   day of   19

Rule 101 (1)

Form 22

Originating Summons for Alteration of Maintenance Agreement after Death of One of the Parties

In the High Court of Justice
   Family Division
     (Divorce)
   [District Registry]
      In the Matter of an application by   under
       section 36 *of the Matrimonial Causes Act* 1973

Between   Applicant[s]
and   Respondent[s]
   Let   of   attend before Mr. Registrar   in chambers at the Divorce Registry, Somerset House, London, WC2R 1LP, [*or as the case may be*] on   day, the   day of   19   , at   o'clock, on the hearing of an application by   that the agreement made on the   day of   19   , between [the applicant and]   who died on the   day of   19   , [and the respondent] should be altered as shown in the affidavit accompanying this summons so as to make different [*or contain*] financial arrangements.

Dated this   day of   19   .

This summons was taken out by   [Solicitor for] the above-named applicant[s].

To the Respondent.
Take notice that:—

1. A copy of the affidavit to be used in support of the application is delivered herewith.

2. You must complete the accompanying acknowledgment of service and send it so as to reach the Court within 8 days after you receive this summons.

3. [*If the respondent is a personal representative of the deceased:* You must also file an affidavit in answer to the applicant's application, containing full particulars of the value of the deceased's estate for probate, after providing for the discharge of the funeral, testamentary and administration expenses, debts and liabilities, including the amount of the estate duty and interest

thereon, and the persons or classes of persons beneficially interested in the estate, with the names and addresses of all living beneficiaries and stating whether any beneficiary is a minor or incapable, by reason of mental disorder, of managing and administering his property and affairs.]

[*Or, if the respondent is not a personal representative of the deceased:* You may also file an affidavit in answer to the application].

[*Add, in either case:* The affidavit must be filed by sending or delivering it, together with a copy for the applicant, so as to reach the Court within 14 days after the time allowed for sending the acknowledgment of service.]

4. If you intend to instruct a solicitor to act for you, you should at once give him all the documents which have been served on you, so that he may take the necessary steps on your behalf.

Rule 103 (1)

Form 23

Originating Summons for Maintenance out of Estate of Deceased Former Spouse

In the High Court of Justice
    Family Division
        (Divorce)
[District Registry]
   In the Matter of an application by   *under*
          section 26 of the Matrimonial Causes Act 1965

Between   Applicant
and   Respondent
Let   of   attend before Mr. Registrar   in chambers at the Divorce Registry, Somerset House, London, WC2R 1LP, [*or as the case may be*] on   day, the   day of   19 , at   o'clock, on the hearing of an application by   that provision for her maintenance be made out of the estate of   of   , who died on the day of   19 , on the ground that he has not made reasonable provision for her maintenance after his death.

Dated this   day of   19
This summons was taken out by   [Solicitor for] the above-named applicant.
To the Respondent.
TAKE NOTICE THAT:—

[*Continue as in Form* 22]

Appendix II

COUNTY COURT RULES 1936

23

Originating Application

Order 6, Rule 4 (1)

[General Title—Form 1]

I,

of [*state address and occupation of applicant*] apply to the Court for an order in the following terms:—

[*here state the terms of the Order to which the applicant claims to be entitled*]

The grounds on which I claim to be entitled to the Order are:—[*here state the grounds upon which the Order is claimed*]

The names and addresses of the persons upon whom it is intended to serve this application are:—[*here state the names and addresses of the persons intended to be served*]

or It is not intended to serve any person with notice of this application.

My address for service is:—[*here state the applicant's address for service*]

Dated this   day of   , 19   .

(Signed)

Applicant.

FORMS NOT PRESCRIBED

Notice of Application

In the   County Court

No. of Plaint

Between   Plaintiff

and   Defendant

TAKE NOTICE that I intend to apply to the Judge [*or* Registrar] of this Court at   on   the   day of   19

at   o'clock for [*Here state nature and grounds of Application*].

Dated this   day of   19   .

Plaintiff
Defendant.

To the Registrar
and to the Plaintiff.
Defendant.

[*N.B.—Prints of the above form may be obtained from county court offices, and are there known under number Ex. 23.*]

Form D635

Practice Direction, [1973] 1 All E.R. 192

Affidavit of Means and Questionnaire

No.   of 19

DIVORCE REGISTRY

Between   Petitioner

and   Respondent,

and   Co-Respondent

I

of

make oath and say that the answers to the questions below are true to the best of my knowledge information and belief and that they are a full and accurate statement of my means.

Save as set out in the said answers I have no capital or income.

---

1) What is your present occupation?
   If you are not now employed, give details of your last
   employment and any trade or professional qualifications.

---

2) What is your current gross income from:-
   a) your employment, trade or profession
        i) normal   per year (month) (week)
        ii) overtime or other special receipts   per year (month) (week)
   b) pension or annuities
   c) interest on bank or savings deposits
   d) building society interest
   e) dividends
   f) any other source
   *(So far as possible show all receipts in respect of the same
   period of time: i.e. give all weekly and monthly or all annual
   amounts. Show all receipts as* gross *amounts before deduction
   of tax where possible: where not possible, indicate that the
   amount shown is the net amount received).*
   Do you receive any benefits in kind, such as free
   accommodation, use of car, etc.?   If so, give details

---

3) What National Insurance contributions are paid by you?   **per week**

---

4) Are there any, and if so what, other expenses, which are
   necessary to enable you to earn the income set out above?

---

5) a) What was your gross taxable income during the last complete
tax year (6 April to 5 April) from your employment, trade
or profession including overtime or other special
payments and taxable benefits?
   b) What was your Income Tax liability during the
last complete tax year?
   *(Where figures for the last complete tax year are not
available, give them for the last year for which they are
available. In the case of a fluctuating income give also
the figures for two or more preceding years).*

6) What do you claim to be your necessary expenses of
providing yourself with a place to live in, such as rent,
rates, water rate, mortgage interest and re-payments,
premium on endowment insurance used as collateral, etc.?

7) What maintenance payments (if any) do you make to or
receive from your (former) wife/husband including any
payments to or for any child and including school fees?

8) Are any payments to which question 7 refers made
   a) under a Court order (give Court, date and details of order)
   b) under an enforceable agreement (give date and details)
   c) voluntarily?

9) What payments (if any) do you receive from the   **per week**
Department of Health and Social Security by way of
supplementary pension or supplementary allowance?

10) What family allowance (if any) do you receive for   **per week**
a child or children?

11) Was the former matrimonial home
   a) rented
   b) owned (i) by you
          (ii) your (former) husband/wife
         (iii) jointly by you and your (former) husband/wife?

12) a) Is the former matrimonial home still occupied by you or
your (former) wife/husband or by both of you?

    b) If it is owned by you or your (former) husband/wife or by
you both jointly, at what do you estimate its present value?

    c) Is it subject to a mortgage? If so, give details of the
mortgage, including the rate of any repayment, the amount
outstanding and the date at which re-payment will be
completed.
If there is any collateral security in the form of an
endowment assurance, state the surrender value of
the policy.

---

13) Do you own any car(s)?   Yes/No
If yes, what is its (their) make, model and year of manufacture
and what do you estimate its (their) present value?

---

14) What other assets do you have, such as cash at bank, savings
bank accounts, premium savings bonds, building society
account, stock and shares, reversionary interests, etc.?
(give details and present value)
Include any house property owned or in which you have any
interest, jointly held property and articles of substantial
value such as jewellery or furniture.

---

15) a) Apart from any liability set out in the answers to questions
8 and 12 what other unpaid debts are at present due and
payable by you including hire purchase debts?
Also give particulars of any judgments against you.

    b) Do you have any life or endowment assurance policy
other than any set out in the answers to question 60?
If so, give details including amount of annual
premium and date of maturity.

---

16) *(to be answered only by respondents to applications for
financial provision)*
If a decree absolute has been made, have you re-married?
If a decree has not been pronounced or made absolute,
do you intend to re-marry if one is made?
Do you provide for your wife/husband on re-marriage
or will you provide for your intended wife/husband by
way of accommodation, living expenses or otherwise?
Do you provide for any other person? If so, give particulars.

In either case, has the wife/husband, intended wife/husband
or other person any means?
If so, state briefly what they are.

---

17) Are you a member of any pension or superannuation
scheme (other than State Insurance)?   Yes/No
   a) give details
   b) would your (former) husband/wife have been
     entitled to any benefits at your death in the
     absence of a decree absolute?   Yes/No

---

18) Is, to your knowledge, your husband/wife
a member of any such scheme?   Yes/No/Don't know
If so, do you think you will lose any benefits by
reason of a decree absolute, and if so, what?

---

19) Is there any other reason which you wish to urge
against paying maintenance or are there any
other matters which you wish to raise in
connection with this application?

Continue on next page if necessary

===

No.   of 19

DIVORCE REGISTRY

Between

Petitioner

and

Respondent

and

Co-Respondent

===

Affidavit of means of

===

Date of swearing :

Solicitors for the

PART 2

PRECEDENTS

Part 1 of this Appendix contains some of the Forms prescribed by the Appendix to the Rules. There follow in Part 2 of this Appendix some examples of pleadings and other documents required in matrimonial proceedings. These Precedents, and some Notes upon them, are as follows:—

No. 1. This is an example of a wife's petition in reliance upon her husband's adultery. Like the other precedents of petitions in this Part of the Schedule, it follows the order laid down in Form 2 in the Appendix to the Rules (see *ante*, p. 396). Paragraph (3) is based upon the fact that the domicile of one party alone suffices to found jurisdiction, although the other spouse is domiciled elsewhere. The parties are of modest means, the husband being employed as a motor mechanic, and the financial position is complicated by the fact that there are two young children of the family and the husband is already living with another woman. For this reason it would be pointless to pray for such orders as those for a secured provision, a lump sum payment or a transfer of property. It is likely that, should he marry the other woman and there are children of that union, both families will be driven to rely upon Social Security Benefit, but that is no reason why the petitioner should not pray for, and be granted, periodical payments for herself and the children. The breakdown of the marriage is clearly irretrievable and for this reason Form 3, the certificate of the wife's solicitors with regard to reconciliation, will certify that they have discussed this possibility with the petitioner but have not given her the names and addresses of those qualified to help her to effect a reconciliation. It would be useless: she has forgiven him once and cannot be expected to do so again.

No. 2 is an example of Form 4, the Statement of Arrangements for Children (see *ante*, p. 398), which must be filed with the petition set out in the first precedent. It should be noticed that the woman with whom adultery is alleged has been made a co-respondent, and that the details required in paragraph (1) are fuller than those which were at one time necessary.

No. 3 exemplifies a wife's petition in reliance upon conduct such that she cannot reasonably be expected to live with her husband. The particulars which follow paragraph (9) indicate the behaviour of which she complains. The husband is a wealthy man and in his position would not wish to face the publicity resulting from defending the petition. Paragraph (8) indicates the terms upon which the parties have agreed. It should be noticed that the prayer does not seek an order for custody of the child Richard, since he has reached the age of 16, but does pray that the agreed terms, or such other terms as the court shall think reasonable, shall be included in the orders of the court. Having regard to

419

the nature of the wife's allegations and the financial circumstances, this petition has been settled by counsel, who has signed it. It must be accompanied by the prescribed Forms 3 & 4.

No. 4 is a husband's petition in reliance of five years of life apart for which he was mainly, if not entirely, to blame. It should be noticed that paragraph (8) contains his proposals for the support of his wife if a decree is granted. Since the terms proposed have not been agreed, Rule 8 (3) requires the petition to be accompanied by an affidavit by the petitioner giving brief details of his means and commitments. This affidavit can conveniently follow the Form given on p. 415, which will obviate the necessity of a more detailed affidavit at a later stage. This will include particulars of the provision which he is making for the lady with whom he is living and their illegitimate child. Form 3 will also be required, but not Form 4, since there are no children of the family.

Unlike the cases of May Day in **No. 1** and Martha Wotherspoon in **No. 3**, the case of Samuel Weller is a defended case. His wife's answer is illustrated in **No. 5**, in which she raises the defence, under the Act of 1973, s. 5, that the dissolution of the marriage will result in grave financial hardship to her and that in the circumstances it would be wrong to dissolve the marriage. She relies mainly upon the loss of the chance of acquiring a widow's pension under the contributory pension scheme of the company by which her husband is employed and upon financial difficulties resulting from her disablement by arthritis. Since the case is to be defended, counsel has been asked to advise, has settled the answer, and has signed it. On the answer being filed, the case will be transferred to the High Court.

It is by no means clear that the court will regard this case as one of *grave* financial hardship, though it might well do so. Should this defence fail it will still be open to the wife to apply to the court under section 10 (2) of the Act of 1973 to consider her financial position after the divorce in order to ensure that the decree nisi shall not be made absolute unless the court is satisfied that the financial provision for her is fair and reasonable or the best that can be made in the circumstances. This application should be made by Notice in Form 12, see *ante*, p. 406, which can (and in this case should) also be filed before the hearing of the case.

It is in fact plain that whether or not a defence under section 5 will succeed the terms proposed by the petitioner in paragraph (9) of No. 4 are inadequate, and have been deliberately made so in order to illustrate the results of unsatisfactory proposals. Provision might be made for the wife's position should her husband predecease her by the sale of his house (The Old Forge) and use of the balance of the purchase money, either alone or with the whole or some part of his investments, to purchase an annuity for her. In any event, having regard to her disability and the duration of the marriage, the periodical payments proposed seem insufficient.

The double threat of a defence under section 5, and an application under section 10 (2) of the Act of 1973, may well lead the husband to reconsider and improve his offer and enable the wife to discontinue her defence.

No. 6 exemplifies a husband's petition for nullity alleging in the alternative his wife's wilful refusal to consummate the marriage and her inability to do so. The correct wording of the prayer in view of the provisions of the Nullity of Marriage Act 1971 (which are now embodied in the Act of 1973) is a matter on which there is no authority.

No. 1

Wife's Petition for Divorce in reliance upon Matrimonial Causes Act 1973, s. 1 (2) (a) (Adultery)

IN THE EATANSWILL COUNTY COURT
No. of Matter:

THE PETITION OF MAY DAY shows that:—

(1) On the 1st day of October 1962 the petitioner, May Day, was lawfully married to Albert Day (hereinafter called the respondent) at the Parish Church in the Parish of Eatanswill in the County of Mercia.

(2) Since the said marriage the petitioner and respondent have cohabitated at No. 21 Broad Street, Eatanswill in the County of Mercia.

(3) The petitioner is domiciled in Scotland and the respondent is domiciled in England and Wales. The petitioner, who is a secretary, resides at No. 21 Broad Street, Eatanswill aforesaid and the respondent, who is a motor mechanic, resides at Rose Cottage, Muddlecombe in the County of Wessex.

(4) There are two children of the family now living, namely June Day who was born on the 13th day of June 1965 and Thomas Day who was born on the 28th day of November 1966.

(5) No other child now living has been born to the petitioner during the marriage.

(6) There have been no previous proceedings in any court in England and Wales or elsewhere with reference to the marriage or to any children of the family, or between the petitioner and the respondent with reference to any property of either or both of them, except that on the 22nd day of March 1969 in the Eatanswill Magistrates' Court the respondent was adjudged guilty of adultery with April Showers and an order was made granting custody of both children to the petitioner with reasonable access by the respondent and the respondent was ordered to pay £4 a week for the maintenance of the petitioner and £1.50p a week for the maintenance of each of the said children. The parties resumed cohabitation on the 1st day of March 1971.

(7) There are no proceedings continuing in any country outside England and Wales which are in respect of the marriage or are capable of affecting its validity or subsistence.

(8) No agreement has been made or is proposed to be made between the parties for the support of the petitioner or the said children.

(9) The said marriage has broken down irretrievably.

(10) Since the resumption of cohabitation in 1971 the respondent has committed adultery with April Showers and the petitioner finds it intolerable to live with the respondent.

(11) In August 1971 the respondent and April Showers stayed together for a week-end at the Old Bush Hotel, Muddlecombe in the County of Wessex and the respondent committed adultery with April Showers.

(12) From January 1972 to the date of this petition the respondent has lived and cohabited with the said April Showers at Rose Cottage, Muddlecombe aforesaid and has frequently committed adultery with her.

The petitioner therefore prays:—

(1) That the said marriage be dissolved.
(2) That she may be granted the custody of the said children of the family.
(3) That the respondent may be ordered to pay the costs of this suit.
(4) That she may be granted the following ancillary relief

    (a) an order for payment of maintenance pending suit
    (b) a periodical payments order in respect of herself and each child of the family respectively.

(Signed) *Dodson and Fogg* (Solicitors for the petitioner)

The names and addresses of the persons who are to be served with this petition are Albert Day and April Showers, both of Rose Cottage, Muddlecombe, Wessex.

The petitioner's address for service is
    C/o Messrs Dodson & Fogg,
        Bank Chambers,
            2 High Street,
                Eatanswill,
                    Mercia.

Dated this 21st day of February 1974.

No. 2

Petition of May Day for Divorce. Form 4
Statement of Arrangements for Children

IN THE EATANSWILL COUNTY COURT
No. of Matter:

BETWEEN

MAY DAY	..	..	..	..	..	..	.. *Petitioner*
and							
ALBERT DAY	..	..	..	..	..	..	.. *Respondent*
and							
APRIL SHOWERS	..	..	..	..	..	.. *Co-respondent*

STATEMENT OF ARRANGEMENTS FOR CHILDREN

The present arrangements for minor children of the family under 16 are as follows:—

(i) Both June Day and Thomas Day live with me at No. 21 Broad Street, Eatanswill in the County of Mercia which is a modern house with three bedrooms. The only other occupant of the house is my sister Elsie Smith, and I myself look after the children, with her assistance.

(ii) Both children attend the Eatanswill Church of England School.

(iii) The respondent undertook to pay me the sum of £10 per week to cover the maintenance of myself and the children of the family and the rent payable in respect of No. 21 Broad Street Eatanswill. He has failed to make these payments regularly and I have been compelled to seek Social Security Benefit.

(iv) No arrangements have been agreed with the respondent for access to the children of the family but when he has wished to see them I have allowed him to do so on condition that he is not accompanied by April Showers. His visits have been infrequent at intervals of about 6 to 8 weeks.

The arrangements proposed in the event of a decree being granted are as follows:—

(i) The said children will continue to reside with me at 21 Broad Street, Eatanswill as aforesaid, unless the payments made to me and my part-time earnings as a secretary prove insufficient to provide for the rental of £5 per week in addition to our maintenance.

(2) The children of the family will continue to attend the Eatanswill Church of England School until they reach the age at which they will attend the nearest available Comprehensive School. The grant of a decree will in no way affect these arrangements.

(3) Unless reliance is to be placed upon Social Security Benefits my own earnings will not suffice to enable the above arrangements to continue in the absence of an adequate order for periodical payments by the respondent.

(4) I have no objection to proper provision being made for reasonable access by the respondent to the children of the family, for whom he plainly feels affection.

The said children are not suffering from any serious disability or chronic illness or from the effects of any serious illness.

They are not under the care or supervision of a welfare officer or officer appointed by a local authority or other person or organisation.

(Signed) *May Day*

(Petitioner)

No. 3

Wife's Petition for Divorce in reliance upon Matrimonial Causes Act 1973, s. 1 (2) (b) (Conduct making life together unreasonable)

IN THE EATANSWILL COUNTY COURT
No. of Matter:

THE PETITION OF MARTHA WOTHERSPOON shows that:

(1) On the 1st day of April 1954 the petitioner, Martha Wotherspoon, was lawfully married to Marmaduke Wotherspoon in the Abbey Church in the Parish of Eatanswill in the County of Mercia.

(2) Since the said marriage the petitioner and respondent have cohabited at the Manor House, Eatan Peverill, near Eatanswill aforesaid.

(3) The petitioner is domiciled in England and Wales. The petitioner, who has no occupation, resides at the Cedars, Shiptown-by-the-Sea, in the County of Wessex, and the respondent is a company director and resides at the Manor House, Eatan Peverill aforesaid.

(4) There are three children of the family now living, namely Thomas Wotherspoon, who is over the age of 18, and is a child of the respondent by a previous marriage, Richard Wotherspoon, who was born on the 30th day of September 1957 and is receiving full time instruction at the Eatanswill High School and Harriet Wotherspoon who was born on the 19th day of July 1960.

(5) No other child now living has been born to the petitioner during the marriage.

(6) There have been no previous proceedings in any court in England and Wales or elsewhere with reference to the marriage or to any children of the family, or between the petitioner and the respondent with reference to any property of either or both of them.

(7) There are no proceedings continuing in any country outside England and Wales which are in respect of the marriage or are capable of affecting its validity or subsistence.

(8) The following agreement has been made between the petitioner and the respondent.

(i) that the petitioner should seek a decree of divorce on the ground that the marriage has irretrievably broken down by reason of the respondent's behaviour and that respondent shall offer no defence to such a petition.

(ii) that custody of the said child Harriet should be granted to the petitioner the respondent to be allowed reasonable access to the said child.

(iii) that the respondent should pay to the petitioner maintenance pending suit and periodical payments thereafter at the rate of £4,000 per annum less tax. Of the periodical payments the sum of £1,500 per annum less tax shall be secured.

(iv) that the respondent should make periodical payments to the petitioner at the rate of £600 per annum less tax for each of the said children Richard and Harriet, should pay their school fees and reasonable medical and holiday expenses.

(v) that if either or both the said children are successful in obtaining a place at a university the respondent should pay their fees and continue to make the other payments mentioned in paragraph 8 (iv) above for their maintenance, medical and holiday expenses until their courses are completed.

(vi) that the respondent's house The Cedars, Shiptown-by-the-Sea should be transferred with its contents to the petitioner absolutely.

(vii) that upon the making absolute of the decree the respondent should pay to the petitioner a lump sum of £10,000.

(viii) that the respondent should pay the costs on a solicitor and own client basis of and incidental to the proceedings and the making of this agreement.

Save as aforesaid no agreement or arrangement has been made or is proposed to be made between the parties.

(9) That the said marriage has broken down irretrievably.

(10) That the respondent has behaved in such a way that the petitioner cannot reasonably be expected to live with the respondent.

PARTICULARS

(i) That from towards the end of 1971 the respondent has habitually drunk to excess and particularly after so doing has abused and used violence towards the petitioner.

(ii) That on numerous occasions he has failed to return home from his office in London for several days without giving the petitioner any reason for so doing or any indication of his whereabouts.

(iii) That on occasions too numerous to mention he has returned to the matrimonial home in a drunken condition.

(iv) That in December 1972 the respondent attacked the petitioner, striking her so many blows with his fists that she fell to the ground and was compelled to seek medical treatment.

(v) That on New Year's Eve 1972, in the presence of guests in the home, he taunted her with cowardice in respect of the incident mentioned above, pelted her with food and poured wine over her.

(vi) That on the 21st day of April 1973 he again violently attacked her, threw her out from the home and left her injured in the garden with cuts and bruises and a broken wrist, whereby she was compelled to leave him taking the said children Richard and Harriet, who had witnessed the incidents in December 1972 and April 1973, with her.

The petitioner therefore prays

(1) That her said marriage may be dissolved.

(2) That she may be granted the custody of the said child Harriet.

(3) That the respondent may be ordered to pay the costs of and incidental to this suit.

(4) That she may be granted ancillary relief on the terms agreed and set out in paragraph (8) of this her petition or otherwise such orders for maintenance pending suit, periodical payments and a secured provision for her own support and that of said children Richard and Harriet, a lump sum payment and a transfer of property order in respect of The Cedars aforesaid, as the court may think just.

(Signed) *John Harddriver* (Counsel for the petitioner)

The name and address of the person who is to be served with this petition is Marmaduke Wotherspoon of the Manor House, Eatan Peverill, near Eatanswill, Mercia.

The petitioner's address for service is c/o Messrs Dodson and Fogg, Solicitors, Bank Chambers, 2 High Street, Eatanswill, Mercia.

Dated this 21st day of February 1974.

No. 4

Husband's Petition for Divorce in reliance upon Matrimonial Causes Act 1973, s. 1 (2) (e) (Five years' separation)

IN THE EATANSWILL COUNTY COURT
No. of Matter

THE PETITION OF SAMUEL WELLER shows that:—

(1) On the 15th day of July 1944 the petitioner was lawfully married to Mary Weller (hereinafter called the respondent) at the Register Office in the Parish of Dingley Dell in the District of Eatanswill in the County of Mercia.

(2) The petitioner and the respondent have cohabited at The Old Forge, Dingley Dell, Eatanswill aforesaid.

(3) Both the petitioner and the respondent are domiciled in England and Wales. The petitioner is a works manager and resides at Flat 5, Tower Court, Wimbleton in the County of Wessex: the respondent is unemployed and resides at the Old Forge, Dingley Dell aforesaid.

(4) There are no children of the family now living.

(5) No other child now living has been born to the respondent during the marriage so far as is known to the petitioner.

(6) There have been no previous proceedings in England and Wales or elsewhere with reference to the marriage, or between the petitioner and the respondent with reference to any property of either or both of them.

(7) There are no proceedings continuing in any country outside England and Wales which are in respect of the marriage or are capable of affecting its validity or subsistence.

(8) No agreement or arrangement has been made or is proposed to be made between the parties for the support of the respondent.

(9) The petitioner proposes if a decree nisi is granted to make the following financial provision for the respondent

(a) That the petitioner shall continue to pay to the respondent the sum of £800 a year less tax by equal quarterly instalments.

(b) That the respondent shall be permitted to live for the rest of her lifetime in the Old Forge, Dingley Dell aforesaid, which property is owned by the petitioner, who will discharge the interest upon the mortgage of that property and continue to pay the rates and the cost of essential repairs to the property.

(10) The said marriage has broken down irretrievably.

(11) The parties have lived apart for a period of at least 5 years immediately preceding the date of this petition namely since the 4th day of October 1965, when the petitioner left the matrimonial home.

(12) Since the month of October 1965 the petitioner and the respondent have lived together for 2 periods not together exceeding 6 months, namely from the 4th day of July 1966 until the 10th day of September 1966 and from the 8th to the 27th days of December 1970, of which periods no account should be taken.

The petitioner therefore prays

That the said marriage may be dissolved.

(Signed) *A. Fogg* (Solicitor for the petitioner)

The name and address of the person who is to be served with this petition is Mary Weller, the Old Forge, Dingley Dell, Eatanswill, Mercia.

The petitioner's address for service is c/o Messrs Dodson & Fogg, Solicitors, Bank Chambers, 2 High Street, Eatanswill, Mercia.

Dated this 9th day of June, 1974.

No. 5

Answer of Mary Weller to Petition of Samuel Weller based upon five years of separation.

IN THE EATANSWILL COUNTY COURT
No. of Matter:

BETWEEN
SAMUEL WELLER .. .. *Petitioner*
and
MARY WELLER .. .. *Respondent*

The respondent in answer to the petition filed in this suit says:

(1) That there is no agreement or arrangement made or proposed to be made between the parties to this suit for the support of the respondent.

(2) The respondent admits that the parties have lived apart for a continuous period of five years immediately preceding the presentation of the petition.

(3) The respondent opposes the grant of a decree nisi to the petitioner on the ground that the dissolution of the marriage will result in grave financial hardship to her and that in all the circumstances it would be wrong to dissolve the marriage.

(4) The allowance of £800 per annum less tax proposed to be made to her was fixed at the date when the petitioner deserted the respondent in October 1965 and has not been increased since that time.

(5) It takes no account of changes in the cost of living since 1965 or of the fact that, although the respondent was then able to obtain employment as a secretary, she is now aged 55 and disabled by arthritis from obtaining that, or any other, employment.

(6) The proposal of rent free accommodation in the Old Forge, Dingley Dell, Eatanswill in the County of Mercia is unacceptable because the respondent's disablement increasingly compels her to live on the ground floor and she is likely in the future to be compelled to make use of a wheeled chair, whereas the Old Forge is a building of two storeys with inconvenient steps and passages, in which her disablement will create insurmountable difficulties.

(7) Should the said marriage be dissolved the respondent would forfeit her right to a pension as the widow of the petitioner under the contributory pension scheme of his employers, Nuts and Bolts Limited. The petitioner has made no proposal to compensate her for loss of this potential benefit nor does he appear to possess such capital resources as would enable him to do so.

(8) The petitioner has since January 1971 been living with, and committing adultery with, Rachael Wardle at Flat 5, Tower Court, Wimbleton in the County of Wessex and is the father of her child James, who is illegitimate. The dissolution of the said marriage would confer upon Rachael Wardle and her said child James financial benefits which take no account of the physical disabilities of the respondent or the contribution made by her to the petitioner's welfare by looking after the home and contributing to the household expenses during their 20 years of life together.

The respondent therefore prays

that the prayer of the petitioner be rejected

(Signed) *V. Helpful* (Solicitor for the respondent).

The name and address of the person who is to be served with this answer is Samuel Weller, c/o Messrs Dodson & Fogg, Solicitors, Bank Chambers, 2 High Street, Eatanswill, Mercia.

The respondent's address for service is c/o Messrs Helpful & Handy, Solicitors, 41 North Street, Eatanswill, Mercia.

Dated this 3rd day of July 1974.

No. 6

Husband's petition for nullity alleging in the alternative his wife's wilful refusal or inability to consummate the marriage

IN THE EATANSWILL COUNTY COURT
No. of Matter:

THE PETITION OF ALBERT WINKLE shows that:

(1) On the 12th day of May 1973 the petitioner went through a ceremony of marriage with Maria Winkle, then Maria Crab (hereinafter called the respondent) at the Parish Church in the Parish of Eatanswill in the County of Mercia.

(2) After the said ceremony of marriage the petitioner and the respondent lived together at the Gables, Dingley Road, Eatanswill aforesaid.

(3) Both the petitioner and the respondent are domiciled in England and Wales. The petitioner is an architect and lives at the Gables, Dingley Road, Eatanswill aforesaid. The present occupation and residence of the respondent are unknown to the petitioner.

(4)
(5)
(6) } As in paras. (4) (5), (6), (7) and (8) of No. 4.
(7)

(8) The said marriage has never been consummated.

(9) Such non-consummation is due to the wilful refusal of the respondent to consummate the marriage in that during the first 14 days after the marriage the respondent refused all attempts by the petitioner to have sexual intercourse with her and thereafter until she left the matrimonial home in August 1973, withdrew to a separate bedroom of which she kept the door locked and refused to permit the petitioner to attempt to have sexual intercourse with her.

(10) In the alternative the respondent has at all relevant times been and still remains incapable of consummating the marriage. The petitioner will ask the court to infer that if the respondent's refusals to have sexual intercourse with the petitioner were not wilful they were due to some physical or psychological inability to have or to permit such intercourse.

The petitioner therefore prays that the said marriage may be annulled.

(Signed) *John Harddriver* (Counsel for the petitioner)

This petition is to be served on Maria Winkle whose present address is not known to the petitioner.

The petitioner's address for service is c/o Messrs Helpful and Handy, Solicitors, 41 North Street, Eatanswill, Mercia.

Dated this 14th day of June 1974.

INDEX

446

Index

NULLITY,
children—
additional powers as to, 183–184, 357–361, 374
custody and education, 179–183, 358–359, 374
financial provision for, *see* financial provision, *infra.*
natural parent(s), rights of, 182
property adjustments for, 121 *et seq.*, 342–343
matters affecting, 145–148, 343–344
protection and welfare, 179 *et seq.*, 357–361, 374
statements as to arrangements for, 398
unsatisfactory arrangements, restriction on decrees, 57, 147–148, 184–186, 357–358
wards of court, 183, 358
conflict of laws, 81, 82, 102–103, 338
decree of—
absolute, making, 246–248
notice of application, 405
appeals, 294, 296
children, legitimacy of, 68, 370
defences, 75–78
post-1971 Act, 79–80, 338
domicile, effect on, 82
effect of, 66–68
financial provision on, *see* financial provision, *infra.*
grounds, 68–75
post-1971 Act, 78, 337
history, 1, 4
interventions, 61, 245–246
nisi, proceedings after, 246–248
overseas, recognition of, 102–103
domicile, based on, 102–103
residence, based on, 102–103
unsatisfactory arrangements for children, effect on, 57, 147–148, 184–186
void marriage, for, 66, 77, 337
declaration under R.S.C. contrasted, 72, 78
declaratory, 66
void or voidable, validation of, 185, 370
voidable marriage, for, 66–68, 79, 337
retrospective effect before 1971 . . . 66–67
financial provision—
avoidance of transactions to defeat, 177–178, 248, 251–252, 354–355
bankruptcy, effect of, 170–171, 351
capital gains tax, 150
child of the family, for, 113–115, 341
ancillary financial payments, 113–115
arrears, 162–163, 167–169, 322
back-dating of, 114
duration of order, 115, 347–348
lump sum payments, by, 114, 115, 116
matters affecting, 145, 343–344
meaning, 113, 363
pending suit, 114, 248, 341

NULLITY—*cont.*
financial provision—*cont.*
child of the family, for—*cont.*
periodical payments, by, 114, 115, 116, 242
property adjustments, for, 121 *et seq.*, 248, 342–343
secured periodical payments, by, 114, 115, 116
variation and discharge of orders, 158–162, 248, 348–350
death of former spouse, after, 115–120, 212, 314–317, 323
form, 413
secured periodical payments, 116
estate duty, liability for, 150
maintenance agreement—
alteration of, 172–176, 212, 352–353, 410–413
restricting right to apply for, void, 51, 60, 172–173, 351
overpayments, recovery of, 163–165, 212, 350–351
change of circumstances, 163–165, 350–351
remarriage, unaware of, 163–164, 355–356, 371
procedure, 246 *et seq.*
property adjustments, by. *See* PROPERTY RIGHTS
spouse, for, 109–113, 341
ancillary financial payments, 109–113
arrears, 162–163, 350
back-dating of payments, 110
duration of order, 110, 111, 347
lump sum payments, by, 110, 111, 112
matters affecting, 131, 343–344
pending suit, 107–109, 248, 343–344
periodical payments, by, 110, 111, 112
property adjustments, by, 121 *et seq.*, 248, 342–343
remarriage, effect of, 111, 162, 163–164, 347, 355–356, 371
secured periodical payments, by, 110, 111, 112, 116
security for, nature of, 112
variation and discharge of orders, 158–162, 248, 348–350
taxation, 149–150
foreign element in, 80–83, 102–103, 338
grounds of—
age, under, 1, 69, 78, 81, 337
bigamous marriage, 1, 69, 78, 337
consent, lack of, 1, 70–72, 78
Act, effect of, 75–76, 337
ratification, effect of, 76, 79
consummation—
incapacity, 72–73, 337
wilful refusal of, 73–74, 337
drunkenness, 70
duress, 71–72, 78
Act, effect of, 78, 79, 337
ratification, effect of, 76, 7

VOIDABLE MARRIAGE—*cont.*
  nullity decree—*cont.*
    lack of sincerity a bar, 76–78, 79
      statutory bar, replaced by, 79, 338
    parties only may petition, 67
    post-1971—
      marriage valid until annulment, 66, 338
      transactions, effect of Act, on, 67
      remarriage before annulment, bigamous, 67
    pregnancy *per alium*, 75, 78, 337
    ratification replaced by statutory bar, 76, 338
    unsoundness of mind, 74–75, 78
      lucid interval, marriage in, 70
    valid until annulment, 67, 338
    venereal disease, respondent suffering from, 75, 78, 337
    void marriage distinguished, 66

W

WELFARE,
  children, of, 179 *et seq.*, 359–361, 374
    court not satisfied with arrangements for, 57, 147–148, 184–186, 360
  judicial separation, 63

WIFE. *See also* SPOUSE
  agency of necessity, abolition of, 64, 108, 156, 189
  ancillary relief, distinction from husband in relation to, 4
  costs—
    legal aid, unsuccessful petitioner, 188
    liability for, 189–190
  domicile, 86, 98
  indirect contributions by, 202–203
  magistrates' court order, application for, 152
  matrimonial home, rights of occupation, 203–207
  necessaries, husband liable for, 64, 189
  wilful neglect to maintain, 151 *et seq.*, 271

WILFUL NEGLECT TO MAINTAIN,
  adultery, conducing to, 3, 53, 278
  agency of necessity, abolition of, 156
  appeals, 294–295
  applications based on, 256–258, 345
    forms, 408–410
    magistrates' court, in, 271
  arrears, recovery of, 162–163
  avoidance of transactions to defeat claims, 177–178, 354–355
  children—
    custody of, 182, 359
    natural parent(s), rights of, 182
  discharge of orders, 158 *et seq.*, 161–162
  final orders, 156–157
    arrears, 162–163
    duration, 157
    overpayments, 163–165, 350–351
    variation and discharge of, 158 *et seq.*, 161–162, 348–350
  grounds for application, 152–155, 345
    husband, by, 152, 271, 345
    obligation to cohabit, dependent on, 154
    separation agreement, effect of, 155, 173
  interim orders, 156, 346
    arrears, 162–163, 350
    overpayments, 163–165
    variation and discharge of, 158
  jurisdiction, 151–152, 271–272, 345
  maintenance agreement does not bar action for, 155, 173
  overpayments on change of circumstances, 163–165, 350–351
  polygamous marriage, action not maintainable where, 88–89
  procedure, 256–258
    forms, 408–410
  property adjustments, no power to make, 156
  summary of provisions, 151
  variation of orders, 158 *et seq.*, 161–162, 348–350
    death of person liable, after, 161, 349
    restrictions on, 159